AT THE REQUEST OF

MR. ~~William D. MacDonald~~

*we are pleased to send you
a complimentary copy of this
book for your consideration
as a basal text for your
classes*

THE LIST PRICE IS $ 5.50

HOUGHTON MIFFLIN COMPANY

UNDER THE EDITORSHIP OF

William F. Ogburn

A Study of RURAL SOCIETY

JOHN H. KOLB · COLLEGE OF AGRICULTURE · UNIVERSITY OF WISCONSIN

EDMUND deS. BRUNNER TEACHERS COLLEGE · COLUMBIA UNIVERSITY

Fourth Edition

HOUGHTON MIFFLIN COMPANY · BOSTON · NEW YORK · CHICAGO
DALLAS · ATLANTA · SAN FRANCISCO · The Riverside Press Cambridge

Original drawings by Aaron Bohrod, *Artist in Residence,*
University of Wisconsin

We Dedicate This Book
to the Youth of
Rural America
Whose Intellectual and
Spiritual Powers and Desires
Will Determine Her Future

Editor's Introduction

THE AUTOMOBILE TODAY is a much better vehicle of transportation than was the Model T Ford in 1912. Kolb and Brunner's *A Study of Rural Society* now, is a better book than it was in 1935. Improvement of an innovation is the key characteristic of the process of progress. Textbooks that are not improved cease to be used, and are forgotten.

Rural Society in its various editions has been studied by the youth of our colleges for nearly a fifth of a century. It is pleasant to think that these many tens of thousands of students and other readers have thereby been made wiser, happier, and that their lives have been more useful. The continued popularity of this textbook in rural sociology is no accident; for the authors have, between new printings and new editions, been busy with note-taking on new researches, with record-keeping of new developments, and with their own original studies in order to make their book more useful to the young people of our country.

The most apparent change is in the presentation. The authors have taken advantage of the contributions in visual education. There are more charts and drawings. Particularly valuable are the five original drawings and the many pictures selected from a very large collection, each to represent an important idea. Most tabular material has been broken into small, simple tables, easy to read. The writing has been made readable by a generous use of concrete terms and descriptive illustrations. This attractive exposition means that this newest revision will appeal to a larger number of students, especially those who consider taking a first-year course in rural sociology in their sophomore or junior year.

The authors have made their chapters challenging to the student's mind with ideas which will stimulate him to do his own thinking, to compare the contributions listed in the selected bibliographies, and to search his own experience for answers to the questions raised. Often writers who are original thinkers and contributors to their science, as Professors Kolb and Brunner are well known to be, tend to present mainly their own theories and researches. But in this book, readers will find a balanced and comprehensive presentation of the system of the many different contributors to the structure that is now rural sociology.

Rural Society is also an improved book because of its new content. It contains the results of new findings that researchers have made since the previous revision. These additions to knowledge are a considerable body of materials. Timely is the new chapter on rural society in other lands. Since World War II the people and the government of the United States have become internationally minded. Our boys have fought in strange lands and distant places. Here in India, for instance, where I am writing, county agricultural agents from the U.S.A. are teaching the peasants how to increase the production of their small family farms. The bibliography on rural life in foreign countries is believed to be unique in texts on rural sociology.

Welcome too, are the new data from the 1950 Census of the United States. These are important in this census because of a new classification of urban and rural populations which gives a truer picture of rural communities unmixed with suburban areas of city dwellers and which makes possible a better study of town-country relations. The book covers completely the school as a social institution and education as a social force in rural society, making it especially suitable for teachers' colleges.

Finally, drawing on their many years of teaching experience, the authors have added a brief chapter on the use of the book. It provides many practical suggestions and is full of sound advice. An early reading of this chapter will prove exceedingly helpful to teachers and students alike, as well as to all other readers.

It is a pleasure to present the 1952 model of *A Study of Rural Society*.

WILLIAM F. OGBURN

Contents

The authors urge that Appendix One — "The Book — What It Is, How to Use It" — be read before the rest of the volume because here will be found the material which usually appears in the Preface.

ix

PART FOUR · INSTITUTIONAL ARRANGEMENTS   281

A Study of

RURAL SOCIETY

1 What Is Rural Society—Why Study It?

AMERICA, DESPITE HER HUGE CITIES, IS A nation of rural backgrounds and traditions. Few are the families of native stock that do not trace back to the soil within two or three generations. The democracy so widely cherished is soil-born. Many social attitudes have their roots in the experiences of frontier and farm.

Notwithstanding the great industrial zones, agriculture is still a very important part of the nation's total economic life. More capital is invested in it than in any other type of enterprise. It gives employment to more persons than any other single industry; indeed, it is exceeded by only two major occupation groups in its share of the nation's gainfully employed. Its purchases keep the wheels of industry turning a fifth or more of the time. Its products load the majority of freight cars outside of the East. Its surpluses make up an important fraction of our export trade even in peacetime. And, of course, its soils bear and sustain the crops and livestock that answer the daily prayer for bread.

The human side of agriculture. Soils, crops, and livestock are the concern of the physical sciences related to agriculture, but there is also a human side to agriculture. The tiller of the soil and his family and those who care for his immediate physical, social, and economic needs are at least as important as the soil and its products. In short, successful agriculture has three concerns: farming as such, the efficient, profitable marketing of the products of the farm, and living the

good life. To overlook any one of these three is dangerous for the individual farmer and for society. The aim of better farming is to secure better returns. The objective of better business is to support or achieve security, justice, culture, education, and all those personal and social satisfactions that enter into winning the final objective of human effort, better living. Neither efficient farming nor plentiful profits in themselves guarantee better living. There is still the question of the human material and its capacity to measure up to the standards that better living demands. Consequently, the study of rural society and of the human element in agriculture is one of vast importance.

In the expansion period of national development this fact, axiomatic as it seems, was given little attention. It did not achieve official recognition until 1908, when President Theodore Roosevelt appointed his now famous Country Life Commission. The classic report of this commission marks the real beginning of the country life movement in the United States. It dealt with the conditions, needs, and aspirations of rural people. It pointed out both deficiencies and assets in rural life and showed how rural social institutions, such as school and church, could be improved. These and other institutions gradually began to respond to the challenge of this report to play their part in the vast changes of the next decades.

It is the purpose of this book to examine the whole complex of social arrangements,

1

group characteristics, traits, and institutions that are concerned with rural living and go to make up rural society.

Rural Society

Its people. In any consideration of rural society, then, the people composing it are a basic consideration. America was once, of course, entirely rural. Up to our entry into World War I it was half rural, and even today the percentage is well over one third. From these rural people has come a crop more important than any other: perhaps half the boys and girls born into rural homes in the last two generations migrated to the city and thus replenished the less fertile urban population. These matters are given detailed attention in Part One of this text.

Its institutions. A study of rural society is also concerned with a study of social institutions and social relationships and their changes, with reasons for such changes. The school is a social as well as an educational institution; the church is social as well as religious, and so with others. This is to say that basic interests such as education, religion, health, government, and the like, institutionalize themselves in organizations through which persons coöperate in achieving their expressed ends. These organizations influence and are influenced by the community. Much of the life of rural society flows through them.

Its groups. There have been those who argued that citizens of rural society were individualists, living alone and caring little for friend or foe. Evidence for this conclusion is hard to find. Even the hardy pioneers took their families with them or soon acquired them. "Neighbor" became a trenchant term, setting off in sharp relief those who were entitled to friendly confidence from those who were regarded as strangers

or "foreigners." Neighborhood groups and family groups have played and continue to play important roles in the more personal drama of rural life. Modern facilities for travel and communication permit rural people to seek companionship on the basis of special interests. In fact, so specialized have some of these special interest groups become that concern is expressed in some quarters lest families, communities, and even personalities be pulled apart. For this reason, questions of community organization and integration are most timely. Parts Three and Four consider the groups and institutions of rural life.

Its wealth. The consumption of wealth becomes an important consideration, fully as significant as its production and distribution. This has for some time been clear to rural leaders, and in these days when the federal government is so largely devoting its efforts to balancing the production of goods and their consumption, it is probably self-evident. The consumption of wealth in any community may be an aid in analyzing its standards of living. The distribution of expenses within the total income available indicates the values that are held by the family or community.

But the matter goes deeper. American economic society is organized on the basis of the profit motive, however variously that term is defined, and this has resulted in a certain mode of life. It accounts, for instance, for the protection society affords the institution of private property, which in rural society is so closely associated with land possession, and for the insistence of business upon "free enterprise." One has only to consider the contrasting attitude in present-day Russia to realize how completely different attitudes toward wealth and its consumption, profits and their making, possession and use, change drastically the social arrangements, laws, and institutions of a people so far as they relate to these things. Thus the whole consumption of wealth, not only of food, clothing, and shelter within the home, but of those social utilities including education, religion, recreation, and welfare within the community, must be considered in any study of rural society.

Its policies. Planning and policy-making have always been functions of any society and must probably become even more important. In planning for rural America, a study of rural society is essential, for policy-making requires knowledge of the situations and agencies involved in the plans. The naïve assumption that any group of persons will fall in with any plan about which they have not been consulted and which has not taken the social situation into account has been proved false so often in history that its survival is one of the world's mysteries.

Tradition plays its part here. Despite the lowest cotton price in years, the head of a large plantation in the South, scion of a family of distinction in his state, remarked in 1932, "The Lord meant this country to grow cotton. It's done so for two and a half centuries. Why should I change?" Religion and nationality play their parts also. Japanese have never competed with wheat-growers on the Pacific Coast. Their excursions into agriculture were confined to specialties requiring intensive hand cultivation, the stoop-and-squat labor so largely required in their rice paddies at home.

Sentiment, too, plays its part. It may seem a common-sense matter for isolated families in the Ozarks or on the sterile soil of some dry-farming area to avail themselves of a plan to move elsewhere. But perhaps they share the pioneer's love of solitude, perhaps they have a deep attachment to the familiar scenes of their home, perhaps life gains in zest because of their constant battle to outwit Nature and wrest a living from soil never intended to support human life.

Perhaps the little community is one bound by religious ties and settled in such a place to keep itself "unspotted from the world." Such social and socio-psychological considerations will, if not taken into account, upset the best-laid plans.

Social Change

All society is caught in the grip of social changes of considerable moment and velocity, and rural society is no exception. No one, of course, can predict how long this period will continue. In such times of adjustment, much of the surface interest is naturally captured by political changes, nor are these unimportant. But political arrangements are but a device for expressing social judgments. Public opinion often changes before shifts in the political scenery occur. More fundamental are economic changes, and more important are changes in attitudes and philosophies, registering profound shifts in convictions. With these latter come changes in the social processes themselves.

For these reasons Part Two considers the social economics of agriculture and the changes in thought and action taking place in this sphere of rural life. The sociologist has no professional concern with the management of a farm coöperative. He is, however, concerned with the growth of economic coöperation in rural America as a social movement; with the fact that in many respects organizations for economic coöperation are affected by the same factors and in somewhat similar ways as are rural organizations for noneconomic coöperation; and with the social implications of economic coöperation. It is important to grasp this distinction. Social science is the poorer because of the assumption on the part of some of its practitioners that anything somewhat economic is wholly economic. Sociology has much to contribute through adequate analysis of social aspects of economic events, movements, and organizations. It can, if it will, breathe the breath of life into the "average man" of statistics and into any impersonal aspects of economics.

Characteristics of Rural as Compared with General Society

Thus far in this introductory discussion no definition or characterization of rural society has been attempted. It is important, before going further, both to define and to note some of the distinctive characteristics of rural society in order to recognize why it should be studied apart from society in general and, in a sense, contrasted with it.

For many decades the United States Census counted as rural the farm population, other than the few thousands living within the boundaries of cities, and all the nonfarm population living in centers of less than 2500. With the census of 1950 a change was made. Incorporated places of 2500 or more are still counted as urban. To this urban population has now been added (1) the densely settled urban fringe around cities of 50,000 or more, and (2) unincorporated places of 2500 or more inhabitants. This reduced the rural population in 1950 to about 54,600,000. Had the 1940 definition been used, the figure would have been some 7,000,000 higher. For the most part the new census definition is used in this book, though rural affiliations of urban places are considered.

Natural environment. Most obvious in a comparison of rural and urban society is the immediate environment. Rural people have space, especially farm people. Once this meant isolation, but that has been greatly reduced by modern invention. The "fruited plains" stretch away from the door of the farm home, over which trees cast their protecting shade in summer and from which, perhaps in the distance, tower "the purple mountain majesties." Even in villages and towns there are trees, gardens, lawns, detached houses. Nowhere are there the narrow streets, sky-reaching buildings, elbowing crowds, snarling traffic, and the congestion, noise, and turmoil of the city.

The rural scene shifts, of course, according to soil and topography. Here it is level, there rolling, yonder hilly. Here there is black loam, there sandy soil, or again the firmer texture of shale or lime; there waving grain, yonder regimented rows of fruit trees, elsewhere fluffy cotton or myriad vegetable plants. Except along trunk highways, none of the earth is hidden by the solid concrete with which man protects the earth's surface from the scarring pressure of mechanized transportation.

Climate, too, plays its part. The graceful date palm never courts the breezes where they bear any touch of the North. The sun of the plains is just enough for the grain, but its greater generosity to the South and Southeast produces cotton or perhaps citrus fruit. Alfalfa yields to man five or six times a year in frostless areas, once or twice in regions mantled by snow and ice a third of the year. The machinist, the typist, the clerk, the banker, carried to and from work, perhaps, beneath the ground in roaring subways, pursue their accustomed tasks without regard to wind or weather. The farmer and even the villager fit their task to Nature's mood and the rhythm of the seasons and by the same token shift to a certain extent their attitudes and organizational programs. In short, rural Americans are close to Nature. Urban Americans have built an artificial structure to escape Nature so far as possible. Even where cities have saved oases of trees and open spaces whither their inhabitants may crowd to remind themselves of what the country is like, Nature is, so to speak, artificially on exhibit.

The family, a unit. In rural society people live in close proximity to their work. They can see the fields and orchards where they toil. They can hear the animals and chickens that are theirs to tend. They are never out of sight of their enterprise. For this reason the family has an absorbing common interest. Father, mother, and children are associated with living things, plants and animals, in the task of feeding the world. Every meal has the possibility of being a staff conference. Commutation is a word unused in the daily vocabulary of the rural family. Its members do not scatter to widely diversified tasks in different parts of the community by means of various sorts of transportation. In the rural world the individual adapts himself to the family situation. In the urban, the family adapts itself to the individuals that comprise it.

The family is, therefore, a supremely important rural social unit. In the economic life of the city family means little, but in the country it means much. Especially in older communities actions, achievements, and mistakes are judged in the light of the community's knowledge of the family unto the third and fourth generation. Measurably, though to a less extent, this is true in social relationships as well.

Rural organization simple. The physical spaciousness of rural life makes for a far lower density of population and restricts the number of human contacts, although not their depth. Conversely, within the community local group organization is simpler and not so highly specialized as in the city. Invariably the larger the community, even in rural terms, the larger the number of organized interests and agencies there are. But local rural communities do not possess medical and bar associations, councils of churches, and specialized trade groups, as do cities. If these and others exist at all, they are on a county basis.

Country and village, separate but united.

The chapter thus far has several times differentiated between farm and village and yet has included both as belonging to rural society, as indeed the United States Census does by its definition. What are the relations between these two great elements in rural society?

In many parts of the world, notably in the Orient, this distinction cannot be drawn. There the agricultural village is the home of the farmer. From it each day he trudges to his fields. To it each night he returns, to mingle with his neighbors or join the village elders as they discuss community affairs. In many parts of Europe, too, this age-old pattern still persists. It is to be found chiefly where farms are small and easily reached. It is appearing again in certain restricted areas of specialized farming where farms are comparatively small in the United States and where they can be reached quickly by automobile. This is especially noticeable in a few citrus-fruit centers on the Pacific Coast.

This, too, was the American pattern in early colonial days, but soon the huge tracts of land to be had for the taking and clearing spurred men to venture to live upon the broad acres they could not well reach daily from the village. It was in the Americas that agriculture first meant isolation for the farmer and his family. For a time it seemed as if the agricultural village was thereby doomed. The self-sufficing plantations of the South seemed to show the trend. They needed but one center to a county, and the county seat came to be something of what the market town is to much of the Orient today, a place where the farmer went periodically for the relatively rare goods and services he could not supply for himself.

Self-sufficing agriculture did not continue in the United States, however. Specialization set in, as will be seen later. More and more the farmer needed a nearby center where he could secure supplies, clothing, medicine, and other professional services. As time went on, the farmer was spurred by the automobile, which reduced the time required to cover the distance from farm to town, and tended to use his village more and more. It became increasingly a social as well as an economic center, and rural America has shifted its capital from the crossroads hamlet to the village or town. This dualism in the structure of the rural community, accompanied by a high degree of integration and division of labor, is another of the distinctive characteristics of rural society.

Rural America and the great society. In broad strokes these paragraphs characterize rural society, with its more than twenty-three million persons on farms and more than thirty-one million in villages and other non-farm territory. But, as stressed throughout this text, rural society is an integral part of the great society, and while countryman and cityman live under different circumstances, they are inevitably interdependent. Indeed, the lure of those things the countryman has by virtue of his location and occupation sends thousands of urbanites into the semi-rural suburbs of our metropolitan areas.

Why Study Rural Society?

The study of rural society is a practical as well as a scientific pursuit. It supplies a knowledge of the importance of rural America in the national life, of the rural heritage of that life, and of rural-urban-relationships. It shows the importance of social forces, groups, and organizations and the parts they play in national and community life. It furnishes, if not techniques, at least clues for the understanding of places where one works and lives and, indeed, of the backgrounds of associates and friends.

These values grow out of such a study only if the attitude toward this subject of rural society is that of the student, of the scientist who seeks facts and understanding, laying aside, so far as possible, preconceptions and adopting instead an objective approach. Such values may accrue to members of both rural and urban society. A study of rural society should give to rural residents a better understanding of the life about them which they are all too likely to take completely for granted. Rural leadership to be effective today needs the attitude of the student. City dwellers should benefit from a study of rural society if they come to recognize more fully the real interplay and interdependence of the great rural and urban forces which, working together, may realize the dream of America, but which, pulling apart, may tear her asunder.

TOPICS FOR DISCUSSION

1. List and describe very briefly five distinctive characteristics of rural society.
2. Make a list of what you consider the six chief deficiencies or problems in rural society today. How does your list compare with that of the Roosevelt Country Life Commission of 1908?
3. Rural society is said by some writers to be "individualistic." What do they mean by this? What do you think of this explanation?
4. What are the chief reasons for a study of the social and consumption relations of agriculture as compared, for example, with its production or distribution problems?
5. What social forces have been released by science and invention during the past ten years which are producing social changes and posing social problems in rural society?

REFERENCE READINGS

Adams, James Truslow, *The Epic of America*. Revised edition. Boston: Little, Brown, 1933. An excellent statement regarding the influence of the frontier upon American life.

Galpin, C. J., *Rural Life*, chap. III. New York: Century, 1918. A classic statement of rural social problems.

Griswold, A. Whitney, *Farming and Democracy*. New York: Harcourt, Brace, 1948. A reappraisal of interrelationships in the light of the last 150 years.

Roosevelt Country Life Commission, *Report of Commission on Country Life*. New York: Sturgis & Walton, 1911. Read especially the first fifty pages. An important and historic document giving rural social problems their setting in the national life.

Williams, J. M., *Our Rural Heritage*. New York: Knopf, 1925. An interpretation of the backgrounds of rural life, especially from the New England viewpoint.

Rural People – Their Distinguishing Characteristics

People are the vital and distinguishing feature of any society. They give it life and meaning. In American rural society, people are distributed over the landscape on separate farms and in scattered villages and towns. Because of unique cultural backgrounds, they have certain characteristics which set them off from other people.

In this part of the study, people are considered as units which may be counted, arranged on area maps, and classified as to age, sex, and family size. This is known as the demographic aspect of a society. Elsewhere people are studied in terms of their personal and group relations and as participating members of organizations and social institutions.

Mobility is a distinguishing characteristic of rural people in the United States. They have moved from East to West, and back to East again, from country to city, and back to country areas. They have literally been "on wheels."

PART ONE

Rural People – Their

2 Cultural Origins and Rural Regions

PEOPLE CONSTITUTE THE ELEMENT that gives the breath of life to the social structure. The structure itself evolves from the complexity of cultural heritages and experiences, of mores and acquired social habits which any given unit of population possesses.

American Cultural Origins

Culture is a broad term. It encompasses the attitudes, faiths, values and sanctioned ways of life; the habitual ways by which people coöperate in an organized and systematic fashion to achieve their mutual desires and objectives, including the ways they make a living; accepted modes of communication; and the material vehicles by which the culture is made effective. Understanding of the dominant elements in the culture of any community, group, or nation is indispensable equipment for anyone who works with people, since each individual reflects and conforms to the expectations of his culture and the community or given social structure as a whole mirrors the cultural patterns of its members. Indeed, the culture itself sets the limits within which an individual or subgroup may deviate from accepted norms and values. There is far less liberty of action and belief in a small, closely knit, isolated neighborhood in the Ozark Mountains than in a rural community long subjected to the urbanizing influences of specialized and commercialized agriculture. Rhode Island was founded because the seventeenth century Congregationalists of Massachusetts could not make room within

their value system for Roger Williams' views on baptism;[1] and two centuries later the Mormons for similar reasons migrated to, and founded, Utah.

There is great cultural diversity in a population as large as that of rural America. Interaction takes place, modifications in social behavior occur. The culture is a changing process, never quite the same but never wholly losing the heritages of the past. This is true also in single communities. The larger the number of cultural influences that have gone into the make-up of a given community, the broader its experience and the more fluid its local culture is likely to be. The converse is also true. This explains some of the differences between communities on the West Coast of the United States and other communities in the Midwest or the East, where the bulk of the population has sprung perhaps from a single racial group.

Any group is influenced not only by its physical environment but also by the national climate of opinion. Viewed from the air, the physical structure of communities founded by German migrants in eastern Pennsylvania or central Wisconsin is closely similar, even in the architecture of churches and barns, to communities of similar origin in South Australia or Queensland. The policy and creed of churches in such com-

[1] Only recently did the Massachusetts legislature repeal the law, long a dead letter, that any resident of Rhode Island could enter Massachusetts only on pain of death. For different cultural reasons the same penalty could once be meted out to Connecticut farmers bringing their products to New York City markets.

munities are closely akin. Cultural practices in agriculture may be similar, but will show differences forced by variations in climate and soils. Attitudes show far greater diversity.

It is necessary, therefore, before considering the social arrangements, institutions, and behaviors within any society to understand something about the people themselves. Their origins, characteristics, distribution, and attitudes, as well as their interaction with their environment, are important.

This is especially true in rural America. While many areas, such as Australia, New Zealand, the islands of the Pacific, and to a lesser extent Holland, Scotland, and Egypt, are relatively homogeneous (well over 90 per cent of the population of the first-named of these lands is of English origin), the population of rural America is composed of many diverse strains, each of which originally had its own culture. Some groups attempted to set up cultural "islands" and preserve their accustomed ways of life; but slowly the changed environment and the unique place of the United States in the world undermined the cultural foundations of such groups and forced adaptations. It was not until the late 1910's and early 1920's that religious services in the mother tongue were largely abandoned in areas settled by some German groups.

Over a period of years the population of rural communities often became quite heterogeneous, with two or more racial stocks represented. The various cultures interacted, but some traits of each almost always remained and are clearly discernible. Such cultural impedimenta have to be taken into account in all local planning. This interaction and the influence of the total environment — physical, social, and economic — resulted in the evolution of a societal structure describable by no other term than American. For instance, the Portuguese in Barnstable County, Massachusetts, retain

their Catholic religion and marry largely within their own group, but they join the same coöperatives, trade at the same stores, send their children to the same public schools as do the descendants of the first settlers, the English. Almost every nation in the world has had a part in the development of our present rural society, some, of course, more than others. The contribution of a few of those races whose influence is still traceable and vital will be briefly examined.

The English. Two predominating English strains founded our first agricultural colonies, the country gentleman and the yeoman. The former settled in the South, and the latter left his impress chiefly in New England. From the beginning the South concentrated on export crops, first tobacco, later cotton. The history of the section is closely linked with the story of cotton and tobacco; in fact its very agricultural geography is determined by them. The South was not tilled so much by small holders as it was divided into large estates or plantations, which were mostly self-subsisting. The plantation form of agriculture was a direct descendant of the old English manor. Since cotton and tobacco required cheap labor, a slave economy arose, accompanied by an enormous influx of Negroes which continued for 250 years. Except for the political necessity of a county seat, the self-contained plantation had little if any need for the services of towns and villages. This accounts for the fact that the number of southern villages per hundred square miles is today only half that in the northern colonial states.

The yeomen settled for the most part in New England, and to some extent in the Middle Atlantic states. They were freeholders and participated in the great westward migration toward the cheap virgin land that was so different from that which their European forebears had tilled and exploited for centuries. The lure of these large holdings seduced the imagination of these men and in effect did away with the immemorial agricultural village in which their ancestors had resided, from which they had gone to their fields in the morning and to which they had returned at night.

In America agriculture became isolated for the first time, and the result was the solitary homestead set in the midst of the farmer's acres, miles from the nearest town, although families on adjoining farms often formed closely knit neighborhood groups. This pattern came to characterize American agriculture. Indeed, under these conditions vestiges of the early doctrine that community well-being under a regulated economy was more important than the profit of individual enterprise remained chiefly, although not wholly, in New England. There regulations provided for market places, common pastures and woodlots, and even for town planning.

It is difficult now to realize how revolutionary this change was historically and to appraise its influence in the pioneer's development of such qualities as self-reliance and rugged independence, which contributed immensely in North and South alike toward the drive for national liberty. This may account in part for the intense individualism that for decades characterized the economic, social, and religious life of the United States. Nevertheless, as will be shown in Part Three, the village could not be entirely dispensed with, and today it has become the service station for the farming population. The historical fact that the village came after settlement on the land is of great importance to present-day village-country community development.

In time the stream of yeomen divided. Some, as we have seen, migrated to the West, and traces of their influence can be found today in many middle and even far western states. Some, turning southwest in search of a kindlier climate than New England's, were marooned in the Appalachian Highlands and the Ozarks along with many southern emigrants. Even today in the more isolated sections of these areas, one finds many household arts of pioneer days and hears English words which have passed out of currency everywhere else. Other New Englanders forsook agriculture for the sea and in their famous clipper ships carried the American flag and American trade over the seven seas, contributing in this way to the economic development of the young republic.

The Scotch and Irish. Another racial stream came from Ireland, driven out in the middle of the last century by successive crop failures and other economic maladjustments. The Irish settled from Maryland northward, for the most part in nonrural areas. The North-Irish and Scotch-Irish, who came earlier, established a considerable number of farming communities in Pennsylvania and northern Maryland, and their descendants are still living in scores of communities in those states, each settlement possessing its two-century-old Presbyterian church and other relics of Irish and Scotch pioneering.

The Dutch. The Dutch, two of whose progeny have occupied the White House in this century, were rather more important in urban than in rural American development.

The Germans. The Germans, whose cultural contributions are very significant, came in two waves, the smaller from southern Germany in the eighteenth century and the larger from central and northern Germany in the century following.

The first are the so-called Pennsylvania Germans, sociologically a highly interesting race. Originally extremely poor and tenacious of their Germanic traditions, they remained for nearly two centuries an almost alien group, not only in southeastern Pennsylvania where they first settled, but wherever they chanced to migrate. They took their form of religion with them when they migrated, and in their churches and parochial schools their dialect has been preserved in many places until this day. Moreover, they invariably clung to the limestone soil to which their ancestors were accustomed in the German Palatinate. These people fled to America partly because of untoward economic conditions, and partly to safeguard their religious liberty and avoid joining the German State Church.

The bulk of the North-German immigration, greatly stimulated by the German Revolution of 1848 and the conditions that produced and followed it, took place between 1836 and 1886. These people were agrarians, and settled for the most part in the west north central states.

The Scandinavians. The Scandinavians — Swedes, Norse, and Danes — also contributed much to rural America. The Swedes originally settled in New Jersey in colonial times but the middle of the nineteenth century saw immigrants of all of these nationalities arrive in force. They settled largely in the north central states, especially Minnesota and Wisconsin. Like their German neighbors, they were farmers.

For a time the East regarded the rapid settlement of the frontier by people of alien tongues as highly dangerous, but opposition began to fade when these immigrants responded wholeheartedly to the northern spirit during the Civil War. They did, however, change the local scene. Places whose English names still betray their New England origin have been engulfed by Germans and Scandinavians and postoffice rosters now often reveal no English stock. The Congregational Church was replaced by the Reformed or the Lutheran. The parochial school was introduced. The *Verein* became the leading social organization. Only the

American forms of government and the physical structure of the community persisted.

Other nationalities. The flood of immigrants, especially from southern and southeastern Europe, increased enormously with the turn of the century, but for the most part these people settled in cities. The Czechs, who came earlier, did settle on the land, as did some of the Italians and Poles, especially in the East. These people, and the French Canadians who poured into Vermont and New Hampshire, and the Portuguese, who still dominate some types of agriculture in eastern New England, introduced their diverse social elements. So, too, the Mexican has invaded the Southwest, though more as an agricultural laborer than as a farmer.

The blending of these various racial streams with American rural life has been widespread and far-reaching in effect. In many communities now apparently typically American, close study discloses influences, attitudes, and cultural deposits which reflect diverse racial origins, an understanding of which is essential to an understanding of the community itself.

Local manifestations of cultural heritages will, of course, vary even within the same nationality group and between adjacent communities. Peter Munch gives an interesting illustration of this in his study of two Norwegian communities in Wisconsin settled about a century ago.[2] The two were similar in many ways, both belonging to the Lutheran church, both sharing many values and customs of the mother country. One, however, was in a mostly uninhabited section, while the other was in close contact with the "Yankees" of the county seat, an Irish settlement, and some Germans. The latter group departed sharply from the

[2] "Social Adjustments Among Wisconsin Norwegians," *American Sociological Review*, December, 1949, pp. 780–787.

social status system of the mother land; in fact, it "came with the definite idea of establishing a democratic society on the basis of genuine American ideas of liberty and equality." Thus, despite similarities, the acculturation process proceeded at quite different tempos in the two communities. Any professional worker who approached these two groups with a single stereotyped idea of "the Norwegian community" would be seriously in error.

All cultural groups in the United States have been exposed to the technological and material aspects of our civilization. The coming of electricity, for instance, changed the social habits of many villages, making it easier to secure illumination not only in homes and on streets, but also for public meetings in schools and churches. Even here cultural values have affected the acceptance of many modern inventions. Some branches of the "plain people" of southeastern Pennsylvania, for instance, still require their members to dress in sombre colors and their men to use hooks and eyes instead of buttons on their clothes; automobiles and tractors are taboo.[3] This is an extreme case but it makes the point clear. The Amish are a special, or closed, social system. Ogburn and Nimkoff have characterized them as a folk society.[4] They probably deserve this characterization more than most rural communities or groups, though their life and their response to outside influences have produced a more complicated social structure than would be found among more isolated folk societies, for instance, in South Pacific islands.

Obviously, all members of the nationality streams mentioned, or others present in rural America, did not remain where they first settled. They spread far and wide, mingling with new people, contributing and assimilating cultural and ethnic heritages. Today the actual number of foreign-born on farms and in villages of the United States is relatively small and, because of immigration laws, is declining; but the record of achievement of immigrant farmers, as shown in the United States Census tabulations and in field studies, is highly significant.[5]

Regional Characteristics of Rural America

The basic culture of a community or social group is also influenced by its general geographic location. Many social customs and behaviors result from the interaction of people and their environment. Certain broad areas within which there are important similarities of thought and action have come to be recognized, both in the United States and in other countries, as regions. Definitions given to the term "region" are many and frequently indicate the special interest of the author. This is natural, as the concept has validity for several social sciences. The sociologist is especially interested in such elements as homogeneity of economic and social structures influenced by environment and demographic factors and cultural differentiation from neighbors.

Concept of region useful. There can be no question as to the usefulness of the concept "region." Data on comparable items for various regions make vivid the contrasts existing in the United States. However, with any given region, no matter which classification is used, there will be wide fluctuations from the regional average or norm in many counties and communities. On one or more indices a state in a given region may resemble a state in another region even more

---

[3] Edmund deS. Brunner, *Cooperation in Coopersburg* (New York, 1915), and Walter Kollmorgen, *The Old Order Amish of Lancaster County, Pennsylvania* (Washington, D.C.: Bureau of Agricultural Economics, 1942).

[4] William F. Ogburn and Meyer F. Nimkoff, *Sociology* (2nd ed.; Boston: Houghton Mifflin, 1950), p. 291.

[5] Edmund deS. Brunner, *Immigrant Farmers and Their Children* (New York: Institute of Social and Religious Research, 1929).

than it does its own neighbors. The preponderance of such similarities determines its regional assignment.

Use of regional concept increasing. The use of the regional concept has increased considerably in the last thirty years. The excellent studies of the National Resources Committee, initiated in the early 1930's, made much of regional planning and stimulated interest in regional matters. These studies indicate that many conditions and problems overlap state lines, that they affect and are the concern of regional groupings of states, and that necessary action therefore must also transcend state lines. Various departments and agencies of the Federal Government use over a hundred different regional classifications, many of which vary only slightly. The regions of the Federal reserve banks and of the Farm Credit Administration are illustrations. More important for our purposes is the crop area classification used by the Department of Agriculture. Many corporations, and social agencies like the American Red Cross, have regional offices, though these are chiefly for administrative purposes.

The practical utility of regional classifications, the similarities of conditions and problems among contiguous states, the speed of modern communication, and the great reduction in travel time brought about by modern transportation, have led some political scientists to propose that the number of states be reduced from forty-eight to six or twelve. Unquestionably the trend is toward an increasing use of regional divisions for planning and administration. By the same token the subject of regionalism becomes increasingly significant.

Some regional classifications. It is important, therefore, to consider both the origin of the concept and some of the regional classifications which have value for rural soci-

ology. It was the rural sociologists who first used the concept of region as a tool for analysis. In 1920 Dr. Warren H. Wilson proposed a nine-region classification of the United States, and Brunner and Morse used this in several national studies.[6] Professor Mukerjee of the University of Luchnow, India, issued a text on this subject in 1924.[7] Among other things this study indicated in terms of India the relation of region to food, race, and social types, as well as the correspondence between social and economic indices within the same region as compared with different regions. These latter elements proved significant in Brunner's study of Korea.[8]

The most ambitious research in regionalism was carried on by Howard Odum and his staff at the University of North Carolina.[9] Using hundreds of indices, they divided the country into six regions of from four to twelve states each. These they called, "The Six Major Societal Group-of-States Regions," approximating "the largest available degree of homogeneity measured by the largest number of indices available for the largest possible number of purposes." These regions are given in Figure 1. Perforce Odum used state units, since the data were not available in any other form. But he properly says that boundaries between regions overlap and often are fluid. This fact and certain important differences within Odum's regions led to efforts to develop a finer screen. The most detailed effort along this line was a study by A. R. Mangus.[10] Using

[6] Cf. especially their *Town and Country Church in the United States* (New York: 1923).

[7] *Regional Sociology* (New York: D. Appleton-Century, 1924).

[8] *Rural Korea: A Preliminary Social and Economic Survey* (New York and London: 1928. Tokyo: 1929).

[9] Cf. Howard W. Odum, *Southern Regions of the United States* (Chapel Hill: University of North Carolina Press, 1936) and H. W. Odum, and Harry E. Moore, *American Regionalism* (New York: Holt, 1938.

[10] *Rural Regions of the United States* (Washington, D.C.: Government Printing Office, 1940).

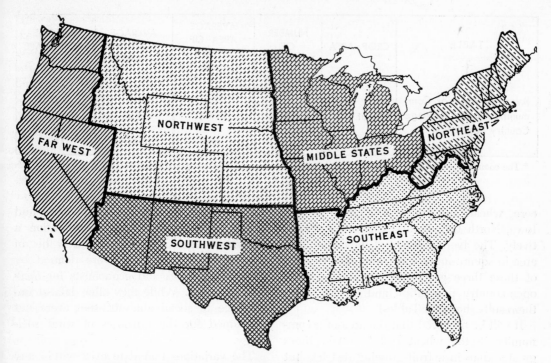

Figure 1. The Six Major Societal Group-of-States Regions.

As used in *American Regionalism*, by Howard W. Odum and Harry E. Moore, Henry Holt & Co., N.Y., 1938. Source: U.S. Department of Agriculture, Bureau of Agricultural Economics.

only indices available in the census on a county basis, he delineated 264 rural cultural subregions which he combined into 34 general rural cultural regions and 37 general rural-farm regions. Mangus's delimitation of subregions goes further than any other scheme in revealing the significance of relatively minor, though important, differences among groups of counties within a state, or sometimes spanning state lines. In that respect it is the most useful classification, but it is based on 1930 data. With the many changes since that time, it needs to be brought up to date now that 1950 census results are available.

A regional classification based on eight types-of-farming areas, developed by the Bureau of Agricultural Economics of the United States Department of Agriculture

(Figure 2, p. 20), is highly important and has been given extensive treatment by two recent sociology texts.[11] Long ago one of the present authors pointed out that types of farming have important effects on social conditions.[12] This may be illustrated by reference to two factors, the community area and the open-country population of the community, both discussed elsewhere in this text. Where factors of topography and proximity to cities did not appear, small groups of villages were selected from the

[11] Cf. Carl C. Taylor and associates, *Rural Life in the United States* (New York: Knopf, 1949), chap. XIX–XXVII, inclusive, and Charles P. Loomis and J. Allan Beegle, *Rural Social Systems* (New York: Prentice-Hall, 1950), pp. 249–306.

[12] Edmund deS. Brunner, G. Hughes, and M. Patten, *American Agricultural Villages* (New York: Harper, 1927), chap. XI.

TABLE 1 Average Area of Communities and Average Country Population	CROP AREA	NUMBER OF VILLAGES *	AVERAGE AREA OF COMMUNITY (Square Miles)	AVERAGE COUNTRY POPULATION	PERSONS PER SQUARE MILE
	Corn	10	80.0	1640	20.5
	Wheat	9	294.4	1908	6.5
	Citrus	6	40.0	1443	31.1

* The communities selected for this table were as nearly as possible one-crop communities.

corn, wheat, and fruit belts, encompassing Iowa, North Dakota, and California respectively. The average extent of the community area in square miles was computed for each of these three groups and compared with open-country population and density, with the results shown in Table 1.

It will be observed that the area of a community in the wheat belt is seven times greater than in a fruit-growing district, but that the density of population in the latter is five times that of the former. As far as factors of transportation or topography are concerned, there is no reason why the California communities should not be larger. The average number of farmers served does not vary greatly, regardless of the size of the village. This is largely because other centers spring up, each serving its own closely integrated group of farmers.

As Taylor and his associates point out, [13] "the way in which the people of any given rural area make a living is one of the major components of the culture of that locality." The way the work in any given crop area is done, seasonal demands, the type of special-interest farm organizations to which the operators belong — these and other factors are importantly influenced by the type of farming.

But these crop areas, as Taylor also indicates, are not definitive of all social phenomena. Many cultural traits are independ-

[13] Taylor, *op. cit.*, p. 331.

ent of them. Some states in the corn and wheat belts began school consolidation a generation ago. A few have barely begun this policy. These areas were defined by physical scientists and economists *for their own purposes*. While they offer data of importance to social analysts, they were not developed for the purposes of rural sociology.

The variations bound to exist within any large region, however defined, have been mentioned. A few illustrations in terms of major types of farming regions may be useful. Much of both Wisconsin and New York are in the dairy area. However, in 1940 New York was 82.8 per cent urban, Wisconsin, 53.5 per cent. In New York the rural non-farm population was larger than the farm, in Wisconsin smaller. Foreign-born and foreign-stock farmers of Wisconsin were largely of northern European origin and Protestant persuasion; in New York they were more of central and southern European origin and Roman Catholic. There have even been sharp differences of opinion between eastern and middle western dairymen as to what was best for the industry as a whole, caused in part by the fact that the easterner sells a larger proportion of his product as fluid milk, and the middle westerner as processed dairy products. Similarly unreconcilable differences among potato growers of Maine, Long Island, Michigan, and Idaho prevented a potato program under the first Agricultural Adjustment Act.

Again, much of both Pennsylvania and Tennessee are placed in the general and self-sufficing farm areas. But culturally there are tremendous differences between these two states. The first was less than one-third rural in 1950, the second barely one-third urban. The first is northern, the second southern, with all these backgrounds imply in cultural heritages. Tennessee has a number of counties lying in the southern mountains, long a well-recognized subregion. Pennsylvania has nothing comparable. Pennsylvania has far more foreign-born and foreign-stock farmers than Tennessee, as well as the special cultural group mentioned earlier in this chapter, the Pennsylvania Germans, but few Negroes. Outside the southern mountain area, Tennessee has a considerable minority of Negro farmers in many counties.

The types-of-farming classification also lumps under "all other areas" 406 counties, over 13 per cent of the total, including sections as diverse as the northwest Pacific coast, the potato section of Maine, the tobacco country of Virginia and North Carolina, and the citrus-fruit section of Florida. Except for the sake of completeness, the combination of such diverse groups in a single category and its use in statistical compilations is sociologically useless. Here again the finer screen used by Mangus proves its usefulness as far as it goes.

While considerable differences could be shown between state units in other regional classifications, this is not an argument against the use of the regional concept. Such use obscures fewer facts than a national average. Regions and subregions are recognized by the man in the street. The Piedmont has meaning to any Virginian or North Carolinian. So has the "tidewater." There are regional variations in speech, art, religious concepts, attitudes toward race problems, and so on. Every four years Americans hear about the "solid South." It is useful indeed to assemble measurable data that corresponds to these loose and popular terms. Among available classifications that which best fits the purpose for which data are presented should be employed. Where possible or important, state comparisons should also be made, and the sociologist must also recognize sub-regional and county differences when called upon to help in social planning.

Census regions and divisions. Still another classification, more familiar than any other, is that employed by the United States Census. Its reports divide the nation into three regions and nine divisions. The regional classification, north, south, and west, is, of course, very broad. The nine divisions are more satisfactory, although, like any other broad-gauge classification, they obscure many variations. These divisions, however, have been used for many decades. Better than any other scheme, they therefore permit comparisons over time — a measurement of trends. Such measurement is extremely important for all social science, since it indicates the way society is moving. For this reason the census divisions are used at a number of places in this text. The distribution of states among the divisions is as follows:

New England: Maine, New Hampshire, Vermont, Massachusetts, Rhode Island, and Connecticut.

Middle Atlantic: New York, Pennsylvania, New Jersey.

East North Central: Ohio, Indiana, Illinois, Michigan, Wisconsin.

West North Central: Minnesota, Iowa, Missouri, North Dakota, South Dakota, Nebraska, Kansas.

South Atlantic: Delaware, Maryland, Virginia, West Virginia, North Carolina, South Carolina, Georgia, Florida.

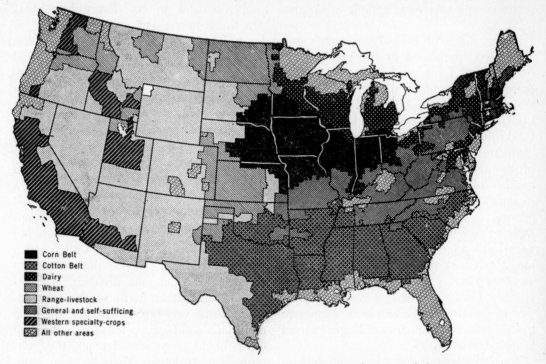

Figure 2. Regionalized Types of Farming in the United States.
(Special Adaptation, 1944). Source: U.S. Department of Agriculture,
Bureau of Agricultural Economics.

East South Central: Kentucky, Tennessee, Alabama, Mississippi.
West South Central: Arkansas, Louisiana, Oklahoma, Texas.
Mountain: Montana, Idaho, Wyoming, Colorado, New Mexico, Arizona, Utah, Nevada.
Pacific: California, Oregon, Washington.

It is also possible to combine these census divisions into a regional classification according to some of the outstanding cultural factors, both social and economic. This permits, where appropriate, the combination of census data by divisions, though with full recognition that, like all other regional classification schemes, boundaries between regions are not sharp but blurred. This scheme, which is not unlike Odum's, is used at some places in this text. The next section of the chapter, therefore, will indicate some of the characteristics of these

regions, presented as vignettes rather than completely. Implicit in these descriptions, as in the concept of regionalism, is the assumption that the underlying characteristics of these regions to some degree account for the differences among the regions as reported under various topics elsewhere in the text.

The Northeast. This region includes the New England and Middle Atlantic census divisions. More than other regions, this one, especially the New England division, shows the influence of the colonial tradition. This is manifested even in its domestic and ecclesiastical architecture. Its agriculture is conditioned by proximity to urban markets, but urban opportunity has drained off more of its youth than elsewhere, so that its farmers are on the average older. But although the

THE GOOD EARTH *Top*: New England (Standard Oil Co., N.J.)
Center: Western Mountain Region (Soil Conservation Service)
Bottom: Midwest (Standard Oil Co., N.J.   Photo by Rotkin)

MECHANIZATION COMES TO THE FARM: WHEAT FIELDS (Top photographs, Standard Oil Co., N.J. Bottom photograph, Extension Service, U.S. Dept. of Agriculture)

STARVED
BY LACK OF
PLANT FOOD

NOURISHED
ON
PHOSPHATE
AND LIME

MECHANIZATION — CORN *Top left:* Field Chopper (Extension Service, U.S. Dept. of Agriculture). *Top right:* Mechanical Corn Picker (Standard Oil Co., N.J.). *Bottom:* Demonstrating the Use of Fertilizer (Extension Service, U.S. Dept. of Agriculture)

COTTON HARVESTING *Top*: The Mechanical Cotton Picker. *Bottom*: Picking Cotton by Hand (Extension Service, U.S. Dept. of Agriculture)

number of farms may continue to decrease in any predictable future, agriculture, and therefore rural life, in this region, have achieved during the last decade or two a relative balance with industry and the city, or at least more of a balance than in other regions. The unique system of town-meeting government is still largely continued. French Canadians and some southern European groups have taken over many of the farms in some areas. Part-time, subsistence, and week-end farming by those with urban occupations, account for a larger proportion of the farms than elsewhere. Suburbanites have taken over much of the land, and their attitudes on local governmental services affect community standards of living. No region has as small a percentage of farm population in the total as this one. In few areas are farmers so likely to have non-farming neighbors.

The Middle West. The Middle West, on the other hand, comprising the East North Central and most of the West North Central census divisions, was invaded by various migratory streams — from the East, from northern Europe, and in some sections from the South — and therefore by various cultures. Its relative lack of cities and its larger farms forced it into cereal farming and thus made it more dependent upon the world economic conditions than any other region except the South. Fluctuations in these conditions have brought wider swings between prosperity and depression than in some other areas. Despite the growth of some large cities and greater industrialization, this region is still agriculturally one of the most important, but urban growth has resulted in significant shifts in farm management. The average size of the farms has steadily increased, but family-operated farms are still the most important type. The proportion of tenant-operated farms is higher than for the nation as a whole. Agricultural coöpera-

tion in the United States originated here. The region has a record of progressiveness and vigor, reflecting some of the characteristics of a pioneer period scarcely a century gone. Rural school consolidation began here. Efforts to achieve what the farmer considered justice to agriculture from the rest of society abound: the Grange movement organized in the 1870's, the Populist movement of the 1880's and early 1890's, the Non-Partisan League, and the Farmers Labor Party of the 1920's, originated here and, except for the Grange, largely remained within the region.

The Northwest. Nowhere perhaps are the boundaries between regions more blurred than between the Middle West and the Northwest. Though corn yields to wheat as the major crop, many social characteristics of the Midwest carry well into the eastern part of the Northwest. But as one leaves the humid western fringe of the Mississippi Valley and enters the Great Plains, conditions change. Dry farming begins and the size of farms increases sharply, with an attendant decline in population density. Further to the west in the Rocky Mountain states are the range-livestock areas, extending from the Canadian border through the Southwest to the Mexican border. Population per square mile is lower than in any other region except the western part of the Southwest. Some communities have an air of impermanence. The church is weak, but education is well supported and the school is often the largest and most modern building in the community. The median number of years of schooling completed by the rural population is high. Social life is informal but vigorous. The settlers have come from all parts of the United States. This region includes the extreme western part of the West North Central census division and the northern two thirds of the Mountain division. Northwest and Southwest share many characteristics, such as very low density of population, dry farming, and stock raising.

The South. The South includes the South Atlantic and East South Central census divisions, and its characteristics spill over into the southwest or, in census terminology, the West South Central states. It has fewer foreign-born than any other region, but nine tenths of America's rural Negroes are in this region, descendants of those who were originally slaves. It was the first region to export considerable proportions of its two basic crops, cotton and tobacco. Even in colonial times its concentration on a one-crop agriculture made the region vulnerable to economic fluctuations. Its agriculture early evolved into the plantation system. Following the war between the states, former slaves became sharecroppers, joined in this status by landless whites. Farm-owner operators were, and are, relatively fewer than in other regions. The two basic crops were hard on the soil. Erosion became serious and still is, though much progress has been made in controlling this threat, which is by no means unknown in several other regions. Because of these and other causes, the region has a relatively lower standard of living, especially among the Negroes. Because of the plantation system, so largely self-sufficing, there were comparatively few village centers, mostly county seats. The South includes a large subregion of 250 counties in parts of seven states, the Southern Highlands or Appalachians. Like the Ozark subregion, this one has its own distinctive folklore, dances, and music. Despite many handicaps the South has made much progress materially and socially, since 1920 and especially since 1940. Agriculture is being increasingly diversified. It is an area of great potential resources, physical and human.

The Southwest. This region includes the western half of the West South Central census division and the southern third of the Mountain. As with the Northwest, the eastern boundaries of this region are fluid. The influence of the South is clearly evident in the considerable cotton areas of eastern Texas and Oklahoma. But the Mexican is present in this region and as one goes westward the Negro all but disappears. Texas was once an independent nation. Its history and traditions are thus different from the old South. The quip that Texas, like California, is a state of mind is a popular recognition of these differences. Oil is a considerable mineral resource, and profits of its exploitation, as well as rising land values, have produced a number of modern cities. In proportion to population, there are more metropolitan districts in eastern Texas and Oklahoma than in the South. The western part of this area, New Mexico and Arizona, is largely a range and livestock area, partaking in many ways of the characteristics of the Northwest, and is included by the census in the Mountain division. However, it is significantly different in the proportion of Mexicans and Indians in the population, higher than elsewhere in the nation and clearly reflected in the art, music, and handicrafts of the area. It has a higher proportion of Roman Catholics among its rural church members. Especially in the open country, Protestantism is very weak. The famous Dust Bowl of the 1930's lay largely in this and its neighboring Northwest region.

The caution that the boundaries of any regional classification adopted are not ironclad is illustrated by one village-centered agricultural community in the southeastern part of the Southwest region, where climate and irrigation made possible the growth of such crops as citrus fruit, melons, and early spring vegetables for winter sale in the North. Cotton-growing had disappeared by 1924. The population was drawn from many regions, farms were small, churches varied, and even architecture and speech were affected by the new conditions. Field workers described it as a California village set down in the Far South. Southern mores were on the defensive, and southern traditions were not binding on the community. The Mexican, rather than the Negro, furnished the farm labor. In population growth, school construction, farm ownership, and per-capita retail sales, this community ranked either first or second among thirty agricultural villages studied in the South. Even regional influences, powerful as they are, exercised no unimpregnable control. This illustration suggests that regional boundaries themselves may not be fixed for all time.

The Far West. This region includes the Pacific census division. It is an area of great variety. California alone has approximately two hundred different agricultural products and is properly classified by the Bureau of Agricultural Economics as a specialty-crop area. Irrigation is highly developed here, especially in the southern part. There are more corporation farms and other large-scale agricultural enterprises than in other regions and, by the same token, proportionately more wage labor in agriculture. Agricultural coöperation is very well developed. The growth of large cities throughout the region has enlarged markets for farmers, but large quantities of some agricultural products are still sent to eastern states. Industrial expansion has been very rapid. In fact, the whole region is the most rapidly growing in the United States, having gained almost 50 per cent in population between 1940 and 1950. California is now the second state in the Union

and has a smaller proportion of farm population than the Middle Atlantic census division. This population growth has come more by migration from other states than by natural increase, in which respect California especially ranks quite low among the states.

Oregon and Washington differ in some significant respects from California. They raise a smaller number of crops. Some sections, especially the central and eastern parts of these states, are more like the Northwest than like the rest of the Pacific region in important particulars. Throughout most of the Far West the standard of living is high but clearly reflects over-all regional characteristics: the public schools are excellent, the county strong, the church weak.

Summary. This chapter has described briefly some of the racial streams, now largely assimilated but still distinguishable and significant, which have contributed to American rural society and culture. It has described various schemes for classifying the nation into major societal areas called "regions." These are a significant aid in any analysis of rural life, despite wide variations within and among them.

It is time now to consider the rural people who live in these regions on farms and in villages. How many and how important are they in the national scene? What has brought about the present distribution of our rural population? Why has urban population forged ahead of rural? What of the future trend regarding population? These questions will be answered in the next chapter.

TOPICS FOR DISCUSSION

1. Trace the early settlements in your county. Where did the first settlers come from? What racial groups did they include?
2. Compare your county or state on selected

items with divisional or regional totals in the census of population and agriculture and explain the differences.
3. Locate your own subregion in Mangus's *Rural Regions in the United States.* Compare 1950 with 1930 and explain any trends discovered.
4. Should matters of regional concern be han-

dled by regional organizations or by coöperation among the states? Defend your point of view in terms of your own general region.

REFERENCE READINGS

Jensen, Merrill, ed., *Regionalism in America*. Madison: University of Wisconsin Press, 1951.

Loomis, Charles P., and J. Allan Beegle, *Rural Social Systems*. New York: Prentice-Hall, 1950. A summary of the Taylor and associates study listed below.

Mangus, A. R., *Rural Regions of the United States*. Washington, D.C.: Government Printing Office, 1940. The most detailed delineation of regions and subregions.

Odum, H., *Southern Regions*. Chapel Hill: University of North Carolina Press, 1936. This and the following reference are the first detailed studies of regions and their differentiation. Uses far more indices than any other.

Odum, H., and H. E. Moore, *American Regionalism*. Chapel Hill: University of North Carolina Press, 1938.

Taylor, Carl C., and associates, *Rural Life in the United States*. New York: Knopf, 1949. The most complete description of the social characteristics of type-of-farming regions extant.

Educational films are listed at the conclusion of many chapters and in the Bibliography on Rural Life in Foreign Lands. These films have been tested for educational value either by the Bureau of Visual Instruction at the University of Wisconsin, Madison, or by the Institute of Adult Education, Teachers College, Columbia University, New York City, or both.

Most of the films can be secured from your state university or college film rental library or from local commercial rental libraries. To save space, symbols are used, "S" for sound and "C" for color. Numerals signify the number of minutes the picture requires.

FILMS

And So They Live (Rural South). S, 24. University, Washington Square, New York.

Far Western States. S, 11. Encyclopedia Britannica Films, Inc., Chicago.

The TVA. S, 22. Tennessee Valley Authority, Knoxville.

The U.S.A. Regional films on New England, Midwest, Northwest, Southeast, Southwest. Each S, 20 to 22. United States Films, New York.

Westward Movement. S, 11. Encyclopedia Britannica Films, Inc., Chicago.

3 The Mobility of Rural Population

MIGRATION FROM EUROPE to the rural areas of America, which began almost as soon as the first colonies were permanently established and which continued to the close of the last century, is by no means the only migrational influence in rural America. Once the nation was firmly established, the ceaseless movement of people hither and thither across the continent was of even greater importance.

America's Great Migrations

Before 1930 this movement was characterized by two drifts, one westward, the other toward the cities. The former came first and was the more important for many decades. The latter began slowly at the beginning of the nineteenth century, but in the fifty or sixty years prior to 1930 it gradually became more significant than the westward trek.

Westward ho! Westward expansion began in colonial times. The English who settled Plymouth, Cape Cod, and Boston, penetrated to the Berkshires in a few decades, to central New York by 1800, and thence continued to move westward. So with other groups. Indentured servants of early Virginia planters, after serving their time, pushed up the Virginia rivers toward the west. In Washington's day the site of Pittsburgh was the western outpost of the European emigrant. Expansion accelerated with time, led by frontiersmen of the Daniel Boone type, in whose wake followed hardy pioneer farmers like the parents of Abraham

Lincoln. So it continued until the comparatively recent days of homesteading, the frontier and the center of population moving farther west every year.

The frontier. The frontier left a tremendous mark on American life, rural and urban. Pioneering involved ceaseless, unaided struggle. Land had to be cleared and cultivated; civilization with its well-established and comfortable institutions was left behind. Neighbors were few and far between. Only the strong, the fittest, survived. Migration meant a definite break with Europe, the parent continent, and a repudiation of the eastern United States, whence the earlier pioneers had come. Later, as noted in the previous chapter, many immigrants from northwestern Europe went directly to the Midwest.

The frontier drive had many motivations. Doubtless no single motive influenced any one person to head westward. Love of the new and strange and the zest of adventure played their part. To others the frontier offered an escape from personal dilemmas. There were also strong currents of democratic aspiration in the early nineteenth century, the ideals of which seemed more easily realizable in the West than in the older East. Certainly the economic motive was strong.[1] Cheap western land, the chance to

[1] The influence of the frontier on America has been well discussed by the historian Frederick Jackson Turner in his *The Frontier in American History* (New York: Holt, 1920). See also James T. Adams, *Epic of America* (Boston: Little, Brown, 1932) chaps. IV, V, VI, and *Westward Expansion: A History*

become monarchs of vast acres, lured the masses. Land was wealth in those days, as in all agrarian civilizations, and these migrants were Europeans or descendants of Europeans who, accustomed to the meager holdings of continental peasantry, were willing to make any sacrifice to obtain and hold these vast acres of the West.[2] A movement similar to this was that from China proper and Korea into Manchuria, which between 1900 and 1930 brought a fifteen-fold increase in the population of this fertile empire which then totaled thirty million people.

Westward expansion carried 3,500,000 people into the eastern Middle West, including Iowa and Minnesota, between 1850 and 1860. The importance of this enormous mass migration, as indeed of all interstate migrations, is recognized by the United States Census, which since 1870 has attempted a rough measure of the migrational force by noting how many people are living in states where they were not born. For example, by 1870 one twelfth of all persons born east of the Mississippi were residing west of it — two fifths of the West's six-million population. Horace Greeley's slogan, "Go West, young man!" described a national movement.

The period ends. In 1890 one tenth of those born east of the Mississippi, about 4,500,000, had crossed it, and almost another million was added by 1910. Thereafter the pace slackened, both because free land was getting scarce and because of the rise of the

"industrial frontier" in the East. The 5,200,000 Easterners reported living in the West in the 1930 Census constituted but a sixth of all western population, and less than one thirteenth of all living Easterners. By 1940 the number of Easterners living west of the Mississippi River had actually declined by half a million and was but 5.5 per cent of the total number of Easterners. Indeed, the movement had reversed itself, and the flow was toward the East; by 1940, 1,920,000 Westerners were living east of the Mississippi, about 272,000 more than in 1930 and nearly a million more than in 1920. Interestingly enough, the proportion of all native Westerners living in the East was also 5.5 per cent. The westward migration 1940–50, already noted, was largely to industrial centers.

Long before 1940 a definite pattern with respect to migration had begun to develop among the census divisions. In 1870 the proportion of the population residing in the West North Central states but born in other census divisions, was almost one half — only slightly below the Pacific division, where it was just over half. By 1940 the proportion had dropped to 13.8, but as would be expected, the Pacific continued above half. On the other hand, New England and the Middle Atlantic states attracted a slowly growing proportion, but the former stabilized at less than 8 per cent in 1900 and the latter at close to 10 per cent in 1930. The South Atlantic and East South Central divisions also had less than 10 per cent, but the former has been slowly increasing each decade since 1870, the latter decreasing. In the Mountain states 37.8 per cent of the population in 1940 had been born elsewhere; in the East North Central and West South Central, about one in seven. Preliminary 1950 census data indicate that these trends continued throughout the 1940's.[3]

of the American Frontier by Ray Allen Billington with the collaboration of James B. Hedges (New York: Macmillan, 1949).

[2] See Herbert Quick, *Vandermark's Folly* (Indianapolis: Bobbs-Merrill, 1923), for an excellent description in fictional form of American migration and its motives. See also sections of Phillips, *Life and Labor in the Old South* (Boston: Little, Brown, 1931) for family case histories based on old records and materials relating to the causes of migration and the experience of migrants from the Old South.

[3] It happens that detailed analysis of interstate and interdivisional migration is one of the last

Migrations are more than movements of people. Along with the baggage stowed in the prairie schooner were transported distinctive social and cultural ideas: ideas of local government, of community organization, education, architecture, even modes of speech and superstitions. The farther west the pioneers traveled and the more they mingled with natives of other regions and countries, the more their traditional personal and social mores were modified by environmental and social contacts.

Some differences resulting from migration. Among results credited to westward migration is the idea of "rugged individualism," by which alone the pioneer survived and which has only recently, and perhaps temporarily, been more or less abandoned. Furthermore, the pioneer had his share in our continuing "splendid isolation" from the rest of the world, in the face of rather intricate economic and cultural ties with all lands. The westward movement gave us our great dramatic era of railroad-building, the by-product of which was the creation and growth of towns and villages. The rapidity of agricultural and transportation development increased the value of land and helped create a speculative attitude toward it. The necessity of having governmental units of manageable areas resulted in our three thousand local counties, tens of thousands of townships, and hundreds of thousands of school districts. These divisions are less necessary now than in the last century, since today the fast-moving automobile has replaced the horse and a plane can span the continent in a few hours. Frequently, therefore, throughout this volume problems and conditions will be discussed which have their roots in an age that is past, outmoded

by the rush of inventions but persisting as part of a tradition or because social inventiveness lags behind mechanical discovery.

Interstate Movement of Farm and Rural Non-Farm Population

The 1940 census made a more detailed analysis of migration than had ever been done before, covering the period 1935–39.[4] Since no comparable data are likely to be available soon in as much detail, some attention will be given to this analysis.

Americans a mobile people. One clear impression from these data is that Americans are still a mobile people. In 1940 one person in every eight over five years of age was living in a different county than in 1935, a total of almost sixteen million persons. This movement of population continued at an accelerated rate during the 1940's, especially after the end of World War II. Thus the census reported after a sampling study that 8,335,000 persons moved across county lines between April 1, 1948, and April 1, 1949,[5] or 5.6 per cent of the estimated population. Similar results were obtained a year earlier. Even allowing for underenumeration in the 1935–39 period, it would appear that the rate of internal migration in the United States in the late 1940's was at least double that of a decade before. The preliminary results of the 1950 census confirm this conclusion, since 6.2 per cent of the population aged one year and over were enumerated in a different county when the census was taken, April, 1950, from that in which they had lived the year before.[6] At this rate,

---

major topics on which the census reports each decade. Such preliminary data as are available appear later in this chapter.

[4] Four volumes of analysis were subsequently issued, *Internal Migration in the United States, Social Characteristics of Migrants, Economic Characteristics of Migrants,* and *Age of Migrants* (Washington, D.C.: Bureau of Census, 1944 to 1945).

[5] Series P–20, No. 28, March 17, 1950.

[6] Series PC–7, No. 3, April 30, 1951.

within a decade well over half the population would move, at least across county lines. Almost half of these remained within the state of their residence, but two in every ten moved to a contiguous state. Three in every ten, however, made longer moves to noncontiguous states.[7] As compared with the late 1930's, the proportion of people migrating longer distances doubled.

The behavior of rural and urban people in interstate migration differs in degree. When measured in 1920, 28 per cent of all city dwellers were born in states other than those in which they resided at the time of that census. The comparable rural figure was 18.5 per cent. In 1940 18 per cent of the urban population were found living in a census division other than that in which they had been born, and 26.6 per cent were living in a different state. For the rural non-farm population the respective proportions were 14.6 and 22.5 per cent. Only 8.4 per cent of the rural farm population were living in divisions other than that of birth, and only 13.4 per cent in other states.

This same trend continued in the 1940's. In the year prior to April 1, 1949, only two farm people moved across county lines for every three non-farm people. Two thirds of these farm migrants stayed within the state. About one fifth went to a contiguous state and only 14.7 per cent to a noncontiguous state. Of the total non-farm population, 36.8 per cent moved to noncontiguous states in this year and only 42.3 stayed in the same state. One explanation of these differences is that migration for a farmer involves more than for any other worker. He must either move a considerable amount of machinery and perhaps livestock in addition to his household goods, or he must sell out. Even so, a majority of the farm population who migrate move to another farm — 50 per cent between 1935 and 1939, and 58 per cent in 1949–50. This was also true of the

[7] Series P–20, No. 28.

large majority of the farm families who moved within the same county in 1948–49.

In passing, it should be noted that farm labor, as would be expected, is far more mobile than the farmers. Almost two thirds of the farm operators who moved in the year prior to April 1, 1949, stayed within the boundaries of their state. This was true of slightly less than half of the farm laborers. However, if state lines were crossed, both groups favored noncontiguous over adjoining states — farm operators about two times out of three, farm laborers by only a slight margin.

Some studies of migration by state college of agriculture experiment stations, and also data on the distance moved, suggest that some of the migration of population in the United States is similar to a wave-like movement. Farm people go first to villages. Villagers choose towns. The move to a city is often not made directly in one step.

By way of summary, Table 2 gives the proportion of migrants between April 1, 1949, and the same date in 1950 for farm and rural non-farm populations. It will be noted that there were fewer migrants among the farm group and that for both groups there was least migration in the Northeast and most in the West. It is clear that Negroes were less mobile than whites in the South. Considering that these are figures for just one year and that internal migration was also heavy in previous years, the task of schools, churches, and social agencies in getting acquainted with, and extending service to, new population appears considerable, especially in the West and among southern whites.

Farm — Non-Farm Population Movement

As previously noted, the farm population of the United States stood at just over 24,500,000 at the end of 1950, a loss of practically 25 per cent, or 8,000,000, from the

TABLE 2 — Proportion of Farm and Rural Non-Farm Populations Living in Different County on April 1, 1950, from April 1, 1949, by Census Regions	REGION	FARM	RURAL NON–FARM
	Northeast	3.9	6.2
	North Central	4.6	7.2
	South: Total	4.6	8.3
	South: Non-White	2.8	6.5
	West	7.4	11.9

Source: Preliminary report, Seventeenth Census of the United States, 1950, Series PC–7, No. 3, April 30, 1951.

high point in 1916. More than half of this loss was registered in the 1940's. Part of it was due to the change in the census definition of farm, to be discussed later. This figure is the net after considering the movement of farm population to cities and towns and of urban and town population to farms and the rural farm excess of births over deaths.

There is a great deal of such movement. Gross migration from farms to cities and towns from 1930 to 1950 came within 5.6 per cent of equaling in numbers the total farm population of 1940. Table 3 gives the details.

The county story. This rural-urban migration has been selective as to territory and has seriously drained some rural counties originally organized on the basis of the population they had or thought they could reasonably expect. In every census period but one since 1920, more than 1000 counties have lost in population. The exception was the depression decade of the 1930's, when fewer than 900 registered a drop. Between 1940 and 1950, 1510 of our 3070 counties showed a decline in population, nearly half by 10 per cent or more. Of the 1560 gaining, all but 170 added 10 per cent or more, and about 500 gained 20 per cent or more. More than four fifths of the national population increase took place in the 168 standard metropolitan areas. (The Pacific Coast also gained heavily, about 50 per cent.) Their growth was 14,653,382, or 21.2 per cent. Interestingly enough, however, the rate of growth outside the central cities of

TABLE 3 — Estimated Population Movement to and from Farms (In thousands)	DURING YEAR	TO CITIES * FROM FARMS	TO FARMS FROM CITIES *	NET MOVEMENT TO CITIES
	1920–24	8,701	5,370	3,331
	1925–29	10,735	7,770	2,965
	1930–34	7,176	6,578	598
	1935–39	6,816	4,044	2,772
	1940–44	9,180	3,934	5,246
	1945	1,081	1,684	−603
	1946	1,343	1,077	266
	1947	1,554	914	640
	1948	1,301	1,178	123

* "Cities" here includes towns and villages. The net loss by migration from farms is therefore greater than the loss to the total rural population, as it includes migrants from the farm joining both the urban and rural non-farm groups.

Source: *Farm Population Estimates* (Washington, D.C.: Bureau of Agricultural Economics, United States Department of Agriculture).

these districts was more than twice that within them.

Who Are the Migrants?

With population movements of such scope it is important to consider whether or not those who migrate have distinguishable characteristics.

The areas of greatest mobility of farm population correlate highly with percentage of tenancy and share-cropping, and somewhat in recent years with untoward climatic conditions. Tenants move from two to six times as frequently as farm-owners. Presumably migration of this sort, counting those who move within the same community, affects more than a million farm families in some years. Although such migration is often undertaken in an effort to improve economic conditions of the family, such constant shifting calls for constant readjustment on the part of the family as well as on the part of social institutions and communities. There are clearly social losses too subtle to measure with precision, and the change is frequently an economic gamble as well. In the long run it might be better in an average situation for the community or county to seek to so improve conditions that some of the incentive to migrate would disappear.

Education influential. Education was also a factor in migration. In the 1935–39 period more than half the rural migrants twenty-five to thirty-four years of age with eight grades of schooling or less moved to other farms, whereas this was true of only 35.7 per cent of high school graduates. Just over half the college graduates migrating stayed in rural territory, about one third on farms. Very small proportions of college graduates in this age group on farms moved, as compared to those in cities and rural non-farm territory. Possibly rural college graduates make their initial choices more care-

fully than others. Possibly also the number of graduates of agricultural colleges in farm areas account for this.

Beyond this there is a tendency for those in the lower educational groups to migrate to, or remain in, rural non-farm or farm areas. That one explanation for the migration of these people is economic is shown by a rank-order correlation of plus .51 [8] between gain or loss in state population by migration of the native born and the support of education per classroom unit. There is a tendency for people to move from areas where the level of educational support is below the national average to those states where it is above. From an educational point of view, the more progressive states, cannot afford to be unconcerned about the general level of education elsewhere. Migration could well nullify the effects of their superior educational programs.

The other side of this picture is that a disproportionate number of urban migrants to farms had eighth-grade education or less, usually sixth-grade or less. The seriousness of this situation lies in the fact that agriculture has become a skilled, not to say specialized and scientific occupation. Large proportions of poorly educated migrants fail as farmers, although they may subsist as farm laborers. The idea held by some that the relief problem of cities in the 1930's could be solved "by sending the unemployed to the land where they could raise their own food" was completely fallacious. Scores of studies by state colleges of agriculture and the rural research unit of the WPA proved this. Moreover, these urban migrants, because of their low capital resources, gravitate to the poorer land, often marginal or worse.[9] The type of farming operations carried on by these poorly educated urban mi-

[8] This coefficient is 3.5 times the standard deviation of r.

[9] Cf. Edmund deS. Brunner and Irving Lorge, *Rural Trends in Depression Years* (New York: Columbia University Press, 1937), pp. 75–76.

grants presents a social and economic hazard. These ill-prepared farmers are not competent, for instance, to safeguard their soil adequately from wind and water erosion, and land thus unprotected often becomes a menace to adjoining farms.

Sex differences a factor. Studies of rural migration have invariably shown that females migrated a year or two younger than males and were more likely to go to the city. This is confirmed by the 1935–39 data. The ratio of males to females among all farm migrants was 109.8 to 100, but among those who migrated to the city, there were only 92.5 males to 100 females. Indeed, from 1935 to 1940 farm girls seem to have bypassed the village to a greater degree than previous studies of specific localities would have led one to expect. Among farm migrants who went to rural non-farm territory, the ratio was 112 males to 100 females. Among those farm migrants who migrated to other farms, this ratio rose to 118 to 100. This same situation existed with respect to the rural non-farm migrants. Here there were 101 male migrants to every 100 females, but of the group which went cityward there were again only 92.5 males to every 100 females. The situation here described held nationally with relatively slight variation in every region.

Age a factor. In city and country alike, it is those in the early years of their productive life who are more likely to migrate than others. Nationally about one fifth of those eighteen to twenty-four years of age moved, at least to another county, in 1948–49. With the males, however, a considerably larger proportion of the twenty to twenty-four year olds than of those eighteen and nineteen migrated. Among the females the younger group migrated in slightly larger proportion than the older and in sharply higher proportions than the males of the same age.

In the 1935–39 period the most migratory group among the farm population were the twenty to twenty-four year olds, with the twenty-five to twenty-nine year old group in second place. Each successive age group contributed fewer migrants than the one below it.

Reasons for migration. There are many reasons for migration. They vary according to age, sex, and time, and sometimes show regional variations. In the 1930's many left the farms because of low returns, high taxes, and drought. Others craved richer educational, social, and cultural opportunities. But the social scientist probes beneath these replies. His answers are that, first of all, land lost its importance as a means of livelihood, that more alluring and profitable means of subsistence were found in the cities. In 1820, agriculture, the leading American occupation, absorbed two thirds of those gainfully employed; in 1950, less than one sixth. In the intervening 120 years, manufacturing and trade surpassed agriculture in national importance; but more of this elsewhere.

Moreover, mechanization decreased the need for manpower on the farm and helped to increase the efficiency of those who remained. Indeed, many tasks, such as butter and soap-making and butchering, were transferred from farm to commercial institutions, often located in town or city. Many such impersonal factors influenced migration. Depletion of soil fertility through erosion and in other ways, discussed in another chapter, played its part also. An opportunity on the land waned, it waxed in the city.

When depression strikes, migration to cities, especially of rural youth, slackens. When industrial recovery sets in, the stream flows cityward once more.

Results of rural-urban migration. The great movement to the city had far-reaching results in both city and country. Those who left their rural homes, quite naturally, took their mental furniture with them, and the influence of the frontier lingered in their blood. Although the city liberalized them, provincialism was not entirely eradicated. Consider, for example, their churches, which remained, according to many studies by H. Paul Douglass (mentioned in another chapter), nothing but oversized country institutions. Our city school term, to take another instance, is that of the farmer, vacations coinciding with the time when the farmer's children are most needed in the fields. Our taxation system, too, is still largely of agrarian origin. If, then, there has been urbanization of the country, there has been also ruralization of the city, and that to such an extent that some authorities believe that the rural heritage is a fundamental determinant of our national psychology.

We are most concerned, however, with some of the rural results of this migration, which were in some cases unfortunate but more often beneficial if we look at the picture as a whole. If there had not been freedom of movement in the United States, if there had not been through most of the last half century economic opportunity for rural youth in an expanding urban industry, these youth would have backed up on the land. The result would have been either the growth of a class of landless farm laborers or a steady reduction in the size of farms as they were subdivided to make room for each new generation, and a lowered standard of living among the rural population, farm and non-farm alike. A further result could only have been reduced production per agricultural worker, since the smaller farms could not have afforded to apply modern technology.

The city profits. Migration has obviously contributed to the economic and social wealth of the city, both directly and indirectly. Its youth (most of the migrants were between fifteen and twenty-five) was a considerable addition to the manpower of the city, which thus obtained a horde of people whom it did not have to educate, since they had been educated in their original homes. Cities probably bore less than half the cost of educating, feeding, clothing, and providing medical service for the young men and women who went to work in their commerce and industries between 1920 and 1950. It has been estimated that in many years the cost of educating and raising the rural youth who migrated to the cities, plus the net sums that left the country for the city in the settlement of estates, often amounted to 20 per cent of the annual net farm income.[10] There are no recent comparable estimates, but even with the increased farm income of the 1940's, with the increased migration, the figure is certainly over 12 per cent. This amounts to an indirect subsidy of the city by the country and therefore lends cogency to the argument for the equalization of educational opportunity and costs by means of state or possibly Federal subsidies. This matter is discussed further in another chapter. Furthermore, the influx of so many people stimulated urban building trades and raised land values.

Of course, the growth of cities has made for a comparable increase in domestic demand for the food and other goods the farmer produces. Hence, even with respect to the effects of demographic trends, we are brought face to face with one of the key facts of American society, the interdependence of all major groups.

[10] O. E. Baker, "Rural-Urban Migration and the National Welfare," *Annals of the Association of American Geographers,* June, 1933.

TOPICS FOR DISCUSSION

1. Trace from census reports the contribution of other states to the population of your own. Do the same for the farm population.
2. Which group in your state — rural farm, rural non-farm, or urban — shows the greatest mobility? Is the balance in favor of or against your state? How do you account for this?
3. What were the causes of the rural-urban migration?
4. Select one community you know. Where have families gone who have left this community? Did they sell or rent? Who took their places? Trace young people who left when unmarried. Where did they go? Why? Education? Present occupation? Trace, if possible, the effect of these changes in population on one or two social institutions.
5. When 1950 census results are fully available, compare the 1935–39 trends with those of 1949–50.
6. Trace the moves of your family, or some family well known to you, as far back as you can. Give the motives for each major change in location.
7. Secure and analyze any studies of population mobility made by the department of rural sociology of your college of agriculture. Compare these with national or regional trends.

REFERENCE READINGS

Agricultural experiment station bulletins. Two thirds or more of the state college of agriculture experiment stations have made population studies covering trends, characteristics, and mobility — in all, well over a hundred titles. Students are urged to secure copies of these from their own or neighboring states.

Anderson, W. A., *Mobility of Rural Families.* Ithaca: Cornell Agricultural Experiment Station, June, 1934.

Annals of the American Academy of Political and Social Science, "World Population in Transition," 237, January, 1945.

Baker, O. E., "Rural Urban Migration and the National Welfare," *Annals of the Association of American Geographers,* June, 1933.

Brunner, Edmund deS., and J. H. Kolb, *Rural Social Trends,* chap. 1. New York: McGraw-Hill, 1933.

Brunner, Edmund deS., and Irving Lorge, *Rural Trends in Depression Years,* chap. III. New York: Columbia University Press, 1937.

Galpin, C. J., and T. B. Manny, *Interstate Migrations.* Washington, D. C.: United States Department of Agriculture, 1934.

Goodrich, C., B. Allen, and M. Hayes, *Migration and Economic Opportunity.* Philadelphia: University of Pennsylvania Press, 1936.

Goodrich, C., B. Allen, and M. Hayes, *Migration and Planes of Living.* Philadelphia: University of Pennsylvania Press, 1936.

Holbrook, Stewart H., *The Yankee Exodus: an Account of Migration from New England.* New York: Macmillan, 1950.

Lively, C. E., and C. Taeuber, *Rural Migration in the United States.* Washington, D. C.: Government Printing Office, 1939.

Sixteenth Census of the United States, 1940, Population; Internal Migration in the United States, Social Characteristics of Migrants, Economic Characteristics of Migrants, Age of Migrants.

Stanbury, V. B., *Migration into Oregon.* Eugene: Oregon State Planning Board, 1938.

Thompson, Warren, and P. K. Whelpton, *Population Trends in the United States,* chap. II. New York: McGraw-Hill, 1933.

FILMS

Growth of Cities. S, 11. Encyclopedia Britannica Films, Inc., Chicago.

Westward Movement. S, 11. Encyclopedia Britannica Films, Inc., Chicago.

4 Changing Patterns of Fertility, Residence, and Age

THE TWO PREVIOUS CHAPTERS have discussed the origins and distribution of our present rural population and the great migratory movements within our boundaries affecting that population. But nothing has been said of the characteristics of that population. It is to this subject that the discussion now turns.

To the uninitiated it is sometimes surprising how many important clues on the characteristics of given population groups the forbidding statistical tables of the census volumes furnish the sociologist seeking to explain social behavior. Sharp variations in divorce rates, for instance, are evidence of varying mores in regard to this moot subject. An area with a large proportion of its population under twenty-one years of age is likely to have problems and attitudes in educational matters different from those of a community or section with fewer children and more older people. Where males outnumber females in the population, the whole social situation is different from where the reverse is true. The discerning student of census reports has, then, an exciting exploration ahead when he turns to them for indications that help him either explain or discover revealing facts about people. Like many explorations, however, the way is none too easy.

Until 1930 the census had divided the population of the United States simply into rural and urban. In 1926 studies of unpublished census results proved that there were significant differences between farm and rural non-farm population groups.[1] This two-way division of rural population was adopted by the census in 1930. It disclosed that the decline in rural population which had been reported was due to the loss in the number of Negroes and foreign-born farmers and that the rural non-farm population was increasing. In fact, between 1920 and 1930 the rate of gain for this part of the rural population was 16.1 per cent, two points higher than the national rate of growth. Between 1930 and 1940 the rural non-farm population gained 14.5 per cent, double the national rate.

Comparisons are difficult to make for 1940 to 1950 because of the change in the definition of rural and urban, explained in Chapter 1. On the basis of a recent census release [2] giving urban and rural populations without dividing farm and non-farm (and giving effect to the 1940–50 decline in the farm population, also affected by changes in definition), the authors estimate a gain of about one third in the rural non-farm population as defined in 1940. Even with the change in definition, which transferred over seven and a half million persons from the rural to the urban category, there were nearly thirty million rural non-farm residents, a gain of close to 10 per cent.

The most significant fact with respect to the 1950 rural non-farm population is that

[1] Cf. C. Luther Fry, *American Villagers* (New York: Institute of Social and Religious Research, 1926).

[2] Series PC 3, No. 10, February 16, 1951.

TABLE 4	REGION	URBAN	RURAL NON–FARM	RURAL FARM
	United States	63.7	20.6	15.6
	Northeast	79.5	15.5	5.0
Per cent Distribution of Total Population by Residence and Regions, 1950 *	North Central	64.1	19.0	16.9
	South	47.8	26.3	25.8
	West	69.5	20.9	9.6

* Because of the drastic differences made by the new definition of rural and urban no comparisons over time are given.

Source: Bureau of Census Series PC–7, No. 2, April 30, 1951.

it now for the first time exceeds the rural farm population. It includes 20.6 per cent of the population of the United States, while the rural farm has 15.6 per cent. Farmers, who once were the majority in the nation, are now not even the larger portion of the rural population, having only 43.1 per cent.

The regional distribution varies widely, as Table 4 shows. It is clear also that even in the South the rural non-farm now exceeds the farm population. Up to 1940 more than half the states were more rural than urban. In 1950, using the old definition, this was true of 22; by the new definition, of 17.

That these trends will continue is shown by the census estimate of October 26, 1951, that in the year following the 1950 census and ending April, 1951, the farm population lost over a million persons and stood at 23,276,000.

Implications of rural non-farm growth. The rapid increase in the numerical and proportional importance of the rural non-farm groups compared to the farm population raises several questions. Should the schools of country, village, and town agricultural areas, for instance, expand their vocational education curriculum for boys beyond the agriculture now being offered? If this is necessary, how shall such expansion be financed? Should the extension services of the colleges of agriculture definitely plan to serve all rural people, as many are doing, instead of confining their programs to the farm population? If they do, what changes need to be made in the programs of agricultural extension services and in the training of their personnel? Will the growing coöperation of farmers and villagers in social and economic life and the increasing tendency for all rural life to be organized around villages and towns be accelerated or hindered? In either case what will be the political implications? Will the farm bloc become an all-rural bloc? Will the village, especially if industry decentralizes, throw in its lot with the city or will it become powerful by holding the balance of power, under leadership not yet developed? In view of this situation what is the best policy for the city, the state, and the nation to follow in relation to proposals affecting public policy and emanating from either or both of the great rural population groups? Should the United States Departments of Agriculture, Commerce, and possibly Labor, develop sections that would give attention to the rural non-farm aspects of their major divisions in some such way as the Department of Interior has already done in the rural section of the Office of Education?

With the growing social and economic importance of the rural farm population, to places of 2500 to 10,000 population, will such centers, at least those that are not chiefly suburban or industrial, become more or less rural in their economic and social services, their attitudes, and their sympathies in the future? If they become more rural, should the census of population change its dividing line between rural and urban from 2500 to 5000, or restore the former division at 8000, or even adopt the census-of-distribution practice of including together as "rural and small town" everything under 10,000 population? These and other similar questions are matters that will be of increasing concern in the next fifteen or twenty years. Their importance is made manifest by the census revelation of the growth of the rural non-farm, or village, population and by the research and sociological analysis, summarized in another chapter, that indicate the growing interrelationships of the rural farm and non-farm groups. Clearly, then, the fact that the rural farm and non-farm populations show varying trends is important both in itself and because of the questions it raises.

Rural farm and non-farm population contrasts. It must be remembered, however, that the rural non-farm population has no such single occupational interest as has the farm group, diverse as agriculture is. It is made up of many elements with sharply different economic backgrounds. The bulk of this population lives in incorporated non-urban centers of less than 2500. With the new definition it is certain that a larger proportion of these than ever before are agricultural villages, those whose chief function is to supply goods and services to a tributary farming population. Many of these incorporated places are hamlets of less than 250 population, described in another chapter and having only very limited functions. The next largest group of rural non-farm persons live in unincorporated centers of village

size and in unincorporated hamlets of which, on the basis of atlas place names, there are over 30,000.

Hundreds of thousands of persons reside in territory immediately adjacent to villages, towns, and small cities. They belong, to all intents and purposes, to these municipalities. Other large numbers live in the uncounted crossroads centers with fewer than twenty-five persons, too small to list in an atlas. Others are lumberjacks, tearoom and roadhouse proprietors, clergy of open-country churches, teachers, and many persons who commute to villages, towns, or cities. Some of them are part-time farmers. It will be interesting to discover in the following pages whether these differences in population groups are associated with differences in the composition of population as revealed by the census. Chapter 13 gives a more extended discussion of this situation as it affects villages. Here the purpose is simply to review the general situation as a background for the comparisons of rural farm and non-farm populations which follow.

Rural non-farm population older than farm. Not only are there sharp differences in rates of growth and diversity of location between rural farm and non-farm populations, but there are also many diversities in the make-up of their populations. Rural non-farm people are, on the average, older than those on the farms. In most age groupings above twenty years, the proportion in the total population for the rural non-farm exceeds that of the farm.

It will also be seen from Table 5 that both these rural population groups reflect the national trend of the 1940's toward an increased proportion of older people and of children. For the first time the proportion of children under five years of age in the rural non-farm population, at least in terms of the preliminary census report, now exceed that of the rural farm. Nationally there

		RURAL FARM Per Cent			RURAL NON–FARM Per Cent		
	Age Group	1920	1940	1950	1920	1940	1950
TABLE **5** Age Distribution for Rural Farm and Non-farm Population	Under 5 years	12.7	10.0	11.4	11.6	9.3	11.9
	5– 9	13.1	10.4	11.1	11.2	9.1	10.4
	10–14	12.7	11.2	10.8	10.0	9.3	8.7
	15–19	10.4	11.1	9.3	8.6	9.2	7.4
	20–24	7.9	8.3	6.3	8.4	8.6	7.2
	25–29	6.8	6.9	5.6	8.2	8.5	7.9
	30–34	6.0	6.0	6.0	7.3	7.9	7.6
	35–44	11.2	11.3	12.6	12.8	13.1	13.4
	45–54	8.9	10.4	10.8	9.4	10.5	9.8
	55–64	5.8	7.8	8.6	6.4	7.4	7.4
	65–74	3.1	4.7	5.2	4.1	5.0	5.4
	75 and over	1.3	1.9	2.3	2.0	2.3	2.9

Source: Fifteenth and Sixteenth Census of the United States, 1930 and 1940. Preliminary 1950 report, Series PC–7, No. 1, February 25, 1951.

were almost six million more youngsters under five in April, 1950, than there were ten years earlier. This means a tremendous added strain on school facilities in the period immediately ahead. Despite the great gain in the urban birth rate, this will also be a rural problem. The rural population is 36.2 per cent of the nation's total, but it contains 39.1 per cent of those under five years of age.

Perhaps the best way to indicate the differences among the three major population groups within the regions is to compare the median age of the population, which shows clearly the relative youth of the farm population in all regions but one, as follows:

The same trends operated among the Negro group until 1940 and then reversed. The median age of Negroes was younger than of whites. Between 1930 and 1940 the median age of rural non-farm Negroes rose from 23.6 to 25 years, and of the farm group from 18.6 to 19.8 years.

These figures make it easy to understand that rural adults have more children to support in proportion to their numbers than urban. The ratio of adults to those twenty years of age and under is also a rough indication of this fact. It is 172 to 100 for the cities, 125 to 100 for the rural non-farm, and 77.6 to 100 for the farm population.

Despite the large increase in the number

		URBAN	RURAL NON–FARM	RURAL FARM
TABLE **6** Median Age of Total Population by Residence and Regions, 1950	United States	31.5	27.8	26.0
	Northeast	33.0	29.6	29.9
	North Central	31.7	30.6	28.7
	South	29.4	25.1	23.3
	West	31.7	28.1	27.9

Source: Preliminary Report 1950 Census, Series PC–7, No. 3, April 30, 1951.

of children in the 1940's, the median age of the population continued to gain through the decade of the 1940's, as has been noted, though at a slower pace than from 1930 to 1940. The rural non-farm median is raised by the numbers of farmers who retire to rural villages.

Social significance of age. This aging of the population of the nation as a whole, as well as in rural America, has certain rather important implications. In census terms, at least, our young nation was built by youth. It was the adventurous and the youthful who followed the westering sun to the Pacific, who grappled with the frontier, settled and exploited the Midwest, conquered the Rockies and tamed the Far West. As a population ages, it loses some of the traits of youth. It becomes conservative, less hospitable to new ideas, and it values security above all else. An aging population amidst the problems of the postwar world may then be a disadvantage unless its normal results can be combated by adult education, which will be discussed later. The aging of the population is also responsible for interest in legislation for old-age security through pensions.

In terms of the agricultural village this picture is reduced to miniature scale. A considerable portion of the inhabitants must conserve their resources. They seek peace, not opportunity; quiet, not life. They are likely to dwell in the past. They see little necessity for change or improvement. They are frequently out of sympathy with youth. Moreover, their relative financial security and their greater leisure sometimes give them a disproportionate voice in the affairs of the community and its social organizations.

Rural farm population has more children. The lower average age among the rural farm people proves that children make up a larger share of the whole group than among the rural non-farm group. Taken together, however, these two groups, comprising our total rural population, include 42.7 per cent of the nation's children under fifteen years of age against 36.2 per cent of the total population. Put another way, less than one quarter of the urban population is under fifteen years of age, as opposed to one third of the rural farm and 30.9 per cent of the rural non-farm. This has great significance for the nation and its educational system and gives to rural education a significance often underestimated. This matter is discussed in another chapter.

During the 1930's the rural farm population produced over 160 per cent of the number of children needed to sustain this population group at the 1930–40 level. The comparable figure for the rural non-farm residents was 115 per cent. In contrast, the urban rate was less than 75 per cent. In these figures lies the proof of the familiar statement that rural America is the seedbed of the nation. Indeed, the urban deficiency in 1940 was so great that the net reproductive index for the nation was only 97 per cent. There was a spurt in the birth rate during the earlier years of the war, and although it was generally expected that the rate would decline again by a few years after the war, in harmony with a recognized trend for the last 150 years, this decline has not taken place.

The popular explanation, which undoubtedly has some validity, is that prosperity of all major occupational groups in the nation has sustained the rate. Threatening times have also been associated, historically and in many nations, with a rise in the birth rate. None the less, a measure of the decline in the first four decades of the century is important, if only to note the varying reactions of our population groups and to gain some idea of the level to which the birth rate could sink if the present behavior of the popula-

TABLE 7		1935–40			1930–35			1905–10		
		RURAL FARM	RURAL NON–FARM	URBAN	RURAL FARM	RURAL NON–FARM	URBAN	RURAL FARM	RURAL NON–FARM	URBAN
Adjusted Net Reproduction Rate by Regions and Periods	U.S.	1661	1150	726	1632	1150	747	2022	1499	937
	N.E.	1406	1035	715	1349	1049	756	1426	1439	1033
	N.C.	1452	1146	753	1425	1115	759	1834	1451	963
	South	1812	1211	712	1802	1250	742	2199	1591	764
	West	1559	1174	726	1473	1116	690	1848	1459	807

Source: *Sixteenth Census of the United States*, 1940, *Differential Fertility 1940 and 1910*, Table 7. Adjusted rate of 1000 is equivalent to the maintenance of a stationary population.

tion were reversed. For this reason Table 7 is inserted. It shows that the several regions all behaved in similar fashion in this respect. It also makes clear the necessity for rural-urban migration; the lower urban reproduction rate furnishes opportunity for "surplus" rural youth to find jobs in the cities. For the 1941–6 period the net reproduction rate for the United States was estimated by the census at 976 for cities, 1359 for rural non-farm territory, and 1928 for farm — increases over the previous five years of 34, 18, and 16 per cent respectively.[3]

The same trend is shown when a more easily calculated measure is used, the number of children under five years of age per thousand women aged fifteen to forty-nine. This comparison is given in Table 8.

[3] Bureau of the Census, *Differential Fertility: June, 1946*. Series P20, No. 8.

The data here for the two earlier periods, as in the previous table, are standardized for marital status and underenumeration. Those for 1950 are not, being based on preliminary tabulations. The pattern is the same. There are proportionately more young children in the rural farm than the rural non-farm group, and both exceed the urban population by large margins. There is also far less variation among regions in urban population than in the two rural groups. The stake of the nation, and especially of the cities, in rural children is again apparent. Yet the larger educational and health responsibilities of rural America are clear.

Negro pattern differs. The data given concern the total population. In the South a considerable proportion of the residents in both rural and urban territory are Negroes.

TABLE 8	REGION	1950			1940			1910		
		RURAL FARM	RURAL NON–FARM	URBAN	RURAL FARM	RURAL NON–FARM	URBAN	RURAL FARM	RURAL NON–FARM	URBAN
Number of Children Under 5 Years of Age per 1000 Women 15 to 49 Years Old, by Regions, 1950, 1940 and 1910	United States	525	523	383	462	344	238	623	489	357
	North-east	425	441	354	391	312	244	379	432	380
	North Central	519	457	402	398	339	238	554	466	345
	South	554	522	389	509	367	236	712	546	353
	West	485	542	406	422	338	227	557	459	297

Source: *Sixteenth Census of the United States*, 1940, *Differential Fertility, 1940 and 1910*, Table 6. Necessary to maintain stationary population, 368. 1950 data computed from preliminary census reports of the *Eighteenth Census of the United States*, Series PC–7, No. 1 and Series PC–3, No. 7.

Among the urban and rural non-farm populations of this group in 1940, the number of children under five years of age for every one thousand women fifteen to forty-nine years of age was less than for the whites. This reflected to a considerable degree the much higher infant and child mortality rate among Negroes than among whites. By 1950 Negro ratios were higher than white in all population groups, although the 1950 ratios are unstandardized and the preliminary census results show an abnormal age distribution among Negro women of childbearing age. This was undoubtedly caused by migration out of the South, especially the rural South. Preliminary 1950 census tabulations indicate that the North and West have 50 per cent more non-whites under twenty-one years of age than in 1940.

These tables record very interesting, perhaps profound, changes in the attitude of Americans in city and country alike toward the desirable number of children for a family to have. The low point of child production in the whole history of the United States was reached during the depths of the depression in the 1930's. The cities especially were falling short, some of them by more than one third, of producing enough children to sustain their populations. The net reproduction index for the nation as a whole dropped below 100. Demographic discussion was concerned with when and where the rate would stabilize. Pessimists dated the arrival of a stationary population in the United States at between 1955 and 1960. Those more hopeful and under somewhat different assumptions estimated 1975 to 1990. In terms of the steady decline in the birth rate for the previous century or more, these discussions were warranted.

It was recognized at once that World War II would interrupt this trend, but as has already been pointed out, contrary to expectations the years after the war have shown little change in fertility patterns, despite the spread of knowledge of how to space the birth of children, which was one explanation of the earlier decline in the rate, especially during the latter half of the 1920's and the 1930's. There are strong indications from the preliminary 1950 census returns and in earlier sampling studies that the rise in the birth rate in the 1940's occurred chiefly among those groups whose fertility was previously lowest, the urban, better educated, middle- and upper-income, classes. The rural South, long the region with the highest birth rates, showed smaller rates of increase. Though rural America still produces more children than urban, its lead has been reduced. What the 1950's will bring forth is a demographic puzzle of great interest.

Have youth reached peak numbers? Youth had, as a result of long-operating population trends in the United States, reached its peak of population for the age years sixteen to twenty-four in 1940, when there were about 24,000,000 persons in this age group, 1,500,000 more than in 1930. However, there were only 22,400,000 in the five-to-fourteen-years age group, over 2,000,000 less than in 1930. It is not surprising, therefore, that the 1950 census reports a decline of 13 per cent in the number of youth fifteen to nineteen years of age and over 2 per cent in the twenty-to-twenty-four-years group. The two made up 12.6 per cent of the population in 1950, as against 18.2 per cent in 1940. But this decline will be stopped after 1954 as the babies of the 1940's reach the upper teen ages. The Office of Education estimates that the low point for the eighteen-to-twenty-years group will be reached in 1953 with 6,233,000. By 1960 there will be 7,407,000, and after 1966 the number will exceed 10,000,000 by a considerable margin. Assuming the same population movements in these ages as in the five years after World War II, there will still be more rural youth of college age in that year by several hundred thousand than in the twenty to twenty-four year old division in 1950.

What may be involved in migration and for agriculture is indicated by two earlier studies. During the depression a rough proportion of two and one-half males were reaching maturity in the rural farm population for every farm made vacant by the death or retirement of the operator. The Bureau of Agricultural Economics estimated in December, 1944, that in the decade 1940 to 1950 there would normally become available only three-fifths as many farms as there would be young men reaching twenty-five years of age. In other words, the replacement ratio was 167 to 100. In every state in the South the replacement ratio was higher for whites than for Negroes, regional averages being 195 and 175 respectively. The lowest replacement ratio rates were found in the Pacific states (123) and in New England (124); higher rates were in the South Atlantic states (192) and in the East South Central states (190). In Utah and in eight southern states the rate was over 200. New Hampshire was the only state where the ratio was as low as 100. Even with the heavy demand of the armed services' for youth, there were enough youth left on farms to fill the "vacancies."[4]

Marital status. The marital status of the population also bears on the situation discussed in this chapter. The proportion of single persons fifteen years and over in the United States declined slowly for a number of decades up to 1940 and rapidly in the next decade. The proportion of males of this age unmarried in 1940 was almost one third. The preliminary 1950 census indicates that this has dropped to 26.8 per cent. Comparably, the proportion of unmarried women

[4] Conrad Taeuber, *Replacement Rates for Rural-Farm Males Aged 25 to 69 Years, by Counties, 1940–50* (mimeographed).

fifteen and over dropped from over one fourth to 20.8 per cent.

Historically, a larger proportion of women than men are married among the rural farm population than the urban, with the rural non-farm falling in between. This is due to the sharply different sex ratios. There are 109.1 males for every 100 females among the rural farm group because of the larger proportion of young women who migrate. In the city this ratio is 94.1 to 100. Indeed, for those fifteen and above, the rural farm ratio is 111.8 and the urban, 91.7. For the same reason there are proportionately fewer married men among the farm population than among the urban. As is pointed out in another chapter, the proportion of divorces among the farm population is lower than for the urban in all census divisions by one third to one half. Again, the rural non-farm falls between. This reflects the greater stability of rural families and in some areas a more conservative attitude toward divorce.

Rural population more homogeneous. Another significant characteristic of the rural population is its greater homogeneity as compared with the urban. Only 2.4 per cent of the rural farm population were foreign-born in 1950 as against 3.6 in 1940. Comparably, the proportion in the rural non-farm population dropped to 3.5 from 5.5 per cent. The urban proportion was 6.4. Cities contained slightly more than five sixths of the foreign-born in 1950. The farm foreign-born come largely from northern Europe, have been in this country a considerable time, and are therefore well assimilated into American life. Rural America, except for some industrial villages and a few neighborhoods in the Northeast, has no counterpart to the Little Italys, the Ghettoes, and the similar foreign communities of the cities. Therefore, its social organization and political life is less divided by racial lines than is the case in cities.

The Negro. In the South the Negro is an important element in the rural population, although he is seldom foreign-born. In 1940 more than one half of the nearly 13,000,000 Negroes were rural, and approximately half of these were on farms. By 1950 the effect of the migration of Negroes to the North and West and to southern cities was startlingly evident: of the less than 15,000,000 Negroes, only 34.7 per cent were rural. Of these the great majority were still in the South, migration to other regions having been largely to cities. Of the 5,400,000 rural southern Negroes in 1950, 57.7 per cent were on farms. They comprised, as they did in 1940, about a fourth of the South's population.

In this region the Negro population is more separate in its social organizations than are the foreign-born in the cities. They have their own schools, churches, and social organizations. Space is lacking to analyze in any detail the census records for this one race, but such an analysis would show somewhat distinctive population characteristics, a few of which run counter to popular supposition; it would record a great cityward and northward migration; and it would reveal the struggle of the Negro toward security through landownership and his disproportionately crushing losses of the depression as well as the steady building up of a business and professional group from his own race to serve his own people. In comparison with the social and economic institutions of the white race in the South, those of the rural Negro appear poor and inadequate, though there has been marked improvement, especially during the 1940's. In view of the status of the Negro eighty years ago, the progress has been indeed considerable.

To summarize, the farm population, then, as compared to other groups, has proportionately more children, more males, more single men, fewer single women, and more homogeneity.

TOPICS FOR DISCUSSION

1. Compare the growth or decline since 1920 of the urban, the total rural, and the rural farm and non-farm population in your state. Account for the results you discover. (*United States Census of Population*, 1950, 1940, and 1930, State Tables.)
2. Make a list of the states and census regions which have gained and of those which have lost farm population since 1920. Explain.
3. Make a simple chart showing the proportion of farm, of village, and of urban population in each of the following age groups: under 15 years; 15 to 44 years; 45 years and over.
4. Discuss two or three important social implications of age and sex distribution, first of farm and second of village population as contrasted with urban.
5. Compare net reproduction rates and number of children born to women 15 to 49 years old for rural farm, rural non-farm, and urban groups in your state or region. (See census references under Reference Readings.)
6. Trace the trends in size of farm families by census regions, states, or counties and explain this trend.

REFERENCE READINGS

Anderson, W. A., *Population Trends in New York State, 1900–1940*. Ithaca: Cornell Agricultural Experiment Station, 1942.

Brunner, Edmund deS., and J. H. Kolb, *Rural Social Trends*. New York: McGraw-Hill, 1933.

Clark, C. D., and R. L. Roberts, *People of Kansas*. Topeka: State Planning Board, 1937.

Fry, C. L., *American Villagers*. New York: Harper, 1926.

Mangus, A. R., *Rural Children and Youth in Ohio*. Ohio Agricultural Experiment Station, Columbus, 1945 (mimeographed).

Sixteenth Census of the United States, 1940, Population, vol. 4, *Characteristics by Age*, Part I, U. S. summary, 1940. Comparable data from *Seventeenth Census, 1950* (forthcoming).

Thompson, W., and P. K. Whelpton, *Population Trends of the United States*, chaps. I, X, XI. New York: McGraw-Hill, 1933.

United States Census, *Differential Fertility 1940 and 1910* (2 vols.), Washington, 1943 and 1944.

Vance, Rupert B., *All These People: The Nation's Human Resources in the South*. Chapel Hill: University of North Carolina Press, 1945.

See also population sections of any standard rural sociology and population censuses of the United States, especially 1920, 1930, and 1940.

Population studies by departments of rural sociology in state colleges of agriculture will be especially valuable. See note under Reference Readings for previous chapter.

5 Psychological Characteristics of Rural People

Because of the popular feeling, among city people at least, that rural people are in some way inferior to or at least different from their city cousins, it might be pertinent at this point to inquire into the matter of rural and urban psychological characteristics. First, scientific data now existing with regard to this question will be analyzed and second, certain matters of common observation will be presented.

That the rural population is in a measure distinct from the urban has been reiterated in this book; but the distinction has been almost entirely from the point of view of economic and social relations. This chapter will try to focus attention on psychological aspects of the differences between the farmer and the villager, and between them both and the city resident.

Conditions make such comparisons difficult. It is important at the outset to warn against pitfalls of such a discussion. American culture in the present century has shown a steady progress toward standardization. As a result of the amazing achievements in the fields of transportation and communication, the continent has been narrowed to the extent that the Pacific is now only a few hours away from the Atlantic by plane, and a radio broadcast can be heard simultaneously in California and on the East Coast. Time has been annihilated and space diminished. Both rural and urban people are responding to a greater number of stimuli than ever before. They listen to the same coast-to-coast broadcasts, ride in the same automobiles, witness the same movies, have the same advertisement thrust at them in their daily papers, from billboards, and from barn and store walls. They eat the same breakfast food, buy the same coffee, smoke the same cigarettes, and what is more, wear clothes of the same cut and style. There is now no cleavage in much of the United States between the provincial and the urbanite such as there still is in any European country.

In the matter of language, our dialects have tended to run together, so that the rustic and the sophisticate, Westerner and Easterner, not only as a rule read the same literature but understand each other readily. Contrast with this a pocket-sized country like England, or a larger one like Germany, where the man from the North understands with difficulty the man from the South, and where the provincial with his peculiar dialect often speaks what amounts almost to a foreign language in the ears of the townsman. The chasm between rural and urban in more backward countries like Hungary and Italy is even wider: there the peasant affects a particular mode of dress, speaks a dialect distinct from that of the city, and the amenities of his daily life are far removed from those of his town or city cousin.

Are Americans all alike? In a democratic country such as ours the tendency has always been toward a leveling of all classes, a fact which is proved by the usual taunt thrown at America by visitors when they say, "Your land is all alike. Every town is like the next.

Every Main Street resembles every other Main Street." Far from being a taunt, this statement is an illustration of the fact that we have leveled out at least the material aspects of our civilization; our towns, villages, and cities are alike — the town is only the village multiplied, and the city is only an expanded town — because we have spread the good things of life to a great extent all over the country. For example, concrete roads and widespread use of electricity, to mention only the most obvious instruments of civilization, penetrate most rural areas as well as cities. All classes, the pauper who accepts relief in the crowded tenement, and sometimes the farmer as well, may enjoy central heat, inside plumbing, and running water.

Similarities apparent. Our enormous natural resources and relative prosperity have tended to equalize the rural and urban, so that no longer is the distinction as clear-cut as in the days of William Dean Howells or Mark Twain, whose uncivilized country types are now remote and antiquated. If you read a novel of farm life like *As the Earth Turns*, which depicts the process of assimilation of foreign-born farmers in so Americanized a section as New England, you are at once aware of the amazing equalization of our racial and economic groups, and you notice especially how much our farmers, particularly the younger ones, resemble our city residents. Their scheme of life duplicates, more than is possible in other lands, that of their city relatives. They do the same things — go to the same kind of dances and parties, indulge in the same social games, and conduct their domestic or commercial affairs in much the same fashion as the townsman, villager, or cityman.

The chief reasons for *rapprochement* between the urban and rural, as before intimated, are our educational system, our facilities for communication and transportation, and the mobility of our population. Our country schools follow the lead of our city schools and disseminate generally the same type of education; even many of their extracurricular activities are similar. Our newspapers tend to print the same news in city and country — a major scandal receives the same exaggerated treatment in the paper of Centre City as in the New York dailies. Again, the farmer's son goes to the city, acquires some of its veneer, and when he returns for a visit or protracted stay, leaves some of it with his family. In what ways, then, are rural and urban psychological characteristics different?

In spite of these centripetal forces of standardization, certain attitudes and qualities peculiar to rural people have not yet been ironed out nor, perhaps, will they ever be. Although the appellation "farmer" no longer has the same precise, almost contemptuous meaning it had fifty years ago, when the heroes of all rustic novels ran off to the city to get rid of their opprobrious characteristics, the word still stands for more than an occupational group. Certain behavior patterns more characteristic of farmers than others have remained, and as we shall indicate, some of them are admirable.

Measuring Rural Intelligence

Many psychologists have attempted to prove that there is a visible objective difference between the rural and the urban mind. They conducted numerous studies in the earlier days of the testing movement to bring out the fact that the native intelligence of the country resident not only differs from, but tends to be inferior to, that of the cityman. These investigations are fraught with so many dangers — since intelligence is one of the most difficult of all human characteristics to isolate — that we must study the results with great care and try to indicate wherein they are fallacious. In later years interest in this problem has died down. *Psychological Abstracts* records no recent significant studies.

Defining intelligence. Probably few persons under twenty-one in this country have escaped having their intelligence measured. Tests purporting to do this have been printed and used by the million in our public and private schools, colleges, and universities. The result has been that the I.Q., the intelligence quotient, has become one of the most widely used scientific terms. From this the reader might infer that doubtless the psychologists have discovered an infallible technique for the precise evaluation of each individual's intelligence. But such a conclusion should be held in abeyance until the psychologists are better able to isolate and define *intelligence*.

Strange as it may seem, some textbooks devote enormous space to intelligence testing and its results without defining intelligence. Others remark that there are different kinds of intelligence, such as social and intellectual and mechanical, and give theories about and criteria for judging intelligence.[1] Some admit that intelligence is not easily defined and attempt several definitions, as Dashiell does.[2]

Psychologists themselves are beginning to recognize the dilemma. George Stoddard in 1942, writing of "New Light on Intelligence," [3] pointed to the evidence, now indisputable, that the I.Q. score can change and can differentiate between "potentiality and actual delivered power." It is only the latter that can be measured. Doctor J. L. Anderson's presidential address for the 1944 meeting of the American Psychological Association stressed the importance of knowing the environment of the subjects of psychological studies, its quality, force and uniformity, and to what extent the subject had reacted or responded to it.

Sociologists, who have to deal with people in the mass, and who must take account of individual intelligence and try to apprehend group intelligence as well, will perhaps prefer the simple and workable definition of Sorokin and Zimmerman: "Intelligence is that combination of mental factors which the individual is supposed to use in achieving some aim or goal in life or the ability to adjust himself adequately to a new situation." [4] They point out that there is disagreement as to the respective contributions of inherited and environmental factors in intelligence, and conclude that "it is probably a composition of the two certain innate abilities polished by the environments both mental and social." In essence, the best definition of intelligence is that it is the ability to learn.

Beyond question, the results of so-called intelligence tests, have a high correlation with school achievement and with certain types of success in life, although, of course, this correlation can be interpreted to mean either that the tests simply measure school achievement in a different way or that intelligence is responsible for the scores made in both tests and school subjects. But though of great practical value in the schools, they are far from infallible in all cases. Our concern with them is to discover what they reveal when rural and urban people are compared.

Prerequisites for comparative testing. In

---

[1] Cf., for instance, W. C. Trow, *Educational Psychology* (Boston: Houghton Mifflin, 1931), pp. 137ff.

[2] *Fundamentals of General Psychology* (Boston: Houghton Mifflin, 1937), p. 342. Dashiell's conclusion is eminently worth remembering: "*That* the methods of examination [of intelligence] get at some ability has been abundantly shown, even if *what* they get at remains in doubt. The ability can be isolated in fact if not in words. And, in any case, there is some point to the claim that 'measurements should precede definition.' "

[3] *Proceedings Iowa Academy of Science*, XLIX, 51–60.

[4] *Principles of Rural-Urban Sociology* (New York: Holt, 1929), Part III, p. 234.

order to attain some degree of accuracy in measuring two groups, it is necessary to equalize as many factors as possible and reduce the number of variables, some of which, considering that the subjects are usually children, are chronological age, social and economic status, environment, language, amount and type of schooling, size of family and order of subject's birth, and occupations of parents. For instance, a comparison of rural and urban intelligence based on New York City school children and the children in an all rural county in Mississippi introduces many more variables than a comparison of these rural children with the children of Jackson, Mississippi's largest city. In other words, scores obtained in these tests are largely invalidated for purposes of group comparison when the environment of any one group varies sharply from that of the other. This seems self-evident, but has often been overlooked, especially in some of the earlier attempts to compare rural and urban intelligence.

Rural and urban intelligence test scores compared. Most of the studies have been carried on with school children, both because measurements are of great value to the schools in the general study of their students, in many problems of grading, program guidance, and adjustment, and because the younger the subject, the more pristine his intelligence and the less he is likely to be influenced by variable environmental factors.

In the twelve or fifteen years prior to 1929, about forty such studies were made — important because of the standing of their authors, the techniques they used, or the results obtained — in which the intelligence of rural people, almost exclusively children, was measured and compared with similar urban scores. More than two thirds of these tests placed rural children below urban, and a large majority of the investigators believe that the difference is a measure of difference in the native ability or intelligence of the two groups, a difference many of them explain by the assumption that the rural-urban migration deprived the country of many of its more intelligent children. In view of the huge size of the rural-urban migration, to say nothing of its causes and consequences, discussed in preceding chapters, this is a vulnerable assumption. When we examine it critically, a number of questions arise which, in the judgment of the authors, seem to throw doubt on, if they do not entirely vitiate, the conclusions of those psychologists who claim that there are innate differences between rural and urban intelligence.

What is rural and urban? It is shown in Part III of this text that rural and urban are no longer clear-cut divisions. Rural characteristics vary markedly according to distance from the city, as measured by concentric tiers of counties. Furthermore, during the periods of high migration, if the assumption that only the superior migrate to the city were true, the inclusion of such migrants of school age would distort the urban results wherever many of these former rural children were present. Strictly speaking, the latter should have been separated from older residents in scoring tests. Such a procedure was actually followed in a small Iowa city by Hornell Hart, who procured a difference of $2.3 \pm .6$ in the score of 248 children from farms compared with 447 from the city. This difference may have been influenced by several variables. Nothing is known of the reasons why the families of these rural children moved to town. If they migrated in order to get better educational opportunities, the chief variable would then be the type of school from which the farm children came. But they may have migrated also because of their failure on the farm, in which case another important variable would be introduced, rendering the difference of 2.3 of little significance in the main problem of determining whether, as a generality, rural children are inferior in intelligence to urban children.●

Moreover, some psychologists have no adequate definition of the terms rural and urban. One study counted all places over 1000 population as urban, although in places up to 10,000 there is a considerable proportion of open-country children in village and town schools, as a later chapter shows. In several other studies, places of from 2000 to 3400 were included in the urban category. This confusion of terms results in the introduction of varying proportions of farm children in urban enrollment and invalidates the results for comparative purposes.

Importance of homogeneity. An important factor in group intelligence testing is that of homogeneity. The rural farm population, having relatively few foreign-born, few Negroes except in the South, and hardly any Orientals except in California, is far more homogeneous than the urban population in general. This homogeneity extends in great measure even to the rural non-farm element, which can be classified in fewer occupational groups than urban workers. The meaning of all this is that stimuli arising from such variables as environment and occupation are less diversified among rural than urban children. As will be shown later, however, the urban population undoubtedly contains more persons of distinction than the rural.

Influence of occupation. When tests are given in bona fide rural and especially open-country schools, the comparison with urban scores resolves itself into a comparison of the children of one or a few occupational groups with those whose parents belong to many occupational groups. Perhaps the fairest and most scientific method would be to divide both rural and urban children according to the occupations of their fathers, comparing, for example, the offspring of farmers with those of laborers, professional men, and so on. But even such a separation would not get rid of the fact that a majority of rural and urban test scores do not take into account differences in the efficiency of the schools attended by the children of both groups, as well as differences in experience and cultural opportunity.

Differences in schooling. For example, the urban school term, as noted in another chapter, is somewhat longer than the rural. Urban teachers are older, more experienced, and better trained than rural. It seems quite likely that these phenomena influence intelligence test scores even when, within the rural group, one-room and consolidated schools are compared. Such variations in educational opportunity clearly affected the measurements in the study conducted by Baldwin, Filmore, and Hadley, who gave the Stanford-Binet Test to 253 children in one-room schools and to 425 of comparable age in consolidated schools with the following results: [5]

		Percentage		
		Below		Above
	I.Q.	Av.	Av.	Av.
1 room school	91.7	.43	.47	.10
Consolidated	99.4	.23	.54	.23

The authors' commentary follows:

The differences between the main I.Q.'s on the first examination of the one-room and consolidated school children, analyzed statistically by age groups, six to fourteen inclusive, are found to be significant at all ages except seven and eight. This likeness among the school children continues the similarity found among the pre-school children at all ages in the two communities and suggests that rural children are much alike in the pre-school and early school years, but with the advance in age some in-

[5] *Farm Children* (New York: Appleton-Century-Crofts, 1930), pp. 238ff.

fluence that produces differences begins to operate . . .

It is obvious that there are a number of variables at work here and that differences in scores cannot safely be attributed to the single factor of intelligence. This agrees with the conclusion of a study of nearly five thousand rural children located in two eastern and two middle western states.[6]

Environment influential. If this conclusion is sound when rural children are measured and compared according to type of schooling, it seems clear that when rural and urban groups are compared, the variables are multiplied and the difficulty of measuring intelligence increases. But since, as indicated, environment begins to become increasingly important with age, some clue to the solution of the problem may be had by measuring children of a younger age. Acting on this assumption, the Iowa Child Welfare Research Station tested seventy-two rural and seventy-two city babies matched for chronological age. No significant difference was found in the results, but on these tests there were five subtests in which rural children succeeded earlier than city children, and seven subtests in which city children succeeded earlier than those living on farms.[7] The authors of this exhaustive study conclude that at no age do rural children in one community differ strikingly from those of another or from the general mental level, while rural and urban children seem to be equal in intelligence until the age of five.[8] This suggests a bias in those cognate tests of children of a higher age level where differences between rural and urban develop.

Testing experiences. On the whole, intelligence tests often measure acquaintanceship with types of experience which are more largely urban than rural,[9] and with, on the whole, book knowledge rather than experience. The alleged inferiority of any group over another may, therefore, perhaps be laid to the instruments used in testing rather than to any innate differences in the groups themselves. This conclusion was reached by M. E. Shimberg, who conducted an *Investigation into the Validity of Norms with Special Reference to Urban and Rural Groups,* in which two information tests, *A* scaled to the experience of rural children and *B* to that of urban children, were taken by both rural and urban subjects. Some questions overlapped. On the urban-scaled test, rural children, as compared with urban, were about one year retarded; on the rural-scaled test, the opposite situation was found. The author concludes:

Test *A* is more specialized in favor of rural children than Test *B* (or any standard test) which is specialized in favor of the urban children.

From the same analysis we produced evidence that questions "fair" to a certain group cannot be selected *a priori.* This was also affirmed by submitting our questions to fourteen rural superintendents who, despite their unusually rich experience, were unable to designate correctly (in a fairly large percentage of the cases) which questions favored the rural children.

An analysis of current standard group tests shows that a large part of the material required is informational in character. So, our results may be said to have some application outside the narrow sphere of individual information tests.[10]

[6] Cf. Edmund deS. Brunner, *Immigrant Farmers and Their Children* (New York: Harper, 1929), chap. III.

[7] Baldwin, Filmore, and Hadley, *op. cit.,* pp. 233–234.

[8] *Ibid.,* pp. 234–238.

[9] An interesting case of bias comes from a test made by a university in a fishing village known to the authors. Among others, the word-association technique was used. Following the word *rain* the pupil was supposed to write *umbrella.* Practically all put down instead the word *slicker,* signifying oilskins, which offer almost complete protection from wet weather. This reply was scored wrong.

[10] For a full report of this study see *The Archives of Psychology,* XVI, Nos. 99–104, chap. VII.

Some of the items in the rural test follow:

Name the young of the sheep, cow, horse.

Name *three* states in the United States where cotton is raised.

Why is it necessary to limit the hunting season?

In what part of the day are the shadows longest?

How can you tell poison ivy by looking at it?

How many pecks are there in a bushel?

Of what use are insects to flowers?

Name *five* wild flowers.

Why does seasoned wood burn more easily than green wood?

Tell one way of finding the age of a tree.

From what does maple sugar come?

Name *two* birds that stay North in the winter.

How can you keep milk from souring?

Give one reason for the rotation of crops.

Name *five* crops.

What kind of dairy cow gives the richest milk?

Why are crops hoed?

Name *two* differences between the barks of birch and oak trees.

The Army tests. It is necessary to consider the Army tests of World War I in passing because they have often been used to support the contention of the backwardness of rural intelligence. These tests have unfortunately been misused in many ways by scientific popularizers ever since their publication. The Army tests were narrowed to a search for prospective officers. Farmers rated "low average" on them, while officers of the engineering corps, with just such a background as the tests would favor, rated highest with a classification of "very superior intelligence," an inevitable conclusion. Moreover, probably the less efficient farmers and farm laborers took the test in disproportionate numbers, since most of the owners and tenants were exempted from the draft in order to raise food.

School paces. There have been numerous studies, for both scientific and practical pur-

poses, of retardation and acceleration among school children which show that there is somewhat more retardation in rural than in urban schools. This, however, contributes little or nothing to solving the problem of differences in rural and urban intelligence. It simply shows that conditions well known to be handicapping many rural schools, such as lower average attendance chargeable to weather, short terms, ungraded classes, poorly trained teachers, and other things described in another chapter, tend to retard rural pupils.

Achievement scores. For the reasons mentioned above, grade achievement in rural schools usually lags behind that of the city in some of the traditional subjects by as much as a year or a year and a half. This has been proved by numerous studies, but again it casts no reflection on rural intelligence *per se.* Progress made even in numerous one-room schools under the best conditions and methods, gains of two or three years in a single school year, as shown in another chapter, are sufficient reproof to those who blame rural intelligence for retardation rather than inferior schools.

This discussion of tests has been extended, for many people have only a vague conception of the subject because of the incompleteness of these early studies. But what of more recent studies? To answer this question, all studies bearing on the subject of rural-urban intelligence listed in *Psychological Abstracts* from 1940 to early 1950 were examined. It would appear that the methodology used was more refined than that of earlier studies, but still the results are inconclusive, as perhaps should be expected. In several studies there were positive, but very low, correlations between intelligence and size of community of residence. The authors give as explanation the interpretations stated earlier in the discussion. Other studies, such as the one by Dr.

D. S. Oberlin, based on general information possessed by Delaware school children,[11] find no significant differences between rural and urban children.

In this connection an extensive urban study is important. In 1922 Professor E. L. Thorndike of Teachers College, Columbia University, began a study of nearly nine hundred boys who graduated from the eighth grade of New York City schools in that year. These same boys have coöperated in frequent periodic follow-up studies for twenty years. Among other significant findings, the check included a subgroup of individuals with I.Q.'s approximately equal in 1922. Of this group, those who never went beyond the tenth grade of schooling scored 103 in 1943. Those who completed the junior year of college or better scored 115. Education apparently made the difference, not in the innate ability of the individuals, but in the release and use of those abilities.[12]

A recent approach. One important study bearing on this point, while it does not concern rural-urban comparisons at all, raises serious questions as to the validity of the ten most widely used tests of "intelligence," and for essentially the same reasons that the authors of this text question them. The study in question was made under the auspices of the Committee on Human Development of the University of Chicago.[13] It was concerned with a comparison of children of "higher" and "lower" occupational groups, the latter including many children of foreign background and Negroes. On the basis of standard tests children of higher occupational groups made much the higher scores. But experiences encountered in the field studies dealing with these same children raised questions. It was found that the higher scores of the "superior" group were associated with the type of vocabulary used in the tests and the stronger motivation with respect to them.

A new test was therefore devised dealing "with experiences about equally common in all occupational groups of American children . . . phrased in words and pictures equally common in the social environment of all groups." This test had ten sections, some of which involved understanding physical principles, memory processes, drawing inferences from given relationships, perception and description, discrimination, critical process, and general inductive and deductive reasoning.

The authors summarize their results thus:

Although the lower occupational white group was on average nearly eight I.Q. points below the upper occupational white group, the high occupational group showed definitely superior performance on only one of the nineteen problems used, while the lower occupational group showed small but consistent advantage on three. On the test as a whole the lower socio-economic white group earned slightly higher average scores at age 6, and equalled the performance of the upper socio-economic white group at each of the other three ages. A lower socio-economic Negro group, which averaged nearly twenty I.Q. points below the high occupational white group, equalled the performance of the high occupational white on seven . . . and at ages six and seven on ten . . . of the nineteen items.

The present discussion is not meant to indicate that rural children are more intelligent than urban, but that accepted measurements of intelligence by achievement tests underrate the average mental ability of rural and especially farm children and that, therefore, to conclude from these tests that rural children are innately inferior to urban is wholly

[11] *Delaware State Medical Journal,* XIII (1941), 133–135.

[12] Cf. Irving Lorge, "Schooling Makes a Difference," *Teachers College Record,* May, 1945, pp. 483–492.

[13] This study is reported on in preliminary fashion by Dr. Allison Davis and Dr. Robert Hess in the *National Education Association Journal,* November, 1949.

IRRIGATION *Top*: Turning the Valve which Controls a Pond Constructed for Recreation, Wildlife, Fish, and Irrigation, Washington. *Bottom*: A Potato Field, Utah. (U.S.D.A., top photograph by Swartz, bottom by Ackerman)

Top: Abandoned and Eroded Farm, Oklahoma (Standard Oil Co., N.J.). *Bottom*: Contour Strips, Pennsylvania (Soil Conservation Service, U.S. Dept. of Agriculture)

Top: Contoured and Irrigated Potato Field, Idaho. *Bottom*: Flood Control and Recreation Reservoir in Thickly Populated Area of Ohio (U.S. Dept. of Agriculture)

Top: Transporting Migrant Labor. *Center*: Migrant Farm Labor Camp. *Bottom*: Farm Labor Exchange. (U.S. Dept. of Agriculture)

unwarranted, especially in view of the proven equality between rural and urban children of preschool age.

The testimony of Who's Who. A number of investigators have studied the biographies of distinguished Americans as presented in *Who's Who in America* to determine whether rural areas are producing their share of eminent figures.[14] The conclusion has been that the city has given birth to a disproportionate number of talented people: Visher, taking 1870 as the nearest census year to the birth of persons listed in *Who's Who* for 1922–23, found that cities, towns, and villages had 30 per cent of the population but contributed 74.1 per cent of the celebrities. The rest were born on farms.

This fact is interesting and valuable as far as it goes, but it contributes little to the problem of separating urban and rural intelligence. *Who's Who* inevitably selects those whose type of achievement puts them in the public eye, and perhaps specifically the eye of the urban public. For example, a middle western farmer who developed a new, highly valuable, and much used variety of corn, who has been an officer of one of the largest state farmers' organizations and is prominent in his state, was not listed in *Who's Who* for 1922–23. Many similar examples could be produced from a perusal of *RUS* — the rural *Who's Who*.[15] It seems safe to conclude with the eminent psychologist, Professor E. L. Thorndike, "That cities give birth to an undue proportion of great

men does not in the least prove that city life made them great; it may prove that cities attract and retain great men, whose sons are thus city born."

The whole problem of innate mental capacity, as we have attempted to suggest, is shrouded in mist. Trustworthy evidence has not yet been produced to prove that rural and urban people have marked differences of cerebral ability; where such differences ostensibly appear they can be traced to environmental and particularly to occupational sources, to acquired rather than inherited attitudes and thought patterns.

If this be true, it is time to turn to the second phase of our problem and seek to discover in what respect, despite the cyclopean forces for standardization and equalization in America, rural and urban people differ, and deduce the social significances of such variations. Precise terminology cannot be used in such a discussion, for social psychology is in its infancy, and wholly adequate group measuring tools have not been forged.

Attitudes of Rural People

At the outset it must be recognized that an analysis of rural traits is difficult not only because of the paucity of reliable studies in the field, but also because in few other realms is generalization in terms of all rural people more dangerous. The truck farmer of the eastern states, for example, is in frequent and often daily contact with storekeepers, middlemen, and commission merchants, transports his perishable produce daily by automobile, and cultivates acres intensively. His experience is quite different from that of the wheat-grower, whose single, nonperishable crop comes slowly to maturity, who handles it by machine and not by hand, sells it in one or at most a few transactions, ships it by railroad, and rarely comes into close contact with the whole machinery

[14] Cf. especially, C. R. White, "The Cityward Drift of Population in Relation to Social Efficiency," *Journal of Social Forces*, November, 1923; S. S. Visher, "A Study of the Place of Birth and of the Occupation of Fathers of Subjects of Sketches in *Who's Who in America*," *American Journal of Sociology*, March, 1925; and J. McK. Cattell, "The Distribution of American Men of Science," *Science*, XXIV, 658–665, 699–707, 732–742; XXXII, 633–648.

[15] Compiled by L. H. and E. Z. Bailey (Ithaca, New York, 1930).

of marketing. Both of these persons have widely different experiences from the southern Highlander, who coaxes a precarious existence from his rocky hillside, consuming much of what he raises and selling little, and whose contacts with the "outside" are few and far between. Thus we see that the attitudes and many of the traits of these types would vary almost as much as their economic experiences; yet all are farmers.

The investigator who knew only the last type might announce that farmers are highly individualistic, and in terms of his experience he might be correct. The investigator whose experience was limited to the citrus-fruit growers of Southern California would, on the other hand, conclude that farmers were highly coöperative.

Such differences in the experience of farmers show clearly in their attitudes on public questions. The support of prices of cereals entering into poultry feed was often denounced by eastern poultrymen in the latter half of the 1940's. Some local farm organizations in New England during World War II passed resolutions asking Congress to import beef from the Argentine Republic, but the cattlemen of the mountain states were and are bitterly opposed to any such proposal.

Sharp differences occur even within a single state. In the spring of 1950 the Ohio Farm Bureau Federation conducted a poll among its members on questions related to national agricultural policy. Thirty per cent felt that there should be no government price guarantee. Others, in almost equal proportions, wanted the Brannan or a similar plan, flexible price supports depending on supply and production costs, or price support to prevent farm income from reaching depression levels.

In any study of rural attitudes case histories are illuminating. The farmer who declared in 1924, when asked to join a flourishing coöperative, "I'll be blanked if any-body's going to tell me when to sell my berries," was voicing the virile individualism that had characterized his forebears for three centuries in their struggle against the wilderness and the sea. The same man, when he capitulated to the coöperative in 1934, had changed none of his innate, inherited characteristics. He was simply bowing to experience. Certainly part of the equipment of the rural sociologist, teacher, or social servant should be to understand the motives and histories of the traditions and attitudes he seeks to change.

Some attitudes measurable. Effort to reduce general observations about rural psychological traits to some factual basis are proving to be significant. Thus in his *Experience Worlds of Southern Mountain People*,[16] Taylor Matthews showed clearly that there were differences in attitudes, knowledge, and experience between those in the village center and those in more isolated pockets of the valleys leading into the villages. Leland Stott's interesting findings in his *Personality Development in Farm, Small-Town and City Children*,[17] are based on careful research procedures. One important observation follows:

The farm home setting appeared at a disadvantage in the area of social relationships. Two of the personality variables, namely, resourcefulness in group situations and ethical judgment, had particularly to do with facility and discrimination in social relationships. The farm group ranked lowest in both of these variables. The city and town groups averaged about equally but both were significantly superior to the farm group. These differences, however, were almost wholly contributed by the girls.

16 (New York: Teachers College Bureau of Publications, 1927). Cf. also James E. Montgomery, "Three Southern Appalachian Communities: An Analysis of Cultural Variables," *Rural Sociology*, June 1949, pp. 138–148.

17 (Lincoln, Nebraska: Agricultural Experiment Station, 1939).

Anderson has also been studying the opinions of high school youth, university women, and adult rural residents, both farm and non-farm, on the values of rural living.[18] This study included both city and rural youth and involved reactions on a five-point scale, from strongly favorable to strongly unfavorable, to 143 value statements. The results are too detailed to summarize. Many would be expected. Rural youth were more favorable to rural life than were urban. Rural boys were slightly more favorable than girls. Retired farmers were more favorable than any other group.

This underlines one important fact. Whether the study relates to public issues or to the values of rural life, the discovery of declared opinions is only a first step. It may define the educational problem for those who seek to change opinions or attitudes, but it does not answer the question of how to do this. This question cannot be answered until it is known why people think as they do or hold the values they assert. To find this out involves an examination of cultural heritages, experiences, and beliefs. For instance, in the Ohio poll referred to earlier, were those who favored something like the Brannan plan the county committeemen of the Production and Marketing Administration of the United States Department of Agriculture? Were those who favored no supports large-scale, debt-free farmers? Were those who simply wanted to prevent a recurrence of the depression conditions the ones who had suffered most in the dark years of 1930–33? How far were the results of this poll influenced by the types of farming in which the respondents engaged?

Effects of different types of farming. It is possible to trace from the behavior of groups of farmers over periods of years

changes in attitude, at least in regard to agriculture itself. The traditional American farm was once as self-sufficient as it could be made, but now in many parts of the country a single money crop is the main objective. The change has produced attitudes largely unknown before. It has converted the farmer into something of a speculator and mercantilist. He acquires attitudes which sometimes begin to color other types of behavior. Diversification of money crops in turn brings other experiences. It is possible that types of agriculture are related to temperamental qualities in those they attract.

Despite new material on attitudes the samples used, contrasted with the size of the total farm population, are so small that he is a brave man indeed who declares, "Thus the American farmer thinks." We know that there are factors in the farmer's occupation which influence his behavior and attitudes. This is inevitable, and the same principle holds true for all other groups.

Influence of weather. There is also a possible relation between weather or climate, which plays so large a part in agricultural life, and the temperament or philosophy of those who till the soil. Perhaps this is one reason why the peasants of such countries as China and India appear fatalistic in some of their attitudes. Again, agrarian life, which is linked so closely to the primal mysteries of Nature, of wind and weather, sky-changes and earth-changes, tends to bring out man's primordial instincts, his superstitiousness and leaning toward the supernatural. Perhaps that is why in some regions of the United States rural people are more religious and orthodox than city dwellers. It may also explain the lack of enthusiasm which the less informed farmer often evinces for scientific methods: he knows that capricious Nature too frequently upsets the best-laid plans of men.

[18] W. A. Anderson, *A Study of the Values in Rural Living*, Part II. (Ithaca: Cornell University Agricultural Experiment Station, 1949).

Coöperative attitudes. The American farmer has often been described as highly individualistic; yet now, as will be shown in another chapter, a majority of commercial farmers are members of coöperatives and considerable percentages of all farm products sold are marketed coöperatively. If such a record had been achieved by industry, perhaps the "coöperative commonwealth" and the "new social order" of some of our social prophets would be nearer than they seem. The great progress of agricultural coöperation since 1915 certainly represents a marked change in attitude, a process in which it is possible to detect some of the formative elements. There was originally resentment against middlemen and processors, a tendency to unite against their menace, a growing understanding of the weaknesses of old marketing procedures. Then came organization and education by leaders to stir the great mass of unaroused farmers. Time was given, though sometimes not enough, to effect necessary modifications in the old, stubbornly persisting individualism. But the sense of need for collective action grew. Those with common interests, such as citrus-fruit, apple, milk, and butter producers, were the first to capitulate; and the success of these and of movements toward combination among employers and laboring men in industry accelerated the general coöperative movement, which although it still leaves much to be desired, is an excellent illustration of how attitudes are changed and how alleged rural resistance to change was overcome by rural people themselves, frequently against outside opposition.

Religious attitudes. There appear to be certain distinctive rural religious attitudes, such as the orthodoxy just alluded to, though again generalization is dangerous. While rural church members are doubtless more orthodox than urban, this probably holds true only within certain regions. Judging by indirect evidence only, the rural people of the Pacific Coast, and more certainly those of New England, are further from the traditional beliefs and interpretations of Christian Scripture than is true, for instance, in the urban South.

Methodist prohibitions against dancing, theater-going, and card-playing became dead letters in city churches long before the denomination as a whole allowed the issue to be settled on the basis of principle and the conscience of the individual. There is some evidence that the individualism attributed to rural people, because of their relatively greater degree of isolation, has made rural religion more "clannish" in its denominational allegiances, using that word in the sense of a closed cultural system. Certainly councils of churches arose in cities before they did in states, and in the more urban states, or those whose religious administration was controlled by urban agencies, before the others.

Other rural characteristics. Other traits can be observed in the behavior of rural people which may not necessarily coincide with their expressions of values. Except among share-croppers and in areas of high and shifting tenant operation, attachment to the land is a characteristic of farm and even village people. Among some groups this is apparent even in the everyday idioms of speech. Patterns of exchange of work, or of borrowing tools and supplies, discussed elsewhere, give practical evidence of the value which rural people set on neighborliness. A helping hand is usually offered to a family in need, and any who withhold such assistance are subject to neighborhood criticism. Such behavior was apparently becoming less common prior to World War II, since it was interesting and significant that in areas where the neighborhood leader plan was successfully operated during World War II, many rural people expressed gratification at the resurgence of neighborliness and expressed the hope that it would continue. Finally, as is shown in the chapter on the family, rural people place great value on family cohesion and loyalty. This is true throughout the western world and even more true of the Orient.

On the other hand, rural people often claim to possess attitudes and beliefs which their behavior contradicts. They frequently assert that "every man's as good as another around here," yet their behavior toward each other indicates a recognition of differences in status. The plantation-owner's daughter would not think of "dating" a sharecropper's son, although her brother might go 'possum hunting with him.[19]

Changing social attitudes. This text has already given evidence and will give more, of changing social attitudes. Thus the growing coöperation of farmer and villager and the increasing importance of the village and town as the center of the twentieth-century rural community, described in the discussion of the modern rural community, are evidences that the old antagonistic attitudes between these groups are passing. With growing acquaintanceship and mutual experiences these are being replaced more and more by coöperation. Moreover, social attitudes have been changed in other particulars, notably in education. Once school work always gave way to farm work if the children were needed at home. Today this is the exception, not the rule. Similarly the changes in social organization, described in another chapter, indicate changing attitudes and fashions as to the objectives of organized social life.

In the last two decades two rural and one

generally circulated women's magazine have submitted questionnaires to subscribers on such questions as divorce and the employment of contraceptive devices. The "liberal" attitudes of rural women on such questions surprised the editors. As the studies were repeated over the years, the attitudes among rural women grew even more liberal. In the latest studies there was little difference among urban, farm, and rural non-farm groups, and none that were statistically significant among the variously defined "younger women."

Rural-urban inferences. We shall now advance some hypotheses which may account for the differences in rural-urban social attitudes already noted.

To begin with, the city resident has a broader range of experience than the country man. He sees more people, is thrown into more situations, and is exposed to a far greater number of environmental action patterns which leave their mark on his reflexes and habits. Consider the amount of transportation he endures — subways, buses, trolleys, automobiles; he has greater access to information and knowledge through libraries, lectures, museums, theaters, concert halls, art galleries, and the like. On the other hand, his direct, occupational experience is more limited than that of the farmer or villager. He is confined, perhaps, to one or a few mechanical operations, to a counter in a store, a desk in an office.

Thus rural people may have fewer non-occupational or worldly experiences and therefore a narrower basis for judging them. On the other hand, their wider range of occupational activities might make them more eager for facts, more resistant to superficial theories or propaganda. Moreover, the outdoor nature of his work makes the farmer, and to some extent the villager, sterner, more virile, persevering, and patient than those in many urban occupations.

---

[19] Cf. James West, *Plainville, U.S.A.* (New York: Columbia University Press, 1945) for a full discussion of what he calls the class system in a midwestern community.

These hypotheses could be illustrated with case histories, but even illustrations must be used with discretion and in terms of the background and experiences of particular groups. It is evident, however, that the lives of rural people, as indicated at the beginning of this chapter, are more and more reacting to common national forces.

Rural people have been put into instant touch with the stream of world events. Isolation has been almost eliminated. Some rooted habits have been changed, others acquired, especially in villages — for example, the remodeling of old one-family houses into apartments and the appearance of rural beauty parlors, unknown before 1925. Sales of labor-saving devices have multiplied; seasonal foods, for example, are now carried all year round in many rural stores.

Some observers assert that rural life, especially village life, is being completely urbanized. This is true only to a certain extent. In the superficialities of life, such as dress and other areas earlier enumerated, urban fashions set the pace in rural communities; in more intangible matters, morals, ideals and religion, such a conclusion cannot yet be accepted.

A personal experience illustrates this point. One of the authors recently spent several days with a state Production and Marketing Administration chairman. This man was equally at home in his well-appointed, efficient office, in the conference rooms, dining room, and cocktail lounge of a large city hotel, on his 232-acre farm, at a neighborhood meeting on farm labor, at the Rotary Club, and at the church in his trade-center village. But throughout, the core of his interest and indeed the inspiration for his work was the welfare of his farm and the farms of his neighbors.

Differences exist and will continue. The country is zealous in its identity, and although it bends before exterior cultural forces, it always does so reluctantly. It is doubtful, indeed, if country and city, urban and rural, will ever be so completely leveled as to lose their group identities, even in the face of the annihilation of space, time, and class. In the questionnaires just alluded to, the suggestion that rural people were blindly accepting urban habits met with a storm of protest. Ruralites felt that those who believed this had "a very limited understanding of rural America," or were "unable or too provincial to conceive of the advanced conditions of the average village."[20]

The conclusion seems to be that so far as evidence exists, the psychological traits of rural people are not inherited but molded by their experiences. Rural psychology is distinctive in great measure from urban despite a great leveling force at present operating in our country; it differs from region to region, from community to community. These differences are in part cultural. Yet there is a good deal of similarity between city and country; people move from one to the other with ease and adjust themselves without undue disturbance. Basic human qualities are doubtless practically the same wherever folk live, move, and have their being.

[20] Cf. a survey in 1930 of *The Small-Town Woman's Reactions to Urban Customs,* by a class in Sociology at Teachers College, Columbia University: (Chicago, Colonial Press, 1930).

TOPICS FOR DISCUSSION

1. Summarize the psychological characteristics which Sorokin and Zimmerman attribute to rural people.

2. Discuss these characteristics in terms of your community, presenting evidence for or against the conclusions of Sorokin and Zimmerman.

3. Outline either the affirmative or negative argument for a debate on the question: "Re-

solved — that city people are more intelligent than rural."

4. Trace evidences of urbanization (or ruralization) of attitudes you have observed in your community.

5. Report results of any studies made by the department of psychology in your institution on the comparative intelligence or achievement of urban and rural school children.

6. Account for any changes in the attitudes of your community on one or more specific issues, paying special attention to the influences of communication.

7. Examine a rural population group (a) as to ancestry, (b) as to the demonstrable persistence of ancestral ideas.

REFERENCE READINGS

BOOKS

Baldwin, B. T., E. A. Filmore, and L. Hadley, *Farm Children*. New York: Appleton-Century-Crofts, 1930. The most thoroughgoing study of many of the matters covered in this chapter.

Matthews, Taylor, *Experience Worlds of Southern Mountain People*. New York: Bureau of Publications, Teachers College, Columbia University, 1937.

Rice, Stuart A., *Farmers and Workers in American Politics*. New York: Columbia University Press, 1924. Especially Chapter 7.

Sorokin, P. A., and C. C. Zimmerman, *Principles of Rural-Urban Sociology*, Part III. New York: Holt, 1939. Assembles a large amount of data from United States and abroad.

Williams, James M., *Our Rural Heritage*. New York: Knopf, 1925.

Williams, James M., *The Expansion of Rural Life*. New York: Knopf, 1926. These two books are a careful pioneer study in rural social psychology, based on two New York state townships.

ARTICLES AND PAMPHLETS

Armstrong, Clairette P., "A Study of the Intelligence of Rural and Urban Children," *Journal of Educational Psychology*, IV (1931), 301–315.

Davis, Allison and Robert Hess, "What About I.Q's?" *Journal of the National Education Association*, November, 1947, pp. 604–605.

Grigg, Austin E., "A Farm Knowledge Test," *Journal of Applied Psychology*, 32: 452–455 (1948).

Jones, H. E., H. S. Conrad, and M. B. Blanchard, "Environmental Handicaps in Mental Test Performances," University of California, *Publications in Psychology*, V (1932), 63–99.

Olcott, M. T., *Rural Psychology: A Partial List of References*. Washington, D.C.: Bureau of Agricultural Economics, 1939.

Shepard, E. L., "Measurement of Certain Non-Verbal Abilities of Urban and Rural Children," *Journal of Educational Psychology*, XXXIII, (1942), 458–462.

Shimberg, M. E., "Investigation into the Validity of Norms with Special Reference to Urban and Rural Groups," *Archives of Psychology*, XVI, Nos. 99–104, chap. VII.

Smith, M., "An Urban-rural Intellectual Gradient," *Sociology and Social Research*, XXVII (1943), 307–315.

Stoddard, G. D., "New Light on Intelligence," *Proceedings of Iowa Academy of Science*, XLIX (1942), 51–60.

Stott, Leland, *Personality Development in Farm, Small-town and City Children*. Lincoln, Nebraska: Agricultural Experiment Station, 1939.

Terry, Paul W., and Verner M. Sims, *They Live on the Land*, chap. X. Bureau of Educational Research, University of Alabama, 1940.

Worbois, G. M., "Changes in Stanford-Binet I.Q. for Rural Consolidated and Rural One-Room School Children," *Journal of Experimental Education*, II (1942), 210–214.

PART TWO

Making a Living in
Rural Society

Making a living is a major enterprise in every society. Traditionally, farming has been the principal means of making a living in American rural society. However, in 1950 half the rural families, and more than half in some regions, were not engaged in farming as a main enterprise. They were living in villages, on the fringes of cities, or even in the open country, earning their living in such non-farm but related occupations as processing and marketing farm products, retailing and wholesaling consumer goods, or working in industrial plants.

In its human and social aspects agriculture involves private property in land and a country environment for the family home. And this environment involves a variety of contacts. While homes are located on separate farmsteads, many relations bind farm with farm and family with family. Coöperatives are important in such interfarm-family bonds. Likewise, farm and non-farm, and even urban, families are interrelated in the many technical processes of an industrialized and commercialized society. In America, science and technology have taken over agriculture, but elsewhere in the world two thirds of the people are still dependent upon traditional farming methods.

Agrarian culture is best typified by the man on his land — with his buildings, his animals, and his machinery — the man at the heart of his homestead.

6 The Agricultural Enterprise— Social Implications

THE MEANS OF LIVELIHOOD men choose affect and mold their social contacts, their personal habits and conditions, their community attitudes, and social organizations. A farmer mingles with farmers more than with other occupational groups. He joins a farmers' organization, not a labor union. He looks at issues from the point of view of their effect upon agriculture. For all these reasons we must consider the social contributions of agriculture and the social implications of the business of farming.

It is important to realize not only that there are these social implications but also that the economic behavior of men is in a large sense social behavior. The vast organizational mechanism, from local to Federal levels, which administered the one-time Agricultural Adjustment Administration, now the Production and Marketing Administration, is nonetheless a social institution because it operates in the economic field. Local committees of Soil Conservation districts now are joined in a national association, with the objective of furthering the cause of soil conservation and promoting the interests of the Soil Conservation Service. In furthering these aims, this association behaves as sociologists would expect a social institution to behave. It meets problems of building group morale, of relationships with other agencies, and of welding diverse cliques within its membership into an effective whole.

Other illustrations will be given in this and the three following chapters.

Agricultural Development

Agriculture, of course, is a highly diversified field. Farms vary in size from the few acres of a subsistence homestead to square miles; they vary in type from the intensively cultivated irrigated tracts of the Pacific Coast fruit-grower to the grazing lands of a Montana rancher. Crops grown in one section of the country may be unknown to another. Wheat and cotton are not neighbors, and citrus fruit is a stranger to Maine potatoes. Moreover, capital invested in farms varies, as do the operator's tenure, his attitudes about and participation in agricultural coöperation, and his credit needs. All these factors have reacted upon him in the social organization of rural life.

The remainder of this chapter, therefore, attempts to catalogue briefly some of these essentially economic factors, to point out a few of their social implications, and to indicate significant differences among the various regions of the nation that are associated with differences in agricultural procedures.

The Agricultural Enterprise

It is helpful at the outset to gain some idea of the magnitude of the agricultural enterprise in terms of number, value, and types of farms.

Number of farms decreasing. Strange as it may seem, it is possible to give the num-

ber of all farms in the United States only if
we are quite explicit in our definition of a
farm.

The 1950 census reports a total of
5,379,043 farms, a decline of nearly 500,000
since 1945 and of over 700,000 since 1940. In
1950, however, the census changed its definition of farm. Previously a place of three
acres or more was counted as a farm without qualification, and any place of less than
three acres was classified as a farm if the
value of its agricultural production was
$250 or more. In 1950 places of three or
more acres were classified as farms only if
agricultural production, exclusive of home
garden, had a value of $150 or more in
1949. Places of less than three acres were
counted as farms only if agricultural products *sold* had a value of $150 or more. The
census estimates that a maximum of 200,000
of the decline between 1945 and 1950 is
attributable to the change in definition.

Another estimate of the number of farms
is obtained by examining the preliminary
data from the 1950 census of population.
Each person was asked what job he or she
held during the census week. On this basis
4,523,000 persons indicated that they were

farm operators, as opposed to 5,143,614 in
1940 — a decline of 12 per cent. Making
allowance for the fact that these data come
from a preliminary sample count, it seems
safe to conclude that at least one person in
seven enumerated by the agricultural census
as a farm operator did not so regard himself,
since his major affiliations were with another
occupation. The new census definition
would therefore seem to move in the direction of greater accuracy. Agricultural census
release AC 50–3 reports that on practically
three farms out of ten, other family income
exceeded the value of agricultural products
sold.

It is safe to assume that these farmers
with other occupations have relatively small
holdings and small agricultural incomes.
Statistically, however, this puts them in the
same class as the full-time but underemployed farmers whose incomes are substand-
ard and whose holdings are below average.
Obviously, these two groups have quite different problems and represent indeed distinct social patterns. The whole significance
of social patterns in farming will be discussed later.

In this whole discussion we are forced to

| | DIVISION | 1950 | 1940 | 1930 | 1910 | PER CENT CHANGE | |
						1910–50	1940–50
TABLE	United States	5,379	6,097	6,288	6,361	−15.4	−11.8
	New England	103	135	125	189	−45.5	−23.7
9	Middle Atlantic	297	348	357	468	−36.5	−14.6
	East North Central	885	1,006	966	1,123	−21.2	−12.0
Number of Farms	West North Central	983	1,090	1,113	1,110	−11.4	− 9.8
by Divisions	South Atlantic	957	1,019	1,058	1,112	−13.9	− 6.1
(In thousands)	East South Central	912	1,023	1,062	1,042	−12.5	−10.9
	West South Central	780	964	1,103	943	−17.4	−19.1
	Mountain	105	233	241	183	6.9	−12.6
	Pacific	267	276	262	190	28.8	− 3.3

Source: *United States Censuses of Agriculture*, 1930, 1940, and preliminary estimates, 1950. A latter release, Nov.
25, 1951, estimates the total number of farms at 5,384,000.

use census data because there is no information dealing only with holdings considered farms by the operator. Even on this basis, as is clear from Table 9, not only did the number of farms decline in every census division between 1940 and 1950, but the rate of decline has been far more rapid in this decade than it was in the period 1910 to 1940. This would be true even if the definition of farm had not been changed. The most recently developed regions, those in the West, continued to show gains up to 1940, but they too succumbed to the national trend in the last decade.

Not only did all divisions show a decline in number of farms from 1940 to 1950, but also all states except North and South Carolina and California. Where there was a gain, in no case was it as much as 3.5 per cent. Between 1945 and 1950 every state lost, and in most cases by a larger number than could possibly be explained by the change in the definition of a farm.

Size of farms enlarging. Since the total farm acreage in the United States has tended to remain about the same or even to show small increases over recent decades, it is obvious that the average size of farms has been increasing.

In the statistics dealing with the size of farms can be traced, from one point of view at least, the fascinating history of the development of the American continent. The first settlers, their backs to the Atlantic, met and seized the opportunity to slake their immemorial hunger for land. It was to be had for the taking and clearing. Pioneers pushing westward took two centuries to reach the Pacific. Size of farm meant little in those early days, but as the pioneering period ended, the changing size of farms began to reflect both changes in farm management and the fact that most of the available land had been settled. In 1900 farms in the United States averaged 146 acres and only

148 in 1920. The effect of gasoline-powered farm machinery and other factors enabling the farmer to work more acres then began to register in the statistics. The 1930 average was 157 acres; the 1940, 174. There was a further gain to 190 by 1945, shared in by almost all the states except those in the South other than Florida. The midcentury point found the average standing at 210.5 acres.

This represents a gain of over 43 per cent in the average size of farms in the United States since the beginning of the century. It also means that under average conditions within any given area, such as a county or a community, the number of farms was correspondingly reduced and with it the number of farm families tributary to, and helping to support, a given village or town center. Here too is one explanation of the decrease in open-country schools, discussed in another chapter; of the fact that some small villages have slipped back into the hamlet class; of the enlarging service and community areas of other centers; and of the complementary functions of many of the remaining centers, noted in other chapters. Such trends reflect the adjustment of social and economic institutions to changing technological and physical conditions.

It must be remembered that the influence of such factors varies greatly among the regions and states and even within states and counties. The irrigated sections of California, for instance, as well as many vegetable-raising areas near cities, have small, compact farms and intensive cultivation. Dry farming and stock raising make for very large farms. Thus the average acreage of farms in Wyoming is over 4 square miles (2700 acres), but in the East South Central states it is still under 100 acres and many counties average less than 75, because of the still considerable number of small farms operated by Negroes and poor whites.

Size of farm is one indication of popula-

	CENSUS DIVISION	1920	1930	1940	1950
TABLE **10** Average Acreage per Farm by Division and By Type of Operator	United States	148.2	156.9	174	210.5
	New England	108.5	114.3	98.9	192.5
	Middle Atlantic	95.4	98.0	96.6	
	East North Central	108.5	114.7	113.0	
	West North Central	234.3	238.6	251.6	
	South Atlantic	84.4	81.6	90.8	142.6
	East South Central	75.0	68.6	75.3	
	West South Central	174.1	166.7	267.9	
	Mountain	480.7	652.5	821.9	689.1
	Pacific	239.8	231.2	280.6	
	Type				
	Owner	162.2	173.3	124*	
	Tenant	107.9	115.0	132	
	Manager	790.8	1109.1	1830	

Source: *Fourteenth Census of the United States*, 1920, V, Table 12, p. 37. *Fifteenth Census of the United States*, 1930, "Agriculture Summary for the United States, 1929 and 1930," Table 3, p. 24, and Table 7, p. 30; *Census of Agriculture*, 1940, and 1950 Series AC 50-3 No. 09.

*Figure for owner. Part-owner operates 235 acres.

tion density, which is obviously low in a region where single farms average more than a square mile. Small farms mean compact rural communities, large ones the reverse. These differences indicate also great differences in the size, strength, frequency, accessibility, and administration of schools, churches, libraries, and similar social institutions. Transportation of pupils is obviously a problem in an area of huge farms and low population density. Churches, as will be seen later, are weak and at a disadvantage under such conditions. Table 10 compares the average acreage per farm for the various census divisions.

Younger countries unique. In passing it is significant to note that there are vast differences among the nations of the world in number of acres per farm and of crop land per capita. Many of the acute problems of the world's statesmen stem from this fact. In the main, the more recently settled countries have the largest farms and practice a less intensive agriculture. Farms in Canada are larger than those in the United States. In Australia the "stations," as they call what

to a North American would be ranches, are measured not by acres but by square miles and in parts of Queensland and elsewhere run into thousands. In one area of so-called "closer settlement" being developed in New South Wales in the 1930's, the tracts ran from 1000 to 1800 acres. Comparably, in the wheat and cattle areas of the Argentine, holdings are very large compared to the United States.

In Europe, on the other hand, in most countries twenty-five acres is a very respectable farm. When Czechoslovakia divided its large estates into farms for the peasants after World War I, the average holding was less than this. Even in Denmark and Sweden farms average less than twenty-five acres.

But to the Oriental outside Manchuria and a few other places such a farm would seem spacious indeed. The average farm size in Japan is two and one half acres; two thirds of these farms are less than this, and only about one tenth exceed five acres; in China and India farms average little more. This means intensive hand cultivation, low income, and very high land values with reduced opportunity to earn a return on the capital investment. It also explains in part why in many countries the farmer is a village dweller who walks to his holding each day, returning at night. More serious, it often means a slender margin between barely enough food and famine. Some European countries are not even self-sufficient as to food. Imports are necessary from younger countries with ample land resources.

Small farms numerous in the United States. This is not to say that there are no small farms in the United States. There are many, and until 1950 each census showed more than the previous one. The decline between 1945 and 1950 was due in large part to the changed definition of farm, but even so, many counties in all regions showed increases in the number of farms under ten acres. In 1920, 12.3 per cent of all United States farms had less than twenty acres. By 1940 this had risen to 17.5 per cent. The 1950 figures, to which the new definition is applicable, was 17 per cent. These smaller farms in all regions are usually located near large towns and cities. As another chapter shows, there is a definite relationship between size of farm, type of agriculture, and distance from the city; and the farming area near the city partakes of more urban characteristics than that farther away.

Large farms increasing. As would be expected from the data on average size of farm, the number of holdings of five hundred acres or more has also gained. In 1900 this group contained one third of the acreage and comprised 2.6 per cent of all farms. By 1945 these two figures had become 50.7 and 4.9 per cent. In 1950 large farms were 5.5 per cent of total. Their share of the acreage also increased somewhat.

A disproportionate number of these large farms are to be found in the Mountain and Pacific census divisions. In 1950 they had over half of all the farm units of this size in the United States. Especially in the former division the huge areas of single farms are due to stock raising, and much of the acreage is devoted to range for the cattle. As a group, these large farms, especially those of one thousand acres or more, have far smaller proportions of crop land than any other size group. In many counties less than 1 per cent of the land in farms was reported as crop land in the 1950 census, and only about 10 per cent for the two divisions. This country, along with some of the Southwest, has contributed the cowboy tradition to American folk lore. It has its own songs and tall tales. The high point of the year here is the round-up, not the corn husking bee or the harvest home festival. The economic base is so different that on occasion the cattlemen have stood for agricultural policies opposed to those of other farm groups. In the early days there was often sharp conflict between the stockmen, who wanted an unfenced range, and those who were interested in crops and a settled agriculture.

A tri-modal distribution of farms. Farms between the two extremes just discussed have shown less change in the last half century than the others. This group includes the great bulk of family-operated farms in the United States. It develops, therefore, that farms in the United States can be classified in a tri-modal distribution. At the present time there are approximately three million farms with less than 100 acres and an average of between 40 and 50, something over two million averaging about 225 acres, and about a hundred thousand very large-scale enterprises averaging more than five square miles in area. The social patterns which appear in these groups, especially the first two, will be discussed at length later. But they involve certain significant questions with respect to part-time farming on the one hand and large-scale farming on the other, and these matters should logically be discussed at this point.

Part-time farming. As the term suggests, part-time farmers, while maintaining their connection with the soil, augment their incomes by nonagricultural employment. There seems to be a clear relation between type of farming, rurality, and proportion of farmers engaged in nonagricultural pursuits. One study showed, for example, that in Ohio only 8 per cent of the heads of farm families in the most rural areas studied had any outside employment, while in the most industrial farm sections 27 per cent had nonagricultural occupations.[1] A study of a central New York community showed 17.8 per cent of the males in open-country area had nonagricultural occupations.[2] In some Massachusetts and Connecticut towns the proportions ranged from one half to two thirds.

On the basis of a so-called master sample drawn from the 1945 census of agriculture, the United States Department of Agriculture estimated that there were in that year 602,200 part-time farms and 987,300 nominal farms with an average gross value of product of $574 and $264 respectively.[3] These would account for more than a fourth of all farms enumerated in that year and a half of the low-income farms averaging under one hundred acres. Most of the reduction in number of farms resulting from the new 1950 definition would fall in these categories.

One check of part-time farming is the number of days the farm operator works for pay away from his own farm. Since 1929 more than one farmer in four has reported

[1] Lively and Beck, *Movement of Open Country Population in Ohio* (Columbus: Experiment Station, College of Agriculture, Ohio State University, 1930), Bulletin 467.

[2] Melvin and Kensler, *A Partial Sociological Study of Dryden, New York* (Ithaca: New York College of Agriculture, Cornell University, 1930).

[3] *The Agricultural Situation*, December, 1948, pp. 1–4.

such employment. The New England, Pacific, and Middle Atlantic divisions exceeded one in three, and nine states exceeded two in five. The three southern divisions fell below the average largely because only two Negro farmers obtained off-farm employment for every three white. The average off-farm employment was for 97 days in 1934, 137 days in 1939, 184 days in 1945. Employment in war industries influenced the last figure.

The economic importance of part-time farming seems to be increasing. In 1950 approaching one fourth of all farm operators, according to preliminary census tabulations, reported that they had 100 days or more of such employment and this despite the revised definition of a farm.

As a rule farmers working off their farms less than fifty days are employed on other farms. The more days a farmer labors away from his farm the greater the likelihood that he is engaged in nonagricultural work. Sources of such employment are varied. Many farm homes put up "Tourists Accommodated" signs. Some open roadside markets, gas stations, or eating places. Other farmers drive school buses, haul local milk, or operate city or town milk routes. Some run sawmills or do road work. A number are always poorly paid preachers. A few take summer boarders.

Large-scale farms and mechanical agriculture. The great expansion in the number of large-scale farm units has been made possible by vast increases in both variety and efficiency of gasoline-powered farm machinery, especially the tractor. The number of these, in thousands, for selected years is given by the Bureau of Agricultural Economics of the United States Department of Agriculture as follows:

1920–	246	1945–	2,422
1930–	920	1947–	2,800
1940–	1,545	1950–	3,825

In the same period the horse and mule population declined from almost 26,000,000 to about 7,500,000. The Automobile Manufacturers Association has recently stated [4] that, counting all vehicles, mechanical power on farms is ten times that in all industry combined. Though improved seeds, better soil uses, and many other gains resulting from research have helped considerably, mechanization is probably the largest single factor in the gain in gross farm production per worker from 1910 to 1950. Taking the years 1935 to 1939 as 100, this index has gone from 80 to 141. The same phenomenon has been observed in Australia, where mechanization has also gained tremendously. If the period from 1920 to 1948 is considered as 100, the productivity per worker of the rural labor force was 98.8 in the 1920's, 115.4 in the 1930's, and 133.0 in the 1940's.[5]

Obviously it is the large-scale farms which can best afford to mechanize. Many important social and socio-economic results flow from this process, which are worth considering briefly here.

The enlarging farm size made possible by farm machinery forces many people off the land, as we have already noted. Man-hour requirements per acre or per unit of production have been decreased, often from 70 to 90 per cent. We called attention earlier to the difficulties farm population declines pose for social institutions like schools and churches, organized on the assumption that the pattern of farming as it existed from 1890 to 1920 was permanent. The spread of mechanized agriculture has clearly helped school consolidation, as already indicated.

An examination of census data shows that disproportionately large decreases in rural farm population under twenty-five years of age often coincide with great increases in farm mechanization. It has become harder for young people to get started in farming because increased acreage and cost of machines involves an almost prohibitive capital investment. Where there are fewer young farmers, there are fewer children, and the average age of farm operators increases.

Mechanization began in the wheat belt and in some areas may be close to having run its course. It has now spread to most other crop areas, most recently to the South. Two illustration of some of the results noted above are typical. A cotton planter in the Mississippi Delta had 160 share-cropper families on his land. When he purchased 22 tractors and 13 four-row cultivators, he let 130 families, about 700 people go, retaining only 30 and these on a day-labor basis. On another much smaller holding of about 2200 acres, 35 tenant families were evicted, 180 persons, and the farm was operated by a few able-bodied single men and machines. In the latter case the families moved to the trade-center village and applied for relief. In the former some followed this policy, but many others headed for California.[6]

Mechanization reduces costs. As a single illustration, a Mississippi study based on 1949 price relationships showed a per-acre cost for cotton of $1.04 with mule power, 63¢ with a two-row tractor, and 37¢ with a four-row tractor.[7] The process of mechanization therefore means difficulty and often poverty for those displaced, but larger profits for operators who remain, and hence the probability of a higher standard of living. However, where mechanization reduces population it costs more per family to maintain community services at the level supported by a larger population.

---

[4] *Automobile Facts,* Vol IX, No. 1, January, 1950.
[5] Derived from tables in the *Quarterly Review of Agricultural Economics,* January, 1950.

[6] About 200,000 distressed migrants entered California from 1936 to 1940. Despite the breaking of the 1934–36 drought the flow of these people has barely slackened.
[7] James P. Gaines and Grady B. Crowe, *Workstock vs. Tractors in the Yazoo* (Mississippi) *Delta* (Mississippi Agricultural Experiment Station), Bulletin No. 470, March, 1950.

As farms add acres and machinery, the farmer becomes more dependent on money to conduct his operations. Even though he raises as much of his own food as before, the proportion of his total product marketed commercially increases. Even the servicing of his equipment calls for cash outlays. He thus becomes more dependent on others, so mechanization and commercialization help to increase the interdependence in a society.

Corporation farms. One aspect of large-scale farming is that conducted by corporations. Large-scale farms are often treated as synonymous with corporation farms, though they actually are not. Kansas, for instance, has a number of highly mechanized family holdings of two thousand to six thousand acres. Unfortunately the census gives no data on corporation farms as such. The only clue is in the number of farms operated by managers, which, however, include many estates. The number of such farms has fluctuated widely. The high point was in 1920, when there were 68,449. In 1940 the number was 36,351; in 1945, 38,885.

Between 1945 and 1950 the number of managed farms appears to have declined sharply, indeed by exactly 40 per cent in the first two thirds of the states first reporting.

The situation under discussion is especially important in the two western census divisions, which have about two thirds of all the land in managed farms. It comprised more than a fifth of the western region's farm land but less than 4 per cent of crop land in 1945.

There have been many prophecies that the trend is toward extensive large-scale farming, probably on a corporation basis. Wherever it does come, the problem created in the community is acute. An Iowa village paper thus described the operations of a 24,000-acre corporation farm:

Each tract in the group is operated as a single field and is planted to a single crop in a rotation program. In the working of its present holdings, the company employs seventy-five general purpose tractors, nineteen combined harvesters and threshers, fifteen two-row harvesters, seventy-five plows, forty grain drills, and associated equipment. This machinery is transported over a hard surfaced state-road system by means of ten motor trucks with semi-trailers capable of hauling three tractors to a load. Field machinery is entirely equipped with electric lighting to permit twenty-four hour operation when necessary.

This company maintains no livestock, has removed from its holdings boundary fences, groves, and often buildings, and employs only unmarried men. Under such conditions village hardware and implement dealers and repairmen naturally fear the ruin of their business. Village social institutions would also be greatly altered if this procedure became general.

On the other hand, one of the oldest corporation farms in the United States has found it profitable, after years of experimentation, to employ only married men and to make both the conditions of operation and of living as similar to those of normal farming as possible.

Other problems of giant farms. Corporation farming brings other problems. Heavy capital expenditure for equipment is required, and new techniques must be learned. Moreover, problems of industrial relations arise, for often the agrarian is not a docile employee. In Hawaii and in California, despite higher wages and many indirect benefits, there have probably been more strikes by farm labor over the years than in all the rest of the nation put together.

The issues of large- versus small-scale farming go deeper than these considerations, as has already been intimated. While generalizations cannot be made from a single study, a survey made by the Bureau of Agricultural Economics of two California communities of equal size and growing the same crops is of interest. One was large-scale, farms averaging 497 acres with 80 per cent of the farm labor force wage hands. The other was a family-farm community with farms averaging 57 acres. Its population was almost one-fourth larger, but on a per-acre basis its returns were much larger. Its retail sales were 70 per cent higher than in the large-scale farm community. It had over twice as many stores and services, much better schools and housing, and a far more varied and active community life. Probably as a result, it had little delinquency, a serious problem in the large-farm community. In a more intangible sphere, the testimony of businessmen and professional workers indicated that there was a much finer community spirit in the small-farm area than in the larger one.[8]

Facts on the size of American farms indicate a growing specialization in agriculture. Small farms, intensively cultivated and given over largely to truck and fruit or to part-time farming, will doubtless stay and probably increase. The very large farm, also slowly gaining in numbers and acreage, will be used for those crops that lend themselves to machine cultivation. Finally, the old type of medium-size general farm, though slowly declining in relation to the total number, is not likely to disappear in

[8] Walter Goldschmidt, *As You Sow* (New York: Harcourt, Brace, 1947).

any predictable future. The first two types, wherever they appear in force, are working changes in the traditional pattern of rural social organization, and they will continue to do so.

Value of Farms

Total investment. Judged by the proportion of the nation's area devoted to it and by the number of its separate units, agriculture is not only a major enterprise, but judged by its capital values it is our most important industry. In 1920 the total value of farm lands, buildings, and equipment was over $73 billion, of which $57.3 billion was in land alone. The agricultural depression carried total valuation of land and buildings back to about $48 billion by 1930 and to $32.8 billion in 1935, a decline of more than 50 per cent in capital values in fifteen years. This terrific deflation was one of the chief concomitants of the depression. It brought great suffering to farmers, their families, and communities and, by drying up of their purchasing power, affected the whole economy.

Since the 1940 census there has been an increase in the value of farms as dramatic as the deflation. The annual *Balance Sheet of American Agriculture*, prepared by the Bureau of Agriculture Economics, gives the value of farms on January 1, 1950, as $127 billion, with outstanding liabilities of $12.4

TABLE 11 Estimated Value per Acre of Farm Real Estate, by Division (1909–14 = 100)	CENSUS DIVISION	1920	1930	1935	1940	1950
	United States	170	115	79	84	193
	New England	140	127	104	106	163
	Middle Atlantic	136	106	85	90	172
	East North Central	161	96	68	78	194
	West North Central	184	109	68	65	163
	South Atlantic	198	128	93	107	255
	East South Central	199	128	93	112	298
	West South Central	177	136	91	99	225
	Mountain	151	102	70	78	176
	Pacific	156	142	101	108	199

Source: Bureau of Agricultural Economics, *The Farm Real Estate Market*, May, 1951.

billion. Even valued at 1940 prices, farm assets rose from $53.8 to $76.8 billion in the decade, and the equity from $43.7 billion to $64.4 billion, or 47 per cent. In every census division save the East North Central, the index of average value per acre in 1951 exceeded the land boom figures of 1920, as Table 11 shows. This table also illustrates the wide fluctuations which have taken place in the last generation.

It will be seen from Table 11 that the decline in the per-acre value of farm real estate after 1920 was most drastic in areas devoted to export crops and to general farming. Regions engaged in dairying and in raising truck, fruit, and other specialized products, grown for the most part in proximity to cities and in the more industrialized areas, suffered least. Although Table 11 shows that the rebound has been stronger where values were most depressed, it also suggests the vulnerability to disaster of one-crop and export-crop areas. Such drastic changes obviously have their social effects on the communities concerned. One of the most important of these effects is related to a cultural trait — the urge for the possession of land and ever more land, going back to the hunger of the agrarian for a stake in the land. The result in our society has been

to capitalize increased farm income in increased land values. This puts the purchase of land into competition with alternative policy, namely, the use of larger profits to procure a higher standard of family and community living. Percentage earnings on capital invested are thereby reduced, with a high or overcapitalized value made more vulnerable to depreciation when the price level for farm products declines. This trait also fails to give weight to the fact that while land is essential to farming, the share of land in the total capitalization is less important than it once was, because of the larger share of capital that must be invested in equipment.

Values per farm. Obviously, the average value of a farm also fluctuates. As Table 12 shows, it dropped from $10,284 in 1920 to $5518 in 1940. This was a measure of the depression deflation. From this point there was a steady rise, especially rapid after 1945, the 1950 figure being $13,642.

Factors affecting farm values. Various factors affect the value of individual farms, even though size and soil fertility of two given tracts may be approximately equal. Farms near markets are more valuable than

TABLE 12 Average Value of Farm Land and Buildings per Farm and per Acre	DIVISION	AVERAGE VALUE PER FARM			AVERAGE VALUE LAND AND BUILDINGS PER ACRE		
		1920	1940	1950	1920	1940	1950
	United States	$10,284	$5,518	$13,642	$69.38	$31.71	$65.26
	New England	5,860	5,478	11,510	54.00	55.38	93.94
	Middle Atlantic	7,061	5,858	11,733	73.99	60.62	108.59
	East North Central	13,371	7,289	16,894	126.87	64.53	131.26
	West North Central	22,307	8,065	17,581	95.22	32.05	66.97
	South Atlantic	4,488	3,099	7,475	53.20	34.14	70.07
	East South Central	3,484	2,272	5,566	46.44	30.16	65.15
	West South Central	6,316	4,388	12,069	36.27	21.10	44.85
	Mountain	12,958	7,623	26,496	26.96	9.27	23.62
	Pacific	19,941	11,720	30,603	83.16	50.82	112.36

Source: *United States Census of Agriculture*, 1935, III, *ibid.*, 1940, *ibid.*, 1950.

those farther away. This is true not merely in connection with the major sources of consumption, the cities, but also within communities where, as a rule, farms near the village and town center and located on good roads, especially hard-surfaced ones, are more valuable than those farther away and on poorer roads. Obviously, also, the better the soil the higher the value. It frequently happens that there are important social correlations to this fact. Numerous field surveys have shown that farms well located as to community center, roads, and soil are more likely to be represented in the membership of churches, farm bureaus, coöperatives, and other social and economic organizations than those not so well located. So, too, children from better located farms more often attend high school.

Again, farms in older and better established areas and those devoted to highly specialized or well diversified products, such as fruit and truck, are usually more valuable, at least on a per-acre basis, than farms in more recently developed areas, in one-crop or general-farm regions.

Erosion a serious difficulty. A final factor of increasing importance needs to be mentioned, namely, erosion. It is easy to assume that land is a permanent factor, but this is not true with respect to top soil, which can be washed or blown away. The geographer Russell Smith once even raised the question as to whether or not this is a permanent country.[9] In North Carolina, for instance, more than twenty years ago county agents reported that fifteen years after the timber had been cut from the lumbering areas of that state, this land, which had produced some of our finest forests, had to be abandoned for agricultural purposes because of erosion. Tests made along railway rights of way and in adjoining fields in Iowa show that an appreciable proportion of the fertile

[9] Cf. *Survey Graphic*, September, 1928.

soil of these fields has disappeared — some of it blown clear to the Atlantic, as in the dust storms during the drought of 1934.

There is no greater threat to land values than erosion, and it is a problem created largely by human behavior. Fortunately, however, considerable progress has been made in soil conservation in the last decade or so. In some areas, though not in all, there was a new overdraft on soil resources during World War II, but it is to be hoped that the soil conservation program will be fully resumed as soon as possible. This is an important item on the agenda of rural adult education.

The importance of this matter is not adequately recognized. The phrase "mining the soil" is often used in discussions about soil conservation and tenancy. Failure to sustain land productivity, eventually is reflected in changing land values. But for the most part farm management and farm accounting take no account of the slow deterioration of soil productivity. In short, dollar gain to a landowner may be partly or wholly fictitious if the productive potential of his land is being gradually reduced.

This issue may be presented in a dramatic way. We have a huge synthetic rubber-producing capacity developed during World War II. There are those who go so far as to say that we should buy little or no natural rubber in the future. Instead, they say, we should grow grain, turn it into alcohol, and the alcohol into rubber. But grain crops are hard on the soil. Apart from the effect of such policies on the standard of living of millions of persons in areas where rubber grows naturally, persons who were allies of ours in the world struggle, it cannot be asserted that synthetic rubber will be "cheaper" than natural rubber until the cost to the soil from such a policy is determined. Soil is, but should not be, taken for granted. Large social issues, as well as economic, emerge at this point — issues that affect not only rural society, but also the nation and the world.

Farm Income

Farm values represent capital investment. How well does this capital serve the farmer in terms of the income he is able to secure? In gross terms this income represents receipts from the sale of all farm products, from which actual expenses of farm operations must be deducted. The resulting figure is further reduced by allowance for return on the capital investment and, the amount earned by the labor of the farmer and perhaps his family. National figures on these items are given in a subsequent chapter, and the uses to which this net income is devoted are discussed in the chapter on standards of living. Here we are concerned only with returns per farm, with differentiating between labor income and the return on capital investment, as the agricultural economist must.

Farm income fluctuates widely. Income per farm varies according to size of farm operation and level of prices within any given crop year. The 1945 census of agriculture reported that 47.2 per cent of farms had a gross cash income of under $1000. The Bureau of Agricultural Economics estimated that in 1946, 45.2 per cent fell in this category.[10] In 1948 the Bureau of the Census put 25.2 per cent of farm families in this category.[11] The whole picture is shown by the following data:

Gross Cash From Income	Census of 1945	B. A. E. 1946	Sample Census 1948
$ 0–$ 999	47.2	45.2	25.2
1000– 4999	39.0	37.1	64.0
5000 and over	13.8	17.7	10.8

[10] Nathan M. Koffsky and Jeane E. Lear, *The Size and Distribution of Farm Operators' Income in 1946* (Washington, D.C.: Bureau of Agricultural Economics, September, 1950).

[11] *Income of Families and Persons in the United States: 1948.* Series P. 50, No. 6, February 14, 1950.

The Bureau of the Census, in its 1948 study, estimated the median cash farm income per family at $2036. This compared with $3551 for urban families and $2954 for rural non-farm. Cash is, of course, not the only source of income on farms. The farm family has its home and consumes some of its own products. In 1948 these items were estimated at $604 per farm, or, if the value of products used is calculated on the basis of what they would have cost at retail, at $1063.[12] While the total figures on this basis give farm families an income of about $3100, it must be remembered that production expenses have not been deducted.

The agricultural census for 1950 in its preliminary report stated that exactly one tenth of the farms reported no products sold in the previous year. One third sold less than $1000 worth. The sales of 30 per cent fell between $1000 and $4000. Eighteen per cent exceeded $4000 but sold less than $10,000 worth of products. Slightly less than 9 per cent had sales in excess of $10,000. Of the farms enumerated in 1950, however, only 68.2 per cent were commercial farms. Of these not quite one third had sales in excess of $5000. Not quite one fourth fell between $2500 and $5000.

Low-income families. On the basis of these data, one might conclude that agriculture is a poverty-stricken occupation. There can be no doubt that there is a disturbing amount of poverty in rural America. These data, however, should be corrected to allow for the large number of farms which, as shown earlier, are part-time, residential, or other special types, and which therefore have non-farm sources of income.

Data given earlier in this chapter report the number of days farm operators worked off their farms. The Department of Agricul-

[12] Joint Committee on the Economic Report, Eighty-first Congress, First Session, *Low Income Families and Economic Stability* (Washington, D.C., 1949), pp. 38–39.

ture and the National Bureau of Economic Research, in a joint research project, have studied this non-farm income of farmers. They found that the considerable group of farm families reported by the 1945 census and the 1946 Bureau of Agricultural Economics study as being without cash farm income averaged almost $2000 per farm of non-farm income. The fourth of the farm families reporting less than $500 cash income from products raised averaged $658 a year from nonagricultural income. To these figures again must be added rental value of homes and value of home-grown products used by the family.

The Joint Committee on the Economic Report made an effort to estimate the actual number of rural families seriously underemployed.[13] They concluded that about one million farm families on small-scale units, with an able-bodied operator and little or no outside income, had a gross value of products of under $1500, and perhaps 600,000 more, similarly situated, had from $1500 to $2500. Seventy per cent of the former and 58 per cent of the latter were found in the South; less than 5 per cent were in the western region. The Committee notes that their calculations were made on the basis of 1944 data and that prices have risen since then. The social problems of rural poverty are centered in this group of farms. Every region has some of this type, though in varying degree. The joint Committee on the Economic Report finds that about half of these low-income farm families were headed by a female or a non-white male, the latter of course largely Negroes.

Income of commercial farms. Repeated studies have found that American farms in the upper-income half produce close to 90 per cent of the commercially sold food and

fibre. It is these farms which furnish the bulk of the local tax money and whose operators are the most important group in American rural life. Professor Wayland's study, summarized later in this chapter, shows the median value of products for the three types of commercial family farms in 1944 to be as follows:

	North	*South*
Large commercial family farms	$12,861	$11,372
Median commercial family farms	4,774	4,270
Small commercial family farms	1,734	1,488

More important historically, are farm income studies by the Bureau of Agricultural Economics over time and based on careful accounting on a small sample of farms. These data are given in Table 13.

The balance sheets of these farmers show clearly the variation due to fluctuating prices and costs and to various types of farm management. The effects of drought and depression can also be read in these figures. Thus the Department of Agriculture estimates a fifty-fold variation in the net income of corn belt cash grain farms between the lowest and highest years of the last twenty. Table 13 gives some indication of how the commercial family farm has fared.

These ups and downs, especially the latter, which affected every type of farm, explain some of the political pressures farmers have brought to bear on Congress. Though the poultryman and the grain farmer may disagree about the price of feed, they are at one with all other agricultural commodity groups in desiring that there be safeguards against a repetition of the long agricultural depression.

It must be recognized that the income data given in Table 13 are based on a sample. Individual farms within the same state or commodity type may vary widely.

[13] Committee Report, Eighty-second Congress, First Session, *Underemployment of Rural Families* (Washington, 1951), Part II.

TYPE	1932	1936	1940	1944	1946	1948	1950
Dairy							
Central New York	$597	$1,204	$1,480	$3,804	$4,538	$5,821	$4,274
Southern Wisconsin	524	1,280	1,589	4,621	5,832	7,171	5,263
Corn Belt							
Cash grain	212	2,458	2,755	6,926	11,089	12,598	10,148
Hog-beef fattening	518	965	2,208	5,766	10,042	11,873	10,303
Hog-beef raising	270	479	1,462	3,128	6,056	7,258	6,142
Hog dairy	392	1,384	1,490	3,291	6,941	7,171	5,420
Spring Wheat							
Wheat-corn-live stock	116	165	1,384	5,403	7,718	8,666	5,301
Wheat-smallgrain-live stock	−126	−89	1,232	5,793	8,450	8,468	6,757
Wheat-roughage-live stock	260	−255	1,123	4,524	7,677	7,601	4,829
Winter Wheat							
Wheat	−27	1,393	1,100	7,245	11,846	9,839	8,861
Wheat-grain sorghum	−156	1,214	1,561	10,768	9,960	12,287	6,824
Cotton							
Southern plains	673	815	1,473	3,772	3,249	3,950	5,969
Black Prairie	433	1,298	1,251	2,034	2,458	3,166	3,351
Delta	255	1,128	829	2,065	2,426	3,507	3,073
Cattle Ranches							
Intermountain	1,229	1,963	2,775	4,910	6,722	10,842	8,835

TABLE 13

Net Farm Income, Commercial Family-operated Farms by Type for Selected Years

Sources: Bureau of Agricultural Economics, United States Department of Agriculture, *Farm Production Practices, Costs and Returns*, Statistical Bulletin 83 (Washington, D.C., October, 1949), p. 106 and *Farm Costs and Returns, 1950, with Comparisons* (May, 1951), p. 2.

Net income as here used was computed by subtracting cash expenditures, excluding interest paid on borrowed capital, from the sum of cash receipts, government payments, perquisites, and net change in inventory.

Thus the fourth annual report of the Southeast Wisconsin Coöperative Farm Management Association, covering 1949, reported an average labor income for 35 farms with 80 acres or less of harvested cropland of $2247, and of $3929 for 93 farms with more than 80 acres. Yet the top fifth of the small farms averaged $4281, or more than two thirds that of the large farms. The lowest one fifth of the large farms averaged only $713.

Comparably, there are wide variations among states. From 1920 to 1931, inclusive, the leading state in terms of yearly cash income per farm was California, which averaged seven times as much income as the

bottom state, Mississippi. In 1944, though Mississippi's average gained over 80 per cent, California averaged almost twelve times as much. In 1944 just one third of the states enjoyed an average per-farm cash income of over $5000. But one more than a third averaged less than $3000.

These facts and the data in Table 13 exhibit the range of individual agricultural enterprise. They also indicate the great complexity of conditions facing schools in utilizing local situations in their teaching, especially agriculture, and the difficulties of the extension service in planning its programs for farmers. This is equally true of other social agencies. These facts show the importance of the Farmers' Home Administration and its work with low-income farmers, which is told about in another chapter.

Some general considerations. In terms of the entire nation, the gross income of agriculture since 1910 has varied from $6.4 billion in 1932 to $35 billion in 1948. Net income has shown an even greater variation. It fell to $1.83 billion in 1932, barely $300 per farm, but reached a peak of $17.8 billion in 1947. In 1950 the net figure was over $13 billion.

In considering these data on net agricultural income, receipts from nonagricultural sources, whether earnings, rent, interest, or social security, must not be forgotten. The Joint Committee on the Economic Report estimates the average net non-farm income of farm families in 1946 as $946.[14] If this estimate is accurate and if there were approximately the same number of farms in 1946 as the 1945 agricultural census reported, the non-farm income of American farm families was $5.67 billion, a handsome addition to the $15.01 billions of net agricultural income. This estimate gains support from the 1950 census results which show that well over one fourth of all farmers reported that their income from non-farm sources exceeds their receipts from the sale of farm products. Indeed, if five midwest states are eliminated the proportion approaches one third. This is but one more indication of the interrelatedness of the rural and urban elements in our society.

Interestingly enough, through many good and bad years, agricultural income and total industrial wages have shown practically a one-to-one correspondence. While no casual relationship has been demonstrated, this fact is at least another indication of the interdependence of our society.

The Occupations of Farm People

Agriculture is of course the chief occupation of gainfully employed farm people. In recent decades, however, members of the farm population have increasingly engaged in non-farm pursuits, though continuing to live on the farm and often to help in farm work in their free time.

Agricultural employment less important. Before presenting data on this subject it is interesting to note that nationally agriculture has declined steadily in importance among the major occupations, as measured by the proportion of the labor force it employs. In 1870, when there were half as many farms as in 1930, 24 per cent of the gainfully employed were farmers and almost as large a proportion, 23.1 per cent, farm laborers. Thus nearly half the gainfully employed were agriculturists. There was a very slight increase in the proportion of farmers by 1880, but from then on a steady decline set in. By 1950, according to the census, only 15.8 per cent of all those gainfully employed were classed as farmers or farm laborers. In other words, in eighty years the proportion of those employed in agriculture declined by more than half, despite a numerical gain of several million persons in the farm population. Nevertheless, when males alone are considered, 14.2 per cent were gainfully employed in agriculture in 1950 and another 1.5 per cent were regular, but unpaid, family workers; only two other major occupational groups included more workers. Even so, this total of 15.7 per cent was sharply lower than the 23 per cent reported in 1940.

Although Negroes made up only 9.8 per cent of the population and one seventh of those gainfully employed in agriculture in 1940, they accounted for 46 per cent of the

[14] Committee Report, Eighty-second Congress, First Session, *Underemployment of Rural Families* (Washington, 1951), p. 41.

TABLE 14	OCCUPATION	MALES Per Cent Total	FEMALES Per Cent Total
Per cent Nonagriculturally Employed Persons by Sex and by Major Categories for Farm Population: 1940	Professional and semiprofessional	5.1	22.2
	Proprietors, managers and officials	9.7	2.9
	Clerical and sales	9.0	15.0
	Craftsmen, foremen, etc.	19.6	0.5
	Operatives	29.4	15.2
	Domestic service	0.9	34.7
	Protective service	1.1	—
	Other service workers	2.4	7.9
	Laborers	22.6	1.4

Source: Computed from *Sixteenth Census of the United States*, 1940, Vol. III, *The Labor Force*, Part I, Table 59. Agriculturally employed persons and small numbers reported as employed but occupation unknown eliminated.

drop in employment between then and 1950. Among the Negro labor force the proportion operating farms or employed for wages in agriculture declined from 26 to 15.9 per cent.

In our culture agriculture is a man's work. In 1940 less than 152,000 women were reported as farmers or farm managers. By 1950 the number had fallen to 126,000.[15]

All major occupational groups represented in non-farm work. In 1940 just over two million members of the farm population were employed in nonagricultural occupations, seven tenths of them males. Since the Seventeenth Census of the United States has not yet reported on occupation by residence, Table 14 summarizes the 1940 findings.

Over 80 per cent of the professionally employed women in the farm population were teachers. Teachers were also the largest single group among the males in this category — 44 per cent. No other single subgroup contained as many as 10 per cent, though clergymen neared this proportion. Retail trade establishments were the largest subgroup among the proprietors of both sexes in the nonagriculturally employed farm population. This outlet also took the largest proportion of the clerical workers. The largest proportion of machine operators for both sexes was found in the various textile-worker subgroups. The use of the automobile brought about great changes in rural employment as shown by the fact that one fourth of the farm females employed in the "other service group" were waitresses. In addition, over 10 per cent were cooks in restaurants, inns, or other public eating places. So other details reflect the changing social customs and conditions of the American scene. Some of these will be commented on later in the analysis of the rural non-farm village population and its functions.

While, as noted, detailed data on occupations are not available for 1950, it is highly significant that the number of persons within the farm population employed in nonagricultural pursuits increased to 2,779,000 by 1950, or by more than one third. This was in spite of the changed definition of farm. The census estimates a further increase of 56,000 persons so employed in the year following the 1950 census enumeration, despite a decline of almost 850,000 persons in the labor force dwelling on farms in that period.

Social Patterns of Farming

It is apparent that agriculture presents a wide variety of conditions, whether judged

[15] Data in this section from Preliminary report of 1950 census, Series PC–7, No. 2, April, 1951.

by size of farm, income tenure, crops raised, or any other pertinent measure. Formulators of social policy have called increasingly for facts that would differentiate significant groups of farms and farmers. The Bureau of Census has responded to some extent, but available data still fall short of the need. The Farmers' Home Administration, for instance, is particularly charged with some types of assistance to low-income farmers. There is no way of determining, however, from published census results whether the low-income farmers of a given county are underemployed on inadequate acreage or whether they are largely part-time cultivators whose income from the farm is but a fractional part of their total earnings. Comparably, there are important economic, social, and demographic questions, among others, which cannot be answered from the published data. This was recognized by the Joint Economic Committee of the Eighty-first Congress in its study of low-income families.

In 1944 several economists of the United States Department of Agriculture drew attention to this "Need for a New Classification of Farms." [16] They proposed five categories based on size of the farm enterprise in terms of value of product, days of wage labor employed, number of days the operator worked off the farm, and age. They also attempted an estimate of the number of farms falling in each of these categories. They did not, however, describe the characteristics of each type beyond the few which entered into their definitions.

The family unit has been the predominant social unit in the operation of agricultural enterprise in the United States. Because of this, in 1947–48 the Columbia University Seminar on Rural Life began a study of the family farm in the United States. From its early work the hypothesis arose that there

[16] Benedict, Elliot, Tolley and Taeuber in *Journal of Farm Economics*, November, 1944, pp. 697 ff.

were definable social patterns in farming. With the coöperation of the Bureau of Agricultural Economics and the Agricultural Division of the Bureau of the Census, and after inspection of 1945 census data, the ten social patterns described below were determined on the basis of the social unit operating the farm, family units or employer-employee units, functions of the enterprise, and scale of operations, the latter two being broken down into four subcategories each. These patterns are briefly described below.

Pattern 1: *Employer Farms* — Units which employed more than one and a half man-years of labor a year, were market oriented, and had a gross value of products of $8000 or more.

Pattern 2: *Large Commercial Family Farms* — Units operated primarily by family labor, market oriented, and with a gross value of products of $8000 or more.

Pattern 3: *Medial Commercial Family Farms* — Units operated primarily by family labor, by operators under 65 years of age, market oriented, and with a gross value of products of $3000 to $7999.

Pattern 4: *Residential-Commercial Family Farms* — Units whose operators were 65 and over *or* who worked off their farms 100 days or more a year, and whose gross value of products ranged from $3000 to $7999.

Pattern 5: *Part-time Farms* — Units whose operators worked off their farms 100 days or more, utilized family labor primarily, and whose gross value of products ranged from $250 to $2999.

Pattern 6: *Elders' Farms* — Units whose operators were 65 and over *and* who worked off their farms less than 100 days a year, and whose gross value of products ranged from $500 to $2999.

Pattern 7: *Subsistence Farms* — Units whose operators were under 65 years of age, worked off their farms less than 100 days a year, whose gross value of products ranged from $500 to $2999, and the major portion of whose products were used on the farm rather than sold.

Pattern 8: *Small Commercial Family Farms* — Units whose operators were under 65 years of age, worked off their farms less than 100 days a year, whose gross value of products ranged from $500 to $2999, and the major portion of whose products was sold rather than used.

Pattern 9: *Residential Farms* — All units with gross value of products ranging from $1 to $499, except those whose operators worked off their farms 100 days or more and had farm products valued at $250 to $499.

Pattern 10: *Nominal Farms* — All units with no farm income reported except those which were placed in other patterns as the result of inspection.

Patterns 1 and 2 were differentiated by the type of social unit involved in farm units. Patterns 3 and 4 were operated on the same scale but were differentiated by function, with Pattern 3 farms being full-time commercial operations, while Pattern 4 farms were part-time, elders', or subsistence farms. Patterns 5, 6, 7, and 8 were operated on the same scale with function serving as the differentiating factor. Patterns 9 and 10 were differentiated by scale of operation, and Pattern 10 included those farms with no farm income but which are farms by virtue of the census definition.

When these patterns were defined, a sample was selected by the sampling specialist of the census from the Middle Atlantic and East North Central divisions in the North and the South Atlantic and East South Central divisions in the South, distributed equally in each region among the types. These four census divisions contained 55 per cent of the nation's farms in 1945. Data from the agricultural, population, and housing censuses were used.[17]

Differences between regions and among patterns significant. Statistically significant differences were found between each pattern of farming and every other pattern in two thirds or more of the variables in almost 90 per cent of the sixteen items used in the South and in over 90 per cent of the fifteen items used in the North. In only one case, the comparison between medial-commercial and residential-commercial farms in the North, were there statistically significant differences in less than half the variables. In both regions these two patterns were more nearly similar than any others.[18] The data with respect to most of these variables for both North and South appear in Tables 14 to 16. These tables are complicated. The data, however, are so significant they will repay study.

It seems clear that the variables used to differentiate social patterns of farming and that the data with respect to these patterns reveal relationships and differences obscured by the system of classification used by the census. Some of the conclusions to be drawn from these data follow.[19]

1. The comparisons of large commercial family farms with employer farms in both the North and the South revealed that family units with adequate capital resources produced a gross income comparable to a large segment of those farms relying on hired labor. The highest gross income farms were exclusively employer farms, but approximately three fourths of the employer farms were operated on the same scale as the large-scale family farms. The specified expenditures on employer farms were two to three times as high as those for large com-

---

[17] Cf. Sloan R. Wayland, *Social Patterns of Farming* (New York: Columbia University Seminar on Rural Life, 1951). In addition to this printed report of

82 pages the detailed results of the study are filed in typescript in the Columbia University Library. This entire section is based on this work.

[18] *Ibid.*, Table 4, p. 76.

[19] The remainder of this section is quoted, with editorial changes, from Professor Wayland's study, *op. cit.*, pp. 77–82.

TABLE 15

Farm Operation Characteristics of Ten Social Patterns of Farming, North and South

CHARACTERISTICS		PATTERN									
		1	2	3	4	5	6	7	8	9	10
Median Value of Products	N.	$16,208	12,861	4,744	4,429	699	1,231	738	1,734	205	....
	S.	$14,668	11,372	4,270	4,249	591	1,125	816	1,488	271	....
Median Capital Resources	N.	$32,982	29,824	12,537	11,666	4,151	5,093	4,032	7,391	3,726	3,354
	S.	$30,000	11,668	6,145	9,595	1,900	2,568	2,087	2,238	1,569	1,853
Median Value: of Mechanization	N.	80% over $2,500	64.7% over $2,500	2,006	1,809	197	249	312	837	132	59% = 0
	S.	52% over $2,500	800	432	507	85	129	166	100	63	54% = 0
Median Cash Wages Paid	N.	63.3% over $2,000	329	139	199	33	37	30	47	30	27
	S.	65.3% over $2,000	180	166	280	30	31	32	34	26	26
Median *Specified Expenditures	N.	$4,541	1,219	614	628	160	169	159	234	140	132
	S.	$4,773	913	571	693	140	156	150	172	133	133
Median Acres Harvested	N.	152	154	104	91	10	30	21	45	9	8
	S.	143	51	43	43	9	20	20	27	7	6

* Cash wages, cost of seeds, plants, trees, livestock and poultry, lime, etc, and feed.
Source: Sloan R. Wayland, *op. cit.*, pp. 24–26.

81

TABLE
16

Percentage Distribution of Farms for Ten Social Patterns of Farming by Tenure and Type of Farming, North and South

CHARACTERISTICS	PATTERN									
	1	2	3	4	5	6	7	8	9	10
Tenure: North										
Owner	90.0	54.0	67.3	89.3	84.0	90.7	85.3	80.7	88.0	80.0
Cash and Share-cash Tenants	2.7	16.0	6.7	3.3	12.7	2.7	6.7	6.0	6.7	7.3
Share Tenants and Croppers	6.7	26.0	22.0	6.7	2.0	6.0	6.0	12.0	2.7	6.7
Others	.7	4.0	4.0	.7	1.3	.7	2.0	1.3	2.7	6.0
Tenure: South										
Owner	86.7	65.3	50.0	76.0	80.0	75.3	72.7	44.0	66.0	61.3
Cash and Share-cash Tenants	4.0	4.7	8.7	4.0	12.0	4.7	8.0	8.0	9.3	12.0
Share Tenants	5.3	13.3	16.0	11.3	1.3	5.3	7.3	15.3	10.0	8.0
Share Croppers	2.0	13.3	20.7	8.0	4.7	10.7	9.3	30.0	8.7	14.0
Others	2.0	3.3	4.7	.7	2.0	4.0	2.7	2.7	6.0	4.7

PATTERN

CHARACTERISTICS		1	2	3	4	5	6	7	8	9	10
Median Age of Operator	N	49.4	45.5	46.5	.....	46.1	.....	50.1	48.9	55.5	50.5
	S	47.5	48.2	44.1	45.4	45.4	.....	47.2	42.4	51.5	46.1
Median Age Household Members	N	35.1	28.0	26.7	39.9	17.8	68.2	23.5	36.1	37.0	38.7
	S	32.3	24.5	18.3	31.6	18.2	46.3	23.8	21.9	25.0	20.8
Fertility Ratio	N	395.3	541.6	554.5	478.9	639.2	181.8	734.9	571.4	468.8	615.4
	S	524.4	453.8	629.9	510.4	616.7	403.8	610.0	541.3	800.0	900.0
Mean Size of Family	N	4.01	4.03	4.35	3.60	4.56	2.68	4.58	3.40	3.03	3.31
	S	4.02	5.20	5.37	4.50	4.72	3.37	4.39	4.22	3.95	3.63
Percent Operators Non-white	S	3.3	8.0	18.7	14.7	12.0	26.0	9.3	36.0	26.7	17.3
Mean Level of Living Index	N	2.72	2.54	2.30	2.53	2.07	1.90	1.64	1.83	1.76	1.29
	S	2.23	1.67	1.26	1.63	1.05	.69	.67	.69	.77	.34
Median Value Home-Used Products	N	$482.	$442.	$418.	$358.	$304.	$223.	$516.	$249.	$122.	.....
	S	487.	497.	487.	474.	431.	375.	550.	317.	185.	.....
Percent Adults Reporting Off-Farm Work	N	4.9	5.3	7.1	18.9	39.8	5.3	13.5	10.5	23.0	27.3
	S	5.4	5.1	5.3	15.5	38.8	7.2	7.5	4.1	15.4	17.4

TABLE 17

Farm Household and Family Living Characteristics of Ten Social Patterns of Farming, North and South

83

mercial family farms, a large portion of which was the price of labor that family farms largely provided from their own households. With the continued development of equipment for the family-operated farm, it is clear that large-scale operations in all types of farming may be engaged in by family units. While support of family farms by federal legislation is a moral and political issue, the choice is not between large-scale employer farms and small-scale family farms.

2. The concept of "family farm" has been divided into a number of subtypes, some commercial units and some noncommercial or quasi-commercial. For the three commercial family farm patterns some distinctive characteristics were revealed.

a. In both North and South the three levels of commercial family farms had the least favorable tenure status of the ten patterns. In the North the proportion of ownership decreased as the scale of operation increased, whereas in the South the reverse was true. It appears that the decline in the proportion of tenant-operated farms, discussed in the next chapter, has occurred more largely among part-time, residential, and other agriculturally less important patterns than among commercial family farms.

b. For both North and South the large and medial commercial family farms had much more regular age-sex distributions than the small-scale units. The holding power of family farms, operated on a scale to permit a higher level of living for the young adult population, was substantially better than on units operated on an inadequate scale. If the agricultural ladder were working efficiently, the younger operators might be expected to be found in the small commercial family farms. However, they were well represented in both large and medial commercial family farms. With the range in ages represented in these patterns, it is apparent that placement in these patterns was not a function of position in the family cycle to any great extent. Another measure of holding power was the relatively greater size of households on the larger commercial family farms.

c. Larger scales of operation for family farms did not decrease the degree of reliance on the farms for goods for home consumption. In fact, increased mechanization and scale of operation resulted in an increase in the per-capita consumption of home-used products.

3. Several interesting relationships between northern and southern farming were revealed.

a. Pattern by pattern, the value of products for the North and the South were similar. However, the capital resources of southern farms were about half those of northern patterns, except for employer farms.

b. Although the value of products for northern and southern patterns were not significantly different, the level of living for households in corresponding patterns was substantially different. Since some of the facilities which go to make up a level of living are usually community functions, individual farm income may not make possible certain changes in level of living without major outlays of funds. The relationship is even more marked for the southern nonwhite operators, whose value of products did not differ significantly from that of white operators, but whose level of living was substantially lower. The northern farms operating on the lowest scale had a higher index of level of living than those southern farms operating on the middle scale.

c. Although the tenure class of sharecroppers is usually associated with small-scale operations, one eighth of the large commercial family farms and one fifth of the medial commercial family farms were operated by sharecroppers, and a corresponding proportion in each pattern were share-tenants.

d. While non-white operators made up about one quarter of the farm operators in the South, the proportions of non-white operators on employer farms and large commercial family farms were only 3.3 per cent and 8 per cent respectively. The highest proportions of non-white operators were found in Patterns 8 and 6, small commercial and elders' in which 36 per cent and 26 per cent were non-white operators.

4. Part-time farm operators (Pattern 5) in both regions were concentrated in the 33–54 age bracket, with only a negligible proportion 65 and over. Part-time farm households had a high fertility ratio, a low median age of household members, and a relatively high average size of households. Their off-farm work made possible a somewhat higher level of living than other households with similar farm income. However, their level of living did not approach that of medial commercial family farm households.

5. Elder farmers were apparently small and medial commercial family farm operators who had reduced their scale of operation, since their capital resources and types of farming were comparable to the commercial farms. However, elder farm operators were in a better tenure position than others operating on a similar scale in both the North and the South.

There are many implications growing out of these data. Obviously, each type will re-quire different sorts of educational assistance from an extension service. The contrasting behavior of the age patterns among commercial farmers is clearly of importance to schools where any one pattern is dominant in the community. The ratio of school population to total will vary considerably and no blanket formula can be applied. Comparably, health needs and programs will differ according to which pattern is numerically the most important. The contrasting behavior of North and South on a number of items indicates that no nation-wide generalizations on these or other points can be made. Factors such as these, were research results available, would doubtless qualify some of the generalizations in the following discussion of "Man and His Land."

Summary. This chapter has shown something of the great size and complexity of American agriculture. It has indicated the diversity in the scale of farm operations and noted that these diversities have influenced the social and economic structure and organization of communities. It has revealed that both high- and low-income farms are to be found in all regions and that many farmers are not wholly agriculturists. Finally, it has indicated that out of this complicated, complex agricultural enterprise in the United States, it is possible to distinguish definite social patterns.

TOPICS FOR DISCUSSION

1. Conduct a panel discussion on the advantages and disadvantages of corporation and family commercial farms.
2. What changes in farm practice have taken place in your home community within the last generation? How were these changes brought about? Were they part of any well-defined social movement, local or national? Were they related to changes in transportation facilities, or to the growth of cities?
3. Trace the changes in the average size of farms in your county or state since 1910 and explain the changes.
4. Explain the divergencies in average income per farm between the six highest and the six lowest states. Are these differences "natural"? Defend your opinion.

5. Conduct a field trip and identify farms visited according to the social patterns they represent.
6. Report on the procedures and results of some soil-conservation measures in a district known to you.
7. Write a case history of a family farm which has been operated by the same family for three or more generations.

REFERENCE READINGS

Consult any standard text in agricultural economics for further data on major items discussed.

Johnson, G. W., *Wasted Land*. Chapel Hill: University of North Carolina Press, 1937.

Lord, R., *Behold Our Land*. Boston: Houghton Mifflin, 1938.

McWilliams, Carey, *Factories in the Field*. Boston: Little, Brown, 1939.

Osborn, Fairfield, *Our Plundered Planet*. Boston: Little, Brown, 1948.

Renne, R. R., *Land Economics*. New York: Harper, 1947.

FILMS

Life on the Modern Farm. S, 17. March of Time, New York.

Muddy Waters. S, 8. United States Department of Agriculture, Washington.

Soil Erosion. S, 7. March of Time, New York.

The River. S, 33. United States Department of Agriculture, Washington.

7

Man and His Land

Land Tenure

THUS FAR the discussion has proceeded without mention of the arrangements by which farms of a given size, value, and productive power are operated. Land is valuable, of course, only because on it men find shelter and employment and from it food and fiber can be raised and minerals extracted. It is the foundation of life. But land has value only in its relation to people. Land is, of course, owned. To be useful it must be operated, which means labor. Because it is wealth, it can be taxed for certain purposes. For the same reason, it is a capital resource which can be used as security for borrowing money. This very recital indicates the importance of both social uses of land and social policies with respect to land. Men have evolved two major relationships by which they are associated with specific plots of land from which they can produce needed agricultural commodities. The *owner* possesses his acres, controls them, and is the sole beneficiary of their productivity after his expenses are met. The *tenant* lives upon and cultivates land that belongs to another individual, with whom he shares both the proceeds of his toil and usually the responsibility of management.

The hunger for land. There are few races that do not display a desire for land, and the more rural races are the stronger this desire usually is. To the peasant, land represents ultimate security. Agrarian unrest has often developed where a growth of commercialization caused the tillers of the land to lose their complete control of it, as will be shown in a later chapter.

Causes for rise of farm tenancy. The American tradition has always been one of landownership, largely because, for nearly three centuries after the first settlements on the Atlantic seaboard, so much land was available for so little money. Even yet there is no pressure of population on the land such as one observes in the Orient. The so-called tenancy problem did not present itself in this country until after the Civil War, and when it came it was directly associated with the declining quantity of good land available for homesteading under federal grant.

But there was at least one other cause for the rise in farm tenancy in the United States. Young men desiring to be farmers and not possessing sufficient capital to buy a farm sought one they could work on shares. Conversely, elderly farmers desiring to retire sought to rent their farms, often to their own sons or nephews. The blood tie, therefore, was prominent in early tenant arrangements, and though its importance decreased, even as late as 1930 one fifth of the farm tenants were related to their landlords. This national average was brought down by the South, where the proportion is less than one tenth. In the Middle West, Middle Atlantic, and New England states it was nearly one third. There are no subsequent national data on this point, though some surveys show that kinship is still important in these three regions.

It was the prevalence of the kinship factor in the early development of farm tenancy, along with a few other factors such as the tenant's desire to be.free to climb the agricultural ladder from tenancy to ownership when possible, that is responsible for the short lease, usually one year, which prevails in many sections. Such short leases facilitated speedy adjustments within the family when necessary, but they are frequently considered socially disadvantageous when the tenant is not related to the landlord, since the necessity for an annual renewal of the lease makes for insecurity and removes some of the incentive to conserve soil and property.

The agricultural ladder. In the United States the rise of a young farmer to full ownership of his land has been likened to climbing a ladder. The usual pattern is that he begins as a helper for his father or a hired hand cn a neighbor's farm, saves enough to become a tenant, and finally buys his own farm. In time two additional rungs were added. One was that of a mortgaged owner, the other that of part-owner or part-tenant. Actually thousands never go beyond the first rung, many leaving farming entirely. During the depressions of the 1890's and 1920's some owners had to step down a rung or two. In the last decade the high cost of land and equipment has made the ladder more like a mountain for some, and new devices have been tried to keep the farm in the family, of which more later.

In this matter of farm tenancy three rural sciences meet. To the soil scientist, tenancy has become almost synonymous with "mining" rather than cultivating the land. To the economist, tenancy means the problem of having a farm support more than one family. The sociologist is interested in the effect of tenancy and its arrangements on the tenant and the social life and institutions of his community.

Growth and decline of farm tenancy. The growth of farm tenancy in the United States has been uneven. When first measured by the census in 1880, it was found that 25.6 per cent of the farms were tenant-operated. Ten years later the proportion had risen to 28.4 per cent.

During the closing decade of the nineteenth century began the rapid rise in the price of farm land which lasted for thirty years. Tenancy also rose apace, among many other reasons because it then took longer for a prospective owner to accumulate sufficient capital to purchase a farm. The proportion of tenant-operated farms increased by more than one fourth, and stood in 1900 at 35.3 per cent of the total.

Many felt that this was an alarming portent in American life. By the end of the first quarter of the twentieth century, 38.6 per cent of American farms were tenant-operated, according to the 1925 agricultural census. The next five years saw a more rapid increase than any previous decade, to 42.4 per cent of the farms in 1930 and more than half the farm land. This was one result of the agricultural depression of the 1920's. From then on, however, the proportion of farms operated by tenants declined, very slowly at first, to 39.7 per cent in 1940, then more rapidly, to 31.7 per cent in 1945 and 26.7 per cent in 1950. This decline to practically the levels of 1880 is a reflection of the high prices for farm products during the 1940's, which enabled many tenants to buy their farms.

These national data conceal a number of important differences. Tenancy has always been relatively higher in the southern region than elsewhere because of the concentration of Negroes and share-croppers. In 1930 this region had one half the nation's farms but three fifths the tenants. The dramatic decline in the rate of tenant operation of southern farms from 55.5 per cent in 1930 to 40.4 per cent in 1945 and 34.0 per cent in 1950 is associated with the decline in the number of share-croppers and the increase in wage labor and mechanization. This decline was in turn accelerated by the reduction in cotton acreage under the Agricultural Adjustment program, and the attendant increase in diversification and new patterns of farm management. The middle western states have also had high ratios of tenant operation. Here one cause was the higher cost of farms, and another was the relatively large number of business and professional people in small cities and towns who purchased farms as investments and hence desired tenant operators. Such farms were not available for sale to tenants desiring to climb the agricultural ladder. The proportions were 34.0 in 1930, in 1945 29.2 and 23.1 in 1950. The other census divisions have always had relatively few tenants, but their proportions increased slightly between 1930 and 1940, and then declined.

In considering these data, reference to Professor Wayland's study of the *Social Patterns of Farming*,[1] discussed at some length in the previous chapter, makes it clear that tenancy has decreased least in those patterns which best represent the traditional family farm in the United States. The family farm, owner operated, represents one of the values held by rural people, and every national farm organization has repeatedly endorsed this ideal. Yet it is evident that farms in this social pattern have lagged behind others in improving the owner-tenant ratio of the last years. Even the agrarian prosperity of the 1940's has not solved this problem, though the situation shows improvement.

Trend in tenure studies. A long-time look at the situation confirms this conclusion. From 1880 to 1940 for the United States as

[1] Sloan R. Wayland, *Social Patterns of Farming* (New York: Columbia University Seminar on Rural Life, 1951).

a whole and for every census division, the number of owners in each thousand males gainfully employed in agriculture has declined. In the same period the number of tenants has increased for the United States as a whole and for all but the New England, Middle Atlantic, and Pacific divisions; the number of laborers has gained except for the South. These data are summarized below.

Year	Owners	Tenants	Laborers
1880	547	187	266
1900	474	256	270
1920	451	283	266
1940	414	273	313

Source: Carl C. Taylor, Louis J. Ducoff, and Margaret J. Hagood, *Trends in Tenure Statistics of Farm Workers in the United States since 1880* (Washington, D.C.: Bureau of Agricultural Economics, United States Department of Agriculture, 1948), p. 1.

Social effects of tenancy. If, as appears, the ratio of tenant-operated farms among the family-commercial patterns of farming has been slow to decline, it is important to examine the social effects of tenancy. If tenancy is a function of industrialism, it is an inevitable phenomenon of the present state of development in the Western world, yet there are many who maintain that land-ownership is one of the strongest bulwarks of national safety. However, the United States has in the past placed powerful assistance at the disposal of those who crave their own stake in the land and it may do so again, not only by advancing credit, but possibly by carrying out some of its developing policies for land utilization.

Whether an unavoidable accompaniment of industrialism or not, areas of high tenancy differ from areas of high ownership in certain respects. The social scientist is interested in these differences, and the conditions they create are frequently problems for the rural educator, social worker, and clergyman.

There have been numerous studies of this point. As the chapter on standards of living shows, tenants are likely to have a somewhat lower standard of living than farm owners, at least as measured by the proportion possessing telephones, automobiles, musical instruments, bathtubs, electric lights, furnaces, and other conveniences. In these respects the tenant who is related to the owner of the farm makes a better record than the tenant who has no such tie.

These facts do not necessarily discredit either tenants or tenancy. The tenant is usually younger than the owner. He has not had an opportunity to acquire all the conveniences of life. He is perhaps trying to save for a first payment on his future farm. Moreover, he is more likely than the owner to have young children.

Effects on community usually adverse. When all allowances are made, however, it is clear that the social consequences of a high proportion of tenant-operated farms in a community are unhappy. Studies made by the Institute of Social and Religious Research seem to show that such effects begin to appear when the ratio of tenant- to owner-operated farms exceeds one in five.

Up to this point, for instance, the proportion of tenants belonging to church and social organizations is approximately the same as that of owners. Beyond this point, the differences become more pronounced. For example, in middle western counties where 50 per cent or more of the farms are tenant-operated, only one third as many tenants as owners are listed as active church members. Although these figures may vary with the type of organization, the trend is the same for lodges, farm bureaus, and all important types of social organizations.

An obvious corollary follows: In tenant-dominated communities all types of social organizations tend to be weaker and less progressive than in localities in which owners

preponderate. One obvious reason for this lies in the insecurity of the renter's tenure. If he operates under a short-term lease he is not sure how long he will remain in the community. He hesitates to form ties until he feels more certain of permanence. Eventually, perhaps, he habituates himself to living more apart from organized social life than does the owner who, because of his capital investment, is likely to be more securely anchored to the locality and therefore more interested in its social life.

Another reason for the less satisfactory condition of social organizations where tenants form a considerable fraction of the population frequently lies in the phenomenon of absentee landlordism. Inevitably absentee landlords become interested chiefly, if not exclusively, in the return from the farm. Community betterment, especially if it raises taxes, is unwelcome and hence opposed. When taxes consume a large part of the landlord's income, such an attitude is understandable.

The unfortunate social consequences of farm tenancy are especially noticeable in the South, where the problem is also complicated by the large number of share-croppers. But even elsewhere class distinctions between tenants and owners occur, since the two groups often belong to different churches, lodges, and other social organizations.

Who owns the land? [2] The discussion thus far leads to the question who owns the farm land of the United States. In 1946 over 85 per cent of it belonged to individuals. Two thirds of the owners were farmers, and they held seven tenths of the individually owned acreage. One in twelve was a retired farmer. This group in the aggregate had one tenth

[2] Data in the following three paragraphs taken from B. T. Inman and W. H. Fippin, *Farm Land Ownership in the United States* (Washington, D.C.: Bureau of Agricultural Economics, United States Department of Agriculture, 1949), p. 51.

TABLE	REGION	TYPE OF OWNERSHIP			
		Individual	Corporate	Public	Other*
18	United States	85.4	5.6	4.9	4.1
Percentage of Land in Farms by Major Types of Owners, United States and Regions, 1945	North East	96.3	2.9	0.3	0.5
	North Central	94.0	2.1	2.7	1.2
	South	88.5	7.4	2.3	1.8
	West	69.1	8.1	11.7	11.1

* Three fourths of this is Indian land.
  Source: B. T. Inman and W. H. Fippin, *Farm Land Ownership in the United States* (Washington: Bureau of Agricultural Economics, United States Department of Agriculture, 1949), p. 51.

of the land. Three per cent of the owners were housewives. Of the remaining fourth of the owners, two in five were business or professional persons who held one seventh of the acreage; three in five were clerical workers or laborers, whose holdings accounted for only one acre out of 20, frequently averaging less than 30 acres. Less than half of the clerical workers and more than two thirds of the laborers lived permanently on their land. Presumably, these farms were near towns or cities which had disproportionate numbers of residential and part-time farmers. Probably also many of the holdings of these two occupational categories would not be classified as farms under the new 1950 definition of farm.

Eighteen per cent of all of the above land-owning individuals were landlords only, while another 15 per cent farmed some of their land and rented the rest. Over half of the first group and about two fifths of the second were dependent upon rent from this land for the principal source of their income.

Farm land not owned by individuals was divided among corporations, public authorities, and all other types. As Table 18 shows, there were wide regional fluctuations. It is probable that some of the corporation land was held by incorporated family farms. It is significant that despite the large number of farms acquired by insurance companies and banks by foreclosure during the long depression of the 1920's and 1930's, less than 6 per cent of the farm land of the United States was corporation owned in 1946. Many of these were operating corporations. On the other hand, 3 per cent of the persons having title to farm land owned 41 per cent of the acreage in the hands of individuals. Much of this was western grazing land, but every region showed some tendency toward concentration of ownership. The slow but steady increase in the number of farms of one thousand acres and over shown by the censuses of the last half century indicates that this concentration is increasing.

This fact illustrates a contradiction in the values held by Americans. On the one hand, there is the belief that farm land should be owned by those who till the soil in family-sized units. On the other hand, under our philosophy of free enterprise we believe that any individual may acquire as much land as he wants and can pay for. Only in the Territory of Puerto Rico is there a limitation on the maximum number of acres (five hundred) any individual or corporation may own. This is a matter of national land policy. It raises the question as to whether measures are needed to strengthen or facilitate family farm ownership.

Strengthening the family farm. The announced objective of a number of laws dealing with agriculture enacted by Congress in the last two decades has been to strengthen the family farm. The Under Secretary of Agriculture, Clarence J. McCormick, speaking before the assembly of the Food and Agriculture Organization in June, 1951, declared this to be our national policy and urged land reform as a major activity of the organization and its member governments. How far has this policy been implemented?

One early effort in this direction was that of the Homestead Act to enable settlers to acquire farms on generous terms. While the purposes of this act were frequently abused, it was measurably effective so long as large areas of public land remained unsettled. At present, despite continued agitation for its repeal, there is a 160-acre limitation on farm land acquired from the Federal Government. A few states have laws exempting homesteads from seizure for debt. Farm credit legislation and the Agricultural Adjustment Act of 1933, discussed elsewhere, as well as other legislation of the 1930's, was aimed to help family farms.

In 1937 Congress set up the Farm Security, now the Farmers' Home, Administration. It was charged, among other things, with helping selected tenants to purchase farms through loans. Low interest rates and repayment of principal in from twenty to forty years were provided, together with some guidance in farm management. This tenant-purchase program is akin to comparable programs in several other countries, notably in Ireland, where over a period of some decades the proportion of owner-operators among the total farm population was increased from 3 to 97 per cent.[3]

The program of the Farmer's Home Administration and its predecessor for aiding

selected tenants to become owners is in the nature of a demonstration rather than an ambitious program to eliminate tenancy among American farmers. Thus far it has reached only about sixty thousand farm families and is financially assisting over four thousand additional tenants each year. To date, over 98 per cent of the payments have been made when due, and only six of the first ten thousand purchase loans have been defaulted. This compares favorably with the general farm credit situation discussed in a later chapter.

Several organizations, notably several insurance companies, have adopted the same plan in financing the large number of farms it was necessary for them to acquire by foreclosure during the agricultural depression.

Broader aspects of the problem were attacked by a presidential tenancy committee, which reported in 1937. It planned in some detail for a Farm Security Corporation to help tenants toward ownership and made suggestions as to rehabilitation work. Other recommendations were designed to discourage land speculation, to improve lease contracts and landlord-tenant relations, to relieve small homesteads of taxation, and to safeguard civil liberties. The need for improved education and health services was also stressed. Several state commissions appointed by governors have made reports agreeing in the main with the proposals just noted. One state report went so far as to propose higher tax rates where several farms are under one ownership. One state, South Carolina, has conducted a highly significant demonstration in one county in improving landlord-tenant relations. This has been accomplished by joint meetings under Extension Service auspices, at which problems and difficulties were discussed frankly. As a result tenant houses have been improved, home gardens started, and production has improved.

These proposals have not been translated

[3] Cf. Elizabeth Hooker, *Readjustments of Agricultural Tenure in Ireland* (Chapel Hill: University of North Carolina Press, 1938).

into effective operation; in fact, they have been ignored by Congress save for the important exception of the tenant-purchase program of the Farmers' Home Administration. But the fundamental fact is that no long-time national policies for agriculture can wholly succeed, whether they relate to prices, soil conservation, or production adjustment, unless some of the basic problems of tenancy are solved. Such policies would be handicapped by a pattern of land tenure that promises little security, and therefore little incentive, for millions of farm families. Such conditions make migration from the land inevitable. Certainly some of these youth should migrate, but if the present situation continues, the more able children of tenants will be forced to seek opportunity elsewhere, away from the farm land which needs their vitality.

There is no possibility of expanding the tenant-purchase program to enable eligible tenents to become farm owners. The cost to the Government would run into billions. The answer appears to be not only in the proposals of the Presidential Committee on Farm Tenancy, but also in new legislation that would protect tenants. Such legislation might provide for longer terms for leases, compensate the tenant for making improvements to land and buildings, and protect him from undue control in his farm-management program. Such provisions are written into law in a number of countries, notably England, which for over sixty years has had agricultural legislation far in advance of that which exists at present in any of the United States. On the basis of the experience of these other countries, it is safe to claim that such legislation, adjusted to the American situation, would prove a powerful incentive for the tenant to conserve rather than to mine the soil, induce more farmers' sons to remain in agriculture, result in a more careful selection of tenants by landlords, and improve the level of the community itself by giving security and therefore stability to the tenant and his family.

Our future farmers. The foregoing proposals relate largely to present tenants and their situation. Of late increasing attention has been given to the problem of maintaining the family on the farm over generations.

About a third of the individual owners of farm land in 1946 had acquired their acres through gift or inheritance or by a combination of these with some purchase money. One in ten had bought all their land from relatives. Except for a few who had homesteaded, the rest, more than half, had had to purchase all their land from persons unrelated to them.[4]

There are two phases of one problem here. It is difficult for a young man wishing to farm to acquire sufficient capital to purchase a farm unless he is assisted by his family. The great increase in the price of land and equipment and necessary restrictions on the proportion of farm value that can be borrowed, create the danger that the prospective farmer will be content with too small an acreage and find himself underemployed. One alternative is for farms on the market to be added to the holdings of a contiguous farmer, accelerating the trend toward larger units.

The prospective farmer who has his family's farm available is in a better position. However, if there are other heirs, he usually has to buy them out and hence meets the same basic problem. Nevertheless, an Iowa study shows such a person gains some advantage in the family situation, though his advancement to ownership status is often delayed.[5]

A new agricultural ladder? The state col-

[4] B. T. Inman and W. H. Fippin, *op. cit.*, pp. 33–42.

[5] Robert A. Rohwer, *Family Factors in Tenure Experience* (Ames: Iowa State College, Argicultural Experiment Station, 1950), Bulletin 375.

leges of agriculture have begun to study the problem of keeping the farm in the family. Coöperating committees have been set up in several regions. Some devices tried by farm families in order to keep the farm in the family have been explored. Among these are family farm-operating agreements and father-son farm agreements.

As some agricultural economists see it, the new ladder begins with project agreements such as those involving 4-H Club or Future Farmers of America projects. The next step would be a formalized apprenticeship, often with a monthly wage allowance to the son, from which he meets his own expenses. The third rung would be a partnership, which would begin the necessary transfer arrangements. Finally would come the assumption of full ownership.

Where more than one son desires to continue in farming the problem is more difficult unless the enterprise is large enough to warrant a partnership. In some cases the family farm has been incorporated.[6]

There has not been enough experience to date to determine which of a number of methods is best in each of various situations which might arise when a family farm must change hands. The amount of research and the general interest in the problem is evidence that a social need has been recognized. The various experiments under way indicate that rural society is feeling its way toward new devices that will satisfy the high value placed on land ownership by the operator's family and in keeping the farm in the family over the generations.

There are situations, of course, in which keeping the farm in the family may work counter to other values and desires, for instance, education for a son or daughter, or the entrance of a son into an occupation which greatly interests him and for which he has more aptitude than he has for agriculture. Any arrangements worked out to meet the general problem must obviously be only for those who desire to use them.

Farm Labor

Regardless of tenure status, farms obviously cannot be operated without labor. Like everything else in agriculture, the farm labor situation has changed rapidly in the last half century. Since family farms make up the great majority of the units in American agriculture, it is not surprising that the great bulk of labor is supplied by the farm operator and members of his family. Only one farm in five employed any wage labor at the peak of the 1948 harvest season.[7]

Types of farm labor. Traditionally the "hired man," like the "hired girl," on the nineteenth-century farm was a neighbor, perhaps a less fortunate neighbor, perhaps the child of another farmer serving as an apprentice. Such workers were "one of the family," whether they looked forward to operating their own farm or were more or less permanently attached to the employer. They served on a twelve-month basis.

There are still farm laborers of this type, though they are no longer the chief group, nor is there a complete absence of the social distinction that seems once to have existed. Mechanization was an important reason for this change, even on dairy farms, since it has increased the amount of work the operator can do and lessened his dependence on others outside the family.

Large-scale farms still employ labor on a permanent or semipermanent basis. These include the pineapple and sugar plantations

[6] Edmund deS. Brunner, *Case Studies of Family Farms* (New York: Columbia University Seminar on Rural Life, 1949).

[7] Bureau of Agricultural Economics, *Wages and Wage Rates of Hired Farm Workers* (Washington, D.C., 1950).

of Hawaii, the huge vegetable farms of California and some other areas, cattle ranches, and dairy farms with more cows than the farm family can care for. The average April, however, finds only about 150,000 farms with three or more workers, though this number considerably more than doubles by September.

A farm labor group of increasing importance is seasonal workers, defined by the Department of Agriculture as employed less than 150 days a year. This group has two main divisions. There are the migratory workers who follow crops from south to north as they mature, or who leave the cities to work within a more limited area and on only one, or a few, crops. The other seasonal workers come from within the area, often the same community, in which they work and labor for only a few weeks, usually at harvest. Industries in a number of smaller cities in the Northeast arrange their production schedules or inventory periods in order to release employees for farm labor when crops mature. Under such arrangements the same people often return to the same farm year after year. Fruit and vegetable farms, especially but not exclusively small ones, make large use of this type of labor.

There are two other categories of seasonal workers. Custom workers, often small farmers with machinery, hire themselves and their equipment to others. Their earnings include cost of labor and machinery, and because these are not separable are not included in farm labor data. There are also "crews" who work in a group or gang and divide the wages paid, usually equally. These are relatively small classes.

The agricultural labor force. In April, 1950, slightly more than two million persons fourteen years of age and over gave their occupation in the last week of March as farm laborers. Several hundred thousand

of these were then unemployed.[8] Counting the farm operators and managers, the total gainfully employed labor force of agriculture was 6,536,000 persons at the time of the 1950 census. A year later the census monthly report on the labor force estimated just under 6,400,000 persons employed in agriculture, excluding unpaid family labor. The picture for the week September 3–9, 1950, at the height of harvesting, was reported by the same source as follows:

Self-employed (i.e., farm operators)	4,358,000
Employed for wages	1,918,000
Unpaid family workers	1,535,000
Total agricultural labor force	7,811,000

Such monthly labor force reports of the Bureau of the Census are necessarily only estimates. This is the difficulty with all the farm labor data. The demand for help is governed by progress of crops. A cold spell retards maturity, a hot spell accelerates it. The beginning of cranberry picking in southeastern Massachusetts, for instance, is usually the first week in September. In the last few years it has been as late as mid-September and as early as August 24. Any enumeration as of the first week in September in this area would be considerably affected by such fluctuations. The willingness of local people to put in a few weeks at harvest also varies according to the need to "save the crop" and the desire for some extra money. During World War II thousands did farm work at rush periods for patriotic motives. In the course of a year about 2,250,000 persons are involved in this group of local nonmigratory workers. It is also well known that hard times, whether local or national, increase applications for farm jobs.

The core of the hired labor force is probably best estimated by the number of persons employed on a monthly wage. Based

[8] Bureau of the Census, Series P–50, No. 29, May 2, 1951.

on estimates by the Bureau of Agricultural Economics and the 1945 census of agriculture, these amounted to 740,000 in 1944, employed by about 500,000 farms. Only about 8 per cent of these farms had three or more hired hands. In terms of the entire year, however, 625,000 farms — 10.3 per cent — employed workers on a monthly wage at one time or another through the year. Thus even this criterion shows wide fluctuation and the number with year-round employment has declined since 1944. The President's Commission puts the number of year-round employees at 600,000 and estimates that 400,000 more have "regular" farm employment of 150 to 250 days.[9] The first of these groups is naturally the most stable and, along with short-term local help, the least involved in the problems discussed in the pages following.

Need for farm labor decreasing. Changes in agricultural technology are reducing the need for farm labor, which is becoming an ever more hazardous occupation from the economic point of view. In 1931 almost half the hired farm workers had full-time employment and 70 per cent could count on eight months or more. The comparable figures for 1949 were less than one fifth and 40 per cent. All census divisions shared in this decline. Conversely, in 1931 only 11 per cent of the farm help were employed for short periods — two months or less; in 1949 the figure was 27 per cent.

Migratory labor problems acute. The unhappy lot of migratory farm labor has aroused a great deal of concern in recent decades. Their wages, housing and living conditions, hiring and employment practices, have all come in for severe criticism by church organizations, social agencies, and even the press. In 1950 the New York *Times* ran a series of daily articles on the problem, and in June of that year President Truman appointed a Commission to study the subject. Several states have similar bodies. The situation is complicated by the fact that some farm laborers are not American citizens. During World War II and in some of the succeeding years considerable numbers — over 90,000 in 1944 and again in 1945 — were legally imported to ease the war-induced farm labor shortage in some crops. Since then thousands, especially Mexicans, have entered the United States illegally to compete for agricultural jobs.

How many migrants are there? On the basis of records of placements in farm jobs of all categories during World War II, it may be estimated that about five million farm jobs were filled in 1949.[10] Possibly that many persons were involved, many of whom worked only a few weeks near their homes. This same study states:

From various sources, it is estimated that there were approximately one million migratory farm workers in the United States at some time during the year, not including an unknown number of Mexican nationals who had entered illegally and were still in the country in December when the survey was made. (It is believed that persons residing illegally in the country would not have been reported to the survey enumerators.) This total involved a little more than 500,000 domestic workers and a little under 500,000 Mexican nationals, who were not in this country in December of that year.

The President's Commission estimates one million without qualification.

[9] President's Commission on Migratory Labor, *Migratory Labor in American Agriculture* (Washington, D.C., 1951). Unless otherwise noted, all data in this section are drawn from this report.

[10] The Bureau of Agricultural Economics in *Migratory Farm Workers in 1949*, page 4, says "persons" not jobs. Many persons, especially migrants, have more than one job in a summer. This survey was based on a sample of 25,000 persons.

Migrant and non-migrant farm laborers compared. Differences in age and sex distribution of migrant and non-migrant farm workers were not large. The latter had a higher percentage of persons seventeen and under and sixty-five and over. About half of the migrant men and two thirds of the non-migrants gave farm work as their chief activity. This was true of less than one fifth of the migrant women and only one tenth of the non-migrant.

Of the migratory farm workers covered, the proportion who were living in urban and rural non-farm localities at the end of the year was much greater than was true among the non-migrants. Urban residents accounted for 27 per cent of all migratory workers compared with only 12 per cent of non-migrants. Farm residents made up 67 per cent of the non-migratory workers but constituted only 44 per cent of the migratory workers.[11]

Wages of farm laborers low. Farm labor is not well paid. In 1949, migratory workers averaged $5.60 a day, when employed, non-migratory just under $4.00, according to the President's Commission. Counting non-farm work, the former averaged $739 a year, the latter, $818. Three quarters of the migrants' annual earnings came from farm work, of the non-migrants, four fifths. Deducting males employed 24 days a year or fewer, migratory workers averaged 98 days of farm and 37 days of non-farm employment a year. The comparable non-migratory group had 165 days of farm and 25 days of non-farm work. Twice as many non-migratory workers are employed 250 days or more a year as migratory. These non-migrants, of course, have some perquisites not available to migrant workers. Many receive lodging and meals. Full-time workers with families usually have the use of some land for a home garden.

[11] *Ibid.*, pp. 4 and 5. Rural non-farm workers are evidently not included in these figures.

Some idea of the value of these perquisites, and also of the trend in farm labor wages, can be had by comparing average cash wages by the month with and without meals for September, in 1945 and 1948.

Monthly pay
without meals, 1948 — $133.70
1945 — 108.30
with meals, 1948 — 98.10
1945 — 76.60

There was considerable variation among the regions in this particular. In both years the Northeast and North Central states were below, but close to, the average; the West well above; and the South way below. Thus, in 1948 the average farm hand in the West received $135.40 a month with meals, $191.90 without. Comparable figures for the South were $66.90 and $93.60.[12] Obviously, these wages are far below those of industrial workers. Between 1948 and 1951 cash wages on an hourly basis have increased slightly but have declined in purchasing power about 10 per cent. The President's Commission states that in 1910–1914 hourly earnings of farm workers averaged 67 per cent of those of factory workers, but only 37 per cent in 1950. They also point to regional "inequities" in farm wages, which have widened over the years. Table 19 shows average farm wage rates for the various regions for the past forty years.

Reason for low farm wages. There are many reasons for these low wage rates in agriculture. One is the fact that tens, if not hundreds, of thousands are employed for only brief periods. They are not dependent upon these jobs and look on them merely as a means of supplementing other income. As noted earlier, the President's Commis-

[12] Bureau of Agricultural Economics, *Wages and Wage Rates of Hired Farm Workers*, p. 19. Cf. also statement by Louis Ducoff at the Annual Agricultural Outlook Conference, October 30, 1951.

TABLE	REGION	AVERAGE FARM WAGE RATES PER HOUR		PERCENTAGE, EACH REGIONAL WAGE RATE ABOVE OR BELOW THE NATIONAL AVERAGE WAGE	
		1910–14	1949	1910–14	1949
19	New England	$0.15	$0.66	+23	+20
	Middle Atlantic	.14	.61	+30	+11
	East North Central	.13	.59	+25	+ 7
Average Farm Wages	West North Central	.14	.65	+40	+18
	South Atlantic	.09	.42	−31	−24
	East South Central	.09	.38	−32	−31
	West South Central	.11	.51	−16	− 7
	Mountain	.16	.66	+48	+20
	Pacific	.21	.90	+52	+64
	United States	.14	.55		

sion estimates the number of these seasonal non-migratory workers at 2,250,000.

Improvement in technology is another reason. In 1949 we produced 27 per cent more than in 1940, with 5 per cent less labor. Obviously the demand for labor is not as acute as it was ten years ago.

The President's Commission lays part of the blame for low wage rates on the competition of foreign labor imported in sufficient amounts to depress the market in some areas. It says:

It appears to us significant that the regions in which farm wages are well below the national average and have been so for 40 years are those regions containing the States in which the major portion of the postwar foreign labor contracting has centered. Florida has been the principal user of British West Indian contract labor and Texas has been the principal user of Mexican contract labor. Both States have wage rates much below the national average. We cannot, therefore, escape the conclusion that demand for foreign labor in these States is in part, at least, due to the desire to keep low wages from rising.

Pursuing this point further, the Commission points to a specific situation, illegal "wetback" Mexican labor, so called because the illegal entrant wades or swims across the shallow Rio Grande River. The Commission says:

The wetback is a hungry human being. His need of food and clothing is immediate and pressing. He is a fugitive and it is as a fugitive that he lives. Under the constant threat of apprehension and deportation, he cannot protest or appeal no matter how unjustly he is treated. Law operates against him but not for him. Those who capitalize on the legal disability of the wetbacks are numerous and their devices are many and various.

It then points out how "graphically and dramatically" wages reflect the impact of the wetback traffic. In the lower Rio Grande valley daily wages for cotton chopping were $2.25. The farther from the border, the higher were the wages, ranging as one went northward from $3.00 to $5.25. In 1950 the cotton growers of the lower Rio Grande Valley "got their cotton picked for approximately one half the wages paid by the average cotton grower of Texas." Furthermore, the vast majority of these workers are un-organized.

Social effects of low wages serious. The last twenty years have brought an increased realization of the fact that the lot of the farm laborer is not only hard, but that it has resulted in social wastes and problems of real magnitude. This is especially true of migrant and other seasonal workers not em-ployed in their home communities.

While there are some sanitary and well run labor camps, much of the housing is insanitary in the extreme. One Texas wit-ness told the President's Commission, "I have seen, with my own eyes, people living in these shacks and sheds, getting their water to use, drink, and cook with out of irrigation ditches, no type of sanitary facili-ties, bathing, or toilet facilities of any kind within sight; living in shacks that I wouldn't put a horse in." A deputy labor commis-sioner of California said, "I have seen lots cleaner and better houses for chickens than I have seen for human beings in the Im-perial Valley."

Obviously, such conditions affect health. The infant mortality rate for the twenty-eight counties of Texas on or immediately adjacent to the Mexican border in 1948 was 79.5 per thousand live births. The state rate was 46.2.

The Commission points out:

In California, the state-wide average infant death rate from diarrhea, enteritis, and dysen-tery is 1.8; for Imperial County, it is 12.9. In both Texas and California an overwhelming pro-portion of infant deaths from these causes is known to be in families of Mexican origin.

Disproportionate rates of death and disease are not confined to children alone. Reported diseases for the entire population in the areas of wetback traffic in Texas are unfavorably high as may be noted in the following comparison where the extent of those diseases listed is shown as a rate per 100 thousand population:

Disease	Texas — state-wide average	Texas — 28 border counties
Tuberculosis	76.4	122.9
Dysentery	312.0	1,554.1
Syphilis	199.8	323.3
Malaria	37.4	126.1
Typhoid	3.7	6.5

Many of the migrants move in family groups. The constant movement interrupts the education of the children. If these chil-dren are not themselves employed in the fields, at best they stay briefly in a local school and then move on with their families. Even in areas where farm labor is more settled and is concerned only with some one crop, the children who work frequently lose two or three weeks at the beginning or end of the school year. As a result their educa-tion is retarded, and this fact has its obvious cost to society. In one North Carolina county the rural school supervisor dis-covered that retardation, plus the loss of state aid which was then paid on the basis of days of pupil attendance, cost the county more than the children earned by their work.[13]

The problem of child labor in agriculture is not as severe as it was twenty-five years ago, but in October, 1950, the United States Department of Labor found 53,000 children 10 to 13 years of age working 35 hours or more a week in the fields, and nearly 100,000 working from 15 to 35 hours. Eighty-six thousand of these children were not enrolled in school.[14]

Remedial measures few. These conditions have disturbed observers who are aware of their implications. Certain church mission-ary organizations have tried for years to bring spiritual, recreational, and health serv-

[13] An unpublished research paper by Ann Cherry, done at Columbia University, 1929.

[14] Release of United States Department of Labor, January 24, 1951.

ices to migrant workers. Growers have learned to appreciate these efforts and to coöperate, but the total amount of such work done in relation to the need has been small. On the Pacific Coast the Farm Security Administration had an extensive program, including both portable and permanent camps for housing workers, with very low rental charges. Some health service was given, and in some camps there were recreational and even educational programs. This program has now been discontinued, though some of the camps are leased to groups of growers.

Labor unions have attempted organization. The two national labor organizations, the American Federation of Labor and the Congress of Industrial Organizations, have attempted to organize farm workers, but without much success. The "hired hand" type of worker regards himself as on the first rung of the agricultural ladder and like the short-term non-migratory worker is uninterested in unionization. There has been great heterogeneity in language, color, and race among workers on many corporation farms. Labor union dues were high for agricultural workers. Urban union members have had little actual interest in rural wage earners. Traditional labor union techniques, designed for dealing with skilled, immobile, industrial workers, were not applicable to unskilled, highly mobile rural laborers. Still more important, many of these workers were too close to destitution to risk striking.

Nevertheless, some steps have been taken. Although it is still weak, farm labor has won some of the average of twenty strikes a year which have disturbed agriculture for the last two decades.[15] Most of these have been in the highly commercialized fruit and vegetable areas of the West and in Hawaii, but

[15] Harry Schwartz, *Seasonal Farm Labor in the United States* (New York: Columbia University Press, 1945).

the Southern Farmers Tenant Union has also conducted strikes. In California and a few other states there have been inspection and supervision of farm labor camps and an effort made to enforce certain minimum standards. The experience with foreign workers during the war has been valuable.

Conditions improved during World War II. Ironically, governments agreeing to send farm workers to the United States insisted on guarantees with respect to wages and living and sanitary conditions which were not applicable to native workers. Since the end of World War II conditions have deteriorated, but not without vigorous protests by labor unions, churches, and other agencies. Hence the appointment of the commissions already mentioned.

The commission appointed by President Truman thus sums up the situation:

We do not find that people become migrants primarily because they want or like to be migrants. Nor do we find that any large portion of American agrucultural employment necessarily requires migrant workers. The economy of this Nation has a great deal of seasonal employment other than that in farming. Yet it is only in agriculture that migratory labor has become a problem of such proportions and complexity as to call for repeated investigations by public bodies.

The fifty-six recommendations of this commission are a statesmanlike approach to remedying the situation. Among other things, its report calls for a federal committee on migratory labor, placing first reliance on the domestic labor force; no contracting for foreign labor except under intergovernmental agreements; adequate enforcement of legislation governing illegal alien labor; placement of migrants by the United States and state employment services or by licensed contractors; amendment of the Labor-Management Relations Act of 1947 to cover employees on farms; instruction of farmer employers in labor relations by the

Extension Service; minimum housing standards; inclusion of farm labor in all applicable provisions of the Social Security Act; supervision of working and living conditions by the United States Public Health Service and appropriate state agencies; enforcement of the 1949 child labor amendment to the Fair Labor Standards Act; and an adequate program of education for migratory workers and their children by schools and the Extension Service.

TOPICS FOR DISCUSSION

1. Hold a class panel discussion on whether corporation farming will benefit American agriculture and rural life.
2. Should legislation give special consideration to maintaining the family farm? Defend your opinion.
3. Should the number of acres any individual or corporation may own be limited by law? Defend your opinion.
4. If there is more than one heir to a family farm, what arrangements should be worked out to keep the farm in the family?
5. What are the causes of farm tenancy? How may they be removed?
6. Does the concept of the agricultural ladder apply in your community? Give instances.
7. Should farm labor be unionized? Defend your opinion or conduct a panel discussion.
8. How were farm labor problems handled in your community during the war? Did the procedures used affect the handling of postwar farm labor problems? If so, how?
9. Is the family farm a valid and feasible concept in an industrialized economy and commercial agriculture?

READING REFERENCES

Tenancy:

Ackerman, Joseph, *Farm Tenure Conference.* Chicago: University of Chicago Press, 1947.

Bercaw, Louise, *Farm Tenancy in the United States.* A selected list of references. Washington, D.C.: Bureau of Agricultural Economics, 1937.

Brunner, Edmund deS., *Case Studies of Family Farms.* New York: Columbia University Seminar on Rural Life, 1949.

Farm Foundation, *Bulletins and Other Published Material on Farm Tenure.* Chicago, Farm Foundation, 1950. A mimeographed bibliography of contributions from colleges of agriculture of the North Central states.

Hoffsommer, Harold, ed., *The Social and Economic Significance of Land Tenure in the Southwest States.* Chapel Hill: University of North Carolina Press, 1950.

Inman, Buis T., and William H. Fippin, *Farm Land Ownership in the United States.* Washington, D.C.: Bureau of Agricultural Economics, United States Department of Agriculture, 1949.

Rohwer, Robert A., *Family Factors in Tenure Experience.* Ames: Iowa Agricultural Experiment Station, 1950, Bulletin 375.

Salter, Leonard A., *Land Tenure in Process.* Madison: Agricultural Experiment Station, Wisconsin State College of Agriculture, 1943.

Schuler, Edgar A., *Social States and Farm Tenure.* Washington, D.C.: Bureau of Agricultural Economics, 1938.

Taylor, Carl C., Louis J. Ducoff, and Margaret J. Hagood, *Trends in the Tenure Status of Farm Workers in the United States, 1880–1940.* Washington, D.C.: Bureau of Agricultural Economics, United States Department of Agriculture, 1948.

Timmons, J. F., and R. Barlowe, *Farm Ownership in the Midwest.* Ames: Iowa Agricultural Experiment Station, 1949, Bulletin No. 361.

Farm Labor:

Ahearn, Daniel J., Jr., *The Wages of Farm and Factory Laborers, 1914–1945.* New York: Columbia University Press, 1945.

Collins, Henry H., Jr., *America's Own Refugees.*

Princeton, N. J.: Princeton University Press, 1944.

Cullum, R. M., F. C. Folsom, and D. G. Hay, *Men and Machines in the North Dakota Harvest*. Washington, D.C.: Bureau of Agricultural Economics, Federal Security Administration, April, 1942.

Ducoff, Louis J., *Migratory Farm Workers in 1949*. Washington, D.C.: Bureau of Agricultural Economics, United States Department of Agriculture, 1950.

Ducoff, Louis J., *Wages of Agricultural Labor in the United States*. Washington, D.C.: United States Department of Agriculture, September, 1944 (mimeographed).

Governor's Commission on Human Rights, *Migratory Agricultural Workers in Wisconsin*. Madison, 1950.

Governor's Committee on Agricultural Labor Resources, *Agricultural Labor in the San Joaquin Valley*. Sacramento, California, 1950.

Holmaas, Arthur J., *Agricultural Wage Stabilization in World War II*. Washington, D.C.: Bureau of Agricultural Economics, United States Department of Agriculture, 1950.

McWilliams, Carey, *Ill Fares the Land*. Boston: Little, Brown, 1942.

President's Commission on Migratory Labor, *Migratory Labor in American Agriculture*. Washington, D.C., 1951.

Among others, the following state colleges of agriculture have made one or more studies of the social and/or economic problems of farm labor: Delaware, Iowa, Louisiana, Michigan, New Mexico, New York, Washington.

FILM

Share Croppers. S, 7. March of Time, New York.

8   The Social Function of Land

THE PREVIOUS CHAPTER has discussed the arrangements under which a man can operate land for agricultural purposes and the situation of those whom he employs to assist him. This chapter is concerned with some of the social functions of land, especially as it supports the activities of society through taxation, and as it furnishes the security by which the owner can borrow needed capital. Finally, some of the more specific social uses of land are discussed.

Taxation

Taxation is the oldest device by which society has paid for its collective activities. For centuries land, as the basic source of wealth, has had to bear the burden of supporting the enterprises society conducts. This tax base and the income derived from it influence directly the scope of various social utilities such as education, public health, and welfare, as well as fire and police protection, road-building and upkeep, and many other essentials of modern living. Taxation thus has sociological importance, although it is primarily an economic subject.

The rise in taxes. Rural America spent generously of its income in the 1910's and early 1920's for improved schools, roads, and other social services; through bond issues by local municipalities and counties it mortgaged its future profits as well. As a result local taxes mounted rapidly, almost dou-

bling between 1917 and 1930.[1] Following this they declined, but rose again after 1944 as war-deferred needs of school districts and local and state governments began to be met.

The farmer pays his taxes in money, but his money represents bushels of wheat or corn, bales of cotton, quarts of milk, pounds of butter or wool, and so on. When prices of products the farmer sells decline, it takes more of whatever commodities he produces to pay each dollar of taxes. This fact caused very real difficulties during the agricultural depression, as will become apparent. For this reason the subject of taxation has been given considerable attention, especially in the decades of the 1920's and 1930's, when it was studied by about a score of colleges of agriculture. The outstanding conclusion of these studies was that the farmer paid taxes which were disproportionately high in relation to his income because of assessment practices with respect to his primary asset, land and buildings.[2] It was found,

[1] In terms of index numbers the rise in farm taxation, using certain significant years, is as follows:

1913	100	1934	178
1918	137	1940	183
1920	244	1945	199
1925	270	1949	296
1929	281	1950	311*

* Preliminary estimate.

Source: Bureau of Agricultural Economics, Washington, D.C.

[2] For a summary of fifteen of these studies, cf. Whitney Coombs, *Taxation of Farm Property* (Washington, D.C.: United States Department of Agriculture, February, 1930), Technical Bulletin 172.

103

for instance, that in Indiana in 1928 farm taxes absorbed two fifths of the rental income and city taxes one fifth. In Michigan between 1919 and 1925, even if the so-called upper peninsula is excluded, farm taxes took 52 per cent of the net income of the average farm. In Pennsylvania, farmers spent 13 per cent more of their earnings for taxes than did the state as a whole, including the farmers.

Taxation is therefore a practical problem for the school superintendent, the librarian, and the social worker, all of whom are concerned with the task of keeping such social utilities at maximum efficiency. Studies by the Institute of Social and Religious Research have revealed numerous instances where enthusiasm for a new school building, community house, or other public building resulted in saddling the community with so large a debt that all other social improvements had to be postponed indefinitely.

Taxes: How much and what for. During the years 1909 to 1914, taxes on farm real estate averaged $184,314,000; including personal property taxes they totaled nearly $213,000,000. By 1929 the total levied for these items exceeded $640,000,000, about 10 per cent of net farm income before taxes. By 1942, improving prices brought farmers into income tax brackets but also held the total tax bill to 6.6 per cent of net income. Since that time the local tax bill has increased sharply. It crossed half a million in 1946 and jumped to $823,209,000 in 1950, a sixth higher than in 1948. Income taxes between these two years, however, dropped from practically a billion to $640,000,000 in 1951. All taxes again totaled about one tenth of net income.

The Department of Agriculture uses two other measures of taxes levied on farm real estate, namely taxes per acre and per $100 of value. It took the two decades from 1890 to 1910 for taxes to go from 13 cents to 19 cents per acre. By 1920 they were 51 cents and reached a peak of 58 cents in 1929. The subsequent decline carried the figure to 36 cents by 1943, but the previous peak was again reached in 1948 and went to an all-time high of 64 cents in 1950. Taxes per $100 of value on farm real estate were 50 cents in the years 1909 to 1914, $1.30 at the 1930 peak, and just over $1.00 in 1950.

Regional fluctuations in these figures are considerable, especially on a per-acre basis; the low region, the Mountain states, currently collects only 18 cents an acre, and the high region, New England, about $1.70. On a value basis the spread is only fourfold, from 54 cents in the West South Central division to slightly over $2.00 in New England.

It is important to remember that taxes are a device by which the payer purchases services he would otherwise not have. In other words, he gets a return for his money. Once taxes are sanctioned by society, however, he has no option in the matter. Society, by its action, holds any given tax-supported service so essential to the general welfare that all must pay for it, whether directly benefited or not. Thus no childless couple can avoid the school tax. It is safe to say, however, that were there no school in a given community, the value of the property would suffer, since this is a service on which Americans place great value. In normal communities, on the average, education is the largest single item of tax expense, averaging over one fifth of the total, and much more in rural America. Roads and debt service each take about a seventh, welfare an eleventh, protection and health each more than a twentieth.[3]

The very mention of some of these services indicates changing conceptions of what government should do. It was well

[3] United States Department of Agriculture, *State and Local Government Finances in War Times* (Washington, D.C., 1942).

into the nineteenth century when health became a budget item, even in cities. The item appeared then only because, first, enough people were convinced that it was more costly to do without the service than to pay for it, and, second, because there was enough wealth, *i.e.*, the production of goods and services, to meet the cost. One of the tragedies of underdeveloped rural countries is that wealth is not available for supplying all the services which would benefit the society. It is specially important, therefore, for social planners to give priority to those services which will give the greatest returns for society.

Results of high taxation. To expand services beyond this point is dangerous. "The power to tax is the power to destroy." Even the United States discovered this during the agricultural depression. The Bureau of Agricultural Economics of the United States Department of Agriculture estimates that between March 15, 1925, and March 15, 1931, 109 of every thousand farms in Montana were sold for taxes. In North Dakota, the number per thousand was 86; in South Dakota, 66; Virginia, 70; Kansas, 17. Nationally, the proportion from 1926 to 1935 was 78.7 farms per thousand. Since 1940, by way of contrast, this rate has exceeded two per thousand only in that year and has frequently been about one. The very contrast indicates the necessity of wise handling of the tax structure.

Taxation problems deeply rooted. The bulk of income for local and county government is raised by a tax assessed on value of land and buildings. This tax is very ancient and was devised and worked well when the world was largely agricultural. But as wealth came to be more and more a matter of stocks, bonds, savings accounts, and other forms of less tangible and readily concealable property, nonconcealable assets like land and buildings began to bear an increasingly disproportionate share of the tax burden. Moreover, the property tax cannot be shifted to the consumer as can taxes on coal, gas, long-distance telephone calls, and the like.[4] The retention of the general property tax on the present basis long after the conditions that called it forth have changed is an interesting if not irritating example of the well-known lag between changing conditions and entrenched or traditional social practices.

Assessors inexpert. Further difficulty lies in the fact that the property tax is usually inexpertly assessed by local officials who have had little or no training, and the result, naturally enough, is great variations and irregularities. Differences of over 100 per cent in per-acre assessed valuations on nearly identical farms lying within the same township are not unusual. Every study has shown a tendency for the assessment on small properties to represent a higher proportion of full value than on large ones. Similarly, the poorer the land, the higher is the ratio of assessed to true value. In poor land areas the reason for this is obvious. Government services are becoming increasingly standardized, at least as to minimum requirements, and it costs more per family and in proportion to wealth to support them in a poor county than in a rich one. As we shall see later, the same problem confronts the church.

Expanded functions need more money. That the Government requires larger funds for operation now than it did a generation ago is obvious. School enrollments are much higher, terms are longer, and children stay in school for a greater number of years. Better qualified teachers have been de-

---

[4] In some states the problem is further complicated by assessing an added sum based on the potential value of possible subsoil minerals.

manded and secured. All public services, including government services, cost more when population density is low. As the country is now organized, a multiplicity of units and small-scale operation is required. This multiplicity, a legacy from the period of pioneer agriculture and relative isolation, creates by itself a huge problem, as will be seen elsewhere.

State aid. Because of these and other aspects of the situation, there has arisen a demand for the support of a number of social utilities on a state-wide or federal basis. Roads are now recognized as a state and national obligation. Increasingly, states rather than the counties have assumed responsibility for bridges. There have also been significant increases in state assistance to local schools, as another chapter shows. Half the states have now given up the right to share in the proceeds of taxes on real and personal property, which is also a help to the local municipalities. But though progress has been made, the problems of taxation of rural America are still far from solved.

Credit the Basis for Security on the Land

Wealth represented by land is not only an important basis for raising the tax money which society needs to carry on its business, but it is also the basis of security by which the landowner can borrow money for capital expenditures. Furnishing the farmer with both long- and short-term credit has long been a major problem in the rural world. The conditions of securing credit have become a primary concern of those seeking to stabilize agriculture and to raise farmers' standard of living in all lands.

In Korea, for example, under Japanese domination the average farmer paid 30 to 36 per cent per annum for any money he borrowed. In a group of 4400 families in Tozen, Korea, average indebtedness approximated the annual gross income per farm. In other communities interest equaled the total expense of farm operation.[5] In China the situation was about the same, in India even worse. Frequently the result of obligations incurred was peonage for the family. The burden of debt often held back whole communities.

It is no wonder, then, that in both India and Pakistan the governments newly created in 1947 moved early to curb both the charges and the power of moneylenders and sought to reform provisions for state loans to farmers which existed under the British connection. Understandable, too, is the lack of confidence of Chinese peasants in market-town moneylenders, against which the Communist regime moved far more ruthlessly than the new governments in India. It is evident that rural debtor-creditor relationships, in addition to their economic aspects, have had deep-rooted social and political implications everywhere.

Like most of the newer nations sharing the western cultural heritage, the United States, Australia, and Canada have never had as serious credit problems as nations of the Orient, but even so, difficulties have arisen. The American farmer claims that the banking system and credit machinery has failed to take care of agriculture since the days of Alexander Hamilton. In all three countries an urban East has been accused of exploiting the agrarian West, and the conflict has affected other policies than those of credit.

Differences obviously exist between agriculture on the one hand and commerce and industry on the other. A store or an industry offers not only its property as security, but what is more important, its current stock of goods and products which can be readily

[5] Cf. Edmund deS. Brunner, *Rural Korea* (New York and London, 1928), p. 27 ff.

converted into cash. Many types of farming, however, such as wheat, corn, hops, and cotton, have no steady source of income throughout the year. Receipts are concentrated in short periods, and if payments of interest fall behind, the creditor has only the farm as his security. Because farms cannot be sold as readily as store goods or corporation bonds listed on a stock exchange, farm loans are known as "non-liquid."

As the nation grew, farmers needed more credit. When free land through homesteading came to an end the price of land increased and the prospective farm owner had to borrow. Moreover, as agriculture became mechanized, the farmer needed to purchase machinery which was usually so expensive that he could not pay cash for it. Hence the increased need for credit, in addition to the perennial necessity of borrowing for current expenses when funds ran low between crop sales. This need was formerly supplied by mortgage companies, insurance companies, and later by banks with costs to the farmer frequently ranging from 8 to 12 per cent. There was constant agitation for lower charges and better terms.

The federal government steps in. Finally, in 1915, over bitter opposition, a federal credit agency was set up in the Federal Land Bank. Its twelve regional banks made loans to farmers through local associations of ten or more members, of which there have been almost five thousand. These banks are now part of an elaborate system within the Department of Agriculture, the Farm Credit Association, which makes credit available to farmers and their co-operatives at an average of not much over 4 per cent. Even so, except during the agricultural depression, the majority of loans to farmers have been made through private banks, insurance companies, and individuals.

The rise of mortgage indebtedness. Reasons for insistence of farm leaders on legislation of this type are clear from the record. From 1900 to 1935 loans on owner-operated farms alone almost tripled. Farms mortgaged also increased greatly — from about one in four in 1900 to more than two in five in 1940, though regional variations were wide. The farmer's equity in his holding declined correspondingly. The West North Central states had 54.4 per cent of their farms mortgaged on average to 51.3 per cent of their value.

Depression and foreclosures. The unhealthiness of this situation became all too apparent with the depression. In 1931, 13.3 of every thousand farms suffered foreclosure. In the ten years from 1926 to 1935 almost 22 per cent of all farms were foreclosed. Adding sales because of delinquent taxes, the equivalent of one farm in every three in the United States was up at forced sale in that decade.

It must be remembered that when a farmer loses his farm he also loses his home, that increasing debt and interest payments are taken directly out of money available for family living unless income is increased by the same amount, and that when agricultural prices fall while payments on interest and principal of debts remain stationary or increase, the standard of living falls. In few if any other businesses are economic and social considerations so intimately interwoven as in farming. Moreover, if farm bankruptcy means leaving the community, as it often does when the rate of foreclosure is high, the community itself suffers from the migration of population — often leaders — and consequent declining support of its institutions.

It is not surprising that in many states agrarian unrest increased in 1932 and 1933. In many places there was organized resistance to foreclosure sales, which were sometimes actually stopped. In other instances, ridiculously low bids were made by neighbors, and other bidders were escorted from the sales.[6] It was this situation which led to expansion of federal credit legislation in 1933. Interest rates on federal loans were reduced, annual payments on principal temporarily waived, and additional loans authorized. An interesting bit of social organization was undertaken under the authority of this legislation. Debt conciliation committees were formed in each county as had previously been done in Canada. The function of these committees was to review the indebtedness of a hard-pressed farmer, attempt to adjust it equitably, even to scaling it down, and to avoid foreclosure if at all possible.

Interestingly enough, Australia and New Zealand passed credit legislation closely resembling our own, and a number of other countries in both Europe and Asia took legislative measures to assist hard-pressed farmers. This is another evidence of the world-wide character of some rural problems.

Situation today not critical. Today the situation is no longer critical. Farm indebtedness was reduced somewhat by liquidations during the depression of the 1930's and rapidly during the high prices of the 1940's. Though the trend has been slowly upward since 1948, the estimated long- and short-term debt of the United States farmer in 1951 is only about $10 billion against a total asset value of $130 billion. Rising land prices, of course, account for a considerable fraction of the gain in assets, and at the same time the purchasing power of the dollar has declined. But the balance sheet of American agriculture looks better today than at any other time in this century.

Are credit problems permanently solved? Such a happy situation offers an opportunity to survey the situation calmly and determine whether or not the shock of another deflation of land values can be met. To this end the Farm Foundation and the BAE have coöperated with thirteen Midwest colleges of agriculture through a regional committee in a careful study of land credit arrangements.[7]

The report points to some danger spots in the current situation and draws attention to the vulnerability of agriculture to weather fluctuations and variations in demand, both beyond the control of even the most capable farmer. It holds that private credit facilities are patterned primarily to meet industrial and commercial needs. It points out that farming is still predominantly a family enterprise, but that inadequacy in the credit system may be "a barrier to owner-operation of economic units" and that if so "there is justification for removal of the barrier." It holds that even a small number of foreclosures are an economic liability to the community, to say nothing of the social loss the sociologist would stress. It makes twelve proposals for further adjustments in credit legislation. Among these, it would give preferred status to delinquents from external causes as opposed to those delinquent from managerial inefficiency; it urges long-term contracts with flexible terms geared to the business cycle; it would hold prepayments in good times as a reserve to apply on subsequent payments if delinquency threatens.

It is clear that the device of credit is a social invention of great importance. Rurally it has been used to help persons toward farm ownership, which many Americans believe represents the acme of security. During the depression, when thousands of urban unemployed were fleeing from cities

---

[6] Edmund deS. Brunner and I. Lorge, *Rural Trends in Depression Years*, pp. 40–44, for illustrations of resistance to foreclosure sales and of farm strikes.

[7] *Improving Land Credit Arrangements in the Midwest*, AES Bulletin 651 (Lafayette, Ind.: Purdue University, June, 1950).

to what they felt was the security of the land, the very security which land had represented to agrarian people the world over was being undermined. But the socio-psychological attachment to the idea that land means security is very strong. Not only is it responsible for the legislation concerning farm credit in our own and other lands, but it is also a social justification for that legislation. The laws passed indicate an acceptance by society of the principle that farmers should have credit on terms roughly comparable to other businesses but adjusted to the peculiar needs of agriculture and thus becoming a stabilizing influence in rural society.

Social Uses of Land

Most of the matters discussed in this chapter raise fundamental questions of long-time social policy, especially as to the use of available agricultural land resources. Tenure practices too often have resulted in antisocial exploitation of the soil, just as there has sometimes been antisocial exploitation of labor. Comparably the tax system, which was ideally suited to the period when the great proportion of all wealth was land and the buildings erected upon it, has now become less suited to a period when other and less visible sources of wealth have come to represent the larger share of our national assets.

So, too, as already suggested, there have been credit policies which, because of pressure upon the debtor, have similarly resulted in the abuse of his fundamental asset, the soil. But this asset is also the basic asset of the nation. Except for the Homestead Law, which after the Civil War made the public domain available to settlers under easy terms, the United States had no national land policy for many years. Development was in private hands. Areas were boomed and settlers exploited purely for profit, some-

times in ways which created problems because the land was not adapted to the uses to which its promoters put it.[8] The matter gained urgency during the depression when titles to millions of acres reverted to the Government; often when put up at tax sales, these acres found no bidders. Increasing attention began to be paid to this problem during the administration of President Hoover. The Roosevelt administration gave it further consideration, making proposals for the removal of population from poor land to more fertile areas.

State policies. Prior to this, two states, Wisconsin and New York, had formulated land policies more forward-looking than any previously attempted. They recognized that if certain land uses result continually in family poverty, in rural slums, in uneconomic costs for mediocre schools, roads, and public services, a public danger or even a social menace is created. In Wisconsin land is being zoned, much as cities are, for particular purposes. Stranded families have been removed to better locations, and the state compensates counties to some extent for areas converted into state forests.

National policies. During the depression of the 1930's the Federal Government made a number of attacks on this same problem. Some soil conservation and much soil and forest improvement work was done by the Civilian Conservation Corps. The Resettlement Administration resettled about twenty thousand families, largely from submarginal lands, on good soil.

But the problem is far wider than this essentially relief measure. As a result of various programs in soil conservation and land utilization, the Department of Agricul-

[8] Cf. Edmund deS. Brunner, *Immigrant Farmers and Their Children* (New York: Institute of Social and Religious Research, 1929), for examples of both good and bad development; cf. especially pp. 31–40 and 138–54.

ture has purchased several million acres of submarginal land. Some of it is used to help farmers shift from wheat to stock farming and to prevent overgrazing. Here the aims are agricultural adjustment and soil conservation. Other projects involve building dams for water conservation, reforestation, and recreational facilities. The last-named developments have meant building picnic shelters, bathhouses, bathing beaches, fireplaces, parking areas, park roads, docks, and similar facilities. The construction of dams has created several large lakes for the runoff of water and to provide the surrounding population with long-needed recreational facilities.

Such projects, multiplied manifold in scope, are also to be seen in the TVA, the dams in the Columbia River Basin such as Grand Coulee and Bonneville, the comparable enterprises along the Colorado River, and the beginnings of developments in the Missouri River Valley. Such large-scale enterprises help greatly in flood control, generate electric power in great quantities, and furnish water for irrigation purposes. Some of this water will make available for agriculture large tracts of fertile soil hitherto unusable because of deficient rainfall. This means an influx of population into areas practically uninhabited before, building new communities, and organizing their social agencies and utilities. In the case of the Columbia River basin, an interdepartmental committee of the Federal Government has made a series of studies covering every aspect of the problem of building farms and communities where none existed before.

No longer is all nonindustrial and nonresidential land conceived of as potential farm land. It is being used increasingly for private and public recreational purposes, such as, for example, national and state parks and the beginning of county parks. Reforestation, not merely for commercial purposes, but to prevent erosion and for flood control, is another important use of land and one too long neglected in a country which is paying a heavy price for the planless destruction of its timber.[9] The problem of land utilization is enormous, and any public policy concerning it cannot ignore its broader social considerations and values. There cannot be too much emphasis upon human aspects in program-building. If it cannot provide adequate social as well as economic life for rural people, no land policy can succeed.

It is quite clear from previous chapters that some parts of rural America have lagged behind others and that they have fluctuated according to economic conditions and, in part, according to the vagaries of nature. Thousands of farmers are tied to holdings too small to produce an adequate livelihood, however loosely that term is defined. They are therefore underemployed. By the same token they fail to produce sufficient capital surplus to enlarge their operations. Migration is heavy from areas where there is a large concentration of such farms.

It has been proposed that in addition to programs to assist farmers, such as price supports, marketing agreements, soil conservation benefits, and a tenant purchase program, there be "labor-mobility assistance loans" to help farm families operating at, or near, a subsistence level to migrate to a non-farm location if they desire.[10] The United States Employment Service would be enlisted to secure jobs for such migrants.

The Rural Commission of the Australian Ministry of Post-War Reconstruction proposes just such a procedure, with many safeguards for state and settler alike, as a result

[9] In many countries timberland is more carefully guarded. About half a century ago Japan, for instance, decreed that no tree could be cut unless another was planted and that not more than 5 per cent of a stand could be cut in any one year.

[10] Leonard K. Schoff, *A National Agricultural Policy* (New York: Harper, 1951), pp. 48–52.

of bitter experience with their land-settlement program after World War I. The whole focus of their report is to raise the rural standard of living. New Zealander and Australian alike would emphatically reject the charge that this was socialism. It simply grows out of their long experience with crown lands, an experience the United States did not share. For that very reason, among others, an American equal of crown lands, if proposed, would be emphatically rejected.

Others have proposed that it is as logical to regulate the number of farmers according to the needs of the nation as to adjust crop production to national and world demand. As long ago as 1938 the President's Advisory Committee on Education proposed an Occupational Outlook Service to guide both vocational choices of youth and the advice of vocational teachers and counselors.

The fact that proposals like these are seriously advanced evidences a growing concern with the inequities in rural life attendant upon the shift from an agrarian to an industrial economy. It recognizes also the increasing interdependence of the various elements in our economy. Advocates of such policies argue that they are more regardful of the national welfare, both in human and economic terms, than present practices, for their intent is the maximum use of human capacities.

The pros and cons of these proposals are not pertinent to this discussion. The point is that an area of maladjustment and tension has been recognized and the problem viewed in both economic and social terms. Its recognition has led to proposals for change. Such proposals, as befits a democratic society, will be debated. They may or may not lead to social action expressed in law. This illustrates one process by which social change occurs. It assumes that there is no reason why society cannot accelerate social processes for the benefit of the general welfare.

A more familiar illustration is the matter of farm tenancy. To achieve the American ideal of land-ownership, a large segment of the farm population has burdened itself heavily with debt. To close estates, ancestral acres are often sold. Possibly there are better ways. When one sees the hundreds of millions of dollars subtracted from farm income through interest charges which flow mostly to cities, the question arises as to whether, after all, every family in each generation should acquire full title to its farm by the usual purchase procedures. The arrangements in certain European countries by which farms remain in the same family for generations might be studied with profit. Do they offer any suggestions for America? The Farmers' Home Administration tenant-purchase plan should also be studied; at very low interest rates on federal loans it assumes a two-generation process before full ownership is achieved.

Our tenancy arrangements, discussed in the previous chapter, grew naturally out of our social situation. Once they made sense, but the situation has changed. It surprises an American to discover that in New Zealand a very efficient and prosperous agriculture is more than one half operated by tenants and that few, if any, of the social and economic problems attendant upon tenancy in much of the United States are present. This is because a very large proportion of tenants are operating crown lands. Their acres belong to the state. They have life tenure if desired. Their sons can succeed to the leasehold. The leases safeguard the fertility of the soil and encourage initiative and enterprise on the part of the operator.

The point for us is that once the concept of the social use of land is accepted, as our society by legislation shows it has, it becomes apparent that some of our accustomed practices, long culturally sanctioned, under today's changed conditions are no longer producing the expected results.

This fact raises questions. Other democracies facing similar problems have attempted different solutions. As the social importance of our basic resource, the land, becomes clear, so does the stake of society, both rural and urban, in land policy. And there is no economic policy which does not have social results, nor is there any social policy which lacks economic implications.

TOPICS FOR DISCUSSION

1. Secure local governmental unit financial statements (county or village) for 1940, 1950, and 1930 if possible. What changes in function have taken place as evidenced by changes in proportion of funds spent for major purposes?
2. Determine whether appropriations for governmental purposes have increased in proportion to increase in agricultural income as reported by the 1950 census.
3. Compare total per-capita cost of government for selected counties for census years with per-farm income.
4. If you needed a farm mortgage would you apply to the Farm Credit Administration, your local bank, or a private credit agency? Explain your answer.
5. If possible, get estimates from local officials of the amount of unpaid taxes on farms since 1930. Record these figures and explain what you have found out about them.
6. What has been the experience with respect to farm mortgage loans by federal agencies in your county?
7. What types of aid by your state government have been initiated in the last twenty years to assist local municipalities?
8. Should the Federal Government offer special credit arrangements to family-operated farms?
9. How far should the interest of society in proper use of the land limit the individual in the management of his acreage? Defend your opinion.

REFERENCE READINGS

On all topics in this chapter, especially farm credit, see discussions in any recent standard text in agricultural economics.

Coombs, Whitney, *Taxation on Farm Property*. Washington, D.C.: United States Department of Agriculture, Technical Bulletin 172, February, 1930. See also the state studies by colleges of agriculture reviewed and summarized in this book.

Lancaster, L. W., *Government in Rural America*, chap. VI. New York: Van Nostrand, 1937.

National Planning Resources Board, *Tax Delinquency and Rural Land Use Adjustment*. Washington, D.C., 1942.

Renne, R. R., *Land Economics*. New York: Harper, 1947.

9   Coöperation — Rural Society's Middle Way

WE HAVE FOUND in previous chapters that the economic aspect of rural society is far from static. It changes, and the changes force adjustments. In this chapter attention is directed to one adjustment attempted by farmers themselves — the coöperative movement. This movement has a history in the world of more than a century, and in the United States of over eighty years. The coöperative movement is sometimes called "the middle way." It has proved to be a desirable alternative both to corporation agriculture and to collectivized agriculture as practiced in Russia. It provides the strength and economic power and efficiency of large corporations, but at the same time it helps to preserve the traditional family-operated farm.

Mutual insurance companies the first coöperative effort. The first manifestation of economic coöperation in rural United States was in the farmers' mutual fire insurance companies. The earliest of these were organized soon after the beginning of the eighteenth century, and many of them are still functioning. There were in 1950 1802 such companies with over $25,000,000,000 of insurance in force. Their average net rates are lower than those of regular insurance companies, and their experience with losses is more favorable. For many years the premium income has exceeded losses by from 50 to 75 per cent.

Among farm coöperatives, in recent years there has been a large expansion in the insurance field, promoted by various state Farm Bureaus, notably in Ohio. Most types of insurance are now written, including life, automobile, and accident. These modern coöperative companies have had a phenomenal growth, and are substantial concerns in the insurance field today.

Basic principles of the coöperative movement. The earlier farmers' mutual companies did not practice all the principles laid down by the famous Rochdale pioneers, who founded the first consumers' coöperative in Rochdale, England, in 1844, with a capital of $140. These principles provide, among other things, that each member of a coöperative shall have one vote, regardless of the number of shares he holds; that dividends shall be based on patronage rather than on investment; that such dividends as are paid on shares shall be nominal and limited; that membership shall be open to all without restriction because of race, creed, or color.

Credit unions develop. A second area for coöperative effort has been the credit union, organized to supply short-term small loans at low cost to farmers. This movement is also growing rapidly in cities, but all unions holding a federal charter are supervised by the Farm Credit Administration, regardless of location. The use of local associations of ten or more farmers as local agencies of the Federal Land Bank was, of course, an extension to the credit field of the coöperative principle. However, the coöperative credit unions are in some ways more interesting to rural society than are these associations.

Like the early locals of the coöperative marketing associations, these credit unions were based on neighborhood or community ties. In other words, there was face-to-face association among the members. They have usually known one another through many relationships for some time. Again, a certain amount of social control was exerted in this way. Loans for purposes of conspicuous consumption are not approved by most credit unions. In many parts of the Orient this has been an especially valuable feature of such groups. Loans are granted for productive purposes and frequently to tide a member over some personal or family emergency; wasteful expenditures are discouraged.

The credit union movement is well known in India, China, and Japan, and to a lesser extent in Europe, as will be noted later. In the United States its growth dates from the depression of the 1930's. The members of a credit union make small payments, usually monthly, to its capital, and it lends funds in small amounts at reasonable interest rates to members for approved purposes. About forty states now have laws which permit the organization of credit unions. In 1934 a Federal Credit Union Act was passed which makes it possible for such an organization to be incorporated in any state. Over four thousand unions now have a federal charter and the number is increasing steadily.

All told, there are now over 10,600 credit unions in the United States, over half of them urban, with close to 4,000,000 members. The average membership is 225, with savings by members of over $10,000, or more than $40 per member. The average loan is less than $100. There have been few failures of credit unions and the per-member loss in these cases was very small. It is significant that at a time of great economic and financial stress the coöperative features of credit unions attracted such wide interest and support from people of small means.

But coöperation as practiced by farmers is far broader. It has been applied to marketing and buying and is a far-flung enterprise. Moreover, it is in essence social, based on mutual trust of the coöperators and is largely, though not exclusively, governed on the principle of one man one vote, regardless of the number of shares an individual may hold in a given coöperative enterprise. Most marketing coöperatives deal with one crop, such as citrus fruit, cheese, cotton, and the like. Any producer who cares to may join, but joining involves the obligation to market his crops through the coöperative organization, which acts as sales agent for each member, pooling the products received and thus having more power in dealing with purchasers.

Development of the coöperative movement. The coöperative movement among farmers in the United States began soon after the Civil War in a time of disturbed conditions, new needs, and problems arising out of postwar deflation. At the start, and for some decades, it was largely a neighborhood matter. A few farmers would combine in manufacturing a cheese, or a community group would finance and manage its own wheat-elevator or creamery. With the coming of the twentieth century the movement gathered momentum. The first successful large coöperative, that of the citrus-fruit growers of California, gave promise of organizing a considerable area. Small local coöperatives were federated into large powerful organizations. By 1915 there were over 5100 coöperatives in the country, engaged in marketing and purchasing products, with a volume of business exceeding $635,-000,000. During World War I and in the following years there was a remarkable expansion, with great campaigns and enthusiastic membership drives. Some of these coöperatives failed as a result of too hasty organization and an uninformed member-

TABLE	YEAR	NUMBER OF ASSOCIATIONS	VOLUME OF BUSINESS	MEMBERSHIPS *
20	1915	5,149	$ 635,839,000	651,186
	1925	10,803	2,400,000,000	2,700,000
	1930	12,000	2,500,000,000	3,100,000
Number and Size of	1934†	10,900	1,365,000,000	3,156,000
Farmers' Cooperatives,	1943	10,300	5,160,000,000	4,400,000
1915–1950	1950	10,035	8,726,000,000	6,584,000

* Gross figures. It is generally thought that, correcting for duplications, over 3,000,000 are members of coöperatives, a majority of the farmers engaged in commercial production on any scale. † Lowest year of depression.
Source: Grace Wanstall, *Statistices of Farmer Marketing and Purchasing Coöperatives, 1947–48.* (Washington, 1950).

ship. The next forward step came under the Federal Farm Board, organized early in the Hoover Administration. The statistics of the movement are summarized in Table 20 by the Farm Credit Administration.

Over the years the trend has been for purchasing coöperatives to increase more rapidly in numbers and membership than marketing organizations, largely because the initial interest was in marketing. The advantage of pooling purchases of farm supplies was seen later. Some purchasing coöperatives have expanded from handling only farm supplies to full-fledged consumer retail stores, and some marketing organizations also purchase for their members. In 1913 better than 19 in 20 of the coöperative associations were marketing organizations which had over 90 per cent of the total coöperative membership and accounted for 98 per cent of coöperative business. In 1948, seven in ten were marketing organizations, with 61.6 per cent of the membership. The Department of Agriculture estimate, after combining the marketing business of all associations and the purchasing business of all, is that the total for marketing in 1949–50 was $6.49 billion, or 74.4 per cent, and for purchasing, $2.23 billion, or 25.6 per cent.[1] This means that in this crop year, between 25

and 30 per cent of commercially marketed food and fibre in the United States was handled by farmers' own organizations.

The United States Department of Agriculture has a record of 26,192 coöperatives being organized between 1863 and 1939, less than two thousand in the nineteenth century. The difference between the present total and the total number organized does not by any means represent the number of failures. Failures have been relatively few since 1910, when the gathering of careful annual statistics was begun, as will be noted later. Rather, in the last quarter-century there have been many consolidations. Small neighborhood groups were federated on a county, often a state or district, basis. Evidence of this and of the strength of the movement is to be seen in the figures just cited, which indicate that although the number of coöperatives has been declining since 1930, actual membership has been increasing steadily. In the troubled depression years of 1930–39 discontinued coöperatives averaged less than one in twenty per year, including those absorbed through consolidation. Moreover, about one half the present associations are a quarter of a century or more old.[2]

[1] Grace Wanstall, *Statistics of Farmer Marketing and Purchasing Coöperatives, 1947–48* (Washington, D.C.: United States Department of Agriculture, 1950, and preliminary report for 1949–50).

[2] The data in this paragraph are largely drawn from R. S. Elsworth, and Grace Wanstall, *Farmers' Marketing and Purchasing Coöperatives, 1863–1939* (Washington, D.C.: United States Department of Agriculture, 1941).

There is evidence that even the federal count of coöperatives is low. Both in 1930 and 1936 field workers studying the 140 village-centered agricultural communities alluded to in this book found about 25 per cent more coöperative associations than were reported for these same communities by the United States Department of Agriculture. These were largely of two types, marketing or purchasing associations that had failed to answer the government inquiries or had escaped the notice of the government, and consumer coöperatives in which the purchasing of farm supplies was a minor or nonexistent element in the total business.

Regional differences in coöperative membership considerable. Table 21 shows that middle western census regions account for over one half of coöperative business, with the Pacific Coast next. It also shows that the movement has spread from these two regions outward, and that though the number of associations and amount of business has grown, other regions are growing more rapidly. These figures must be further evaluated in terms of number of farmers in each region and the size of their agricultural production. In these terms, for instance, the

coöperative movement is stronger in New England than it is in several regions which outrank it in number of members and volume of business.

It is significant that the movement began in the Midwest. This region had a large influx of immigrants from Scandinavian countries who already had experience with the coöperative movement. Especially in Denmark it was so tied in with, and rationalized in terms of, the culture, that it was natural that this aspect of Danish behavior at home should be brought to America, like the Lutheran church and other cultural institutions.

Tenure also affects coöperation. It is apparent from census data that tenure status of farmers has an influence on coöperation. Owners in every region are more likely to do business with coöperatives than are tenants, and among owners, in every region the part owner uses coöperatives more than the full owner. It will be recalled that the part owner also controls more land than the full owner. He is seeking in every way to expand his operations, and rents when he cannot buy or until he can buy. It is perhaps significant that proportionately he makes

TABLE 21 Farmers' Marketing and Purchasing Associations: Percentage of Estimated Business by Geographic Divisions for Specified Periods,* 1913 to 1947–48	GEOGRAPHIC DIVISION	1913	1921	1930–31	1947–48
	New England	2.1	1.9	3.8	3.2
	Middle Atlantic	4.9	7.5	10.2	8.4
	East North Central	16.5	18.1	21.8	24.7
	West North Central	45.1	42.5	32.5	30.8
	South Atlantic	5.7	4.0	5.0	5.6
	East South Central	3.0	.8	2.5	2.3
	West South Central	3.1	5.5	5.5	7.3
	Mountain	2.9	2.8	4.1	4.7
	Pacific	16.7	16.9	14.6	12.8
	Total	100.0	100.0	100.0	100.0

* Most statistics pertaining to farmers' marketing and purchasing coöperatives are now compiled on the basis of the marketing season which includes the period during which the farm products of a specified year are moved into the channels of trade. Marketing seasons overlap.

Source: Washington, D.C.: United States Department of Agriculture, Bulletin 547, 1917, pp. 14–25, and United States Department of Agriculture, Miscellaneous Report 137, March, 1950.

greater use of coöperatives than any tenure group.

The tenant lags behind in every region, especially in the South. However, it must be remembered that under the Southern system the share-cropper turns over his crop to the landlord, who may market it through a coöperative, but the cropper may know nothing of this arrangement, nor does he profit from it. It is often alleged also that Southern landlords are opposed to coöperatives to a greater extent than elsewhere, and will not permit tenants to join them.

Whether one accepts the United States Department of Agriculture data on coöperatives or those of the census, it is apparent from both that the movement is growing steadily, even in the South, where the proportion of members is less than one quarter of that in other regions. Since 1919 the proportion of farm members of coöperatives has doubled, according to the census. In the South it has more than tripled. In sum, the dollar business of marketing and purchasing coöps increased almost fourteen-fold between 1915 and 1948. In the 1940's volume of goods handled roughly doubled and dollar business almost quadrupled.

Types of coöperatives. Many of the 10,035 coöperatives are still local organizations. Others are organized on two bases: (1) federations of locals through which the large organization keeps in touch with its membership; and (2) those organized from the top down, with no local agency. Contact between member and coöperative is direct but largely impersonal. Rural sociologists early pointed out that this was a dangerous procedure because it was in essence less democratic than the federation. More of this type than of the first have run into difficulties or failed. A few of them have constructed local organizations to meet this problem.

Coöperatives in this country are now beginning to follow the European example and to include adult educational programs in the theory and practice of coöperation. This helps to strengthen the organization. Some coöperatives have formed special youth and adult groups, and have developed recreational programs.

Functional types of coöperatives. There is another way of looking at the various types of coöperatives, namely, in terms of functions and services they perform. A partial but reasonably complete summary on this basis is given in Table 22.

Some advantages of coöperative marketing. Through coöperation, the farmer has sought to secure some of the middleman's profit for himself, to reduce marketing costs, to control the flow of nonperishable products to market and thus avoid dumping, to create new markets for certain products both by research and by advertising, and to improve standards of production. Brand names have been adopted and products reaching market have been properly graded, thus protecting the consumer. In short, associated groups of farmers have sought the advantage and profits of the corporation through coöperation.

Opposition met. This growth has not occurred without great opposition. Coöperatives were fought in the courts, charged by powerful financial institutions with increasing the cost of living and interfering with legitimate private enterprise. Today some agencies once opposed are proclaiming coöperation as a panacea for the ills of agriculture, and are chiding the farmer for his too tardy acceptance of the principle. State and federal courts, moreover, have adopted a liberal attitude toward coöperatives.

Since 1944 opposition to coöperatives has arisen on the ground that they held an unfair competitive advantage because of "freedom from taxation." This, of course, is

Making a Living in Rural Society

	TYPE	ASSOCIA-TIONS	ESTIMATED MEMBERS OR PARTICI-PANTS
	Production:		
	Mutual irrigation companies (1940)	4,432	148,496
	Dairy herd improvement associations (1949)	1,787	35,851
	Dairy bull associations (1949)	69	1,133
TABLE	Coöperative dairy-cattle artificial breeding associations (1949)	1,263	316,177
22	Grazing associations (1948)	30	1,311
	Indian enterprises (1947)	205	11,272
Farmers' Coöperatives:	**Marketing and purchasing:**		
Types, Number, and	Marketing (1948)	7,159	3,630,000
Membership	Purchasing (1948)	2,976	2,260,000
Production			
	Financing:		
	National farm loan associations (1949)	1,230	300,000
	Production credit associations (1949)	503	451,118
	Banks for coöperatives (1949)	13	*2,520,108
	Farmers' mutual fire insurance companies (1947)	1,843	3,500,000
	Public Service:		
	Electric light and power associations (1948)	865	2,403,676
	Soil conservation (1949)	2,164	740,000

* Members of associations borrowing from banks for coöperatives. There are some thousands of mutual telephone companies but since the last census of Electrical Industries was in 1937 data are not given.

Source: Grace Wanstall, *Statistics of Farmer Marketing and Purchasing Coöperatives, 1947–48.* Washington, D.C.: United States Department of Agriculture, 1950, page 61.

not true in terms of town, county, and often state taxation. The contention is based on the coöperative principle of patronage refunds. It is contended that in a noncoöperative business these refunds would be classed as profits and be subject to income tax. They are, of course, subject to taxation as part of the farmer-member's income. In Pennsylvania this issue was pressed legally on grounds that state law did not give authority to coöperatives to operate on the basis of patronage refunds. In 1945, the state legislature passed by large majorities three laws safeguarding this right. The grounds for income tax exemption are that the coöperative simply acts as agent for its members and makes no profits for itself. Regulated investment trusts operate on the same basis. Only

about one half of the coöperatives elect to meet the requirements for this exemption, partly because of restrictions on the amount of reserves that may be set up. Such reserves beyond a certain minimum pay the usual corporation income tax.

Legislation has helped. Congress, like the states, has shown a benevolent attitude toward coöperatives, and they have been exempted from federal antitrust laws. In 1926 and 1929 Congress set up machinery to aid coöperatives in developing and expanding, and loans were made available to them through governmental agencies in 1921, 1924, and 1929.

Failures among coöperatives. Failures

among coöperatives compare very favorably with other business failures. Causes of failures and voluntary liquidations were chiefly friction among members, failure to educate or cultivate members, overexpansion, insufficient capital, and too liberal dividend or credit policies. Unfair competition by commercial organizations, while frequently cited, is responsible for only 2 per cent of the failures.

Consumer coöperation growing rapidly. Consumer coöperation has been growing by leaps and bounds in the United States since the great depression, and in this growth rural America has been leading. There are now a large number of central or regional wholesale coöperatives. In some states coöperatives have entered into the processing field. They own a number of refineries and before the war, began to ship petroleum products to coöperatives in Europe. The butter given the highest score by a consumers' research agency for a number of years was processed by a large chain of coöperatives. In wholesaling, processing, and retailing, rural coöperatives began with farm products and supplies, but are increasingly enlarging to include the entire consumer field. Business of coöperatives in all these lines has increased rapidly, even in the worst of the depression. In several of the Midwestern states public schools now teach both consumer and marketing coöperation.[3]

Some Case Illustrations

Many of the coöperatives that purchase supplies and goods for resale to members have greatly increased their business. Typical of these is a concern called Farmers, Incorporated, in a medium-sized Virginia village. Half of the five hundred farmers in the community belong to this organization. In the inter-survey period, 1924 to 1930, business increased about 50 per cent to nearly $170,000 annually. By 1935 there were four hundred members and consumer business alone had increased to $244,000. Since its founding in 1919, dividends to member-stockholders had more than equaled the stock investment.

The case of Rockwell, Iowa. Behind each unit of statistics assembled in this chapter on coöperatives in local communities lies a story of agitation, leadership, education, action, and often struggle. A glimpse of what coöperation means in these terms is given in an account of the oldest grain coöperative in Iowa,[4] written by one connected with it as member and officer for thirty years.

By 1889 in Rockwell, Iowa, there was evidence that grain buyers were acting in unison and not competitively, thus holding down the price paid farmers. There happened to be in the community two men of energy with some experience elsewhere with coöperation. After ceaseless agitation they finally gathered in a granary a group that, after much discussion in the flickering light of a lantern, decided to form a coöperative elevator society.

The businessmen of the town were confident that the step would mean ruin for the community, and the grain trade fought the enterprise by offering higher prices to sellers. This infant coöperative, however, showed from the first the sagacity which has made for its success for more than half a century. It was democratically organized. Any farmer with ten dollars for a share of stock could join and no matter how many shares he held he cast but one vote. Competition from the grain trade was met by requiring members to pay the usual commission to the coöperative even when selling

[3] Cf. the publication, *Cooperation* (Chicago: Cooperative League of America) and its weekly news release for up-to-the-minute news of the movement.

[4] Reuben A. Holman, *Fifty Years of Co-operation* (Rockwell, Iowa: Farmers Elevator, 1942).

to a private elevator, upon pain of losing their other privileges in the society.

These other privileges soon became important, for the society began to handle machinery and then lumber and gave its own members discounts on such business. In ten years this ridiculed coöperative, that had begun business with barely $1000 capital, showed a business volume of over $300,000 a year which, in turn, was doubled within another half decade.

Then a new threat arose. Efforts were made to shut off the urban outlet for coöperatively marketed grain, but some thirty similar societies that had sprung up, following Rockwell's example, combined in a state coöperative association powerful enough to overcome this danger.

In Rockwell itself hogs and livestock were added to the marketing activities and coal, shoes, and clothing to the products purchased for the community. By the end of forty years — that is, 1929 — the society had paid individuals sixty-eight times their original investment. Since then, under a new charter, cash dividends have been limited to 5 per cent annually and other profits have been distributed on a prorata patronage basis.

Several factors contributed to the success of this enterprise, which is still functioning successfully. The management has been almost from the start in the hands of one family, father and sons, men of integrity who refused to be swayed by offers of positions or profits from the grain trade. Other leadership has also been continuous. There were but four presidents and two secretaries in the first forty-odd years of its history. These leaders, as Holman shows in his delightfully simple and human history, have been men of fundamental integrity, and repeatedly in times of crisis their appeal to essential moral principles carried the day. Scripture was often quoted in their meetings. Moreover, the coöperative has been a

stabilizing influence in the community itself, which has seemed to suffer less from migration than many and which has built up a coöperative spirit in many of its other relationships.

Another picture of the rise of the coöperative process is gained from a recent study of fifty midwestern family farms which had been in the same family for three or more generations. There was no organized coöperation, other than exchange of work, among the great-grandfathers of the present operators; six of the fifty grandfathers marketed some or all of their products through a coöperative association. Among the fathers better than two out of five had utilized a coöperative, and in the present generation the ratio has gone up to three out of five. Comparably, the proportion who sold to commission men and/or local merchants declined from two thirds among the grandfathers to about one third among the present generation.[5]

Some coöperative problems. Inevitably the coöperative movement has produced some problems within its own structure which reflect differences in social attitudes among groups within the movement. In the first place, in some of the largest marketing coöperatives there is an observable tendency for some of the problems of big business to appear. One of these tendencies comes from the growing importance of the managerial function and the difficulty of preserving democratic controls, which are the essence of the philosophy of the movement. With this go also the intricacies of employer-employee relationships. Again, it has happened that executives of large coöperatives have displayed attitudes more characteristic of industry than of the coöperative movement. Also, marketing coöperatives have not

[5] Cf. Edmund deS. Brunner, *Case Studies of Family Farms* (New York: Columbia University Seminar on Rural Life, 1949).

always willingly worked with consumers' coöperatives, fearing that their own profits would be adversely affected. Happily, while this problem has not been solved, the two types of coöperatives are developing mutually advantageous arrangements. As consumer coöperatives grow in number and strength, these instances of commercial amity will doubtless increase.

Finally, there is a tendency to expand into processing and even manufacturing. This trend has gone farther in England and Scandinavia than in the United States and appears to be a constructive development. Here it has progressed furthest in the petroleum field, where coöperatives own processing plants, pipe lines, and oil fields.

Agricultural Coöperation World Wide

One of the interesting things about the coöperative movement is its world-wide scope. The International Labor Office estimated in 1949 that there were 800,000 coöperative organizations of all types, both rural and urban, in the world, with 100 million members and an annual business of $33 billion. Almost all governments have some official agency studying, promoting, and advising coöperative societies. Most of them have legislation favoring coöperatives in one or more ways. In a number there are definite ties between coöperatives and government. It is significant that these developments are not confined to any one type of country. The movement is strongest in the countries of northwest Europe, where it originated, in North America, and in other lands sharing in the Euro-American culture. But it has been embraced with enthusiasm in so-called underdeveloped countries which are predominantly rural in their socio-economic structure. This is evidence that similar needs have called forth a similar solution among the farmers of the world. Even the patterns of the institutionalization of the co-

öperative movement among the nations are closely similar.

International agencies helping. The Food and Agriculture Organization has held several regional conferences on coöperatives in the belief, expressed unanimously by member countries, that the movement was "amongst the most effective means by which rural communities in economically less developed countries can be organized to increase production and improve their well being."

The Technical Meeting on Coöperatives in Asia and the Far East, held by the F.A.O. in India late in 1949, urged that member governments promote coöperative societies, arrange tax laws so "as not to discourage" them, provide or arrange for education about them from primary to college levels, grant funds for capital purposes or make grants for specific purposes, organize central coöperative banks, encourage the rapid development of marketing societies, assist in the formation of "multipurpose" coöperatives, and when they exist, utilize them for improving rural welfare.[6]

India. India provides one illustration of the development that has been going on. In 1930, despite some unfortunate failures in the 1920's partly due to overenthusiasm, there were 12,000 coöperative societies in what is now India and Pakistan. A great majority were coöperative credit unions, organized because of the very high interest rates prevailing throughout this subcontinent. In 1948 there were 106,040 coöps of all types, of which 20,780 were noncredit, or almost one in five. The credit societies had a membership of almost 3.5 million.

The government of India is actively en-

[6] Food and Agriculture Organization, *Report of Technical Meeting on Coöperatives in Asia and the Far East* (Washington, D.C.: Food and Agriculture Office, 1950). Cf. Sec. VI, Conclusions, pages 4–18.

gaged in converting credit societies into multipurpose coöperatives. The number of these approximately doubled between 1946–47 and 1947–48 to 18,162, with over five million members. Sales of goods per society at the rate of exchange of that time averaged about $4,300; purchases, $2,200.[7]

India has set itself the ambitious goal of organizing multipurpose societies in half of its hundreds of thousands of villages and of enrolling 30 per cent of the rural population in membership in the 1950's. This goal the Reserve Bank of India suggests will be difficult to attain within the time proposed, partly because of the inability to find and train the staff necessary for such an expansion, and partly because in some provinces among the rural population credit seems "the be-all and end-all of coöperation."

China. Coöperation received its initial impetus in China in the early 1920's under the stimulus of the International Famine Relief organization, which in those days was centered largely on credit. Another positive force was the Mass Education, later the Rural Reconstruction Movement. By 1946 there were reported to be over 172,000 coöperatives in China, five times as many as in 1937 and sixty times as many as in 1930. The Nationalist government reported well over 15,000,000 members in 1947. Chinese coöperatives generally fall into seven categories — credit, supply, producers, consumers, markets, insurance, and public utilities. Most of them, however, are credit societies, with agricultural producers and consumers' coöperatives next. Agricultural and handicraft enterprises handled by coöperatives include general farms, animal industries, tea cultivation, cotton-growing, vegetable and fruit-raising, irrigation, textiles, and paper making.

Elsewhere. In 1936 Japan, with a million fewer farmers than the United States, had 15,000 rural coöperatives, including credit unions. During the war these societies were increasingly used for defense purposes. They were reorganized by the Allied Occupation, and the movement seems to be flourishing. Results of great social significance in community terms were early achieved in Korea, per-farm income having more than doubled in some villages, with attendant gain in education and social organization.[8] In North America perhaps the most dramatic results have been achieved in Nova Scotia.

Attitudes toward coöperation. While the success of farmer coöperatives has been considerable, the progress of the movement is, according to many surveys, conditioned by a number of factors largely social in character.

A recent Iowa study, for instance, found that coöperators tended to be between thirty and sixty-four years of age. Noncoöperators tended to be older or younger, had farmed a much shorter or a longer period than members of coöperatives. Coöperators had medium-sized farms, while noncoöperators tended to farm less than ninety-nine acres or more than five hundred acres. Among coöperators, 52.6 per cent had socio-economic status scores on the Sewell scale[9] of between 80 and 89. This was true of only 41.3 per cent of nonmembers, though 3.3 per cent of this latter group had scores of 90 or over, as opposed to 1.5 per cent of coöperators. At the other end of the scale, 10.8 per cent of coöperators, but 17.6 per cent of nonmembers, scored 69 or below. Coöperators were also members of more formally organized social organizations, not including their membership in the coöperatives. Non-

[7] Data from, or derived from, M. G. Mehkin, *Review of the Coöperative Movement in India, 1946–48* (Bombay: Reserve Bank of India, 1950).

[8] Cf. Edmund deS. Brunner, *Rural Korea* (New York and London, 1928), pp. 37–38.

[9] This scale is explained in the chapter on standards of living.

members thus tended to cluster at the two extremes.[10] The Extension Service has found similar tendencies among its constituencies.

These Iowa farmers stated that economic return was the greatest benefit received from their coöps but mentioned half a dozen other advantages, chief of which were doing business with one's own company and the competitive market resulting from the presence of a coöp. Seventy per cent of the Iowa members felt they had definite responsibilities to their coöperative. Forty per cent, however, split their business with the competing organization. An equal proportion stated they had no say in running their coöperatives and, not surprisingly, had never attended an annual meeting.

In an earlier United States Department of Agriculture study, Manny found that entrenched habits, especially individualism, hindered the movement in local communities. In some instances farmers sabotaged their own organization if they thought it to their immediate profit; this usually happened, however, only when the coöperative had not sufficiently educated its members as to its objectives, methods, and ideals. Coöperatives are more successful in enlisting better educated, more experienced, wealthier farmers, and farm owners will join more readily than tenants. Tenants especially hesitate to subscribe to its stock, since they do not know how long they will reside in a community. These facts in themselves suggest some of the obstacles the coöperative must overcome in order to progress.

Quite apart from these matters, coöpera-

[10] George Beal, Donald Fessler, and Ray Wakeley, *Agricultural Coöperatives in Iowa: Farmers Opinions and Community Relations* (Ames, Iowa: Agricultural Experiment Station, Iowa State College, 1951).

tives, wherever they are local organizations or units, provide mutual interest and face-to-face contacts. The coöperative at Rockwell, Iowa, just described, was not a social organization in the strict sense of the term, but no one can read the history of its fifty years without realizing how it has woven itself into the warp and woof of community life. Through it leadership was developed, class distinctions broken down, and mutual trust and democratic processes encouraged. These beneficial results have appeared again and again.

Nationally and locally the coöperative movement is a social as well as an economic force, and it is significant that despite their reputed individualism one half of the American farmers and a majority of those producing commercially have joined one or more coöperative enterprises. Henry A. Wallace has frequently said that a good country church is a great asset to a coöperative even though it cannot be counted on the balance sheet, and that the reverse was also true. He says that Christians and coöperators have learned that the good things of life come by mutual effort. Coöperation is not a panacea for the ills of agriculture, but it is a definite help in most situations. It is an association of individuals who combine their capital and work power in a self-help organization which also has social tasks and aims, especially to improve the standard of living through lowering costs and increasing returns. Coöperatives are social groups, and though instruments of economic progress, they tend to help integrate the communities or groups they serve. They work within the existing framework of society and its regulations *for* their members, not *against* anyone. The individual by his voluntary connection multiplies his own powers by association with a like-minded group.

TOPICS FOR DISCUSSION

1. Find out the proportion of farmers who belong to farm coöperatives in your county.
2. What values has the Danish coöperative movement for the United States?
3. Contrast the coöperation principle with the individual sales principle and the private corporate principle of merchandising farm or other products.
4. Visit and report on the organization, procedures, problems, and accomplishments of some one coöperative.

REFERENCE READINGS

Beal, George, Donald Fessler, and Ray Wakeley, *Agricultural Coöperatives in Iowa: Farmers Opinions and Community Relations.* Ames, Iowa: Agricultural Experiment Station, Iowa State College, 1951.

Childs, M., *Co-operation: The Middle Way.* New Haven: Yale University Press, 1947 (Revised Edition).

Coady, M. M., *Masters of Their Destinies.* New York: Harper, 1939.

Cowling, Ellis, *Co-operatives in America.* New York: Coward-McCann, 1938.

Elsworth, R. H., *The Story of Farmers' Co-operatives.* Washington, D.C.: Farm Credit Administration, 1939.

Kallen, H., *The Decline and Rise of the Consumer.* New York: Appleton-Century-Crofts, 1936.

Kress, Andrew, ed., *Introduction to the Co-operative Movement.* New York: Harper, 1941.

Landis, Benson Y., *A Co-operative Economy.* New York: Harper, 1943.

Turner, Howard Harris, *Case Studies in Consumers Co-operatives.* New York: Columbia University Press, 1941.

FILMS

Rural Cooperatives. S, 24. Castle, New York.

What is a Cooperative? S, 22. Coöperative League of America, Chicago.

When Mankind is Willing. 36. Coöperative League of America, Chicago.

10 Agriculture Adjusting to National and World Economy

THE PREVIOUS CHAPTERS have discussed certain facts of American agriculture and their social significance in terms of situations existing in specified areas and at definite periods of time. Changes over the years have produced difficulties and made adjustments necessary. What happens in the great "out-back" of Australia, on the steppes of Russia, and the pampas of the Argentine in these modern days is often more important to the American farmer and his family than what happened in the next county was to his grandfather. Apparent after World War I, this is even truer today. Therefore, this chapter begins with a quick review of the development of our agriculture up to the opening of World War I and then turns to a discussion of the adjustments that have been attempted since then, especially since 1933.

Agricultural Development

Early agriculture self-sufficient. In early American history agriculture was self-sufficient. The pioneer built his house of logs from the trees which he cleared from his land. He raised his own food, butchered his own meat, churned his own butter, made his own soap. His womenfolk converted the wool from his sheep into homespun clothes. He counted his wealth in acres, buildings, and livestock. He had little use for money. What goods he could not produce, such as coffee and sugar, he often obtained by barter with the nearest storekeeper. Only cotton and tobacco farmers exported their products for cash, and hence for decades they were closer to the current of world affairs than any other agrarian group.

Changes beginning with the nineteenth century. With the startling technological advances of the nineteenth century, however, agriculture began to change rapidly. The railroad opened up the rich lands of the Middle West, and there, as we have seen, the population streamed. Eastern cities grew and needed more food for their population. Western acres yielded abundant crops, and food was transported to the East at such low prices that it was impossible for the New England farmer to compete, since yields from his relatively inferior soil were low and production costs high. Rural-urban migration, discussed earlier, was accelerated by these forces.

The West beckons. The West beckoned always more seductively. Land was to be procured for little more than hard labor. Moreover, the young nation needed capital to build railways and factories — capital it was not producing as rapidly as required. Huge sums were imported from Europe, and payment was made in rapidly multiplying bushels of grain and bales of cotton, coaxed from the soil by multiplying hordes of farmers. Every spike fastening rail to tie in the expanding web of railroads which were opening territory after territory first to the plow and then to the world market was a blow to general farming in New England. The social problems of depopulation began to arise in this region as America spread a bargain counter in food and fiber before world buyers. Frequently production, growing by leaps and bounds, especially as agriculture began to abandon the hoe for the machine, outstripped consumption. Prices were then depressed, and out of such depression grew the Populist revolt, the Bryan demand for free silver in the 1896 presidential campaign, and the national farmers' organization, Patrons of Husbandry, better known as the Grange, still a powerful agency. This was the first important agrarian movement of the modern era.

From 1860 to 1910 farmers increased from two million to six million, and from 1870 to the turn of the century our agricultural exports gained more than fourfold to $1,250,-000,000. By 1895 we were exporting about half a billion bushels of cereals — over three times the 1870 figure.

Transportation changes help expansion. Improvement of long-distance transportation of nonperishable agricultural products and the establishment of an agricultural export trade are vital facts in American history. Farming thereby ceased to be largely a self-sufficing way of life and became instead a business, acquiring something of the nature and spirit of capitalistic enterprise. Gradually it acquired, too, some of the techniques of capitalism. It learned to profit from coöperation and combination. It revised its commercial manners according to the best capitalistic standards. Its credit arrangements, as worked out in the Federal Land Banks, imitated corporation finance.

Specialization changes social arrangements. This shift from a largely self-sufficient type of agriculture to a more commercial one influenced the social arrangements of farming people. It required specialization and therefore made the farmer more and more dependent on the rest of society for primary needs. The farmhouse became less self-contained; it dispensed with its butcher shop, creamery, soap factory, and tailoring establishment. Distribution of specialized crops brought the farmer into contact with world markets. Developments of communication widened not only mental horizons but community boundaries as well. Schools, churches, and other social organizations responded in varying degree to an expanding world. Social and economic factors are inextricably interwoven in the tangled web of forces which changed the farmer's principal market from his own home to the world and moved the center of his world from the neighborhood to the village or town.

Agriculture experiences a painless revolution. In the early years of the twentieth century, the agricultural structure underwent marked changes. In the crop year ending July 30, 1914, our cereal exports were only one third the 1900 figure, or only about one ninth our total production, as opposed to more than one third in the years 1891 to 1895. Among the reasons for this was the great increase in our own population because of the flood of immigrants from Europe, in some years exceeding a million persons. Also, we had come to the end of our free land. Per-acre valuation increased rapidly, raising costs and prices in turn. It was $11.14 in 1850; it almost doubled by 1890, reached almost $40 by 1910, and stood at $69.38 in 1920. We had gone through a gradual and painless, even profitable, revolution despite the loss of a large fraction of our European trade. In retrospect some have called the period from 1900 to 1914 the golden age of American agriculture. Agricultural and industrial products were exchanged on a remarkably stable basis. This pre-war parity the Agricultural Adjustment Act of May, 1933, sought to regain.

Social and economic progress keep step.

In the first decade of our century there was great stimulus on the human side of agriculture. President Theodore Roosevelt appointed his Country Life Commission, agricultural education expanded enormously, the movement for consolidation of rural schools began, and there was agitation on behalf of the country church. Economic gains of the period were reflected in improved family and community standards of living. But in those years few, if any, noticed that the price of land was rising out of proportion to the productivity of that land and to the price indices of agricultural commodities. The seeds of the social and economic agricultural problems of the 1920's and 1930's were being slowly sown, obscured in large part by the European war which soon engaged the whole world.

The effects of World War I. The war stimulated American agriculture tremendously. The slogan "Food Will Win the War" echoed throughout the land. The American farmer responded to it by both increasing efficiency and expanding acreage.

After the war European demand fell off rapidly as Europe strove for agricultural self-sufficiency, for reasons both of national defense and of economic security. After 1929 Europe expanded her agricultural operations beyond prewar levels,[1] not wholly because she wanted to stop purchasing from us but also because she was in our debt. By 1929 other nations owed us a billion a year in interest. The inevitable result was that by 1931 and 1932 we sold Europe less than half as much as we had averaged in the two decades prior to 1930.

Production for vanished markets. Yet the American farmer went on producing for the same market, and moreover, instead of planting fewer acres, he sowed more. The

[1] The world surplus of wheat in 1933 just about equaled the total increased production in Europe.

total net production of agricultural commodities in the United States in 1932, despite unfavorable growing conditions, was 4 per cent above the average for the period 1919–27.

This was not sheer perversity. The farmer had to meet fixed charges such as freight rates, taxes, and interest, which remained stationary or increased. Each individual farmer argued that, as one told the United States Department of Agriculture, "A man has to raise twice as many hogs at three cents as at six cents to stay in business." With six million farms in the United States all trying their best to stay in business, this attitude is understandable, even though it contradicts the old theory of supply and demand.

Causes of agricultural difficulties. The difficulties of agriculture began in 1920–21 with the postwar depression. Industry recovered in 1922–23, but agriculture did not, partly because of the drop in the export market and high fixed charges such as interest and taxes. But there were other causes. The food habits of the nation were changing; our annual consumption of cereals, for instance, declined nearly 100 pounds per capita between 1909 and 1930. The number of acres required per person per year for food dropped from 3.2 to 2.7, or more than 15 per cent. Our rate of population increase had also slowed down. The number of mouths to feed was not increasing as fast as before.

Moreover, farmers used more machine and less animal power. From nearly 27,000,000 horses and mules on farms in 1918, the number dropped to 17,300,000 in 1933 and lost another 10,000,000 by 1950. These vanished animals had eaten the products of millions of acres now released for other uses.

Furthermore mechanization and greater scientific knowledge had tremendously increased the efficiency of agriculture. In the decade 1922–31 agricultural production per worker was about 22 per cent greater in volume than in the decade 1912–21. Canada, Argentina, Australia, and the Soviet Union had been similarly influenced. Surpluses became a world phenomenon.

Agricultural adjustment has, for all these reasons, been a difficult process. Powerful forces let loose in agriculture cannot be changed as easily as a factory can be shut down. Between 1929 and 1931 steel production was cut 85 per cent, but agriculture cannot act so abruptly. Its production problems are unique; plant and animal biology and the care of soil are involved. Farmers, however, seemed about to succeed in their effort for readjustment to the new situation when, in 1929, the world-wide depression began and agriculture, along with other basic industries producing raw materials, suffered tremendously, with its previous problems still unsolved.

Measuring the damage. One means of measuring what these developments meant to the American farmer is a statistical tool for determining the ratio of what the farmer received for his products to the cost of what he needed to buy. The years 1909 to 1914, when the relationship was remarkably steady, were represented by 100. Fluctuations in the relationship as shown by the index numbers can be taken as one indication of the purchasing power of the agricultural producer. The results of this computation for five-year periods and certain key years within them follow.

1909–14	— 100	1935–39	— 86
1915–19	— 111	1940–44	— 101
1920–24	— 89	*1943*	— 119
1921	— 82	1945–49	— 109
1925–29	— 92	1950	— 100
1930–34	— 71	1951	— 107
1932	— 64		(estimated)

In passing, it is well to note that the agricultural depression was world-wide and that it was especially severe in nations which, like our own, were largely industrial. Reduced to index numbers, the curve of the price of rice in Japan in the 1920's resembles that of wheat in the United States. Comparable indices in New Zealand and Australia also resemble that of the United States. The Canadian farmer was also in trouble.

Three phases of the agricultural depression. The tabulation above makes quite clear three phases of agriculture's long postwar depression. First there was the severe shock of the collapse of European demand and the recession of industrial activity in 1921–22. The second period, from 1923 to 1929 inclusive, was characterized both by a vain struggle to regain the prewar price relationship between industry and agriculture, and, toward the end, by the beginnings of a new stabilization. The third phase is that marked by the world-wide economic depression covering the years 1930 to 1933. In the last-named year a new period began under the new national administration. The index turned upward, and it became a matter of national policy to restore the 1909–14 relationship. These years were called the parity period.

Serious results. What the long agricultural depression did to farm income and farm values in foreclosures and tax sales has already been noted. Indirect results were also serious. Tens of thousands of farm families lost their homes. There was serious social and economic dislocation in thousands of communities. At the worst point nearly ten thousand rural schools failed to open. In many more, teachers were partly paid or received no compensation. Churches and social welfare agencies, which in the 1920's had just begun to remedy their long neglect of rural America, suffered severely. About one fifth of the six hundred county public health units were discontinued. Farm families cut their purchases to the barest minimum. As a result two federal agencies independently estimated that six to seven million urban workers became unemployed. Obviously the collapse of the farmer's purchasing power affected merchant, manufacturer, clerk, and laborer as well. There was even sporadic violence in some rural sections, overt resistance to foreclosure sales or to shipping farm products at prevailing prices. The growing interdependence of our society was again demonstrated.

One may well wonder what the historian of another century will say of the early months of 1933. In the world's richest nation perhaps a fourth of the able-bodied wage-earners of four years previous were eager for work that was not to be had. Thousands of them, their reserves gone, shuffled in city bread lines. Meanwhile, great piles of grain were rotting in the Middle West, fruit went unpicked on California trees, and heavy-hearted farmers were pouring milk into rivers, all because there was no one with the money to buy.

The Agricultural Adjustment Act

The farmers turned to political action early in the 1920's, but several bills to alleviate the situation were vetoed and the one finally approved was ineffective in meeting the growing emergency of 1931–32. But as a result of the socio-political movement for "justice for the farmer" or "parity for agriculture," the farmer assisted in bringing a new administration into power.

The first piece of agricultural legislation of this new administration, the Farm Act of 1933, introduced vast changes into American farm practice and has important sociological ramifications. It represents, too, our first nation-wide effort to exert social control over a highly individualistic occupation, agriculture; and as such, it will probably always have historic significance.

How the law operated. This act empowered the government to adjust production to effective demand in order to restore the farmer's buying power; to finance and readjust farm mortgages and interest payments; and to bring about controlled inflation. The heart of the law was the first provision.[2] The goal was to restore the relationship between the prices the farmer received and those he paid that existed between 1909 and 1914. This is the "parity price." Behind all our complicated modern price system, we are still bartering one thing for another, bushels of wheat and corn, quarts of milk, or pounds of rice, for shoes, radios, or medical care. When we exchange on even terms, trading goes on steadily. But when trading gets too one-sided, agriculture and industry together head for trouble.

The Secretary of Agriculture was to arrange with individual farmers of seven specified crops to reduce their acreage or production by a predetermined amount not to exceed the proportion that exports normally had been of any given crop, and to compensate them either by rentals or by direct benefit payments. Land not used for these seven crops was to be fallow or planted with soil-conserving crops. The amount of payments was supposed to be such as to give the farmer the buying power for his produce he would have received for it in the five years before World War I. This meant, if the law achieved its objective, that the farmer would receive as much in exchange for a bushel of wheat or corn or a bale of cotton as he did in the years 1909 to 1914. Funds for these payments were raised by small taxes on the processing of the crops included. Crop plans were put into opera-

[2] The Second Section became the responsibility of the Farm Credit Administration, discussed elsewhere.

tion only after approval by the farmers concerned. The act was broadly conceived and gave wide powers to the Secretary of Agriculture so that, as conditions changed, changes could be made within certain limits. Benefit payments were to cease when any commodity achieved parity.

Social implications significant. A number of significant social implications flowed from this act. In the first place, in harmony with our culture, the participation of any farmer in the plan was voluntary. This is important to note, since in practically all other democracies of the world that have experimented with marketing or production controls, such as Great Britain, Denmark, the Union of South Africa, and Australia, the plan proposed became mandatory on *all* producers as soon as a given proportion of growers or the acreage had agreed to the plan.

Huge proportions of the farmers concerned coöperated in the program. No crop program became effective unless approved by producers of that crop. The various referenda, especially before the Second Agricultural Adjustment Act of 1938, were carried by majorities ranging from 90 to 98 per cent of the ballots cast. The significant thing here was the unanimity of farm opinion and also the high degree of interest evidenced. American farmers may be, as is often claimed, individualistic, but from whatever motives, they acted practically as a unit in this matter. This is significant and may become more so. If agriculture should begin to speak as a unit in national affairs, as business and labor often do, it will unquestionably become more powerful and more vocal in nonagricultural as well as in agricultural policies.

Of equal significance is the fact that the administration of the plan and the checking of compliance with the agreement was done by township and/or county committees of farmers elected by the farmers of the area

concerned. These committeemen were paid a nominal daily fee for time they worked. Supervising state committees were also made up of farmers. A real effort was made to tie the operation of the act to the people concerned. This brought the Federal Government into a closer relationship to the individual farmer than ever before and often through a neighbor; this was a device new to political science, and its significance is not as yet fully appreciated.

The sociological effects of this innovation upon the social and institutional organization of agriculture should not escape attention. A new group of professional farm workers has arisen from the ranks of the farmers themselves, comparable to the development within the ranks of labor. A quarter of a century ago this group was small, represented only by the few persons on the staffs of large state or national farm organizations. Not only are these staffs larger today and their organizations more powerful, but they have been joined by farmers selected to represent their fellows in the multiplying relationships of farmers and government. Inevitably the processes of building a new social institution began. In a few instances the process went further than in others and had to be restrained by administrative edict from the office of the Secretary of Agriculture, commanding the farm committeemen to stay within the law. Sociologically, the most important element in this enterprise was building the local organization on the basis of neighborhood and community face-to-face acquaintance-ship.

Subsequent history. The later history of this effort to protect the position of agriculture in the total economy can be quickly told, since the changes did not affect general philosophy or organization. The Supreme Court declared the tax feature of the first act unconstitutional. Subsequent acts tied some of the benefits to soil conservation and provided for support prices implemented by government loans at the support level with the crop as security for the loan. If the price declined below the support level, the government took the security as satisfying the loan. If a serious surplus developed, quotas were permitted, when approved by a two-thirds majority of the producers, and could be adjusted upward or downward. With the coming of World War II, production goals were substituted for quotas; the machinery of the Agricultural Adjustment Act, now the Production and Marketing Administration, was used to spur the necessary increases in some crops. New legislation greatly extended the number of crops covered and guaranteed the farmer protection for two years after the end of the war, since many farmers altered farm practices radically and at some cost to meet war needs.

Criticism of the farm acts. Since the passage of the very first agricultural adjustment act there has been criticism of the philosophy implicit in this series of laws. It has been argued forcefully that the use of a historic base period, especially one now so far in the past as 1909–14, gives the farmer a hidden advantage because it takes no account of the advances in technology which have greatly reduced production costs. Several farm organizations, many agricultural economists, and Secretary of Agriculture Charles Brannan, in the plan which bears his name, have proposed a sliding base period, such as the decade preceding each crop year.

The validity of parity as a continuing index has been impaired by Congress, which once directed that labor costs should be omitted and later, when these costs had risen greatly, ordered them included. Congress has also repeatedly set the loan level or support price above that suggested by the Department of Agriculture. There has been some correction in the current act, in that the support price of the basic commodity will be lowered as the supply above normal increases.

During inflationary periods legislation comes under fire because parity is not a constant, but a relationship. If the farmers' costs rise, parity prices must rise to compensate, and support levels rise with them.

The unevenness of benefit payments among various crops and states has been criticized. Per-capita receipts for 1936 to 1939, inclusive, were almost forty times as large in the top state as in the bottom one. In this period nine states received more than $100 per capita, but half got less than $50 and about half of these less than $25.[3] The argument here is essentially one of welfare. It is frankly admitted that no legislation either enacted or proposed, benefits in an appreciable degree the million or more underemployed and poorer farmers.

What are the objectives of agricultural policy? In effect the parity concept has different meanings. There is an ethical concept implied in the criticism by Professor Smith and his colleague. The term also has powerful political connotations. Parity to the farmer is what the slogan, "a living wage," is to union labor. Third, there are dollar and cent parity prices of specific commodities, used in the administration of the various farm acts and in setting support prices. The economic provisions are viewed as the means to achieve the ethical objectives. These, in turn, arise from our cultural background and out of the value it places upon equality.

These meanings relate in turn to somewhat different objectives. One aim of agricultural legislation might be to diminish poverty within agriculture. Another would

[3] T. Lynn Smith and Ralph W. Roberts, *Journal of Farm Economics*, August, 1941, pp. 608–618.

be to safeguard agriculture from the results of mass industrial unemployment or of a new agricultural depression. Finally, there is the aim to increase incomes of farmers during periods of full employment. This last seems to be the position of the most powerful farm organizations, though behind that objective is the memory and the fear of the terrible depression and of the sharp fluctuations in farm income.

Those who stress the last objective point out that business and organized labor have comparable aims. But here the danger arises that as large groups compete for improved shares of the national income the general welfare will be forgotten. This is a consideration the sociologist cannot neglect in terms of values involved, even though he dispassionately analyzes the struggle in terms of the sociology of group power and power systems.

Farm organizations and agricultural policy. That there is such a struggle is self-evident. Farmers very properly have their own national organizations comparable to those of business and labor. The largest of these is the American Farm Bureau Federation. Originally farm bureaus were formed in counties as local groups to coöperate with the Extension Service. These soon federated into state organizations and soon after World War I into a national organization which naturally soon began to express opinions on legislation of concern to agriculture. It has maintained an office in Washington and has become a very powerful body with more than one and a half million members. Although no analysis of its membership has been made, it is popularly supposed to represent the larger commercial farmers. Many state units conduct social, educational, and recreational programs within their units. Nationally, however, the major concern of the Federation is agricultural policy.

The Grange is the oldest of the farm groups. Since its membership is on a family basis, its local units have always given attention to social programs. Far from unconcerned about agricultural policy, it has from the beginning emphasized education.

The Farmers' Union is the smallest of the national farm organizations, though its membership runs into some hundreds of thousands. It is supposed to represent the smaller commercial farmers more than the other two. It has supported actively many measures of Roosevelt's New Deal. It was the first farm organization to urge the inclusion of farm labor under the provisions of the Social Security Act. It endorsed the Wages and Hours Act. It has well-developed local programs in many places, especially in coöperatives and youth and adult education, and it has made many suggestions for strengthening the family farm. It has frequently differed from the other two organizations. In other words, agriculture does not always speak with a united voice.

Freezing patterns of farm management. Another very fundamental criticism arises from the tendency of legislation to freeze the pattern of American agriculture in its present form. It is one thing to declare that "policies to limit output must be reversed all along the line," as the Land Grant College Association postwar policy report did. It is something else to demand that farmers should be protected or subsidized in raising unlimited quantities of any crop beyond the capacity of nation or world to absorb the production. Several farm organizations are charged with having in effect taken this latter position, especially by some labor and consumer groups. Thus at the insistence of senators and congressmen from the cotton states, the price of American cotton has been held above world prices for some years with legislative help. This has encouraged the production of cotton elsewhere, and also the use of synthetic fiber. Only war has saved the government from accumulating huge quantities of cotton.

North America and Australia have more improved acres per worker in agriculture than any other areas of the world. Especially in cereal crops they are therefore a dependable source of food in war, but normally they are surplus-producing areas. The solution for such surplus-producing farm groups would appear to be freedom of trade and perhaps subsidies to export their products to needy countries, as, for example, the United States sent wheat to China during the 1930's. But if, as seems likely after a few crops, there are still unusable surpluses, there will be need for controls. There is no social sense in producing what is not needed when other commodities are needed much more.

For instance, the South could profit by a diet containing more of the so-called protective foods. As Selective Service records show, many were rejected because of physical conditions caused by bad nutritional habits. This was not at all peculiar to the South, though the incidence was greater there. Millions of people in the nation are ill-fed.

Just as land taken from unsalable crops in the 1930's was sowed with other crops which were more needed and more soil-conserving, so it may be wise to make comparable shifts in our farm management. There is nothing sacrosanct about the present patterns of our agriculture. They must be molded to the needs of society based on the newer findings of science.

Can we raise enough? In 1929 the United States Department of Agriculture conducted a study to determine whether the United States could raise enough to give its people a nutritionally adequate diet if the average yearly income per family should be raised to $3000, twice what it was in that prosperous year. It found that only in cereals and potatoes were we producing enough to meet the demand under such conditions. The study was ridiculed as theoretical and useless. But during the recent war, and indeed since, with average per-family incomes close to and often well over $4000, America had to resort to food rationing in order to send to war-torn countries as much food as we had often exported in peacetime. The dramatic fact is that for the first time in our modern industrial history Americans had enough money to buy the diet they craved, the protective foods and proteins often denied to the poor. Statistically, America was better fed in the war years than from 1935 to 1939. High incomes produced the scarcity of wanted foods.

This fact has many implications. One is that the farmer has a high stake in industrial prosperity. It has brought him good income in the same way that industry prospers when the fifty million people on farms and in service-station hamlets, villages, and towns have money with which to buy industrial products.

Another is that, if they have the means, Americans will buy costlier and better foods.

A third is that in our interdependent society it is essential for agriculture, labor, and industry to join hands in maintaining a prosperous America.

A fourth is that under such conditions it is far wiser to adjust farm management to demand than to subsidize less valuable and less nutritious crops. That is the best type of agricultural adjustment, though it may require some subsidy while the change-over is being made. It is simply an agricultural equivalent of industrial reconversion.

Just as no policy of farm management or economics is without social results, so no type of agriculture is without its cultural roots which help hold in place the soil of tradition. Education or government, or both, must stimulate and inspire the needed action.

What of the problem of agricultural adjustment? Prosperity cannot be assumed. In appraising future policy it is essential to recall the historical review given earlier, and the cost to American farmers of the long-continued agricultural depression. It was a cost measured in drastic reductions of purchasing power, resulting not only in lowered standards of living on the farm, but also in greatly increased unemployment in the cities. It was a cost measured in hundreds of thousands of evictions of farm families from their lands and homes, in disrupted communities, and in hundreds of millions of dollars in direct relief or remedial measures of various types. It was a cost measured in ten thousand bank failures and the wiping-out or impairment of the savings and equities of the more prosperous and stable portion of the farm and rural non-farm population. It was a cost measured in the closing of thousands of rural schools, depriving children of education and contributing to a lowered educational status for our population. It was a cost measured in the abandonment or reduction of work in agricultural and home economic extension services, in public health, and other social fields. The social and economic costs are incalculable. Therefore, the stake of nation, city, and country alike in agricultural prosperity is very high.

It is the costs of this depression which explain efforts of organized farmers to protect their economic position. This is understandable and legitimate. It must not be forgotten by those who criticize efforts in this direction, even when such efforts seem to harm other groups in the economy.

In terms of the general welfare, however, certain other things must be remembered. Since 1941 the parity index has consistently been above 100 with the exception of a few months, though there have been commodities which were well below parity. There have also been years when producers of some commodities, such as cotton, potatoes, and beef, enjoyed unparalleled returns. Farmers today are very much a minority group in the labor forces of the nation. Neglect of the principle of the general welfare could arouse damaging opposition even to legitimate programs in aid of agriculture. As an earlier chapter shows, the standard of living of farmers and of rural communities has improved markedly in recent years. Net and gross farm incomes have exceeded anything experienced before the 1940's. Even so, it is doubtful whether agriculture's share of the total national income as compared with its share of the population, is as large as in 1909–14. Struggles over policy are therefore sure to continue.

Retention of the parity principle, however defined, is a solution which will obviously receive much support. It has been with us for two decades. It was used to help agriculture, but also to help the nation by helping the farmers, who form such a large segment of society. There will be other proposals, such as announcing in advance of the crop a price which the government will support or guarantee, as is done in New Zealand. This would enable farmers to plan and business to have some assurance as to probable spending ability of farm and village people. Such a device could also become an instrument of social policy. Putting attractive "forward prices" on needed crops and less attractive prices on surplus crops would give farmers a powerful incentive to shift to crops which are more in demand. Government subsidies to consumers in the form of aid for school lunches and a revival of the prewar food-stamp plan could support either of these policies. One official proposal has been to let all but the few basic crops seek their own level and to make compensatory payments to farmers based on a percentage of parity.

It is not for this text to advocate any specific solution or solutions, but it is highly important to point out these issues, to stress the inevitability of adjustments, and particularly to emphasize that, though the policies to be adopted are economic in nature, profits or losses accruing must be measured in social terms as well, for they have social results of great magnitude. Man was not made for money; rather money was invented by man as a tool for his use.

TOPICS FOR DISCUSSION

1. From the agricultural census secure information as to quantities of chief crops raised in your state in 1900, 1920, 1940, 1945, and 1950.
2. Compare over a number of months the prices of various kinds of goods the farmer sells (such as cattle, cotton, vegetables, etc.). Are prices of farm commodities going up as fast as prices of manufactured commodities?
3. Make a study of your own or some nearby neighborhood to see how much it has been affected by the agricultural depression and the Agricultural Adjustment Act.
    a. Interview men and women engaged in various types of work in order to determine their attitudes toward the agricultural situation. Go through local newspaper files and study the Farm Act in relation to what local people have had to say about it. •
4. Conduct a class debate on the subject of the Agricultural Adjustment Act, such as, "Resolved: that the Agricultural Adjustment Act retarded national recovery," or, "Resolved: that the Agricultural Adjustment Act was unfair to urban America."
5. Contrast the functions performed by the pioneer and the modern farm family in gaining a livelihood.
6. Discuss and evaluate the various proposals for basic agricultural legislation by the national farm organizations, Secretary Brannan, agricultural economists, and others from the point of view of the general welfare.

REFERENCE READINGS

American Farm Economic Association, *Readings on Agricultural Policy*. Philadelphia: Blakiston, 1949.

Beard, C. A., *The Rise of American Civilization*, chap. XXII. New York: Macmillan, 1927.

Black, John, *Parity, Parity, Parity*. Cambridge: Harvard University Press, 1942.

Blaisdell, Donald C., *Government and Agriculture*. New York: Farrar and Rinehart, 1940.

Brandt, Karl, *The Reconstruction of World Agriculture*. New York: Norton, 1945.

Brunner, Edmund deS., and J. H. Kolb, *Rural Social Trends*, chap. II. New York: McGraw-Hill, 1933.

Gold, Bela, *Wartime Economic Planning in Agriculture*. New York: Columbia University Press, 1950.

Nourse, E. G., J. Dewis, and G. Black, *Three Years of the Agricultural Adjustment Administration*. Washington, D.C.: The Brookings Institution, 1937.

Reports of the Secretary of Agriculture, 1934–1951. Washington, D.C.

Schafer, J., *The Social History of American Agriculture*. New York: Macmillan, 1936.

Schmidt, Carl T., *American Farmers in the World Crisis*. New York: Oxford University Press, 1941.

Schultz, Theodore W., *Agriculture in an Unstable Economy*. New York: McGraw-Hill, 1945.

Schultz, Theodore W., *Redirecting Farm Policy*. New York: Macmillan, 1943.

FILMS

Land and Life. S. To be released late in 1951. Tennessee Valley Authority, Knoxville.

Magic in Agriculture. S, 28. Ethyl Film, Standard Oil of New Jersey, New York.

Power and the Land. S, 44. Rural Electrification Administration, Washington.

PART THREE

Group Relationships

Groups give society its form and substance. Various means of personal association and group systems of human relations make for a measure of social stability and toughness. On the one hand, they result in certain accepted values and modes of behavior; on the other, they help keep fresh and healthy the growing edge of a society, making it responsive to change. Communication is vital in this process.

In American rural society, despite a good deal of nostalgic regard for the tradition of independence and individualism, groups have always played and continue to play determinant roles. Although individual families of course settled on separate farms, the settlement was often in closely-knit neighborhood groups. Unlike the pattern in most other world societies, in America villages and towns came later. Now, farmers and villagers are forging newer forms of town-country community relations. Special interest groups are becoming strong and varied. Former differences between rural and urban groups are diminishing. Interdependence is therefore the theme in the study of contemporary group relationships.

White collar and blue, farmer, merchant, and chief, all meet freely and frequently in this kind of interdependent, dynamic rural society.

11   Rural Families

FAMILIES remain the firm foundation of our American society. This is true despite all the population changes described in previous chapters, the general downward and recent upward trend of birth rates, increase of divorces, world wars and depressions. The latest census reports from which materials are drawn for this chapter make this fact quite clear. Families are important groups in any society, but especially in rural society. The farm family is the working unit as well as the living unit. Any country scene is convincing evidence of this, for there in one cluster stand the house and the barn surrounded by smaller buildings and yards, and the fields beyond. The whole layout is called the "homestead" and it has a social connotation which means far more than such terms as "farm," "factory," or "store." These family groups are more isolated physically than are urban families, although they may not be isolated socially, as some have assumed. Many intimate contacts are maintained with neighbors and with relatives.

The village family resembles the farm family in many respects. Its dwelling and place of business are not far apart; the two may even be in the same building. Both home and business are located near neighbors and relatives with whom associations are personal. Judged by various characteristics, the village family stands between the country and the city family.

The family can be defined as a genetic group bound by kinship and marital ties. It is a group consisting of father, mother, and children, living together under one roof.

Many times rural households are not so simply composed. A grandfather or maiden aunt may be living there also, or perhaps a younger family is living with the parents. There may be hired help or summer boarders also, and consequently it is necessary to distinguish between the immediate natural family and the larger household.

The younger family may live in a separate house on the same farm, on an adjoining farm, or in the same village as the parents. There may also be married brothers or sisters, aunts or uncles. In this case it is the "great family" of relatives and kinsfolk. Frequently the great family is of more importance than is the individual family in matters of social control, in perpetuating attitudes, and forming opinions. This is especially true if its members live in the same locality and thus form the neighborhood group.

Family groups, like other groups in society, have their own social institutions such as home, standards of living, household systems, marriage, and divorce. Some of these will be considered in later chapters, but it is the family as a social group to which attention is given here. In common with other groups, families are not static but dynamic, always changing, adjusting, and readjusting to their own internal as well as to their external environments.

The Early American Family

As a background against which to view changes in the more modern rural family, a brief sketch of the earlier or pioneer family is drawn. Longer perspectives are useful in periods of seemingly rapid and radical changes. Literature abounds with stories of early settlement. A sort of "myth" has been built, sometimes deliberately, about the "early American family." It has its variations, from region to region, from New England to southern plantation and western pioneer, but in essentials it is much the same.

Land — private property in land — stands out in dramatic fashion as one of the important features of early American agricultural and family life. Questions of land, utilization, taxation, and possession, continue to be dominating issues, as, for example, the land-planning policies of the New Deal. In the settlement days before and after the Homestead Act of 1862, ownership of land was the symbol of a domestic economy, whether for the Pennsylvania farmer, the western pioneer, or the southern planter. As Dr. Wilson [1] has phrased it, "the household farmer owned his home. He built upon his farm a homestead which represented his ideal of domestic and family comfort. He built for permanence. So far as his means permitted, he provided for his children and for generations of descendants." This relationship of land, family, and home is the background for many writers' interpretations of country life. It may be Whittier's *Snow-Bound*; Hamlin Garland's *Son of the Middle Border*; Gladys Hasty Carroll's *As the Earth Turns*; or Louis Bromfield's *The Farm*. This relationship represents the "social origins" of the rural family.

Self-maintenance with a sense of isolation is another characteristic of the early rural family. The importance of this fact to agriculture and the business of farming will be detailed in a later chapter, but for the family and its household, it is the tradition which has been passed on in such stereotypes as "independence," "individualism," "integrity," and the like. Without doubt the roots of this tradition extend back to the Old World. Stories of the struggle of pioneer families attempting to maintain themselves economically, socially, and religiously, serve as contrasts for those who today are striving to remake rural society by such means as coöperative marketing, community organizations, or larger parish churches. How strange it sounds to hear Mr. Wright [2] telling of his early family experiences in Otsego County, New York, in 1848. "Our new home was in a comparative wilderness; not a house was in sight. The nearest neighbors on the south and east lived over a mile from us. On the west, the nearest lived three fourths of a mile, and on the north over one fourth of a mile; and a thick dark forest intervened." Today these would seem like near neighbors, too near, perhaps, for some kinds of commercial agriculture. The swing away from the idea of self-maintenance in some quarters of highly specialized production has been very wide, but like so many extremes, it has swung back again until one finds that the idea of family-farm is one emphasis within the present planning for agriculture. There can be little doubt that the early isolation and the sense of independence did much to magnify the importance of the family and to intensify its relationships.

Kinship, with a sense of solidarity, was another important bond in the framework of the early family. This feature stands at least in partial contrast to the former, but it is questionable whether such complete independence or such entire isolation as some writers have suggested really did exist. A sense of kinship, of continuing a line of common descent, must have been a sustaining force in those pioneering experiences.

[1] Warren H. Wilson, *The Evolution of the Country Community* (Rev. Ed.; Chicago: Pilgrim Press, 1923), p. 22.

[2] H. C. Wright, *Human Life: Illustrated in My Individual Experience* (Boston, 1849).

Moreover, kinsfolk tended to settle in small clusters or neighborhoods, as will be described in the next chapter. The pioneer family of Footes in Vermont, for example, sent some of its branches to New York, or "York State," as it was called. They, in turn, sent younger members to Ohio and to Wisconsin; and so on to Iowa and to California. No one individual family went alone; it was always in company with others, aunt or uncle, brother or sister, or cousin. Communication and contacts were relatively frequent. Letters flowed freely, and annual or semi-annual visits were made, even though it did take almost a week to return by team and buckboard from Iowa to Wisconsin. Fealty to kinsman, then, is one of the great heritages of the early rural family. This bond of the great family was a strong influence. To what extent it is a factor which can still be counted upon, and to what extent it has been dissipated by the greater mobility and by what may even be termed the larger independence of the modern family, is a problem for the student of modern rural society to consider.

Characteristics of Rural Families, Significant Changes

Present-day rural families need to be considered against the background of the early American family. This is true because one who would understand rural society or would endeavor to change it must know not only those forces and processes related to the past, but also those which can be utilized for the future. The rural family, of course, must be considered as a usual family, not as something different and distinct; yet it does possess certain characteristics which can be identified and which are useful for our study. Four of these will be considered here.

In the midst of its occupation. A striking characteristic of the farm family, and to a lesser extent of the village family, is that it lives in the midst of its occupation. Its residence is as fixed a part of the layout as are the barns, fields, or fences. The family and its homestead, together with the farm and its farmstead, make up the living and the working unit. This, then, is the physical and the social environment in which the farm family group lives and works.

The village family included in the term "rural" is not so different in its setting. As is the case with so many village characteristics, the village family stands midway between farm and city families, partaking of the nature of each but having traits of its own. It is not uncommon for a village retail or repair business to be conducted as a family responsibility and for the living quarters to be in the same or in an adjoining building. It is common indeed for the family to own the land on which is found its house, its garden, and even its business establishment.

The occupational environment puts all the members of the family group into close contact with each other. It is in this world that the group develops and builds up its modes of behavior and its institutions and traditions. Acquaintance with this world is best gained by contact with those who live in it. Brief extracts from case stories, written by college students, of their own home are therefore given.[3]

I believe my father should be considered an average father, judged by the standards of his community. He always seemed to me to put far more thought on having the best corn crop, the largest potatoes by the Fourth of July, etc., than he did on disposing of them to the best advantage. The income for the family was not adequate for the standards which were my mother's goal. There were times when I wonder how she

[3] C. E. Lively, *Readings in Rural Sociology*, I, "Life in the Farm Family" (Mimeograph by H. L. Hedrick, Columbus, Ohio, 1933).

contrived to manage as she did and give us the opportunities she did. We always had plenty of good food, but my mother's ingenuity, industry, and instilling the necessity for care of materials into us were the factors which for years solved the problem of comfortable and attractive clothing for her large family.

My mother and the girls in our family did very little work in the fields, which was rather singular, since there were so many girls and only one boy, and since it was customary for women to work in fields. We, the girls, helped pick up potatoes, and pick sweet corn several summers when my father had contracted some for a canning factory. My mother did much work in the garden, always raised many chickens, and helped milk until brother assumed the task.

It is this sort of family life which has influenced students of the family to conclude that rural families have developed characteristics of their own. LePlay, the great French scholar of family life, places a great deal of stress on what he terms "successful families," upon the sentimental attachment or relationship which exists between the family group and its homestead or its "hearth." Thus at least one of the features of the early family seems to have extended its influence through the years to the present, namely, the organization of a family occupation about the utilization and possession of land.

Close family relationships. Since agriculture is operated on the family plan, close working relations within the family unit are essential. These relationships assume a characteristic solidarity and cohesion. They influence family life at many points. For example, there is the importance of home-produced food; there is the constant pressure upon the family income to meet farm operation expenditures, and the urge to pay off the mortgage or to buy more land. This competition will be considered more fully in the chapter on family standards of living. Illustrations are found in the family case

stories reported by students, and quoted from sources to which previous reference has been made.

When I look back now, I am sure she, mother, was overburdened. I think she was so busy caring for the physical needs of her children, that she did not have time to enjoy them. Much of her care of the younger children fell to me, since I was the oldest and a girl. Even yet I feel a deep responsibility for the other children, and find myself eternally planning and deciding for them, when there is no need and they would many times prefer that I did not.

Father had the greater say-so. He did not consider mother his inferior. She belonged in the house and he over the place in general. He didn't consider her his equal in some cases for the reason that he did transact most of the business. Furthermore, mother wasn't interested in details. Mutually, they both decided to make things go, and they did go. Mother did not feel inferior to father and she never felt that he expected her to feel so. She knew that he knew what he wanted and both were interested in making things go. So they worked together. Even with all the drudgery they enjoyed working together and going places together.

Women and children are especially involved in this close working relationship. Their situation is quite in contrast with that of urban families where the father leaves the home early in the morning for office or factory and does not return until the evening meal. Furthermore, the family-type of husband, wife, and children is much more frequent in rural areas than in cities of a hundred thousand or more population. In cities there are many more husbands and wives living alone, and more family units without children or with only one child.

An interesting formula of interpersonal relations in the family has been devised which indicates that with the addition of each person to the family group, the number of persons increases in simple, whole numbers, while the number of personal interrelationships within the group increases in the order of triangular numbers.[4] For example, the first child increases the number of persons in the family by one, but it increases the number of personal relationships by two; that is, from one to three. Another member would increase the number of persons to four, but the personal relationships from three to six, that is, increased by three. This has important implications for the larger rural families because of the many potential personal contacts.

It is significant that professional workers in agriculture, whose business it is to assist with management and economic problems, should recognize the importance of coöperation of wives in the farm and family enterprise. They report that since no exact measure of her coöperation was possible, they chose for comparison seventeen families in which coöperation was evident and seventeen in which there was least evidence of it. The average labor earnings showed a difference of $915. This might seem too great a difference, but it is even more significant that farm operators themselves ranked the coöperation of their wives second on a list of fifteen items which they regarded as most important in the success of the farm.[5] At least it is evidence of the close relationship of family and farm. Farm management can be stressed and home management can be emphasized, but encompassing the two is family management; farming is a family affair.

The close relationship of the family in its farming and its homemaking is becoming more generally recognized in many professional circles, but it is doubtful that the implications are fully realized. A home economics worker [6] stresses the point that dur-ing the early organization of this work there was a tendency to "carve up" the family into three parts: the farmer, the homemaker, and the children. "We lost sight," she says, "of the fact that the family is a social and economic unit with coöperative relationships. Certain things are to be done by the man, and there are certain things to be done by the women, but both are homemakers. So are the children."

The closely knit relationships of the family carry over into the rural situation of which it is a part. Many studies and observations confirm this. For example, in a study of family resettlement it became evident that in the internal relations among the family members, their attitude toward one another and toward the farm, as well as the interfamily relations with neighbors, might easily become a handicap which would preclude successful adjustment of the family with the land.[7]

Women are assuming a greater amount of leadership in rural organizations than in the earlier days. In some localities they now hold about 50 per cent of the offices, and incidentally, their education in terms of schooling is about two years more than that of the men in similar positions. But of even greater significance is a conclusion that the cultural backgrounds of the locality and of family relationships themselves were important factors shaping the future trend of rural social organizations.[8]

---

[4] James H. S. Bossard, "The Law of Family Interaction," *American Journal of Sociology*, January, 1945.

[5] Wilcox, Boss, and Pond, *Relation of Variations in the Human Factor to Financial Returns in Farming* (Minneapolis: University of Minnesota Agricultural Experiment Station, 1932).

[6] Maggie W. Barry, "Rededication to Truth," *Ex-*

tension Service Review (Washington, D.C.: United States Department of Agriculture, June-July, 1944); Ava B. Milam, "Strengthening Home Economics Stakes," *Journal of Home Economics*, XXXIV, No. 10, December, 1944.

[7] George W. Hill, Walter Slocum, and Ruth O. Hill, *Man-Land Adjustment*, Research Bulletin 134 (Madison: University of Wisconsin Agricultural Experiment Station, February, 1938).

[8] E. L. Kirkpatrick, J. H. Kolb, Creagh Inge, and A. F. Wileden, *Rural Organizations and the Farm Family*, Research Bulletin 96 (Madison: University of Wisconsin Agricultural Experiment Station, November, 1929).

In New York similar conditions were found. Dr. Anderson [9] reports that participation in organization activities is a characteristic of the family as a whole and that the best approach in promoting such family participation would be through the mother, since she exhibits the trait more than other members of the family. This is to say that if the mother becomes a participant, her influence is likely to spread to other family members, thus encouraging their participation.

More family units in proportion to total adult population. The early American family was part of a domestic economy, and the rural family in its close contact with its occupation has continued this system to a greater degree than have families in other areas of our society. It is to be expected, therefore, that in relation to the adult population more family units are found in rural than in other sections of society. This is true because country people marry earlier in life, the union is less frequently broken, and there is a tendency for the unmarried and those left by broken marriages, either by divorce or death, to migrate. The latter is especially true of country girls and women. The country simply is not a hospitable place

[9] W. A. Anderson, "Social Participation and Religious Affiliation in Rural Areas," reprint from *Rural Sociology*, IX, No. 3, September, 1944.

for single persons, especially for unmarried girls and women.

In 1950, of the 38,800,000 families in the United States, 5,600,000 were on farms, 7,700,000 in rural non-farm areas, and 25,500,000 in urban areas.

The percentage distribution of families in the three residence categories for the four major regions of the country are shown in Table 23. The general distribution follows very closely that of the total population.

Regional differences directly reflect the variations in farming situations. Only in the South does the proportion in rural areas approach 50 per cent, and even here the larger percentage is with the non-farm rather than farm families.

On the average, more rural people than urban marry in age groups fourteen years and over, but averages tend to obscure important differences among areas of residence and between men and women as Table 24 indicates.

The lower percentage of married farm men seems an exception to the generalization that more rural than urban people are married. This disparity is related in differences in the sex ratios of the rural farm population as explained in the chapter on changing population patterns. In farm areas where there are proportionately more men, the percentage of married women is high; in cities, the reverse is the case.

TABLE 23 Per cent Distribution of Families by Residence, Urban and Rural, and by Region, 1950.	REGION	PER CENT DISTRIBUTION BY RESIDENCE			
		Total	Rural Farm	Rural Non-Farm	Urban
	United States	100.0	14.5	19.8	65.7
	Northeast	100.0	4.5	14.7	80.8
	North Central	100.0	16.1	18.6	65.3
	South	100.0	23.5	25.1	51.3
	West	100.0	9.4	20.4	70.2

Source: 1950 Census of Population, Preliminary Report, Series PC–7, No. 3, Table 6, April 30, 1951.

TABLE 24 Per cent Distribution of Marital Status of Men and Women 14 Years and Over, by Residence.	RESIDENCE	PER CENT MARRIED	
		Males	Females
	United States	67.8	65.5
	Rural farm	64.0	70.7
	Rural non-farm	67.9	69.8
	Urban	68.7	63.3

Source: 1950 Census of Population, Preliminary Report, Series PC–7, No. 3, Table 4, April 30, 1951.

Selective migration has much to do with the characteristics of rural family composition. City conditions and opportunities attract certain kinds of people, which is only another way of saying that farm or country life is unfavorable to some people. Girls, for example, leave farm homes more frequently than do boys and about two years younger. Those who remain marry earlier than the boys. Conclusions from special studies indicate that children of tenant farm families and of owner families with lower incomes are more likely to leave than others. A large majority of single, widowed, and divorced women are quite sure to leave the country for village, town, or city.

Children, a distinguishing characteristic. Children are most characteristic of the rural family; in fact, they are the most distinguishing factor in rural society. The country produces children, the city consumes

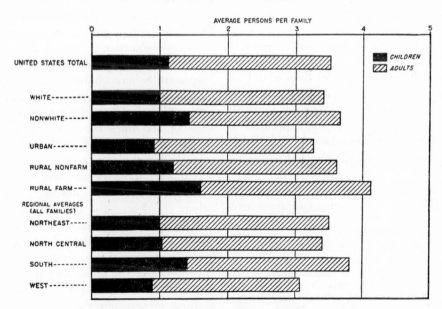

Figure 3. Average Number of Persons per Family, by Color, Residence, and Region, 1940.

Source: Sixteenth Census of the United States, 1940, *Population*, IV, Part I. Characteristics by age, marital status, relationship, education, and citizenship.

them; this has been a fundamental consideration in the rural-urban relationship during the past half century. However, with the shift of young families with children toward the fringe of cities, with the proportion of children under five years of age greater in the rural non-farm than in the farm population, and with other changes, this previously accepted relationship is due for review.

One hundred and sixty years ago, in 1790, the size of the family household in the United States was 5.7; a hundred years later, it was 4.9; fifty years later, in 1940, it was 3.8. This means fewer than two children per family, while under the rates of mortality for that year it was necessary for the average to be three in order to maintain a stationary population. For urban areas the average family size in 1940 was 3.6 persons; for rural areas it was 4. These and other averages for that year are shown in Figure 3. By 1950 the average size of households was 3.4; in the urban census classification it was 3.3; in the rural non-farm, 3.5; in the rural farm, 4.0.[10]

The average-size household showed smaller differences from region to region and from rural to urban in 1950 than it did in 1940. The South had the largest size in both years, namely, 3.6 in 1950 and 4.0 in 1940. The only region which did not experience a decline during the decade was the West, which remained at 3.2. Analysis of age composition and mobility indicates that many thousands of households of young adults with children of early school or preschool

[10] Comparisons are difficult, since in the 1950 census definitions for both family and rural were changed. A family was defined as "a group of two or more persons related by blood, marriage, or adoption, and residing together." A household included "all of the persons, without regard to relationship, who occupy a house, an apartment, or other group of rooms, or a room, that constitutes a dwelling unit." The number of households in the 1950 reports may be regarded as comparable with the number of "families" or "private households" shown in the 1940 census reports.

age moved to the West during those ten years. Rural farm households were larger than urban or rural non-farm in every region.

Since 1930 the decrease in size of households in metropolitan centers was more rapid than in the general urban classification and especially than in the suburban fringe areas. This can be explained by the movements of young families from both city and country into those fringe areas, and by the high proportion of children found there. It also explains the higher proportion of young children in the rural non-farm than in rural farm population, even though the latter had larger households.

In 1950 the percentages of children under five years of age in terms of all ages, for the three residence categories were as follows: rural non-farm, 11.9; rural farm, 11.4; urban, 10.4; total population, 10.8. It is important to note that the per cent for the rural farm is below the rural non-farm. This is a reversal of earlier trends.

In the North and West children under five years increased at more rapid rates between 1940 and 1950 than any other age group. A surprising change also took place in the Northeast, where children under five years increased 59 per cent, while the total population increased only 10 per cent, a difference of six times the rate. As previously shown, this fast growth of the child population during the war and in postwar years was among those classes where birth rates were previously the lowest, namely the urban, the white, the better educated, and the higher income classes. These are the classes which are relatively large in the northeast region of the country. This change is evidence of the equalizing process taking place in family patterns. In general, the marked increase in the number of young children in the population is the product of higher birth rates and of reductions in infant mortality, both of which may be reflections of enhanced values accorded children in

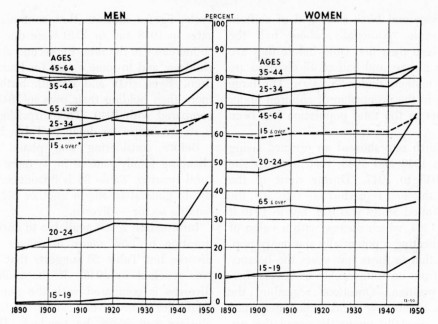

Figure 4. Per Cent Married at Ages 15 and Over, by
Sex and Age Groups. United States, 1890 to 1949.

Source of basic data: Various reports by the Bureau of the Census, reported by *Statistical Bulletin,* Metropolitan Life Insurance Company, XXXI,
No. 7, July, 1950.

family life within our present cultural
system.

*Changing characteristics of general family
patterns.* There are not only more families
in our society in absolute numbers but also
in proportion to the whole adult population.
In the last fifty years population about
doubled, while families have about tripled.
The number of married people is at an all-
time high, higher than in any other country.
In 1947 two million couples were married —
fourteen marriages for every thousand population.[11] Nearest to this rate were New
Zealand and Czechoslovakia, with about
eleven per thousand. Not only do more
people marry, but they marry younger than
anywhere else in the western world. Half
of the male population is married before 24

[11] Louis I. Dublin, "The Truth About American
Marriages," *Parents' Magazine,* December, 1948.

years of age, and the female before 22 years;
three fourths of both before 30 years. In
Ireland, for example, at 30 years of age only
a third of the men and about half of the
women are married. In Norway the average
age of marriage for women was 26 years and
for men, 29 years.

The age group in the United States which
showed greatest change for both men and
women was 20–24, as Figure 4 indicates so
strikingly. Among the women in this age
group the rate rose from 47 per cent in 1890
to 51 per cent in 1940, then jumped to 68 per
cent in 1949. The increase for women in
every age group under 45 years was greater
in the last decade than in the previous half
century. Such a boom in marriages has depleted the number of single persons in the
population, as the chapter on population
changes has shown.

These dramatic changes lead to questions

of marriage and birth rates and of shift in family cycle. Nationally, about half the women bear their first child before they are 23 years of age, and half of all children are born to mothers under 28 years. The large increase in the proportion of children under five years to the total population has been noted.

The birth rate showed an upward swing between 1940 and 1943, then a sharp rise from 1945 to 1947. During most of the thirties the net reproduction rate for the whole United States was 978, but in 1946 it rose to 1364, which means, with a value of 1000 indicating a potentially stationary population, that in these few years the balance turned from an unfavorable to a very favorable position. Questions regarding the duration of this new trend immediately start debate, especially among the population authorities themselves.

Recent releases of vital statistics give every evidence that the upward trend of birth rates is continuing. The number of babies born in the United States during the first five months of 1951 showed a major increase over the same period the previous year and approached the all-time record set in 1947. Indeed, the increase continued through the rest of the year, and 1951 set a new record. Of greatest significance in terms of personal relations in the family

cycle, figures indicate that continued high rates in 1948 and in 1949 were due mainly to increases in the rates for second and third children, and to some extent for fourth children. Even sixth and seventh births were more than holding their own in 1949 when compared with 1940. This surprising trend is shown in greater detail in Table 25.

Before considering one phase of the changing family pattern in its more strictly rural bearing, Table 26 is introduced to indicate general trends in another highly debatable sector — divorce.

Information is not available to answer the question of how many marriages end in divorce but Table 26 suggests that a peak was reached in 1946. If the number of divorces is compared with the number of marriages in any given year, misleading conclusions can easily be reached. Divorces granted in any one year apply to marriages which occurred over many preceding years. For example, in 1945 there were about thirty-one divorces granted for every hundred marriages which took place in that same year. This seemed to give rise to the "one-in-three" idea or that a third of all marriages ended in divorce, which was far from the facts. It simply meant that thirty-one couples were divorced for every hundred couples married in that particular year. It did not tell how long the divorced couples had been married,

	BIRTH ORDER	1949	1948	1947	1940
TABLE	All births	105.2	104.8	110.1	73.5
25	First	36.0	39.2	46.0	27.5
	Second	31.8	30.5	29.6	18.6
Live Birth Rates by	Third	17.0	15.8	15.1	10.2
Birth Order: United	Fourth	8.4	7.7	7.6	5.9
States, 1940, 1947–49	Fifth	4.5	4.3	4.3	3.7
	Sixth and Seventh	4.5	4.4	4.4	4.3
	Eighth and over	3.5	3.4	3.4	3.8

Birth order refers to number of children born alive to mother. Rates per 1000 estimated female population 15–44 years of age. Figures other than "total" exclude data for Massachusetts. This state does not report birth order. In computing rates by birth order, births of order "not stated" in states other than Massachusetts have been distributed.

Source: Release August 3, 1951, FSA–C65, Federal Security Agency, Public Health Service, Washington 25, D.C.

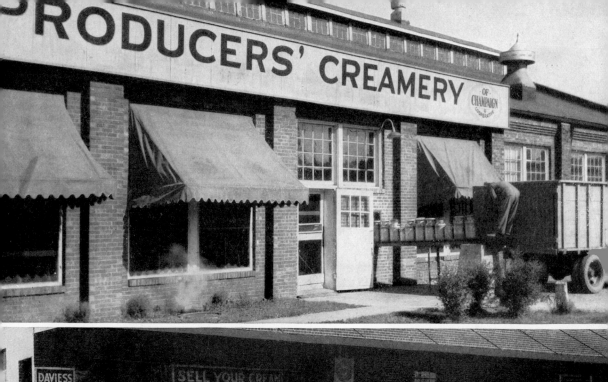

THREE TYPICAL FARMERS' CO-OPERATIVES *Top*: Producers' Creamery. *Center*: Daviess County Farm Bureau. *Bottom*: Farmers Exchange. (U.S. Dept. of Agriculture)

TRANSPORTATION OF FARM PRODUCTS *Top*: Transporting Tea, Ceylon (Plâté Ltd., Office of Foreign Agricultural Relations). *Center left*: Mule Carrying Bananas, Central America (Standard Oil Co., N.J., photo by Collier). *Center right*: Bringing Crops from Fields, Okinawa (U.S. Army). *Bottom*: Primitive Wheelbarrow, Colombia, S.A. (Standard Oil Co., N.J., photo by Collier)

Top: Passengers and Freight Jam Bus to the City, Central America (Standard Oil Co., N.J.). *Bottom left*: The Farmer Goes to Market (U.S. Dept. of Agriculture). *Bottom right*: Modern Roads Bring City Consumers to the Farm

Top: Main Street, Pacific Northwest. *Center*: Small Village, Southwestern United States (Photos, Standard Oil Co., N.J.). *Bottom*: Country Neighborhood, Vermont (Photo by A. Devaney, Inc., N.Y.)

	YEAR	MARRIAGE RATE	DIVORCE RATE
TABLE	1949	85.5	10.8
	1948	98.0	11.3
26	1947	106.8	13.7
	1946	120.7	17.8
Marriage Rates per 1000 Un-			
married Females * and Divorce	1945	84.5	14.5
Rates per 1000 Married Fe-	1944	76.8	12.1
males, 15 Years of Age and	1943	83.8	11.0
Over: United States for Specified	1942	93.6	10.1
Years.			
	1941	88.8	9.4
	1940	82.9	8.7
	1939	73.9	8.5
	1938	70.8	8.4

* Includes never married, widowed, and divorced.

Source: Vital Statistics-Special Reports-National Summaries, XXXVI, No. 2, June 5, 1951. Federal Security Agency, Washington, D.C.

or what proportion of those married that year might be expected to stay married.

Changing patterns among farm-operator families. The general trend of family pattern in the United States has been from the traditionally large family with a minimum of family limitations and high fertility rates, through a long period of transition covering many decades, to the small family with widely accepted limitations and consequent low fertility rates. Margaret Hagood, authority on population trends and student of census materials, states as her opinion that only a relatively small proportion of the nation's families have not made a substantial shift from the very large family pattern.[12] The extent to which this shift has occurred in various kinds of families and in different regions is a problem of absorbing interest.

It might be assumed that the farm family would be the last or the slowest to make the transition, especially those of the lowest income status. Earlier studies indicated that the number of children in the family are in-

versely correlated with family income, that is, the greatest number of children were found where there was the least income. This is but another way of saying that in the past there has been a concentration of children in low-income families. In fact, nearly half the children were to be found in the relatively few large families of comparatively low income. The farming sections with the largest families were those in the cotton South, the Appalachian and Ozark Mountain areas, the Lake States cutover, and the Mexican border.[13] Among Oklahoma completed farm families, differences in family size were found to be related not only to socio-economic status but also to education of parents, to migration, and to residential backgrounds.[14]

In order to examine the conditions of farm families more thoroughly, Dr. Hagood based her study upon special tabulations of the 1945 Census of Agriculture. She applied the

[12] Margaret Jarman Hagood, "Changing Fertility Differentials," *Rural Sociology*, XIII, No. 4, December, 1948.

[13] Thomas J. Woofter, Jr., "Children and Family Income," reprint from the *Social Security Bulletin*, VIII, No. 1 (Washington, D.C.: Social Security Board, January, 1945).

[14] William H. Sewell, "Differentiated Fertility in Completed Oklahoma Farm Families," *American Sociological Review*, IX, No. 4, August, 1944.

fertility of women between the ages of twenty and forty-four in terms of the number of children under five years of age to the farm population, dividing the number of farms into seven classes by economic size. These seven classes were analyzed for all the states, which were divided into nine geographic regions. The results showed a rather mixed picture; in some states there was a positive relation between family size and economic class, and in others a negative relation; in still others there were no clear-cut relations. At least the older assumption of large family associated with poor farm was not borne out.

Certain geographic differences did appear. In the southern states the negative relation between family size and economic class was more common, while in Ohio and New York the opposite trend was more clear. Since these two states showed a marked departure from the traditional relationship of family size and economic status, a more intensive study was made of them. In both states the higher income families showed greater increase in fertility from the depression to the prosperous war years than did the lower-income families. In Ohio the high-income fertility ratio increased by 20 per cent, while the low-group ratio went up only 2 per cent. In New York the corresponding changes were an increase of 17 per cent in the high and a decrease of 2 per cent in the low group. Certainly these different income-group families responded differently to economic conditions than could have been expected on the basis of former trends.

This kind of study opens the door to studies of other influences which bear upon family patterns. As suggested in the conclusion of the report, among such factors must be included the attitudes and desires of the parents themselves, the satisfactions which they anticipate and actually experience in parenthood, the ability they feel to pay the early costs of children, and their sense of security in being able to support children to maturity and to educate them in accord with their standards. This course of discussion leads at once to considerations of the family cycle and to those human values which are inherent in educational, religious, political, and economic ideals, and which relate to other aspects of the cultural setting of which the family group is an integral part.

Family Cycle and Fundamental Functions

One of the most far-reaching implications of the trends just traced is that while two generations ago only about half of the married couples in this country could hope to survive to the age when their last child left home, in 1940 about half could expect to live for eleven years, nearly a fourth of their married lives, after the last child was matured and ready to start his own family cycle. Early marriage and early parenthood give children an opportunity to grow up while parents are still relatively young. The chances of losing a parent through death, separation, or divorce are less. Young parents can be enriched and nurtured emotionally by association with their children, and they can look forward to enjoying their grandchildren.[15]

Family cycle has special social significance. The family group cannot be considered as static; it moves through a characteristic cycle. The family is formed by the original pair, man and wife, and for them it is a voluntary association. Children are born and grow up in an involuntary association, a genetic group. Following its formation the family develops, increases in size and complexity, and then declines as some of its branches start their own cycles.

The social significance of considering family cycles is important for students of

[15] Adapted from Louis Dublin, *op. cit.*

society as well as for those who are associated with families professionally, such as medical doctors, teachers, pastors, welfare workers, recreation leaders, agricultural agents, and home economists. Among professional workers there is too often a tendency to expect all families to respond equally to a currently offered program. For the researcher it is all too easy to come to conclusions by cross-section studies which catch all families in some general category at the same point in time but at very different stages of their life cycles. Therefore various ways have been devised for equating age differences such as the fertility ratio, or the adult male equivalent, in comparing food budgets.

For families themselves the implications of the cycle are also far-reaching. The distribution among items in the budget must undergo significant change. Very often the needs are more demanding than the current income can meet, but they cannot be set aside or postponed. The change in needs is frequently slower than shifts in family resources. Planning and saving or borrowing are necessary. Daily decisions made by the farm operator or the village merchant have deep implications for long-term success or failure, since they must try to balance the input and the output involved in the total family career. It was pointed out in a recent study of family-type farming that the future resources of a whole state are dependent upon the ways farm people manage their family careers.[16]

Another point of social significance is the way family cycles frequently affect a whole neighborhood or community situation. A majority of the families may move through their life cycle together, all growing old and retiring at about the same time or all taking over their farms or businesses and having their children within a few years of each other. A school board, for example, especially if its members' children are grown up, may not observe the large group of preschool children coming along. Therefore, they may make decisions which are short-sighted and which must be revised unless they are irrevocable. Local leaders may become confused as to why some of their plans fail, since they may not be adjusted to the prevailing family cycle in the community. Different stages in the cycle reveal different interests and different motivations.

Impressive changes in the general family cycle. During two generations, between 1890 and 1940, the median age at marriage decreased two years. There was a sharp drop in the number of children, from 5.4 to 3.1. The median age of the wife bearing her last child was reduced from 32 to 27 years, and her age when this child was married went from 55 to 50 years. Because of the reductions in mortality rates, the age at which the husband and wife might be expected to die rose from 53 to 61 years.

These and other changes shown in Figure 5 have tremendous consequences for many aspects of society such as welfare, security, housing, recreation, education, health, and standards of living, to be considered in later chapters.

Stages in the development cycle of rural families. In rural families the cycle of development ordinarily requires about twenty-five years. Each stage brings its own unique requirements. The four chief stages are recorded in terms of the children rather than the parents, as is shown in Figure 5. There is the preschool stage, when the children are under six years of age; the grade-school stage, when the children are six to thirteen years of age; the high-school stage, with children fourteen to eighteen years; and the

[16] Erven J. Long and Kenneth H. Parsons, *How Family Labor Affects Wisconsin Farming*, Research Bulletin 167 (Madison: University of Wisconsin Agricultural Experiment Station, May, 1950).

1940

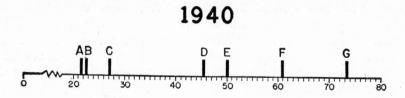

1890

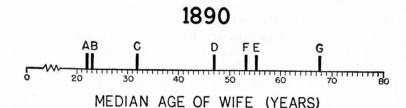

MEDIAN AGE OF WIFE (YEARS)

<u>CODE</u>   <u>STAGE</u>

A....*MARRIAGE*

B....*BIRTH OF FIRST CHILD*

C....*BIRTH OF LAST CHILD*

D....*MARRIAGE OF FIRST CHILD*

E....*MARRIAGE OF LAST CHILD*

F....*DEATH OF HUSBAND, IF FIRST*

G....*DEATH OF WIFE, IF LAST*

Figure 5. Stages of the Family Cycle in the U.S.

Source: Paul C. Glick, "The Family Cycle," *American Sociological Review,* XII, No. 2, April, 1947.

all-adult stage, with children nineteen years or more of age.[17]

Two other stages in the cycle might be mentioned. The pre-child period, which for the majority of farm families was found to be short, since the family usually increased in size within the first or second year; and the post-child period, reached after all the children have left home and the family is again composed of the parents. Most farm families of the post-child period, however, were found to contain at least one grown son or daughter who was helping with

[17] Kirkpatrick, Tough, and Cowles, *The Life Cycle of the Farm Family in Relation to Its Standards of Living,* Research Bulletin 121 (Madison: University of Wisconsin Agricultural Experiment Station, September, 1934).

the farm or housework. Such families were thus classed in the all-adult group. The average size of family increased from 4.1 persons in the preschool stage to 5.1 persons in the high-school stage and returned again to 4.1 persons in the all-adult.

(1) *The preschool family* is a young family in a double sense: it has existed a relatively short period of time, and usually its operator and homemaker are between twenty-five and thirty-five years of age. Preschool families, in contrast to those in other stages of development, spend more time in reading and listening to the radio, and they are usually more interested in community affairs.

In the depression period many farm families were unable to meet interest and tax payments. Children's illnesses went without professional medical care or doctor bills went unpaid. This became a major family problem, not only from the standpoint of the future health situation of the children, but also in family relationships because mothers of preschool children made it very clear that in their minds children were more important than unpaid interest or delinquent taxes. When money became more plentiful in the war period, the greatest expansion in family expenditures was for medical care, especially among a group of relatively low-income farm families, as will be detailed in the chapter on home and standards of living.

(2) *The grade-school family* is similar in many respects to the preschool family, although, of course, the parents are older. It, too, is making sacrifices to climb the "agricultural ladder," is finding it difficult to meet interest and tax payments, and has relatively high expenditures for medical care.

In talking about plans for the future, parents in this stage of development are primarily concerned with education for the children. The family will have to make provision for these future educational needs at the sacrifice of many other things including even immediate housing improvements, as was indicated in a conversation with a Mrs. Roth, who is the mother of children in grade school. Her ambition for her two children is a high school education. In addition, she wishes her son to go to college to learn to be a "real farmer." She stated that neither Mr. Roth nor she went to high school, but "no matter what happens, the children are going because they need it and must have it." This story is a good illustration of the projection upon the children of the unfulfilled educational desires of the parents. Such projection is more likely to be characteristic of the family with younger children.

(3) *The high-school family* presents a decided contrast to the two earlier stages. In this period the family is larger than at any other stage, reaching its maximum size of 5.1 persons, and obviously, children or adolescents constitute three fifths of this family. In this group the labor of the boys and girls is a substitute for hired help. Wants in the high-school stage are many and varied. They make themselves felt in expenditures for clothing and advancement goods and services for the children. In rural areas it is necessary for the children to go to the neighboring village high school and this involves either expenditures for transportation or for board and room. In addition, expenses for advancement goods take the form of relatively high outlays for reading materials, organization dues, and recreation. Hours spent in reading and listening to radio programs at home drop for this group as compared with the others.

Since the amount of cash available for family living in this group is not necessarily more than at the other three stages of family development, the relatively large amounts spent for clothing and advancement must result in curtailment of expenditures for other goods and services. This reduction occurs in such items as furnishings, household operation, maintenance of health, and insurance.

(4) *The all-adult family* has greater expenditures for family living than any other group. This indicates not only that the wants in this group are greater and more diverse than those at the other stages of development, but also a greater tendency to gratify them. Relatively large expenditures are made by families in this stage for clothing, furnishings, schooling, reading matter, church support, recreation, and personal goods.

Often the all-adult stage of development is a period when anticipated wants on the part of the parents for the children are fulfilled, at least in part. The children are educated, have positions, may have been married, and very often are beginning another family cycle.

Three fundamental functions remain — emphasis shifts. The family is a primary group characterized by common residence, economic and social coöperation, and reproduction, as has been stressed throughout the chapter. It is a universal human grouping found in every known society.[18] It is likewise a group of interacting personalities deeply imbedded in a cultural setting. There are the husband-wife, parent-child, child-child, family-farm, and family-neighbor relations. The peculiar role of the family as a group is that of working out some semblance of harmony among these various interrelations.

In times of rapid change and transition, such as have been traced briefly here, there are those who despair of the future of the family and predict that it will go the way of Greek and Roman families — toward disintegration.[19] There are others who are exponents of greater democracy within the family, of more deliberate effort in meeting crises, and of adjusting the forms but keeping the content, namely, the fundamental functions of family.[20] Professor Burgess, for example, rejects the viewpoint that the family is declining and will eventually disappear. He turns his back on the idea that the family must retain those highly institutionalized forms which characterized much of American life during most of its history until World War I. He suggests that emphasis be turned to making adjustments from autocratic to democratic relationships, from external forces to internal bonds of affection holding families together, and from reliance on custom and tradition to more deliberate preparation for marriage and family life.

Three chief functions of the family may be briefly enumerated by way of summary before considering its cultural setting in society.

A first family function is preserving and protecting human life. This involves the multiplicities of homemaking, housekeeping, child care, and living. Though modified in many of their forms and mechanics, as the chapter dealing with the home and its standards of living will show, these still remain dominant activities of rural families. During depression and war years, rural families and their households became more self-reliant and more self-asserting by necessity. During the more recent and prosperous years, many household conveniences have been acquired, housing has been improved, and forms have changed; but family life goes on, and children appear in ever-increasing number.

If this function of protecting life is to be given primary consideration, the family must prepare in advance before swinging into that cycle where these responsibilities are heaviest. Unless this can be done to a much greater extent than at present, the wide differences in the economic and social situations of families can be offset only by some kind of group or public responsibility. Only in this way will it be possible for every child to be well-born and guaranteed an equal chance in beginning life.

A second function of family is perpetuating the race and caring for the sex relationships. The rural family has certainly distinguished itself in the first part of this function, as has been amply proved; no adequate

[18] C. P. Murdock, *Social Structure* (New York: Macmillan, 1949).

[19] Carle C. Zimmerman, *Family and Civilization* (New York: Harper, 1947); and "The Family Farm," *Rural Sociology*, XV, No. 3, September, 1950.

[20] Ernest W. Burgess, "Achieving a Stable Family in an Unstable Society," from a summary of the University of Kentucky Institute on Family Life (Lexington, July 7–9, 1947); and Joseph K. Folsom, *The Family and Democratic Society* (New York: Wiley, 1943).

basis for comment on the second part exists. Comparative studies on divorce may be of some little value, but certainly marital felicity goes much deeper than that. The rural family continues to have a real measure of stability. Field studies, however, indicate rather clearly that domestic tranquility is not universal even in the country. Further studies are needed to show trends and to point to ways and means for attaining a greater degree of success in marriage. Studies have been made in some urban situations.[21]

A third great function, or rather, perhaps, group of functions, has to do with personality in the cultural and affectional relations. Members of a family need some sense of security, of status or group solidarity, and quite as important, they need to cultivate facility in relating themselves to other groups such as neighborhoods, communities, and to the Great Society itself. It is difficult to consider this function unless some idea of goal or direction is introduced. It means raising the question of what values need fostering in rural life and what services the family can render to achieve them. The obvious answer would seem to be children. In adopting its Children's Charter, the White House Conference pointed out that every phase of child life affects the welfare of society itself. Similarly, the Committee on Recent Social Trends concludes that the future of the family will depend more and more on the strength of its affectional bonds. As we have seen, the rural family is distinguished by children. Children are the prime objects of affection; thus the circle would seem complete.

There is evidence of a growing recognition of the importance of this personality function in family life. It is most readily observed in the fields of education and research. In periodicals such as *Parents' Magazine* there is a notable increase in the articles dealing with family life. In schools and colleges the number of courses which deal with marriage and the family is increasing. In an index of research projects the emphasis is shown to have shifted from economic and legal problems of the family to those of its human relations, interaction of husband and wife, and of parents and children.[22]

Gunnar Myrdal, the Swedish authority on population who was called to this country to study interracial problems, suggests that children are the central clue to individual and to family happiness, a means to the healthy development of personality in the various members of the family, including the children themselves.[23] The implications of such a premise are far-reaching. If children were really considered important and were given a position of high value in both personal and social plans and in both private and public measures, more of the problems facing a society in transition would be solved.

The Great Family in Its Cultural Setting

Rural families have been considered in different references: in the pioneer period, in the current scene, in comparisons over time, in changing life cycles, and in their fundamental functions in society. If the idea has crept in that the family or the household are somehow isolated, units apart, or complete integers which can be calculated separately, then vigorous corrections must be made. Just as personalities are at the basis of the family group, so individual families are closely knit by threads of kinship, marriage, and association with other families. A whole philosophy of family has been built

[21] Ernest W. Burgess, and Leonard R. Cottrell, *Predicting Success or Failure in Marriage* (New York: Prentice Hall, 1939).

[22] Meyer F. Nimkoff, "The Family," *American Journal of Sociology*, May, 1942.

[23] Gunnar Myrdal, "Population Problems and Policies," *Annals of the American Academy of Political and Social Science*, May, 1938.

by the analogy of the trunk and its branches. This is to the effect that an individual family sends out branches when its children marry and in turn have their own children. The network of relationship is known as the "family tree." The point for present emphasis is that families are part of a larger kinship association — the great family. This is one of the significant legacies of the pioneer family and one of the important characteristics of the modern rural family.

The great family is the standard pattern in many other parts of the world, far more powerful in determining attitudes and behavior than the nuclear family of husband, wife, and their offspring. This is especially true in the Orient, where the conflict between the West and that deeply seated eastern conception of the family is one of the cultural clashes of this century. An illustration of the size and character of great families within single households is found in the report of a recent study of a group of Chinese families. The percentages of families with relatives living in the same household were given as follows: male heads 98, sons 60, grandsons 18, daughters 51, granddaughters 13, daughters-in-law 31, mothers of head or wife 23, brothers 15, brothers' wives 11.[24]

Thomas and Znaniecki, in their study of the Polish peasant in America, found that this larger family group — the great family — "had an integrity and a self-sufficiency providing the materials out of which personalities and careers of its members were built." [25] "We found," they said, "that land hunger and status were the drive within this group, and accounted for the intensity with which pursuits were directed and carried on. That is to say, the individual was predetermined by the habits of this group." No

one familiar with rural society can doubt the importance and the influence of this larger group of relatives by blood or marriage, even to the third and fourth generations. The great family is the custodian of the culture, the traditions, and the ideals of the society in which it is indigenous. Evidence of this fact is accumulating in many recent studies of rural society. Some adaptations from conclusions of such studies will be given to provoke discussion about reasons and implications and to make comparisons with other situations.

In *adopting farm practices*, the value on individual freedom in the Danish group tends to facilitate the acceptance of new practices by making a relatively complete break in operations between father and son, thus leaving the son free to make his own adoptions. In the Polish group, quite in contrast, the transfer of the farm from father to son is a gradual process. The son becomes the owner when he has demonstrated to his father that he can operate the farm in the manner in which tradition has proved most effective.[26]

In *acquiring a farm* there is a relationship between the operator's security on his land and the extent of familism in his great family. By statistical tests, the association is not close but in an area so uniformly prosperous and so commercial in its farming methods it is remarkable that any significant relationships were found at all.[27]

In *determining intermarriages* the tendency was found to increase with second and third generations of foreign stock. For five ethnic groups the proportion of inter-

---

[24] Ta-Chen, *Population in Modern China* (Chicago: University of Chicago Press, 1946).

[25] W. I. Thomas and Florian Znaniecki, *The Polish Peasant* (New York: Knopf, 1927).

[26] Harald A. Pedersen, "Cultural Differences in the Acceptance of Recommended Practices," *Rural Sociology*, XVI, No. 1, March, 1951.

[27] Robert A. Rohwer, *Family Factors in Tenure Experience: Hamilton County, Iowa, 1946*, Research Bulletin 375 (Ames: Iowa Agricultural Experiment Station, July, 1950).

marriages was highest among the Anglo-Saxon in Nebraska and Wisconsin, while Scandinavians ranked first in New York. Germans were second in Nebraska and Wisconsin, and third in New York.[28]

In *influencing family fertility*, nationality background and religious affiliation, especially when taken in their combinations, are obviously important factors in explaining differential declines. German-Catholic families held first place in fertility ratio in both 1875 and in 1940, even though that ratio dropped 40 per cent. In contrast, the fertility of German-Lutheran families, while nearly as high in 1875, had gone down 65 per cent, to fourth place by 1940. Norwegian families declined 58 per cent.[29]

In *making occupational choices* rural adolescents reflect "ideological notions" which prevail in American life. Their verbal responses indicate that they possess the personal and the social attributes consistent with the values current in their society.[30]

In *moulding the social structure* of rural communities, the existence and the persistence of cultural differences among family and locality groups are of profound importance, especially in times of crises.[31]

Neither the small family nor the great family are sufficient for meeting the needs of personalities in modern rural society. Other contacts and other associations are required, and they are being experienced on an ever-widening scale. This leads to further exploration of group relations in that society.

[28] Edmund deS. Brunner, *Immigrant Farmers and Their Children* (New York: Doubleday, Doran, 1929).

[29] Douglas G. Marshall, "Farm Family Fertility," *Rural Sociology*, XV, No. 1, March, 1950.

[30] Margaret L. Bright, "Occupational Choice Behavior: An exploratory study," Ph.D thesis, University of Wisconsin, 1950.

[31] Lowry Nelson, "Inter-marriage among Nationality Groups in a Rural Area of Minnesota," *The American Journal of Sociology*, XLVIII, No. 5, March, 1943.

TOPICS FOR DISCUSSION

1. Compare and contrast the manner of early farm family settlement in New England, in the Old South, in the Middle West, and in the Far West.
2. Does a greater proportion of rural or city people marry? Which marries younger? Which has more children per family? Give your explanations.
3. How does the life cycle of farm families differ from that of village or city families?
4. Study the trends in rural divorce in your county or state, either from the census or from local court records. What accounts for the upward swing?
5. Explore the idea that family success and happiness are based on companionship and affection, and that children have cultural and psychological importance. How are these ideas related to the principle of democracy? If put more fully into practice, how might they influence divorce rates, birth rates, public health, and housing policies?
6. Give the best example you know of a "great family." What influences does it exert upon individual families and upon the personalities of younger members?

REFERENCE READINGS

American Journal of Sociology (entire volume) "The American Family," LIII, No. 6, May, 1948.

Anderson, W. A., *Marriages and Families of University Graduates*, Ithaca, N. Y.: Cornell University Press.

Arensberg, Conrad, *The Irish Countryman*. New York: Macmillan, 1937.

Becker, H. F., and R. Hill, *Marriage and the Family*. Boston: Heath, 1942.

Bowman, Henry A., *Marriage for Moderns*, 2nd edition. New York: McGraw-Hill, 1948. The McGraw-Hill Text-Film Department has five 16mm sound films and five 35mm silent filmstrips which were prepared in coöperation with Professor Bowman. The sound motion pictures follow the book, presenting the problems of courtship, marriage, personality types, choice of mate, marriage-career conflicts, adjustments in marriage, etc. The five 35mm filmstrips are for use in discussion of the problems featured in the moving pictures.

Brunner, Edmund deS., "Education and Marriage," *Teachers College Record*. New York: Columbia University, May, 1948.

Burgess, Ernest W., and H. J. Locke, *The Family*. Cincinnati: American Book Co., 1945.

Fitzsimmons, Cleo, and Nellie L. Perkins, "Patterns of Family Relationships in Fifty Farm Families," *Rural Sociology*, XII, No. 3, September, 1947.

Foster, Robert Geib, *Marriage and Family Relationships*. New York: Macmillan, 1950. A text for courses in marriage and the family.

Groves, E. R., *The Contemporary American Family*. Chicago: Lippincott, 1947.

Hill, Reuben, "The American Family: Problem or Solution?" *American Journal of Sociology*, LIII, No. 2, September, 1947.

Landis, Paul H., "Sequential Marriage," *Journal of Home Economics*, XLII, No. 8, October, 1950. Analysis of the frequency and character of remarriages.

Mead, Margaret, "Family," *Ladies Home Journal*, September, 1949.

FILMS

Choosing for Happiness S, 14. Analysis of possible mates in contemplating marriage. McGraw-Hill.

Family Circles S, 29. Problems of the modern home — raising children. McGraw-Hill.

Family Life S, 11. Problems due to mismanagement of time, money. *Coronet*.

Marriage Today S, 22. Dramatic treatment of the ideals and goals to make marriages successful. McGraw-Hill.

This Charming Couple, S, 19. Frequent cause of broken marriages. McGraw-Hill.

12 Country Neighborhoods

BEYOND THE FARM FAMILY GROUP is the country neighborhood group. The question "What is the name of the neighborhood in which you live?" often brings an answer such as Wheeler Prairie, Spring Valley, Pierceville, or Pumpkin Hollow, which is just as definite and full of meaning as the family name. Neighborhoods are made up of groups of families whose members know each other well and who recognize each other by their first names. Frequently these neighbor families are close relatives or members of a great or extended family, as suggested in Chapter 11. Very often too, they are associated in school, in church, in some local social organization, or in informal activities.

In stricter phraseology, a neighborhood is the first group larger than the family which has social significance, and which has some sense of local unity. Both geographic and psychological factors are involved. It is a locality, a vicinity of recognized and localized associations; it is a group with primary, face-to-face relations. There is greater interaction among families within the neighborhood group than with families outside of it. In rural society propinquity continues to be important in group formation, and as elsewhere, primary relations are basic in influencing personality and in exerting social control. Neighborhoods can be considered as small communities which are characterized chiefly by limited size and highly developed primary relations. Primary relations are also found in other forms, as described in the chapter on interest groups.

It was Charles H. Cooley [1] who gave this primary group concept its force and its clarity, and it is sure to be useful for a long time in studying human society. By primary groups he meant those groups which are personal, intimate, or face-to-face in character; they are primary because they are fundamental in forming the social nature and the ideals of the individual. In fact, Professor Cooley said that personality cannot exist without such association or fellowship. Human nature is but a trait of primary groups, he insisted. Among the more important phases of this kind of group life, he enumerated the family, the neighborhood, and the play group. It is the country neighborhood to which attention will be given in this chapter.

The neighborhood has played its part from the time when country people first formed themselves into more or less permanent settlements and established themselves on specific areas of land. In most European rural societies, which formed the cultural background of early American settlers, the agricultural village was the center of settlement and primary group relationships. In Russia it was the *mir;* in Scandinavian countries, it was the family estate; in Norman England, the manor. Concepts corresponding to neighborhood are found in many languages, such as the English *neighbourhood,* the French *vicinage,* the Spanish *vecindario,* the German *nachbarschaft.* It is the state or condition resulting from the personal inter-

[1] *Social Organization,* (New York: Scribner, 1925), chap. III.

action, the process of settling down into a recognized form, which is expressed by the "ship" in relationship, the "schaft" in *nachbarschaft*, and the "hood" in neighborhood. Close interfamily relations were characteristic of all these earlier forms of rural group organization just as they are in the system of homesteads on separate farms which developed later in American rural society.

Early Neighborhood Settlements

In New England the village form of local social economy was continued on the European pattern. Residences were clustered around the "common." At the center were the squares for church, school, and town hall. Barns and sheds were on the home lot with the house. The tillable lands were adjoining, but extending back into the open, often in rather narrow strips. Beyond lay the meadow land and frequently the wood lots.[2] In many ways the New England town with its town meeting and village-centered social life was the primary group. Its influence was widespread, for many of its social institutions and ideals were carried westward, although for many reasons the centralized village pattern was not transplanted.

In the South the plantation was to all intents and purposes the primary locality group. Its origins can be traced more or less directly to the old English manor of lords and country gentlemen. The plantation plan lent itself to large-scale, single-crop farming, to a slavery system of labor, and subsequently to tenants and croppers.[3] Both the social and the economic life of the area were organized about the plantation and carried on as a unit enterprise. It might range in

[2] For a fuller description see Anne B. MacLear, *Early New England Towns* (New York: Columbia University Studies in Economics, History, and Public Law, XXIX, No. 1).

[3] C. O. Brennan, *Relation of Land Tenure to Plantation Organization*, Bulletin 1269 (Washington, D.C.: United States Department of Agriculture).

size from six or eight families to more than a hundred. There were the plantation buildings, the commissary, often the school, the large dwelling house, and the coterie of small cottages and cabins. The planter and his family were, of course, the dominant figures in the group and represented the aristocracy of southern society.

In the Middle West and Far West the separate-farm, neighborhood settlement was most common. Individual farms were settled by families who went out to get land and to seek their fortunes. They settled in groups on adjoining farms and were bound together by such ties as kinship, common nationality, the same educational, social, or religious purposes. When the neighborhood was composed largely of a kinship group or of the great family such as described in the preceding chapter, a very closely knit organization was formed. Topography and crop or forest cover were also important. Some of the earlier settlers sought the "oak openings," or moved directly into the timber so that they might have building material and fuel. They looked for springs or streams to supply water for themselves and their livestock. Mutual aid, exchange of work, building bees, social affairs, schools, and churches soon became organized. If adjoining settlements were made by those of different cultural backgrounds or nationality, and unlike purposes, group lines were drawn a little closer. School district boundaries were gerrymandered so as to include only the in-group. But the arbitrary township lines laid out by the surveyor and carefully executed on the checker-board pattern would not yield to the social or group design. Herein may lie at least one of the reasons for the impotency of local government organized on the township basis.

Country neighborhood settlement and social organization went on quite independently and often prior to small town settlement. The latter sprang up to render certain special types of services which the neighborhood could not organize for itself, such as transportation, banking, merchandising, and certain forms of manufacturing. Villages or towns were often populated by more heterogeneous groups, unrelated in blood or ideal to those of the country neighborhood. These differences became the basis for some of the lack of understanding between town and country, and even for conflicts which developed a little later, when mutual relationships became more important and when the newer transportation and communication systems tied town and country more closely together. Unlike the New England plan, midwestern and western villages were incorporated as municipalities, thus withdrawing from the township unit and leaving the country group on its own.

In the pioneer fringes neighborhood settlement continues westward and northward. C. A. Dawson describes the process in the Peace River district of Alberta and British Columbia.[4] He describes how the individual settlements of Fairview and Grande Prairie preceded the railroad; how they set up one-room schools with a six-month term; how whole families go to all-night dances, putting the small children to sleep in a space set aside for the purpose; and how informality and kindliness prevail. These two settlements are simply examples of the old neighborhood primary group formation process. Dawson goes on to point out that the next stage is soon reached, when there is a greater diffusion of culture, urban influences are felt, and the later settlers demand greater accessibility to the town with its stores, clubs, theaters, hotels, and athletic teams. With a division of interests there is a realignment in primary group organization and the beginning of secondary forms of contact. Very similar

situations were found in Beaverhead County, Montana, and in Union County, New Mexico, and in other areas of relatively recent settlement.

What Neighborhoods Are, Why They Persist, How They Change

One of the interesting and important findings in various studies of local groups in rural society is the persistence of neighborhoods. Many have predicted that this form of local group organization is a thing of the past because of the greatly increased facilities for communication and travel, the greater mobility of both country and city people, and the loosening of kinship and nationality ties. There have been changes, to be sure; there are fewer neighborhoods than formerly, yet many activities continue to center in them. Changes toward greater flexibility and adaptability are the very conditions for their survival.

Characteristic activities in neighborhoods. Neighborliness implies certain obligations and a sense of interdependence. This does not mean complete friendliness; there can be "bad" neighbors as well as "good" neighbors, and conflicts can be bitter by the very reason of close personal contacts. It does mean that there is real communication; "a web of habits" and "a pattern of expectation" are built up over time.[5] "My neighbor" is an expression which has real emotional content. This was particularly true in the pioneering days of the frontier, but it continues to be so and offers a clue to better understanding of the process of interaction of persons and groups.

On the more objective side, it is contacts which hold neighbors together. Working together built up neighborhoods. This is only

[4] *Pioneer Settlement* (New York: American Geographical Society, 1932), chap. VI.

[5] Lyman Bryson, ed., "The Communication of Ideas" (New York: Institute of Religious and Social Studies, distributed by Harper, 1948).

natural, since during settlement days or during the first period of a group's existence, joint effort was directed toward constructing those common forms of life which would endure. Many of the early settlers did not rest until their ideals and values had been embodied in a school, a church, and a social organization with a constitution and officers. They often built the school and church buildings with their own hands in the celebrated building bees which made for friendliness and which determined leadership and other roles in the group. They frequently presided over many of the functions of these fundamental social institutions in the absence of professional leadership or in the intervals between visits of the itinerant or "saddle-bag" teacher and pastor. It is not surprising, then, that these institutions as well as others often continue beyond the period of their usefulness, or that sometimes they remain as vital symbols.

Activities characteristic of present-day country neighborhoods are still those centered about the school, church, local store, social and economic organizations, as well as in relations of kinship and exchange of work. Evidence is found in reports of recent studies.[6] Variations are wide among different geographic regions and type-of-farming areas. For example, in the Far West church-centered neighborhoods are not as frequent as elsewhere, and nationality or kinship patterns are not as important as in the Middle West. In an earlier nation-wide study including 140 town-country community areas, two thirds of the neighborhoods in the Far West were characterized by combinations of school and some social or economic activity.[7]

In wheat or livestock areas where settlement is sparse, neighborhoods are larger in area and smaller in number of families. Highways are usually straighter and more level than in some parts of the Middle West and South, however, so that measured in time units, the contacts may not be much different. In those sections of the Middle West where dairy farming predominates, locality determines many contacts, formal and informal, for sociability, education, religion, trade, and coöperative organizations.

Through the corn belt, church, school, and nationality groups are important in the open country. In Hamilton County, Iowa, for example, 108 country neighborhoods were found in 1949, composed of from 8 to 37 families, or an average of 19 families. (See Figure 6.)

In the South and in some border states, church and school are still centralizing influences in neighborhood life. In addition, there are often strong bonds of interfamily visiting and informal gatherings at country stores or amusement places. Contacts are determined to quite an extent by physical accessibility and by class and occupational lines. Paralleling the white neighborhood patterns are those of the Negroes. A recent research report indicates that the neighborhood continues as the most meaningful local group for rural Negro families. Their social, educational, religious, and organizational

[6] Merton D. Oyler, *Neighborhood Standing and Population Changes in Johnson and Robertson Counties, Kentucky,* Bulletin 523 (Lexington: Kentucky Agricultural Experiment Station, August, 1948); Paul J. Jehlik and Ray E. Wakeley, *Rural Organization in Process,* Research Bulletin 365 (Ames: Iowa Agricultural Experiment Station, September, 1949); Ronald B. Almack and Lawrence M. Hepple, *Rural Social Organization in Dent County,* Research Bulletin 458 (Columbia: University of Missouri, August, 1950); S. Earl Grigsby and Harold Hoffsommer, *Rural Social Organization of Frederick County, Maryland,* Bulletin A51 (College Park: Maryland Agricultural Experiment Station, March, 1949); Frank D. Alexander and Lowry Nelson, *Rural Social Organization in Goodhue County,* Bulletin 401 (Minneapolis: Minnesota Agricultural Experiment Station, February, 1949); Donald G. Hay, Douglas Ensminger, Stacy R. Miller, and Edmond J. Lebrun, *Rural Organizations in Three Maine Towns,* Maine Extension Bulletin 391 (Orono, June, 1949).

[7] Edmund deS. Brunner and J. H. Kolb, *Rural Social Trends* (New York: McGraw-Hill, 1933).

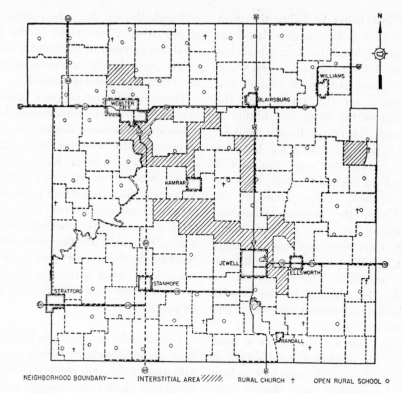

NEIGHBORHOOD BOUNDARY--- INTERSTITIAL AREA////// RURAL CHURCH + OPEN RURAL SCHOOL o

Figure 6. Neighborhoods of Hamilton County, Iowa, 1947.

Source: Paul J. Jehlik and Ray E. Wakeley, *Rural Organization in Process,* Research Bulletin 365 (Ames: Iowa State College Agricultural Experiment Station, September, 1949).

activities are still mainly at the neighborhood level. Because there are few strong outside ties with town or village centers, the neighborhood also functions after the general pattern of the white town-country communities.[8]

The kinds of contacts by which local primary groups are delineated are only the means for bringing about group integrity. Obviously similar activities have different meanings in various situations. Borrowing tools or exchanging work in areas of highly commercialized or large single-crop farms

[8] Charles P. Loomis, *Studies of Rural Social Organization in the U.S., Latin America and Germany* (East Lansing, Mich.: State College Book Store, 1946).

have little relevance for determining social relations or for indicating neighborhood solidarity. The important objective of our study is not a scheme of classification for groups but rather some understanding of processes in terms of personality reactions and group action.

The story of Rogers Hollow neighborhood. To give a clearer and more vivid picture of neighborhood activities and of how the various influences work together, a case is given from the Otsego County study. Rogers Hollow is an open-country neighborhood in the west central part of Unadilla Township. The activities of the neighborhood center around the schools, a Grange, and a Friends

Church, the last being probably the most important in giving the neighborhood its identity. The neighborhood fair, which has been held each fall for the past eleven years, includes the school districts of Idumes and Unadilla Center on the north and the Meeker district on the south, in addition to the two school districts in Rogers Hollow. The Grange is stronger than it has been for several years. About five years ago interest in it declined to such an extent that the meetings were held at the homes of the members. Under the present leadership, however, interest has again revived. There are now fifty-three members, and meetings held twice a month at the Grange hall have an average attendance of twenty-five to thirty people. In addition to the regular meetings, dances and parties are held in the hall about once a month.

The Friends Church is the center of most of the life of the neighborhood because of the able leadership of the resident pastor. The church has slightly more than a hundred members, an average attendance of about fifty people at church, and an enrollment of forty to forty-five people in the Sunday School. The membership is well organized, having two young people's societies, the Penn Helpers and the True Blues, each of which holds a regular monthly meeting; a Missionary Society which meets every month at the homes of the members, supplemented by an annual public meeting and entertainment in the community house; a Ladies' Aid Society, at present combined with the Home Bureau unit, which also meets regularly. There are also monthly church nights. The 4-H Club for boys and girls, directed by the minister, has about twenty-two members and usually meets once in four weeks at the community house. In 1929 Rogers Hollow united with Rockdale, Guilford, and East Guilford, all of which are in Chenango County, in the formation of a larger parish, a movement which

will undoubtedly strengthen all the churches of the area. Every child in the neighborhood is a member of the Sunday School, and nearly every family is represented in either the church or Sunday School.

There is a young people's branch of the Woman's Christian Temperance Union and a Loyal Temperance Legion for the school children. Both the Farm Bureau and Dairymen's League have local organizations which hold about two meetings annually. As a result there is a social party or meeting of some kind every week in the year, and often two or three meetings in the same week. This is by far the most active neighborhood in the county and is an excellent example of what a country church with a resident pastor can contribute to the life of its people.

The hamlet-centered neighborhood. A type of neighborhood which merits special attention is the one centered about a small residence cluster of usually not over 250 people and having one or more local institutions. This type of center is commonly known as a hamlet. In all of the areas studied, this type of neighborhood was found. Although population changes were not great in the interval between the studies, the relationships of these small centers to the surrounding country areas were different. In the earlier studies they had frequently been classed as centers for a village-country community, but in the interim they had slipped down into another classification; they could not possibly be considered the center for a town-country type of community group. They were usually found within the service areas of some larger urban center but to all practical purposes were similar to open-country neighborhoods centered about one or two local institutions such as school, church, or store.

Westville, a hamlet neighborhood. Located in Cherry Creek Valley, Westville is halfway between Middlefield and Milford. At the center there are nineteen houses, a garage, a general store, two sawmills, a Grange hall, a grade school, and two churches — one Baptist with a resident minister, and the other Methodist, served by the minister at Milford. Milford, about four miles south, has the high school and is the trading center except for drygoods and women's ready-to-wear, most of which are bought in Oneonta. The only organizations connected with the churches are the two Ladies' Aid Societies; neither church has a young people's organization. The average attendance at church services is about twenty people. The Home Bureau has a local organization with twelve members, but interest in the work is not very strong because most of the members belong to one of the Ladies' Aid Societies or to the Grange. The only organizations for the young people are the Boy Scout troop, with six members, organized by the minister, and the local 4-H Club with twenty-two members.

The Grange is probably the most important factor in the life of the neighborhood. It has 126 members and meets every two weeks in the Grange Hall, with an average attendance of approximately fifty. It recently organized a degree team which has been instrumental in maintaining the interest of the younger members. During the winter social parties are held after the regular meetings and each member is allowed to bring one guest. The Grange membership area is somewhat larger than the immediate neighborhood, extending as far as Middlefield on the north and Milford on the south. Westville is the most active of the hamlet centers of the county and is a good example of that type of neighborhood.

Why social institutions and combinations of contacts are important. As is so evident in the cases of Rogers Hollow and Westville,

established institutions are among the strongest forces holding neighborhood groups together. As suggested earlier, one of the ambitions of many pioneers was to establish a local school, church, or social organization. Once established, the institution has great power in keeping people together. It is tangible evidence of group achievement, a symbol of common objectives and accepted values. Naturally, then, neighborhood boundaries frequently determined the character of school districts, church parishes, social organization affiliations, or the trade areas of a country store, tavern, blacksmith shop, or garage. In later years these patterns fixed by the institution's influence tend to mold the character of the neighborhood itself.

In this New York county where Rogers Hollow and Westville are located, it is quite evident that churches and Granges are typical of the older institutions in both open-country and hamlet neighborhoods. Organizations such as Home Bureau, social club, and 4-H Club, are most characteristic of the recent years.

Evidence that activities are often found in combination is also significant. It means that neighborhood life is not unicentered but focuses about multiple interests, some common to all, some special and overlapping, and some even conflicting. The process of reconciling differences and reaching measures of consensus may indicate the turning point between persistence and obsolescence. In the restudy of neighborhoods in Dane County, Wisconsin, it was found that the most frequent combination was three functions or activities, occurring in about half the cases.[9]

Educational, economic, and social was the most frequent combination; educational, religious, and social, the second; educational,

[9] J. H. Kolb and D. G. Marshall, *Neighborhood-Community Relationships in Rural Society*, Research Bulletin 154 (Madison: Wisconsin Agricultural Experiment Station, November, 1944).

religious, and economic, the third. Greatest stability seemed to occur in the neighborhoods where these combinations were found. For example, the social function played an important part when in combination with the educational. It served as a kind of catalyzer, giving the combination its power and vitality. When it was ineffective, neighborhoods tended to lose their active characteristics. In other words, when a school was only a school, little in the way of group influence was evident. But when the school also became a social center, then neighborhood strength could be expected. Similarly, when nationality or kinship bonds combined with religious activities, a group solidarity was created. When all four functions were locally united, then a neighborhood could hardly fail to appear in the "active" category.

Thus combinations of activities in a neighborhood group suggest that there is a process of cumulation, a piling-up of the functions making for group cohesion. Such groups can be characterized not only by the lateral or geographic dimension and the primary or personal dimension but by a third dimension of group depth or intensity.

Persistence of neighborhoods and related factors. Evidence gathered in numerous studies indicates that the types of neighborhood groups exhibiting the greatest tendency toward persistence are the following: first, those integrated about one or more local institutions; second, those interrelated with formal or informal patterns of interfamily visiting, sociability, exchange of work, or other forms of social activity, each as was described in the last section of the chapter; third, the hamlet type of neighborhood by reason of larger and better organized systems of education and other service institutions. One can be quite safe in saying that those country neighborhoods which do persist are more the result of deliberate

group action and social adjustments, of stimulated common interests, and of organized activities than of depending largely upon proximity of residence, physical isolation, or pioneering traditions.

Some examples are cited for purposes of comparison with local situations. In Covington County, Mississippi, it is reported that the church remains the chief integrating force in the majority of neighborhoods, but that neighborliness itself and mutual coöperation within such small groups are still prized virtues.[10]

In an early study of Boone County, Missouri, forty out of fifty-nine neighborhoods persisted, while fifteen new ones were found. Besides local institutions, informal social contacts and family neighboring continued. In Otsego County, New York, the movement from neighborhood to town-country community forms of rural organization had proceeded further than in many other parts of the nation, but some open-country and hamlet-centered groups did persist.

In Dane County, Wisconsin, neighborhood organization had developed in early settlement days. Such factors as topography, nationality, and activities centered about school, church, store, and tavern, were strong when the first study was made in 1921. Neighborhoods reached their peak numerically by 1931; by 1941 there had been a leveling off. Of those remaining active, however, three fourths had continued throughout the twenty-year period. There was a decrease of about 20 per cent in the total number during the second ten years. This was about the same reduction reported for the Middle Western states as the result of a larger nation-wide study for a similar period of time.[11]

[10] H. Hoffsommer, "The Relation of the Rural Church to the Other Rural Organizations," *Social Forces*, XX, No. 2, Dec., 1941, pp. 224–232.

[11] J. H. Kolb and Douglas G. Marshall, *Neighbor-*

During the depression period, many neighborhoods throughout the country gave up, victims of general discouragement and despair. On the other hand, economic difficulties and social insecurities were the very factors which brought others into greater activity. Families were determined to satisfy their social necessities and to share their limited resources in their own home localities. Such families soon found themselves bound together by mutual aid and exchange of work. They joined in home-talent effort such as music, drama, recreation, and group discussion of local, state, and national problems.

When the war came, many neighborhood groups sprang into renewed activity all along the home front. Under local voluntary leadership and with the stimulus of agricultural extension services, they formed civilian defense units. They assumed responsibility for the rapid circulation of information, for stepping up production, and for better utilization of existing food, machinery, and labor.

Population mobility and transportation changes important. These factors operate both internally and externally in neighborhood affairs, as is well illustrated by the westward movement of the frontier. Wave-like movements brought New Englanders or "Yankees" from the East; then came the Germans and Scandinavians from Northern Europe, and later the Swiss, Polish, and some Italians. Each time a wave moved over an area, readjustments in group arrangements had to be made. Churches were among the first institutions to come and the last to go. In more recent years migration caused a lapse in neighborhood activities,

both in areas which lost population and in other areas where the influx was so great and so rapid that existing neighborhoods could not assimilate the newcomers. The former situation was particularly noticeable in regions crossed by the hundredth meridian and the latter in large sections of the Far West.

The introduction of hard-surfaced roads and expanded ownership of automobiles are other factors disturbing locality groups. Local efforts augmented by county, state, and federal aids have gone far toward bringing a good road to every farmer's gate. These highways have opened new group opportunities to both country and city people; traffic moves in both directions. Choices can be made more freely than formerly. Changes have taken place, to be sure, but as we have shown, many local neighborhoods and social institutions still have a surprising vitality. Whenever new ways of making contacts or making them more frequently are instituted, rearrangements in social and group affairs are necessary. Farm-to-market roads built during the depression proved a disturbing element to neighborhoods that had experienced a degree of isolation. Thus there was a heavy decline in neighborhoods in Pennsylvania where the state administration attempted to keep its promise of "getting the farmer out of the mud." Results were akin to those of earlier years when hard-surfaced roads upset the life of neighborhoods that lay in their paths.

Increased facility for moving about does not necessarily mean disintegration of all local or all primary groups, however. It may even strengthen them by permitting greater selection of members, larger variety of activities, and wider contacts with other similar groups. In a word, rural groups under modern conditions are more voluntary associations than formerly. An illustration of this fact was found in the Missouri county

hood-Community Relationships in Rural Society, Agr'l Exp. Station, Univ. of Wis. Research Bulletin 154 (Madison: University of Wisconsin Agricultural Experiment Station, 1944); Edmund deS. Brunner and J. H. Kolb, *Rural Social Trends.*

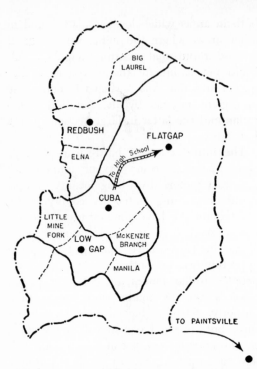

Figure 7. Neighborhoods and Communities in the Sample Area of Magisterial District 4, Johnson County, Kentucky.

Source: Merton D. Oyler, *Neighborhood Standing and Population Changes in Johnson and Robertson Counties, Kentucky,* Bulletin 523 (Lexington: Kentucky Agricultural Experiment Station, August, 1948).

as has been suggested, locality and special organization or interest group arrangements may develop together. Modern facilities for communication and travel may increase outside contacts, but they may increase the local contacts at an even greater rate.

Impersonal factors related to persistence of neighborhoods. The influence of impersonal factors can be illustrated by the cases of Johnson and Robertson Counties, Kentucky (Figure 7). Differences there among families in their neighborhood standing were found to be correlated with such characteristics as levels of living, occupation status, educational levels, housing conditions, and whether they had an automobile, telephone, and radio.

Another illustration can be cited from the Dane County restudy. Out of some twenty such factors tested, three were found to be especially significant for differentiating neighborhood activeness and inactiveness. These were length of residence, tenure status, and nationality similarity of the families within the neighborhoods. It must be emphasized at once that these three factors were correlated; that is, they act together as a sort of social complex. It became evident in the course of analysis that a greater or a lesser proportion of any given factor would tend to accelerate certain neighborhoods toward active or inactive status.

Toleration points were, therefore, worked out for each of the three factors. This is only another way of saying that active neighborhoods can "tolerate" a certain proportion of tenants, of families with short periods of residence, and families with a certain degree of similar nationality background. A change in any one factor may not be sufficient because it may be offset by a higher proportion of another. However, if all three tend toward their toleration points, then the neighborhoods in question are likely to show signs of inactiveness. By this

which was restudied. In a careful recording of all social contacts for the people of a village center and each of the surrounding eleven school districts, it was found that the annual per capita visiting contacts for the village were 170; for districts adjacent to the village, 108; and for districts not adjacent, 126. Furthermore, it was pointed out that the local visiting or neighboring contacts were 2.7 times as numerous as were the special-interest or organization contacts, both inside and outside the district, and that special-interest or special-activity contacts are more likely to be outside than inside the district in a ratio of three to two. Therefore, toleration test, neighborhoods could expect to remain active, provided their tenancy rate was no higher than 28 per cent, the proportion of their families less than twenty-five years in residence no larger than 42 per cent, and provided the families of similar nationality background represented not more than 64 per cent of all their families.

It seemed especially significant that neighborhoods in which at least 36 per cent of the families had mixed or indefinite nationality backgrounds were more likely to be active than those with 64 per cent or more of their families of similar and recognized backgrounds. This is contrary to some popular opinion, but it points to interesting possibilities for future neighborhood development and change. It should be added that if an active neighborhood had families of similar nationality background, it was more apt to remain active if those backgrounds were German rather than Scandinavian. Figure 8 gives the comparisons.

Full explanation of the differences shown in Figure 8 cannot be given because they are not known, but apparently during periods of settlement and in early stages of group formation similar nationality backgrounds may help to hold groups together. In later periods, when other cultural values and different group tenets are being taken over, too much similarity of nationality may be detrimental to keeping groups active. Preliminary findings in the studies of nationalities in the state indicate that different nationality groups react differently, both in the character of their adjustments and in the time required to make them.

Such findings suggest that a certain amount of social change within a neighborhood is compatible with activeness — persistence.

Cases illustrating influence of nationality. Three case stories show the influence of the nationality factor in terms of deliberate efforts made or not made in the process of accommodation. In a Norwegian settlement a son of one of the two or three remaining "Yankee" families, a Sutcliffe, was to marry the daughter of a local Norwegian family. The marriage was accomplished by and with the full consent of the local pastor. He was not particularly troubled by mixed marriages; consequently, he helped to add this young family to the neighborhood and to his church.

In a predominantly German settlement the Seston sisters, country school teachers of New England stock, became members of the

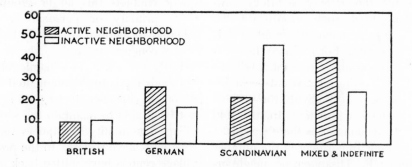

Figure 8. Comparison by Percentages for Nationality Backgrounds of Active and Inactive Neighborhoods.

Source: Kolb and Marshall, *op. cit.* (footnote 11).

local church. Their disclaimer that it was no longer a "German" church was quite right. The congregation, by majority vote, had previously withdrawn from one synod and joined another which a few years before had deliberately changed its name to the American Lutheran Synod. The German language was no longer used in the local church, except for a few special services or funerals.

In a third neighborhood situation the reverse process was in effect. One nationality group was in the majority and its elders held rigorously to traditional standards in education, religion, and recreation. Many of the sons married girls from other localities since they did not participate to any extent in local social activities. They had been away from the neighborhood at one time or another during the war or the depression. They did not establish their homes there because, as they put it, they did not feel their wives would "fit in very well." Here was a group without flexibility, defensive and resistant to change. But time seems to have a way with such a group. As indicated on the scale of "active" to "inactive" neighborhoods, it stood well down toward the inactive end.

Important changes and direction of trends. The general direction of changes in country neighborhoods may be briefly summarized thus: First, some groups do disappear or lose those elements found in definitely active groups. For example, in Dane County, Wisconsin, about one third fell out of the active class during a twenty-year interval. In the New York county the proportion was somewhat greater. In the 140 village-country communities there was a net decrease of about 16 per cent in the number of neighborhoods. Disappearing neighborhoods may retain their form; they may even appear active. But they tend to take the direction of decadence.

Second, new groups appear or old ones become active again. They assume characteristics which by all the refinements of analysis make them comparable to the older and the more readily recognized groups. These newer groups, however, are more often the result of deliberate organization, promotion, or voluntary association. They are centered generally about certain interests such as social activity, drama, or club programs. They are less dependent upon tradition, nationality, locality, or religious purpose than the older ones.

Third, there is a tendency for neighborhoods to retain or to assume only certain kinds of functions. They are less self-sufficing than some were at the time of the earlier studies, whose traditions carried back to settlement days, and whose strong nationality or kinship bonds were often sheltered from outside influences by the topography of the country. Open-country neighborhoods retain their schools and churches, but also take on certain social activities and give up certain economic services. Specialization has set in, although this trend has been somewhat checked in more recent years.

Fourth, neighborhoods in the immediate vicinity of small towns or villages tend to give way first. Their functions are slowly assumed by the larger town-country community unit. Because of freer and more frequent contacts this larger group becomes more primary or personal in character, whereas formerly it was likely to be largely of a secondary order.

Fifth, the number of hamlet-class neighborhoods tends to be augmented by the addition of village-centered groups that have not been able to maintain the standing of a village community. Distances measured in time units have shrunk. In the process some village centers have settled back to a hamlet status. As was pointed out earlier, they are not essentially different from the more nearly open-country groups centered about two or more local institutions. This trend was very evident in the case of the New York county, and in the 140 town-country communities distributed over the nation.

Sixth, neighborhoods tend to form, or older ones to readjust, in the suburban fringes of city centers. In the case of Madison, Wisconsin, many of the fringe families' occupational and special service contacts are urban-centered. However, many of their personal, primary contacts such as visiting, exchange of work, and informal group associations are oriented within the locality. Church affiliations are split three ways: in the city, in the village of Sun Prairie (2260 population), and in an adjoining active country neighborhood, Pump-

kin Hollow. The resulting neighborhoods are similar to those found in more strictly open-country areas. The situation is illustrated in Figure 9. Small incorporated villages or city subdivisions are likely to be interspersed between neighborhoods in this urban fringe. Under the new census definition, some neighborhoods in urban fringe areas or even small incorporated centers, are counted as urban population. However, despite change of category, such groups will continue to link together people of urban and of country backgrounds.

Neighborhoods may resist change. When primary groups as neighborhoods become

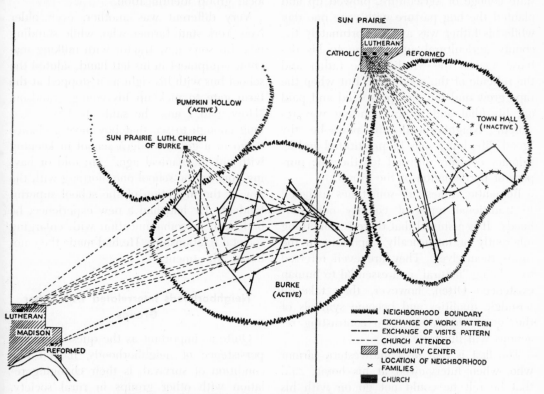

Figure 9. **Neighborhood in an Urban Fringe Area.**

Source: J. H. Kolb and Douglas G. Marshall, *Neighborhood-Community Relationships in Rural Society*, Research Bulletin 154 (Madison: University of Wisconsin Agricultural Experiment Station, November, 1944).

rigid and resist change, they may contribute to frustration of personalities. Little objective evidence can be produced on the point, since few studies have given attention to it. What evidence there is can be found associated with groups becoming inactive through failure of young men to return with their wives to establish homes, as suggested in the case story. Other examples have been encountered in the course of field work in neighborhood studies, when sons of farmers have actually run away from home rather than stay and be dominated by traditional standards of behavior.

There is the case of the daring youth who, after attending a short winter course at the state college of agriculture, plowed up and planted the hog pasture with rape one day while his father was away. Fortunately the county agricultural agent came to his defense against the wrath of the father and the ridicule of the neighbors. But when the rape grew and the pigs prospered and paid off, his filial and group standing was restored. Neighborhood life may be the "good" life, but it may be prostituted and its primary controls misused for the sole purpose of perpetuation of the group.

Romantic values are sometimes assigned to traditional types of country neighborhoods. It is assumed that there is something inherently or intrinsically important in the forms themselves. They are even referred to as being "natural" and essential to human existence. Often, however, they take on nostalgic qualities and become symbols of the "good old days." Two contrasting reactions will illustrate.[12]

The first is that of a midwestern farmer who, when interviewed at his home, said that he felt he could not go on with his farming if he did not see the country school-

house across the road each morning as he went to the barn to milk. The school had been closed for nearly two years. The flag no longer waved from its short pole. The question of sale and removal of the building had come before the recent school meeting but had been voted down by a narrow margin. This same farmer told of seeing the school bus pass his house each morning soon after he finished his breakfast. He said he regarded the bus as an intrusion from the outside, the symbol of some foreign influence from the county seat or the state capitol, or somewhere, he didn't just know. But he didn't like it, that he did know. He could not make the emotional transition from the local group identification.

Very different was another, even older New York state farmer who, while standing near his son's new tractor with milking machine equipment in his left hand, saluted the school bus with his right as it stopped at the farm gate to pick up his young grandson. "How glad I am," he said, "to have lived long enough to see that boy have a chance to go to a good, modern school in keeping with our mechanical age." He told of having gone to the school one morning with the boy at the invitation of the school superintendent. He had had a new experience; he had been in communication with enlarging societal relationships. He had made the emotional adjustment.

Neighborhoods Interrelated with Other Groups

Quite as important as the question of the persistence of neighborhoods, indeed one condition of survival, is their changing relation with other groups in rural society. No doubt physical and social isolation will continue to play their parts in holding some country neighborhoods together; but as population mobility continues, and as means for communication and transportation improve,

[12] J. H. Kolb and LeRoy J. Day, *Interdependence in Town and Country Relations in Rural Society*, Research Bulletin 172 (Madison: Wisconsin Agricultural Experiment Station, 1950).

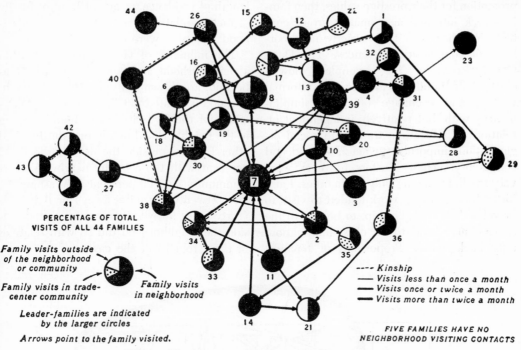

Figure 10. Visiting Among Families of White
Plains Neighborhood, Charles County, Maryland.

Source: L. S. Dodson and Jane Woolley, *Community Organization in Charles County, Maryland*, Bulletin A21 (College Park: University of Maryland Agricultural Experiment Station, January, 1932).

other factors will become more important. First to be examined are the interrelations of neighborhoods with various localized patterns of family visiting, exchange of work, and informal associations, and second the larger community consisting of town or village and country relations. The rural community itself becomes the subject for a later chapter.

Interfamily visiting and exchange-of-work patterns. Different social contacts have different meanings in different situations and, as explained earlier, exchange of work, tools, machinery, and even labor may have little significance for determining primary relations in the large wheat or livestock

farming areas. In dairy and small truck farming areas it is quite different. Evidence seems to be accumulating that informal interfamily contacts of visiting, exchanging work, and mutual aid may perform important functions of catalyzing the more formal contacts within a neighborhood in order to give it cohesion. They may operate without reference to established neighborhoods, or they may play a part in interrelating neighborhoods and communities.

A hypothesis may be suggested that (1) as country neighborhoods tend to become larger or hamlet-centered, (2) as they become more institutionalized in terms of church, school, or social organization, and (3) as they persist by deliberate effort and promotion for their prestige values, then families seek informal and smaller group contacts in other than their strictly neighborhood or community references. The Dane County restudy, for example, showed clusters of families carrying on informal visiting and exchange of work simultaneously with, but relatively independent of, relations of education, trade, and social organizations important to neighborhood and community. These clusters however were very small, averaging only six families. Families who exchanged work tended to visit, to be related through kinship, to belong to the same church, and to be of similar nationality background. Proportions of tenancy,

length of residence, or age of head of family — factors related to activeness in neighborhood groups — were of little significance.

The influence of visiting patterns within a neighborhood and community as well as beyond, are shown in Figure 10. This neighborhood is located in Charles County, Maryland. Of the forty-five white families living in the neighborhood nearly one third visited other families outside the neighborhood, 12 per cent with those in the nearby Waldorf community, and 20 per cent in Washington, D.C. (twenty-five miles away) or Baltimore (forty miles away). Those who visited outside the neighborhood did so with relatives in three fourths of the cases.

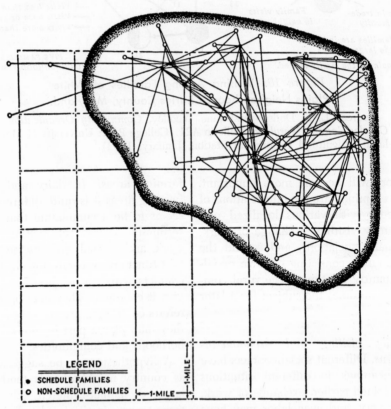

LEGEND

● SCHEDULE FAMILIES
○ NON-SCHEDULE FAMILIES

1-MILE

Figure 11. Most Garden Valley Families
Exchanged Work with Several Neighbors.

Source: Hill, Slocum, and Hill, *Man-Land Adjustment,* Research Bulletin
134 (Madison: University of Wisconsin, February, 1939).

Exchanging work played an important part within the Garden Valley neighborhood in northern Wisconsin, (Figure 11) where twenty-one families lived. At the same time, informal visiting ties related the majority of these families to a community focused in Alma Center, a village located about two miles from the southern border of the neighborhood.

A much more dramatic story of the multirole character which informal family contacts may play is shown by the visiting pattern of fifty-six families in the Komensky neighborhood. This is a Bohemian settlement located in the same general area of Wisconsin as Garden Valley. Families in this neighborhood were so well bound together by ties of kinship, visiting, exchange

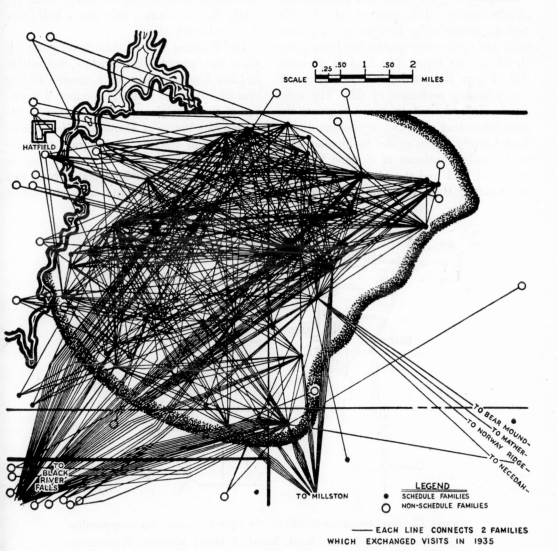

Figure 12. Komensky Neighborhood Families Visited Many Neighbors.

Source: Hill, Slocum, and Hill, *op. cit.*

of work, and mutual aid, that they weathered the depression far better than the majority of surrounding families. Nevertheless, as Figure 12 shows well, they were also related by strong visiting ties to families in Black River Falls, the town-country community center and county seat about eight miles down the river.

Building neighborhoods and communities simultaneously. The process of simultaneously interrelating families in neighborhood and community groups has been going on for a long time. The case of Pleasant Hill (Figure 13), in the state of Oregon, is a step-by-step recitation of this. The most clearly defined, and in many respects the most interesting open-country community in Lane County, has its center on Pleasant Hill, twelve miles southeast of Eugene between the Coast Fork and the Middle Fork of the Willamette. Here the five neighborhoods

of Evendale, Coastfork, Enterprise, Trent, and Pleasant Hill join in supporting the oldest open-country high school in Oregon.

There is no feeling of diversity of interests between the people at the center and those on the outskirts of the high-school district; the church, the hall, the cemetery, and the high school border the road at dignified distances which make it clear that here is no thought of an organized town. Until recently the store was a mile and a half from the blacksmith shop.

The Pleasant Hill neighborhood grew up about the farm of Elijah Bristow, first settler in Lane County. Bristow, a veteran of the War of 1812, was a sturdy pioneer, a member of the Disciples of Christ, father of fifteen, and a native of Kentucky. He went to California in 1845 as an emigrant from Illinois. In 1846, he went to Oregon and in 1848 took a donation land claim, built the first house in Lane County, and later asked

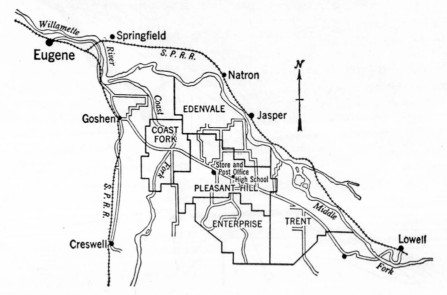

Figure 13. Five Neighborhoods in the One Pleasant Hill Community.

Source: Country Church Work Board of Home Missions, Presbyterian Church in the United States, *A Rural Survey of Lane County, Oregon,* 1916. Report of the State Planning Board, *A Study of Natural Communities in Three Oregon Counties* (Portland, May, 1937).

the Legislature for permission to name his farm Pleasant Hill.

Bristow and his family possessed this fertile land with a thoroughness which must be considered the most significant factor in establishing the unity of the Pleasant Hill community. They initiated and for many years controlled the religious and educational activities of the community. For more than fifty years, the center of the Pleasant Hill community remained where Bristow made the first settlement. The stones of the chimney of his house are now preserved in a memorial watering trough in front of the post office, only a few hundred yards from the site of the original building. In the spring of 1910, when the site of the Union High School was definitely fixed, the real center of the district may be said to have moved somewhat.

The high school was established in 1907. When the County Superintendent and some members of the faculty of the University of Oregon proposed to organize the first open-country high school in Oregon, the five districts comprising the neighborhoods of Evendale, Trent, Coastfork, Enterprise, and Pleasant Hill voted without any serious opposition to make the experiment.

Union High School Number One is the strongest force now operating to hold the Pleasant Hill community together. It was established just in time; otherwise, the community would even now be breaking up, following a tendency toward disintegration that becomes more noticeable as the farms fill up with people who knew not Elijah and who owe no allegiance to the Christian Church. From the first the high school has offered four years of work. For six years it has graduated at least seven students annually, and holds within its student body practically the entire high-school population of the district, some forty young men and women.

In a middle western state where dairying interests are dominant and where some country neighborhoods continue strong, a school reorganization plan is evolving which attempts to build both neighborhood and community relations. The argument runs that not every country center can hope to have a complete educational system, including both elementary and secondary schools. If it is a strong country neighborhood center, it may have an elementary school of six grades, with two or three teachers. For high school facilities, both junior and senior, it would need to be part of a larger group unit. Or, if the center is a small village with a well integrated country constituency, it may have a six-grade elementary school and a three-grade junior high school. But again, it would be part of a larger community group for its three-grade senior high school. Thus in a town-country community relationship, one administrative system may include a network of interrelated patterns such as one or more country neighborhoods, one or more small village-country groups, and the one larger town-country community.

A practical and ingenious device for interrelating neighborhood and community in a school reorganization plan following the principle suggested above should be cited. The first thing the supervising principal did after a school reorganization was effected was to have telephones installed in the school buildings in the ten active country and hamlet neighborhoods which were to retain their elementary schools. The ten schools became branches in the integrated system. This plan of intercommunication became the symbol for the new intergroup relations of country neighborhoods with the town-country community. The plan of organization is shown on the accompanying map of the reorganized school district, Winneconne, Wisconsin.

The implied theory in these illustrations is that each group and its own institutions, just as each person and his own contacts,

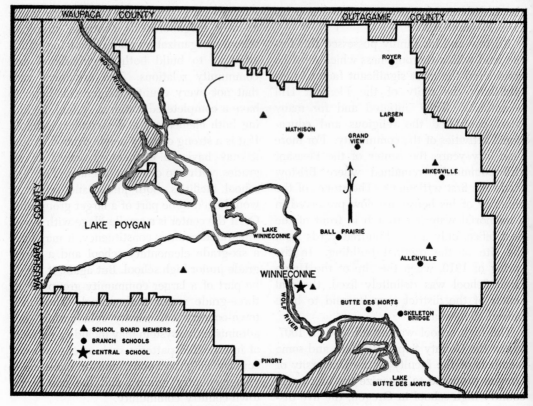

Figure 14. Town-Country Community School District with
Ten Neighborhood Branch Schools, Winneconne, Wisconsin.

gain their importance and receive their meaning not through reference to themselves alone, but also from their relations with others. People do not "belong" to separate groups, one at a time, but to a number of interrelated groups all at the same time. Wholesome personalities do not develop within the confines of single communities or become well integrated by limited contacts of even primary groups.[13] Persons play different roles in various groups. This idea was expressed many years ago in Miss Follett's call for group organization as a

basis for new methods in politics. She said, "The reason we want organization is not to keep people within their neighborhoods, but to get them out.[14] It is not that she would have people abandon their neighborhoods, but rather by means of them to relate themselves to the larger society of which they and other such groups are a part.

In conclusion, some country neighborhoods come into active being, some become inactive and disappear, and many live on. Changes and readjustments are characteristic of those that do continue. The evidence is clear that neighborhoods can be revived or new ones formed. When they are

[13] This point of view is not shared fully by some other authors, for example: Lloyd A. and Elaine F. Cook, *A Sociological Approach to Education* (New York: McGraw-Hill, 1950), p. 50; and William F. Ogburn and Meyer F. Nimkoff, *Sociology* (2nd ed.; Boston: Houghton Mifflin, 1950), pp. 113 and 300.

[14] M. P. Follett, "The New State," *Group Organization the Solution of Popular Government* (New York: Longmans, Green, 1918), p. 249.

needed, they tend to appear. Primary personal contacts can be made, and families can meet, discuss problems, and determine what to do. Tenants can be helped into ownership of their farms. New families or sons and their wives can be encouraged to move to the neighborhood. Those of like nationality backgrounds can be given opportunities for meeting more freely with those of other backgrounds. Country neighborhoods can be interrelated with larger communities.

Young people, especially, can be introduced to the ideals and attitudes of primary groups and to the cultural values of the society of which the group is a part. This can be done directly by personal association or by means of the expressive arts — drama, music, folk dancing, literature — ". . . man consciously . . . hands over to others, feelings he has lived through, and other people are infected and also experience them." [15] This is important. An emotional continuity "from one generation to the next is one of the outstanding features of man's life in society." [16] It gives society a certain "toughness" so that it does not break apart readily and is not swayed by every passing opinion.

The purpose of neighborhood integrity is not to keep people hemmed in or protected from the rest of society. Rural groups are not hedged about by mutually exclusive boundaries; they are intermeshed with other groups. Moreover, the only group culture which can have vitality is one which is poured out — given away.

Furthermore, primary contacts are not confined to country neighborhoods. "In our kind of society, being little bound by place, people easily form clubs and fraternal societies based on congeniality which gives rise to real intimacy." [17] Such relations are readily formed in school, at work, or at play. They are found in "interest groups" which abound in rural society and likewise within urban areas.[18]

Personal contacts of farm families with village families are also multiplying so that the web of group relationships in rural society enmeshes not only country families and neighborhoods in its design, but also villages and communities and even cities.

[15] Leo Nikolaevich Tolstoy, *What is Art?* (Rev. Ed.; New York: Oxford University Press, 1942), p. 385.

[16] Kimball Young, *An Introductory Sociology* (Rev. Ed.; New York: American Book Co., 1939).

[17] Charles H. Cooley, *Social Organization* (New York: Scribner, 1925).

[18] Neighborhood development within urban areas is an interesting phase of recent city planning and of urban research. See for example, Eschref Shevsky and Molly Lewin, *Your Neighborhood, a Social Profile of Los Angeles* (Los Angeles: Haynes Foundation, 1950); Theodore Caplow and Robert Forman, "Neighborhood Interaction in a Homogeneous Community," a report of studies in Minneapolis-St. Paul metropolitan district and in University Village, a student housing project of the University of Minnesota, *American Sociological Review*, XV, No. 3, June, 1950; Richard Dewey, "The Neighborhood, Urban Ecology and City Planners," *American Sociological Review*, XV, No. 4, August, 1950.

TOPICS FOR DISCUSSION

1. Draw an outline map of a rural or an urban situation with which you are personally acquainted, locating the following:
   a. The home with which you are acquainted.
   b. The boundaries of a recognized neighborhood.
   c. The location of the important social and economic institutions with which this home has regular contacts.

2. List in order of their importance the factors which have created the neighborhood you have outlined above, or if there is no such recognized grouping, the factors which have prevented such an arrangement.

3. Characterize and give reasons for changes which are taking place in primary or per-

sonal groupings in present-day society, first rural and second urban.

4. What forces are tending to integrate, and what to disintegrate, country neighborhoods?
5. Why do neighborhoods with local social institutions such as church, school, or club tend to persist longer than those without institutions?
6. What functions do you think country neighborhoods may well render in the future?

REFERENCE READINGS

Cooley, C. H., *Social Organization.* New York: Scribner's, 1912. See early chapters for an excellent statement and definition of primary social groups.

Hoffsommer, Harold, and Herbert Pryor, *Neighborhoods and Communities in Covington County, Mississippi.* Washington, D.C.: United States Department of Agriculture, July, 1941.

Kolb, J. H., *Trends of Country Neighborhoods,* Research Bulletin 120. Madison: University of Wisconsin, Agricultural Experiment Station, 1933. A restudy of rural primary groups.

Mayo, Selz C. and Robert McD. Bobbitt, *Rural Organization: A Restudy of Locality Groups in Wake County, North Carolina,* Technical Bulletin 95. Raleigh: North Carolina Agricultural Experiment Station, September, 1951.

McMurray, J. Donald, Fred R. Keeler, and Donald F. Rehl, *Rural Neighborhoods and Communities of Ross County, Ohio.* Agricultural Extension Service, Ohio State University, and United States Department of Agriculture, coöperating, August, 1941.

Nichols, Ralph R., and John S. Page, *Community and Neighborhood Areas Lincoln County, Oklahoma.* Washington, D.C.: United States Department of Agriculture in coöperation with Oklahoma Joint Land-Grant College, B.A.E. Committee, May, 1941.

Nichols, Ralph R., *Locating Neighborhoods and Communities in Red River Parish, Louisiana.* Washington, D.C.: United States Department of Agriculture in coöperation with Louisiana State Extension Service, April, 1941.

Winchester, Frank, *Rural Neighborhoods and Communities in Thirteen Kentucky Counties, 1941: Size, Population, and Social Structure,* Bulletin 450. Kentucky Agricultural Station, June, 1943.

Reports of the five original studies of country neighborhoods:

Baumgartel, Walter H., *A Social Study of Ravalli County, Montana,* Bulletin 160, University of Montana Agricultural Experiment Station, 1923.

Kolb, J. H., *Rural Primary Groups,* Research Bulletin 51. Madison: University of Wisconsin Agricultural Experiment Station, 1921.

Morgan and Howells, *Rural Population Groups,* Research Bulletin 74. Columbia: University of Missouri Agricultural Experiment Station, 1925.

Sanderson and Thompson, *Social Areas of Otsego County,* Research Bulletin 422. Ithaca: Cornell University Agricultural Experiment Station, 1923.

Taylor and Zimmerman, *Rural Organization,* Bulletin 245. North Carolina Agricultural Experiment Station, 1922.

FILM

Experimental Studies in Social Climate of Groups. S, 30. The Lewin study. Iowa University.

Top: Typical Town-Country Community, France. *Bottom left*: Small Town, U.S.A. *Bottom right*: Multilane Expressway Uniting Rural and Urban Communities (Photo by Squire Haskins, Dallas)

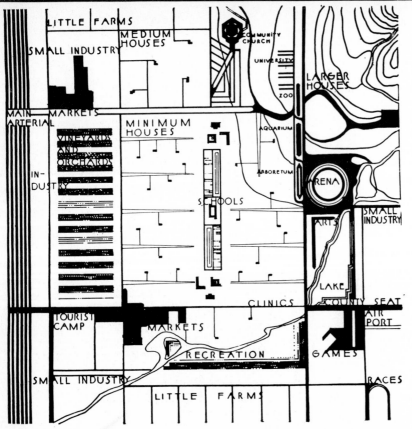

FRANK LLOYD WRIGHT'S DE-SIGN FOR "BROADACRES" *Top*: Section of Model, with View of Civic Center; Neighborhood Park and Acreage Farms at Right. *Bottom*: General Plan, Four Sections, Each One-fourth Section One Mile Square. (Courtesy, Frank Lloyd Wright, Taliesin, Spring Green, Wisconsin)

RURAL HOUSING *Top*: Tenant Farmer About to Move to New Home; Old Cabin in Foreground, New in Background (U.S. Dept. of Agriculture). *Bottom left*: Acadian Cabin, Louisiana (Standard Oil Co., N.J.)

RURAL HOUSING *Top*: Southern Plantation Home, Louisiana (Standard Oil Co., N.J.). *Bottom*: Northern Farm Home (Extension Service, U.S. Dept. of Agriculture, photo by Ed Hunton)

13 Agricultural Villages and Small Towns

BETWEEN THE COUNTRY AND THE CITY are villages and small towns, sharing the nature of both, but having distinguished characteristics of their own. Rural society, as the previous population analysis has shown, is divided into two main parts, farm and non-farm. The non-farm represents an increasing element, now even larger than the farm, but one frequently neglected in discussion of rural society. About two thirds of the rural non-farm population is made up of people living in nearly 80,000 villages and hamlets. It also includes people on acreages not within the census definition of "farm," and others living in rural territory but working in towns or cities. Included in our discussion are the more than 3,000 towns and their almost 15,000,000 people. Thus, in this chapter we are concerned with nearly one quarter of the nation's population.

Strictly speaking, a village is a population center ranging in size from 250 to 2500 people. A hamlet is a smaller center. Towns are here defined as centers of 2500 to 10,000 population, and are therefore included in the urban category of the census. Hamlets, villages, and towns may or may not be legally incorporated as municipalities. Unless they are incorporated or have more than 1000 population, they are not enumerated separately in the 1950 census. Furthermore, hamlets and villages located within areas of defined urban influence, such as the 168 standard metropolitan districts, are included in the urban rather than the rural non-farm census category.

"Can the village and small town come back?" is a question often raised in popular discussions of urban developments. The facts indicate that they have never been away. They continue to play an important part in rural society. They not only maintain but increase their proportionate share of the total population, even with a shrinking farm proportion. Apparently they do have a chance in a modern society of improved highways and automobiles, radios, television, and metropolitan newspapers, of chain stores and national advertising. Before considering the extent to which villages and towns are holding their own and what part they are playing in rural life and agriculture, it is important to examine their origins and backgrounds.

Historically Considered, Other Country Comparisons

Agricultural villages more often than not have been the form of settlement and the residence centers for rural people, including farmers, in Europe, Asia, and much of Africa and South America. They were the primary locality groups in those societies, as the previous chapter on country neighborhoods has suggested. In New England and in limited regions of the West, this plan of settlement was followed by the North American pioneers. In most other parts of the country, however, the village or small town had other origins. Settlement was first made on individual farms in neighborhood groups; village or town centers came later as an adjunct to the agricultural enterprise, performing

181

services of communication, transportation, trade, and industry. Or, as was often the case in midwestern and western settlements, the centers were deliberately established and made the spearheads of railway develop-

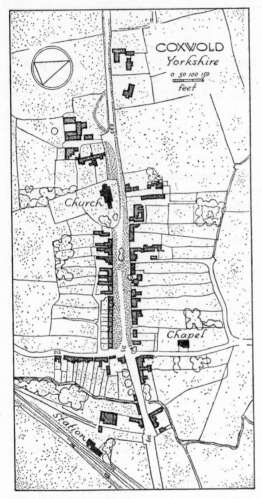

Figure 15. Coxwold, Yorkshire (200).

At the junction of five roads. The main street, climbing up from a small stream with wide sloping green verges, is dominated by the church at the top of the rise. Views in and out are all closed. A few narrow fenced front gardens, but houses mostly on the street line. Stone; roofs of stone-slabs and pantiles. Source: Thomas Sharp, *The Anatomy of the Village* (Harmondsworth, Middlesex, England: Penguin Books, 1946).

ments into new territory in order to stimulate further settlement and provide new business. It is reported that one railroad company, whose tracks traversed a particularly fertile agricultural state, actually "planted" towns at five-mile intervals along its right of way to develop its own volume of business. The fact that farms came first and villages and towns were settled later in this country distinguishes American rural society from that of much of the rest of the world.

Village and town centers, however started, soon became centers of business more than social groups or residence centers for farm families. Business enterprises as small-scale manufacturing, wholesaling, fishing, or mining — in addition to retailing, marketing, and transporting — began to accumulate. Social distinctions were made between town and country people. The nucleated agricultural village failed to transplant to American soil.

In this failure Professor N. S. B. Gras believes that America suffered a great social loss.[1] In Europe as elsewhere, he emphasizes, close proximity has meant the development of such daily social contacts as group singing or dancing and various other forms of social activity. "Such things," he says, "lead to rural amenities and to rural art of which America has had all too little." In similar manner, he suggests that coöperation in social affairs prepares the way for coöperation in the business phases of agriculture, which in this country has grown slowly and with many setbacks. This is due mainly to the fact that farms in America were too large to be compressed into a village form of organization. It is of interest, however, to find that in periods of emergency when farm families have pushed too far out toward the margins, and must be relocated, when city workers, without employment, are encouraged to move to the country, or new settle-

[1] *A History of Agriculture* (New York: Crofts, 1925), chapter II.

ment is contemplated, a centralized plan is considered by those who make policies. For example, in the Columbia River settlement project a plan of farm layout was proposed which gave small frontages on the highway and greater depths of fields, so that families might live relatively near together. Here was a set-up reminiscent of the French line village or the English roadside village.

In the English tradition. The English villages have long occupied a central place in the affections and the traditions of both countrymen and townsmen. While they vary considerably, two principal types can be identified: the roadside and the squared.[2] The roadside village is much more common and consists of a string of houses, shops, inns, and other buildings standing side by side along a highway. It is generally located at a junction of roads as the diagram of Coxwold in Yorkshire shows so well (Figure 15). The buildings are close to the sidewalk and street and give the villages their distinctive character.

The squared type of village is usually quite irregular in shape and may vary from a roughly square to a triangular form. At its center or in the "square" may be a point of interest or accent such as a small market, a central green, a telephone kiosk, or a village hall. This is the form generally followed in what are currently termed Planned Villages, as shown in Figure 16. Informality in form and individuality in buildings is attempted so far as possible, though some believe that these characteristics cannot be accomplished arbitrarily. In general, however, these planned villages are within the main stream of the English village tradition.

The Oriental Village. The Japanese village of Karako, in the central part of the Kanto Plain about fifty miles from Tokyo,

shows quite a different plan. The village was settled about 300 years ago by families who were related in an extended or great family system. In 1948 there were 939 households, of which 749 were farm households. The social structure of the village takes its form from this early family system. The dwellings are in compact locality groupings which center around shrines as well as economic and social arrangements. Two fifths of the area is in forest, which is practically all privately owned. Figure 17 shows the location of the paddy fields along the river, which must be controlled by levees extending through the village.

Japanese villages, more than 10,000 of them, are pervasive throughout the entire land area of the country. They are highly institutionalized and form the local units of a strongly centralized governmental organization. Each village is composed of local units known as *buraku*, most of which were once separate villages. The present system has been in effect about sixty years and came about in response to efforts of the central government to have fewer and more effective units of local administration.[3]

The New England pattern. Following the English tradition, New England villages and towns were laid out as social and residence centers quite in contrast with what later came to be known as the "Western business" type. They were frequently built about a piece of ground known as the "common," with prominent blocks given over to public buildings, schools, and churches. A simple plan illustrating the triangular type with a town common is seen in Figure 18. Other types, according to F. A. Waugh, are the wide-street type, as represented by Northfield, and the quadrangular type as represented by Amherst. Definite planning was done in advance and an effort was made to

[2] Thomas Sharp, *The Anatomy of the Village* (Harmondsworth, Middlesex, England: Penguin Books, 1946).

[3] Arthur Raper, "Recent Changes in Japanese Village Life," *Rural Sociology*, XVI, No. 1 (March, 1951).

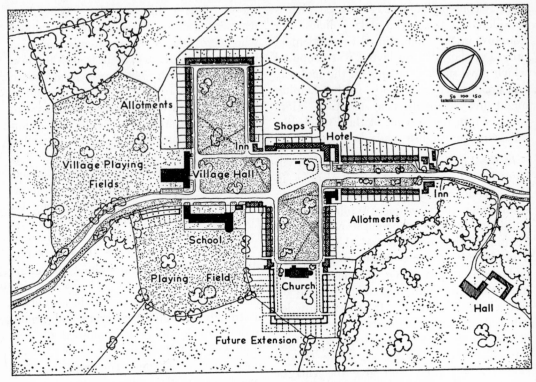

Figure 16. A Plan for a New Village.

Note the interplay of shapes, and the considered siting of the main buildings. Source: Thomas Sharp, *The Anatomy of the Village* (Harmondsworth, Middlesex, England: Penguin Books, 1946).

have the village a pleasant and attractive place to live in.

Many villages and town centers in this region are still not legally incorporated or set apart socially from the surrounding country territory. Center and country were united in this New England town form of democratic government. Towns or townships, in the geographic sense, are not regular or checkerboard in plan as in many parts of the Middle West, but follow natural boundaries such as divides and drainage basins. Frequently there is more than one center in the town, perhaps a larger market center and several smaller places a few miles distant, with separated dwellings in ribbon-like fashion along the joining highway. Thus there

might be a Troy Center, an East Troy, and an Old Troy.

During the earlier years before scattered settlement on separated farms, all families lived in the center. Farm families would have their barns and other buildings near their houses, with garden plots nearby. Farther away would be the cultivated fields, and still beyond were the pastures, sometimes owned and used in common, and the wood lots. This pattern still prevails in some New England villages.

The Mormons were the only early settlers who carried the pattern west — over the Allegheny Mountains and the Great Plains to Utah. The idea was fortified with the religious concept of the "City of Zion" and

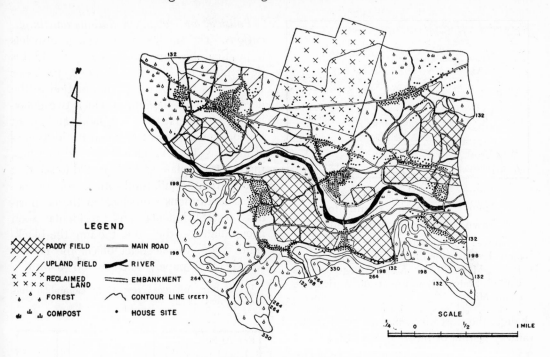

LEGEND

⧓ PADDY FIELD	═══ MAIN ROAD
⫽ UPLAND FIELD	⌇ RIVER
× × × × RECLAIMED LAND	═══ EMBANKMENT
⸋ FOREST	⌒ CONTOUR LINE (FEET)
⸋ COMPOST	• HOUSE SITE

SCALE

Figure 17. Karako-Mura, Saitama Prefecture.

Source: Arthur F. Raper, *The Japanese Village in Transition*, Report No. 136 (Tokyo, Japan: General Headquarters, Supreme Commander for the Allied Powers, November, 1950).

modified to conform to a regular terrain. The plan called for a rectangle one mile square, divided into blocks of ten acres; these were cut into dwelling lots of one-half acre, permitting twenty houses to the block. Streets were eight rods wide, intersected at right angles, and extended north and south.[4]

The Western business style. Small manufacturing, retailing, marketing, transportation, and communication were among the important early business enterprises about which villages and towns were built in the Middle West and the West, in order to service extensive agriculture. Their layout was severe and utilitarian in character. Streets

[4] Lowry Nelson, *The Mormon Village, A Study of Social Origins* (Provo, Utah: Brigham Young University Studies No. 3, 1930).

were square cornered, or strung along a railroad track or a river. More recently much has been done to beautify and improve this rectangular "business" arrangement by setting aside blocks for parks and playgrounds, by constructing public utilities, and by encouraging private plantings and landscaping (Figure 19).

As suggested elsewhere, the functions determined in large measure the location of the centers. It may have been a fork in a river where cargoes had to be divided; a place where transfers from water to land or land to water had to be made. It might have been a division point where carload lots were broken up for smaller shipments or where train crews were changed and repairs made in the roundhouses. Highways and railways radiated from these centers. Communication agencies were there — the telephone ex-

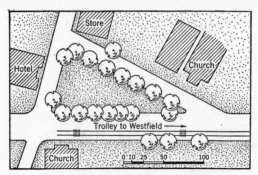

Figure 18. Triangle Type of Town Common, Huntington Town Common, Massachusetts.

Source: F. A. Waugh, *The Town Common*, Extension Bulletin 7 (Amherst, June, 1916), Massachusetts State College and the United States Department of Agriculture coöperating.

change, the post office and its rural route, a railway station or bus depot, and the weekly newspaper. The convergence of this network of transportation and communication at these centers will be seen to be significant when we examine town and country relations in the next chapter. Services performed at the centers bear a recognizable relationship to their size and the character of their populations as well as to the distances between centers.

In the Middle Colonies there were modified forms of the village system and the business type. In Virginia and states further south, a kind of manorial plan developed around the large plantation and the separate Negro village or "quarters."[5] In the Southwest the Spanish built a type of village center around a plaza, which corresponded to the New England village "common." For the inland towns this was rectangular and at the center of the pueblo; elsewhere it might face a waterfront.[6]

[5] L. C. Gray, *History of Agriculture in the Southern States to 1860* (Washington, D.C.: Carnegie Institution of Washington, 1933).

[6] Frank W. Blackmar, *Spanish Institutions of the Southwest* (Baltimore: John Hopkins University Press, 1891).

Political and social separations and implications. The small town or village also has a political background and origin. In his description of *A Hoosier Village*, Professor N. L. Sims tells of a typical situation in the early history of Indiana in which two enterprising pioneers took up land and went about organizing a county seat for local government.[7] They divided their land into lots, made a town plan, and proceeded to see that a courthouse, jail, and other county political institutions were located there. Business establishments and residents soon accumulated — the store, the inn, the blacksmith shop, the abstract office, the county weekly newspaper, and so on — until a

[7] *A Hoosier Village* (New York: Columbia University Press, 1912).

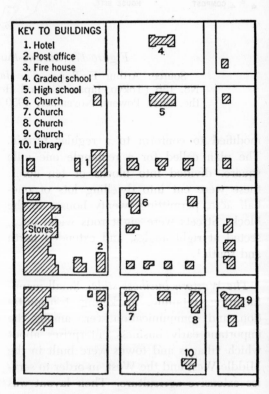

KEY TO BUILDINGS
1. Hotel
2. Post office
3. Fire house
4. Graded school
5. High school
6. Church
7. Church
8. Church
9. Church
10. Library

Figure 19. The "Business" Type of Village, with Straight Lines and Square Corners.

Source: H. Paul Douglass, *The Little Town* (New York: Macmillan, 1921).

thriving political center was established. The influence of county-seat functions and patterns remains very important and easily recognized. Officials of many recently constituted agencies, county, state and federal, have set up their offices and make their homes in county-seat towns. These centers grow faster than other comparable centers of the same size group. It is estimated that in the decade from 1940 to 1950 they showed a rate of gain nearly twice that of non-county-seat centers.[8]

Another traditional element in the background of the village and small town has even greater political and social significance; that is its legal separation from the surrounding township. This legal and social severance has far-reaching consequences in any consideration of town and country relations. In the early country neighborhood settlement, there was a certain assumption of independence. In the incorporated municipality there was often an attitude of superiority, a facing away from the country, often toward the city.

Similarly certain social institutions came to belong to and, in the minds of people, be associated with villages and towns such as the high school, the library, hospital, theater, and park. These institutions built by town and village people do not "belong" to country people. Country people use them, but it is "by leave" or by invitation of the town or village people. C. J. Galpin pointed out the inconsistencies of the situation when he began to study town and country relations.[9] He called attention to the fact that all too often the banker, storekeeper, and blacksmith (now the garage man) knew the farmer as "the goose that lays the golden egg." His money was good and necessary,

and his good will must be retained. But to incorporate him into the stream of village or town life was another matter. He did not share in the control and responsibility of the institutions he patronized. He even stood on "other people's streets." The embarrassment was mutual. The farmer paid so much money into the town through trade that he felt he ought to have some consideration, yet he contributed so little directly toward some of the social institutions that the villagers did not consider his rights very compelling. And the legal separation of village from township and town form of government has added to the confusion.

To be sure, this social separation of townsmen and countrymen is not unique to America. It still pervades many European countries whose agricultural populations have peasant backgrounds. Antagonisms persist and town-country coöperation is difficult to achieve, both there and here.[10] Some of these traditional attitudes carried over into the American scene already complicated by its own heterogeneous backgrounds. They are revealed in town-country school controversies, in religious divisions, and in town conflicts with country coöperatives.

Today, greatly improved facilities for travel and communication — physical inventions of the modern age — have increased enormously the freedom of movement and thought for both farmers and villagers. They have also changed and improved details of the general situation, but they have not met the central problem. Social inventions are needed for its solution. Villages and towns continue to need the country and its agricultural wealth, and the country needs the village and town social and educational institutions even more than formerly. Country people are not so dependent upon any one center for business services as they once

[8] Edmund deS. Brunner, "Village Growth, 1940–50," *Rural Sociology*, XVI, No. 2 (June, 1951).

[9] *The Social Anatomy of a Rural Community* (Madison: Wisconsin Agricultural Experiment Station Research Bulletin 34, 1915), p. 25.

[10] Thorstein Veblen, *Absentee Ownership and Business Enterprise in Recent Times* (Viking Press, 1923), chapter VII, "The Country Town."

were. In fact, village and town business leaders generally recognize that today the range of choice has expanded and that retail trade, in the majority of cases, now follows high-school attendance, which is a recognition of the social function of rural centers. A rural community is therefore in formation, a collation of small town or village and country, arising out of their interdependencies and their mutual needs, but not yet recognized in the legal structure of the day. It is time then to consider in detail the place of the village and town in our modern rural society and their power to survive and to perform needed services.

Hamlets, Villages, Towns — How Many? Growing or Declining?

Trends in population growth for the United States as a whole have been traced in other chapters. Growth in the decade from 1940 to 1950 exceeded all expectations. For the first time in census records, the non-farm population exceeded the farm in the rural classification. The question is, what is happening to the villages and small towns of rural America; are they holding their own in this general upward sweep? Popular attitudes toward these smaller centers, especially prior to the last decade, were often somewhat derisive or patronizing. During the boom years of large city development, the small town seemed to offer very little to those who appeared ambitious and adventuresome. But all this has changed. Now there are those in these smaller centers who feel sorry for those who continue to live in the big urban centers. Conditions have also changed in the smaller centers, as a later section of this chapter and the next chapter will indicate. There have been improvements in housing, education, and recreation. Isolation, which characterized village life of earlier days, has largely disappeared, thanks to radio, television, improved high-

ways, and increased numbers and kinds of motor vehicles.

Growth of village and town centers is rather uneven in that the larger village centers are increasing at more rapid rates than the smaller ones. Also those near urban, especially large metropolitan, centers are gaining more rapidly than those more remote. The latter tendency will be analyzed in the chapter on rural-urban relationships. Surburban villages have been sorted out in the tabulations presented in this section of the chapter in order to give a truer picture of current developments in rural society itself. Population trends will be given here in terms of three large categories: hamlets, villages, and towns.

Hamlets — incorporated and unincorporated. Hamlets have been arbitrarily defined as centers of less than 250 population. Many are crossroad or neighborhood centers. A more adequate definition proposed by the geographer Glenn T. Trewartha includes certain minimum numbers and kinds of aggregated dwellings and business establishments, but special studies are required to meet this test.[11]

Census reports include legally incorporated places of this size, but to include the unincorporated centers special analysis is required, using such other sources as published atlases or almanacs. Table 27 represents the results of such special studies for the two decades 1920–40, the latest available.

Incorporated hamlets have shown a remarkable stability both in numbers and in population during the twenty-year period. Their population has approached but never exceeded a half million. Some hamlets gained enough in one decade to put them into the village class in the next. For ex-

[11] "The Unincorporated Hamlet — One Element of the American Settlement Fabric," *Annals of the Association of American Geographers*, XXXIII (March, 1943).

TABLE 27	YEAR	TOTAL		INCORPORATED		UNINCORPORATED	
		Number	Population	Number	Population	Number	Population
Hamlets — Incorporated and Unincorporated, Number and Population, 1920–40	1940	58,818	3,922,037	2,847	463,565	55,971	3,458,472
	1930	55,135	3,579,648	2,982	486,204	52,153	3,093,444
	1920	65,298	3,879,438	2,436	415,162	62,862	3,464,276

Source: 1940, Sixteenth Census of the United States, Population vol. 1, Table 5, by states; 1930 and 1920, Fifteenth Census of the United States, Population, vol. I, Table 5, by states. Special analysis of unincorporated places from 1943 edition of Rand McNally Atlas and Dun and Bradstreet reports by Douglas G. Marshall. See his article "Villages in the United States," *American Sociological Review*, II, No. 2, April, 1946.

ample, of the 507 incorporated between 1910 and 1930, about one fifth had moved up into the village category by 1940.

Unincorporated hamlets reached their peak in about 1920, leveled off between 1920 and 1930, but increased somewhat in both numbers and population in the decade 1930 to 1940. Many may have disappeared or moved into the incorporated or the village classification, but many new ones came into existence. As pointed out earlier, much depends upon definition, but there is little evidence to suggest that these are a vanishing type of population center in our rural society. They are built around the institutions characteristic of country life; general stores, filling stations, taverns, schools, and churches.

Villages — incorporated and unincorporated. Villages represent a larger segment

of the rural population than do hamlets. However, it is from the growing hamlets that they are replenished and given some of their increase. They are also a rather heterogeneous class, extending from 250 to 2500 in population and including the incorporated and unincorporated, the agricultural, the industrial, and some suburban. While a much larger proportion of villages than hamlets are incorporated, nevertheless those unincorporated held their own in both numbers and population in the twenty-year period between 1920 and 1940. (Table 28). This is the latest complete analysis available. As in the case of the hamlets, these unincorporated villages must be studied from other than census sources, except those having populations of 500 to 2500 in 1940. For these the Sixteenth Census made a special report.

Incorporated villages also exhibited great

TABLE 28	YEAR	TOTAL		INCORPORATED		UNINCORPORATED	
		Number	Population	Number	Population	Number	Population
Villages — Incorporated and Unincorporated, Number and Population, 1920–40.	1940	19,359	13,780,990	10,441	8,879,112	8,918	4,901,878
	1930	19,367	14,309,607	10,451	8,697,249	8,916	5,612,358
	1920	19,440	13,925,033	10,422	8,556,387	9,018	5,368,646

Source: Regular census releases for incorporated places. Special Census release for unincorporated places 500 to 2500 in 1940 and special analysis by Douglas G. Marshall, *op. cit.*

TABLE 29 Proportion of Villages 1000–2500 Population Gaining or Losing, 1910–1950	DECADES	GAINING 10% OR MORE	NEITHER GAINING NOR LOSING 10%	LOSING 10% OR MORE
	1940–50	47.6	46.8	5.6
	1930–40	43.9	47.0	9.1
	1910–30	38.7	55.3	6.0

Note: In 1940–50 suburban villages were not counted.

stability during the twenty-year period. There was a net gain in numbers if those which moved into the town class of over 2500 population between 1930 and 1940 are compared with those of the urban which slipped back into the village classification. It is estimated that a million villagers did pass into the town category in that decade. In the same decade, 90 villages were disincorporated, but 406 of the incorporated hamlets moved up into the village category. There is every evidence that incorporated villages not only held their own but made a proportionate contribution to the growing segments of the urban as well as the general population increase. When larger villages are analyzed according to size groups, it is apparent that they were growing more rapidly than the smaller ones.[12]

Unincorporated villages were somewhat fewer in number than the incorporated ones but contained only about half the population. Like the unincorporated hamlets, however, these villages held their own in both numbers and population in the decade from 1930 to 1940. When combined with the incorporated, the total was about 20,000 places and a little less than 14,000,000 people in 1940. This population represented 24 per cent of the total rural population and 51 per cent of the rural non-farm population. This meant that one in four of the people in rural

society, and every second person in the rural non-farm group, was a villager.

More recent trends among medium and large non-suburban incorporated villages. From an analysis made of preliminary releases of the 1950 Census, it is evident that the trends just traced have continued, even with accelerated strength.[13] Medium and large villages, 1000 to 2500 in population and non-suburban in character, enjoyed a greater amount of growth in the decade from 1940 to 1950 than in any previous decade since 1910, when separate tabulations were first made. Table 29 gives the percentage gaining or losing 10 per cent or more through the four decades from 1910 to 1950.

Almost three out of four of these villages, or 73 per cent, showed some growth; and nearly half, 47.6 per cent, grew more than 1 per cent per year in the last decade. It must be remembered that strict comparisons from decade to decade cannot be made because suburban centers were not included in the 1940–50 tally; if they had been, over half, or 51 per cent, would have shown the 10 per cent rate of gain. There were, however, some differences among the various census divisions, as Table 30 shows.

Only the Middle Atlantic and West North Central divisions showed less than one half their medium and large villages growing more than 10 per cent in the decade. The

[12] Edmund deS. Brunner and T. Lynn Smith, "Village Growth, and Decline," *Rural Sociology,* IX, No. 2 (June, 1944).

[13] Edmund deS. Brunner, "Village Growth, 1940–50," *Rural Sociology,* XVI, No. 2 (June, 1951).

TABLE 30	DIVISION	NUMBER OF VILLAGES	GAINING		LOSING	
			over 10%	0.1–9.9%	over 10%	0.1–9.9%
Proportion of Non-suburban Villages 1000–2500 Population Gaining or Losing, 1940–50 by Census Divisions	Middle Atlantic	428	45.6	26.7	7.0	20.7
	East North Central	580	50.5	29.6	6.0	13.9
	West North Central	542	37.5	30.8	5.1	26.6
	South Atlantic	417	57.1	29.7	3.1	10.1
	East South Central	238	62.2	16.0	6.1	15.5
	West South Central	364	56.3	22.8	5.5	15.4
	Mountain	169	56.2	15.4	13.0	15.4
	Pacific	144	75.8	13.8	3.4	7.0
	United States *	2,882	47.6	25.4	5.6	16.6

* Excludes nine places showing no change in population and suburban places as defined, also New England.

Source: *Rural Sociology*, XVI, No. 2.

Pacific States showed the greatest growth because of the large migration to that area. Almost half of the villages which lost more than 10 per cent were in two divisions — the Middle Atlantic and Mountain. Much of their decline can be accounted for by declines in the population of mining towns.

Villages, like other census aggregates, do not stay put; they move in and out of defined categories. Thus, as Table 31 shows, 382 villages rose to the town classification from 1940 to 1950, and were counted as urban.

There were 94 places which became incorporated and were listed for the first time in the size group 1000 to 2500. Two thirds of these were in the Southern region and over one fourth in the Far West. In addition, nearly a score of towns dropped down into the village class. Thus, to compensate for the 382 non-suburban villages which passed into the urban category, as against 316 from 1930 to 1940 but including the suburban, the medium and large village group received 664 accessions.

More recent trends among small incorporated villages. Table 31 indicates the dynamic qualities of some small villages. It will be observed that 554 villages of less than 1000 population had grown into the medium or larger village class between

TABLE 31	DIVISION	NUMBER VILLAGES TO URBAN	NUMBER SMALL TO MEDIUM OR LARGE	VILLAGES GAINING	
				over 10%	0.1–9.9%
Number Villages Becoming Urban; Number Small Villages Becoming Medium or Large; and Rates of Gain, 1940–50 by Census Divisions	Middle Atlantic	49	54	83.4	16.6
	East North Central	58	116	85.5	14.5
	West North Central	29	72	83.3	16.7
	South Atlantic	62	95	95.8	4.2
	East South Central	34	54	94.1	5.9
	West South Central	72	77	97.3	2.7
	Mountain	25	36	97.1	2.9
	Pacific	53	50	94.0	6.0
	United States *	382	554	91.3	8.7

* Exclusive of New England.

Source: *Rural Sociology*, XVI, No. 2.

TABLE	DIVISIONS	NUMBER OF VILLAGES	GAINING over 0.1—		LOSING over 0.1—	
			10%	9.9%	10%	9.9%
32	Middle Atlantic	488	39.1	29.7	7.2	20.5
	East North Central	1500	43.8	25.7	9.6	16.5
Proportion of Incorpo-	West North Central	1727	22.3	22.7	23.4	28.8
rated Villages 250–	South Atlantic	756	42.3	23.5	14.3	17.5
1000 Gaining or Los-	East South Central	382	31.6	19.9	19.6	25.7
ing, 1940–1950 by	West South Central	566	30.4	18.4	33.2	16.8
Census Divisions	Mountain	355	34.6	19.1	26.0	19.1
	Pacific	152	64.5	13.8	9.9	9.2
	United States*	5906	34.8	23.1	17.9	21.1

* New England and suburban centers as defined in *Rural Sociology*, XVI, No. 2 are not included.
Source: Special Tabulation of Preliminary Releases, 1950 Census, Series PC–8.

1940 and 1950. Nine tenths of those which passed this 1000 mark increased at the rate of one per cent or more per year for the decade. The Northern three divisions lagged behind this average, while the Southern and Western exceeded it. In the previous decade, 1930 to 1940, there were 10 per cent of the 7224 small villages which gained from 25 to 50 per cent and almost 4 per cent increased more than 50 per cent in population.

Small villages which did stay in the same class, plus those which came up from hamlets, are included in Table 32, distributed by Census Divisions and by their rates of gain or loss.

Gains among the small villages are not as great as those observed among the medium and larger villages. This differential rate of growth was noticeable in earlier decades but now represents a definite trend. There are some differences among divisions, as the table shows. The process of differentiation among village centers will be described and interpreted in the following sections of the chapter.

More recent trends among unincorporated villages. The 1950 census enumerated unincorporated villages when their population equaled 1000 or more. Their numbers declined, compared with the previous decade, partly because of the increased tendency of village centers to form legal municipalities and partly because of shifts in mining and manufacturing. There is still a sizeable number, but they are difficult to study, since they are not included in detailed census analyses. A disproportionate number of unincorporated places are in the South, especially textile centers.

Towns — incorporated and unincorpo-

TABLE	DIVISIONS	NUMBER OF VILLAGES
33	Middle Atlantic	196
	East North Central	99
	West North Central	7
	South Atlantic	222
Number Unincorporated	East South Central	68
Villages 1000–2500,	West South Central	62
1950 by Census Divisions	Mountain	47
	Pacific	100
	United States (exclusive of New England)	801

Source: Special Tabulation of Preliminary Releases, 1950 Census, Series PC–8.

TABLE	SIZE CLASS	TOTAL		INCORPORATED		UNINCORPORATED	
		Number	Population	Number	Population	Number	Population
34 Towns — Incorporated and Unincorporated, Number and Population, 1950	Total	3,013	14,604,868	2,645	13,068,196	368	1,536,672
	2,500 to 5,000	1,174	8,123,192	1,092	7,560,499	82	562,093
	5,000 to 10,000	1,839	6,481,676	1,553	5,507,697	286	973,979

Source: Census of Population, 1950 Preliminary Counts, Series PC–3 No. 8, July 11, 1951. Washington, D.C.

rated. During the first fifty years of the century, nearly 2400 of the more rapidly growing and larger villages increased their population beyond the 2500 mark and became "towns." This number is equivalent to about four fifths of all the places reported by the census in the classification of 2500 to 10,000 population in 1950. Table 34 shows that there were over 3000 such centers, with a population of nearly 15,000,000 people.

Towns in the table are shown in two size groups, and incorporated and unincorporated are listed separately. Together they represent nearly 10 per cent of the total population and more than 15 per cent of the "urban." Their number, as well as their population, has been growing rather steadily during the last thirty years, as Table 35 indicates, although the rates of both have increased in the last ten years.

Some of the towns recorded in the previous table lie within the 168 standard metropolitan areas, and as such are "urban." Many others are still agriculture-centered to a high degree. This is more especially true of the smaller ones and those located in farming regions. Like the larger villages, they have many relations with country people. Some of these relations are represented by trade and social contacts and are somewhat less personal than those usually found in the smaller centers; yet they are increasingly important as agriculture tends to become more and more mechanized and industrialized. These service contacts, to be described in the next section, are more specialized than those of the village, and they are easily recognized by such institutions and functions as wholesaling, central credit agencies, flexible processing plants for agricultural products, other industries, daily newspapers, theaters, hospitals, and county courthouses.

Characteristic Types, Changing Functions of Villages and Towns

The question whether villages and small towns are growing and maintaining their proportionate share in the general stream of population increase has been answered in the affirmative. However, their functions are changing. "Small towns must sink or swim,"

TABLE	YEAR	NUMBER	POPULATION
35 Incorporated Towns — Trends in Number and Population, 1920–50	1950	2,645	13,068,196
	1940	2,387	11,707,805
	1930	2,183	10,614,746
	1920	1,970	9,353,530

Source: 1940, Sixteenth Census of the United States, *op. cit.;* 1930, *ibid.,* vol. 1, Population Table, Table 10, p. 26; 1950, *op. cit.*

is the warning carried editorially in a national magazine circulating among small centers. This means, of course, that changes and adjustments are essential in a dynamic society. The place of the village and small town in modern America is not typical of the rest of the world, as was explained earlier in this chapter. Agricultural villages in most other countries were, and many still are, residence centers for farmers as well as for villagers. There were also other types of centers not related directly to agriculture, as for example the industrial, seaside, and holiday villages of England.

In parts of Australia and in some South American countries the major division in "rural" population is often between larger market centers and the open country. Intermediate small towns and villages are relatively unimportant. There is evidence of such a trend in the predominantly agricultural areas of the United States. Larger villages grew disproportionately to smaller ones in the decade 1930 to 1940, and the trend continued into the next decade. The opposite trend appears in some sections of the East and the Far West, where small centers are growing at more than average rates, especially as units in or near large suburban and industrial developments.

In North American rural society there has been a close population relationship between the village or town center and the surrounding farm area, as the next chapter will explain more fully. This relationship has been reasonably constant among the various crop areas. Dr. H. Paul Douglass pointed this out in his early study of small towns in Iowa.[14] He suggested that rural people, including farmers, have villages and towns as their numbers and their means warrant, as they "can afford them." He meant that rural people look to such centers for various economic and social services which they need and for which they can pay. There is economy in this system of division of labor, as the English economist, Adam Smith, pointed out many years ago. Villages and towns have made a secure place for themselves and constitute a definite group in our rural society. But processes of differentiation continue until various types of centers can be distinguished and different functions characterized.

Various types of village centers. Not all villages in rural society can be considered agricultural villages, oriented to rural life. In a ten-county region of North Carolina, 126 villages and hamlets were found. Nearly three fourths were designated agricultural, the others industrial and suburban. Table 36 shows their distribution according to size groups.

Agricultural villages were smaller in population than all villages, but the study shows

[14] *The Little Town* (New York: Macmillan, 1927).

TABLE	POPULATION SIZE CLASS	NUMBER OF CENTERS			
36 Size-types of Villages and Hamlets, North Carolina Subregion, 1940		TOTAL	AGRICULTURAL	INDUSTRIAL	SUBURBAN
	All classes	126	89	22	15
	25– 99	44	41	0	3
	100– 249	37	27	5	5
	250– 749	26	11	11	4
	750–1,249	10	5	3	2
	1,250–2,499	9	5	3	1

Source: Whitney, Vincent H., "Economic Differences Among Rural Centers," *American Sociological Review*, XII, No. 1, February, 1947.

that they have a larger average number of business units than the others. As they increase in size, they have greater specialization in types of stores. This tendency was found earlier in a study of a larger number of agricultural centers representing the main regions of the nation.[15] It is suggested that agricultural villages can be considered as open centers. They are frequented and patronized by farm families in the surrounding territory. To make the size classes strictly comparable, the farm population should be added. Industrial villages can be characterized as closed centers largely dependent upon their own people for support. Suburban villages can be described as attached centers, chiefly places of residence for those engaged in commercial or industrial activities in a nearby city.

Industrial villages. While it is agricultural villages with which we are mainly concerned, it should be recorded here that industrial villages are a distinct type. According to an earlier study their population was younger, with more males and children and fewer widows than in agricultural villages. There were fewer contacts with the hinterland, because of such locations as lumbering areas, and because of independent interests. Their average trade area is only four square miles, and there are only half as many stores as in the agricultural village. Farmers do not frequent their churches, farm children do not attend their schools. One eighth of their employees come from farm homes. Life is ordered by the factory whistle and the decision of an often distant and unknown executive. Industry dominates the social organization of the community, in which there is often a high degree of paternalism, never found in agricultural villages. In the South, where textile mills have been imported into agricultural

villages, a great gulf usually exists between the old population and the new, which lives on "the mill hill." Mill-workers and agrarians are served by different churches, although of the same denomination. So far from uniting industry and agriculture, the average industrial village has bred social estrangement.[16]

Industrial villages can be differentiated from agricultural villages when they are absorbed by one or more manufacturing enterprises to the exclusion of almost all other activities. By that criterion and on the basis of the study to which reference has just been made, it was estimated that approximately one village out of four can be classified as "industrial," having no direct connection with agriculture and not dependent upon it. This does not mean that factory industries are lacking in other villages, including those closely related with agriculture. Such industries, however, are likely to be smaller, more diversified, and more dependent for both raw material and labor upon the surrounding locality and its farmers. This phase of the industrial enterprise in rural society will be considered presently.

Who are villagers and towsnmen? Village populations, compared with those of farm and city, represent a midpoint in many features, a point which both farm and city populations seem to be approaching. In some respects villagers are more like country people than city people; in others the reverse is true. Consequently village populations may typify the nation's population as the trend toward fewer and fewer sharp differentiations noted throughout the discussion

[15] Edmund deS. Brunner and J. H. Kolb, *Rural Social Trends* (New York: McGraw-Hill, 1933).

[16] For a full discussion of the problem based on a nation-wide field survey of seventy industrial villages, see Brunner, *Industrial Village Churches* (New York: Harper, 1930), especially chapters I to V and the Appendix, pp. 175–181. See also T. J. Woofter and E. Winston, *Seven Lean Years* (Chapel Hill, North Carolina: 1939), pp. 113–116.

tends to stabilize. This hypothesis need not weaken an observation made earlier, that villages have been in existence in American rural society long enough to have developed some of their own distinguishing characteristics.

Analysis of population data prior to 1950 indicates that people who live in the smaller villages related to agriculture are more likely to resemble the farm population than the urban. On the other hand, larger villages, especially those over 1500 in population, are more likely to show city than country patterns. All villages have fewer extremes of tenancy or illiteracy, and smaller proportions of foreign-born, than urban centers. The fertility ratio for children under 10 years of women aged 20 to 45 was higher for villages than cities but lower than for farms.

The main differentiating factor was the high proportion of old people; it may be suggested that the village is rural society's "old folks' home." Except in certain areas of the South where the population is fairly normal in age distribution, the disproportion of old people in villages was general. The excess was due in major part to older persons moving in from the country areas, since there was no significant difference in death rate at the various age levels between the two populations.

A comparison has been made between growing and declining agricultural villages.[17] The conclusions as to age structure were that the greatest difference was in the age group under 10 years in which growing villages had a larger proportion than declining ones. The second greatest difference was in the group 20 to 30 years of age in which the growing villages had substantially larger proportions. In every age group beyond 40 years the declining village had the larger proportion.

[17] David Jenkins, *Growth and Decline of Agricultural Villages* (New York: Bureau of Publications, Teachers College, Columbia University, 1940).

Large villages and small towns tend to resemble each other, and to have more urban than rural population characteristics. There was an excess of females, especially single, widowed, and divorced women. In this respect they outranked even the cities. There was a marked excess of aged persons of both sexes. This may be one factor accounting for the high death rates in towns of 2500 to 10,000, which will be recorded in the chapter on rural health. In brief, larger villages and small towns have a slight deficiency of children, a marked deficiency in the early working ages, and an excess of aged people.

What villagers do, functions of villages and towns. Agricultural villages and towns are more than aggregations of people struggling to "hold their own" or to improve their positions from one census count to another. Their ability to continue as centers depends largely upon the functions rendered their own residents and those who live in the countryside, farmers and non-farmers. As the next chapter will show, there is a close correlation between size, characteristics, and functions — between who village and town people are and what they do. We are concerned here with the occupations of the people in such centers and the kinds of business institutions and industrial agencies found there.

General occupational distributions of all non-farm rural people are given in Table 37 for 1940, the latest year for which such data are available.

"Operators," the high ranking class for males, includes manufacturing, 7.3 per cent, and mining, 6.3 per cent. Within the manufacturing classification all textiles account for 2.3 per cent. Among female operators, manufacturing is twice as high, 14.8 per cent, two thirds in textiles. The second high class for men is crafts and foremen, mechanics being 3.3 per cent and carpenters 2.7 per

	OCCUPATION	MALES	FEMALES
TABLE **37** Per cent Distribution of Employed Persons by Major Occupation Categories for Rural Non-Farm Population, 1940	Total	100.	100.
	Operators	24.6	18.2
	Craftsmen, foremen	17.3	0.7
	Other laborers	13.7	1.2
	Proprietors, managers, officials	12.4	5.8
	Clerical and sales	10.0	20.7
	Professional and semi-professional	6.1	16.1
	Farm laborers	5.7	1.2
	Other workers	3.6	12.0
	Protective service	3.1	0.0
	Farmers and farm managers	2.0	0.2
	Domestic	0.6	23.4
	Others not reported	0.9	1.6

Source: *United States Census, "The Labor Force," United States Summary*, III, Part I, pp. 84–86.

cent. When proprietors, managers, officials, and clerical and salespeople are combined, the ranking for men is third, but for women it becomes first. Retail trade for men represents 5.4 per cent. Saleswomen are 6 per cent, stenographers, secretaries, and typists, 5 per cent, and other clerical, 4 per cent. All farmers do not live on farms, as the table shows; some live in villages and manage farms or work as farm hands; together this group represents 7.7 per cent of males.

Among the women, domestic service ranks first in the table, but second if a combination of clerical, sales, and proprietary is made. Operators stand third, a wide classification which includes 2 per cent beauticians and manicurists. The fourth rank among women is professional, with 16.1 per cent, teachers representing 10.9 per cent. Teaching for men is only 1.4 per cent.

Occupations of those classified more strictly as villagers, especially in agricultural regions, can be grouped into five main categories.

(1) *Manufacturing.* It may surprise some to find manufacturing high on the list of village occupations. This is partially accounted for by the rather inclusive census definition which includes such artisans as carpenters, masons, and seamstresses, as well as those employed in industrial plants.

Industries connected with food assume an increasingly important place in every agricultural region. Food processing plants of every kind are tending to move into larger villages and small towns. The trend is typified by the larger canneries or flexible dairy plants built in such centers to replace the neighborhood or small village units. This is a phase of the centralizing process which is taking place in rural society. It is associated with similar movements among such social institutions as schools and churches. When the food group of occupations is combined with lumber, tobacco, textile, and paper-mill groups, they represent nearly two thirds of the total, indicating a direct association with agriculture and forestry.

(2) *Trade or merchandising.* Trade showed a tendency to increase in total number of employees and in percentage when compared with the other occupations during the period studied. This is but further evidence of growth and ability of villages to maintain themselves as centers in the face of urban competition. Shifts in this retailing function in respect to kind of retail agencies and size of centers will be discussed later.

(3) *Domestic, personal, and professional services.* The increase in domestic, personal, and professional employees is an important reflection of the concentration within village centers of those institutions and services which are more and more needed by people living in the village and in its country community areas. Schools, libraries, hospitals, and churches are, of course, examples of institutions that employ professional people, while the increase of such establishments as restaurants, beauty parlors, pressing and cleaning shops, and tourists' service agencies accounts for the definite increase of those in the personal services. Much restaurant help is classed as domestic and is needed because of our mobile society.

(4) *Agriculture.* The number employed in agriculture who maintain a residence in village centers fluctuates. This is partially the result of a lessening demand for farm laborers because of the increasing use of machinery. In some regions it is due to the fact that fewer farmers retired to live in the village, especially during the depression. Recently the movement was resumed in some regions. It is estimated that in 1950 about 4.8 per cent of farm operators were not living on farms but presumably in towns or villages.

(5) *Transportation.* Transportation is an excellent illustration of the function of the village in rural society. Transportation agencies assemble for primary processing the food products and raw materials destined for local or distant consumption and then transport them to other manufacturing centers or to city wholesalers and retailers. Conversely, transportation agencies bring to the village for distribution those things needed for local consumption or required in farming, trade, and industry.

Industry in agricultural villages and towns. Two of the five functions enumerated above will be considered briefly,

namely industry and trade. Thus far a majority of rural industries are related to the soil-processing of food and fibre. The idea of a closer union of agriculture and industry, urged during the depression, has recently been revived. As suggested elsewhere, this has frequently been advocated for periods of crisis. The idea is commonly held that the introduction of industry would furnish needed employment and might take up the slack when wartime or defense production demands weakened. An opinion also expressed in many rural communities is that the local economy should somehow be balanced, made reasonably complete or self-sufficient. The view is that there should be local employment opportunities for all residents, weekly payrolls to supplement farm income in order to support local trade. But these opinions run counter to the trends discussed throughout this study of rural society. Interdependence, not local self-dependence, is the dominant trend of the day.

The present situation in respect to industry in village and town centers is uneven from one region to another, and the future is uncertain. There is evidence that food processing is being centralized in the larger centers, as mentioned before. The extent to which industry not related to agriculture will be decentralized is important for the future of rural society. There are indications that the trend has begun under stimulation of depression experiences and the more recent urge for dispersed production and civilian protection. However, the merger of agriculture and industry is far from complete in rural America. In some rural areas industrial workers and the increase of workers in other non-farm occupations have introduced a kind of "third estate" in addition to the traditional farm and village or small town occupations.

During the depression years, many variations in rural industries occurred.[18] Not

[18] Edmund deS. Brunner and Irving Lorge, *Rural*

only were the units small but their life cycles were short. Frequently there was insufficient capital, poor planning, and competition from newer and larger plants. Villages seeking a payroll auxiliary often launched questionable schemes introduced by outside promoters. Those factories which did succeed, although not as important as trade in volume of business, did put money into the local retail tills, and unlike trade, even into farmers' pockets by buying raw materials from them.

Factors in the success of rural industries are worthy of notation. The recruiting of an appreciable fraction of labor from farm homes, and the purchase of local raw materials, made the factory a potent influence in community life. Local investments, well distributed, and local control made for adherence to the industry rather than the opposite. As in the agricultural villages, no labor trouble was experienced, although the opposite was true in industrial villages, as mentioned above. This general survey makes clear that as in the case of stores, these local industries were institutions of some social as well as economic importance. If industries increase in rural areas there will be an increase also of certain socioeconomic problems involving such problems as wage rates, conditions of labor, and employer-employee relations.

The importance of such social and community relationships is illustrated in many recent studies. For example, after thirty years, a non-agricultural industry became an accepted part of the local community in one county-seat town in an intensive dairying region.[19] About 100 skilled employees and a small group of business executives were employed, and the majority owned their own homes. They found regular places in local civic and social organizations. They have made real contributions to the cultural life of the community through their leadership in music. They have little contact, however, with the farm segment of the community relationship except as their children mingle freely with town and country children in the local schools.

Another community, not quite so fortunate but located in the same region, has four industrial plants. At the time of the study, nearly 60 per cent of the labor force were not local residents but came daily to work by bus lines from a radius of twenty miles. The plants did not furnish employment opportunities for farm youth, and only 10 per cent of the employees reported previous farm experience. About 50 per cent had completed a high school education. Some of the plants had been located there on the basis of personal or casual choice rather than because of careful planning in relation to community conditions. One owner had spent a summer in the vicinity, liked it, and decided to move his factory there. In another case, ownership and management were highly centralized in a person who did not assume civic responsibilities and who threatened "to move the whole works" whenever displeased with decisions made by local authorities. In a third case, a public relations man for one of the industries was elected to the public school board. When issues came before the board by which he thought his company might be embarrassed, he was inclined to take a position of compromise and continue the uncertainty over when and how to expand local educational facilities.

A factory, especially in any small center, is something more than an employment opportunity; it is a social system.[20] Recently

---

Trends in Depression Years (New York: Columbia University Press, 1937). A survey of village-centered agricultural communities, 1930–36.

[19] J. H. Kolb and Leroy J. Day, *Interdependence in Town and Country Relations in Rural Society* (Madison: Wisconsin Agricultural Experiment Station, Research Bulletin 172, December, 1950).

[20] William Foote Whyte, *Industry and Society*, report by Committee on Human Relations in Industry, organized at the University of Chicago (New York: McGraw-Hill, 1946).

there has been a transition from an earlier type of family- or individually-owned and managed factory to corporation management, with its board of directors, executive managers, and labor union. Moreover, such an organization is not simply one person working for another, but a series of working and associating relationships. There are prestige and status differences such as white-collar, blue-collar, foreman, and "top boss." These are important not only in the work behavior within the factory, but in the social and economic relations within the town-country community.

Trade in agricultural villages and towns. It was estimated from a recent survey by *The American Press* that nearly a third of all retail sales were made in towns and villages of less than 10,000 population and that one third of the purchases by farmers in addition to their small-town buying were made in cities of 50,000 population and over.[21] Such estimates may not be accurate in detail or for any one region, but they do suggest confirmation of trends being reported here, namely the growing strength of villages and towns, and the increasing spread of farmers' business activities. These trends are not of recent origin but are evident from studies going back as far as 1910. It was found in a detailed survey of 140 agricultural villages located in all regions of the nation that the average number of commercial establishments had increased from 44.0 in 1910 to 56.2 in 1930.[22] The important feature in this trend was the 43 per cent increase in retail outlets. The largest gain was in privately owned stores. The number of chain stores had remained constant. The multiplication of retail shops was observed even among the small villages and those not

[21] Richard Roley, "Farmers Need Advice," *National County Agent and Vo-Ag Teacher*, VI, No. 10 (October, 1950).

[22] Brunner and Kolb, *Rural Social Trends* (New York: McGraw-Hill, 1933).

gaining in population. Village size, however, was a vital factor not only in the number of stores but more especially in the kind of commercial enterprises found. For example, two fifths of the villages under 1000 population had no furniture stores. The larger villages had 6.5 apparel stores, compared with 1.5 for the smaller centers.

Many influences were involved in these trends. One reason for the ability of many agricultural villages to hold their own even during the depression was the fact that a new generation of merchants had taken over. In many instances the sons of former proprietors had introduced modern merchandising practices and newer selling techniques. Younger people had also introduced many of the personal services formerly associated with urban life or had given former services new names or accommodations, such as beauty parlors, mortuaries, gourmet and delicatessen shops, soft-drink and dairy bars, liquor stores, bakeries, chiropractic clinics, tonsorial services, automotive accessory shops, and new-method cleaning establishments.

World War II changed some of this as older men and women, including wives of soldiers and sailors, carried on many village mercantile enterprises. More recently the former trend was resumed and younger merchants, veterans of the war, were in evidence on the "main street" of many villages and towns. They were also making their presence felt in elections to village councils and school boards.

Competition and stimulation of the "chains." Concern with chain stores was acute during the thirties. Nearly a dozen states levied special taxes on them, although the constitutionality of such taxes had been attacked. There was local press and radio propaganda against the chains. Agricultural villages and small towns had been invaded by chains of all kinds: grocery, clothing, drug, and tobacco stores, gasoline stations, and even banks. Grocery and clothing units were most frequently found in agricultural trade centers, and the invasion was mainly in larger places. Two thirds of the centers studied which did not have chains were under 1000 population.

What were the consequences? Some of the local merchants who could not adjust to the chain competition simply gave up. Sons of former proprietors, who had expected to become proprietors themselves, hired out to the chains instead. However, private merchandising did modernize, and the number of outlets increased. "If the chains beat us, it is our own fault," was the conclusion expressed in many centers where merchants had made adjustments. One kind of adjustment was the development and rapid growth of independent coöperatives or voluntary chains, as they were sometimes called. Merchant members bought coöperatively, used group advertising and chain merchandising techniques. In about 1936 the proportion of commercial chains in the agricultural villages studied stabilized with an estimated 5 per cent of the retail units but about 10 per cent of the business.

Differentiation in types of centers and specialization in kinds of functions. It should be evident that villages and small towns have participated proportionately in the general step-up which has characterized modern society, especially in recent prosperity years. This time farmers have shared in the up-swing, so that much of their "embarrassment" on the streets of their trading centers has disappeared. Their incomes, their clothes, their cars, their children in school, or the hairdress of their wives do not suffer by comparison with those of the merchants, the artisans, the teachers or even the bankers. Their range of choice has greatly expanded and they frequent more centers than in the horse-and-buggy days. Mer-

chants and other small-town business people realize this change. They have organized "buy-at-home" campaigns. They have sought to enlarge their trade areas by direct-mail advertising and shopper-service sheets mailed to every R.F.D. boxholder in their areas. They have bettered their merchandising and their credit practices. They have organized themselves into businessmen's associations although in relatively few instances have they recognized the modern farmer as a "businessman" and made him full partner in their community development plans.

The trends thus traced literally have become social movements in which the processes of differentiation and specialization are playing significant roles. This means that certain villages and town centers become characterized and recognizable by the specialized kinds of services they render. As the next chapter will indicate in more detail, certain kinds of services tend to belong together, since they require about the same volume of business, number of people, and extent of area.

In agricultural hamlets the general store continues as the most common service institution. Many such neighborhood stores, along with local garages, filling stations, machine repair shops, and taverns, have taken their share of the farmer's prosperity dollar.

Small villages are becoming differentiated from larger ones, as previously shown. One index of this process is the greater proportion of social contacts compared with trade contacts, as illustrated in Figure 20, from the study of town and country relations, Walworth County, Wisconsin.

Care must be exercised, however, in attempting to draw any clear-cut distinction between social and trade contacts. Merchandising, especially in small centers, is much more than a business transaction; it is a social function as well. There is the sharing

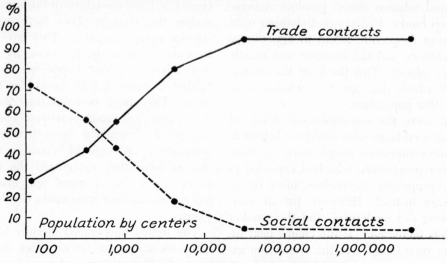

Figure 20. **Trade Contacts and Social Contacts.**

The two curves intersect at centers of about 600 population. Population shown along the horizontal base line is in terms of a logarithmic scale in which multiples of ten occupy equal intervals. Source: John H. Kolb and LeRoy J. Day, *Interdependence in Town and Country Relations in Rural Society*, Research Bulletin 172 (Madison: University of Wisconsin Agricultural Experiment Station, December, 1950).

of experiences, the exchange of information and opinions among friends, neighbors, and associates, farm and non-farm alike. Similarly, contacts in the coöperative, the creamery, the small industry, the tavern, the barber shop, or the beauty parlor are more than passing economic affairs; they are the social "stuff" whereby human relations are patterned into group relationships.

Differentiation among smaller and larger centers is further demonstrated by the shift in the proportion of businesses which has come about in recent years. This process is shown by the study of business agencies in North Carolina trade centers from 1910 to 1940 (Figure 21). While 41 per cent of such centers still had only one to four businesses in 1940, the bar chart shows a significant shift in proportions when going from very small to small, medium, and large centers during the thirty-year period.

The kinds of agencies and professional

services in larger villages of 1750 to 2500 population are given in Figure 22 taken from an early study in New York State. There were some differences between the two size classes but no significant ones. Important differences did appear when compared with smaller villages.

The process of differentiation continues as we move on to towns and compare their position with urban centers. One very specialized kind of trade contact is used to illustrate this, namely women's best dresses and coats. Figure 23 shows the amount of specialization which takes place among eighty farm family buyers whose address was Urbana, Ohio, Rural Route No. 2. Urbana is a town of about 8000 people; Springfield, six miles away, had 70,000; and Columbus, twenty-eight miles distant, over 306,000 population.

The same tendencies are encountered elsewhere, wherever comparable studies have

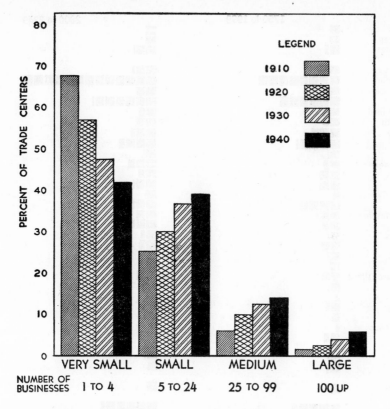

Figure 21. Shift in Number of Businesses in North
Carolina Trade Centers, from 1910 to 1940.

Source: Albert Ferris, "How Far to Town?," *Research and Farming*
(Raleigh: October, 1949).

been made. One more example from another region is summarized as follows:

Group activities of the farmers have long been shifting townward. This has been facilitated by the improvement of roads, the increased use of automobiles, and the location in the county-seat town of the local representatives of agricultural agencies. The small rural village is becoming a neighborhood convenience center for farm people, rather than the shopping center it was in earlier days. It often remains the focus of social activities, with the larger town used for special services. After several years of makeshift adaptations, beginnings of larger school district reorganization are appear-

ing, and the shift of members to village or town churches.[23]

In summary, the trend of the times is toward specialization, which is resulting in a certain degree of differentiation among village and town centers of varying sizes and types. This results in a high degree of interdependence, not only of town or village and country, but of smaller centers with their surrounding communities and larger centers

[23] A. H. Anderson, *Population Distribution and Rural Services in the Northern Great Plains* (Fort Collins: Colorado Library Bulletin no. 18, July, 1947).

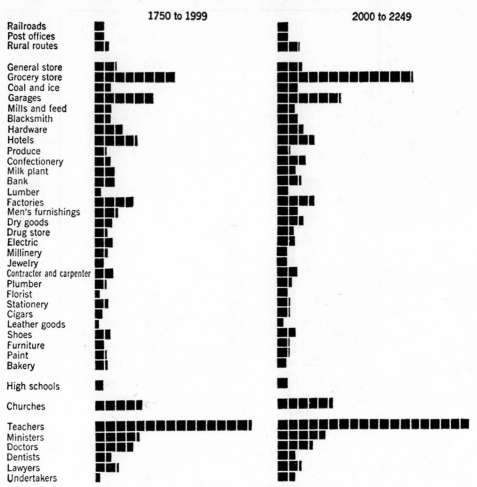

Figure 22. Economic Agencies and Professional People in
Two Classes of Villages, 1750 to 1999 and 2000 to 2249.

Source: Bruce L. Melvin, *Village Service Agencies* (New York, 1925).
Bulletin 493 (Ithaca: Cornell University Agricultural Experiment Station,
August, 1929).

with their tributary communities. Individuals and families, farm and non-farm, in rural society today have associational contacts within a number of group arrangements simultaneously, as the next chapter on rural communities will show. Sinclair Lewis' "Main Street" has joined the rest of the world.

Since village and town functions are changing, readjustments are imperative as

the price of survival. Every village or town should find it advantageous to discover its niche in the changing pattern and then organize its life and activities accordingly, not attempting to be self-sufficient but to become an effective unit in the larger interdependent plan. Evidences of such comprehensive planning are difficult to find in this country. Beginnings are being made in respect to special functions such as educa-

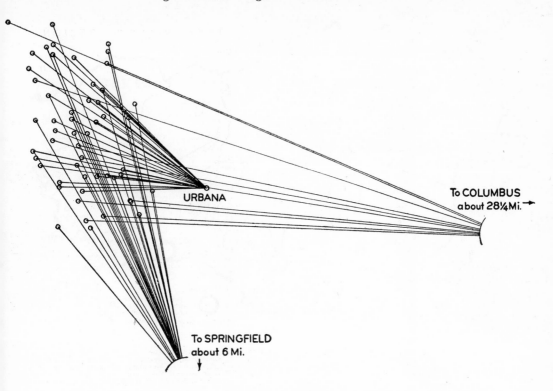

URBANA

To COLUMBUS
about 28¼ Mi.

To SPRINGFIELD
about 6 Mi.

Figure 23. Usual Places of Purchase for Women's Best Dresses and Coats by Country Gentleman Subscribers, RFD No. 2, Urbana, Ohio.

Seven scattered lines were omitted from original chart to focus attention on the three centers most patronized. Source: *Where Farmers Go to Buy,* Release No. 79 (Philadelphia: *Country Gentleman,* Research Department, June, 1949).

tion, recreation, hospitals, and rural coöperatives, as other chapters suggest. Perhaps trails will be blazed in England, one proponent of the village system of settlement. As indicated at the beginning of this chapter, the trends described here follow in general pattern the interdependence of small country villages with larger market towns, as found in England as well as in China.

The Town-Country Act of 1947 authorizes a planning committe for each County Council in England to survey and plan with respect to its future development. How such an over-all plan might appear is indi-

cated by this proposed pattern for the Tay Valley region. As Figure 24 shows, four types of centers are suggested: (1) Major specialized commercial, educational, and health services and large-scale industry; (2) Minor specialized services, agricultural market, and general industry; (3) Localized services, rural industry and agricultural processing center; (4) Basic social group related to primary school.

Thus the basis has been laid for the discussion of the next chapter in those town or village and country relationships known as rural communities.

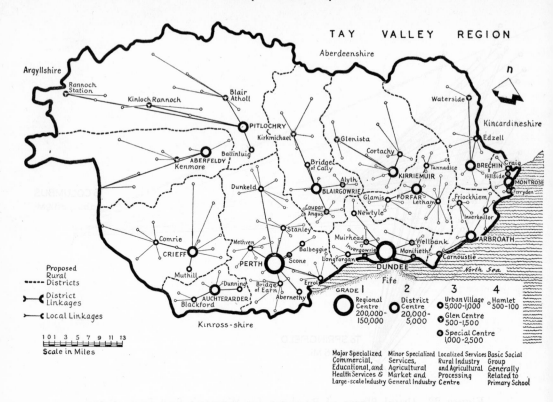

Figure 24. **Proposed Settlement Pattern.**

Source: G. P. Hirsch, "Country Towns: Their Function in the Rural
Pattern," *Town and Country Planning* (Oxford, England: May, 1951).

TOPICS FOR DISCUSSION

1. Sketch the stages of development and change
through which some village or small town
with which you are personally acquainted
has gone.
2. Account for the fact that village and open-
country neighborhood settlement occurred
separately in the Middle West.
3. Describe the New England and the Southern
form of group settlement and organization.
4. Make a list of all incorporated places in your
home county, indicate gains or losses in
population of each for the decades from 1930
to 1940 and 1940 to 1950. Is there any
tendency toward growth or decline to be
associated with certain sizes of places? Explain.
5. Which types of retail establishments are

tending to leave, which to remain in, and
which to come into agricultural villages?
Give your explanation.
6. Enumerate the factors which seem to influence where farm people trade. How do these
differ from those influencing village people?
7. What problems and what benefits come to
local communities by reason of chain stores
or chain banks?
8. What types of industry are likely to come to
agricultural villages and small towns? Give
your reasons and cite evidence.

REFERENCE READINGS

Brunner, Edmund deS., *Village Communities.*
New York: Doubleday, Doran, 1927.
Brunner, Edmund deS., G. S. Hughes, and

Marjorie Patten, *American Agricultural Villages.* New York: Doubleday, Doran, 1927.

Bunin, Ivan, *The Village* (authorized translation from the Russian by Isabel F. Haygood). New York: Knopf, 1923.

Fry, C. Luther, *American Villagers.* New York: Doubleday, Doran, 1926. Report of census study of American villages and village populations showing growing importance of the village in rural life.

Hicks, Granville, *Small Town.* New York: Macmillan, 1946. A description of what people in a small New England town talk about, their opinions, religion, education, economic patterns, and political life.

Kent County Council, *A Planning Basis for Kent County Council,* County Hall, Kent, Eng.: County Hall, Maidstone, 1948. Map of village interconnections.

Knight, W. D., *Subsidization of Industry in Forty Selected Cities in Wisconsin, 1930–1946,* Wisconsin Commerce Studies, I, No. 2. Madison: University of Wisconsin Bureau of Business Research and Science, 1947.

Kolb, J. H., *Service Relations of Town and Country,* Research Bulletin 58. Madison: University of Wisconsin Agricultural Experiment Station, December, 1923.

Kolb, J. H., *Service Institutions of Town and Country,* Research Bulletin 66. Madison: University of Wisconsin Agricultural Experiment Station, December, 1925.

Leonard, Olen E., *The Role of the Land Grant in the Social Organization and Social Processes of a Spanish American Village in New Mexico.* Nashville, Tenn.: Vanderbilt University Press, 1950.

Munch, Peter A., *Landhandelen i Norge* (*Country Trade in Norway*). Oslo, Nor.: Halverson and Larsen, 1948. Monograph reporting a study of country and village stores and trade centers.

Poston, Richard W., *Small Town Renaissance: A Story of the Montana Study.* New York: Harper, 1950.

Redfield, Robert, *A Village that Chose Progress: Chan Kom Revisited.* Chicago: University of Chicago Press, 1950.

Sanders, Irwin T., *Balkan Village.* Lexington: University of Kentucky Press, 1949.

Thomas, F. G., *The Village.* England: Oxford Press, 1943.

Vaile, Roland S., ed., *The Small City and Town.* Minneapolis: University of Minnesota Press, 1930.

Wilder, Thornton, *Our Town.* New York: Coward-McCann, 1938.

Williams, J. M., *An American Town.* Published privately, New York, 1906. An early study of a New England town.

Wilson, Warren H., *Quaker Hill.* Published privately, New York: 1907. A study of a New York country community from 1728 to 1880.

Yang, Martin C., *A Chinese Village: Taitou, Shantung Province.* New York: Columbia University Press, 1945.

FILMS

Hometown, U.S.A. S, C, 22. Description of life in a typical small town. *Look.*

Town. S, 11. A cross section of the average American community. New York University.

14 Rural Communities

Because of the still developing web of communication and transportation, there is an intermesh of town and country relationships. Just as the country looks increasingly to the village or town for many services, such as education, recreation, and merchandising, and just as the village or town is more and more depending upon the country for trade, raw materials, and patronage of its institutions, so the two in this reciprocal relation are becoming the town-country community of modern rural society.

As a matter of fact, many social trends which are developing in rural life today are closely linked with the whole question of village stability or growth which was considered in the last chapter, and with this growing interdependence of village or town with country. The areas of social, business, and educational contacts are expanded beyond neighborhood boundaries. Farmers and villagers are mingling as citizens of a larger community. This has fundamental importance for many of the movements which are to be discussed in later chapters. We shall consider, for example, the consolidation of country schools, the leadership of high schools, the reorganization of retail merchandising through principles of specialization, and the institution of the larger parish plan for churches by use of this town-country community idea.

America is becoming an older country; the frontier escape is no longer possible, and the result is the necessity for group organization and social planning which will make that mature life more satisfying. This emerging community which encompasses both town and country has many possibilities; hence we shall, in this chapter, focus our attention on a careful analysis of community areas and relationships. With the opening of the West under the Homestead Act, the method of settlement was largely on separate farms in neighborhood groups, as explained earlier. Villages and towns sprang up as business and institutional centers. Finally the integration of these two elements of rural society began.

Ideas About Community

The community and the family are the only social groups found universally. This broad and forceful generalization is made by Professor C. P. Murdock of Yale on the basis of a recent cross-cultural survey in which materials dealing with more than 150 different cultures from every part of the world were analyzed and summarized.[1] Community and family, he says, occur in every known human society, but nowhere on the earth do people live regularly in isolated families. Rather, everywhere territorial propinquity supported by diverse other bonds unites at least some neighboring families into larger groups, whose members maintain close personal relationships. These close working relationships may be considered communities.

[1] *Social Structure* (Glencoe, Ill.: Free Press, 1949); Yale Anthropological Studies 1945 and "Feasibility and Implementation of Comparative Community Research," *American Sociological Review*, XV, No. 6 (Dec. 1950).

Community groups vary widely, of course, with different modes of livelihood and with various cultural backgrounds. They may assume the form of villages, as in many parts of Europe, Asia, or even South America, or they may be composed of families living on separated country homesteads but clustered about some village or small town. In the modern North American scene, a kind of compromise is emerging. Families on dispersed farms or other country places are interrelated with some local village or town center through bonds of communication, education, religion, recreation, selling, and buying.

Students of society are constantly stressing the fact that social control operates most effectively within relatively small community groups, and that primary attitudes and public opinion are developed through them. They emphasize that both size and location are important, since there appears to be a negative correlation between close personal contacts and large numbers of people in widely scattered homes. Just how large, in numbers of families and in extent of land area, a community can be and still be a community group is an important question. It is one which must be considered as plans are made for the development of highway and other communication systems, and for the reorganization of local social institutions such as schools, churches, stores, factories. However, local institutions and other forms of social organization can be definitely influential in expanding social control and in changing attitudes.

One of the first, if not the very first, American student of rural society to write about this emerging rural community of country and village or town was Dr. Warren H. Wilson. He described the community in terms of a "team haul."

People in the country think of the community as that territory with its people, which lies within the team haul of a given center. . . .

Social customs do not proceed further than the team haul. Imitation, which is an accepted mode of social organization, does not go farther in the country than the customary drive with horse and wagon. . . . The team haul which defines the community is a radius within which men buy and sell. . . . It is the radius of social intercourse. Within this radius of the team haul families are accustomed to visit with ten times the frequency with which they pass outside the radius. . . . The community is the larger social whole outside the household; a population complete in itself for the needs of its residents. . . . It is a man's home town.[2]

It is not surprising to find the idea of self-sufficiency in the definitions of a community written a generation ago when rural life was more isolated than now, but it has led to an over-emphasis upon the community as a mutually exclusive group. For example, Dr. Butterworth also described the "true" community from this same point of view.

A true community is a social group that is more or less self-sufficing. It is big enough to have its own centers of interest — its teaching center, its social center, its own church, its own schoolhouse, its own Grange, its own library and to possess such other institutions as the people of the community need.

Much more recently and in theoretical terms, the idea is expressed that individuals live most of their lives within some one community, and that most of their "meaningful experiences" occur there. It is emphasized that "a community is unlike a neighborhood in that a person could spend his whole life within its boundaries, if he so wished.[3] How such a group hermitage could be arranged in a dynamic modern society, even if one should wish it, is difficult to imagine. Recent studies of rural society, some of which will be reported later in the chapter, develop

[2] Wilson, Warren H., *The Evolution of the Country Community* (Boston: Pilgrim Press, 1912).

[3] Lloyd A. and Elaine F. Cook, *A Sociological Approach to Education*, 2d ed., (New York: McGraw-Hill, 1950).

quite a different view, namely, that rural people are actually living in a variety of local groups, even communities, all at the same time.

It was Dr. C. J. Galpin who first invented a method for locating and mapping the rural community and who coined the term "rurban" to describe it. He presented an analysis of the American community as an interrelationship of town and country people together with their institutions. The following paragraph is recognized as a classic statement of the community idea in rural society:

It is difficult, if not impossible, to avoid the conclusion that the trade zone about one of these rather complete agricultural civic centers forms the boundary of an actual, if not legal, community, within which the apparent entanglement of human life is resolved into a fairly unitary system of interrelatedness. The fundamental community is a composite of many expanding and contracting feature communities possessing the characteristic pulsating instability of all real life.[4]

Dr. Galpin made his first community study in Walworth County, Wisconsin, but the origin of the idea goes back to an earlier survey of Belleville, Jefferson County, New York. When, as a young man, he was teaching in the academy there, he undertook a survey of the surrounding agricultural community. In reporting this study before the first Wisconsin Rural Life Conference in the spring of 1911, he said:

This stretch of land impressed me with its social front, with its variety of social activities, with its real progress made by the voluntary association of many small amounts of surplus labor and capital, and I decided to map the social topography of this whole community, at least as far as it was definitely organized, in order that I might discover the clue to its solidarity.

It was found that twenty-seven organizations center in the village. . . . No organizations except district schools were found in the open country. Village and open farming country form a community of homes which seems to be a sort of social drainage basin beyond whose border every home drains off into some other basin.

The big discovery of this survey is the fact of a real rural community and also pretty clearly the area of this community with its bounding lines. It appears that this community takes in parts of four townships, and ignores in its social dealings the voting precincts set by law.[5]

The beginning of this idea of spatial arrangements of social phenomena can thus be seen in the early Belleville study, but the technique for presenting it was revised and greatly improved in the Walworth County study, in which the publication of striking maps, showing the community relations of the twelve centers, attracted wide attention.

Thus, the map became the means for analysis, and "rurban," a general descriptive term. But perhaps a point which is implicit in the foregoing description will bear reemphasis; namely, that in studying any rural community, we must consider not only its physical boundaries, or locality, but also the functions which give it its life as a group. It is the fusing of the geographic or ecological and the psychological or functional elements which gives the community idea its real power and usefulness. To follow this in analysis is not always easy for, unlike the village, the town-country or rural community does not have such an easily recognizable physical base or a definite corporate boundary. Nor are its social functions integrated and united by political organization to the same extent as in the village. In the rural community, associations and social contacts are more voluntary; that is, people are drawn together by common interests of trade or education, recreation or religion. It is a com-

[4] *The Social Anatomy of an Agricultural Community.* (Madison: Wisconsin Agricultural Experiment Station Research Bulletin 34, 1915), p. 18.

[5] *Country Life Conference.* (Madison: University of Wisconsin Bulletin Series no. 472, General Series 308, February, 1911).

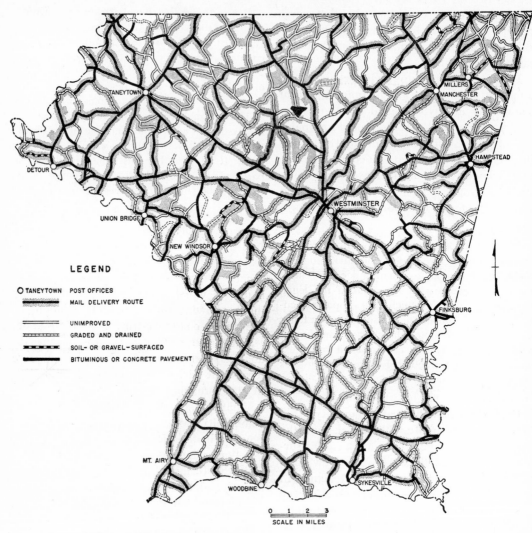

LEGEND

○ TANEYTOWN   POST OFFICES

━━━━━━━━   MAIL DELIVERY ROUTE

══════   UNIMPROVED

┅┅┅┅┅┅   GRADED AND DRAINED

✕━✕━✕━   SOIL- OR GRAVEL-SURFACED

━━━━━━   BITUMINOUS OR CONCRETE PAVEMENT

0   1   2   3
SCALE IN MILES

Figure 25. The Extensive Use of Rural Roads for Mail Delivery.

This 1949 map of mail routes in Carroll County, Maryland, shows that seventy-six per cent of all rural roads are used in delivering mail in this county. Source: S. H. DeVault, *Local Rural Road Use and Benefits in Maryland,* Bulletin A 61 (College Park: University of Maryland Agricultural Experiment Station, November, 1950).

munity of interest, but all interests need not be coterminous. Despite the process of specialization detailed in the previous chapter, there is, nevertheless, a coincidence or a grouping of functions and interests, as the next section of this chapter will demonstrate. Similarly there is a central core which can

be considered the community group. The most recent and satisfactory definition arising out of careful analysis of modern rural life as well as a detailed tracing of the older forms of group living, reads as follows:

A rural community consists of the social interaction of the people and their institutions in the local area in which they live on dispersed farmsteads and in a hamlet or village which forms the center of their common activities.[6]

The locality phase and the interest phase are thus brought together. It may be a little more or a little less of the one or the other. One community may represent an area easily recognized and well defined, with the social interactions of its people rather weak or sluggish. Another may have a high degree of social integration, but its boundaries may be none too clear. "Community," then, with the same root as "common," "communication," and "communion," is a unit of society with three implications: territorial area, interpersonal relations, and some differentiation from other groups.

Patterns of Rural Community Relations

The web of communication suggested at the beginning of the chapter as binding town and country into community relationships is strikingly illustrated by the design of rural mail delivery routes in Carroll County, Maryland, shown in Figure 25. Westminster is the focal point of the system. Taneytown, New Windsor, Finksburg, Hamstead, Manchester, and Millers, while centers themselves, are definitely tributary to the larger center.[7] The pattern has characteristics similar to those found in parts of England and much of the Orient, where small agricultural villages are located at the periphery but within the framework of influence of a central market town.

The general pattern of the village or town-country community is circular; the relation of the land to its center is like that of the outer wheel to its hub. Country people in the tributary area are more closely, al-

[6] Dwight Sanderson, *The Rural Community, The Natural History of a Sociological Group* (Boston: Ginn & Co., 1932), p. 481.

[7] S. H. DeVault, *Local Rural Road Use and Benefits in Maryland* (College Park: Maryland Agricultural Experiment Station Bulletin A61, November, 1950).

though not exclusively, related to each other and with those in the center than they are with those in more distant centers. It is more than a locality relationship, as has been emphasized, for the currents of life and thought of those who live within the area constantly flow together.[8] This is the essential function of communication, since to communicate is to make common.

Patterns of community relations will be shown by use of representative cases; then a summary will be presented in terms of types of centers and their services, together

[8] Galpin, *Rural Social Problem,* Fourth Wisconsin Country Life Conference (Madison: University of Wisconsin Serial No. 711, General Series 515, 1914).

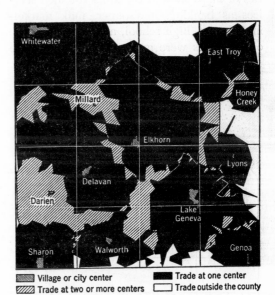

Village or city center | Trade at one center
Trade at two or more centers | Trade outside the county

Figure 26. General Community Areas Indicated by Trade.

Twelve villages and small cities in the county serve as trade centers for farm homes precisely as for villages and city homes trading at the same center forms a rural community. Township lines six miles apart indicate distances. Source: C. J. Galpin, *The Social Anatomy of an Agricultural Community,* Research Bulletin 34 (Madison: University of Wisconsin Agricultural Experiment Station, May, 1915).

with a generalized formula of the factors involved in the patterns.

Community areas indicated by services and institutions. The first studies call definite attention to the growing interdependence of village or town and country in Walworth County, Wisconsin (Figure 26). Generalized community areas delineated by trade are represented in map form. Twelve villages and towns serve as centers for country families, precisely as for those who live in the centers. General trade lines were the best single index for determining extent of community relations at the time of this study.

In the original study of 1913, another series of maps showed the areas for such services as banking, newspaper, milk marketing, church, high school, and library. Some of the maps were grotesque in appearance

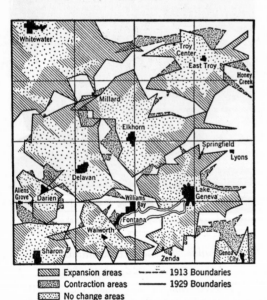

Figure 27. Changes in the
High-School Service Areas.

Source: Kolb and Polson, *Trends in Town-Country Relations*, Research Bulletin 117 (Madison: University of Wisconsin Agricultural Experiment Station, September, 1933).

because certain portions of the country were not included in the service areas, and at other points the boundaries were extended to include only a few family farms. The map of high-school areas, for example, shows that some farms were not included in the areas of some centers, either because of farm children not attending high school or because some of the centers did not have high schools of their own. Even in the early trade-area map, overlapping boundaries were indicated. The influence of differentiation or specialization which will be stressed in the summary can be observed.

Sixteen years after the original study was made, a restudy was undertaken. Expansion was found in service areas when the seven services for each of the twelve centers were carefully compared. No one center, of course, expanded all of its areas, but general expansion took place because of three things: first, there was a more complete coverage of the country, suggesting a greater use of village services and institutions by country people; second, there were encroachments of the larger centers upon territory formerly served by small village or hamlet centers; and third, there was a very appreciable increase in the overlapping of service areas of two or more centers. The library area increased most, while banking and drygoods areas expanded least.

An examination of the whole set of Walworth County maps shows that many service areas are not greatly different in total area from what they were sixteen years before. The majority of changes appear at or near the borders of the old areas, as may be observed in Figure 27, leaving the comparatively large central portions around the larger centers practically unchanged.

A Southern county-seat town and community is St. Matthews, South Carolina (Figure 28), a relatively large center with a large community area. The banking area, however, extends even beyond the community

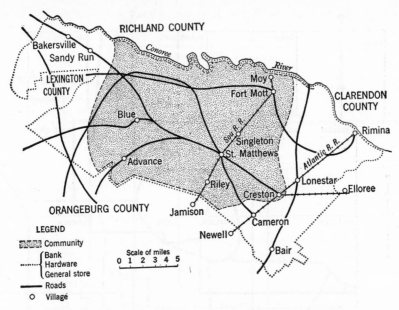

Figure 28. A Southern County-Seat Community.

Large population and possession of the county seat has given St. Matthews a large community area. Its banks exceed even this area and serve the entire county. County lines are, however, effective barriers. Though a neighboring county forces a wedge into St. Matthews County, its banks do not draw many people from the other side of the county lines. Note how all roads lead to the village. Source: Brunner, Hughes, and Patten, *American Agricultural Villages* (New York: George H. Doran, 1927).

area. County boundaries are important in setting the limits of the community area, and highways converging at the center do much to extend as well as to consolidate the area.

Exceptions to the wheel or circular pattern can be found in certain regions where farms, roads, and county lines are laid out on the gridiron pattern with straight lines and right angles because there are few typographical interferences. Hamilton County, Iowa and Ellis County, Kansas are illustrations (Figures 29 and 30). In the Iowa county two kinds of trade relations are indicated, one primary and one secondary. Primary areas are found within the secondary areas, indicating an interdependence of group relations. In the Kansas county the community areas delineated by trade services are larger, while country neighborhoods continue to be the smaller areas of primary relationships.

The general community area and changes in its pattern. In the studies of the 140 agricultural villages, the general community boundary in each case was drawn to include that area from which a majority of the country people came for a majority of their services, such as retail trade, education, or marketing. The boundary line did not necessarily represent exactly the area of any one or more services. Rather, it indicated what could be regarded as the modal area with which any particular service area could then be compared.

Changes in community areas drawn according to the "majority" definition were

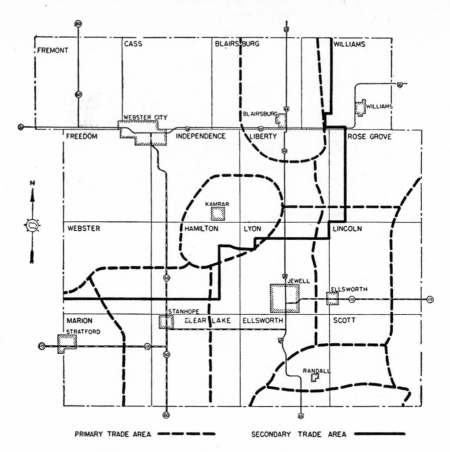

PRIMARY TRADE AREA ▬ ▬ ▬ ▬   SECONDARY TRADE AREA ▬▬▬▬▬

Figure 29. Primary and Secondary Trade
Relationships in Hamilton County, Iowa.

Source: Paul J. Jehlik and Ray E. Wakeley, *Rural Organization in Process,*
Research Bulletin 365 (Ames: Iowa State College Agricultural Experiment
Station, September, 1949).

found in the restudies. Nearly one third of
the community areas had increased significantly between 1930 and 1936. In the Middle West the increases were above this average; in all the other regions they fell below
it. The larger villages expanded their areas
rather more than did the others.

Trade areas were more difficult to determine in 1936 than in the former years of
study, except for such special services as
hardware or banking. General retail trade
tended to be more scattered, and the economic areas for specific villages were less

definite. Areas for regular social and recreation services were more clearly defined
than in the earlier years, but they continued
to be somewhat smaller than the general
trade area. The high school was increasingly
important as a determinant of the community area. More than any other single
service, its area was likely to coincide with
the general community boundary. The importance of this for community organization
will be discussed later in the chapter.

In summary, the American village or small
town is in possession of the major patronage

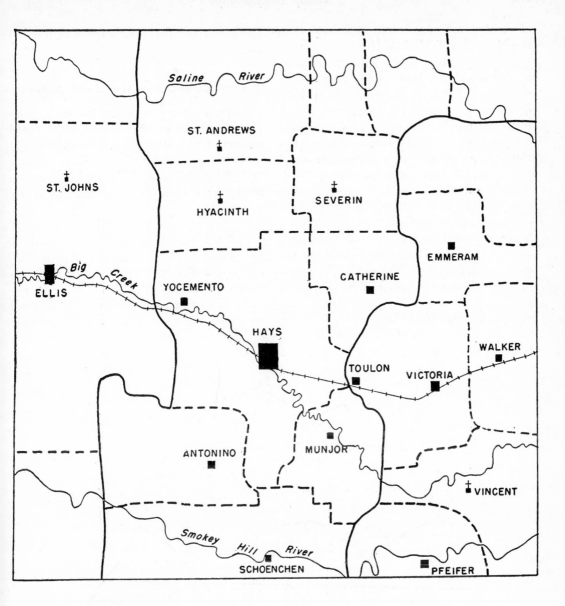

————	COMMUNITIES
– – – –	NEIGHBORHOODS
∿∿∿	STREAMS
✝	COUNTRY CHURCHES

Figure 30. Rural Communities and Country
Neighborhoods in Ellis County, Kansas.

Source: A. H. Anderson and Randall C. Hill, *Rural Communities and
Organizations,* Circular 143 (Manhattan: Kansas Agricultural Experiment
Station, March, 1948).

of rural people for staple groceries, farm machinery, work clothes, hardware, certain types of furniture and clothing, banking, marketing, high school, library, the weekly newspaper, and some forms of recreation. In determining community areas, however, trade lines are less important than they were ten years ago, while the educational, organizational, social, and, to a lesser extent, religious relations are more important. Tendencies for uniting town and country around certain types of functions and institutions, observed and recorded in earlier studies, have continued, but centers of reasonable size and completeness are becoming the rural community centers of today. This is not to say that there is evidence of complete self-sufficiency of any one type of rural community, because the village center is giving way to city centers for such services as ready-to-wear clothing and for specialized

forms of recreation and hospital or medical care.

Rural Communities the World Around

Patterns of similar design but with variations are found in other countries the world around. Unlike the isolated country neighborhoods unique to the Americas, villages and their relations with agrarian people within or outside their borders are nearly universal.

In England. The retail shopping areas of Leeds and Bradford, England (Figure 31), are of a similar pattern to those of Whitman County, Washington. In Leeds there are the market-day customers' areas and the seasonal customers' areas, arranged in concentric circles about the center. Bradford is a smaller center and maintains a secondary

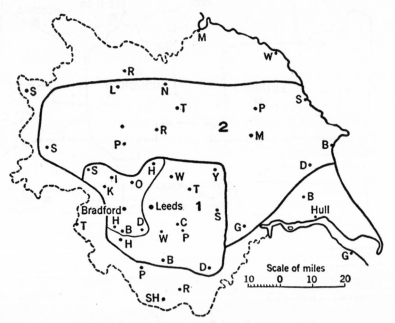

Figure 31. Retail Shopping Areas of Leeds and Bradford, England.

1. Market-day customers' area. 2. Seasonal customers' areas, mainly shopping at Leeds. Source: R. E. Dickinson, *The Regional Functions and Zones of Influence of Leeds and Bradford.* Reprinted from *Geography*, September, 1930.

position in the large area, but has a small
area of its own.

In Australia. A recent study of the country
towns of Victoria shows that the town (and
village by our definition) and the surrounding farm land can be considered as a social
and economic unit. The pattern, however,
is irregular and inconsistent as in other parts
of the world. "The delineation of districts
[areas] was complicated by the illogical distribution of towns and the consequent tendency for districts to overlap; for example,
Dronin and Warragul are only four miles
apart; Dronin is evidently used by part of
the district which also uses Warragul, and
people living in Dronin do much of their
shopping in Warragul." [9]

The authors point out that the war has
complicated the situation even more and suggest that growth and necessary adjustments
will not be a smooth, automatic, painless procedure, but must come as the result of careful planning and effective public education
and action.

In New Zealand. *Littledene* is the story
of a real New Zealand rural community,
though that is not its real name. It is typical
of the country, especially North Island, and
charmingly written, and it leaves no doubt
about the actual social and economic interrelationships of town and country people.
This is fully demonstrated in the occupation
pyramid (Figure 32) showing how Littledene earns its living.[10]

One of the discriminating insights in this
community study is found in a very brief
chapter entitled, "The Great Society and the
Little." The economic depression and the
experience of the war have brought "the

[9] A. J. and J. J. McIntyre, *Country Towns of Victoria* (Melbourne University Press and Oxford University Press, 1944).
[10] H. C. D. Somerset, *Littledene — A New Zealand Rural Community* (New Zealand Council for
Educational Research, 1938).

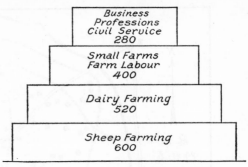

Figure 32. The Occupational Pyramid: How Littledene Earns Its Living.

Drawn to scale, showing the numbers supported from each type of occupation.

Great Society into closer coöperation with
the Little in some unexpected ways." The
young people are learning that to be in-
tolerant with the ways of others is to show
lack of knowledge. One of the interesting
ways this is being learned is through correspondence clubs in which half the pupils
in the upper classes of the local school correspond with children in other parts of the
world, particularly in the United States.

In China. Residences are clustered in the
small villages, but, as Figure 33 shows, there
is the market town with its large market and
trade institutions, its large temple, its new
school, and its railway station. Yao Hwa
Men, the market town, is the community
center for seventy-two small farm villages.
Farmers bring their eggs to the center each
market day and exchange them for the goods
they need. Grain is sold for money at the
grain shop. Each farm village has its own
worship place and the local temples are the
centers for religious activities. The large
worship area covers a radius of twenty-one
li, and the villagers make an annual pil-
grimage to the larger temple at the community center.

Elsewhere in the Orient. The general pattern of China holds for much of the rest of

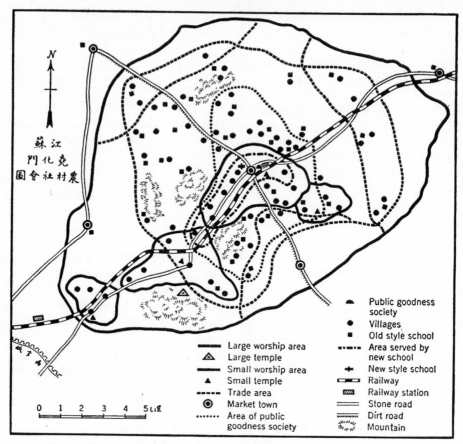

苏江
門化充
園會社村農

▲	Public goodness society
●	Villages
■	Old style school

Large worship area
△ Large temple
Small worship area
▲ Small temple
----- Trade area
◉ Market town
······ Area of public goodness society

·—·—· Area served by new school
✛ New style school
Railway
Railway station
Stone road
Dirt road
Mountain

0 1 2 3 4 5 山里

Figure 33. Service Areas of Yao Hwa Men, Near Nanking China.

The scale of the map is indicated by Chinese li. By using this scale, the distances may be measured from the market center to the different villages. Source: Chiao Chi Ming, *Mapping the Rural Community*, Miscellaneous Series 4 (Nanking, China: University of Nanking, College of Agriculture and Forestry, December, 1924).

the Orient. It grows out of the extreme pressure of population on land, and the consequent small areas of the farms. It is also influenced by the fragmentation of holdings. The area of a single farm operator may consist of from three to six or seven small fields in various parts of the farming area of the village. Under such conditions there is no problem of determining community areas. The farmers live in a cluster of houses at the center. They go out to their fields in the morning and return home in the evening. In a majority of these Oriental communities

the only cattle are work animals, so there is no need for grazing land. The available soil resources cannot support human beings and cattle. The exceptions are in the relatively small areas of low population, such as southeast Asia and parts of Manchuria. As in the United States, there is a direct relationship between population density and community area, and, in the parts of Asia mentioned, between cattle population and area.

In Japan. On northern Hokkaido, the least populated island, farms average five to six times the two and one-half acres of the other islands. There is more dairying on Hokkaido than elsewhere, community areas are larger, and the villages have more services, resulting in less dependence upon the market town.

In Thailand (Siam). As the result of a study in 1930, it was reported that, as a rule, the people are grouped into units which may be described under several headings. The first of these is the village along a stream or river bank; the second is the village scattered among fruit farms on which are homesteads with rice lands beyond; the third is the grouped village of people who farm the surrounding rice fields; the last and least prevalent is the isolated farm.[11]

In Korea. Before the Japanese domination, there were about twenty-six thousand villages, which were very important in the whole scheme of social organization. They formed the central units for communal activities, and were the most characteristic feature of Korean rural life. They were democratic, largely self-contained, and in them family life was deeply rooted.[12] The result of detailed studies of thirty-five carefully selected villages showed that fifteen contained no employed persons except farmers and an occasional policeman, teacher, or preacher. The others had some beginnings of trade, but each made up a social community. The areas of these communities, comprising the village and its fields, varied according to region and population.

The commercial and professional services which an American village offers to the farmers in its contiguous territory are performed in Korea by the market town. There are about 1300 such towns in Korea, in each of which itinerant peddlers every fifth day spread their wares on the sides of the main street for people from villages for miles around to view and buy. Market day is a social institution of great vitality. It takes the place of the newspaper and the lodge. Its frequent recurrence is an economic detriment, as attendance usually means the loss of an entire day's work. The area which these market towns serve is considerable, and quite comparable to the trade area of agricultural villages in the United States, ranging in those visited from 50 to 210 square miles.

In the Pacific islands. The situation, at least among the more primitive societies, and in parts of Africa, is similar to that of the Orient, except that the institution of the market town is less well established, and often is nonexistent. Thus in larger islands like Fiji or New Guinea, there are many communities in the interior whose only contacts outside the village are with near-by villagers. Where there has been some contact with western life, the port towns or cities of the island serve as market towns in varying degrees. In some parts of Africa the location of the village is not fixed. When the soil begins to show signs of exhaustion under the unscientific methods of cultivation, the whole village moves to a new site. Some Indian tribes in North America had this custom.

In some areas of commercialized agriculture, as in the rubber plantations of the Malay States, Africa, and the Dutch East Indies, or the sugar and pineapple plantations of Hawaii, the workers live in village communities under rural conditions, but the plantation usually supplies the function of the market town, and the degree of social organization and sometimes the social utilities available are more complex and more numerous than elsewhere. Western contacts have brought great changes, and some communities are more analogous to the rural industrial communities in the United States.

Two neighbors to the south. In the Argentine, Carl C. Taylor reports that locality groupings range all the way up from geo-

[11] Carle C. Zimmerman, *Siam — Rural Economic Survey, 1930–1931* (Bangkok: The Times Press, Ltd., October, 1931).

[12] Edmund deS. Brunner, *Rural Korea* (New York: International Missionary Council, 1928).

graphically isolated, highly cohesive groups which are easily identifiable as communities or neighborhoods. An even greater number can be classified merely as neighborhoods, and are so transient that an attempt to describe them would be of little value.

Early settlements in the Argentine, unlike those in North America, were not colonies of ethnic groups seeking homes on the land; they were little more than squatters' camps. Immigrants did not come in family groups, but were usually single men. Each new settlement was formed with indigenous Indian groups as nuclei and gradual realignment into semi-agricultural communities. This was facilitated by the rapid mixing of the two racial groups. However, today over 90 per cent of the country's population has its ancestral antecedents in persons who came to the country after 1850. Much good land was allotted before the great tide of these later immigrants arrived; it did not go into family-size farm units, however, but into great holdings running to thousands of acres. Local group patterns had to work against this *estancia* form of farm organization.

Against this historical background, however, the present objective is said to be for the family-size, owner-operated farm. This means a transition from certain types of locality groupings to other types, and there are many variations among the major types of farming areas. In the livestock areas, the large *estancias* do not fit into any neatly patterned locality groups. Such local organization as there is is not for purposes of neighborliness or for community social action, but for convenience of work administration. School, church, and generally town trade centers, are not a part of the *estancia* organization.

In the cereal mixed farming area, locality groups as known in the United States are more or less diffused. The pampa, in which almost the whole cereal belt is located, is an almost flat, unbroken plain with few barriers to communication. Furthermore, none of the nationalities form cliques or retain their old folk-cultures. They have made their adjustments to the agronomic requirements of the area. The uniformity of these adjustments and the flat evenness of the pampa have, as it were, flattened out the social life of the people who live on it.

In other areas where settlement has a fairly long history of family-size farms and where more or less continuous ownership prevails, the usual locality group patterns found elsewhere have developed. Likewise, in areas of geographic isolation, as in the desert oasis settlements like the Eldorado in Misiones, also among the Jewish colonies or in the government-sponsored colonies, local group formation is hastened and highly developed. Especially on the larger oases where population density is great, all three locality groups of neighborhood, local community, and urban centers exist and function as complements each to the other.[13]

From Brazil, T. Lynn Smith reports many similarities between the locality groups of that country and those of North America. One of the reasons for this is that, in the colonization of Brazil as in the settlement of the United States, extensive use was made of single farmsteads. Therefore the farm or *fazenda* stands out as an entity in Minas Geraes as it does in Iowa. Then, the country neighborhood is made up of a relatively small number of families, who live on adjacent farms. The Brazilian village or town, as in parts of the United States, was almost an "afterthought" so far as the early agricultural economy was concerned. It came later to care for the multiplying social and economic needs of rural people. Residences and business places for tradesmen, moneylenders, men skilled in the professions, and workmen of all types are found in the village

[13] Taylor, "Rural Locality Groups in Argentina," *American Sociological Review*, IX, No. 2 (April, 1944).

or town. Here, too, are schools, churches, and recreation institutions. The church is said to be especially important. The farm families who live in surrounding country areas make the village their trading and social center, and in many cases they maintain a "town house" for use on week-ends, holidays, and on occasions of marriages or funerals. The North American expression "go to town" has a counterpart in the Brazilian's "*ir ao commercio*" (go to do business).

There are also differences in relations of rural groups on the two continents. For example, in Brazil the service of the church is more important than trade in delineating community boundaries; therefore the religious areas coincide more closely with those of the general community. As in certain southern portions of the United States, so in Brazil, the village-centered community may embrace large estates, *fazendas,* or plantations which by themselves may be almost large enough to qualify as communities. Often the proprietors have "town houses" in the community center, in addition to their manor houses on the land. It is obvious that the social horizons of these landowners are quite different from those of the laboring classes.

Finally, an increasing tendency is observed for the *municipio*, the Brazilian administrative government unit which would correspond to the North American county, to function as a larger or urban community. Especially in southern Minas Geraes and in Sao Paulo, the local seat of the *municipio* is becoming the economic and social center for rural communities. The fact that Brazil does not allow the *cidade* to separate itself by incorporation from the open country contributes directly to this trend.[14]

An interpretation. Briefly stated, the design and character of rural communities, wherever found, are functions of (1) pressure of population on the land, including systems by which family and farm are interrelated; (2) agrarian practices and traditions, including type of crops and farm management; the factor of crops being related to size of farm. (In the wheat belt, the area of the rural community is seven times greater than that of a community in a fruit-growing region, while the density of population in the fruit area is six times that of the wheat belt.) (3) the degree of impact of industrialization and commercialization upon agricultural and other phases of life, together with proximity of cities; and (4) the region, characterized not only geographically but culturally.

Professor Frederick J. Turner was one of the first to stress this last point in his vivid analysis of the westward movement of the American frontier. Later anthropologists emphasized the whole nexus of value systems which hold groups together, and determine what is important, right, and wrong. The social psychologists and educators gave the community its personality attributes. Viewed against its cultural background, "the community has a pattern. In each of these the individual member can find meanings for his own guidance." [15]

Thus similar conditions produce situations similar to rural community patterns and organizations the world over, and it is possible to distinguish various types ranging from the primitive isolated communities of Africa and the larger islands of the Pacific to the rather highly organized community relationships of country with village and town centers in the United States.

Internal Community Relations

What goes on within its area determines, at least to some extent, the character and

14 Smith, "The Locality Group Structure of Brazil," *American Sociological Review,* IX, No. 1 (February, 1944).

15 J. K. Hart, *Mind in Transition* (New York, 1938), p. 107.

solidarity of the rural community. It must be kept in mind that this community is an emerging, developing group. In the past, rural society was characterized by its country neighborhoods and its village or town settlements, many of which set themselves off by legal incorporation, as was explained in the previous chapter. Now common interests and concerns are bringing the two together.

Many group activities in rural communities may not lend themselves to exact measurement; they are, nevertheless, the very things which give significance to map-making and to tabular analysis. It must be recognized, first of all, that improved travel and communication facilities have enabled country and village people to multiply their contacts in trade, education, recreation, and sociability. Some of these contacts are of the day-by-day character which occur in the market place, in the schoolroom, on the street corner, or in social affairs. Others are contacts of a more fundamental kind, as represented by a condition found in one middle western village of about 1200 population where there were more than 150 village families of retired farmers. In some instances the older children were left on the farm; in others, the younger ones accompanied the parents in order to attend the village school. The retired farmers usually became homeowners in the village, and therefore interested voters, although sometimes reluctant taxpayers. Consequently, lines of cleavage were not so easily found within the village group or between the village and country elements of the community. A further reason for this was that a number of businessmen had spent their childhood on the adjacent farms. Other villagers owned farms and rented them to grown sons of neighboring farmers. So complete had the solidarity become in this community that in 1931 a country neighborhood church, very strong and quite isolated in 1921, had merged with the village church of the same synod, to form one congregational organization. Services were continued in the two places, but the congregations were one. Other local community situations are quite different and "problems" arise.

Status and solidarity in rural communities. The popular way of explaining the problem is that not everyone in a community "counts" the same. This is only another way of saying that not everyone plays the same role, has the same influence, assumes the same responsibilities, participates in the same activities. The extent to which social stratification does disrupt or threaten the solidarity of rural communities cannot be definitely asserted, but a number of most interesting studies of the problem have been made recently.

A "prestige" class rating-chart (Figure 34) was constructed for a New York State rural community. Eleven classes were made on the basis of detailed tests within the community.[16] The characteristics which seemed to distinguish the members of the various classes were (1) nature and extent of participation in formal and informal activities, (2) attitudes regarding certain social questions, and (3) occupation, education, and level of living.

One of the most significant conclusions drawn from a comparison of persons in the various classes was that the concentration of both formal and informal leadership appeared in the upper classes. Fifty-one people were in a position to control most of the formal organizations of the community. The majority of individuals in the lower classes had no organization connections. They had their informal contacts within their kinship groups or in their neighborhoods. It is of importance to note that the social stratifica-

[16] Harold F. Kaufman, *Prestige Classes in a New York Rural Community* (Ithaca: Cornell University Agricultural Experiment Station, Memoir 260, March, 1944).

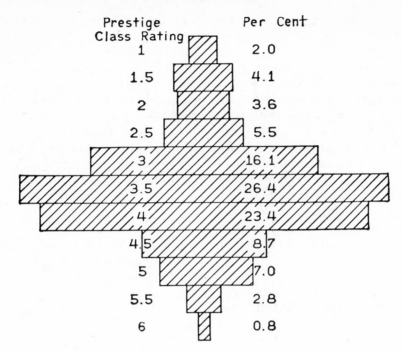

Figure 34. The Class Structure of the Macon Community.

tion was in terms of social participation and social attitudes, many of which were not of a predominantly economic or political nature.

Similar importance was given the place of organizations in rural community relations in other studies. As a result of analyzing the personnel of land-use planning committees in a Kentucky county, the hypothesis was ventured that greatest receptivity to organization programs is found among the "middle" groups of farm people; those on medium-size family farms who engage in a moderate amount of activity in community enterprises are neither apathetic nor highly aggressive in their economic activities, neither wholly detached from family and neighborhood activities nor completely absorbed in them.[17]

Lack of community integration in a Virginia community was attributed to the fact that country neighborhoods were not closely related with the larger community group, that many families, especially those with low incomes, did not participate in activities, and that factionalism was almost a tradition in the community.[18]

Finally, a generalization from such studies of the internal relations of rural community groups should be of great help in better understanding them and working in them. No single factor or set of circumstances determines the responsiveness of persons to the community and its associations. Rather, it is a "network of social influences" among which leadership, organization, and group morale are very important.[19] But leadership,

[17] Howard Beers, *et al.*, *Community Land-Use Planning Committees — Organization, Leadership, and Attitudes, Garrard County, Kentucky, 1939* (Lexington: Bulletin 417, Agricultural Experiment Station, University of Kentucky, 1941).

[18] Edwards, Allen D., *Beaverdam: A Rural Community in Transition* (Blacksburg: Bulletin, 340, Virginia Agricultural Experiment Station, May, 1942).

[19] Hoffer, C. R., and D. L. Gibson, *The Community Situation as It Affects Agricultural Exten-*

as we shall see in the next section, is but one of many group processes — a way of interacting with others.

Similarly, as the result of studying the effects of status on attitudes in a New York rural community, it was concluded that people's attitudes and their group affiliations do not exist in isolation, but in "related patterns" — a pattern of attitudes which appears to concur with certain patterns of group identification. For example: Mr. Jones was conservative in his attitude toward the rights of labor; he believed in a high protective tariff; he was a member of the Republican Party and the local Episcopal church.

Informal grouping arrangements within rural communities. Group solidarity and unity need not be the result of attempts at uniformity or acquiescence in any one plan. Persons assume varying roles in the community as has just been shown, but this process is not simply one of separate individuals relating themselves to the various organizations or activities of the one larger group, the community; they may, and many often do, form themselves into smaller affiliations which in turn may or may not contribute to the solidarity of the whole. One does not attempt to add together these smaller or more informal groupings to arrive at the total larger group. The relationship is much more complex than that. It is a network of interrelations, and unity may be achieved by an emphasis upon the unique rather than the uniform character of the various group relations. This is the formula which Louis Adamic urged as the American contribution to the social culture of the future age. It will be illustrated in the case of the Norwegians in the Prairie community, which follows.

Furthermore, the single person does not acquire his place in the larger community group by climbing up through an imagined hierarchy of small groups, such as the great family, neighborhood, or informal visiting group; he is in fact a participating member of all these group identifications at one and the same time. To be sure, he may not reconcile all such interests into a unity for his own personality or for the groups concerned. This is involved in the problems considered in the previous section.

Communities and neighborhoods, complementary. We have seen that the interrelation of families in neighborhoods and communities is important. Some family contacts come through the neighborhood itself as, when its country school is closed and the officers arrange with the village school board to have the children transported to the village center; or when its country church is yoked with a village church. Other contacts of country-neighborhood people with village or small-town people are direct and personal, as through enrollments in the village high school, membership in village churches, or officership in coöperative business enterprises. Thus the rural community cannot be considered an accumulation of country neighborhoods, nor can neighborhoods and communities be considered as opposing types of relationships; they can be complementary. This kind of pattern was evident in Ellis County, Kansas.

One interesting case is an ethnic group, first and second generation Norwegians in a prairie town and farming community.[20] Although a minority group, they were not under pressure but found themselves free to develop their own social organizations. They were able to maintain an in-group unity with its own cultural heritage and at the

sion Work (East Lansing: Special Bulletin 312, Michigan State College Agricultural Experiment Station, October, 1941).

[20] John and Ruth Hill Useem, "Minority-Group Pattern in Prairie Society," *American Journal of Sociology*, L, No. 5 (March, 1945), p. 377.

same time to achieve a working relationship within the contemporary community.

Tendencies toward community coöperation and conflict. An effort was made to measure the tendencies leading toward coöperation and toward conflict within town-country communities. This was done by the use of materials gathered in the study of the 140 rural communities to which previous reference has been made. Each local community was classed in one of the three categories namely, "coöperative," "neutral," or "in conflict" for each period of study covering an interval of twelve years.

Even if all due allowances are made for personal bias in such a classification, the results point toward a significant trend — that of greater coöperation between village or town and country. More frequent contacts made possible by improved highways are without a doubt an important contributing factor to this. The village had also become a center for many types of activities. Furthermore, farmers had moved into villages, and villagers in many regions had become farm-owners by purchase, inheritance, or foreclosure. The distressed condition of agriculture had done much to create a new sense of relationship and a keener understanding of farmers' problems by the villagers than ever before. Farmers, too, seemed more intelligent regarding problems of readjustment being faced by many businessmen. They had "talked things over." A feeling of mutual interdependence had emerged. This was the explanation given by local community leaders.

Coöperation, however, was not complete. The communities classed as "neutral" left much to be desired, although their number had decreased. Ordinary routine was being followed in the "neutral" communities — going to town, to trade, to market, to church or school — but little was being done to quicken a sense of community interdependence. Things were just taken for granted. In other communities there appeared a tendency among some to guard one's own interests against encroachments, but to remain inactive or neutral in community issues. This might be interpreted as incipient conflict.

Conflict had not disappeared from some of these town and country situations, but it had assumed other forms and features. Sometimes the failure of an attempted mutual enterprise, such as consolidation of town and country schools, produced serious friction. Bank failures, bankruptcy proceedings, or business crises following the financial crash of 1929 exposed old cleavages. More recent conflicts arose over consumer coöperation, rural electrification, relief grants, and demands of organized farmers for parity payments.

In still other situations, tendencies toward conflict were no longer on the older personal basis, but had passed into more impersonal relations, more remotely controlled. An example was the increasing financial and administrative control of local institutions by outside agencies. For stores and banks it was the chain or affiliated organizations; for the marketing agencies it was the coöperative or corporate terminal association; for the newspaper it was the syndicate; for the schools and churches it was the centralized authority of general boards. There were instances where a local representative of the centralized agencies could not seem to gear his decisions and actions with what local people considered to be their local needs. Chain-store managers were charged with a lack of interest in local problems of credit, unemployment, or community organization. School principals were thought to be more sensitive to state or national standards than to local requirements.

Rural communities composed of villages or towns and their surrounding countrysides are in process of developing. They are relationships capable either of fine integration or of controversy. They may constitute the "line of scrimmage"[21] between what is termed the rural and the urban cultures, but they also are a field of rapprochement, as the evidence presented here has amply shown. Conflict need not and often does not lead to disruption, but to closer unity, because issues are clarified and faced. But whether in coöperation or in conflict, rural communities are increasingly fabricating their various strands of life within present-day rural society.

Rural Community Organization — Consensus and Action

Community fabrication requires a degree of agreement and action. The Australians conclude their report of the social survey of country towns by suggesting that community effort is a sort of medley — a mixture of kindliness, bitterness, generosity, meanness. The end is to dispel the antipathy which so frequently exists between the good of the few and the good of the many, and the harm that the many may be indirectly causing in refusing to unite and plan for their own benefit.

It must be emphasized that community organization in present-day North American rural life is almost entirely dependent upon the voluntary, deliberate effort of leaders and citizens. This is in sharp contrast to the village type of economy, described earlier, characterizing much of the rural life of the Orient, Europe, and New England. As has been shown, the modern rural community is permeated with separate institutions and agencies of many kinds and purposes, such as education, religion, recreation, agriculture. Some measure of local organization and coördination is needed.

[21] T. Lynn Smith, "The Rôle of the Village," *Rural Sociology,* VII, No. 1, p. 21 (March, 1942).

The issue is squarely before rural people today, farmers and villagers alike, as to whether they will organize a community of sufficient size and solidarity to give them the social utilities and institutions which they feel they need, and at the same time develop a point of view which will be recognized in larger political, educational, and religious spheres. National and state politics, as well as urban educational and religious interests, have used disorganized rural society too long as a pawn in issues in which local rural interests are little concerned, if at all. If democracy is to be preserved in government as well as in the other great functions of life, rural local opinion and action must be made more effective. Citizens must assume greater part in public policy.

The argument runs even deeper. Some leaders of social thought raise serious question as to whether a civilization can be built apart from local, primary, or personal groups. They claim that social stability does not develop without it and social control is not effective apart from it.

General "lay-out" of the community. The general structure or lay-out of the community must conform in workable measure with the functions to be performed. It was pointed out earlier in the chapter that three factors were associated with service functions in the patterns of group relationship, namely, population, area, and distance. The implication is that to perform essential minimum functions, any community must have sufficient people living in a center and the surrounding accessible area. If one factor is limited — for example, if the population in the center is small — then there must be compensation in the extent or population density of the tributary area. If centers are too close together, they must either combine for certain functions or services, including institutions, or deliberately bulge their areas in opposite directions in order to gain the required space. This is the principle of unit requirements, and simply means that the community must consider its terms of reference in order to organize and maintain certain service agencies and social institutions. In agricultural circles it is necessary to know how large a volume of business is essential to the effective operation of a creamery. It is equally essential that rural communities know what basic requirements must be met in order to constitute a community in contemporary rural society.

Illustrations of such unit requirements are readily available. Some years ago it was determined that within counties of central and southern Wisconsin, at least 1250 people would be required to maintain a minimum enrollment of 100 pupils in high school, assuming that all those of high-school age actually would attend.[22] That number would probably have to be increased because of present trends, but it was calculated that the 1250 people would require an area of about 41.7 square miles when all the centers of 3000 population were excluded, an area slightly larger than the conventional township.

Or, one could start from some other premise, as a committee on postwar agriculture did. Its report states that, as a measure of size and strength, a rural community must be large enough and strong enough to provide not only elementary, but secondary or high-school education, and also some adult education for all its people.[23] The high school, the report insists, must have at least six or seven teachers in order to offer a course of study varied and vital enough to match the backgrounds, interests, and future needs of all rural youth. Teachers, the

committee believes, are the important desiderata in regard to schools. With such a minimum, a locality can readily determine required enrollment by a pupil-teacher ratio, population constituency, yearly budget, tax rate, evaluation of district, and building requirements. If it is unable or unwilling to provide these minimum requirements, it cannot lay claim to being a full-fledged community in its own right; it will need to join with another, do its part, but not attempt to "go it alone."

Internal readjustments. Even in those studies to which reference has been made, where the focus of attention was upon different classes and status, the conclusions are unanimous that there is need of wider participation to increase community identification and consciousness. To neglect this is to miss the whole lesson of our democratic tradition. Moreover, if group experiences and interactions have the power of therapy, as Doctor J. L. Moreno [24] attests for those disturbed or in conflict with themselves or with others, they should also strengthen those normal individuals who would achieve stronger and healthier communities by the ordinary day-to-day and week-to-week associations within their own localities.

Unfortunately, such high ideals are yet to be realized in many a local rural community. On the debit side, some researches report that even churches and schools perpetuate class lines and accentuate differences, thus setting children and their families apart from each other and the common life of the community.[25]

"Generally speaking, the church has lagged in the realignment of smaller centers

[22] J. H. Kolb, *Service Institutions for Town and Country* (Madison: University of Wisconsin, Research Bulletin 66, Agricultural Experiment Station, December, 1925).

[23] *Rural Communities of Wisconsin* (Madison: College of Agriculture, Circular 353, Extension Service, January, 1945).

[24] *Who Shall Survive?* (Washington, D.C.: Nervous and Mental Disease Publication Company, 1934).

[25] Edith Jeffers Freeman, *Social Class as a Factor in the Family Group Relations of Certain New York Farm Families* (Ithaca: Cornell University Abstracts of Theses, 1943).

to form larger and stronger community groups." [26]

"The school occupies an interesting place in this course of events; despite its rational curriculum, it was not the effective cause of change. Indeed, careful perusal of school records shows that there have been no major curriculum innovations in perhaps fifty years." [27]

Opportunity still knocks at the door of the high school. A unique opportunity for leadership in this emerging village or town-country community presents itself to the high school. Ten and twenty years ago retail trade was a ready means for determining boundaries of rural communities. Today retail trade is broken up in its distribution between village or town center to city center, but the high school rises to a place of significance, not only in delineation of community areas, but in determining trade and social contacts. May not the high school, with its courses in agriculture, home economics, commerce, music, drama, and the arts, as well as its regular academic work, become the focalizing institution for both youth and adult in a round-the-year program for the rural communities of tomorrow?

Readjustments are on the way. In the restudy of Walworth County, Wisconsin, covering a span of nearly forty years, the conclusion was reached that a recognized educational system including elementary and secondary schools and libraries might become the one general and public instrumentality to consolidate the trend toward a growing interdependent town and country relationship.

In New York State, the policy for central-

izing rural schools is posited on the theory that they should be community-centered. Dr. Dwight Sanderson, of Cornell University, emphatically stated that if school consolidation is effected on the sole basis of so-called efficiency, either as to cost or curriculum, the importance of the community relation tends to be ignored. He argued that placing the school outside the community setting alienates community interest and control, and that the pupil is in much the same relation to it as the rural patron is to a city department store — he goes to a school which is outside his area of experience and his natural ties to buy a certain type of schooling.[28]

Formal community organization can help. Consensus and action, the goals of community endeavor, can be enhanced, not only by informal means, but by tested social mechanisms of organization and promotion. Professor Wileden defines rural community organization as the deliberate and voluntary coördinating, integrating, and at times subordinating of various interests, activities, even classes within the community, by fixing the emphasis upon common ends and the attainment of satisfactions for all.[29]

Permanent organization is not always necessary. There may be special means for particular objectives. Rural communities in many states have set up planning committees, meetings, or temporary organizations to prepare postwar programs. Formal community organization, on the other hand, may proceed either by direct or indirect method.[30] The direct method is for all members of the

[26] Harold Hoffsommer, "The Relation of Rural Churches to Other Social Organizations," *Social Forces* (December, 1941).

[27] Herbert Passin and John W. Bennett, "Changing Agricultural Magic in Southern Illinois: A Systematic Analysis of Folk-Urban Transition," *Social Forces* (October, 1943).

[28] "Criteria of Rural Community Formation," *Rural Sociology* (December, 1939); E. T. Stromberg, *The Influence of the Central Rural School on Community Organization*, Bulletin 699 (Ithaca: Cornell University Experiment Station, 1938).

[29] A. F. Wileden, *Rural Community Organization* (Madison: College of Agriculture, University of Wisconsin).

[30] Dwight Sanderson and R. A. Polson, *Rural Community Organization* (New York: Wiley, 1939).

community to participate as individuals, in meetings, committees of the whole, or in an organized association with constitution and officers. The traditional form for this direct means is the New England town meeting. The indirect method is framed on the principle of a representative democracy in which a community council is composed of representative groups concerned. The representatives in question may be selected on an area basis, from special-interest organizations, social institutions, age groups, or some agreed combination.

A more formal definition of a community council geared to exigencies of the postwar situation is the following:

A community council is a body of responsible citizens representing the organizations, agencies, and major interests of the community. Its chief functions are to co-ordinate, to plan, to inform, and to act in the interest of the total community. Through a successful council a community can often do for itself what an agency cannot accomplish alone. A good council also increases the amount of social participation and develops leadership. Morale is built by the successful functioning of a council.[31]

Organization presupposes what is popularly recognized as leadership; indeed the two are but aspects of the same relationship. Stable organization is dependent upon recognized responses among those individuals who compose it. This recognition may depend upon personal qualities, social position determined by means of prestige described earlier, or it may be determined by affiliations or other relations which have thus far defied isolation and accurate measurement. In any case, there must be some agreement as to what qualities are to be regarded as "high" or "low," what values or goals are

to be sought.[32] This is at the very basis of group organization. In an organization system different persons represent different roles; some have authority over others; some have obligations toward others, and so on. Leadership, therefore, as was suggested earlier, is a group process in which persons interact with other persons within a recognized relationship of social values.

Inter-Community Relations

The Great Society has its roots not only in "Littledene," New Zealand but in every other rural and urban community as well. No local community exists by itself. This should be clear from the evidence already presented. However, in closing the chapter, a brief discussion of this important and often neglected trend is in order.

Proportion of country people in community areas correlates with size of centers. The Hamilton County, Iowa, situation previously described provides an opportunity to observe not only different kinds of trade relations but also the necessary corollary concerning the numbers of people and establishments involved. There is a positive relation between the number of people in the centers and in their tributary areas. The proportion shifts at Jewell, a center of 1051 people. At this point in an imaginary curve, the two population components of the community are about equal. As one goes toward the smaller centers, the proportion of country people becomes larger. In the other direction, toward the large center, Webster City, the proportion of country people drops to about half the number in the city. The number of agencies climbs steadily from the smaller to the larger centers, indicating specialization and interdependence.

[31] Edmund deS. Brunner, *The What and How of Community Councils* (Washington, D.C.: Extension Service Circular 403, United States Department of Agriculture, March, 1943); *Community Organization and Adult Education* (Chapel Hill: University of North Carolina Press, 1942).

[32] Charles P. Loomis and Douglas Ensminger, "Governmental Administration and Informal Local Groups," *Applied Anthropology* (January-March, 1942).

Kinds of town-country contacts vary with types of centers. The more than 20,000 contacts reported by a representative sample of country families in the Walworth County restudy were distributed among forty-three different centers. The centers ranged from small country or hamlet neighborhoods to cities like Milwaukee and Chicago. When all the contacts are plotted among all centers, the curve rises steeply between centers of 400 and 15,000 but reaches its peak of 50 per cent at 3,000 population. The trade contacts and the social contacts are contrasted in the graph. The social contacts, it will be noticed, have a lower peak of 40 per cent at the 3,000 population point (Figure 35) since there is a larger proportion in the smaller centers and a much smaller proportion in the larger centers. In fact, 16 per cent of

all social contacts are in centers of less than 200 people, and another 16 per cent in centers of between 200 and 500 population. On the other hand, only 6 per cent of the trade contacts take place in centers of less than 500, while 54 per cent are carried on in places of 2000 to 10,000 population.

On the basis of an analysis of contacts, centers can be typed and characteristic clusters of contacts in each type observed as indicated below.

Generalized types of centers correlated with size and services. Just as variations exist in the functions of various centers in rural society, so these differences are also found to be related to the population of the center and to the pattern of the area itself. This is another way of saying that by proc-

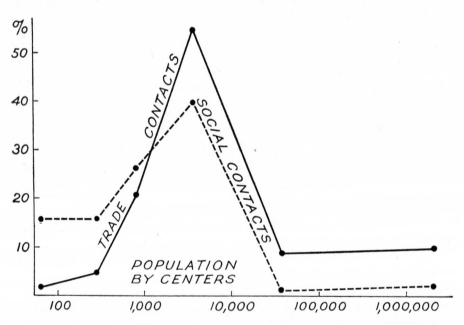

Figure 35. Trade and Social Contacts Distributed Among all Centers.

Trade contacts are more characteristic of the larger, and social contacts of the smaller centers. Population shown along the horizontal base line is in terms of a logarithmic scale in which multiples of ten occupy equal intervals. Source: John H. Kolb and LeRoy J. Day, *Interdependence in Town and Country Relations in Rural Society,* Research Bulletin 172 (Madison: University of Wisconsin Agricultural Experiment Station, December, 1950).

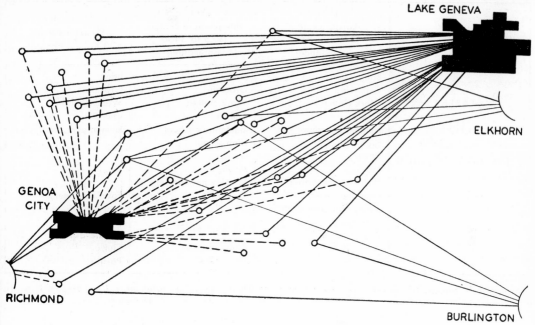

Figure 36. Sociogram showing complementary character in terms of social contacts, of a smaller center, Genoa City, and an intermediate center, Lake Geneva.

Source: John H. Kolb and LeRoy J. Day, *Interdependence in Town and Country Relations in Rural Society,* Research Bulletin 172 (Madison: University of Wisconsin Agricultural Experiment Station, December, 1950).

esses of differentiation and specialization, made possible by greatly increased facilities for communication and transportation, the modern trend is toward the accumulation of certain utilities in certain types of centers. It is possible, therefore, to devise a generalized scheme of classification.[33]

(1) *The single, simple service type.* This type of center is usually an open-country neighborhood or hamlet center where single and comparatively simple or undifferentiated services are performed. The agencies in such centers may be school, church, general store, Grange hall, or repair shop. The

[33] Figures will differ for various regions of the country, but they can serve as a general basis for comparison and discussion of varying situations.

centers usually fall into the hamlet classification; that is, places of less than 250 population.

(2) *The limited, simple service type.* This type of service center may range in size from about 200 to 400 or 500 people. Villages in this class fall short of providing what may be termed a "six-service standard"; that is, having agencies in all of the following groups of services: economic, educational, religious, social, communication, professional.

(3) *The semi-complete, intermediate type.* This type of center averages about 800 to 1000 people with a range from about 400 to over 1200. In certain middle-western states it is the most frequent type. It is intermediate

	TYPE I Larger centers (2400 to 3700 population)	TYPE II Intermediate centers (975 to 3400 population)	TYPE III Smaller centers (600 to 875 population)
TABLE **38** Types of Centers and Characteristic Contacts	Bank Groceries Work clothes Church Elementary school High School Library Movies Weekly newspaper Farm machinery Men's and women's clothing Public dances	Bank Groceries Work clothes Church Elementary school High school Library Movies Weekly newspaper Clubs	Bank Groceries Work clothes Church Elementary school Farm machinery Private dances Clubs Parties

Source: J. H. Kolb and LeRoy J. Day, *Interdependence in Town and Country Relations in Rural Society,* Research Bulletin 172 (Madison: University of Wisconsin Agricultural Experiment Station, December, 1950).

because it stands between the type last mentioned and the larger centers, some of which are county-seat towns. It is semi-complete because it is frequently lacking in fulfillment of the six-service standard. It may have a bus line, but no railroad; a high school, but a small one; a market, but with inadequate processing agencies for raw products. Its trade area is relatively large and its merchandising agencies frequently draw as much as 75 per cent of their business from farm sources.

(4) *The complete, partially specialized type.* This type averages about 2500 or more persons and may range from 1200 to 5000, or just a little over. Its agencies are numerous enough to cover all the more common needs, and differentiated enough to take on specialized characteristics. Its services are often rendered on a less personal basis than in the small centers. Together with its tributary community area, it has some elements of functional self-sufficiency. If the population in the center ranged from 1000 to 2500, within limits and in regions of general farming, one would expect to find

about an equal number of people in the tributary country area.

(5) *The urban, highly specialized type.* This type, which needs further sub-classification, is represented by the larger town and the city. The interests assume larger proportions and are divided into such functions as manufacturing, wholesaling, and financing. They are the centers in which farmers and their wives, as well as villagers, shop when quality, variety, and opportunity for a wide and discriminating selection are wanted. They cannot cater to general trade needs as the small town can; they specialize to a higher degree. The farmer does not look for spools of barbed wire on the city square, but his wife does shop there for some of her choice, ready-to-wear clothing — at least, she likes to do her window-shopping there.

Conventionalized pattern with the four factors involved. In order to generalize the situation still further, a graph was drawn to indicate the service areas surrounding the various types of centers. For the smaller

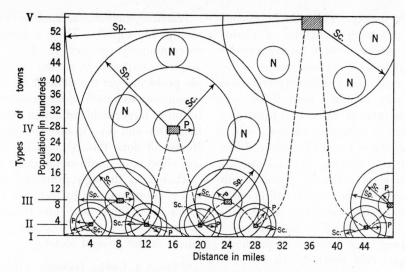

Figure 37. A Theoretical Graph Indicating the Interrelation of Rural Group Areas and Types of Service Centers.

Type I. Single service (neighborhood or hamlet). *Type II.* Limited and simple service (small village). *Type III.* Semi-complete or intermediate (village or small town). *Type IV.* Complete and particularly specialized (town or small city). *Type V.* Urban and highly specialized (city). P. Primary Service Area; Sc. Secondary Service Area; Sp. Specialized Service Area; N. Country Neighborhood Area. Source: J. H. Kolb, *Service Relations of Town and Country,* Research Bulletin 58 (Madison: University of Wisconsin Agricultural Experiment Station, December, 1923).

places there was very little difference in size between the general community area and the specialized area, if indeed a specialized type of service area was present at all. By contrast, the larger city center does not have the primary or personal area, and its general area is relatively small, while its specialized area extends far out to include most of the areas of the smaller centers. Neighborhoods or hamlet centers appear near the periphery of the larger community areas, while they tend to cluster on the outskirts of the larger city.

It should be evident, therefore, that an association does exist in this pattern of service relationships which involves four factors: first, size of center in terms of population; second, type of center in terms of its aggregate institutions and agencies; third, size

and conformation of the service areas; and fourth, distances between the centers.

A dotted hill-and-valley-shaped line connects the various types of centers in the graph (Figure 37). This line might be considered the "great American highway." Every farmer's gate opens onto this highway, which extends beyond his "home town" to the other centers, large and small. Not only the farmer, but also the villager and the city dweller are using this highway; the traffic is in two directions. The highway, symbol of communication, becomes the means for community as well as inter-community relations.

This is but another way to summarize and to emphasize that rural communities are not for purposes of limiting or fencing in but for introducing and relating their members to the larger society. This can be accomplished by observing principles of comity and of coöperation. Comity means courtesy between equals; coöperation means acting jointly. Some internal community and some inter-community relations must follow one and some the other of these two principles. For example, in religious matters, where church congregations are of widely differing cultural and theological backgrounds, obviously common action is possible only through comity. On the other hand, in enterprises for coöperative marketing and buying or for providing recreation and education facilities, where large volumes of participation and equal cost burdens are essential, then joint action and inter-community coöperation must be undertaken.

Practical successes in such endeavors are multiplying rapidly. There is the story of a six-community project in Utah, for example.[34] Experiences gained in solving simple problems, yet too difficult for any single community to handle alone, soon were transferred to larger fields of action in education, irrigation, and even in one cemetery district. It was all done through organized coöperative effort on a "multi-community" basis.

Therefore, through principles of comity and coöperation, and by means of communication, community and inter-community relations may be social reality and be part and parcel of the general society.

[34] Joseph A. Geddes, *Institution Building in Utah* (Logan: Utah State Agricultural College, 1949).

TOPICS FOR DISCUSSION

1. Consider again a household, rural or urban, with which you are well acquainted. Indicate its location and then, by use of six arrows drawn so as to indicate the direction and distance, show the location of centers to which members of this household go for each of the following services: (You may have to split some arrows if more than one center is used for some services.)
   a. Economic — marketing, merchandising, financing.
   b. Religious — church, religious education, organizations.
   c. Education — school, high school, library.
   d. Social — sociability, recreation, welfare.
   e. Communication — mail service, telephone, newspaper.
   f. Professional — doctor, lawyer, dentist.
2. Draft in general form the general community or service area of the "home town" village you have described in the previous chapter. Sketch the areas of each of the six services listed in the previous exercise if they differ from the general community area. (The general community area shall be defined as that area from which a majority of the families come to the village for a majority of their services.)
3. What does Doctor Galpin mean by "rurbanism"? State your agreement or disagreement with this idea.
4. What difficulties and inhibitions need to be overcome in drawing farmers and villagers into larger community arrangements? Illustrate.
5. Describe in detail an effective plan for rural community organization which you have observed or read about. What are its chief elements of strength, and what are its deficiencies?

REFERENCE READINGS

Arensberg, C. M., *The Irish Countryman.* New York: Macmillan, 1937. An anthropological study.

Brunner, Hughes, and Patton, *American Agricultural Villages.* New York: Doubleday, Doran, 1927. A report of field research of 140 agricultural village communities made in 1924.

Burchfield, LaVerne, *Our Rural Communities.* Chicago: Public Administration Service, 1947.

Chapin, F. Stuart, *Community Leadership and Opinion in Red Wing (Minnesota).* Minneapolis: University of Minnesota Press, 1945. A study of the impact of war. Bulletin 3 in the series, *The Community Basis for Postwar Planning.*

Farm Security Administration, *Small Town Manual for Community Action,* Industrial Series, No. 4, Washington, 1942.

Galpin, C. J., *Rural Life,* chap. IV. New York: Century, 1918. Original study of Walworth County, in which was developed the concept of the rurban community.

Halbert, Blanche, *Community Buildings for Farm Families,* Farmers' Bulletin 1804. Washington: U.S. Dept. of Agriculture, 1938.

Hay, Donald G., and Robert A. Polson, *Rural Organizations in Oneida County,* Bulletin 871. Ithaca, N.Y.: Cornell Agricultural Experiment Station, May, 1951.

Hillman, Arthur, *Community Organization and Planning.* New York: Macmillan, 1950.

Hirsch, G. P., "Rural Social Organization: An Introduction. III. The Methods and Techniques," VI, No. 3. Oxford, Eng.: The Agricultural Economics Research Institute, 1951.

Kolb, J. H., *Service Relations of Town and Country,* Research Bulletin 58, 1923; *Service Institutions for Town and Country,* Research Bulletin 66, 1925; *Trends in Town-Country Relations,* Research Bulletin 117, 1933. Madison: Wisconsin Agricultural Experiment Station.

Kumlien, W. F., *Community School Districts in the Making,* Bulletin 404. Brookings: South Dakota State College, June, 1950.

Leao, A. Carneiro, "Rural Brazil," *Rural Sociology,* IX, No. 2, June, 1944.

Leonard, Olen E., "Bolivian Locality Groups," *Rural Sociology,* XIV, No. 3, September, 1949.

Leonard, Olen E., *Santa Cruz: A Socioeconomic Study of An Area in Bolivia,* Foreign Agriculture Report No. 31, Washington, D.C., October, 1949.

Lindstrom, David E., "Rural Community in Sweden," *Rural Sociology,* XVI, No. 1, March, 1951.

Loomis, Charles P., "Extension Work at Tingo Maria, Peru," *Applied Anthropology,* III, No. 1, December, 1943.

Lynch, Russell W., *Czech Farmers in Oklahoma.* Stillwater: Oklahoma A. and M. College, Bulletin, XXXIX, No. 13, 1942.

Miner, Horace, "A New Epoch in Rural Quebec," *American Journal of Sociology,* LVI, No. 1, July, 1950. A restudy of the community St. Denis.

Morgan, Arthur, *The Small Community.* New York: Harper, 1942. An interesting statement of the place of small communities in our contemporary society by an engineer and administrator.

Sanders, Irwin T., *Making Good Communities Better, Handbook in Social Engineering.* Lexington: University of Kentucky Press, 1951.

Sanderson, Dwight, *Leadership for Rural Life.* New York: Association Press, 1940. A very good beginning analysis from both practical and theoretical aspects.

Sanderson, Dwight, *The Rural Community.* Boston: Ginn, 1932. Note particularly chaps. 1 and 2, 10, 11 and 12, 15 and 16. This is a thorough study of the rural community as a population group.

Sarkar, Benoy Kumar, *Villages and Towns as Social Patterns.* Calcutta: Chuckervertty, Chatterjee and Co., Ltd., 1941. A study in the processes and forms of societal transformation and progress.

Stacy, W. H., *Guides for Building your Tomorrow's Community.* Ames: Iowa State College, Agricultural Extension Service, September, 1949.

West, James, *Plainville, U.S.A.* New York: Columbia University Press, 1945. A detailed study of a local rural community in Missouri. All names including the author's are fictionalized.

Wilson, Warren H., *The Evolution of the Rural Community.* Boston: Pilgrim Press, 1923. A very good discussion of the development or evolution of rural society.

Young, Hsin-Pao, "Agricultural Planning with the Chinese," *Rural Sociology,* March, 1945.

Zimmerman, Carle C., *The Changing Community.* New York: Harper, 1938. A summary of modern trends with excellent case studies of individual communities.

FILMS

Community Resources in Teaching S, 20. Techniques for use of community resources. University of Iowa.

Developing Leadership S, 10. Coronet.

U.S.A. Community and Its Citizens. S, 20. A typical community being surveyed. United World.

15 Rural Interest Groups and Classes

RURAL SOCIETY is made up of many different kinds of groups. As has been shown, neighborhoods, villages, and communities all have their place, but within them or cutting across their boundaries are other groups such as farmers' clubs, homemakers' clubs, 4-H clubs, spray rings, parent-teacher associations, choral and dramatic clubs, young people's and old people's societies, breeders' associations, coöperative buying and selling organizations, informal groups, cliques, congeniality groups, and many, many others. These groups are not characterized so much by their recognized locations as by their activities and the special purposes or interests which they represent.

Interest groups arise out of likenesses and differences in age, sex, occupation, tradition, experience, choice, propensity, intent, and so on. They may be contrasted with locality groups, which have lateral or geographic dimensions whereas interest groups have perpendicular or voluntary dimensions. Locality groups depend upon common life, proximity, residence in a recognized area. Interest groups depend upon polarity, promotion, narrowed concerns, special leadership, directed effort. This polarity implies fields of magnetic influence. When released from locality restrictions, certain people are attracted to certain of these poles of interest. The old phrase "Birds of a feather flock together" conveys the idea very well indeed. Some wag has added, "And they sit a long time," which simply means that when people are thus drawn together into groups of con-

genial interest they tend to want to stay together.

While there is a very wide variety of interest groups in rural society, it is possible to bring them together into generalized types for purposes of discussion. They can be considered in terms of the purposes or functions they seek to serve or the kind of forms or structures they assume. For example, they may be formal or informal in their organization. The more formal are known as associations and usually have officers, a constitution, and an accepted procedure. The more informal are obviously less standardized and take such forms as friendships, coteries, gangs, or cliques. The clique may be considered as a unit beyond the family in social class formation, and like the neighborhood it has primary or personal relations. The emphasis is upon exclusiveness and selectiveness as well as smallness. The extent to which class formation leads on to stricter stratification and definite divisions in rural society is a question which will have to be considered with care, and cannot be fully answered until more evidence is available as the result of more studies.

The parts which small groups such as kinship, visiting, and exchange groups play in neighborhood life have been observed in an earlier chapter; likewise the problems which prestige classes present for those interested in community organization. In this chapter various interest groups will be described in their wider implications for rural society as a whole. Many interest groups have been

239

characteristic of American society from its very beginning.

Origin of Interest Groups

Americans have a penchant for organizations and associations, at least so many foreign critics say. A gibe of one such critic is to the effect that whenever two or three Americans get together, they soon organize, elect officers, adopt a constitution, and appoint committees. Although this is obviously an exaggeration, it does suggest something of the part which organized groups of many kinds have played and continue to play in this country.

A very brief excerpt from just one foreign writer will serve as an illustration. The Frenchman, de Tocqueville, was greatly impressed by the many organizations and societies which were common in an early period. He wrote:

Americans of all ages, all conditions, and all dispositions constantly form associations. They have not only commercial and manufacturing companies in which all take part, but they have associations of a thousand other kinds — religious, moral, serious, futile, general or restricted, enormous or diminutive. The Americans make associations to give entertainments, to found seminaries, to build inns, to construct churches, to diffuse books, to send missionaries to the antipodes. . . . Wherever, at the head of some new undertaking you see government in France, or a man of rank in England, in the United States you will be sure to find an association.[1]

It may well be that this tendency to join hands in the prosecution of common interests is an essential part of a democratic society. Frederick Jackson Turner, the great historian of the American frontier, was quick to see the role which such voluntary groups played in the opening and the developing of new territory by the pioneers. In a characteristic paragraph, Professor Turner says:

From the very first, it became evident that these men had means of supplementing their individual activity by informal combinations. One of the things that impressed all early travelers in the United States was the capacity for extra-legal voluntary associations. This power of the newly arrived pioneers to join together for a common end without the intervention of governmental institutions was one of their marked characteristics. The log-rolling, the house-raising, the husking-bee and apple-paring and the squatters' associations whereby they protected themselves against the speculators in securing titles to their clearings on the public domain, the camp meeting, the mining camp, the vigilantes, the cattle-raisers' associations, the "gentlemen's agreements," are a few of the indications of this attitude.[2]

This tendency toward many forms of organization did not decline with the recession of the frontier. It is a factor of importance in rural society at the present time for, as Professor Turner emphasizes, its origin is not one of tradition and custom, but of initiative and voluntary action. He continues:

It is well to emphasize this American trait, because in a modified way it has come to be one of the most characteristic and important features of the United States today. America does through informal association and understanding on the part of the people many of the things which in the Old World are and can be done only by governmental intervention and compulsion. These associations were in America not due to immemorial custom of tribe or village community. They were extemporized by voluntary action.

Much, but by no means all of this voluntary action took on neighborhood and community patterns in our earlier society, as has been pointed out previously. In a more modern society, group action can assume

---

[1] Alexis de Tocqueville, *Democracy in America* (tr. Henry Reeve, 1876), I, p. 242.

[2] *The Frontier in American History* (New York, Holt, 1921), p. 343.

greater differentiation and associational character. In pioneer neighborhoods, and in small villages and communities, there were so many common interests that group organization could be relatively simple, differentiations few, and nearly everyone could be included in the general plan of activities. As shown earlier, active neighborhoods today are characterized more by planned activities and social institutions than merely by nearness of residence or traditional ways of life. However, field work experiences indicate that many of the newer forms of

interest groups spring from the soil of older neighborhoods. They are found more frequently than elsewhere in social situations where earlier group experiences serve as background for current group life.

Interest Groups in Modern Rural Society

The transfer in emphasis from locality to interest groups, and from generally accepted to contractual forms of association through promotion, is a significant trend. In recent times such associations have been increasing

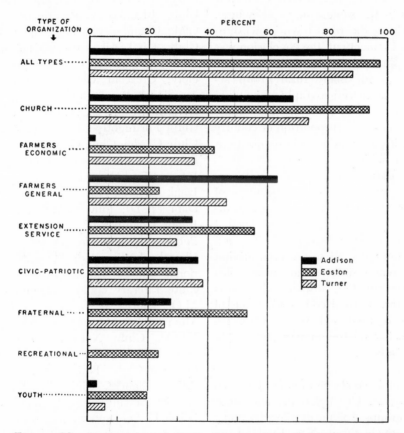

Figure 38. Percentage of Open-Country Households in Selected Maine Towns Participating in Types of Formal Organizations, 1947.

Source: Donald G. Hay, Douglas Ensminger, Stacy R. Miller, and Edmond J. Lebrun, *Rural Organizations in Three Maine Towns,* Maine Extension Bulletin No. 391 (U.S. Department of Agriculture, Bureau of Agricultural Economics, June, 1949).

in number and variety, in strength of control over their members, and in the pressure for privilege which they exert on general society. This has been due not only to greatly improved means of individual communication and transportation but also to the expanded use of techniques for mass communication and propaganda.

The trend is general throughout rural society, although the interests as well as the forms which the association takes may be different from region to region. One might expect this trend in the newer sections of the country, but it was observed in New England about the same time as elsewhere. From a study of the rural town (township) of Lebanon, Connecticut, the conclusion was drawn that similarity of interests is a more workable basis for many rural group arrangements than mere geographical juxtaposition.[3] A more recent study of three Maine towns indicates a high proportion of country families participating in formal organizations even though neighborhoods and communities were reported as important and continuing locality groups. The distribution of participation among the various types of organizations shown in Figure 38 indicates that those which are church-centered are in a strong position while those centered around youth or recreation interests are weak. This represents the situation in many other parts of the country. Formal education, levels of living, and occupational status were reported as being related to participation in these organizations.

Varieties in interests and kinds of groups which they form. Other varieties and kinds of interest groups can be displayed against the comparatively simple New England design. First to be enumerated is a long list of organizations to which adult members of

families in Valley View belong. Valley View, a pseudonym for an interior plains town-country community of about 3000 people, located twenty-six miles from a city of 100,000 population, was settled in 1870 by Czech immigrants and New England "Yankees." Here is the almost unbelievably long list of organizations recorded:

Altar Society; American Federation of Labor; American Legion; American Association of University Women (AAUW); Art Study Club; Auxiliary, American Legion; Auxiliary, Trinity Episcopal Church; Auxiliary, Veterans of Foreign Wars; Bepah Club; Birthday Club; Birthday Pinochle Club; Chamber of Commerce; Child Study Club; Civil Air Patrol; Contract Bridge Club; Cottonwood County Agricultural Society; Crescent Club; Daughters of the American Revolution; Delt Rite Club; D.W.C.N. Club; E.O.T. Club; E.T.P. Sewing Club; Fortnightly Club; Four Acres Bridge Club; Garden Club; Grandma Club; Hillside Pinochle Club; Home Improvement Club; International Order of Odd Fellows (IOOF); Izaak Walton League; Jednota Ceskych Dam (JCD); Jolly Twelve Pinochle Club; Junior Chamber of Commerce; Knights of Pythias; Ladies Aid, Bethlehem Lutheran Church; Ladies Aid, Plymouth Congregational Church; L.C.W. Bridge Club; Lions Club; Literary Guild; M.C. Pinochle Club; M.O. Club; M.S. Club; Mizpah Club; Mom's Club; Mutual Improvement Club; N.O.M. Club; Northside Pinochle Club; O.N.E. Club; Order of the Eastern Star; O-So-Ga Club; Past Noble Grand Club; P.E.O.; Pinochle Club; Priscilla Club; Progressive Sewing Club; Pythian Sisters; Rebekah Lodge; Rotary Club; Royal Arch Masonic Lodge (Masons); Saturday Night Club; St. Joseph Society; S.B.A. Lodge; Sew and Sew Club; Social Twelve Club; Social Wednesday Club; Sorosis; Star Club; Supper Club; T.M.S. Club; Tri Delt Club; Valley View Air Patrol; Valley View Axis Club

---

[3] J. L. Hypes, *Social Participation in a Rural New England Town* (New York: Bureau of Publications, Teachers College, Columbia University, 1927).

(B & PW); Valley View Bridge Club; Valley View Columbia Club; Valley View Men's Glee Club; Valley View Metropolitan Club; Valley View Music Club; Valley View Volunteer Fire Department; Venus Club; Veterans of Foreign Wars (VFW); Wednesday Club; Women's Association, First Congregational Church; Women's Club; Women's Society of Christian Service; Zapadni Cesko Braterska Jednota (ZCBJ); Zephyr Club.[4]

In Virginia the interests about which country groups have formed are classified under three general heads: educational societies, farm organizations, and commodity marketing associations.[5] Among the educational societies are found the Coöperative Education Association, the Parent-Teacher Association, farmers' institutes, homemakers' associations, farmers' evening classes, and numerous educational councils, such as agricultural advisory councils, home advisory councils, 4–H club councils, and high school advisory councils. An analysis of the work of these societies reveals a wide variety of activities and purposes. Although of a special interest character themselves, some of the societies are broken down into highly specialized committees or groups. For example, the Coöperative Education Association has ten standard committees, among them being health, child welfare, roads, agriculture, and citizenship.

Among the more general farm organizations are listed the Farmers' Union, the Farm Bureau, the Grange, and many independent farmers' clubs. The commodity marketing associations are reported to be on the increase in Virginia. They are local in character, but many attempt to cover the state by means of federations or coöperative agreements. The whole development of the marketing associations, especially those organized on the coöperative principle, is a movement of great importance in rural society. In many ways it becomes a first-class illustration of the tendency toward the interest or functional type of organization which is being considered in this chapter. The coöperative form of organization becomes a principle or a pole of interest which attracts some farmers and repels others. The different types of commodities also become a selective factor which draws certain producers together. The following are but a few examples, indicating the extent to which specialization has grown: Valley of Virginia Coöperative Milk Producers' Association, Coon River Tomato Association of the Northern Neck, Rockingham Coöperative Farm Bureau, Inc., Eastern Shore of Virginia Produce Exchange, and Rockbridge Coöperative Livestock Marketing Association.

In this state, furthermore, another whole set of country interest groups and organizations was found. They are Negro organizations,[6] and they, in turn, can be classified into three large types of interests, as follows: agricultural organizations, educational societies, and fraternal or secret orders. In many respects the agricultural and educational organizations parallel those which have previously been described, for there are farmer conferences, 4–H clubs, agricultural extension societies, school improvement leagues, and county fair associations. The fraternal and secret orders have many interesting and unusual features. The interests to which they cater are evidently a feeling of brotherhood, a desire for security, which takes the form of insurance and mutual-aid plans, and a sense of the religious, which expresses itself in ritualism. Organizations of a fraternal nature are, according to the bulletin, most

[4] Wayne Wheeler, *Social Stratification in a Plains Community* (Lebanon, Missouri: Allen G. Everingham, LCSR, October, 1949).

[5] W. E. Garnett, *Rural Organizations in Relation to Rural Life in Virginia* (Blacksburg: Bulletin 256, Virginia Agricultural Experiment Station, 1927).

[6] J. M. Ellison, *Negro Organization and Leadership in Relation to Rural Life* (Blacksburg: Virginia Agricultural Experiment Station, Bulletin 290, 1933).

numerous among rural Negroes. A list of the names of the organizations in the one community of Fairfields, Northumberland County, may convey some idea of a local situation. In this community there are thirteen adult organizations, as follows: Knights of Jerusalem, Court of Queen Esther, Good Samaritans. Lone Star, Edwardsville and Ophelia; Odd Fellows, Bay View and Tranquillity, Household of Ruth, Pride of Lilian, Masons and Eastern Star, and Rock Lee Home Society. It is not unusual to find a half dozen or more such organizations in a single community. Although they bear a variety of strange names, their objectives are practically identical.

Youth group activities. In a recent study of high-school youth in Walworth County, Wisconsin, more than twenty different kinds of activities were identified. The ten most frequently mentioned were 4–H clubs, church societies, social clubs, farm organizations, and groups organized for sports, card playing, social dancing, hunting, and going to the movies. The number per pupil averaged six and ranged from four for country girls in smaller center schools to seven for town boys in the larger centers. There was a regular and steady increase from smaller centers through intermediate to larger centers for both boys and girls.

The activity which easily ranked first in every group was attending movies, with 93 per cent reporting it. For country girls in smaller centers, however, the proportion dropped to 76 per cent. For boys, ball playing and hunting were second and third in popularity; for girls, social dancing was next after movies. Church societies and parties were a strong fourth.[7]

County-wide groups. The tendency for

[7] J. H. Kolb and LeRoy J. Day, *Interdependence in Town and Country Relations in Rural Society* (Madison: Wisconsin Agricultural Experiment Station Research Bulletin 172, Dec. 1950).

local groups to federate on a county basis or for county-wide groups to form is also a recent movement. Examples are found in studies made in Minnesota, Iowa and Missouri. The Missouri list is given here: Dent County Farmers' Association, Women's Progressive Farmers' Association, Junior Farmers Association, Dent County Farmers Improvement Association, Registered Beef Cattle Association, Lake Springs Conservation Association, Chamber of Commerce, American Legion, American Legion Auxiliary, Veterans of Foreign Wars, Women's Federated Clubs, Home Economics Clubs, 4–H Clubs, numerous secret fraternal orders and such public agencies as the Agricultural Extension Service, Farmers' Home Administration, Production and Marketing Administration, Farmers' Production Credit Association, Forest Service, Conservation and Park Board, Social Security, and County Public Health Service.[8]

Some changes and the direction of their trends. In a sample area of five counties in central and southern Wisconsin, 351 country groups were found.[9] They included organizations with seventy-five different names, but about 75 per cent of them can be grouped into twelve classes or kinds. It is evident that such forms as parent-teacher associations, farmers' clubs, community clubs, 4–H clubs, homemakers' clubs, and coöperative associations are among the most popular groups. The ninety-one organiza-

[8] Ronald B. Almack and Lawrence M. Hepple, *Rural Social Organization in Dent County* (Columbia: Missouri Agricultural Experiment Station Research Bulletin 458, August, 1950); Paul J. Jehlik and Ray E. Wakeley, *Rural Organization in Process* (Ames: Iowa Agricultural Experiment Station Research Bulletin 365, September, 1949); Frank D. Alexander and Lowry Nelson, *Rural Social Organization in Goodhue County* (Minnesota Agricultural Experiment Station Bulletin 401, February, 1949).

[9] J. H. Kolb and A. F. Wileden, *Special Interest Groups in Rural Society* (Madison: Wisconsin Agricultural Experiment Station Research Bulletin 84, December, 1927).

	INTEREST CLASSES	ORGANIZATIONS	
		Number	Per Cent
TABLE 39	All organizations *	351	100.0
	Social enjoyment	252	71.8
	Better farming	115	32.8
Interests About Which Groups Formed in the Order of Frequency of Occurrence	Help school and teacher	84	24.0
	Better business	59	16.8
	Young people's interests	59	16.8
	Health and social welfare	41	11.7
	Home improvement	40	11.4
	Public and civic affairs	15	4.3
	General community betterment	13	3.7
	Unite locals	5	1.4
	Mutual improvement	5	1.4
	Help church and preacher	5	1.4

* Obviously the sum of the organizations in the various interest classes greatly exceeds the total number of organizations, because any one organization may fall into more than one of the classes.

tions listed under a miscellaneous item include mothers' clubs, boys' clubs, farm bureaus, fair associations, equity societies, and cemetery associations. The names, however, are often more indicative of the form which the organization takes and may not be a reliable clue to the real activity or the central interest of the group. For example, it was found that a group called a farmers' club was actually a choral society; that a parent-teacher association was a women's social and sewing group, and that a community club was a cemetery association. Because the name did not always designate the interest, the 351 groups were studied at firsthand and then classified according to their real interests.

The twelve major interests or functions about which the groups formed are shown in Table 39. It is quite evident from the table that social enjoyment is an important interest, for it was found to operate in over 71 per cent of the cases. Better farming comes second; the most significant fact, however, is that these groups are not single in interest; the majority of them have two or more interests. This is one of the outstanding characteristics of this type of country

organization. Many have interests which are not highly specialized; that is, several interests are closely associated. Some interests, such as sociability, are seldom found alone.

Preliminary analysis has been made of the changes in these country special interest groups over a fifteen-year period from 1925 to 1940.[10] First, the total number increased by nearly 60 per cent but with variations among counties and kinds of groups. The more specialized women's and youth groups increased, while those of the general family type and men's groups declined. Second, there was a growing tendency for local groups of similar interest to work together on a county or even a state basis. The number of independent organizations decreased and those with state affiliation increased. Third, those types able to secure the services of professional personnel were the ones to gain most in numbers and in strength. The greatest increase on both counts came in those groups organized and sponsored by public agencies, such as 4-H clubs and homemakers' clubs under the Agricultural

[10] A. F. Wileden, *Trends in Rural Organizations in Wisconsin* (Madison: Extension Service Special Circular, January, 1951).

and Home Economics Extension Services. This is a general trend.[11] Fourth, interest organizations develop through cycles. As the cycle nears its completion, new groups evolve, replacing older ones. The general pattern of the cycle is described in a later section of this chapter.

Some interest groups include both farmers and villagers but vary with size of village center. As indicated elsewhere, the restudy of community relations of 140 agricultural villages showed the growing interdependence of country and village people. There was an increase in the participation of country people in the special interest organiza-

[11] Carl C. Taylor, *et al., Rural Life in the U.S.* (New York: Knopf, 1949).

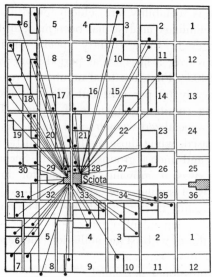

• Homes of those who attended regularly
══ Roads

Figure 39. Area of Influence of the Sciota Community Club of Mc-Donough County, Illinois, 1930.

Source: D. E. Lindstrom, *Local Group Organization Among Illinois Farm People,* Bulletin 392 (Urbana: University of Illinois Agricultural Experiment Station).

tions centered in the villages and towns. This means closer and more intimate personal contacts between the two major classes in rural society — farmers and villagers. Increased country enrollments were also observed in the educational organizations, largely the parent-teacher associations, a corollary of the increased use of village schools by country people, and likewise a compensation for the falling off in such country groups as just noted.

A graphic representation of this interest or functional organization, involving both country and village, given in Figure 39, illustrates a situation in rural Illinois. It shows the selective membership of the Sciota Community Club. The homes of the country members are scattered over two townships, some are as far as five miles from the village center.

A significant relationship was found between the numbers and types of special interest groups and the size of village or town centers. Another aspect of this situation has been described in the chapter dealing with recreation, namely that the smaller villages had fewer organizations and the larger ones more, but the average number seemed to level off at about twenty per village. Their mortality rate increased as the number increased above that figure. In New York State a correlation was found between the population and the number of socio-educational organizations, especially in the dairying and in the fruit-raising counties.[12]

Similarly, in the Australian study of the country towns of Victoria, it was found that more women's organizations were likely to be found in places of less than 1000 population than in the larger centers. Men's and youth organizations, on the other hand, were somewhat more characteristic of the larger villages and towns. Women's organizations,

[12] B. L. Melvin, *Village Service Agencies in New York* (Ithaca: Cornell University Bulletin 493, 1929).

the report states, are the most numerous and the most hardy of all. These organizations have for their main purpose the helping of some cause, interest, or institution, such as overseas mission, hospital, or school; and even those groups which exist primarily for the benefit of the members usually have some helping activity as a secondary function, a characteristic quite like that of the American groups described earlier. Men's organizations in the Australian towns were less numerous and meetings were usually held at night. They were rather a contrast with the women's groups, since the majority of them existed chiefly for the benefit of the members themselves, although their activities were varied and many of them "do good works." Lack of vitality characterized the youth organizations. This, it was thought, was due to the fact that they were so largely founded on the idea of doing good for the young people and training them to social conformity, rather than for their enjoyment.

Generalized scheme for classification. Because of the welter of interests and the varied forms which interest groups assume, it is important to have some scheme of classification whereby local situations can be observed and comparisons made. The following types are therefore suggested to serve such purpose: [13]

Athletic: Baseball, basket-ball, tennis, golf, fishing clubs and the like.

Civic: Organizations designed for the good of the community, such as the WCTU; charitable and welfare agencies or fire departments, when social in character.

Educational: Parent-teacher associations, literary and study groups.

Fraternal: All lodges or secret orders of the fraternal type.

Musical: Bands, orchestras, glee clubs, choral societies.

[13] Edmund deS. Brunner and J. H. Kolb, *Rural Social Trends* (New York: McGraw-Hill, 1933).

Patriotic: American Legion and its auxiliary, G.A.R., Sons of Veterans, D.A.R., W.R.C.

Social: Card clubs, community social clubs, and all other organizations chiefly sociable in purpose, regardless of other minor functions.

Socio-Economic: Farm Bureau, Grange, home demonstration groups, etc.; all businessmen's organizations, service or luncheon clubs.

Socio-Religious: Ministerial associations; social organizations under religious but not local parish auspices, the Young Men's Christian Association, Knights of Columbus and its women's organization.

Youth-serving: All 4-H groups, Hi-Y and Pioneers, Boy and Girl Scouts, Camp Fire Girls, and any others for children and young people except junior lodges.

Some generalized characteristics. As a further guide for observations of local situations and as a kind of summary, general characteristics of the more formal groups found in rural society will be briefly noted. First is their dependence upon promotion and leadership. In many if not most of the cases cited, original motivation, especially for those groups concerned with farm, home, and youth interests, is given by some representative of such agencies as the Agricultural Extension Service, parent-teacher associations, schools, Red Cross or farmers' organizations. Actual promotion and organization comes about by outside promoters working through local leaders. The final task of keeping the organization active and alive rests largely with elected officers and committees. The quality and character of their leadership is therefore of prime importance.

A second characteristic is that most interest groups depend upon a program of activities to accomplish their objectives. Meetings are held, their nature and frequency depending upon what the organization is trying to accomplish. For those groups organized about the social, the educational, or the young people's interests, the meeting usually consists of four parts: an educational program, a social period, a business session, and refreshments. To attempt a general meeting of country people without refreshments would be like trying to run a car without gasoline. Eating and visiting together are prime requisites in the programs of many a congeniality group. Coöperative organizations, of course, give more time and attention to business features, but even they do not completely neglect the occasional picnic or social affair. Activities other than the regular meetings are many and varied, such as poultry culling and tree spraying demonstrations, health clinics and exhibits, plays and pageants, parties and picnics, community and county fairs, debates and discussions, or games and field days. Such activities become the center of attention for the group itself, and they also provide an opportunity for displaying or dramatizing its work before other members of the community.

Now and then an activity may be fostered which is quite out of line with the main interest for which a group has been organized; in fact, it may be done to divert attention from the central purpose. The story is told of a coöperative creamery which was not doing very well in a business way. The directors conceived the idea of holding a dance once a month for their members, hoping that they would have such a good time that they would overlook the financial difficulties. It came to be known as the "dancing creamery."

A third characteristic of interest groups is that by their very nature only certain kinds and numbers of people are attracted to them. It may be redundant to say that interest groups need people who are interested, but the practical implication is important. Leaders are likely to go to one of two extremes. They will either generalize their

programs in order to hold a larger group, and in this way lose the support of the persons most deeply interested, or they will hold too strictly to their original objectives and thus fail to attract sufficient numbers to carry on their enterprise. In other words, there is an appropriate size and kind of organization for certain types of interests. In the business or coöperative field the principle is known as "sufficient volume of business." There is also an appropriate "volume of people," neither too large nor too small, needed to carry on a mothers' club, a choral society or a subordinate Grange. It is not an accident, for instance, that college or university fraternities and sororities average approximately twenty-five or thirty members. A larger unit might be more economical to house, but the limiting factor is the number who can be truly congenial and who are enough alike in interests and propensities to work out a closely-knit, primary, functioning group.

A fourth characteristic of interest groups and organizations is their tendency to federate. This is often undertaken in an attempt to unify the efforts and activities of a series of local organizations within a district or a county-wide plan. The county organization may even precede the locals and then promote and establish them. At other times the federation grows out of already established locals, which combine in a desire for united action and for wider contacts of group endeavor.

The large federation may then seek to gain power and privilege in society. This characteristic is illustrated in the case of the evolution of certain farmers' organizations from country federations to big state and national federations with well-paid personnel and legislative bureaus.[14] On the other hand, the tendency to federate may be considered one form of reconciliation for the

[14] Stuart Chase, *Democracy Under Pressure* (New York: Twentieth Century Fund, 1945).

overlapping and conflicting loyalties which arise in a local situation where there are many interest groups. The process may take place on a community basis, in which case it becomes one of the steps in social integration or "community organization," as it is termed, a problem which has been considered in another chapter.

General life cycle of interest groups. Like other living things, groups follow cycles. These cycles consist of rather definite stages through which they pass, the periods being of long or short duration, according to the nature of the group, its central interest, and its surrounding conditions. The rise and decline of groups and organizations, in the abstract, may be taken for granted by many persons, but when a group with which they are personally associated is involved, it is quite another matter. Students of rural society will do well to watch the cycles of change carefully, not only within those groups of which they are members, but in other special interest groups as well, for such changes are becoming very common. Many such organizations have a comparatively short life cycle, and this is a problem of much concern both to their leaders and to their members. This section presents a sort of composite narrative of what happens in the various periods in the life cycle of rural interest groups. Four periods may be observed. They are: stimulation, rise, carrying-on, and decline.

(1) *Stimulation.* The period of stimulation may come about by direct action or by indirection. In the first instance the purpose is stated openly. This is the rationalized procedure. When sufficient sentiment has been aroused, a union of kindred spirits takes place. Like the chemical reaction, it may be either a rapid or a slow process. It may come quickly at some promoted meeting where definite organization was not anticipated, even by the leaders; suddenly the idea "takes hold," and the movement rises like a wave, carrying the originators far past their channel markers. It may take more time when a certain amount of capital stock must be sold, or when a certain original quota of membership must be signed. Even then there usually is some kind of "drive" or campaign with a certain amount of emotional excitement.

The indirect method of forming an interest group may have its origin in a very successful social gathering. The desire for more occasions in the near future is voiced. A loosely formed organization results. In this case the purposes or interests remain veiled for a time, but gradually take form and become the axis around which further activities revolve.

(2) *Rise.* During the period of rise people who have never thought of organization approve it; they do more; they ask for admission and offer help in getting it started. There are frequent meetings and large crowds. Special meetings are called to decide upon such important matters as a constitution and the election of officers. Enthusiasm runs high. Everything is new and there are plenty of ideas. "Everybody" joins, that is, everyone at the organization meeting who is eligible. There are fewer who join at the next meeting and finally there are no new members.

Meanwhile, the structure of the organization is becoming "set." A constitution is accepted. This specifies that this organization shall meet once a month during the school year. It shall meet at the school house. It shall have four officers: a president, a vice-president, a secretary and a treasurer, to be elected annually at the first meeting in January. Anyone who is "truly interested" may become a member. A two-thirds vote is necessary to change the constitution, which means that it is the fixed code or method of procedure for the organization from that time on.

(3) *Carrying-on.* The crucial time for every organization comes after the promotion period is over and the newness has worn off. This is the period of "carrying-on." By this time the outside promoters have disappeared almost entirely from the scene, and the burden must be shouldered by local people, usually by the officers. From this time on, disillusionment may begin, for often certain promises were made and objectives set forth by the promoters that apparently are not and frequently cannot be fulfilled. Factions develop within the group and conflicts arise.

It may also be discovered at about this time that the group is conflicting with the ideals of other groups, or institutions, such as the school or church. Consequently, they may be denied the use of the school building, or the clergy may forbid their young people to take part. On the other hand, this new group may be trying to do almost the same things as an older group in the same locality. Adjustments are necessary and methods of establishing working relations with these other groups must be devised. If this necessity is ignored, the results are often fatal to both groups.

During this carrying-on period, the changing demands of the membership must be carefully watched. There are seasonal fluctuations in the programs and activities to be considered. People tire after a while even of pie — and even of their favorite kind. Likewise, debates and plays run their course, and something else must be supplied. Suggestions for change are brought before the organization. About half the time, however, the constitutionalists or the fundamentalists win, and the proposed change is not made. If the group will accept the change, it may secure a new lease on life.

Added to the difficulties of this period is the tendency for an organization to grow up with its members. As a new organization, it begins life with people unfamiliar with its ways. They gradually mold it to conform to their ways of doing things. Amateur leaders gain confidence gradually and their efforts become more and more successful. New people coming in later cannot experience this same "give and take" process. They must take things more largely as they find them. This they occasionally refuse to do, particularly those of a younger generation. Thus it is not unusual to find separate organizations for the various age groups, and to see a new organization cycle start with each succeeding generation.

(4) *Decline.* When decline once sets in, there are but two avenues open, other than demise. One is specialization. The old generalized club may become a strictly social club; it may become a women's welfare organization, or a farmers' discussion club. The present tendency is toward more specialized groups. The other avenue is a complete reorganization. For example, women's clubs which were practically inactive have reorganized and become active homemakers' clubs; community clubs have become parent-teacher associations, and equity societies have become coöperative shipping associations.

If disintegration begins in earnest, it is difficult to check without rather drastic measures. An attempt may be made to revive the organization, but revivals are rarely successful during this period. In the minds of many of its members the organization is not really dead, because they still have the constitutuion, the records, and some money in the treasury. It is simply "inactive." There does not seem to be a thoroughly respectable ritual of demise for organizations, and therefore many of them continue far beyond their span of usefulness and after the purposes or interests for which they were originally intended have completely disappeared. The officers say in great anxiety, "Why, we can't have it die on our hands."

"*The road an organization travels.*" If presented diagrammatically, the life cycle just described would appear as drawn in Figure 40. In this chart the time units must not be construed in terms of years, although in some cases they might indicate years. Superimposed on the first curve may be the stimulation and rise periods of other groups. Another group can be expected to appear on a local scene as the first shows a tendency to decline. The question which an organization leader or officer, or, for that matter, a member, may well ask himself is, "Where are we on this road just now?" Each period brings certain problems, and if one's location can be fairly well established, much can be done to anticipate and therefore to cope with the difficulties lurking in the next valley. The skillful leader, like the modern highway engineer, may find that he can fill up the low places by cutting down the crests of the hills.

What of Social Stratification in Rural Society?

The impression can be easily gained from the plethora of interest associations described that rural society and everyone in it are organized to the teeth. There is, however, another side to the story. While some people in some localities may identify themselves with many organizations, there are others who have few or no such affiliations. They simply do not belong; they are not "joiners." Briefly stated, there is an uneven response to interest groups. This leads to questions of what kinds of people are responsive and what kinds are not. Do these differences result in class cleavages in rural society?

Uneven response of rural people to interest groups. The differentiation of rural families by group affiliations has been observed for a long time. But the extent to which this tendency results in social stratification has not been clearly shown. For example, the

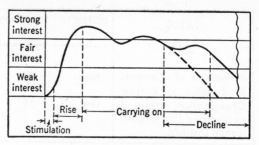

Figure 40. **The Road an Organization Travels.**

Source: Kolb and Wileden, *Making Rural Organizations Effective,* Bulletin 403 (Madison: University of Wisconsin Agricultural Experiment Station, October, 1928).

282 families involved in the 351 interest groups in five Wisconsin counties previously referred to were arranged according to their residence in twelve school districts, six with "high" and six with "low" organization characteristics. They were arrayed from "hundred-per-cent" families in which every member ten years of age or older was affiliated with one or more organizations, to "zero" families having no member in any organization. The variations were striking. In the "high" districts 53 per cent of all the families were in the hundred-per-cent class. In the "low" districts 43 per cent of the families were in the zero class. Table 40 indicates further differences.

Apparently there is something about local situations which fosters or foils interest organizations. Or is it something within families? Many studies indicate that women and girls are affiliated with more groups than are men and boys. There are family patterns of response, and if one were to risk a prediction, it would be that as the mother goes, so goes the family. A practical question can be asked: If a person were to start a new organization, where should he go, to the hundred-per-cent or to the zero families, to the high or the low organization districts?

Variations are found wherever such inves-

TABLE	DISTRICTS	100% AFFILIATION		MEDIUM AFFILIATION		ZERO AFFILIATION	
40		Number	Per Cent	Number	Per Cent	Number	Per Cent
Affiliations of Members of Families in Interest Organizations Arranged as High and Low Organization Districts.	High	80	53	46	21	25	16
	Low	16	12	59	45	56	43

tigations have been made. In the Illinois study, the extent to which persons were affiliated with certain types of organizations ranged from 13 per cent for community clubs to only 3 per cent for farmers' clubs. The Virginia study concludes that the majority of rural people seem to believe in local organizations, but less than 20 per cent give them their active support. In Madison and Union counties, Ohio, it was found that in 610 farm families, 24 per cent had members belonging to lodges, 16 per cent to Granges, 28 per cent to Farm Bureaus, and 33 per cent to 4-H clubs.

A summary of recent studies in several states regarding participation in those organizations promoted by a public agency, the Agricultural Extension Service, indicates that there is a "bottom third," a direct suggestion of some kind of stratification.[15] A wider variation was found among women than among men. In one state, even among those women who participated most in homemakers' clubs, namely those native-born and middle-aged, there were still differences too great to be accidental. As measured by both family income and formal education, the lower third was reached least by organization meetings.

[15] Edmund deS. Brunner and E. Hsin Pao Yang, *Rural America and the Extension Service* (New York: Columbia University, Bureau of Publications, Teachers College, 1949). For a somewhat different discussion of these same data, see pages 344 and 345 of this text.

Women in the various income groups attended meetings as follows:

49 per cent of the women in the upper third,

53 per cent in the middle third,

31 per cent in the lower third.

Attendance in the various educational groups was as follows:

71 per cent of the women with college training,

51 per cent of the women with high school training,

30 per cent of the women with grade school training.

Factors associated with variations in response to groups. Questions constantly arise about the "why" of the wide variations in the responses to group organization. The people directly concerned recognize the condition but can seldom go far to explain the underlying reasons. One hears characterizations of this or that neighbor, or even whole neighborhoods in such phrases as "they belong to everything," "they are always there," "he really supports the club," "she is a born leader."

Careful analysis does reveal certain factors which are related to, or at least associated with, this matter of group affiliation. It cannot be claimed that these factors are directly causal in character, but it can be demonstrated and tested by statistical devices that they are significantly related with the organizational behavior of people. This means that they are present not by mere chance or accidental circumstances. However, they may in turn be the effects of other more basic causes. In the study of those 282 Wisconsin families to which reference has been made correlation was readily found between high organization affiliation and the higher proportions of heads of families who were farm owners with larger incomes, as well as the higher proportions of periodicals taken, books owned, hours spent in reading, radio listening, and other forms of recreation. But who can affirm "which is hen and which is egg," which cause and which effect? The high organization affiliation and the large number of magazines present both may be results of some other parent cause. For practical purposes the important point is that they are related; they go together. There can be little doubt that the whole cultural background, the social experiences within the locality, and the customary family patterns of life have much to do in shaping the organizational response of the people concerned. There is also evidence that the factors do not work singly but in combinations or complexes.[16]

Long ago Professor Giddings of Columbia University coined a phrase to describe differentials in association — "Consciousness of kind." This consciousness, he pointed out, is built up in many ways through personal congeniality, the age cycle in social experiences, and the result of recognized needs. The selectiveness is often carried over when economic status is changed or when there is migration from one community to another.

Education, as measured by years of schooling completed, is almost always associated with participation in organized group activities. This is well illustrated in the case of 2832 adults living in seven counties in Kentucky. The proportion of men and women belonging to interest organizations other than those of a religious character is shown in Figure 41.

Not only are years of schooling associated with memberships but particularly for men, with office-holding. Men with a college education held 115 offices per 100 persons in contrast with only five offices for those with less than eight years of schooling. Other factors going along with education were length of residence in the community, economic status, and tenure. Families of more recent residence, lower income, and in tenant status were negatively associated with both participation and affiliation in formal organizations. This study and many others, such as those cited on problems of community organization, indicate that the selective process carries over into other social relations, such as school, church, occupation, and recreation.[17] Means for measurement of the socio-economic status of families have been devised for study and comparative purposes.[18]

Informal groups even more selective, indicative of social cleavages. There is also great variety among informal, loosely-organized groups in rural society. They are likewise highly selective in character and contribute to or are an indication of one's place or status in society. They are sometimes known as cliques, a word which may have an uncomplimentary connotation. These associations may be congeniality

---

[16] J. H. Kolb, *Trends of Country Neighborhoods* (Madison: Wisconsin Agricultural Experiment Station Research Bulletin 120, November, 1933); Harold F. Kaufman, *Participation in Organized Activities in Selected Kentucky Localities* (Lexington: Kentucky Agricultural Experiment Station Bulletin 528, February, 1949).

[17] Harold F. Kaufman, *Defining Prestige in a Rural Community* (New York: Beacon House, Sociometry Monographs, No. 10, 1946).

[18] W. H. Sewell, *Construction and Standardization of a Scale for Measurement of the Socio-economic Status of Oklahoma Farm Families* (Stillwater: Oklahoma A. and M. Arts Technology Bulletin 9, 1940); and H. F. Kaufman, *Prestige Classes in a New York Rural Community* (Ithaca: Cornell Agricultural Experiment Station Memoir 260, 1944).

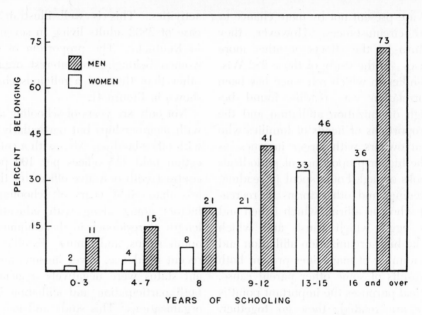

Figure 41. Per Cent of Men and Women in the Survey Population Belonging to Other-than-Religious Organizations, Classified by Years of Schooling.

Source: Harold F. Kaufman, *Participation in Organized Activities in Selected Kentucky Localities,* Bulletin 528 (Lexington: Kentucky Agricultural Experiment Station, February, 1949).

groups capable of wholesome personal relations, although like so many other forms of human association, they can be turned to anti-social purposes, as in the case of gangs with malicious behavior patterns.

As suggested in the introduction to this section, the clique can be considered as a first group beyond the family in class formation, and like the neighborhood, has primary or personal contacts. Some non-academic definitions suggest that cliques are groups of people, noisy in their applause of one another and excited in their exclusion of others. Whatever else they may be, they are closely united by kindred interests. Their members are integrated about some central core of special values. Memberships may tend to become rigid and selective, but there is still sufficient fluidity so that in American rural society at least, there may be social cleavages but not fixed caste systems, such as seem to persist in certain other societies.

Informal groups, cliques, or coteries are found within, among, and traversing the limits of other group formations such as formal associations and locality groups like communities, and certainly rural social institutions. One may venture the hypothesis that as interest groups become more formalized, and as locality groups, even neighborhoods, depend increasingly upon promoted activities, some people, especially young people, slip out from the more formal arrangements or structures. Indeed, they may not enter these established forms at all. Rather, with those of similar tastes they may form congeniality circles or primary groups of their own.

The range in interests and forms of organ-

TABLE 41	RESIDENCE OF FAMILIES	FAMILY PARTICIPATION	
		Number	Per Cent
Participation in Selected Informal Activities, Hamilton County, Iowa	Webster City	87	86
	Village	42	58
	Open country	82	82

ization is much wider for informal than for the formal groups already described. In some situations, informal groups have been identified as, or as parts of, auctions on farms or in villages, birthday, anniversary, or wedding parties, small clusters of people in front of churches after the Sunday morning service or on the corners of "Main Street" Saturday nights. Among adolescents they may be play groups or gangs.[19]

In the Hamilton County, Iowa study, certain "selected" informal activities were classified and comparisons made among city, village, and farm families (Table 41). Kinship ties, nationality backgrounds, work exchange, and sociability were among the factors of selection among such groups. The very informal but named groups were clubs: Every Other Wednesday, Get Together, Wall Street Society, Friendly Neighborhood, Saratoga Sunshine, Thimble Club, Young Married Women, Golden Hour. They ranged in membership from 10 to 35 persons. The number of groups and the proportion of participation in Webster City, a place of nearly 7000 population, varied only slightly from the open country. The village with a substantial number of retired families having members higher in the age cycle restricted

both the number and kinds of informal activities.[20]

"One-third," "one-third," "one-third" — a social rank order. Inevitably there seem to arise indications of differences among persons and families and between localities. There is a tendency to rank them and to assign them a position, a status, within the society of which they are a part. In the Kentucky two-county study three groups are neatly divided into approximately equal size. They are designated as the highest one-third, middle one-third, and lowest one-third. While the highest one-third in rank is simply reported as being associated with the largest proportion of participation in group activities, nevertheless there is an overtone of distinction or prestige. Of this highest one-third, 86 per cent belonged to organizations and 20 per cent held offices. Of the lowest one-third, 50 per cent belonged but only 2 per cent held offices. Other comparisons appear in Table 42.[21]

Ranking people up and down a scale, no matter how it is done, is fascinating. It involves not only a question of prestige but a sense of power. Prestige implies a value which a person possesses, always in relation to other persons. The idea has many interesting and important implications, both theoretical and practical. For example, it was in this framework that leadership, in the discussion of community organization, was

[19] Frank D. Alexander and Lowry Nelson, *op. cit.*; S. Earl Grigsby and Harold Hoffsommer, *Rural Social Organization in Frederick County, Maryland* (College Park: Maryland Agricultural Experiment Station Bulletin A 51, March, 1949); William Foote Whyte, *Street Corner Society* (Chicago: University of Chicago Press, 1943); Frederic M. Thrasher, *The Gang* (Chicago: University of Chicago Press, 1936), 2d ed.

[20] Paul J. Jehlik and Ray E. Wakeley, *op. cit.*
[21] Harold F. Kaufman, *op. cit.*

TABLE 42 The Per Cent of Persons in Two Kentucky Counties Belonging to Organizations and Holding Office, Classified by Social Rank	RANK	NUMBER PERSONS	PER CENT BELONGING TO ORGANIZATIONS		PER CENT HOLDING OFFICE
			One	Two or more	
	Highest one-third	315	45	39	20
	Middle one-third	368	39	29	5
	Lowest one-third	343	34	16	2

implied to be a group process within a recognized scheme of social values. From the various studies described, it seems clear that families considered membership in organizations as carrying prestige. Efforts to gain standing or position sometimes brought conflict with others or within the family or even the personality, if it meant too great a sacrifice of independence. In other instances it seemed to bring about a withdrawal or holding back from group activities.

As Professor Anderson of Cornell has suggested, there is also a kind of self-identification and a projection of family or personal status into a community situation. Families may accept a position in group relations on their own terms of evaluation or one in which they assume others have placed them.[22] This kind of process can render inter-group contacts or general community integration difficult if not impossible, in any fundamental sense. By thus narrowing lines of group participation, certain avenues of information are automatically cut off. Thus communication may be free in the mechanical sense that one can turn the dial on the radio, buy any newspaper on the stand, or go to any motion picture theater on the street, but choices are conditioned by the defined group relations. How far this process of channeling communication and thus

imposing the power of position has gone in our American rural society is debatable.

Special studies in social stratification. Results of studies following the design of Professor Warner in his Yankee City series would indicate that stratification in American communities is rather far advanced and, in some respects, relatively fixed. To display the results of these findings, the neat pattern of the three-thirds used in the Kentucky study had to be broken down into more divisions with greater refinements such as upper-upper, upper-lower, and lower-lower. Detailed report or criticism cannot be included here but a schematic comparison of three such studies is presented for purposes of providing a basis for observation of local situations and for stimulating further discussion and study (Figure 42).[23]

In the Valley View community in which so many different kinds of interest groups were found, ten indices of status were used. They were said to be the criteria by which local citizens determine the positions of their fellows and presumably of themselves within the community. They are: (1) wealth and its use, (2) education and its use, (3) ethnicity, (4) occupation, (5) place of res-

[22] Richard L. Schanck, "A Study of a Community and Its Groups and Institutions Conceived of as Behavior of Individuals." (Princeton: Psychological Review Publications, No. 195, 1932).

[23] Wayne Wheeler, *op. cit.*; W. Lloyd Warner and Associates, *Democracy in Jonesville* (New York: Harper, 1949); M. C. Hill and H. R. McCall, "Social Stratification in 'Georgia Town,'" *American Sociological Review*, XV, No. 6 (December, 1950); August deB. Hollingshead, *Elmtown Youth* (New York: Wiley, 1949).

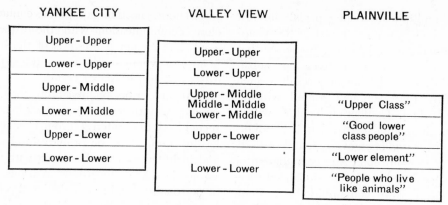

Figure 42. Levels of Social Stratification.

Source: Wayne Wheeler, *op. cit.*

idence, (6) personal behavior and appearance, (7) kinship affiliation and family reputation, (8) religious affiliation and religious activity, (9) association membership and activity, (10) community leadership.

Criticisms of studies of this design have centered chiefly on four counts: first is the placing of too great emphasis upon the indices used for stratifying into classes.[24] There may be other more discriminating variables which should be taken more fully into account. Second is the question of techniques for dividing or separating the classes. Critics object that the class intervals used are too fixed to fit the materials which can be gathered in an empirical study. Third, the question is raised as to the extent that one can generalize about a society from conditions found in separated communities. It is suggested that class positions in any local community may be only local expressions of determinants present in the larger or Great Society; they may be simply local reflection of larger cultural value systems. Fourth,

migration is omitted from consideration. This is said to be especially important in the Jonesville and Elmtown studies (both reported to be the same locality).

Some Conclusions and Implications

Final conclusions regarding the influence of interest groups in the social stratification of rural society cannot be given in any final form. Processes resulting from changes are still too incomplete. However, some implications of these changing group relations can be presented. There are those who are greatly concerned for the future of rural life because of tendencies traced here: the drift from certain personal to more impersonal forms of social contact; from neighborhood and other locality restrictions to the many kinds and character of interest associations; and from what was early considered a relatively equalitarian kind of society to one which appears to some as highly selective and securely stratified into classes. They fear that communities, and personalities too, will be either pulled apart by the many separate group fealties or restricted and controlled in the mounting power structure of a highly commercialized and industrialized society.

It is quite possible that the tendency

[24] Otis D. Duncan and Jay W. Artis, "Stratification Research," *Rural Sociology*, XVI, No. 1 (March, 1951): Paul K. Hatt, "Stratification in the Mass Society," *American Sociological Review*, XV (April, 1950), 216–222; H. D. Pfautz and O. D. Duncan, "Critique of Warner's Work in Stratification," *American Sociological Review*, XV, No. 2 (April, 1950).

toward multiplication of special interest groups which has been traced in this chapter may swing to an extreme. Some say that it has already done so. Extreme specialization and division of labor may result in such complexity that common ground will be difficult to find. Conflicting loyalties within the same individual or overlapping authorities of special *ad hoc* governmental districts may lead to confusion. An accumulation of highly specialized and professionalized services in small rural communities may "bog down" the whole financial structure. These problems are dealt with in the chapters on rural communities and local government.

May there not also be unusual opportunities offered by the very presence of diversities in group arrangements? Many local studies give evidence that much of the functioning of the more formal structures in society, especially of social institutions and agencies, rests upon the internal and informal relations of small groups. Even in the army, with its highly stratified system of authority, a very important part was played in the realm of morale by informal friendship groups.[25] Informal and formal associations as they have been described may be interdependent and even essential to each other. If there is to be group action and accomplishment, there must be social organization. Some freedom and independence may be sacrificed but some may be gained. Stress should be placed upon the adjustability and the flexibility of organizational struc-

ture. There is need for continuous contact and close communication with the expanding needs and changing interests of the human beings for whom and by whom the structure exists and has its social being.

In regard to personality, Professor Cooley points a way through the seeming maze. He recognized that interest groups as well as locality groups can be primary in character and included play groups along with neighborhood and family groups. Various facets of personality can be smoothed and polished by varied group contacts. Fortunately all of life need not be confined to one locality in these days of rapid travel. Problems there will be, but personality and group problems existed in the days of pioneer neighborhoods too. Different times bring different problems but they also bring opportunities for development.

Professor J. K. Hart [26] describes mutual relationships of different interest groups and personality in the following statement: "Every membership in a new group brings some distinctive new touch to the personality of the individual. If he can find his way around the range of humanizing groups, he will thus find his way around into all the distinctive phases of humanity and he will become a complete human being."

The range of interest group organization in rural society extends beyond rural limits into urban society to form one phase of rural-urban relationships, the subject of the next chapter.

[25] Samuel Stouffer *et al.*, *The American Soldier: 1, Adjustment During Army Life* (Princeton: Princeton University Press, 1949).

[26] "Belonging to Too Many Groups," *Survey* (March 15, 1924).

TOPICS FOR DISCUSSION

1. Write a case history or life story of an interest group or organization which you know by first-hand contacts, such as a social club,

a parent-teacher association, a coöperative marketing organization, a young people's society, a fraternity or sorority. Give special attention to the following points.

   a. Reasons and circumstances surrounding its origin.

b. How members are recruited.

c. What kind of leaders are chosen.

d. Plans for keeping members loyal.

e. Difficulties with other groups.

f. Conflicts within the group.

g. Readjustments made to overcome difficulties.

h. Evidences of permanence or decline.

2. Make a list of all the social organizations such as community club, Grange, Union, Farm Bureau, parent-teacher association, 4–H Club, etc., which have members in a rural locality with which you are acquainted. Do you think there are enough, too many, or too few such organizations there? Give reasons for your answer.

3. Outline the social and the organization plan and policy of one of the national farmers' organizations, such as the Grange, Farmers' Union, Farm Bureau, or of a state or national breeders' association.

4. Enumerate and discuss briefly the social forces which have given rise to special interest groups in rural society.

5. What problems do interest groups create for a local community? Trace the steps by which special interest groups may lead to social stratification in rural society or (the reverse process) how special interest groups may prevent class formation.

REFERENCE READINGS

Anderson, W. A., "Family Social Participation and Social Status Self-Ratings," *American Sociological Review,* June, 1946, pp. 253 ff.

Anderson, W. A., *Some Participation Principles: Their Reactions to the Programs of Rural Agencies,* Bulletin 731. Ithaca, N.Y.: Cornell Extension Service, September, 1947.

Bales, Robert, "Set of Categories for the Analysis of Small Groups Interaction," *American Sociological Review,* April, 1950. Presents symbol system and schedule classification for use in recording small group interaction, in terms of problems of orientation, control, decision, tension-management, integration.

Davis, Kingsley, and Wilbert E. Moore, "Some Principles of Stratification," *American Sociological Review,* April, 1945, pp. 242–249.

Draper, C. R., and Daniel Russell, *Rural Organization in Val Verde County, Texas,* Miscellaneous Publication 71. College Station: Texas Agricultural Experiment Station, March, 1951.

Guetzkow, Harold, ed., *Groups, Leadership and Men.* Pittsburgh: Carnegie Press, Carnegie Institute of Technology, May, 1951.

Hay, Donald G., and Robert A. Polson, *Rural Organizations in Oneida County, New York,* Bulletin 871. Ithaca, N.Y.: Cornell Agricultural Experiment Station, May, 1951.

Hepple, Lawrence M., and Margaret L. Bright, *Social Changes in Shelby County, Missouri,* Research Bulletin 456. Columbia: Missouri Agricultural Station, March, 1950.

Hibbard, B. H., *Marketing Agricultural Products.* New York: D. Appleton, 1921. Part II has a brief statement of the origins and development of the various farmer organizations as Grange, Alliance, Equity, Union, Farm Bureau.

Hill, M. C., and H. R. McCall, "Social Stratification in 'Georgia Town'" *American Sociological Review,* December, 1950.

Jennings, Helen, *Sociometry of Leadership,* Sociometric Monograph No. 14. New York: Beacon House, 1947. Discussion of sociogroups and psyche-groups, the community being the former. Leadership is interpersonal.

Kirkpatrick, Kolb, Inge, and Wileden, *Rural Organizations and the Farm Family,* Research Bulletin 96. Madison: Wisconsin Agricultural Experiment Station, 1929. Report of a study of rural organizations from the standpoint of the family and its individual members.

Komarovsky, Mirra, "The Voluntary Associations of Urban Dwellers," *American Sociological Review,* December, 1946.

Useem, John, P. Tangent, and Ruth Useem, "Stratification in a Prairie Town," in Wilson and Kolb, *Sociological Analysis.* New York: Harcourt, Brace, 1949.

Wing, D. C., "Trends in National Farm Organizations," *1940 Year Book of Agriculture,* Washington, D.C.: United States Department of Agriculture.

16   Rural-Urban Relationships

AT THE END of the highway that runs past farmers' driveways through villages and towns is the city with its smokestacks and its jagged sky line. The traffic on this great American highway moves toward the city, but it also moves toward the country. It is not simply a physical highway for the transportation of goods and people, but an open channel of communication for the interplay of ideas and attitudes. Fifteen to twenty years ago students of rural society were not so conscious of this interaction between rural and urban life; they were more concerned with the cityward drift of country people. Recent studies of social trends show that a second important focus for the two great social movements of centralization and decentralization is not the city itself but the surrounding suburban areas. As earlier chapters have shown, the other focus is the contemporary town-country community which is developing in rural areas.

Thousands upon thousands of country people go to the city daily for employment but keep their country residence. Many urban people have their residence in the country and travel to their urban employment. Direct and indirect contacts have multiplied in recent years. Direct contacts of farm, rural non-farm, village, and small-town families with urban centers occur through full or part-time employment, purchasing, marketing, entertainment, and visiting. Conversely, city dwellers are in closer touch than formerly with rural affairs through ownership of farms, country recreation, visiting, and travel.

More subtle indirect contacts between city and country have likewise multiplied and are re-determining the form and content of rural as well as urban society. Media of communication — radio, moving pictures, daily newspaper, and weekly or monthly magazines with their uniform national advertising — are attempting to dominate both rural and urban societies. Many means of social control and policy-making are also inherent in plans for binding local institutions such as banks, stores, churches, and schools into centralized organizations with headquarters and leadership often urban-centered.

Finally, the great flow and ebb of millions of country people into the cities and back again is making profound changes in rural-urban relationships. This mobility and these contacts have continued long enough to make many general differences between rural and urban centers less pronounced than formerly. Changes and adjustments are evident in merchandising practices, in type of agriculture, in forms of social activities, and even in those population characteristics by which rural and urban were formerly distinguished. Now many differences may be found within urban or within rural populations which are greater than those existing between the two. Hence the old division of society into rural and urban has less and less meaning as a method for comparison and study. Rural and urban are becoming relative terms which

261

can be scaled by gradients outward from a city center or inward from a country area.

Rise and Decline of City Centers. Formation of Metropolitan Clusters

Long-time perspective is necessary for viewing changing rural-urban relationships. This can be found in the great dynamics of population mobility described in an earlier chapter, and in the dramatic story of the rapid rise of great American cities and their more recent expanding metropolitan areas. The proportion of the nation's population classed as urban nearly doubled in the half century from 1880 to 1930. For each of the decades in that period there was an ever-increasing concentration of people in city centers and their immediate environs. In 1940 the Sixteenth Census reported that 47.6 per cent of the nation's people were living in the 140 metropolitan districts, each with a city center of at least 50,000 population. The 1950 Census reported 168 "standard" metropolitan areas, each with at least one city of 50,000 or more, and contiguous counties which were "deemed to be economically integrated with that city." These areas contained more than 55 per cent of the total population, nearly 84,000,000 people.

Included within them, however, is territory radiating from 20 to 50 miles, with a population which by former census definition would be termed "rural." Surely it is an important turning point in the history of American society when large city-centered areas contain more than half the total population. But it is the tributary territory which has grown significantly, not the city centers. As later sections of this chapter will indicate, not only the population but the social and economic relations in these outlying areas possess characteristics not strictly urban or rural in the traditional meanings of those terms. A new and emerging rural-urban relationship is evident.

The rapid rise of cities and the aggregation of people and socio-economic activities within and around them are not matters of haphazard arrangement. There was a tendency for such aggregations to occur along waterfronts, in port cities, especially along the Atlantic seaboard, and in the Great Lakes region, along inland transportation routes, particularly where there were necessary "breaks" in the system. The breaks come at assembly and distribution points, where there were transfers from water to rail routes, where car lots have to be broken, and at division points.[1] These assembly and distribution points must also have their hinterlands of production and consumption. Large city concentrations were impressive during the two decades from 1910 to 1930. The great Empire State Building in New York City, with its shaft reaching skyward a quarter of a mile, is a symbol of the age of city building.

Reversal of trend in city concentration. During the industrial debacle of 1929 and the 1930's, cities literally spewed their accumulated millions back into the country. Some of the results of this reversal of population trends are recorded in the census reports for 1940. Central cities within the 140 metropolitan districts grew only 6.1 per cent during the preceding decade, less than the rural increase of 6.4 per cent and less than the total national growth of 7.2 per cent. But for the first time in American history, as much as 29 per cent of the large cities of 100,000 or more people experienced a population decline.[2] Four of the ten largest cities actually lost population, and a fifth remained

[1] C. H. Cooley,, "The Theory of Transportation," *Publications of the American Economic Association,* IX (May, 1894); and Edward Ullman, "A Theory of Location for Cities," *American Journal of Sociology,* XLVI, No. 6 (May, 1941).

[2] J. M. Gillette, "Some Population Shifts in the United States," *American Sociological Review,* vol. V, no. 5 (October, 1941).

practically stationary. The reverse trend can in no sense be interpreted as the beginning of the end of urban growth, but rather as a forerunner of new patterns of population distribution.

In the decade from 1940 to 1950, the decline in the growth of city centers slackened but did not stop. The 106 cities of 100,000 population or more increased 12.3 per cent, compared with 14.3 per cent for the country as a whole. The changes varied widely, from a decline of 11 per cent to an increase of 257 per cent. Eight of the ten largest cities, excluding Los Angeles and Washington, D.C., showed an average increase of only about 6 per cent, less than half the national rate. The really significant trend was the increase in the outlying districts of these metropolitan areas. Nearly half the population growth of the entire country took place there, and the rate approached three times that of the central cities, as the accompanying figures indicate.

Population increase 1940–1950

Areas	Number	Per cent
Total United States	18,186,317	14.3
168 standard metropolitan areas	14,653,382	21.2
Central cities	5,652,053	13.0
Outlying parts	9,001,329	34.7

Source: United States Bureau of the Census, 1950 Census of Population, Preliminary Counts, Series PC-3, no. 3, November, 1950.

In the previous decade, 1930–1940, the rate of increase outside the central cities in the 140 metropolitan districts was 16.9 per cent compared with 6.1 per cent for the cities. This means that a third of the people in the districts were living outside the central cities.

Those cities of the "standard" metropolitan areas in 1950 which were in the middle size range had a greater rate of growth than did those which were larger or smaller. Only in the South did any significant number of central cities increase more rapidly than

	SIZE OF PLACES	TOTAL		INCORPORATED		UNINCORPORATED	
		Number	Population	Number	Population	Number	Population
TABLE **43** Population of all urban places of 10,000 Population or More, Incorporated and Unincorporated, According to Size, 1950	Total	1,257	73,387,779	1,228	72,939,821	29	447,958
	1,000,000 or more	5	17,302,538	5	17,302,538	—	—
	500,000 to 1,000,000	13	9,110,922	13	9,110,922	—	—
	250,000 to 500,000	23	8,131,010	23	8,131,000	—	—
	100,000 to 250,000	65	9,410,440	65	9,410,440	—	—
	50,000 to 100,000	125	8,826,709	125	8,826,709	—	—
	25,000 to 50,000	246	8,644,050	243	8,547,343	3	96,707
	10,000 to 25,000	780	11,962,110	754	11,610,859	26	351,251

Source: United States Bureau of the Census, 1950 Census of Population. Preliminary Counts, Series PC–3, no. 8, January 11, 1951.

their outlying areas. Twenty-five of the thirty-four areas in this class were found in this region. In the South, urban patterns of metropolitan development apparently have not reached the stage so marked in other regions; or another kind of pattern may be in formation because of differences in industrial and communication systems and in general geographic location.

Current concentration in population. The general situation of city populations in the United States can be observed from Table 43.

Cities, strictly defined as places of 10,000 population or more — that is centers larger than villages and towns — numbered 1140 in 1940. Of these 63 were unincorporated and more than a million people lived in them. By 1950 there were 1257 centers of this size, but only 29 were unincorporated and these had less than half a million population. Table 44 shows population distribution and population gains of incorporated cities extending back to 1910.

The gain of 14.7 per cent in the decade from 1940 to 1950 represents the increased proportion of people living in incorporated places of 10,000 population or more, not simply the growth of the centers of that size. There were 180 more such places in 1950 than in 1940. The increased number indicates a trend toward more legal incorporations, since there were 63 unincorporated places of that size in 1940 but only 29 in

1950. The increase was also due to a number of towns moving up into the 10,000 population classification.

The population gain in incorporated centers of 100,000 or more (there were no unincorporated centers of that size) increased one point, to 15.7 per cent between 1940 and 1950. There was a net gain of 14 cities in the class, bringing the total number to 106. Of the 15 cities that passed into the class (only one fell back), nine were in the South and three in the West. The nearly 44,000,000 people living in the 106 cities represent about 45 per cent of the urban population as defined in the 1950 Census.

General population figures, however, give only limited impressions of the relations between rural and urban societies. It is the distribution of the city centers, their size and clustering into complexes or constellations, which give chief point to the discussion.

Metropolitan constellations. The late Professor McKenzie explained that large cities seldom appear isolated or alone, but are nearly always surrounded by clusters of smaller centers of varying sizes with which they are closely related in a sort of complex. These he called "Metropolitan Constellations." The map showing city distributions calibrated for size (Figure 43) indicates the patterns of the constellations. The implication is clear that there are interdependencies and specializations among the centers within any one constellation. While detailed studies

TABLE 44 Incorporated Cities of 10,000 or More, Number and Population by Decades, 1950 to 1910	YEAR	NUMBER	POPULATION	INCREASE IN PER CENT
	1950	1228	72,939,821	14.7
	1940	1077	62,715,897	7.5
	1930	982	58,340,077	30.2
	1920	752	44,904,443	31.6
	1910	597	34,053,318	....

Source: United States Bureau of the Census, Sixteenth Census of United States, 1940, I, Population, Tables 13 and 14, and 1950 Census of Population, Preliminary Counts Series PC–3, no. 8, January 11, 1951.

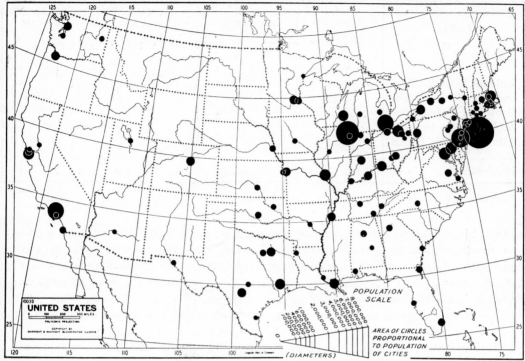

Figure 43. Geographic Distribution of Cities
of 100,000 or More, Calibrated as to Size.
Source: Seventeenth Census of the United States, *op. cit.*

have not been made, it is quite apparent that the same principle of unit requirements found in the relations of smaller centers and their tributary territories are also operative here. It will be recalled that the four factors involved are size of center, type of agencies, extent of areas, and distances between centers.

Population relationships are demonstrated in the interesting analysis made by Donald Bogue of the Scripps Foundation.[3] Table 45 carries the central story. It shows that in the years between 1930 and 1940 only cities lying 65 miles or more from the metropolis were

[3] "Metropolitan Decentralization: A Study of Differential Growth." *Studies in Population Distribution* No. 2, August, 1950 (Oxford, Ohio: Miami University, Scripps Foundation).

able to grow at a rate significantly higher than the total rate. The rural rate, on the other hand, was greatest within the 25-mile radius, and next largest within the 45-mile zone. In the zone beyond 65 miles, where there was a city of 10,000 or more population, growing at more than the national rate, there was also a rural population surrounding it which was increasing at a rapid rate.

Commercial interdependence. Reports of the Census of Distribution show the interrelations of central cities with their satellites and their tributary territories. Services determining the areas of influence are newspaper circulation, banking centers and branches, trade, both wholesale and retail, and manufacturing. Because of rapid motor

TABLE 45	DISTANCE ZONE (Miles)	TOTAL POPULATION		URBAN POPULATION		RURAL POPULATION	
		1930–40	1920–30	1930–40	1920–30	1930–40	1920–30
Ratios of Rates of Urban and Rural Population Growth in Metropolitan Regions to the National Rate of Growth, United States, 1920–30 and 1930–40.*	Central cities	.8	1.6	.8	1.6	—	—
	0–24	1.8	2.1	1.0	2.5	3.3	1.5
	25–44	1.0	.7	.7	1.1	1.2	.4
	45–64	.7	.6	.7	1.1	.7	.3
	65–164	1.0	.4	1.4	1.3	.7	.1
	165 Over	1.1	.8	2.3	1.9	.7	.5
	Total	1.0	1.0	1.2	1.6	1.0	.3

* Population classified by distance from the nearest metropolis.

transport by truck and delivery service, certain functions tend to accumulate in the dominant centers and others to gravitate to the sub-centers. Thus a system of regional economy is evolving whereby a central interdependence is gained in such matters as industries, markets, and financial control. Small cities tend to fit into the region of which they are a part, or if they are too far removed from the large center, they attempt to asume functions similar to those of intermediate cities. Professor Gras describes the process as follows:

Just as the development of towns in town economy displays steps or phases, so does the growth of metropolitan economy illustrate certain steps which stand out more or less clearly. In the first part of the growth we see the prospective center reach out its tentacles by land and sea to secure supplies and to sell goods. It creates a situation and a feeling of dependence, although its means of exploitation are strictly limited. In short, it begins to organize the market. Then comes the development of manufacturing and transportation. In many parts of America these two grew up hand in hand, and with them, but lagging a bit behind, came the close financial knitting together of the whole area.[4]

Taking Chicago as an example, three zones

[4] E. W. Burgess, *The Urban Community* (Chicago: University of Chicago Press, 1926), p. 183.

can be marked off: the first, with a 20-mile radius from the loop, contains 21 smaller cities; the second, 20 to 40 miles out, has six centers; and the third, 40 to 80 miles away, includes 10 cities. A comparison of the average number of persons per store and the average expenditures per store for food, wearing apparel, and general merchandise, indicates that the influence of the central city gradually tapers off.

The tendency to form large metropolitan clusters is not wholly inspired by commerce and industry. Certain other advantages accrue to a center of high specialization and great division of labor. Such centers attract those types of social institutions, and those leaders in the professions, in the arts, and the sciences who contribute to and benefit from highly differentiated services. Large cities possess almost unlimited opportunities for diversification and specialization, for commercial amusements, art galleries, theater and opera ,and for social and professional contacts. These constitute an important corollary attraction or "lure" of the city.

Metropolitan society as a "state of mind." There are those who see this metropolitan development as a rival in economic administration and control to the present political system based upon federal, state, and county units. The city is more than a congeries of streets, buildings, telephones, people and service institutions, as Professor Burgess well points out. He says:

The city is rather a state of mind, a body of customs and traditions, and of the organized attitudes and sentiments that inhere in these customs and are transmitted with this tradition. In other words, the city is not merely a physical mechanism and an artificial construction. It is involved in the vital processes of the people who compose it; it is a product of nature, and particularly of human nature.[5]

If this "state of mind" and "organized attitude" does follow the mechanisms of trade, market, finance, and social contacts out into the larger metropolitan regions as described, then rural society will soon assume vastly different aspects. The mutual impacts of rural and urban ways of life will be considered in the next section, but the point of the present argument is that rural and urban are not separate entities and that students of rural society need to familiarize themselves with the rise, the development, and the influence of cities and metropolitan formations.

Changing Design of Rural-Urban Relationships

It is in the fringe areas of cities and in the outlying districts of metropolitan areas that the design of rural and urban relationships is changing most. The population story has been told in previous paragraphs in terms of the 168 areas known as standard metropolitan areas. It is in the areas immediately outside the cities, where greatest population growth has taken place, that important changes in social and economic relations are occurring and many problems arise. These areas have been designated the "New Social

Frontier" and have many characteristics once ascribed to the West.[6]

Rural-urban fringe. The late Professor George S. Wehrwein used the term "fringe" for that zone surrounding any large city because he said it was an area in transition between well recognized urban land uses and the area devoted to agricultural purposes.[7] This interpretation represents a different conception of rural-urban relationships from that of the early German writer, von Thunen, whose scheme of land-use was a series of concentric circles surrounding a city. All the land beyond the boundaries of the city, he declared to be agricultural. He made no provision for a transitional zone between the rural and the urban. Some recent students of society have also assumed a sharp distinction between "rural" or "urban." This, together with the arbitrary population limits set by early census reports, has tended to obscure recent developments in the rural-urban design.

Improved communication and transportation facilities, together with the expansion of electrification and other public utilities, have encouraged settlements of people in areas contiguous to cities. The movement is two-way. It is an "escape" from congested city centers, a thrusting-out into country areas of certain urban activities or land-uses, some unwanted or "condemned" by city ordinances, and others the result of suburban development or subdivision promotion. On the other hand, it is a movement of farm and village people toward urban opportunities for employment, markets, education, and other social services. For example, in the Madison fringe area, to be described presently, six out of every ten adults were reared on farms or in villages. A third of the

[5] Park and Burgess, *The City* (Chicago: University of Chicago Press, 1925), p. 1.

[6] Solon T. Kimball, *The New Social Frontier — The Fringe* (Michigan Agricultural Experiment Station Special Bulletin no. 360, June, 1949).

[7] "The Rural-Urban Fringe," *Economic Geography* (July, 1942).

families had never lived in the central city or in any other city.

Reports of recent studies make it quite clear that the force of these two movements coming together is making for a new pattern of living which is different from the traditional urban or rural forms. In times of industrial curtailment, for example, the "fringe" or "satellite" areas tend to absorb the shock; families step up their part-time farming activities. In periods of expanding employment opportunities, the city draws more heavily upon this area for workers, and the non-farm activities of the families approach full-time proportions.[8]

This may be the unplanned American counterpart of the plan advocated by LePlay, the French engineer who became social analyst and made studies of family living referred to in a later chapter. He urged families to have some of their members in agriculture and some in industry as a buffer against expected crises. It is an example of the policy urged by the Ford Motor Company since the days of the Model T, namely, "One foot in the factory and one foot on the soil."[9] It is likewise kindred to the idea of Broadacre City, designed by Frank Lloyd Wright and described in the chapter on recreation and the cultural arts.

Problems arise in transition areas. Neither the urban nor the rural social institutions or habits of social life are fully adjusted to the new situation. There are increased demands for more and better school facilities, thus increasing the already heavy tax load on real estate — farms, acreages, lots. Land values rise and the former ways of farming cannot survive. Certain commercial recreational activities are promoted over which local town governments fail to exercise adequate control. City authorities, thinking the solution to be in the direction of expanding the city limits, seek to incorporate adjoining areas. People in those areas resist the attempt and organize their own public services; they even incorporate as villages. Then, between or surrounding such organized sub-units there are likely to be disorganized areas — slums and poverty — endangering the entire rural-urban relationship. There is great opportunity for some political inventions by which the whole situation can develop, the urban center assuming its portion of responsibility and the fringe areas having freedom to assume some local direction and control for certain of their group interests. Families with small children have little concern for "downtown" schools or playgrounds.

The case of Webster, New York. The clashes and tensions that develop in the fringe area are well illustrated in a recent study of what, in 1923 when first surveyed, was an agricultural service station village and its rural community, Webster, New York.[10] Today it is the fringe of Rochester, New York. The process began when the overcrowded condition of the city's high schools resulted in towns within the metropolitan area sending pupils to Webster High School. Soon people from the city began to move to this attractive village. Taking up citizenship, they soon tried to accomplish "reforms," especially in the schools. In a short time there were three distinct groups, villagers who "belonged," the farmers, and the newcomers, known locally as "commuters." The farmers resented interference with their schools, the commuters having in-

[8] Howard E. Conklin, "The Rural-Urban Economy of the Elmira-Corning Region," *The Journal of Land and Public Utility Economics*, XX, No. 1 (February, 1944); W. R. Gordon, *Satellite Acres* (Kingston: Experiment Station Bulletin 282, Rhode Island State College, March, 1942).

[9] Henry Ford, II, address, Annual Convention of the American Farm Bureau Federation, Dallas, Texas, December 13, 1950.

[10] Earl L. Koos and Edmund de S. Brunner, *Suburbanization in Webster, New York* (Rochester, New York: University of Rochester, 1945).

spired a movement for consolidation. The "superior attitude" of the new population, together with their failure to conform to the local mores with respect to exchange of work and borrowing, soon set them apart. The villagers feared for their political dominance, in local government, in the village social organizations, and even in their churches. The commuters complained of the conservatism of the community and resented their exclusion from personal fellowship with "the natives," especially since they had come to Webster because of the importance they placed on rural living and rural values.

The case of Madison, Wisconsin. The situation can be further illustrated by a brief review of a study of the fringe area of Madison, Wisconsin.[11] In the decade from 1930 to 1940, the city itself increased by 16.5 per cent to a population of about 67,000 the metropolitan area, exclusive of the city, increased 69 per cent in the same period. The "fringe" was delineated by use of three indices: (1) proportion of non-farm families to all families, (2) density of non-farm population per square mile, and (3) assessed valuation of land and buildings per acre. The forty-nine township sections thus selected were found to contain a total of 3700 non-farm families. The most striking charac-

[11] Myles W. Rodehaver, adapted from an unpublished thesis, Department of Rural Sociology, University of Wisconsin, and an administrative release to the Madison Area Planning Council, June 28, 1945.

teristic of these families was their large number of children. Children under five years represented 20 per cent of the total population, while those under fifteen were 40 per cent. Only 3 per cent of the people were sixty years of age or older.

Table 46 and Figure 44 show the population distribution by age classes and give comparison with the city of Madison and with the farm population of the county in 1940. The actual size of the immediate family, comprised of head, wife, and children, for the fringe families was 3.8; for the city of Madison, 2.9; for the rural non-farm population of the state, 3.2; and for the state's farm population, 3.7. Such a comparison suggests the importance of more discriminating studies of fertility in rural and urban populations. They might show that the urban population is not "dying out," but that those families with children and going to have children are "moving out" from city centers.

The intermediate or transitional character of the rural-urban zone is further attested by the record of social and economic contacts of the non-farm families in the Madison fringe. Three fourths of the breadwinners were employed in the city. An equal proportion of the families did their "grocery" shopping in the city, not necessarily "on the square," but often in the secondary shopping centers near the city limits. Nine out of ten families used the Madison banks and commercial recreation places. Only six out of ten went to Madison for church services. Seventeen per

TABLE 46 Distribution by Age of Madison Fringe, City and Farm Population of Dane County	PLACE	PER CENT UNDER 5 YEARS	PER CENT UNDER 15 YEARS	PER CENT 25–39 YEARS	PER CENT 60 YEARS AND OVER
	Fringe	20.1	40.0	30.4	3.1
	Madison	6.6	20.1	26.4	10.5
	Rural-farm (Dane County)	8.8	28.1	18.7	10.2

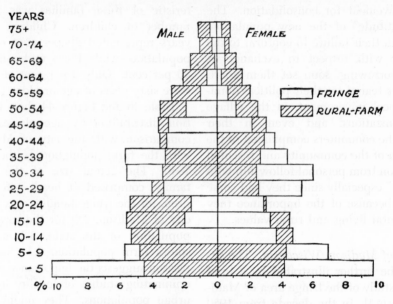

Figure 44. Age-Sex Distribution for Fringe and for Dane County Rural-Farm.

cent had children in the city elementary schools and 13 per cent in high schools. Thus, for many social activities and institutions, such as education, religion, and non-commercial recreation — picnics, outings, parties, children's games — the fringe families focused their efforts outside the city, and in many instances joined with the so-called rural farm families also living within the fringe area or near-by.

Similar conditions prevail elsewhere. Professor Butterworth of Cornell University reports that in 1950 there were 76 one-, two-, and three-teacher schools around Ithaca, a city of about 30,000 population, which were not included in the prevailing central community school systems. About 40 of them contract with the city for most of their grades, nine through twelve. The rest were carrying on independently. It is a sort of educational "no man's land" to which neither the rural nor the urban systems are adapted.

Along the Michigan-Ohio boundary and on main communication lines between Detroit and Toledo is the township of Bedford, another "social frontier." Here traditional rural community life is being shattered. Land is passing from agricultural use to become living space. A youthful and heterogeneous urban population is seeking to work out a new way of life with people of rural background. Many problems remain unsolved and the design of the resulting rural-urban relationship is still none too clear.

Changing relationships extend beyond the fringe. It thus becomes evident, as we examine numerous current situations, that a city does not really end at its legal or corporate limits nor even at the edge of the rural-urban fringe; it influences, and is influenced by, the characteristics and activities of people who live and work in areas beyond. This is the result of continual readjustments, the urban center adapting its functions to a wider circle, and both village and country accommodating themselves to

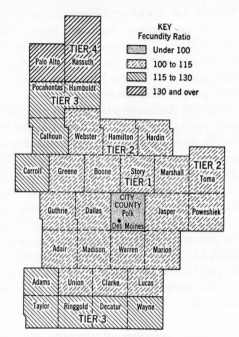

Figure 45. Fertility Ratios in the Des Moines Area, by Tiers of Counties, 1930.

Source: Brunner and Kolb, *Rural Social Trends* (New York: McGraw-Hill, 1933).

greater conformity with the city. A design or pattern of rural-urban relationships is finally formed which can be mapped and studied.

In order to examine such relationships, a plan was devised for the analysis of the concentric zones extending out from cities. Eighteen medium-sized cities scattered throughout the nation were studied.[12]

The Des Moines area: an illustration. To illustrate the type of measurement and the twofold comparison made in a single area, one item has been selected from population data, namely, fertility, and one from agricultural data, value of field crops per acre.

Population fertility may be measured by

[12] For a list of the cities see Brunner and Kolb, *Rural Social Trends* (New York: McGraw-Hill, 1933), chap. V and Appendix D.

taking the ratio of children under 10 to all women between ages 20 and 45. The data for Des Moines show that this ratio is lowest in the city county and increases with each succeeding tier. This is illustrated in Figure 45. A similar relationship existed in both 1910 and 1920. It is also clear that in the city county, and in all the others, the ratio had been falling during the two decades prior to 1930. The points of difference between 1910 and 1930 were greater in the city county than in any other tier of counties except the fourth, but even here the proportionate decrease was not so great as in the city itself. This comparison suggests a graduated influence in the operation of forces controlling birth rate as one moves from the urban county to rural counties surrounding it and illustrates a trend which has continued.

Values of field crops per acre in this Des Moines area are highest in the city county,

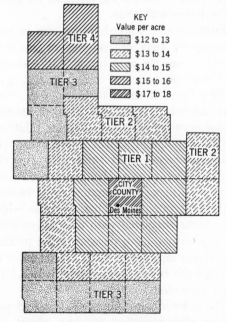

Figure 46. Value Per Acre of Field Crops in the Des Moines Area in 1930, by Tiers of Counties.

Source: Brunner and Kolb, *Rural Social Trends* (New York: McGraw-Hill, 1933).

and decreased with distance in the first three tiers, as shown in Figure 46. The story of agricultural prosperity which culminated in 1920 and the ensuing prolonged depression is told in these figures; the rise and fall of values are certainly abrupt.

Other relationships can be examined in terms of distance from cities and over periods of time.

Summary of the "tier" study; some social implications. It is evident from the prevailing pattern of the Des Moines area and from the study as a whole that the emerging design of rural-urban relationships has two important features of place and time. The first is a gradient character, that is, a gradual variation as the distance from the urban center increases. The second is a tendency to change with time. Population characteristics vary rather definitely as one proceeds away from or toward the city, but the differences lessen with time.

Rural-urban relationships can now be summarized by tiers of counties or zones of mutual influence as follows: City counties and tier one counties were likely to have smaller farms devoted to truck crops, fruit, and intensive dairying. This necessarily means more compact communities, relatively higher population density, and more frequent contacts of all sorts with the city center. The process has continued long enough so that such counties share increasingly those population characteristics which have been associated with the city; namely, fewer children, more persons in the productive age groups, lower birth rates, and so on through the list of comparisons which have been presented.

The story of rural population and its particular characteristics revolves about the tendency of families in the outer rural tiers to have more children. This is evidenced by fecundity and birth rates, by age distributions, and by sex and marriage ratios.

Children are a distinguishing characteristic of farm populations removed from cities. The tendency was more pronounced in the last decade, despite the fact that general differences in this regard between rural and urban people were decreasing.

Although the country is likely to contribute fewer young people to the nation in the future, its share will undoubtedly be disproportionately large for some time to come. The ratio of children to persons twenty to forty-five years of age is greater in the outer rural tiers than elsewhere. These persons may find it increasingly difficult to provide an education commensurate with the city county's, which has a greater proportion of people in this productive age group. This is a problem for consideration in the chapter on rural education.

Changing relations of country and city continue. Evidence gained from many recent studies indicates that rural-urban relationships are continuing to develop according to the general patterns just traced. Fringe areas near city centers are gaining not only in population but in perfecting living arrangements and in procuring social services and public utilities.

The case of Milwaukee, Wisconsin, illustrates the pattern of concentric circle growth extending out from the city but compensating for the lake which acts as a barrier on the east.[13] Twelve thousand families in the outlying area were questioned about why they had moved there. Their answers are summarized in Figure 47. Some of the hoped-for advantages proved illusory, as might be expected, since costs of transportation to and from work ate up gains from cheaper land or lower taxes. It is significant that many reasons relate to children. As in Madison, and in other fringe situations, chil-

[13] Richard Dewey, "Peripheral Expansion in Milwaukee County," *American Journal of Sociology,* LIV, No. 2 (September, 1948).

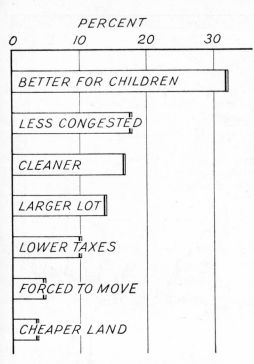

PERCENT

BETTER FOR CHILDREN

LESS CONGESTED

CLEANER

LARGER LOT

LOWER TAXES

FORCED TO MOVE

CHEAPER LAND

Figure 47. Reasons for Moving into Unincorporated Areas of Milwaukee County.

Source: Richard Dewey, "Peripheral Expansion in Milwaukee County," *The American Journal of Sociology,* LIV, No. 2, September, 1948.

dren are becoming an important feature of these regions. Whether families with children move out of cities or whether families have children because they move out is not important to the present argument but the fact that children are found in the outlying areas is highly important. It is sure to influence the character of social organization in these areas and the type of social institutions demanded by families who live there.

Cincinnati, Ohio and Hartford, Connecticut also show the widely expanded influence of a city center. Many indices can be used to illustrate the extent and character of this influence. For Cincinnati the radio audience and newspaper circulation were considered good indicators of the metro-

politan region and its cohesion through communication.[14] Charge accounts in a leading department store spread out over a very large area of influence including twenty-six counties, eight in Ohio, twelve in Kentucky and six in Indiana. This expanded area is indicated in Figure 48.

For Hartford, attention centered in finance and insurance; indeed, the city is referred to locally as "the Insurance Capital of the United States." The commuting pattern of those employed in a single insurance concern is shown in Figure 49. The residences of these workers are scattered over thirty-seven towns (townships) throughout central Connecticut, and the suburbs surrounding the city contain large numbers of such workers. It is these suburban towns which have grown most rapidly during the past twenty years, while the city itself has almost stood still.

Population influences extend to rural areas. As the chapter on population emphasized,

[14] City Planning Commission report, *The Economy of Cincinnati Metropolitan Area, 1946.*

Figure 48. Counties in Which 15 Per Cent or More of "Buying Families" Have Charge Accounts at a Leading Cincinnati Store.

Source: *The Economy of the Cincinnati Metropolitan Area.* (Cincinnati: City Planning Commission, December, 1946).

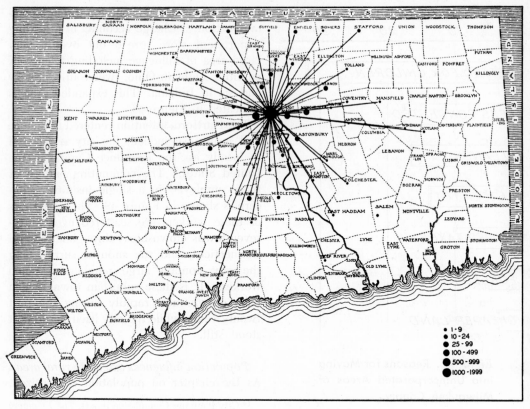

Figure 49. Residences of Workers Employed
in a Hartford Insurance Company, 1948.

The number of workers living in Hartford is not shown. Source: Walter
C. McKain, Jr. and Nathan L. Whetten, *Occupational and Industrial Di-
versity in Rural Connecticut*, Bulletin 263 (Storrs: University of Connecticut
Agricultural Experiment Station, November, 1949).

an increasing proportion of non-farm people
is included within the rural population. The
greatest rural non-farm growth, however, in
the decade from 1930 to 1940, was in the
vicinity of growing cities located in the outlying areas of metropolitan influence. This
would suggest that the process of suburban-
izing was extensive and not confined to
large central clusters. Even counties whose
largest city had a population of only 5000
showed definite increase among non-farm
people. It is suggested that this process might
set a limit to the size of large cities, since the
larger metropolitan regions with the largest

central cities have already declined in relation to other areas. Whatever the future
holds, it is clear that present rural-urban relationships are assuming new and larger importance. They are not restricted to large
and complex metropolitan regions but include all intervening rural-urban situations
even to the town-country community with a
center of 5000 people.

Interaction of Rural and Urban

Certain characteristics have traditionally
been associated with rural and with urban

populations. Questions naturally arise regarding future results of the greater interaction of the two societies. With today's free contacts and increased mobility, will the city urbanize the country or will the country ruralize the city? From the evidence of present trends, there seems to be little immediate likelihood that all differences will be obliterated. There can be no doubt, however, that many of them will be greatly modified. On the other hand, it should be pointed out that there are many common characteristics which are neither rural nor urban. In the great population movements described in an earlier chapter, first from rural to urban before 1929, and then from urban to rural in the following five years, the question is, which traits have been sloughed off and which have been rendered more common? What will be the effects of efforts to decentralize industry and population and of the movement of people, especially non-farming families, to the penumbra of cities, both large and small?

Rural and urban are now more relative terms than earlier, as previously suggested. This is only another way of saying that a process is under way which is modifying wide differences. Since the changing design has been examined, the processes themselves should be studied more thoroughly. A two-way action is involved which, at the risk of over-simplifying and over-popularizing, can be termed "urbanization" and "ruralization." These terms are widely used, but often with so little discrimination that it is important to examine some of their implications.

Urbanization. To urbanize means to transfer the characteristics of a city. Direct and indirect contacts have, without doubt, made country and city more alike in many respects, but to say that the city has deliberately fixed its features upon the country is an exaggeration. The city is not sufficiently organized and unified to do this, although it is quite evident that certain city groups and enterprises have proceeded with this aim in some of their propaganda campaigns. That both country and city are exposed on a grander scale to the influences of mechanical invention, mass production, and centralized control would be a more exact statement. Often the city acts as the earlier laboratory; later it becomes a center of diffusion or propagation. To say that an invention comes out of a city, however, does not prove that it is of urban design.

The clearest evidence of direct rural contacts with urban centers is, of course, in the commercial field, where it is easy to observe and to record. Small centers attract to their general stores only that proportion of families who live within their primary sphere of influence, and the goods bought at such centers pertain directly to the farm or to daily living. When clothing, furniture, and other specialities are purchased, then the larger places have a greater attraction. Central city stores also establish branches in out-urban centers. In these ways some of the apparent differences between the country and the city man have disappeared; both buy at the same stores.

Indirect contacts are more subtle, as emphasized previously. The increase in city practices of finance and control, rural banking, rural storekeeping, and village manufacturing plants was evident when specific rural communities were restudied over periods of ten and twenty years. Social institutions and agencies are not immune to urbanization. Urban influences are playing upon rural schools, and within the local churches the force of administrative boards dominated by urban points of view is constantly felt. Similarly, luncheon clubs, parent-teacher associations, men's and women's clubs, receive from their regional, state, or national offices more and more suggestions unfamiliar to the rural world. Such influences also reach directly into homes by means of modern media of communication, such as newspapers, magazines, radio, and television. The simultaneous exposure of rural and urban families to these pressures can hardly fail to iron out many of the curves of difference, even though listening and reading habits may differ. Differences of opinion and attitude are tending to form about other cleavages in the total society, such as occupations, economic and social status, and special interests.

Ruralization. To ruralize means to impart a rural character or aspect. If there has been urbanization of the country there has also been ruralization of the city. The urban movement reached its height during the first thirty years of the century. Those were the years of city building, the increasing use of the automobile, extension of mechanical power, and of improvement in telephone and radio. It is estimated that in the decade from 1920 to 1930 nearly 20,000,000, and from 1940 to 1949 nearly 15,000,000 people migrated to cities. Certainly these millions did not shed all their ideas, attitudes, and ways of living at the city gates, as some writers have implied in their great emphasis upon the urbanization of the country.

Even superficial observation, as for example the roof-garden of a city apartment house several hundred feet above the ground, provides evidences of ruralization. The roof-garden itself is a reversion to a country form of living. There over the ledge can be seen a front porch, a suspended line with drying clothes, flower boxes gay with color, formalized pines at an entrance across the street, a dog in his runway on another flat roof, and beyond, a cat sunning herself contentedly. In the outskirts, past the "downtown" districts, many other country scenes greet the understanding eye. The more trenchant implications of the rural-urban migration as a phase of rural-urban relationships, which were discussed in an

earlier chapter, have been summarized in a few sentences by Sorokin, Zimmerman, and Galpin. Of the trend to the city, they say, "The characteristics of the rural population are carried into the city by each new generation of migrants. The spiritual and moral convictions, the habits of life, and the personal traits of the rural population, whether good or bad, are constantly being injected into the culture that obtains in the city."[15]

There are many evidences of the influence of rural culture upon urban life. Interesting examples are the rural practices that carry over into the administration and conduct of city churches. By carefully devised measurements, Dr. H. Paul Douglass is able to identify city churches of rural origin and to determine the extent to which adjustments have been made to urban conditions. He suggests that city churches as a group vary all the way from extreme simplicity to great complexity of program, and the explanation he gives is that they are getting away more and more from a rural tradition and moving toward an urban one. He estimates that 25 per cent or more of city churches are no larger and no more highly organized than the average rural church. He concludes that the city church represents an evolution from a rural parent stock, although its immediate ancestor is the town church.[16]

Furthermore, just as the countryman has many direct contacts with city life, so there are an ever-expanding number and type of direct contacts for the city man in the country: contacts of business, pleasure, hunting, fishing, touring, or the more extended associations of a country home, a summer vacation, and visits with rural relatives. It is also estimated that a perceptible amount of agricultural wealth migrates annually to

[15] *A Systematic Source Book in Rural Sociology,* III (Minneapolis: University of Minnesota Press, 1930), p. 534.

[16] *One Thousand City Churches: Phases of Adaptation to Urban Environment* (New York: George H. Doran Co.), chap. IV.

cities through inheritances, as an illustrative study in Ohio shows.[17] Thus rural and urban are bound by many ties. Inventions for communication and the wider use of machines in country and in city are important forces in this process.

Rurbanization. To rurbanize means to bring town and country together *en rapport.* This intermediary process is suggested as an explanation of a present trend. It is not merely a figure of speech to say that midway between country and city stands the village or small town, one hand extending toward the country and the other toward the city. It is rather a description of an actual situation. Likewise, the rurban community of town and country manifests many features of a reconciliation between extreme ruralism and extreme urbanism. And finally, the designation of the village or small town as the mid-point toward which the changing characteristics of both country and city populations are approaching, is a representation of present and probable future trends. Rural and urban societies already tend to resemble each other in many respects, a resemblance which may continue as the expression of modern relationships, and this without undue sacrifice of those unique qualities which have characterized their past and which are needed for their future.

Finally, implications following from the changing rural-urban relationships detailed in this chapter require the attention of the people who live in the country and those who live in the city. Traditionally farmers have had an antipathy to city dwellers. Some experiences of the depression and of the war have seemed to modify this attitude and give increased realization of the interdependencies of agriculture and the business and industry of the city. On the other hand,

issues have been raised regarding prices, wages, tariffs, and labor unions. There have been McNary-Haugen bills, export debenture plans, and the AAA. For the first time some villages have had experience with organized labor. The employees of a small industrial plant in an eastern agricultural village were organized by men sent out from union headquarters. A strike was called. In a middle-western farming community the state labor board exercised its authority in a dispute between the directors of a farmers' coöperative association and its employees. The political reverberations of this action are sure to be heard for many a year. Alignments of farmers and city wage-earners have been attempted, but they seem to fall apart rather easily. In New Zealand a labor party came to power by the votes of farmers, but there is a constant struggle to keep the coalition together in thought and attitude. It is very difficult for a farmer to understand a labor organizer's point of view, and it constantly tests the patience of a labor official to have a farmer stress the importance of land-ownership, low farm wages, and high prices for the food and fiber produced on the farm.

It is futile to think of turning back. The future lies, as Lewis Mumford says so well, in "intelligent participation and understanding at every stage in the process," and the "process" is sure to involve rather fundamental readjustments for both urban and rural society.[18]

Summary of Group Relationships, Some Implications

Discussion of group relations in rural society has extended all the way from families, neighborhoods, villages and communities, and special interest groups, to rural-urban relationships. Families continue to hold a firm and recognized place. There are more

[17] E. D. Tetreau, *Some Trends in Rural Social Organization in Four Ohio Counties* (Columbus: Ohio Agricultural Experiment Station Bulletin 42, November, 1931).

[18] *Culture of Cities* (New York: Harcourt, Brace, 1939).

of them than formerly in proportion to the total population. People marry younger; there are more young children. Country neighborhoods are gaining new significance when related to larger group formations as town-country communities. Special interest groups are increasing in number and strength. Rural communities and rural-urban fringe areas are focal points for two great social movements, centralization and decentralization.

Evidence is emphatic that groups are increasingly interrelated and that people, as persons, move about among them playing different roles as they go. Opportunities for alternative choices and for reasoned decisions have increased. Technical improvements in communication have made this possible but not automatic. It is only through some recognition of and voluntary response to these inter-group experiences that society can have vitality and meaning and that groups can become more than rigid forms and empty symbols for the persons involved.

This interpretation is quite different from that of people having fixed traits and inherent instincts, living in closed groups and always reacting in the same way. It shifts the attention from attempts at definition and classification of groups and persons to an analysis of their functions and the interaction which takes place in certain social situations. Persons and groups are simply two aspects of interaction in any social situation; thus society becomes a vast network of interactive relationships.

The practical as well as the theoretical consequences of this view of people and society are very great. It means that every person must learn his "way around" if he is to keep in actual contact, in the sense of being in communication, in his various groups. It means that group competence can be learned and improved upon, that wholesome and workable group techniques can be acquired just as skills can be achieved and perfected in any manual technique, such as writing, plowing, driving a car, or playing a violin.

This interrelationship means that personal and group developments are complementary and compulsory; one cannot go forward without the other. People are not separate, self-contained integers; they gain their significance by reference to each other, especially in those group relations of family and community which have universal recognition. That each of us is our brother's keeper is not simply a statement of religious principle; it is a social fact.

Similarly, groups are not self-sufficient and mutually exclusive; they also are interdependent and interrelated, and they gain their meaning by reference to each other and to the cultural systems of which they form a part. This means that groups must become flexible; they must encourage readjustments, deliberately seek to find their own places in relation with other groups.

Finally, the interdependence of individuals and groups means that society does not advance by the additions of individual or separate group achievements alone but also by those social processes which build up mutual response, responsibility, and respect. Questions involving personal and group relations of control and freedom in any corporate, democratic society are always pivotal, and usually perplexing. For example, what shall be public policy for farm production or population growth?

Consideration of social groups in rural society and the importance of their interrelationships leads naturally and directly to the whole field of social institutions. Social institutions have their group backgrounds and implications. They are the more formalized and more securely established relationships in a society. They too must have a degree of flexibility and responsiveness to change if they would survive and remain vital in the society within which they have their social being.

TOPICS FOR DISCUSSION

1. Describe and give reasons for such direct contacts between rural and urban people — such as shopping, visiting, and recreation — which you think have increased most in the past five years.
2. Make a list of five city-centered agencies operating in country-village communities. Describe briefly the local system of organization and operation of each. Example: chain store, trade union.
3. Describe any variation which you have been able to observe in driving out twenty miles or more from a medium-sized city in density such as shopping, visiting, and recreation — of country population, types of agriculture, frequency and size of villages, characteristics of the population.
4. How do you account for this gradient pattern of rural-urban relations? What are its practical implications for land-use planning? For curriculum building in high schools?
5. Give the best example you know of farmers and city wage-earners successfully working together, or give an example of a conflict situation and suggest solutions.

REFERENCE READINGS

Angell, Robert C., *The Moral Integration of American Cities*. Chicago: University of Chicago Press, 1951.

Bogue, Donald J., *Structure of the Metropolitan Community*. Ann Arbor: University of Michigan Press, 1949.

Douglass, H. Paul, *Suburban Trends*. New York: Century, 1925. The movement toward decentralizing cities and the growth of satellite cities.

Hallenbeck, Wilbur, *American Urban Communities*. New York: Harper, 1951.

Hauser, Phillip M., "How Declining Urban Growth Affects City Activities," *Public Management*, XXII, December, 1940.

Hoyt, H., "Forces of Urban Centralization and Decentralization; Historical Review of Urban Development," *American Journal of Sociology*, XLVI, May, 1941.

McKenzie, R. D., *The Rise of Metropolitan Communities*. New York: McGraw-Hill, 1922. A social trends monograph.

Shevky and Lewin, *Your Neighborhood: A Social Profile of Los Angeles*. Los Angeles: Haynes Foundation, 1949.

Smith, Mapheus, "Rural-Urban Intelligence Gradients," *Journal of Sociology and Social Research*, XXVII, August, 1943.

Sorokin and Zimmerman, *Principles of Rural-Urban Sociology*, Part I. New York: Holt, 1929. Fundamental relations of the rural and urban worlds.

Thaden, J. F., *The Lansing Region and Its Tributary Town-Country Communities*, Bulletin 302. East Lansing: Michigan State College Experiment Station, March, 1940.

Tomars, Adolph S., "Rural Survivals in the American Urban Life," *Rural Sociology*, VIII, No. 4, December, 1943.

Whetten, Nathan L., and E. C. Devereaux, *Studies of Suburbanization in Connecticut* (I. *Windsor: A Highly Developed Agricultural Area*), Bulletin 212. Storrs: Connecticut State College Experiment Station, October, 1936.

Whetten, Nathan L., and R. F. Field, *Studies of Suburbanization in Connecticut* (II. *Norwich: An Industrial Part-Time Farming Area*), Bulletin 226. Storrs: Connecticut State College Experiment Station, May, 1938.

Whetten, Nathan L., *Studies of Suburbanization in Connecticut* (III. *Wilton: A Rural Town Near Metropolitan New York*), Bulletin 230. Storrs: Connecticut State College Experiment Station, February, 1939.

Whitney, Vincent H., "Rural-Urban People," *American Journal of Sociology*, LIV, No. 1, July, 1948.

FILMS

U.S.A. Metropolis. S, 21. Description of life in the city of New York. United World.

PART FOUR

Institutional Arrangements

Social institutions are the more or less recognized and established ways and means for getting things done collectively in a society. They are indispensable not only in the business of making the living but in doing the living. Institutions relate past and future through the present; they are anchored in the past but must be geared to the future as a condition of survival. The function of any social institution in a changing society is to influence the direction of trends and to readjust to dominant forces of change.

Rapidly changing times call for flexibility in the processes of social institutions and for imagination and courage in formulating policies and programs. This is especially true for rural society today in regard to improving education, expanding health facilities, extending social security provisions, quickening spiritual leadership, developing recreation and the cultural arts, and keeping public agencies, including government itself, responsive to democratic controls.

The country church, its steeple reaching skyward as if to unite heaven and earth, stands as a significant symbol of institutional strength and solidarity in rural society.

17 Standards of Living and the Rural Home

THE STUDY OF SOCIETY is sometimes begun with the great social institutions such as home, school, church, and government. For these institutions seem so tangible and so permanent that they challenge attention at the outset. This procedure, however, seems to be "putting the cart before the horse," as the old adage has it, for it should be quite clear from the preceding discussion that social institutions spring from group experiences and backgrounds and from the desires and traditions of people. They are the results of evolution and change, since to survive, institutions must constantly make adjustments.

In introducing the social institutions of rural society, it should be emphasized at once that the home is not the house, the school is not the building, nor is the church merely the structure with the steeple. The terms and the ideas for which they stand are easily confused. An institution is the more or less regular way a group does things. Habit and custom are important, since people tend to repeat methods of accomplishing their ends until the habit becomes definitely established. Such ways and methods are finally given the sanction of society. They may be society's plan for keeping certain groups in line with accepted social standards.

The school, for example, is the whole social arrangement of teachers and pupils, teachers and parents, and pupils and parents. It has its curriculum, its community relations, and its public policy. The school building is only an external evidence of internal activity.

Similarly, the home with its ways of living, which is the subject of the present chapter, is something vastly more than a house. This truth was evidently in the mind of the popular writer who said, "It takes a heap o' livin' to make a house a home."

The Rural Home as Social Institution and Consumer Center

Characteristics of the rural family group and its chief occupation, farming, have been discussed in other chapters. It is the purpose of this chapter to study the family's ways of living. Such institutional forms of behavior have two aspects, internal and external. Society has never given the family group an entirely free hand in its own internal ways of living. Standards of health, honesty, morality, and many other forms of conduct have been prescribed. Whether internally or externally conditioned, the home with its standards of living is a social institution of primary importance.

Standards of living as a component part of this institution, the home, are themselves social forms of behavior embracing not only consumption of the economic goods — food, clothing, and shelter — but also the consumption or use of the wide range of non-material elements including those spiritual, esthetic, and social amenities which go to make up ways of living. These ways of living in the home can be observed or studied through actual budgetary expenditures, through socio-economic status as reflected in the possession of cultural goods or household conveniences, and in other forms of social behavior such as the participation in social groups or the use of time for recreation, education, religion, or other activities.

Broadly considered, consumption means the converting of gross profits into goods and services for human joy and living. The consuming takes place through the home, and the nature of the consumption is defined through the standards of living. In short, the rural home so conceived is as definitely a consuming institution as the farm is a producing institution, and together they become a mode of living quite as much as a means of livelihood.

"Socially desirable" standards, result of social processes. Standards of living from this focus of the home are obviously group products. They arise out of social experience, and what is finally considered necessary or proper — that is, "desirable" — emerges as regular and recognized. This is the social process of building up a social institution. To be sure, different families have different ways, and these ways are undergoing constant change and adjustment, but this is the dictum of society.

In rural society, where the family group is so important, its ways of living are subjects of vital interest. Through studies of living, some of which will be described later in this chapter, it is possible to observe some of the changes and readjustments going on in the home and also to understand more fully the social processes involved. One may think of the matter as a game of choosing: so much food as compared with so much shelter, or so much recreation, in order to have the sort of home life one wants. This proportioning of the factors of consumption becomes a very complicated affair, and its analysis soon leads one into many questions which cannot be considered here. What are wants? What conditions them? Why do they differ for different people? These are problems with which social psychologists must wrestle.

Some of the results of the proportioning, however, can be seen from the studies. For example, it was found that for farm families within the same state, food costs ranged from 20 to 50 per cent of total expenditures. The explanation does not lie entirely in the amount of income available, but leads back to social customs, to size of family, to values placed upon food as compared with education or religion. The matter of valuing and choosing is one of the most fundamental in human relations. Professor Cooley suggests that all psychical life is in some sense a choosing.[1] He declares that "a system of values is a system of practical ideas or motives to behavior."[2] Behind the whole valuation process, therefore, is this effort of human beings to continue life and to work out their interests in a changing world.

The consumer emphasis in modern life. Thus the rural home and its standards of living are seen to be closely related to other aspects of rural society and to the "Great Society" beyond. Experiences during depression years have given practical demonstration of the importance of this emphasis on consumption.

Consumption, according to Professor Gide of the University of Paris is the final goal or "consummation" of the whole economic process. He says, "The domain of consumption is infinitely rich and as yet half explored; it is from here probably that economic science will one day start anew."[3] Despite this strong statement, he and many other political economists develop their system of economic thought around the concept of production. In fact, as stated elsewhere,

[1] Charles H. Cooley, *Human Nature and the Social Order* (New York: Scribner, 1902).

[2] *The Social Process* (New York: Scribner, 1925).

[3] Gide, Charles, *Political Economy* (authorized translation from the 3d ed., 1913, of the *Cours d'Economie Politique*. Boston: D. C. Heath).

Americans have become well schooled in the production theory of economics, a theory born when recurring famines and other shortages of uncounted centuries pointed to the need for supplying sufficient food and shelter for mankind.[4] In early American life it fitted in with the whole pioneering spirit to which reference has been made. Settlers sought to exploit and subdue the natural resources and to make them produce. There were always hungry mouths to feed in both country and city. The only problem was to produce sufficient quantities; the market seemed always to be calling for more. The government later, through extension service, urged farmers to increase per acre yields through use of more science and better technology. In recent decades such technology has multiplied many forms of production so that now the apparently impossible has happened. Production has outstripped consumption and finds itself caught in the web of a theory which never envisaged such a possibility. Hunger and want are still pressing their claims, but now in a land of plenty.

Rural people are directly concerned with consumption from a second angle. Consumption habits, which in many particulars have changed but little for centuries, can now be altered or even revolutionized in a few months. Production, then, cannot be regarded for its own sake, but as it ministers to consumers' needs and wants, and consumption habits must be studied and even forecast. The science of consumption should be built up by students of society rather than by sales managers.

Finally, from the standpoint of public policy, consumption includes various uses to which wealth is put. It must be admitted that more than once wealth has been amassed where it is not of maximum social usefulness. The question has been seriously raised as to whether consumption, condi-

tioning as it does so many phases of life, is not the next area to which government and private agencies need to turn their attention.

Doctor Galpin emphasized the place of consumption in agriculture and rural life when he said: "The farmer's problem is far from being solely a problem of price for farm products and profits of agriculture. It is a problem also of consumption goods, and for the college to leave this problem untouched and unsolved is to invite a situation in agriculture in which farmers know how to make profits as farmers, but not how to spend their profits as consumers. Such an agriculture is neither stable nor prosperous nor well paid." [5]

Robert Lynd, after an extended study of "The People as Consumers" for the President's Research Committee on Social Trends, concluded his report with the two following significant sentences: "The primary concern is whether the government is prepared to give to the spending of the national income the same degree of concern that it at present bestows upon the earning of that income. Such coherent leadership is needed if schools and other agencies are to educate the consumer in the practice of the fine art of spending money." [6]

Importance of living recognized by rural groups. The practical implications of the consumption emphasis and of the necessity for recognizing standards of "desirable" ways of living are being increasingly appreciated by farm people themselves. There was a time when certain groups of families chose to delay much home consumption until the farm was paid for, or until "it could be afforded." Private property in land was a "motive for behavior," driving the pioneer

[4] Brunner and Kolb, *Rural Social Trends* (New York: McGraw-Hill, 1933).

[5] C. J. Galpin, "Spending the Dollar Wisely in Home and Community" (Address, Thirty-Eighth Annual Convention of the Association of Land-Grant Colleges, Washington, D.C., 1924).

[6] *Recent Social Trends* (New York: McGraw-Hill, 1933), II, p. 911.

westward, as was noted in the chapter on the rural family. The old motto of scarcity economy was, "You can't have your cake and eat it." More recently the living side of farm life has received new recognition, so that the proverb could be revised to read, "You can't keep your cake unless you eat it" — which suggests simply that profits from farming should be converted into standards of living for home and for community. To use an agricultural metaphor, profits should be "plowed back" into the soil of family and community life, rather than into the physical soil simply to induce more production.

Necessity for protecting standards of living has been recognized by agricultural leaders. In the earlier days there was discussion of "eliminating the marginal producers"; more recent thinking stresses the dangers attendant upon sacrificing accepted standards of living by "marginal consumers." A striking statement of this occurs in a discussion of "success" in farming by two English writers. They say:

> But ultimately there is no general success which is not measurable in human values, and most of the success in farming can eventually be measured by the standard of living obtainable and enjoyed by the family. This is not a plea for ostentation, for real standards of living are not to be measured by outside show. . . .

Although the possibilities of the standard of living for individual families over the whole group are largely determined by the common standard of living, this imposes the general limitations on the competition for the requirements of production, especially land and labor, but it also has a great influence on the conditions under which capital is accumulated or obtained. Thus the individual who is willing to sacrifice the accepted standard of living in the competition for either, is a danger to his neighbor.[7]

[7] A. W. Ashby and J. P. Howell, "Success in Farming; Its Nature and Determination," *Journal of Surveyor's Institution,* 1926. Reprinted in *Rural Standards of Living, a Selected Bibliography* (Washington, D.C.: United States Department of Agriculture, Agricultural Economics Bibliography no. 32, August, 1930. Mimeographed).

Concern of society in rural levels of living. Various agencies of government have "stepped into" the rural home and influenced its living in the last decades. Many of the governmental programs are discussed elsewhere and need emphasis at this point only as evidence of the definite concern of society regarding the rural living functions of the home. One way in which the government affects living is through assuming more and more of the former functions of the home, such as education, health, and recreation. Another important means of helping consumers is standardization, labeling and sumptuary legislation, and the enforcement of various food and drug acts.

The Federal Housing Authority and the Rural Electrification Administration have undertaken large programs for the improvement of standards of living through better housing and household conveniences. The significance of these programs for the present discussion is the recognition from the standpoint of public policy and interest that there are certain levels of living below which rural families should not be allowed to go. With such extreme reductions comes the danger to public health and the burden of poor relief, which will be emphasized in the chapter on public health and welfare. It is likewise recognized that levels of living of rural families have a real relation to public policies for land use, credit, and taxation, topics which have been explored in other chapters.

Early Studies of Levels of Living

Although detailed studies of levels of living in the rural home are of comparatively recent date in this country, knowledge of living conditions in general has grown through a series of systematic studies, mostly of urban laborers, dating back at least to the comparisons made by Gregory King for the years 1688 and 1699 for England, France, and Holland. Since that time hundreds of studies have been made. The methods employed have varied considerably, and no one of them singly deserves credit for providing complete help. There are, however, students whose contributions have proved particularly useful as a means of understanding the standards of living in the rural homes of America.

Studies of levels of living become a means or a "tool" for a better understanding, not only of the rural home, but of society itself. Budgets of income, expenditures, and use of time or energy have importance in and of themselves, but they have wider usefulness as a means of studying family organization, discovering social classes, and observing the interaction of family groups with other groups and with the institutions in society.

The Le Play case studies. As a professor in Paris, Le Play started his investigations of family living in about 1830, and for half a century carried on his studies in practically every country of Europe. He would arrange to live with families which he selected as representative of certain types and would stay long enough to prepare a complete case analysis of each family.[8]

Le Play was concerned with the problems arising out of industrialization in the nineteenth century. It was evident to him that there was a close connection between the consumption habits of families and the social policy of a nation. In times of prosperity, if habits of waste and unwarranted expansion of standards of living were allowed, there was sure to be a reaction which would end in suffering. Society should, therefore, in-

fluence families to prepare for the rainy day rather than to hasten its coming. He pointed out that if society's leaders were willing and prompt to act, much suffering caused by wars, industrial crises, and famine could be avoided, and the consequent lowering of standards of living and the disruption of the social classes averted. He made the family his unit for study and investigation. Emphasis was placed on the mores, habits, and institutions which preserve the physical as well as the mental and social well-being of the family.

As was noted in the early chapter on the rural family, Le Play placed a good deal of stress upon the sentimental attachments which exist between the family group and its homestead or its "hearth," as he called it. Therefore, it is not strange that he should seek to analyze the ways of living of the family. He maintained that he who makes a complete analysis of the factors influencing the income and expenditures of a family possesses a complete knowledge of that family. By the use of this case-study method he and his followers made classifications of societies according to types of family organization, and gave explanations of the processes and changes in the society itself. The home, with its ways of living considered as a social institution, was the starting point for Le Play in his study of society.

The Engel statistical studies. In contrast with Le Play, Engel put his emphasis upon the accumulation of data regarding many families. His was a statistical study of what might be termed "mass" consumption. He used some of the original material gathered by Le Play and others, and also the studies of wage-earners in Belgium in 1886 and 1891. By statistical analysis he was able to show relationships between the distribution of the items of the budget and the rise of the family in the social scale. His statements of these relationships have come to be known

[8] Published in *Les Ouvriers Européens* and *Les Ouvriers des deux Mondes*, 1856–1930. The present summary of the early studies is adapted from interpretations made by Carle C. Zimmerman, "Development of Research in Family Living," Scope and Method Monograph; *Research in Family Living* (Social Science Research Council, J. D. Black, editor) pp. 48–56; and "Family Budget as Tool for Analysis," *American Journal of Sociology* (May, 1928), XXIII, p. 901.

as "Engel's Laws" of consumption. The
statements took two forms. The first, which
has received much less attention but which
has significance for the student of society,
was that the importance of food in a
budget was the best single index of the
social position of the family. The second
was that an increase in income was associated with declining proportions of the
budget spent for food, with about the same
proportions spent for clothing, rent, fuel,
and light, and with increasing proportions
for education, health, recreation, and amusements.

Although the relationships suggested by
Engel have been found in general to hold
true for present wage-earning families, as
well as for rural laborers and salaried people,
some revisions and modifications have been
made on the basis of more recent studies in
this country.[9]

The influence of Engel's type of analysis
has been direct in both rural and urban
studies of standards of living. The method
affords an opportunity for observing the
changing behavior of families as they move
up and down the income scale, and also for
making limited comparisons between rural
and urban families. It does not give the
chance, however, for relating the home as
an institution to its own immediate social
environment. Therefore, both the Engel and
the Le Play methods can be used to good
advantage as complements to each other.

American farm family studies. Studies of
farm families in America were much later in
starting than those of wage-earners and low-
salaried groups, but once under way they
increased rapidly. Among the early contributions were the field studies of Warren in
1909, of Funk in 1913, and the writings of
men like Galpin. These publications and the

series of studies which followed have provided background knowledge regarding
ways of living in American rural homes,
especially farm homes.

One of the significant field surveys was a
project of the Bureau of Agricultural Economics, United States Department of Agriculture, directed by E. L. Kirkpatrick. In
this study, data were collected from 2886
white farm families in eleven states, for a
one-year period during 1922–24. The results
secured were believed to represent general
conditions for the country as a whole. Although no other nation-wide surveys were
immediately undertaken, agricultural colleges coöperating with the United States Department of Agriculture have made a great
many local studies which contributed both
to research method and to an understanding
of how farm families live.[10]

Studies of the ways in which rural people
spend their time also afford a clue to their
standards of living. The use of time reflects
the value attached to this or that form of
activity. Such studies offer interesting in-
sight into some of the traditional attitudes
toward recreation, for example.[11]

Finally, the realistic portrayals of rural
life through the novel and drama must not
be overlooked. Only by making use of all
available sources can we come to know
how farm people live and what factors influence their ways of living.

[9] United States Public Health Service Report 35,
No. 48 (Washington, D.C.: United States Treasury
Department, 1920).

[10] Carle C. Zimmerman, *Consumption and Stand-
ards of Living* (New York: D. Van Nostrand, 1936);
Faith M. Williams and Carle C. Zimmerman,
*Studies of Family Living in the United States and
Other Countries* (Washington, D.C.: Miscellaneous
publication No. 223, United States Department of
Agriculture, 1935).

[11] Mary E. Frayser, *Use of Leisure in Selected
Rural Areas of South Carolina* (Bulletin 263, Clem-
son Agricultural College Experiment Station, 1930);
Maud Wilson, *Use of Time by Oregon Homemakers*
(Bulletin 256, Oregon Agricultural Experiment Sta-
tion, 1929); J. O. Rankin, *Use of Time in Farm
Homes* (Bulletin 230, Nebraska Agricultural Ex-
periment Station, 1928).

Recent Trends of Living in Rural Homes

Like any other social relationships in a dynamic society, ways of living in homes change. Generalized statements are therefore difficult to make, and if too general have little relevance to an understanding of particular situations. There are not only changes over time but variations from rural to urban, region to region; in residence with respect to nearness to urban centers; and differences in income classes, tenure, family size and cycle, as well as in community resources for education, recreation, and welfare. Nevertheless, some important impressions regarding rural society can be gained from brief reviews of recent trends, since, as Le Play maintained, there is close correlation between consumption habits of families and society's welfare.

It should be borne in mind that there is not always complete agreement or consistency in the use of such terms as "cost of living," "level of living," or "standard of living." However, "level of living" is understood to mean the ways that groups actually live in a particular time and place, while "standard of living" is the broader term, implying social patterns in the institutional sense, also implying a general standard of norms. In the presentations to follow, levels of living described are in terms of the physical goods and services which particular families use or consume in given periods of time. It is difficult, if not impossible, to get a common physical measure of goods and services; therefore, the common practice is to express items of a family budget in monetary terms. Even this is far from satisfactory, since the buying power of a dollar is not a stable thing when considered in terms of hours of work or bushels of corn necessary to acquire it.

Fortunately for those interested in rural society, many recent studies of family living have considered not only items of expenditure, but have attempted to trace their relationships with other family concerns, such as

mobility, social participation, source of income, housing, and even the use of time. Scales for measurement and comparison of levels of living have been devised. Some are long and complicated, others short and simple, but the purpose is to find measuring techniques with standardized and validated indices.[12] There are also attempts to study and measure the non-monetary items in family living. There is payment in kind, such as eggs, milk, and garden space for the farm laborer or the cash tenant, and there are many items produced by the family itself, whether living on the farm or in the village or town. Finally, there are the numerous factors which contribute to standards of living of families which do not yield to physical measurement at all — trustworthy traditions, attractive settings of woods or fields or mountains, and spiritual qualities attendant upon filial confidence and sense of security.

Family expenditures, 1935–36, base-line for comparisons. A comprehensive study of consumer incomes and expenditures of a representative sample of all families living on farms and in villages, towns, and cities was made for the year 1935–36, under the auspices of the National Resources Committee.[13] One general table from this study can well serve as a basis for making comparisons with later studies. As Table 47 indicates, the pro-

[12] William H. Sewell, "A Short Form of the Farm Family Socio-Economic Status Scale," *Rural Sociology* (June, 1943) VIII, No. 2; "A Scale for the Measurement of Farm Family Socio-Economic Status," *The Southwestern Social Science Quarterly*, XXI, No. 2; *The Construction and Standardization of a Scale for the Measurement of the Socio-Economic Status of Oklahoma Farm Families* (Stillwater: Technical Bulletin No. 9, April, 1940, Oklahoma Agricultural College).

[13] *Consumer Incomes of the United States: Their Distribution in 1935–36* (August, 1938); *Consumer Expenditures in the United States, Estimates for 1935–36* (March, 1939); and *Family Expenditures in the United States, Statistical Tables and Appendices* (June, 1941). Washington, D.C.: National Resources Committee Publications.

	CATEGORY OF DISBURSEMENT	AVERAGE DISBURSEMENTS PER FAMILY			PERCENTAGE OF INCOME		
		Farm Families	Rural Non-Farm Families	Urban Families	Farm Families	Rural Non-Farm Families	Urban Families
TABLE **47** Average Disbursements of Farm, Rural Non-Farm, and Urban Families, 1935–36	Current consumption: Food:						
	Purchased	$187	$352	$492	15.4	25.0	26.5
	Home-produced	286	31	- - -	23.5	2.2	- - -
	All food	$473	$383	$492	38.9	27.2	26.5
	Housing:						
	Money expense	$18	$127	$244	1.5	9.0	13.1
	Imputed value	114	60	70	9.4	4.3	3.8
	All housing	$132	$187	$314	10.9	13.3	16.9
	All household operation	$93	$156	$192	7.7	11.1	10.3
	Furnishings, clothing, automobile, medical care, recreation and other personal and advancement items	$352	$472	$591	28.9	33.5	31.9
	All consumption items	$1,050	$1,198	$1,589	86.4	85.1	85.6
	Gifts	23	44	54	1.9	3.1	2.9
	Personal taxes	3	11	36	.3	.8	2.0
	Savings	139	156	. 176	11.4	11.0	9.5
	All items	$1,215	$1,409	$1,855	100.0	100.0	100.0

Source: *Family Expenditures in the United States*, adapted from Table 40, p. 13, *op. cit.* See volume cited in note 13 for methods of deriving estimates of home-produced foods and other items. The estimates in this table include those receiving some relief during the year.

portion of incomes spent by all families for the various consumption items is surprisingly similar, although the amounts spent by farm families are considerably lower than those spent by urban families, $1050 compared with $1589. However, the proportion of this total used for food, including both purchased food and that furnished by the farm and garden, is significantly higher for farm families, namely 38.9 per cent as contrasted with 26.5 per cent for urban families, and 27.2 per cent for rural non-farm families.

Home economists suggest that when 40 per cent or more of a family's income goes for food, the budget is likely to be out of balance, and other items are necessarily too restricted. The farm family also stands out in the comparisons because of higher proportions of food produced on the farm, especially at the lower income levels. This is

evidence of the household type of economy described in the earlier chapter on the rural family as a social group. However, as the prosperity of the later post-war years overtakes the farm, this distinguishing characteristic tends to diminish with increased buying from stores and bakeries.

Other more detailed tables showed that no budgets were balanced in terms of incomes equaling expenditures for any region, or for any of the three groups of families, below the $1500 income level. Effects of the depression were still being felt, and deficits had to be met from savings, borrowing or from public assistance, either direct or indirect through work projects. This persistent and inelastic demand of the family's standard of living is clearly evident in many other studies, one of which will be reviewed briefly later in the chapter. It suggests that once the family cycle has been started, it must continue, and parents will employ extreme measures to prevent living conditions from falling below minimum standards. During the depression, farm families held to their standards as well as they could and as long as they could. Then savings were consumed and shifts made from "purchased" to "furnished" items. Finally, some families neared levels which clearly endangered not only the families as such, but the public interests as well, so public assistance was provided. It seems paradoxical to record the feeding of farm families, but it was done — in some extreme cases for 90 per cent of the families in certain counties over short periods of time.

Other differences in expenditures were wide when comparisons were made by geographic regions and by income levels, and between white and Negro families in southern rural counties. Expenditures for Negro families, both rural and urban, were significantly smaller for the majority of items at every income level. Two items in a rather large grouping of expenditures bear on topics to be considered in later chapters,

namely recreation and medical care. Among expenditures for recreation for farm families, radio purchases rank first and movies second, but in reverse order for rural non-farm families. Sports and games are a close third for the latter. For medical care, physicians rank first for both farm and rural non-farm families, followed by medicine and drugs, then dentists. Among urban families, expenditures for dentistry follow those for physicians.

Changes indicated by upward trends. By 1941 wartime expenditures had climbed along with increased incomes. As Table 48 shows, farm family expenditures totaled $1374 compared with $1215 in 1935–36, non-farm family expenditures had risen from $1409 to $1470, and urban from $1855 to $2468.

In the light of such increased incomes, it is important to watch what happens to expenditure items in the family budget. For food, the increase for all families represented more than 30 per cent over 1935–36. However, families in the lower income brackets did not increase their total expendi-

	CONSUMPTION ITEM	U.S.	TYPE OF COMMUNITY		
			Rural Farm	Rural non-Farm	Urban
TABLE	Total	2,057	1,374	1,470	2,468
	Food	660	601	513	729
48	Housing	430	236	279	542
	Household operation	88	35	54	120
Average Dollar Expenditures for Major Categories of Consumption of Families with Two or More Persons by Type of Community, 1941	Furnishings	111	73	89	128
	Clothing	251	158	170	308
	Automobile	187	104	152	223
	Other transportation	36	7	15	53
	Personal care	39	20	25	50
	Medical care	91	62	71	107
	Recreation	74	27	36	101
	Tobacco	37	17	26	48
	Reading	18	8	11	23
	Education	17	9	11	18
	Other	18	17	18	18

Source: *Family Spending and Saving in Wartime*, Bureau of Labor Statistics, U.S. Dept. of Labor, Bull. 822, 1945. Adapted from Part III, Table 5.

tures for food beyond the 1935–36 levels, although prices had advanced nearly 6 per cent. With rising prices, the family manager can alter not only the items within the budget but also the quality, and to an extent the quantity purchased. She can also work out different kinds of substitutions. Farm families grew more of their own foods. Expenditures for clothing went up 9 per cent but housing costs and household operations were actually lower than in 1935–36. It is apparent that families do not increase cash expenditures for many items as incomes rise unless they are in the relatively high income levels. Neither rural farm nor rural non-farm families increased their outlays for goods in proportion to price changes below the $1500 income bracket. Thus consumption lags behind income both on the upturn and the down trend.

Greatest differences in expenditures were found for so-called "durable goods" such as household equipment, washing machines, and refrigerators, and for many advancement items which became scarce even in early 1942. These kinds of increases in family budgets occurred in every income group. It was this changing relationship which Engel sought to formulate in his "laws," namely, that as income rises, the proportion of the total spent for food decreased while that for advancement items tends to increase.

The upward trends continued until by 1944 it was estimated that farm receipts had increased 152 per cent over prewar averages. Net savings had increased six times, debts were retired, and studies indicated that expenditure for "many other purposes" beyond ordinary budget items increased very greatly. At that time, farm families were at an all-time "high" of money available for family living.

Current trends — up and down, tendency to level off. The most recent comprehensive survey of farm family expenditures and incomes covers the calendar year 1946. The total spent for family living had advanced to $1629, but the $2000 income level had to be passed before income and expenditures could be balanced and any actual saving was shown. It is significant that in 1947, before decline in incomes began, about half the farm families of the nation still had net incomes of less than $2000. Differences among items in the family budget are not indicated in this study, but special studies extending to 1951 suggest many irregularities. Trends already noted continued, but the tendency was for a general leveling off of the upward curve of expenditures. For example, in the 1950 Agricultural Outlook Conference it was noted that while consumers as a whole had spent a great deal of money during the past two years, there had been a downward trend in 1949, followed by an advance of 9 per cent in 1950. However, due to the change in purchasing power of the consumer dollar, an income of $2500 in 1950 would buy no more goods than $2,000 in 1941.[14] It is of special interest to note that expenditures for durable goods continued high and increased most — automobiles, furniture, household equipment in the order given. Then came housing and the extension of electricity to farms. Special surveys in sample areas of Montana, Kansas, and Minnesota showed substantial purchases of furniture and equipment, including stoves, washing machines, radios and toasters. In Kansas, 70 per cent of the farm families canvassed bought such equipment and spent more than half of the "house-furnishings" budget for these things, a much higher proportion than in 1935–36.

Home production of foods remained important, yet the proportion going for all foods in the total budget was down com-

[14] Gertrude Weiss, "Farm Family Spending," Agricultural Outlook Conference, Washington, D.C., October 31, 1950.

pared with the earlier year. Food purchases had also changed. There was an increase in purchased vegetables such as lettuce, frozen citrus concentrates, ready mixes for pies, cakes, and rolls, and bread already baked. During any average week of 1949 in the four Kansas counties, for example, 94 per cent of the families bought some bread at the store or bakery, although still baking some at home, in contrast to 67 per cent in 1936. It is estimated that one fourth of the urban housewives' food expenditures goes for such foods; the farm housewife may not equal it but former differentials between rural and urban spending for these as for many other items in family living have surely diminished.

It was also pointed out in the Proceedings of the 1950 Outlook Conference that the climb of durable goods within family budgets could not continue indefinitely. While consumers might have more to spend, prices would be higher. Taxes already had increased. Consumer credit, important in the purchase of such goods, was being restricted. Also defense production called for some of the resources that had been used in the production of houses, automobiles, and household equipment.

Struggle of family income and expenditure — critical point? Throughout this discussion it has been evident that many factors influence the levels of family living at particular times and places, but that standards or goals tend to overshadow both time and place. Upward and downward trends have been traced, but whatever the variations, there is always the struggle between income and expenditure. This struggle seems especially acute among farm and village families where, as has been suggested repeatedly, earning a livelihood is a family undertaking. The point will be stressed again at the end of the chapter, but its factual basis should be examined here. Table 49 gives the variations in the two factors, income and expenditure, by the levels of

TABLE 49	AVERAGE EXPENDITURE ON					
	(1) Classified gross cash income	(2) Average income	(3) Farm production	(4) Family living	(5) Farm production and family living	(6) Average savings (or dis-savings)
		(dollars)	(dollars)	(dollars)	(dollars)	(dollars)
Average Expenditures for Family Living and Farm Production, and Average Savings of Farm Families by Gross Cash Income Class, United States, 1946	$ 0– 499	293	353	656	1,000	−716
	500– 999	755	363	759	1,122	−367
	1,000– 1,499	1,261	591	931	1,522	−261
	1,500– 1,999	1,728	792	1,129	1,921	−193
	2,000– 2,999	2,430	1,091	1,462	2,553	−123
	3,000– 3,999	3,463	1,608	1,704	3,312	151
	4,000– 4,999	4,361	2,067	1,942	4,009	352
	5,000– 7,499	5,972	2,854	2,237	5,091	881
	7,500– 9,999	8,519	4,202	2,566	6,768	1,751
	10,000 19,999	12,890	7,745	3,025	10,770	2,120
	20,000 and over	33,585	20,449	5,379	25,828	7,757
	Total	4,330	2,289	1,629	3,918	412

Source: T. Wilson Longmore and Carl C. Taylor, "Elasticities of Expenditures for Farm Family Living, Farm Production, and Savings, United States, 1946," *Journal of Farm Economics*, XXXIII, No. 1, February, 1951.

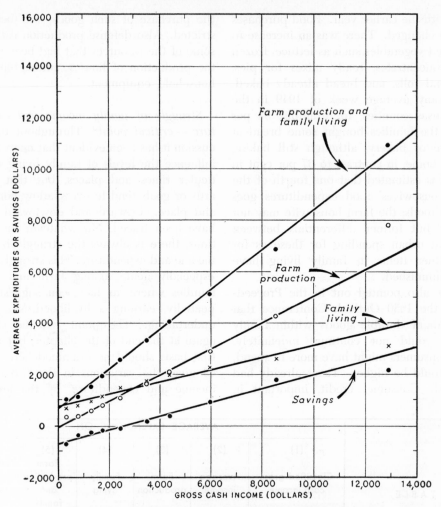

Figure 50. Relationship Between Average Expenditures and Savings and Gross Cash Income of Farm Families of the United States, 1946.

Source: T. Wilson Longmore and Carl C. Taylor, "Elasticities of Expenditures for Farm Family Living, Farm Production, and Savings, United States, 1946," *Journal of Farm Economics*, XXXIII, No. 1, February, 1951.

income. Figure 50 from the same source, shows the relationship graphically.

The critical point, of course, is where the income and the expenditures are equal, the point at which the two curves intersect. Savings are negative below this point and positive above it. The graph shows that it is not reached until the $2700 income level. Questions at once present themselves: how can more than half the families below that

average realize their standards of living, and what can they do in periods of sharp income decline? In the South the critical point was reached at $1900, in the North Central region at $3000, in the Northeast at $4400, and the West at $4900. The findings in this study indicate that farm family living expenditures increase consistently up to, and in some cases one income interval above, the critical point, then decrease in terms of the percentage of total expenditures. Production expenditures do not increase proportionately in terms of total expenditures until living expenditures decline. This rigidity of family expenditure is not only a response to physical needs but to cultural circumstances. As is pointed out in the conclusions of the study, it is not simply the requirement to be clad or even well clad, but to be acceptably dressed by standards of the community in order to move freely and without embarrassment in its educational, religious, and recreational circles that really determines family spending behavior. The tendency is so strong that it influences not only the savings item in the budget but likewise farm production practices and expenditures, and so has a far reaching effect on policies involving the agricultural enterprise of the entire nation.

Measures for comparing levels of living.

The desire of students of rural society to make comparisons and to standardize their findings has resulted in many ingenious devices to measure levels of living. The benefits which derive from the use of such measuring devices in the study of rural society are many, but a word of caution about interpreting results is necessary. Concrete and definite indices are needed for such measurements, but their use may lead to quite erroneous conclusions unless interpreted properly. As was suggested elsewhere, "things" have their own intrinsic values, but they also have symbolic values. As symbols they acquire their meanings within their cultural references. It has been shown for instance, that even such specific figures as $500 or $5000 do not mean the same in terms of patterns of living in two different and separated regions.[15] In another study the money values of products

[15] Longmore and Taylor, *op. cit.*

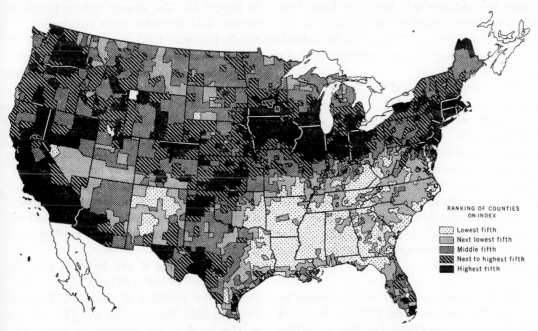

Figure 51. Farm Operator Family Level of Living Indexes, 1945.

Source: Margaret Jarman Hagood, *Farm Operator Family Level of Living Indexes for Counties of the United States 1940 to 1945* (U.S. Department of Agriculture, Bureau of Agricultural Economics, May, 1947).

TABLE 50 Average County Index of Farm Operator Family Living for the United States, Major Regions and Geographic Divisions, 1940 and 1945	REGION AND DIVISION	AVERAGE INDEX		INCREASE 1940 TO 1945	
		1945	1940	Index points	Percentage of 1940 index value
	United States	100	80	20	25
	Northeast	139	115	24	21
	New England	137	115	22	19
	Middle Atlantic	139	114	25	23
	North Central	128	104	24	23
	East North Central	131	109	22	20
	West North Central	125	100	25	25
	South	66	50	16	32
	South Atlantic	65	49	16	33
	East South Central	48	35	13	37
	West South Central	81	62	19	31
	West	125	101	24	24
	Mountain	113	91	22	24
	Pacific	150	121	29	24

Source: Data from the 1940 and 1945 Censuses of Agriculture on four items related to level of living of farm operator families. Value for average county in the United States in 1945 equals 100 in 1940 and 1945 indices.

used by northern and southern farm families were not found to be significantly different, but levels of living for households in corresponding brackets were substantially different.[16]

The components used by Dr. Hagood as an index for comparing levels of living, described below, obviously have different meanings to various groups of families, however useful they have proved in making general comparisons. They are the proportions of households within a defined area such as a county, which have electricity, telephones, and automobiles, and the average value of products sold or traded (after adjustment for changes in the purchasing power of the dollar).

Comparison by place of living. County by county comparisons for 1945 in levels of living for farm operator families, using the indices selected by Dr. Hagood, are shown

[16] Sloan R. Wayland, *Social Patterns of Farming* (New York: Columbia University, 1951).

in Figure 51. The county indices for major regions and divisions with comparison between 1940 and 1945 are given in Table 50.

The average level of living for all counties in the United States in 1945 was selected as the starting point and given the arbitrary value of 100. This does not mean that any particular county with an index score of 100 was perfect, simply that it was at the average level of all counties for that year; an index of 50 means halfway between the general average and "zero." However no county could be rated zero unless all its farmers produced no farm products for sale and did not have household electrical appliances, a telephone, or an automobile.

From the table it can be seen that the average level of living of farm operator families in the counties of the New England states in 1940, for example, was 115 per cent of the level of all families in 1945. The southern states had the lowest levels in both years but gained more on a percentage basis than the other regions. From the map it is

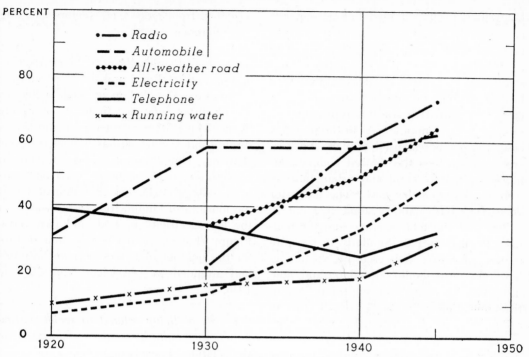

Figure 52. Percentage of Farm Operators Reporting
Specified Family Living Items, United States, 1920–45.
Source: U.S. Department of Agriculture, Bureau of Agricultural
Economics, August, 1947.

evident that the counties in the highest fifth are concentrated in the heart of the Corn Belt, in the small industrial states on the northeast seaboard, and in California.

Comparisons over time point to rising levels. The level-of-living index as recorded in Table 50 rose 20 points from 1940 to 1945, compared with only 5 points during the whole decade from 1930 to 1940, thus indicating a general trend toward greater prosperity. Figure 52 shows the percentage of farm operator families having certain items used in the index for determining levels of living, plus radio, running water, and location on all-weather roads.

All items show upward curves except telephones (there were more in 1920 than in 1945), and electricity shows the greatest increase. Apparently many farm families

consider a telephone a kind of luxury, something to get along without when it is difficult to keep the budget in balance. It was estimated that only 37 per cent of farm families had telephones in July, 1948, about half as many as had electricity. Density of population and distance from city centers were also influencing factors. With this unfavorable situation in view, the Eighty-first Congress provided funds for greater expansion of telephone lines into rural areas to be administered by the Rural Electrification Administration, following policies which proved successful in extending electric lines.[17]

Levels of living related to community social resources. Families and their house-

[17] "Calling Rural America," *Rural Electrification News,* XVI (Washington, D.C., January, 1951).

holds are not self-contained, but are dependent upon the social resources of their communities. Indices devised to measure this relationship indicate this dependence very clearly. For example, an index of the number of doctors per 100,000 persons in a county was used to study a representative sample of 372 counties.[18] As in the previous case, 100 points was used to mark the general average, then the desired comparisons of counties or of rural and urban families were drawn from this base. The index for doctors for farm families stood at about 70 in terms of the total average and for non-farm families at 120. Similarly in the proportion of babies delivered by doctors in hospitals, farm families rated 60 and non-farm, 125. The index showing the portion of the population between 25 and 29 years of age was 60 for the farm and 130 for the non-farm. As in the former cases, density of population in the counties and distance of

[18] Walter C. McKain, Jr. and Grace L. Flagg, *Differences Between Rural and Urban Levels of Living* (Washington, D.C.: Bureau of Agricultural Economics, U.S. Department of Agriculture, January 1948).

residence from cities were factors affecting the differences.

Levels of living influenced by nearness to urban centers. Rural and urban population distributions detailed in an earlier chapter are of direct influence in levels of family living. This is demonstrated by combining a rurality index with various indices of levels of living. Thus Figure 53 shows an increase in the amount of electricity used on farms from 1930 to 1945, but also indicates that the more farm families there are in an area the less electricity is used, and vice versa. Figure 54 shows a strikingly similar picture for the number of babies born in hospitals and attended by physicians from 1937 to 1946.

Levels of living related to social participation and cultural controls. Emphasis on the relation of levels of living to the social situation leads to other interesting comparisons. A study of clothing supplies and social participation of white farm families in twelve representative beats (districts) in

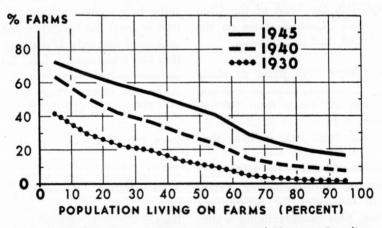

Figure 53. Electricity on Farms in Areas of Varying Rurality.

Source: Grace L. Flagg and T. Wilson Longmore, *Trends in Rural and Urban Levels of Living*, Agriculture Information Bulletin No. 11 (Washington, D.C., December, 1949).

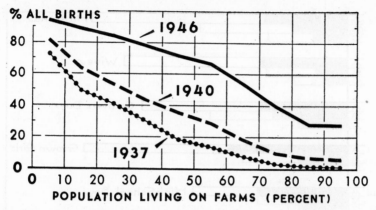

Figure 54. Births in Hospital in Farming Areas of Varying Rurality.

Source: Grace L. Flagg and T. Wilson Longmore, *Trends in Rural and Urban Levels of Living*, Agriculture Information Bulletin No. 11 (Washington, D.C., December, 1949).

Mississippi during 1940 provides an illustration (Figure 55). Here the extended bar for grown girls in families of "A" clothing rank and highest social participation is an excellent illustration of the influence of the family cycle discussed in Chapter 11.

The average number of members is lower for families ranked A or B in clothing than for those classed as C. Social participation figures show that the majority of families with A clothing ranks also have highest social participation. Of families with B and C clothing ranks over half were in the average social participation group. However, a larger proportion of the C than the B families had low social participation. The relationships between incomes or tenure and clothing rank are in line with expectations — low for tenants, high for owners.

From this type of study the important observation is made that clothing is a type of consumer goods which is not primarily used for physical welfare purposes, but rather for "psycho-social" welfare.[19] This means that clothing fulfills a social purpose and that a minimum amount of it is as necessary for social participation in church or school as is a minimum amount of food for adequate nutrition. The social importance cannot be the sole basis of judgment, to be sure, since there are questions of comfort and of age and sex differences. Finally, it may be suggested that personality can find expression in clothing through color and design, and through the social situations in which it is to be worn.

Practical implications regarding food also flow from this kind of social participation analysis. Thus Miss Dickens believes that women are more ready to adopt those food preparations and serving practices which are followed by their neighbors and relatives.[20] This point of view has confirmation in other areas. In a study of food and culture in southern Illinois the conclusion is drawn that dietary changes are associated with degrees of commercialization and contacts between groups such as German and Old American. It is said that differences in food habits as well as in resistance to change

[19] Dorothy Dickens, "Social Participation and Clothing," *Rural Sociology*, IX, No. 4 (December, 1944).

[20] "Food Preparation of Owner and Cropper Farm Families in the Shortleaf Pine Area of Mississippi," *Social Forces* (XXII, No. 1), October, 1943.

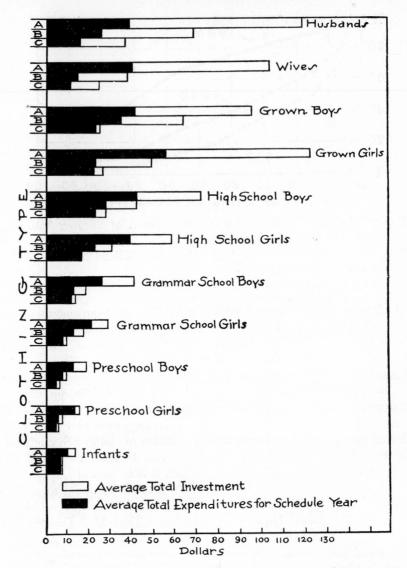

Figure 55. Average Investments in Clothing Inventories and Amounts Expended for Clothing During Schedule Year, by Sex and Activity Groups.

Source: Alice Bowie and Dorothy Dickens, *Clothing Supplies of Socially Participating White Farm Families of Mississippi*, Technical Bulletin 30 (State College: Mississippi Agricultural Experiment Station, June, 1942).

were closely related to the contemporary social scene.[21]

[21] Herbert Passin and John W. Bennett, "Social Process and Dietary Change," *The Problems of Changing Food Habits* (Washington, D.C.: Report of the Committee on Food Habits of the National Research Council, National Research Council Bul-

A study of nutrition among Spanish-Americans in northern Colorado reveals that there

letin 108); and John W. Bennett, Harvey L. Smith, and Herbert Passin, "Food and Culture in Southern Illinois — A Preliminary Report," *American Sociological Review* (VII, No. 5), October, 1942.

is a close relationship between local culture and environment and food habits. This means that any recommendations for improvement in diet must be made in terms of the local situation and with an understanding of the ethnic hiatus between Americans of Spanish-Indian background and Americans of North-European origin.[22]

Electricity changes ways of living in rural society. More electricity on farms and in villages has been one of the most popular and widely publicized trends influencing rural ways of living. "Farms light up," "The more farmers have electricity, the more they use," "REA near its 100 per cent birth-

[22] M. Pijoan and R. W. Roskelley, *Nutrition and Certain Related Factors of Spanish-Americans in Northern Colorado* (Denver: Rocky Mountain Council on Inter-American Affairs, 1943).

day," "Rural electricity needs skyrocketing" — these are among many titles of news stories, agricultural reports, and state bulletins. Without doubt the greatest factor in this trend is the Rural Electrification Administration, created in 1935, when about one farm in ten had electric service. After sixteen years, and with the private utilities expanding their services to rural areas, about 85 per cent of the nation's farms were connected to high power lines. Now the concern of the REA is to make sure that enough power is flowing through these lines to supply the greatly expanded needs, plus its determination to bring telephone service into line with electric service.

The state by state distribution of electric service as of June 30, 1950, is shown in Figure 56. Special sample surveys indicate that a radio and an electric iron are found

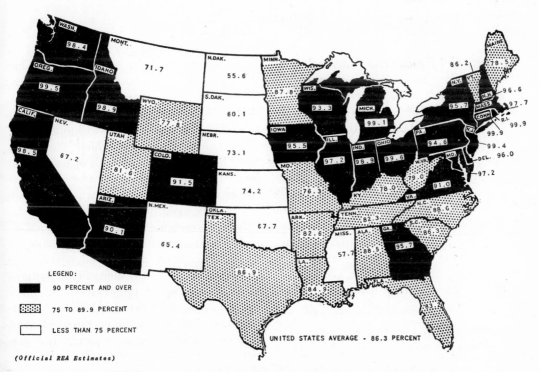

Figure 56. Farms Electrified in the United States.

Source: U.S. Department of Agriculture, Rural Electrification Administration.

in nearly every farm home with electric current. The proportion of washing machines tends to vary widely by areas. In Iowa and the state of Washington, 90 per cent of the farm homes had these appliances, while in Georgia the proportion fell to one third.[23] In the Upper Piedmont area of Georgia, it is reported that 90 per cent of the electricity consumed on farms in 1947 was used for household purposes.[24] In Iowa there were about 99 washing machines, 146 radios, and 108 electric irons for each 100 electrified farms.[25] The market for electrical appliances and equipment (included among the "durable goods" previously noted) is so great that one ambitious marketing agency estimated it to be as high as five billion dollars for the next five years. Such revolutionary trends in the rural economy are, of course, associated with high levels of prosperity but are limited by the possibility of securing needed materials during a defense production period.

The arts and the amenities in rural ways of living. Before concluding an enumeration of "things" which have contributed to the up-trend in levels of living as farm people reach toward the standards they desire, a plea is entered for an improvement in artistic design and greater stress on attractiveness which would add grace to the whole manner of living but which does not lend itself readily to statistical measurement. In many a farm home in Norway, for instance, a piece of art such as an original painting, a wood carving, or a hand-woven fabric, is considered as essential as the cook stove; in Holland, a near-perfect flower in the field,

garden, or window is almost as important as food; in New Zealand, the little library of books and magazines, a buttress for the fireplace, is as generally present as fuel. A "sense of home" may be achieved by even a modest touch of the artistic, and this may appear not only in the different items for living but in their combination and setting. Achieving these touches does not depend solely on the expenditure of money, at least beyond a certain minimum, but upon good taste, deliberate study, and family coöperation.

There can be no question that progress is being made in matters of taste. Since World War II there have been hundreds of thousands of farm and village women in homemakers' extension groups studying interior decoration, and planning outdoor living rooms and beautification of home grounds.

House — symbol of home. Finally, if a single symbol of family living needed to make a home were to be chosen, it would undoubtedly be the house. Durable goods, equipment, and household conveniences are the instruments, the means, in the hands of skillful homemakers — including men, women and children — which may help them to attain their standards of living. But there must be a place to assemble these things into a going concern, where they can be used, enjoyed, and protected.

In new construction, repair, maintenance, and the introduction of modern conveniences, rural housing suffered severely in the agricultural depression. The national government worked diligently to set plans in motion for the relief of too heavy indebtedness on homes, for the encouragement of new construction, and for repairs. However, because of shortages of materials through diversion to war purposes, through some vested interests, and because of delays by many local authorities, a great backlog of

[23] *The Agricultural Situation*, August, 1950.

[24] Oscar Steanson and Joe F. Davis, *Electricity on Farms in the Upper Piedmont of Georgia* (Experiment, Ga.: Georgia Experiment Station Bulletin 263, June, 1950).

[25] Joe F. Davis and Paul E. Strickler, *Electricity on Farms in the Eastern Livestock Area of Iowa* (Ames: Iowa Agricultural Experiment Station Circular 852, September, 1950).

demand for housing was built up. This may be the next major effort in the improvement of living in rural society, since earlier demands for home furnishings and household equipment have been at least partially satisfied.

Establishment of the United States Housing Authority in 1937 marks the first step in the change of public policy in this area of family living. Funds and credit provided for in the Act were used to assist the states and their political subdivisions to alleviate recurring unemployment and to remedy housing conditions and the acute shortage of decent, safe, and sanitary dwellings for families of low income in rural and urban communities.

In its first years, this agency attended mainly to the urban situation, and rural housing projects were undertaken subsequently. Eventually county housing authorities were set up by the various states; these in turn sought the aid of the United States Housing Authority and the United States Department of Agriculture. To secure such help, farms must be approved by the Department of Agriculture as being sufficiently productive, and legal title must be with the Authority. Such plans call for a house costing about $2000, a small orchard, fencing for garden and poultry, a sanitary privy, and a covered well.

Housing Act of 1949, a further help for rural and urban housing. The new law sets the goal of a "decent home and suitable living environment for every American family." The need for this advance was demonstrated by a survey carried on in 1945 by the Department of Agriculture's Inter-Bureau Committee, which found that about one-half of the nearly three million farm houses did not meet the standard of "decent, safe, and sanitary" housing. Overcrowding, usually considered an urban problem, was found to be more prevalent in farm than in non-farm housing. If a single index were to include electricity, hot and cold running water, and an indoor flush toilet, then fewer than one tenth of farm houses could have qualified in 1935–36 according to the Consumer Purchase study used as a bench mark. Therefore, some advance is indicated but much remains to be done.

The 1949 Act includes aid to farm owners to construct, improve, and repair their housing and other buildings. It provides: [26]

1. Loans up to 33 years, at interest not to exceed 4 per cent, to owners of self-sustained farms who are otherwise unable to finance adequate housing.

2. Similar loans, supplemented by annual contributions, to owners whose incomes are not at present capable of repaying a housing loan but which may be brought up to an adequate level through a satisfactory program of farm enlargement, improvement, or adjusted farm practices.

3. Loans and grants for minor improvements and minimum repairs to farm dwellings and buildings on the farm.

4. Loans to encourage adequate family size farms where a farm needs enlargement or development in order to provide income sufficient to support decent, safe, and sanitary housing.

The program reaches out in its operation to local communities and to local authorities. County committees already active in the Farmers' Home Administration, successor to the Farm Security Administration, will certify applications; technical assistance will be provided by the State Agricultural Extension Services.

Progress is being made. The farm home is becoming a more convenient place in which to live, as preliminary reports from the 1950 Census of Housing clearly indi-

[26] Housing and Home Finance Agency, "*The Local Community Job under the Housing Act of 1949*," a bulletin for leaders of local community groups (Washington, D.C., September, 1949).

cate.[27] More than 95 per cent of the houses on farms were one-family, detached dwellings; apartment houses do not flourish in rural areas. Four-, five-, and six-room houses prevailed, the average being 5.1 rooms. This compares with 4.6 rooms for all housing units. About 40 per cent had running water, 27 per cent flush toilets, and almost 30 per cent had bath tubs or showers, a substantial gain over 1935–36. Much must be done if the purposes of the 1949 Act are realized and if farm and non-farm families are to live at parity. Among all dwelling units in the United States, including farms, about 8 out of 10 were reported as having running water, 71 per cent flush toilets, and 69 per cent private bathing facilities.

A survey made in 1947 by the Bureau of Agricultural Economics indicated that 23 per cent of farm families reported that houses were repaired or remodeled, while only 15 per cent cited such operations on other farm buildings. The Department of Commerce estimates a fluctuation in residential farm construction from a low of $26,000,000 in 1932 to $275,000,000 in 1948. The house is finally coming into its own; the barn is finding its appropriate place — in the background.

What of the future? A preview of what the future holds may be found in what northeastern farm families say they want in a new house.[28]

Most houses in this area, they say, are large enough, but space is not conveniently arranged or used to best advantage. A majority want 1- or 1½-story houses with a bathroom on the ground floor. They would like a basement, one porch, a dining room, and well-planned storage facilities. They want more work space to relieve the kitchen of some of the present and traditional services

carried on there. In brief, the house of the future should accommodate the living needs of the modern farm family.

Cultural heritage of housing in rural America. A report on farm and village housing made nearly twenty years ago has one section of current interest devoted to the history of rural architecture in the United States and closes with this significant paragraph summarizing the concerted physical, economic, social, and spiritual interests of a house which is a home.[29]

The house, as a physically conditioning factor, in any setting, makes easy or difficult the formation of habits of order, cleanliness, healthful living, and an appreciation of beauty. It may be an object of pride or embarrassment. It constitutes part of the objective environment in which happy or unhappy relationships within the family grow, and in which the child's personality — fully blossoming or dwarfed — evolves. It is believed that better planned homes, more modernized houses, and an increasing number of flower-and-shrubbery decked yards on our farms and within our villages will stimulate an idealism that can give new values to the economic motive in society, and in the midst of financial depressions hold rural living above the ravages. However, economic achievement cannot be the end for human effort; economic activities fluctuate; the longings of men and women reach for permanency in satisfactions — health, harmony within the home, physical comforts, beauty, and many tangible qualities that give zest to family and individual living.

As a conclusion to these comparisons, it must be emphasized that rural family living cannot be compared in any wholesale fashion with urban or village conditions. The surroundings and the plan of farm life differ from those of the city. The major satisfac-

---

[27] *The Agricultural Situation*, U.S.D.A., Washington, D.C., June, 1951.

[28] *Ibid.*, July 1950.

[29] Committee on Farm and Village Housing (A. R. Mass, chairman), prepared by Bruce L. Melvin and edited by John M. Gries and James Ford. The President's Conference on Home Building and Home Ownership, Washington, D.C., 1932.

tions of farm life, and probably to a lesser extent of village life, can come from many different sources, and may be less dependent upon direct financial income than the major satisfactions of city life. Many farmers have close at hand the things for which the villager or the urbanite is willing to pay well in time or money to get. On the other hand, the urban dweller may be envied by the farmer or villager for his readier access to many of the sources of advancement goods and services. It is possible that with more small-farm machinery adapted to the family-type farm, and with more household conveniences, more young people will remain in or will move to the country. The so-called drudgery of farm life has driven many people away from farms in years past, but with science, machinery, and improved transportation, many of the advantages of the city are now available to country people. In all comparisons one must keep in mind that farm, village, and city modes of living are different, and that mental and emotional reactions are not susceptible of measurement in a way to permit complete comparisons.

Standards of living have both material and non-material aspects; this is one reason why some people prefer farm life to city life. With the greater freedom of movement and contacts outlined in the chapter on rural-urban relationships, it should be easier in the future for those who prefer rural life to choose it. Significant contributions to American attitudes and values can be made by rural people in respect to the non-material but essential elements of home life.

Summary of Factors Influencing Rural Ways of Living

It is not possible, of course, to account for all the changes and differences in ways of living shown by the studies which have been presented, yet some of the factors influencing those ways can be pointed out. Illustrations will be drawn from cases so that ways of living among various types of rural families can be further described. It is well to point out again that actual figures for any one group of families, or for any one year, may mean very little in themselves. They take on importance for the student of society only as they reveal important relationships in the home and in the various social groups of which the family is a part. The factors to be discussed should be thought of as forces or situations which help to determine standards in the home as a social institution and the levels of living in any given time or place. These factors or forces do not act singly, but in various combinations. One element in the complex may be strong or another weak, and they may change with the passage of time and with the cycle of family experience.

The family cycle. The description of cycles of family development in an earlier chapter shows that rural families are constantly in the process of change; the family forms with two persons, children come and eventually go. The period for this full cycle in an average farm family is about twenty-five years. In a study of a group of farm families in Ohio, the period was longer, but the maximum size was reduced after about eighteen years.[30] The demands on the family's budget change with the swing of the cycle. It is not only a question of the number of children to feed, clothe, and house, but of their habits of life, which change with age.

Consideration of the family cycle simply means that a family must anticipate and make preparation for the changing requirements of its members. This means good family management, as will be pointed out.

[30] C. E. Lively, *The Growth Cycle of the Farm Family* (Columbus: Ohio Agricultural Experiment Station Mimeograph Bulletin 51, October, 1942).

It also means that those working with rural families, whether in programs to improve health, education, recreation, or husbandry, also need to understand these changes. Standardized approaches will not appeal to all families in every stage of their cycle. When the family is formed and the first children come, there are strong filio-centric bonds. Calls to community meetings or church services may be met with seeming indifference. At the other end of the cycle, when the family loses its driving force, when the children are grown and gone or are beginning their own family cycle, perhaps on the "home farm," then the motives of the original pair have changed. They are less likely to respond to suggestion of larger profits; they may want more flowers in the family garden or some provision for old age.

Family management. Just as the success of the farm or of a business is more than a matter of farm or business management, so is the success of the household as a consumer center more than a matter of home management in the narrow sense. Both are matters of family management. Different families may spend very different amounts to get approximately the same kind of consumption goods or services. Different items of the budget may give more satisfaction to some families than to others. Standards of living, therefore, become a matter of management quite as much as a matter of income. Making the most of home resources is an important consideration. The truth of this can be seen in the differences in distribution of purchased and furnished goods in the same relative income classes. Good management practices which the family should utilize are budgeting in advance, keeping accounts, knowing how to get one's money's worth in the market through knowledge of products and materials, and understanding the principles of personality development.

Interrelated with income. According to various measures, there does seem to be a correspondence between larger incomes and higher expenditures for family living. Yet there is no evidence that the relationship is a thoroughly automatic one; that is, one cannot reason directly from cause to effect. Larger incomes do not necessarily mean higher expenditures for living, nor do greater expenditures imply actual higher standards of living; they only make them possible.

Changes in a family's ways of living fluctuate less suddenly and less violently with changes in general economic conditions than does income, as was demonstrated in the data presented earlier. Farm families, like other families, tend to hold to certain established standards. They attempt to maintain their accustomed ways of living, even though former sources of income have been cut off; savings are used or debts are contracted in order to carry on the family living. One mother asserted in no uncertain terms that she would see the farm go before she would deny her children the opportunity of an education.

The struggle to maintain standards in a period of decreasing buying power and declining prices has many serious consequences. The evidences were found in increased mortgage indebtedness, tax delinquencies, and lack of upkeep of farm buildings and fences. As one popular writer said, "Farm folks are eating their fences, their barns, and their houses."

These instances emphasize what was evident in the comparisons of expenditures and incomes. There becomes visible what can be considered an American pattern of family living. In it, the interrelations between income and expenditure are, with due allowance for fluctuations, remarkably stable. And this is true for all types of families compared — farm, rural non-farm, and urban. Income is a limiting factor to expenditures and to debts assumed for consumption purposes, as the figures indicate. The counterpart of the interaction is equally true. Standards of living, as they condition family relationships in their social, health, and spiritual aspects, have a definite influence upon the income-getting capacity of the family unit. As has been stressed repeatedly, the family is a working unit. Family units are not isolated, however, as has been emphasized. They make up the general society, not through any process of addition, but in a more organic sense of vital relationships. Society is, therefore, concerned with the welfare of its units. For example, among poorer families a set of forces may be in operation over which the individual family has little control, and society must step in. At the other end of the scale there may be what has been called "conspicuous consumption"; that is, spending for effect, for ostentation, without regard to those standards which concern the welfare of the family or the social groups of which it is a part. Here, too, society exerts various forms of social control, such as taxation, social conventions, public opinion, or even ridicule.

Education of parents. Analysis of the many families earlier described shows that the amount of education of parents, both farm operators and homemakers, makes a difference in the ways of living of the family. Several smaller and more recent studies have verified this conclusion, but they also point to the fact that the schooling of the homemaker is more closely associated with the ways of family living than is that of the farm operator. More education on the part of both parents is associated with greater total expenditure. The proportioning of the various items within the family budget also changes with increased education. For those families whose homemaker has had more than average schooling, the percentage spent for food decreases noticeably, and the percentage for "advancement goods" almost always increases. It should not be argued that education can be measured by amount of schooling, since the character of experience is vastly important; nevertheless, education, even by such comparisons, is a consequential factor in family living. The problem is, how best to educate rural youth for the great adventure of homemaking in modern rural society.

Farm and home — compete or coöperate? Attention to the factors of income, status, race, and education soon poses the larger question of interaction of farm and home; are they strengthening each other or may they be competing? Opportunity for competition seems greater in rural than in urban society, since a smaller proportion of city than farm families is in independent business undertakings. In this case, business would seem to compete less strongly for funds in urban than in farm households. There are many illustrations. Payments on mortgages often absorb more than the amount left from the total farm income after paying farm expenses and family living. Farms are frequently rented or sold on the basis of land rather than housing facilities afforded the family. In fact, in a recent bulletin offering advice in buying a farm, it was emphasized that the farm is the source of income and the house must be considered as of secondary importance.[31] Apparently it was overlooked that farm income, no matter how high, cannot stand alone. It must have family support to give it meaning and purpose, and the family must have an adequate and attractive house if it is to be made a home.

This is an age-old problem, and it has found its way into conventional drama plots.

[31] Walter M. Wilcox and P. E. McNall, *Some Questions to Ask — When Buying a Farm* (Madison: University of Wisconsin, Circular 347, September, 1944. Extension Service, College of Agriculture).

The story is in terms of the proverbial choice between values. The farm boy, back home from the college of agriculture, marries the country girl, but her college training was in the school of music. The first family crisis comes suddenly when unexpectedly they learn that the adjoining forty acres are for sale. Should they buy the forty or the new piano they have just priced? Well, the last scene presents the decision to buy both, because the young man's father plays his characteristic rôle of helping them acquire the land. It also brings an announcement of the prospect of a family heir. Families and their homes are built generation by generation, and that continuity is one of the elements of stability in family life and family living which has been the theme of this chapter and the earlier chapter on rural families.

A danger may arise if farm families overemphasize the advantages of increased income, overvalue their land, or attempt to overextend the margins of farming areas or frankly to "mine" the soil and then move on to another farm. As was suggested early in the chapter, some of this income advantage must be plowed back into family and community standards of living if rural life is to offer continuing opportunities for families.

Granted that agriculture should be efficient and productive, a highly commercialized economy is vulnerable indeed unless it can perpetuate a household policy which will foster children — their health, education, and happiness. If it does not, it will not be more than a generation before its farms will be peopled, although perhaps not owned, by the more fecund, self-sufficient families.

Agitation of market and sales pressure. Agitation of the market through national advertising, direct-mail selling, and the constant pressure of salesmen is surely influencing the ways of living of rural as well as

urban families. The extent and the character of this influence is still largely a matter of conjecture; studies have not extended far enough to give definite conclusions. Also, credit practices and instruments have been expanded through credit agencies and installment buying. In a buying and selling economy, the family feels the impact of a set of forces quite different from those at work when it operated with its own individual spinning wheel, churn, and smokehouse. Securing goods of recognized quality and reasonable price is a first-rate problem for the household consumption manager. Dependence upon merchandising is a major factor in the interdependence of town and country, as a previous chapter has emphasized. The problem for the home manager is, How can she be sure of her market, and how can she know when she is getting the most for her dollar?

Customs and demands of society. Another factor which influences levels of family living is that of custom and the demands of society itself. It may be well to emphasize again that families in their homes are not independent integers; rather, they are associated with other families in other homes and are dependent upon them. Indeed, it is in this way that the structure of rural society is organized. Society has many different ways of making its demands felt. Some are direct; others indirect and subtle. There is that wide range of psychological and cultural factors known as custom, tradition, and conventionality. "It is the thing to do," or, "This is the way our folks have always done it," are powerful means of determining the direction that consumption shall take. They play their part in answering such questions as present versus future spending and in deciding between land-ownership and consumption-goods, to which reference has been made.

Moreover, society has a way of imposing

GOVERNMENT AGENCIES AT WORK *Top*: Tenant Family Applying for Tenant Purchase Loan Through County Agent (U.S. Dept. of Agriculture, photo by Ackerman). *Center left*: County U.S.D.A. Clerk Assists Farmer in Applying for Crop Loan (U.S. Dept. of Agriculture). *Center right*: Farmer Consulting Soil Conservation Agent (Standard Oil Co., N.J.). *Bottom*: Farm Mother Consulting County Public Health Unit Nurse (U.S. Dept. of Agriculture, photo by Madeleine Osborne)

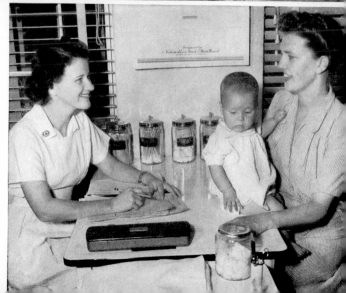

GOVERNMENT AND FARM YOUTH *Top*: County Agent Advises 4–H Club on Stock Selection (U.S. Dept. of Agriculture). *Bottom left*: Demonstrating Poultry Culling to High School Agriculture Class. *Bottom right*: 4–H Calf Club Winner. (Photos, Standard Oil Co., N.J.)

HOME ECONOMICS EXTENSION *Top:* Pressure Cooker and Canning Clinic. *Bottom:* Public Affairs Discussion Group. (Photos, Extension Service, U.S. Dept. of Agriculture, by Ed Hunton and Ackerman)

RURAL EDUCATION *Top*: Future Farmers of America — Vocational Agriculture Class Planting Willow Cuttings to Control Erosion. *Bottom*: Third Grade Art Project in Soil Conservation. (Photos, Soil Conservation Service, U.S. Dept. of Agriculture)

its demands upon families by legislation and taxation. Also, under the rationalization of public policy, general society is more and more directing the functions and services which in the past were largely handled by the family itself, or at least were in pioneer days. As long as the family members as citizens continue to have a voice in the determination of those policies, family and society interests can be reconciled, although they may clash at times.

In the public welfare. This line of discussion leads directly to questions of public welfare. If society imposes its demands, it must also accept its responsibilities. Briefly, this would seem to mean that if there are farm programs, there must be corresponding family programs; if there are land-use planning policies, there must be correlated population policies. If, as is urged in some economic circles, the goal is increased average per capita productivity and therefore need for fewer and fewer people on the land (and the argument should also hold for industry), then there should be some plan for the dis-

position of the "surplus population." Surely another depression should not be necessary to demonstrate the havoc wrought by wresting families from their moorings. People should not be forced to go without food when many producers of food have "surpluses." Surpluses of food and of people at the same time, in the same country, are anachronisms. Correction of this state of things will put this generation to the test.

The urge found in rural people to live well is a great social resource. The determination to improve family as well as community standards of living is clearly discernible to those who know rural America. This struggle may become a challenge as compelling as the conquest of the frontier; might it even become the moral equivalent of war?

All of living cannot be done in the home, however. The recognition of this fact leads to a consideration of those community institutions and agencies with which members of the rural family are increasingly associating themselves. They are subjects for the succeeding chapters.

TOPICS FOR DISCUSSION

1. Give your own definition of consumption. What forces have been at work recently compelling changes in farmers' and villagers' standards of living? What have been the social and community consequences?
2. What items does your family trim first with a declining income? What last? What items does it expand first with an increasing income? What last?
3. How may a farm or village family improve its standards of living without increasing its income?
4. The idea is current that children in the family inevitably lower living standards. Discuss the thesis that children in a family improve both level and standards of living. What are the limitations of this theory? Would it apply equally to both rural and urban families?
5. Secure as accurate information as you can regarding the costs last year of operating the household which you know best. You will need to make estimates when definite amounts are not known. With this information in hand, make the calculations necessary to construct the table outlined below. (It is possible that the ease or the difficulty with which this exercise is done will illustrate the importance of and the problems connected with the whole matter of family standards of living.)

Items of Consumption	Total of Furnished and Purchased		Furnished by Garden, Farm or Store (if Owned by Family)		Total Purchased	
	Dollars	Per Cent	Dollars	Per Cent	Dollars	Per Cent
Total		100		100		100
1. Food						
2. Clothing						
3. Heat, light, fuel						
4. Rent (including taxes, insurance, depreciation on house)						
5. All other operating expense						
6. Health						
7. Advancement						
a. education						
b. recreation						
c. religion						
d. savings						
e. all others						
8. Personal incidental items						

REFERENCE READINGS

Brayne, F. L., *The Peasant's Home, and Its Place in National Planning*. London: The Village Welfare Association, Well Walk, 1949.

Bureau of Agricultural Economics, U.S. Department of Agriculture, *Attitudes of Rural People Toward Radio Service*, Washington, D.C., January, 1946. A nation-wide survey of farm and small-town people.

Cottam, Howard R., "Housing Scales for Rural Pennsylvania," *Journal of the American Statistical Association*, December, 1943.

Cowles, May, Margaret Dickson, and Louise Wood, *Rural Housing Improvement in Southern Wisconsin*, Research Bulletin 161. Madison: Wisconsin Agricultural Experiment Station, October, 1947.

Dickinson, R. E., *The Le Play Method in Regional Survey*. London: The Le Play Society, 58 Gordon Square, 1934.

Garnett, William E., *Farm Housing in Virginia*, Bulletin 417. Blacksburg: Virginia Agricultural Experiment Station, October, 1948.

Hoyt, Elizabeth E., *Consumption in Our Society*. New York: McGraw-Hill, 1938. Contains an important section on consumption and choice.

Kirkpatrick, E. L., *Farmers' Standard of Living*. New York: Century, 1929. A comprehensive treatment of the subject and the first book of its kind.

Kirkpatrick, E. L., *Standards of Living*, Circular 241. Madison: Wisconsin Extension Service, September, 1930. Compilation and interpretation of available publications on standards of living.

Kyrk, Hazel, *A Theory of Consumption*. Boston: Houghton Mifflin, 1923. Statement of the theoretical and psychological backgrounds of consumption.

Lionberger, Herbert F., *Low-Income Farmers in Missouri*, Research Bulletin 441. Columbia: Missouri Agricultural Experiment Station, May, 1949.

MacNaughton, M. A., and J. M. Mann, *Changes*

in *Farm Family Living in Three Areas of the Prairie Provinces, from 1942–43 to 1947,* Publication 815, Technical Bulletin 69. Ottawa: Department of Agriculture, Dominion of Canada, February, 1949.

MacNaughton, M. A., J. M. Mann, and M. B. Blackwood, *Farm Family Living in Lanark County, Ontario, Farm Family Living in Southeastern Saskatchewan, and Farm Family Living in Nicolet County Quebec, 1947–48.* Ottawa: Department of Agriculture, Economic Division.

Mangus, A. R., and Robert L. McNamara, *Levels of Living and Population Movements in Rural Areas of Ohio, 1930–40,* Bulletin 639. Wooster: Ohio Agricultural Experiment Station, March, 1943.

Rush, Donald R., and Olaf Larson, *Farm Resources and Farming Systems Needed to Meet Living Needs of Farm Families.* Washington, D.C.: Bureau of Agricultural Economics, U.S. Department of Agriculture, March, 1942.

Terry, Paul W., and Verner M. Sims, *They Live on the Land; Life in an Open-country Southern Community.* University: University of Alabama, Bureau of Educational Research, 1940.

Thompson, Warren S., "Differentials in Fertility and Levels of Living in the Rural Population of the United States," *American Sociological Review,* XIII, No. 5, October, 1948.

Woodbury, Coleman, *British Housing During the Reconversion Period.* Madison: University of Wisconsin School of Commerce, October, 1947. (Mimeographed.)

Zimmerman, Carle C., *Consumption and Standards of Living.* New York: D. Van Nostrand, 1936. Provides an analysis of the standard of living in all countries and in urban as well as rural society.

FILMS

Building a House. S, 10. Step-by-step processes in the construction of a low-cost, wood-framed, one-family home. Encyclopedia Britannica Films.

Consumption of Foods. S, 10. Food needs and deficiencies of the world's people. Encyclopedia Britannica Films.

Family Life. S, 11. Problems due to mismanagement of time, money. *Coronet.*

Home Magic. S, C, 10. Remodeling an old home. Georgia Agricultural Extension.

Home Management: Why Budget? S, 11. Young America.

18

Education and the Schools

THE AMERICAN PEOPLE are noted for their interest in education and their belief that democratic government makes education at public expense a social necessity. As early as the 1640's the colony of Massachusetts passed two laws requiring that each town (township) tax its citizens for the support of a school. From this beginning public education for all children spread throughout the nation. At first education for everybody did not go beyond the elementary school, but in the last sixty years the opportunity for high school training has become almost universal in most states.

The public school is so universally accepted in western society that it is taken for granted. But in the history of the race it is a fairly recent social invention. In the earliest societies what education the child received was wholly within the family circle. The first step away from the family was the rites which initiated the boy and girl into adulthood at puberty. Tribal traditions, mores, and lore were imparted by the priests. The interest of organized religion in education is thus no new thing. For many centuries after the founding of Christianity education was almost wholly the concern of the Church. The Roman Catholic church and a few Protestant denominations still operate both elementary and high schools.

One index of the progress any people has made in the level of living is the proportion of its youth who are in school. One indication of how far scientific, mechanized agriculture has superceded hoe farming is the disparity between urban and rural educa-tional opportunity. It is no accident that this disparity is very great in nations newly embarked on the road to modernity. Indeed, such differences are observable even in the United States, as we shall see.

In the furtherance of education at public expense the school district was organized. It was supported by families with face-to-face acquaintanceship with one another. The usual district covered only a few square miles. It was a neighborhood institution. It deeply concerned all families, since its function was to extend the training each family group gave to its own child members. Neighborhoods might lack churches or other social institutions, but never a school. Each school district was administered by trustees or directors chosen from among those who lived in the tiny area inhabited by its pupils. Its teacher often boarded with the families of the neighborhood in rotation. Few were the families who were not in direct touch with the district school through the attendance of some child. No wonder that the "little red schoolhouse" lives on in the song and story of the nineteenth century. Although the small school district and its one-room un-graded school are now largely outmoded, as will be shown, it is well to pay tribute to the pioneers who succeeded in placing such an institution within walking distance of almost every six-year-old child.

The Rural School Situation Today

Times changed. As farm families grew smaller and farms enlarged, educational

313

standards were raised. The one-teacher, one-room, ungraded school, even if it had enough children to subsist, became increasingly unable, largely because of limitation in personnel and financing, to satisfy either school administrators or parents. It was handicapped in meeting the demand for an enlarged curriculum and high school entrance standards. The automobile and good roads made accessible the village and town schools, which, it was assumed, usually offered better educational opportunities. The movement for a consolidation of country schools, described later, began. Nevertheless, one-room schools have persisted.

One-Teacher Schools Declining. There were just under 75,000 one-teacher schools at the mid-point of the twentieth century, over 40 per cent of them in the states of Illinois, Iowa, Missouri, Wisconsin, Nebraska, and Minnesota. The last three of these states had between 4400 and 4500 each. Illinois had almost one in ten of the nation's one-teacher schools, but under a school district reorganization law enacted in 1950 will soon have considerably fewer. The other two states exceeded 5000 each. If we add Kentucky and Michigan, which have about 3000 such schools each, these eight states had half of the 1,500,000 children still attending one-teacher schools in 1950–51.

The trend all over the nation for this type of school is downward. In the 30 years from 1918 to 1948 over 121,000 were closed. The rate of decline was quite uniform until 1945, save for some retardation during the worst of the depression of the 1930's and the period of World War II. However between 1946 and 1948, 11,618 one-teacher schools were closed. Today 44 per cent of all schools have only one teacher as opposed to 70.8 per cent in 1918. Only 8.7 per cent of America's teachers preside over such schools, compared with 31.0 per cent at the earlier year.[1]

[1] Walter Gaumitz and David Blore, *The One-*

These statistics indicate changing attitudes of rural people with respect to education. The trend toward larger units is a social movement of considerable proportions, even though it has not proceeded in all states at the same rate. In 1948 Illinois still had 648 one-teacher schools for every 1000 listed in 1918, whereas the neighboring and similar state of Indiana had only 76. Pennsylvania had 279, its neighbor Ohio 54; Vermont had 457 but New Hampshire 140. Such variations indicate in part differences in leadership, in attitudes and social organization, and in part differences in topography and other physical conditions. It is obvious that in areas where farms are very large and population density low, or where the terrain is mountainous, one-teacher schools cannot be readily dispensed with. For this reason the small one-teacher school is not likely to disappear in the foreseeable future, though the number can certainly drop by half.

Other types of rural schools. According to the United States Office of Education it is difficult to present comparable data for other types of rural schools.[2] Oregon, for instance, at least up to 1950, permitted eight different forms of district organization. This is clear evidence of attempts at social experimentation the better to meet the needs of rural children under a variety of conditions.

Some states have shifted from one- to three-teacher schools. Thus, 30 per cent of Colorado's school children attend three-teacher schools, practically all rural. Wisconsin reported 7.2 per cent of its children in two- and three-teacher schools. Perhaps a million children attended schools of this type in 1948.

In October, 1949, the Bureau of the Census estimated that 11,606,000 rural children

Teacher School: Its Midcentury Status (Washington, D.C.: Federal Security Agency, 1950).

[2] *Ibid.*

were attending school. Even with the new definition of rural, the 1950 census shows 11,197,000 in school.[3] Since there were 1,-500,000 attending one-teacher schools, and about a million in two- and three-teacher schools, this means that more than one in five were enrolled in schools with three teachers or less. The other four fifths were in larger schools, consolidated and centralized, or schools in villages open also on a tuition basis to those from the surrounding country-side.

Rural education important. The great importance of these rural schools and of what happens within them needs emphasis. According to the Census over 45 per cent of the children 5 to 14 years of age, inclusive, in the United States lived in rural areas in April, 1950, though the total rural population was only 36.2 per cent of the nation's total. Even allowing for the thousands of those who were undoubtedly attending school in communities of 2500 or more population (urban by census definition) the importance of the rural school to the well-being of the nation is clear.

Rural Education and the General Welfare

Certain significant implications derive from the importance of the rural school to the general welfare. The starting point for this discussion is the unchallenged conviction of the American people that democracy itself rests upon adequate education. How far is that ideal realized in our society? From this point of view comparisons of rural and urban schools are of primary concern. But before making such comparisons it should be noted that in public education, as in other aspects of rural life, there is no such clear-cut distinction between these terms as their use implies. Until the middle

[3] Series P-20, No. 31, April 26, 1950, and Series Pc-7, No. 1.

of the twentieth century a one-room, one-teacher school continued to function in the Borough of Richmond in New York City. There are consolidated schools in rural America which, measured by any of the scales employed by educationists, would score with the best city schools. In some particulars differences among the regions may be wider than rural-urban differences within a given region. Comparisons such as are given below indicate aspects of the problem of providing equality of educational opportunity within the United States. The weight of any factor in a particular state or region can be determined only upon inquiry. Such factors as low density of population, which necessitate either small schools or large service areas requiring transportation, lower per-pupil taxable assets, and other such environmental considerations, will always require different techniques than in the city, despite identity of objective.

Rural and urban schools compared. Over two thirds of the nation's grade and high schools are rural. So are perhaps four fifths of the school buildings and 51 per cent of the teachers. Yet the ratio of expenditure is approximately 60 per cent urban and 40 per cent rural. The per-pupil cost of school operations in rural America in 1947–48, the latest year for which figures are available, was $128; in cities, $199.[4] There has been some increase since then. Comparably, the rural school term averages about ten days — two school weeks — less than the urban

[4] Data from a nation-wide survey of rural education by the New York *Times* with the coöperation of the Office of Education, published March 12, 1951. The definition of rural was based on that used in the 1940 Census. A considerable number of exceptionally well-supported rural-suburban schools were thus included in the rural figure which would have been eliminated under the more realistic definition of the 1950 Census. One of the authors, for instance, lives in a community rural by the 1940 standards. Its per-pupil cost in 1950–51 was two and a half times the average given above.

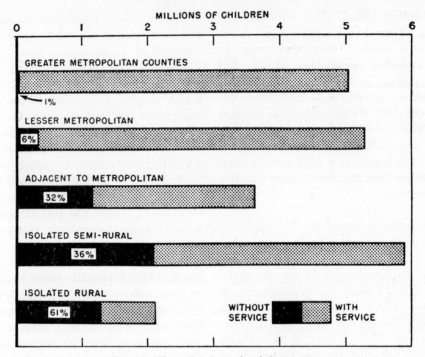

MILLIONS OF CHILDREN

GREATER METROPOLITAN COUNTIES

← 1%

LESSER METROPOLITAN

6%

ADJACENT TO METROPOLITAN

32%

ISOLATED SEMI-RURAL

36%

ISOLATED RURAL

61%

WITHOUT SERVICE   WITH SERVICE

Figure 57. School Medical Services.

Proportion of children aged 5–14 in counties with no organized medical service in public elementary schools, 1946. (A county is said to be without school health service if there is not at least one public elementary school in which children are given a medical examination by a physician.) Source: *Annual Report,* Federal Security Agency, Office of Education, 1949, p. 33.

182 days. However, in 1926 the difference was 38 days.

Another indication of the differences between urban and rural schools, which affect curriculum and services, is given in the results of a study of school medical services summarized in Figure 57. Combining the counties in or adjacent to urban areas, 11 per cent lacked any school health services, as against 36 per cent in semi-rural, and 61 per cent in isolated rural counties. Over three million children were involved in these last two groups.

Rural teachers adversely affected. Obviously the quality, as well as the quantity, of education received in many rural schools is a travesty on the principle of equal opportunity. The younger, inexperienced, and

poorer teachers gravitate to the rural school. The average salary of all rural teachers, in 1942–43, including the better-paid ones in the villages, was only $959, less than half the urban average of $1955, and less than half the salary of civilian employees of the federal government and of manufacturing industries. Forty per cent of all teachers, most of them rural, were paid less than $1200 annually, less than the annual wage of the lowest classification of federal employees. Eight per cent of all rural teachers received less than $600. There are a few predominantly rural states in which the average compensation of all teachers and educational administrators, rural and urban, was less than $1200. In the lowest state the average was $859.

Improvement since then has been encour-

TABLE 51	AGE GROUP (years)	RURAL FARM		RURAL NON–FARM		URBAN	
		1940	1948	1940	1948	1940	1948
Proportion of United States Rural Farm, Rural Non-Farm, and Urban Population in School by Age Groups	6	56.5	89.2	64.5	93.4	79.7	95.4
	7– 9	90.1	94.8	94.7	99.4	96.7	99.6
	10–13	91.8	94.1	95.8	99.4	97.4	99.5
	14	86.1	{82.1	92.9	{94.7	96.0	{97.3
	15	77.4		87.3		93.4	
	16–17	56.8	59.1	67.6	71.7	75.6	76.9
	18–19	23.9	19.8	27.5	23.2	31.7	30.7

Source: Sixteenth Census of the United States, 1940, and Census Report Series P.G.

aging. In 1950–51 the average teacher in rural America received $2200, according to the New York *Times* survey, two thirds as much as his urban colleague and more than double the 1942–43 average. But the slow response of salary increases to rising costs of living during the war doubled the normal rate of turnover, and the increased compensation was not sufficient to keep the supply of teachers equal to the need. Emergency certificates in 1942–43 numbered 37,000. In 1950–51 this had increased to about 65,000 in rural schools, plus about 15,000 in urban.

Proportion of rural children in school increasing. According to the Census of 1940, in every age category there were proportionately fewer farm than village children enrolled in school, and proportionately fewer of both than in the cities. By 1948, to age 17, inclusive, city, farm, and rural non-farm populations all showed improvement over 1940, often considerable, but in some ages the rural farm group lagged behind the others. Table 51 gives the details.

This improvement seems to have continued. According to preliminary reports of the 1950 census, the proportion of children attending school was as follows:

AGE	URBAN	RURAL NON-FARM	RURAL FARM
5–13	82.1	79.9	81.3
14–17	87.5	82.4	78.7

In terms of the total group 5 to 24 years of age, the rural farm group actually led with 63.1 per cent in school, as against 60.4 and 60.0 per cent for urban and rural non-farm groups. These results are the more significant when it is realized that the city, with its far larger number of kindergartens, has many more 5-year-olds in school than the rural areas. It is evident from state reports that the improvement has been very uneven within census divisions. Thus in New York, despite the new definition of rural, 86.4 per cent of the rural population 5 to 13 years of age, and 91 per cent of those of high school age, were in school in 1950, as against 83.4 and 85.5 per cent of the urban group. In Pennsylvania, however, the urban made a sharply better record than the rural.

Some of the improvement in the general situation can be credited to improved education for Negroes. In 1950 the percentage of Negroes 5 to 24 years of age in school was 62.7. For the first two age groups, those in school were but a few tenths of a per cent below the national figures given above.

These data, if confirmed by the complete tabulations, are highly significant, for the rural, and especially the rural farm, improvement has been made against handicaps not present in cities. The United States Office of Education long ago showed that both attendance and enrollment declined, especially among younger children, as distance from school increased. The Negro group, not yet having attained parity with the white in spite of the great improvement of the last years, somewhat lowers the proportions in the high school years, from 14 to 17. In this group the proportions of whites attending school from rural non-farm and rural farm groups are 80.0 and 83.7; of non-whites, 71.7 and 71.4, respectively.[5]

Rural educational status relatively lower than urban. The improvements noted above have, of course, little effect on the median years of schooling completed by adults 25 years of age and over. In 1940 urban native-born whites averaged 9.6 years of school. For the rural non-farm population the median was one year less, 8.6 years; and for the farm population it was 8 years. For Negroes the median years of completed schooling for urban, rural non-farm, and farm adults were respectively 6.8, 5, and 4.1 years.

Despite the progress made in rural education in the last decades, however, there is every indication that there is now

[5] Census release P.C. 7, No. 1, February 25, 1951.

more inequality in education opportunity between rural and urban America than there was at the close of the Civil War, and that the gap between the two became progressively wider between 1920 and 1940. One evidence of this inequality is the median years of school completed by adults in various age groups. Less than a year separates the medians for urban, rural non-farm, and farm persons 35 years of age and over. However, for those twenty to twenty-four years of age, the medians are respectively 12, 10.7, and 8.8 years. Thus in 1940 those in the first half-decade of adulthood in cities had on the average completed high school but the comparable rural farm group had barely passed grade school. The full facts on this are given in Table 52.

It may be said that this is simply the result of migration. But if so, it but emphasizes the problem, for agriculture has become a highly skilled occupation. The food supply of America and the conservation of our basic capital resource, the soil, cannot be left with safety to an ill-educated group. When one recalls the facts on the migration

	AGE (years)	RURAL FARM	RURAL NON–FARM	URBAN
TABLE	Total, 20 and over	8.2	8.7	9.0
	20 to 24	8.8	10.7	12.0
52	Total, 25 and over	8.1	8.6	8.8
	25 to 29	8.6	10.0	11.0
Median Years of School	30 to 34	8.4	9.3	10.3
Completed by Persons				
20 Years Old and Over,	35 to 39	8.2	8.8	9.0
by Age, for the United	40 to 44	8.2	8.6	8.8
States for Rural Farm,	45 to 49	8.1	8.5	8.6
Rural Non-Farm, and	50 to 54	8.0	8.4	8.5
Urban: 1940				
	55 to 59	7.9	8.3	8.4
	60 to 64	7.7	8.3	8.4
	65 to 69	7.1	8.1	8.3
	70 to 74	7.0	8.1	8.3
	75 and over	6.5	8.0	8.2

Source: Sixteenth Census of the United States, 1940.

of rural youth to the cities, urban America's stake in good rural education and other social utilities becomes very plain.

It should be pointed out that there are sharp variations among states and regions in these particulars. Differences are small in the Northeast, larger elsewhere. This again emphasizes the inequality of educational opportunity existent in the United States. The regional comparison is given in Table 53.

From the point of view of national welfare, as well as from that of rural America, these discrepancies are serious. Educational status is lowest in the areas where school support per pupil or per classroom is lowest. The situation feeds on itself, as the relatively slower improvement in the educational status of adults in rural, as contrasted with urban, America shows. The tragedy lies in the fact that in proportion to their wealth the rural states are spending more on education than the richer, urban areas. They get less for their expenditure because they have more children. Some rural states have twice as many children of school age for every thousand adults as have the wealthiest urban states, as the discussion of rural population shows. Everywhere, in terms of population, the rural burden of educating and rearing children is heavier than the urban.

Migration affects the problem. Rural sociology possesses data which can contribute to an understanding of this issue. It is important to realize that in our nation persons reared in one state are quite likely to spend their working lives in another, as the data on inter-state migration, presented earlier, show. It will be recalled that there was heavy migration from states largely rural with a high proportion of children in the population to states largely urban with a lower proportion. More important, in many of the states which contributed heavily to this migration, the schools and other social utilities were below average, as was the educational status of the adult population. These rural migrants to the cities were therefore less well prepared for life in our complex urban society than they would have been if their schools had been better. Their problems of adjustment were severe. This has been reflected again and again in high ratios of unemployment, juvenile delinquency, social casework loads, and other social costs in city wards into which the migrants moved. It would pay cities and the more prosperous states to be more concerned about conditions in those parts of the nation from which they draw large proportions of their own human supply.

The youth who migrate in such numbers to cities are produced, fed, clothed, and

TABLE 53	REGION	RURAL FARM		RURAL NON-FARM		URBAN	
		High	Low	High	Low	High	Low
Highest and Lowest State Median Years of School Completed for Native Whites 25 Years Old and Over for Rural Farm, Rural Non-Farm, and Urban Areas: 1940	New England	9.8	8.6	10.4	8.6	10.7	8.8
	Middle Atlantic	8.4	8.1	8.9	8.3	9.1	8.8
	East North Central	8.2	7.9	8.8	8.5	9.4	8.9
	West North Central	8.4	7.9	8.9	8.3	11.0	8.8
	South Atlantic	8.0	7.2	8.9	7.7	11.3	8.5
	East South Central	8.1	7.1	9.9	7.8	11.7	8.6
	West South Central	8.0	6.3	9.3	8.1	10.6	9.1
	Mountain	9.0	8.2	10.5	7.8	11.5	9.9
	Pacific	8.8	8.6	9.6	9.1	11.4	10.8

Source: Sixteenth Census of the United States, 1940.

given what education they possess in rural areas. In the aggregate the costs of their rearing run into billions of dollars. Those who then spend their productive years in the cities carry a considerable contribution from country to city, a subsidy far larger than the cost of federal aid to education would be to the cities. The national stake in this problem was revealed when disproportionately large numbers of rural youth were rejected for military service during World War II because they were functionally illiterate.[6] Inequalities in educational opportunity were thus revealed as a national liability in time of crisis.

Rural youth concerned. Rural youth is conscious of the situation, of the denial of democratic and equal educational opportunity. In a careful sampling of nearly six hundred Iowa farm youths in 1940, 39 per cent of the girls and 29 per cent of the boys said they disliked farm life because the schools were usually poor. About one fourth of each sex said they would like farm life better if the rural schools were as good as those in the city. Similar data emerge from the studies of the American Youth Commission and several other youth surveys by colleges of agriculture.

Proposals Aimed at Equalizing Opportunities

These comparisons of rural and urban schools, educational opportunity and educational status, clearly indicate inequalities. They have already hinted that part of the problem is financial.

Financial problem acute. As long ago as 1938 the President's Advisory Committee on Education reported a range among the states of from about $25 spent per pupil

[6] Based on county-by-county tabulations of the Columbia University project, The Conservation of Human Resources.

per year to $139, more than fivefold. The United States average then was $74.30. Five out of six of the lower half of the states were considerably more rural than urban. In 1949–50 the six states with the highest percentage of rural school children spent $110 per pupil; the six with the lowest percentage, $222. On the basis of cost per classroom unit, the variation between the top urban schools and the bottom all-rural schools was 1000 per cent in 1940. In both New York and California only about 10 per cent of classroom units received less than $2700 a year. In two highly rural states the top one per cent received less than $2000, the bottom one third, $500 or less. The national median of school support per classroom unit was between $1600 and $1699. Nine states, all heavily rural, had a median of less than $1000. Between 1940 and 1947 there was some increase in dollar support of education, but in very few states did this increase keep pace with rising school costs and the decline in the purchasing power of the dollar. This is clear from the following comparisons of familiar measures of economic health in the United States between 1940 and 1947:

The retail price index went up   79 per cent
Average annual earnings per full-
  time employee in private industry went up   86 per cent
Average income per person went
  up   123 per cent
Increase in pupil costs went up   66 per cent

These findings are illustrated by Figures 58–61.[7]

[7] J. K. Norton and E. S. Lawler, *An Inventory of Public School Expenditures in the United States* (Washington, D.C.: American Council on Education, 1944). And *Still Unfinished: Our Educational Obligation to America's Children*, Institute of Administrative Research, Teachers College, Columbia University (Washington, D.C.: National Education Association, 1948). These per-pupil costs are weighted to put "the various states on a comparable unit basis as to educational load being carried." The picture given is weighted on the favorable side. For technical reasons the rural situation is seriously under-represented.

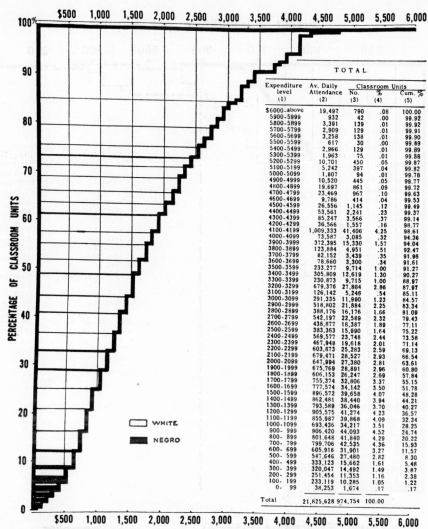

Expenditure level (1)	Av. Daily Attendance (2)	Classroom Units		
		No. (3)	% (4)	Cum. % (5)
$6000-above	19,497	790	.08	100.00
5900-5999	932	42	.00	99.92
5800-5899	3,391	139	.01	99.92
5700-5799	2,909	129	.01	99.91
5600-5699	3,258	138	.01	99.90
5500-5599	617	30	.00	99.89
5400-5499	2,966	129	.01	99.89
5300-5399	1,963	75	.01	99.88
5200-5299	10,701	450	.05	99.87
5100-5199	5,242	397	.04	99.82
5000-5099	1,807	94	.01	99.78
4900-4999	10,520	445	.05	99.77
4800-4899	19,697	861	.09	99.72
4700-4799	23,469	967	.10	99.63
4600-4699	9,786	414	.04	99.53
4500-4599	26,556	1,145	.12	99.49
4400-4499	53,561	2,241	.23	99.37
4300-4399	85,247	3,566	.37	99.14
4200-4299	36,566	1,557	.16	98.77
4100-4199	1,009,333	41,406	4.25	98.61
4000-4099	73,587	3,085	.32	94.36
3900-3999	372,395	15,330	1.57	94.04
3800-3899	123,884	4,951	.51	92.47
3700-3799	82,152	3,439	.35	91.96
3600-3699	78,660	3,300	.34	91.61
3500-3599	233,277	9,714	1.00	91.27
3400-3499	305,809	12,619	1.30	90.27
3300-3399	230,873	9,715	1.00	88.97
3200-3299	679,376	27,864	2.86	87.97
3100-3199	126,142	5,246	.54	85.11
3000-3099	291,335	11,990	1.23	84.57
2900-2999	518,802	21,884	2.25	83.34
2800-2899	388,176	16,176	1.66	81.09
2700-2799	542,197	22,589	2.32	79.43
2600-2699	438,877	18,387	1.89	77.11
2500-2599	383,363	15,990	1.64	75.22
2400-2499	569,577	23,748	2.44	73.58
2300-2399	467,948	19,618	2.01	71.14
2200-2299	603,873	25,283	2.59	69.13
2100-2199	679,471	28,527	2.93	66.54
2000-2099	647,994	27,380	2.81	63.61
1900-1999	675,769	28,891	2.96	60.80
1800-1899	606,153	26,247	2.69	57.84
1700-1799	755,374	32,806	3.37	55.15
1600-1699	777,574	34,142	3.50	51.78
1500-1599	896,572	39,658	4.07	48.28
1400-1499	862,481	38,440	3.94	44.21
1300-1399	793,589	36,046	3.70	40.27
1200-1299	905,575	41,274	4.23	36.57
1100-1199	855,987	39,868	4.09	32.34
1000-1099	693,436	34,217	3.51	28.25
900-999	906,420	44,093	4.52	24.74
800-899	801,648	41,840	4.29	20.22
700-799	799,706	42,535	4.36	15.93
600-699	605,916	31,901	3.27	11.57
500-599	547,646	27,480	2.82	8.30
400-499	333,123	15,662	1.61	5.48
300-399	320,047	14,492	1.49	3.87
200-299	251,454	11,353	1.16	2.38
100-199	233,119	10,285	1.05	1.22
0-99	38,253	1,674	.17	.17
Total	21,825,628	974,754	100.00	

Figure 58. Distribution of Classroom Units According to Level of Expenditure, United States, Current Expenditure per Classroom Unit, 1940.
Source: J. K. Norton and E. Lawler, *The Unfinished Business.*

State aid to the rescue. In most rural communities education is the most expensive single item in the tax budget. Local revenue raised for schools comes largely on the general property tax. Moreover, the wealth of districts varies greatly; there is far more difference between the amount of taxable wealth per child between a mountain district in Kentucky and one in its famous blue grass region than there is between the cost of a minimum adequate program of education in the two districts. It is clear from the figures that support for education varies greatly not only among states but also among districts within the same state. Only aid from the states could effect greater equality of educational opportunity. Such aid has been retarded because of fear of state control. Local people do not relish losing control of an institution as intimately

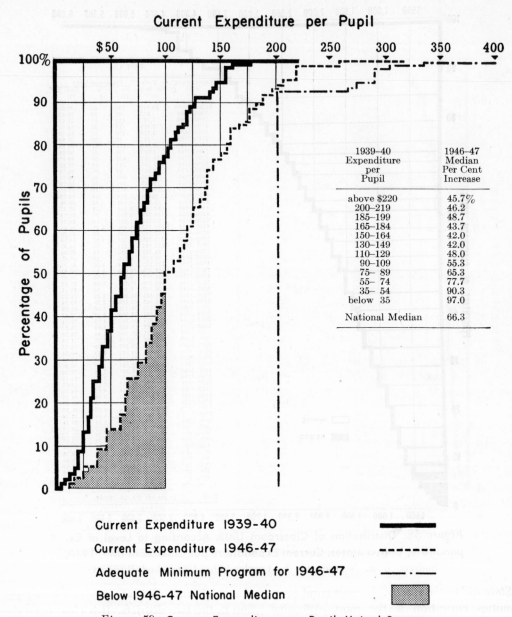

Current Expenditure per Pupil

1939–40 Expenditure per Pupil	1946–47 Median Per Cent Increase
above $220	45.7%
200–219	46.2
185–199	48.7
165–184	43.7
150–164	42.0
130–149	42.0
110–129	48.0
90–109	55.3
75– 89	65.3
55– 74	77.7
35– 54	90.3
below 35	97.0
National Median	66.3

Current Expenditure 1939-40 ▬▬▬▬

Current Expenditure 1946-47 ▬ ▬ ▬ ▬

Adequate Minimum Program for 1946-47 ▬ · ▬

Below 1946-47 National Median ▨

Figure 59. Current Expenditure per Pupil: United States.

Source: Institute of Administrative Research, Teachers College, Columbia University, New York, N.Y.

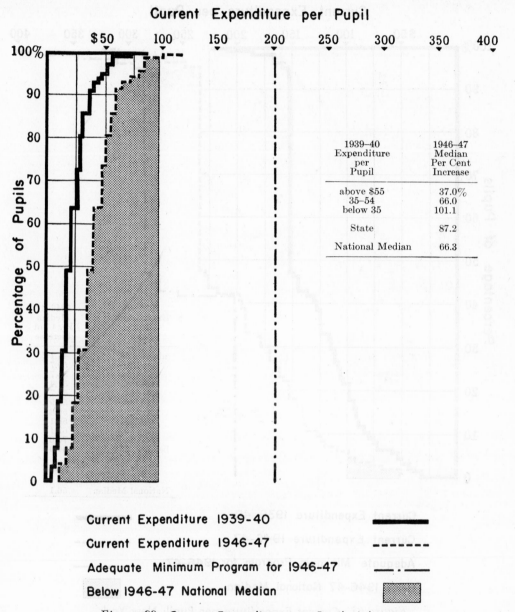

Current Expenditure per Pupil

1939–40 Expenditure per Pupil	1946–47 Median Per Cent Increase
above $55	37.0%
35–54	66.0
below 35	101.1
State	87.2
National Median	66.3

Current Expenditure 1939-40

Current Expenditure 1946-47

Adequate Minimum Program for 1946-47

Below 1946-47 National Median

Figure 60. Current Expenditure per Pupil: Arkansas.

Source: Institute of Administrative Research, Teachers College, Columbia University, New York, N.Y.

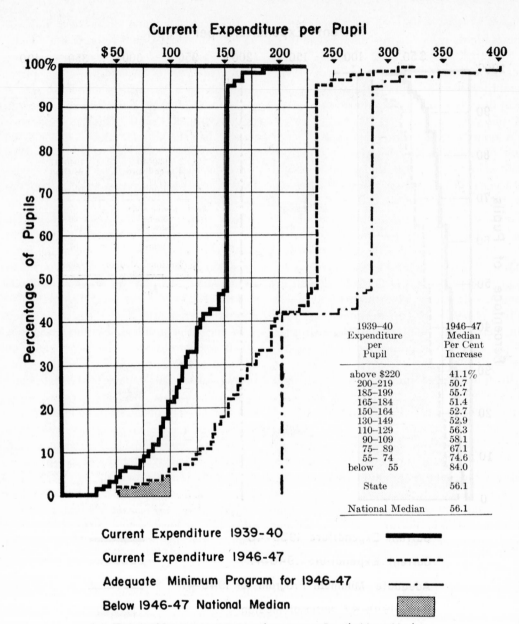

Current Expenditure per Pupil

1939–40 Expenditure per Pupil	1946–47 Median Per Cent Increase
above $220	41.1%
200–219	50.7
185–199	55.7
165–184	51.4
150–164	52.7
130–149	52.9
110–129	56.3
90–109	58.1
75– 89	67.1
55– 74	74.6
below 55	84.0
State	56.1
National Median	56.1

Current Expenditure 1939-40 ————

Current Expenditure 1946-47 - - - - - -

Adequate Minimum Program for 1946-47 —— · ——

Below 1946-47 National Median ▨

Figure 61. Current Expenditure per Pupil: New York.

Source: Institute of Administrative Research, Teachers College, Columbia University, New York, N.Y.

related to them as the school. Local autonomy is highly valued in the American culture.

Nonetheless, state aid to schools has been steadily increasing. In two or three states, notably Delaware and North Carolina, almost the whole burden of education is borne by the state.

A quarter of a century ago only 15 per cent of public school revenues came from state sources. In 1936 the proportion was 29.4 per cent; in 1947–48 it was 39 per cent. In 1950–51 it was estimated that between 43 and 44 per cent of school costs would be met by the states. While this is helpful to harassed local school boards, the fact remains that in 1937–38, state and local revenues for schools represented 3.24 per cent of total income of the states, while in 1949–50 it was only 2.39 per cent. This decline of less than one percentage point represents a drop of 26 per cent in the proportion of income allocated to schools.[8]

In this respect practice in the United States seems to lag behind that in many other democracies. In New Zealand and Australia, for instance, as in other nations of the British Commonwealth, every effort is made to give the rural child the same educational advantages as his urban cousin.[9]

Pros and cons of state aid. The question of increased state aid for schools is arousing much discussion. In some states the argument divides between urban and rural factions. In one eastern state, augmented aid to schools was defeated in the legislature for fifteen years by such a division. City people naturally object to contributing to the cost of the education of farmers and villagers. The latter groups retort that a democracy means equality of educational opportunity, the cost of which should be spread equitably over the entire commonwealth if not over the nation, especially since a large proportion of rural children — approximately half in normal times — become urban residents. They point out that there are great inequalities in the type of wealth taxed for school purposes, which now consists chiefly of real estate. Thus even in one largely urban state, the assessed valuation per child in the eight most urban counties was well over double the figure in the eight most rural counties. On the other hand in one state, Missouri, the state-aid program was the creation of the rural districts which controlled a majority of the legislative votes.

To meet this problem, and the thorny one of state control,[10] the National Education Association has proposed a so-called partnership plan. This assigns to the state chief responsibility for the legal and financial basis of public education. The local district is responsible for operation but assisted with funds and leadership. Educational opportunity is equalized through state guarantee of a "foundation program."

And federal aid? Even the best system of state aid to local school districts does not remove the inequalities in the wealth of the several states available for education. Ever since World War I there has been agitation for federal aid to education, led by the National Education Association. Numerous commissions and committees, some

[8] Professor Francis Cornell, address before the annual meeting of the Association of School Business Officials, September 26, 1950. For details see United States Office of Education Circular 274, *Public School Finance Program of the Forty-Five States* (Washington, D.C.: 1950).

[9] I. L. Kandel, ed., *Rural Education and Rural Society* (New York: Yearbook, International Institute, Teachers College, Columbia University, 1938).

[10] State control of rural education is exerted in the following ways: supervision of building plans and buildings so as to safeguard health and prevent fires while at the same time seeing that an efficient school plant is maintained; formulation of the qualifications for a teacher's certificate; standardizing and often raising local salaries; checking on local educational finances; suggesting curricula and attempting in various ways to put expert service at the disposal of the community.

official like President Roosevelt's Advisory Committee on Education in the late 1930's, have urged that this step be taken. Bills providing for it have been drafted and have frequently passed one house of Congress, but never both.

Opposition to federal aid to education, from which rural education and rural society would clearly benefit directly more than urban, is not on educational grounds. Rather it centers in such things as the dangers of federal control of the schools, the issue whether parochial and other private schools should share in the benefits, distribution of funds where a state operates separate school systems for whites and for Negroes, and in the unwillingness of some in the prosperous states to be taxed for the benefit of schools in poorer states, in view of the fact that education is a generally recognized state function.

The arguments for federal aid to education are closely similar to those advanced in favor of state aid, except that they are couched in national terms. Instead of inequalities in resources among the counties of a state, the stress is on the social desirability of approximately equal educational opportunity for children.

Rural Schools as Institutions

Against this background the discussion now turns to a consideration of the school itself as an institution. This institution is made up of the pupils who are to be taught the accumulated wisdom of the human race in terms of the culture of their own country, the teachers who are to give this instruction, the parents who send their children to the schools and who are therefore more concerned than childless adults, who nevertheless share the financial support of the institution through taxes. This adult public controls the school through the medium of elected directors or trustees, organized usu-

ally as a School Board or Board of Education. Objectives of the school are achieved in large measure by courses of study in a variety of subjects, collectively known as a curriculum, often together with extracurricular activities. The visible expression of this institution is a building commonly called "the school," though obviously a school is both the building *and* what goes on in it. These buildings vary from one-room structures, poor in facilities and equipment, to the ambitious plants of consolidated school districts, with many class rooms, laboratories, cafeterias, and facilities for recreation and large meetings available to both student body and community. Not infrequently such plants include more than one building. The high regard for education in the American culture is shown by the fact that the school building is often the largest structure in the community. In some more recently settled sections of the nation it often dominates all its surroundings.

Small schools or large? We have seen that the small one-teacher school is rapidly declining in numbers but that some tens of thousands of such schools are likely to remain. Thus it is clear that the weight of educational leadership in recent decades has shifted toward larger institutions, so-called centralized or consolidated schools. These combine a number of small districts into a larger one.

Small schools have some advantages. Where population density is not too low or enrollments too slim, the small rural school has some advantages the urban institution lacks. There is far greater opportunity for intimate acquaintance among pupils, teachers, and parents and, if teacher turnover is low, for a prolonged period of contact. This offers many possibilities for socializing experiences and for educational growth. The environment can be more readily utilized and there is more chance for the whole school to join in projects that will promote community betterment and the growth of desirable social traits.[11]

Villages and towns offer almost all the high-school education rural America has. More than half the rural elementary-school enrollment is in village grade schools, and this includes about one fourth of all open-country children. All told, about three fifths of all rural children attend village schools.

Village schools are larger, better equipped, have better trained teachers and longer terms, and spend more money per pupil than do those in the open country. In some states there is little if any difference between village and city schools in many of these respects.

Advantages of Consolidated Schools. A majority of the consolidated schools are also located in or very near the village or town center of the community. As compared with the old type one-teacher school, the first advantage of the consolidated school is a larger building of the type described above. Larger school grounds may also make possible athletic fields, school gardens, and demonstration plots.

In the second place, the broader tax base of the consolidated school makes it possible to hire better teachers than the old districts could afford, and provides not only normal recitation periods but some degree of subject-matter specialization among the faculty. In other words, instead of having a teacher for each grade, the consolidated school can hire a teacher for each subject. In some states there is special state aid for consolidated schools.

Third, consolidation makes possible better administration and supervision than is at-

tainable under the traditional type of rural school.

Finally, the pupils are benefited in many ways. There are enough children to permit adequate grading, to develop group and project work, and to organize many socially significant types of extracurricular activities among pupils of similar ages and interests.

Opposition to consolidation. The real crux of occasional farm opposition to school consolidation is the fact that the individual farmer's tax bill is often increased, since his real-estate holding is larger and more valuable than that of the average villager. As we have seen, real estate is the chief source of school-district local tax funds. A recent investigation in one state, conducted in more than two thirds of all consolidated districts (which include incorporated towns — 191 districts in all) showed that owners of farm property were paying 3.84 times as much per farm child as were owners of town property per town child, $142.40 against $37.12.[12] This, of course, was due to the tax and assessment system, not necessarily to increased school costs. There have likewise been a number of studies showing that consolidation frequently, though not always, reduces the cost of education below what it had been with a multiplicity of one-teacher schools.[13]

Consolidation is opposed for other reasons, too. Parents object to having their children ride in school buses and wait in bad weather for the arrival of the bus. In some localities, where one- or two-room

---

[11] See *Schools in Small Communities* (Washington, D.C.: Seventeenth Yearbook, American Association of School Administrators, 1939), especially chapters 1 and 2; and Julia Weber, *My Country School Diary* (New York.: Harper, 1946).

[12] W. H. Lancelot, *Rural School Reorganization in Iowa* (Ames: Iowa State College, December, 1944).

[13] Howard Dawson and Harry Little, *Financial and Administrative Needs of the Public Schools of Arkansas* (Little Rock: State Superintendent of Education, 1930); Dawson, *Satisfactory Local School Units* (Nashville: George Peabody Teachers College, 1934); Little, *Potential Economics in Reorganization of Local School Units* (New York: Teachers College Bureau of Publications, 1934).

schools had an excellent community program and had become something of a community center, the closing of this school has meant a distinct social loss. Local people feel unwilling to enter as fully into the program of the consolidated school as they did in their own neighborhood institutions. Wise administration of the consolidated school can usually overcome this difficulty.

Regardless of certain disadvantages under consolidation, the behavior of rural people favors it. The study of 140 village-centered rural communities referred to earlier showed that the proportion of farm children in village unconsolidated high schools was only slightly lower than the proportion for consolidated schools. In both cases over half the average enrollment came from farms.

A consolidated school is sure of success if in the initial planning of the district, the boundaries conform to customary areas of association among the people concerned. It is usually asking for trouble if a neighborhood which has long had most of its associations with center X is required to send its children to a new consolidated school in center T.

A program of community service will also help in tying the people to a school. This program may include adult education, or permission for local groups to use school facilities, where not needed by the pupils, for lectures, musicals, plays, or community meetings.[14] So important are these wider functions of the school in the community that in New York centralized schools receive additional funds from the state if they are active in adult education, and community recreation and organization.

Solutions proposed for some problems of consolidation. Recent studies indicate at least two things: the consolidated school is

[14] E. T. Stromberg, *The Influence of Central High Schools on Community Organization* (Ithaca: Agricultural Experiment Station, 1938).

not a final panacea for all the problems of rural education; and transportation of elementary school pupils presents more difficult problems than for high school students. Several measures to solve these problems have been advanced. One of the most important and acceptable involves the consolidation of a number of small schools into administrative units but retention of the schools themselves wherever there are sufficient pupils to warrant it. These are called "attendance units." Neighborhood ties and other factors essentially sociological in nature should be and often are given due weight in determining these attendance units.

Such a plan gives all schools the advantages of better administration and supervision. It also makes possible a richer curriculum than the old type of one-teacher school can afford. The adminitrative unit can employ teachers of art, music, or other subjects, or a school nurse, who will travel from school to school to bring it special services.

Teaching, The Heart of the School

It is obvious that the teacher occupies a key place in any educational system. Because of conditions already described, such as the smallness of many rural schools, the difficulties of financial support, and the small salaries paid, rural schools have long had difficulties in procuring teachers with as much professional preparation as city teachers. The average teacher in such a school naturally looks on a move to a city school as professional advancement. This makes for a turnover of teachers that has been as much as four times as high as in cities. In the National Study of School Finance undertaken by the Office of Education in 1930, a direct correlation was found between economic status of counties and number of years of education beyond high school possessed by its teachers. In the lowest tenth of the counties the average teacher had completed slightly less than a year of college work. In the top tenth the teachers averaged but little below college graduation. There was a regular progression upward in training as economic status improved, from the bottom to the top tenth of the counties. In 1930 only a third of the rural teachers had completed two or more years of normal-school training, as opposed to nine tenths in the cities.

Standards improving. Fortunately the situation has been improving, though in training and salary the rural school teacher is still below his city colleague. The study of 140 communities discussed earlier showed that in 1924 four fifths of the teachers in village centers had had the then traditional two-year normal-school training or more. By 1936, outside the South, 95 per cent were in this category including all regions, two thirds were college graduates; more than one fifth held a graduate degree. The same trend was noticeable in open-country schools, though to a less degree. In 1924 only 4.5 per cent of the white teachers in such schools held college degrees. In 1936 the figure was 21.7 per cent, practically a fivefold increase. Even among Negro open-country teachers, 6.4 were college graduates in 1936, almost none in 1924.[15]

This improvement continued up to 1942, but was interrupted to some extent by World War II. As of 1950–51, the average rural teacher, including both white and Negro, village and open-country, had completed a bit more than two years of college work. The open-country teacher still lags behind in both respects.

There are several reasons for this improve-

[15] It is believed that these data are quite representative of the national situation, as those for the 1930 study agreed within two points with the rural findings of the National Study of the Education of Teachers alluded to above.

ment in the quality of teaching so far as it can be measured by the teacher's professional preparation. One is the improvement in salaries. Considering the differences in the cost of living, it is probable that salaries of village teachers are not far behind those of small and medium cities and that differences in training are also small. Equally important, state boards of education, which hold the power of certification, have been using all their influence to raise requirements for entry into the teaching profession. Furthermore, local opinion and boards of education are increasingly recognizing the importance of well-trained teachers.

In line with these changes, there has been a decided tendency to change two- and three-year normal schools into four-year teachers colleges. It is interesting to note that this improvement in teacher training coincides with improved attendance in and greater holding power of the schools, as well as with stronger extracurricular and community programs. This is not necessarily a matter of cause and effect, but the phenomena are undoubtedly related.

The School Curriculum: A Social Force

The teacher is in charge of the learning process. It is his function to guide the pupil's mastery of the content to be learned and to interpret it so that desirable attitudes and traits will be developed. From the beginnings of organized social life, in tribal ceremonies of initiation into adulthood, the function of education has been to pass on to youth the culture of the society and the attitudes and skills which it encompasses.

Of late, education has been used by governments as an instrument of both social control and social change. Conspicuous examples of this in recent years are in the dictatorships, where teaching in all subjects must conform to the ideology of the regime.

In the United States the federal government has almost no control over the schools. Education is a function of the states, where procedures with reference to what is taught vary widely. Some have state courses of study, but wide latitude is usually given so that content can take local conditions into account. It would obviously be impossible to handle any given unit of a course in the same way in a highly organized city school where subjects are taught by specialists and in the ungraded, one-teacher school where one person teaches all ages and all subjects.

Nonetheless, it must be recognized that even in a democracy education is one of the instruments of social change. It must also be recognized that schools are not completely free from controls in their teaching. Schools assist in social change as they teach new scientific findings and as they explore the functioning of society in courses on civic or social problems. One example of this is given in the next chapter, where the contribution of the Agricultural and Home Economic Extension Service of the state colleges is discussed.

Controls usually take the form of legislative dictation regarding the school curriculum, usually in response to some special-interest pressure group, often acting from the best of motives. The stipulation in one state that any school receiving state aid must give instruction on the coöperative movement is a case in point. Every state has at one time or another enacted legislation concerning the public school curriculum. Schools have in this way been directed to do more than fifty different things, and have been restrained from doing as many more. In one sense these actions represent an expression by society of what it believes an institution it supports should do. But these enactments are often pedagogically difficult to comply with, and in small one-teacher schools sometimes impossible.

It is, of course, not only well-meaning legislatures that are responsible for curriculum changes and difficulties. Educators themselves may be too much influenced by local pressures, or by some new theory not applicable to their local situation. Illustrative of this is the doubling of offerings in commercial education in the 140 villages already mentioned. In the 1930's far more graduates of these departments were turned out than their communities or counties could absorb. Failing marriage for the girls, or finding a job outside their special training, the only market for these skills was in the cities. Such an educational program, therefore, stimulated urban migration, but practically no cases were found where the curriculum of the village school contained any offerings designed to help these migrants adjust to city life. The Rural Project of the American Youth Commission found many instances where such inadequately trained rural young people returned to their home communities because they were unable to adjust to urban life and working conditions.

Educators are fully aware that, next to his association with his family, the child spends more of his maturing years in school than anywhere else. They know how influential the school is in forming his attitudes and his social adjustments. They know that the school's job of producing loyal and understanding citizens for a free and democratic society is both supremely important and very difficult. This can be done better than at present, but it cannot be forced beyond the children's level of maturity.

Even with all the shortcomings in our public education, especially in rural America, it must nevertheless be admitted that no country has ever given so much education to so many.

Modern trends in curriculum building. There are, of course, in the very nature of society and culture in the United States, several philosophies of education. They vary from extreme fundamentalism, which would confine the curriculum to little more than the three R's and a few skill subjects, to an extreme eclectic "progressivism." A discussion of these philosophies as such is not appropriate to a text in rural sociology. The trend in actual curriculum building is, however, important. Despite the technical controversies in the field, it is defensible to describe the modern trend in some such terms as the following.

The school is attempting to teach the various subjects required of it, whether the three R's, history, or family relations, in terms of actual life problems and situations, starting within the experience and knowledge of the pupils themselves. It attempts to lead pupils to fact, action, or conviction by a process of deliberation, of intellectual effort. This process it strives to establish as a method of dealing with each new problem of living and learning as it emerges, and thus to apply it to an increasing number of areas of life as the pupil matures and expands his awareness of the world around him. It recognizes that education itself is a social process. This philosophy, and the methods of learning implicit in it, would apply to all subjects, academic or vocational.

Applying this philosophy. Many surveys in the last thirty years have noted increasing vocational indecision among rural high school youth. Some would say this indicates the need for more guidance. Guidance must be based on aptitude and personality tests and on a study of the individual. The whole guidance movement in education is relatively new. There are few trained counselors as yet, almost none in rural schools, though larger village schools are beginning to attack this problem. The proponents of the philosophy summarized above would advocate more guidance and less inexpertness in offering it. They would also argue that the increase in vocational indecision

may be due to the fact that under the traditional curriculum pupils have never learned how to make important decisions. In this connection a community enterprise in a Virginia village is of interest. Disturbed by the number of youths from the community unable to hold jobs after migrating to the city, a banker organized a group of about twenty professional and business people to study the problem and form a panel from which youth could seek guidance. The school and churches coöperated. The State Employment Service and the State Board of Education coöperated in offering a twelve-session course in fundamentals of guidance for this group.

Another interesting attack on this problem was made in Michigan in 1941. Several state agencies united in a weekend "careers conference" which brought together rural youth and agency leaders at the lakeside camp of one of the organizations. The conferees were its guests. Another agency planned and managed the program. A third furnished a staff member to guide the conference procedures, evaluate the enterprise, and prepare a report of findings. A number of others furnished speakers and consultants. The method of this conference successfully encouraged a large degree of give-and-take and of participation on the part of the rural youth themselves. Finally, the procedure and conference follow-up was designed to produce a maximum of influence on the decisions and activities of the young people after their return home, and to demonstrate to the agency personnel, through participation and follow-up activities of the young people themselves, the scope of the needs to be met.[16]

Implications of migration. The influx of country youth into village high schools re-

---

[16] Edmund deS. Brunner, *Working with Rural Youth* (Washington, D.C.: American Council on Education, 1942), pp. 32–33.

quires a reconsideration of the curriculum in terms of the needs of both farm children and village children. It has been safe to assume in the past that most boys and girls who went to high school would head cityward. But with the vast increase in the proportion of rural youth attending high school, this is no longer a justifiable assumption.

The rural high school, often small, has the difficult problem of preparing its students not only for farm or village life, but also for city jobs and for college. Thus it has four disparate tasks. Many surveys in the 1930's and a few since have pointed out rural youth's dissatisfaction with the traditional curriculum and, on the positive side, the demand for more, better, and different education, especially for more guidance, more effective help in home and family life, a more functional vocational education. This is a colossal order for an institution averaging less than two hundred pupils.

Another facet of this problem has been the steady rise in the age at which children are permitted to leave school. A few decades ago a child could go to work at fourteen years if his parents desired. While a few states still have this limit, sixteen is now the age in most, and one or two require eighteen or high school graduation. This puts more rural boys and girls in school, but raises real problems if the curriculum is limited and slanted to college entrance.

How shall agriculture be taught? For the rural high school, part of the problem resolves itself into the question, shall agriculture be taught according to the philosophy described above, or only as a practical subject, as a thing apart, or integrated with the rest of the curriculum? Shall it be taught so that the farm-bent youth may learn that agriculture has social relations and obligations, involving processes of national and world marketing? Shall he learn that carrying on these processes requires an under-

standing of economic trends and coöperative movements, in addition to the fundamental skills of seed-testing, tree-spraying, and other practical matters?

There are few communities which have not witnessed foreclosure and tax sales, which have not received refugees fleeing from hunger in the cities during the 1930's, or which have not profited from full employment in the cities and unprecedented demands for food from abroad during the 1940's. Causes of these phenomena, measures for meeting and solving the resultant problems, their implications for our national well-being and political organization, cannot safely be omitted in training rural youth, more than half of whom have completed their full-time education when they graduate from high school.

It should be added that in some places vocational teachers have become effective leaders in their communities. They have been instrumental in organizing community coöperative canneries, freezing plants, potato storage or drying plants, and so on. In a number of places these have been located on the school grounds or close to them. Sometimes these enterprises were part of a well-rounded continuing program of community development.[17]

Curriculum and community interaction. One of the best bases for building the school curriculum is the life of the community of which it is a part. The Virginia state course of study is evidence of this, as are a rapidly increasing number of local enterprises. The public school in rural Carroll County, Georgia, operated in coöperation with West

[17] Brunner, *Community Organization and Adult Education* (Chapel Hill: University of North Carolina Press, 1942). Also Brunner, *Working with Rural Youth* (Washington, D.C.: American Council on Education, 1942), p. 54. For a careful appraisal of the whole area of vocational education, rural and urban, see John Dale Russell and associates, *Vocational Education* (Washington, D.C.: President's Advisory Committee on Education, 1938).

Georgia College, is one such place. The whole curriculum is geared to the life and needs of the school and its community. This school has even produced its own textbooks, such as *Let's Plant Grass, Let's Raise Pigs, A Primer on Food, The Doctor Is Coming.* Arithmetic, agriculture, home economics, social studies, all come into these texts. The last named was produced because a plan to immunize pupils against infectious diseases failed when the children became alarmed at the prospect of being "shot," and played hookey the day the doctor was to come. After the book had been studied, more children were on hand when the doctor was expected than on any other day of the session. Furthermore, fathers, mothers, and babies turned up to get their "shots."

In Wisconsin, a Committee on Rural Community High Schools entered into a coöperative experiment with seven schools. After careful study, curricula were revised and made more flexible. Supervised correspondence study was substituted for courses which had very small enrollment. The teachers' time, freed in this way, was used on more important work. Social studies and English classes in one school united in a joint project with such units as "Earning a Living in W——," "How Can I Select a Life Work," "Recreation in W——," "How Can I Best Spend My Leisure Time," "Solving the Problems of Agriculture in America." These schools made community surveys, some limited, some comprehensive, to get local data needed for their classwork. Such surveys affected not only the pupils but also the community. Businessmen, churches, even local government changed policies. Interest grew, and an adult education program developed over a three-county area, especially in current affairs, international, national, and local.

Many other instances of effective integration of school and community in terms of current philosophy are given in a very valuable Office of Education report, *Broadening the Services of Small High Schools.*[18] Programs of this sort point toward a new day in rural education. They show what can be done. They produce social change on the community level.

Extracurricular activities expanded. In discussing the curriculum it should not be forgotten that schools are recognizing the potential educational value of leisure time and have organized an increasing number of extracurricular activities — especially the consolidated and village schools, where numbers permit it, and to a certain extent even in smaller country schools. The chief activity is athletics, now frequently under the control of a director of physical education. Musical affairs have tended to increase too, particularly orchestras and glee clubs. Some larger schools also have bands. The development of music can be traced to the influence of state universities, some of which conduct annual high school band, orchestra, or glee club contests.

Dramatics also has now found a place in many high schools, as has organized debating. There is an increased interest on the part of parents in this forensic and dramatic activity, an interest carefully nursed by the school authorities. There is clearly an encouraging increase in both the open-country and the village part of these communities in the contribution of schools to the social and cultural life of their areas. Poor, discouraging, even bad situations still exist, but the trend is one of improvement and progress. This trend is important, for it shows the broadening concepts of education within the school and the enlarging place of the school as a factor in community life, another evidence of which will be discussed in connection with the social significance of adult education.

[18] Washington, D.C.: Bulletin 1948, No. 9.

Social Factors Condition School Success

The last paragraphs have shown what can be done. Many other instances could have been given. But the fact remains that the contribution of the school can be sharply limited by the socio-economic status of its community. Hence, to function effectively the school must understand its social environment.

One evidence of this is a study by the Committee on Education of the United States Chamber of Commerce entitled, *Education, an Investment in People.*[19] The Committee compared several educational indices, such as current expenses per pupil and median number of years of schooling completed by persons twenty years of age and over, with several socio-economic indices and a derived rate of educational deficiencies. The volume of economic activity and the social indices used tend to rise and fall with the levels of educational expenditure and of educational deficiency.

The conclusions of this study are worth noting. They are:

That education is an essential investment for the advance of agriculture, industry, and commerce.

That every community should ascertain its

[19] Washington, D.C.: 1945.

own education status and economic condition, and set to work to utilize education as a lever for its own advancement.

That the cost of adequate education is an investment which local citizens and business can well afford in increased measure.

That educational programs must be made to apply more directly to the needs of the people.

That cultural education must accompany technical training if the desire for better living is to be developed.

That to maintain a representative republic, business must discover sound methods for the expansion of our dynamic economy.

Another indication, among many, of the relation between good schools and good social conditions is to be found in the census publication *Educational Attainment of Children by Rental Value of Home.*[20] To illustrate the point, a typical item from the voluminous data in this volume is given in Table 54 which shows the percentage of rural non-farm 12-year-olds completing a specified number of years of school according to the rental value of their homes, for the Western census region and for the two highest and two lowest rental categories. At

[20] Washington D.C.: 1945. For a discussion of this data see E. deS. Brunner, "Educational Attainment and Economic Status," *Teachers College Record* (January, 1948).

TABLE 54	NUMBER OF YEARS	TOTAL		UNDER $10		$10–$19		$50–$74		$75 AND OVER	
		U*	R	U	R	U	R	U	R	U	R
Per Cent of Native White Urban and Rural Non-Farm Twelve-Year-Olds Completing Specified Number of Years of School by Rental Value of Homes: Western Region	4 or less	10.5	19.3	35.3	31.4	12.7	16.5	1.8	3.6	1.2	6.9
	5	25.8	28.6	31.0	28.5	35.5	31.7	17.6	20.4	11.3	27.9
	6	43.6	39.6	22.4	31.1	37.1	41.1	49.3	54.3	48.9	34.9
	7	16.2	11.0	9.0	7.5	12.0	9.5	24.6	18.0	28.0	30.2
	8 or more	3.9	1.3	1.8	1.0	2.1	1.1	6.5	3.6	10.4	0.0

* U — urban; R — rural.
Categories omitted, $20–$29, $30–$49.

age 12 a child would normally have completed six years of schooling. The three top lines in the table are therefore a measure of retardation, the two bottom lines, of acceleration. Figures in the other regions are comparable. In all regions the lower the rental value of the home the greater the proportion of retarded children; the higher the rental value, the higher the proportion who are accelerated. At the lowest rental level over half, and at the next lowest, nearly half, are retarded.

This, of course, does not mean that poor housing causes retardation in school, or the reverse. It does mean that conditions of which poor housing is an index are associated with less than an average rate of progress in school. This creates a problem for the school and is one of many indications of why the school as a social institution should be aware of, and interested in, its social environment.

A final illustration may be given. In 1940 two fifths to one half of the farm and rural non-farm young women 18 and 19 years of age, and up to two thirds of those 20 and 21 years of age, who were married, left school with six years or less of education. At all ages up to 54, this less well-educated group showed a higher proportion of marriages broken by separation and divorce than did those with high school or college graduation.[21]

These data also indicate quite clearly that those who would solve social problems simply by asking the school to add a course to the curriculum in this or that problem area are highly unrealistic. For one thing, there is no guarantee that all children will take the course even if it is offered. Making it compulsory does not solve the problem, for a course must be located in some one

year, and the pupil may leave school before reaching that year.

Social stratification among pupils. Perhaps the greatest threat to the assumed objectives of American education lies within the school itself, whether rural or urban, in the social stratification among pupils. The student body inevitably mirrors to some extent the society of which it is a part. Farm children riding daily in the school bus tend to form a social group within the student body. Children from "the other side of the tracks," unable to share fully in the support of student organizations and activities, tend to be set apart. Those who live in the same part of the village, who have played together in one another's yards along the same street, have formed associations even before entering school which are reinforced during the vacation period. In communities where church lines are sharply drawn another element of social stratification is introduced — conspicuously, of course, between Catholics and Protestants. Divisions such as these are sometimes emphasized by attitudes of parents and tend to sharpen in high school. Such social groupings may become detrimental to school spirit as one or another seeks to dominate in the leadership of school organizations and extracurricular activities.[22]

Phenomena of this sort are a reflection of the adult world and should be no surprise to a sociologist. Small associational groups within larger social bodies are found in all societies. In democratic societies counter-influences are also at work which weaken stratification and provide for vertical mobility by freedom to migrate or in other ways. The school itself is one agency contributing to this end, to the degree that it provides equality of educational opportunity. Where

[21] Derived from Bureau of Census, *Educational Attainment by Economic Characteristics and Marital Status*, Tables 37 and 41, pp. 191 ff. and 210 ff. See Edmund deS. Brunner, "Education and Marriage," *Teachers College Record* (May, 1948).

[22] A. B. Hollingshead, *Elmtown's Youth* (New York: Wiley, 1949); W. L. Warner and associates, *Democracy in Jonesville* (New York: Harper, 1949), chap. XII; James West, *Plainville, U.S.A.* (New York: Columbia University Press, 1945).

lines of stratification are sharply drawn and where these are uncritically accepted by school administrators and teachers, the contribution of the school to strengthening democracy and to citizenship education is vitiated.

Summary. This chapter has shown various trends and tendencies of rural public education in our century, with emphasis on developments within the last two decades, during which rural education, like urban education, has made strides. Perhaps the achievements of greatest importance were the consolidation movement and the resulting centralization of educational opportunity for rural people on a community basis. Steady improvement in the professional preparation of rural teachers is recorded. Noted also is an increase in enrollment and attendance, especially in high schools, and a marked tendency for more rural youth, especially from villages, to continue education at college or at other institutions above the high-school level. The movement for a more socialized curriculum is described, and for a closer relation of the curriculum to practical life. Education is shown embracing more and more cultural subjects, in the interests of a fuller emotional and spiritual rural life.

This record, however, has left out of account one highly important and advancing movement in modern education, namely, the instruction of adults. It is gradually being recognized that social and technological change is so rapid that even college education can no longer impart final technical skill in vocational subjects. Much less can it impart a general knowledge sufficient for all adult life in this Gargantuan twentieth century with its revolutionary conception of science and the physical world, a conception involving colossal changes in the social, political and economic fabrics. The issues which disturbed the statesmen of the 1930's, and on which voters had to pass judgment, were unknown or scarcely heard of forty years ago. At that time, for example, the gold standard was unchallenged, the United Nations unborn, war debts unknown, farm bankruptcies and tax sales rare, federal relief for millions of unemployed and agricultural processing taxes and crop control inconceivable — to name only a few of the issues of the last decades. Finally, added to all these, came the more tremendous issues of world organization and of reconversion after World War II. Another powerful force in promoting adult education is increased leisure because of shorter working days made possible by technological advance, involving farm and factory alike. Hence adult education has assumed a remarkable importance, and to this subject the discussion will turn in the next chapter.

TOPICS FOR DISCUSSION

1. The exercises for this chapter will take the form of committee work. The class will be divided into five committees.

   Committee I will present a plan for organizing and administering rural elementary education on a county basis rather than a local district basis.

   Committee II will present a plan for consolidating two or more country district units.

   Committee III will present a plan for organizing and administering a high school on a town-country community basis.

   Committee IV will present a plan for organizing and administering libraries so as to be of greatest service to rural communities.

   Committee V will present a policy including editorial, reportorial, and advertising phases for a weekly newspaper, which will make it of greatest service to both its town and country constituencies.

2. Compare the per capita retail sales for se-

lected villages and towns in a county or selected counties in a state with the per pupil costs of elementary or high schools. Can you discover any relationships? If your state has a county system, compare per farm income with per pupil costs.

3. Should rural high schools restrict their teaching of agriculture to the production and marketing phases? Defend your opinion.

4. List five or six of the most important social changes affecting American rural life and indicate the curriculum implications growing out of each of these changes in terms of either elementary school, junior high school or senior high school.

5. Block out the main outlines of a course of study in high-school civics, sociology, or economics that would meet the point of view expressed in this chapter.

REFERENCE READINGS

American Association of School Administrators, *Schools in Small Communities*. Washington, D.C.: 1939.

Baldwin, B. T., *Farm Children*. New York: D. Appleton, 1930. An investigation of rural child life in selected areas of Iowa.

Bowen, Genevieve, *Living and Learning in a Rural School*. New York: Macmillan, 1944.

Brunner, Edmund deS., and I. Lorge, *Rural Trends in Depression Years*. New York: Columbia Press, 1937, chap. VII.

Clapp, Elsie R., *Community Schools in Action*. New York: Viking Press, 1939.

Committee on Rural Community High Schools, *Adventures in Rural Education*. Madison, Wisc.: State Board of Education, 1944.

Cook, Lloyd Allen, *Sociological Approach to Education*. New York: McGraw-Hill, 1950.

Department of Rural Education of the National Education Association, yearbooks: *Child Development and Tool Subjects in Rural Areas*, 1941; *Community Resources in Rural Schools*, 1949; *Conservation Education in Rural Schools*, 1943; *Guidance in Rural Schools*, 1942; *Newer Types of Instruction in Small Rural Schools*, 1938; *Rural Schools for Tomorrow*, 1945.

Educational Policies Commission, *Education for All American Youth*. Washington, D.C.: National Education Association, 1944.

Langfitt, R. E., F. W. Cyr, and H. Newson, *The Small High School at Work*. New York: American Book Co., 1936.

Lewis, C. D., *The Rural Community and Its Schools*. New York: American Book Co., 1937.

Mort, Paul R., and Francis G. Cornell, *American Schools in Transition*. New York: Teachers College Bureau of Publications, 1941.

Norton, John K., and Eugene S. Lawler, *Unfinished Business in American Education*. Washington, D.C.: National Education Association, 1946.

Office of Education, *Broadening the Services of Small High Schools,* Bulletin No. 9. Washington, D.C.: 1948.

Report of the Advisory Committee on Education. Washington, D.C.: Government Printing Office, 1938.

Smith, M. C., *A Sociological Analysis of Rural Education in Louisiana*. Baton Rouge: Louisiana State University Press, 1938.

Strang, Ruth, and Latham Hatcher, *Child Development and Guidance in Rural Schools*. New York: Harper, 1943.

Terry, Paul W., and Verner M. Sims, *They Live on the Land*. University: Bureau of Educational Research, University of Alabama, 1940, chap. VIII.

Weber, Julia, *My Country School Diary*. New York: Harper, 1946.

West Georgia College, *With Great Awareness*. Carrollton, 1944.

FILMS

Better Schools for Rural Wisconsin. C, S, 29. University of Wisconsin, Madison.

Community Resources in Teaching. S, 20. University of Iowa, Iowa City.

School House in the Red. C, S, 45. Kellogg Foundation, Battle Creek.

School in Centerville. C, S, 20. National Education Association, Washington, D.C.

Way of Life. C, S, 22. International Harvester Co., Chicago.

19

Adult Education

ONE OF THE CHIEF social developments of the depression of the 1930's was a heightened interest in adult education. In a time of rapid spiritual and material change, it is argued, schools and colleges cannot give youth a complete cultural and vocational equipment for life. Technological progress renders some trades quickly obsolete and creates others for which labor has to be trained. World events precipitate problems not envisaged in the curricula of educational institutions a few years earlier, witness the New Deal and its sociological and economic implications, and the huge issues growing out of World War II. Moreover, mankind seems to be on the threshold of greater leisure than has yet been enjoyed by the masses, and if this is realized, there will be sufficient time for adults to continue their education.

These implications for adult education are inherent in some of the broad social trends which have developed in the last generation. But there are still other reasons why adult education is increasingly important. One is the increasing age of the population; there are proportionately more adults than ever before, not only in the United States, but throughout the western world. The median age of the population of the United States in 1950 was 29.9 years, up from 20.9 years in 1880. Moreover, the data on years of schooling in the United States, reported in the previous chapter, showed that many persons left school before they had had courses generally considered of real practical value. Even for those who are well educated the constant expansion of human knowledge leaves many persons with learning which is obsolete. The social function of adult education, therefore, is not only to keep adults abreast of developments in fields as diverse as public policy and nutrition, but also to try to compensate for all too common deficiencies in schooling. Education has become recognized as a continuous process which must go on through life.

Rural adult education abroad. Until recently these factors were perhaps better recognized abroad than in the United States. While there are records of organized adult education programs here going back a century and a third, they were largely urban, and never reached the scope attained in northwestern Europe. An important development there, for instance, was the famous folk school movement, which originated in Denmark over a century ago under the leadership of Bishop Grundtvig and was a potent force in the social and cultural revival of a then discouraged and depressed nation. His movement spread throughout Scandinavia. Its major focus is on older rural youth, though the term is broadly defined. These folk schools have won high praise from many educators. In England, the Workers Education Movement, in which tutors from British universities participated, offered a wide range of subjects, as did the Country Women's Association. The coöperative movement in northwestern Europe early recognized the need not only for training its leadership, but also for broadening the horizons of its members. By the late 1920's the summer schools, institutes, and classes offered in the British Isles alone by this movement rivalled in size and scope the summer schools of the largest American universities.

More recently other countries have fallen into line, since World War II, stimulated by UNESCO. In Mexico, for example, since the revolution, adult education has been an obligation of the schools, especially perhaps in rural areas. Cultural missions have been organized. Their personnel varies but usually includes at least an agriculturist, a home economist, a public health officer, and an arts and crafts or recreational worker. Such a mission will settle for some months in a provincial capital or large town and work with teachers and people in outlying villages. Recently a widespread campaign to reduce illiteracy was initiated. Real pressure was put behind the slogan, "Each one teach one."

In China, Dr. James Y. C. Yen began adult education in 1921. Starting purely as an attack on illiteracy, known as the Mass Education Movement, the program expanded to include health, economic improvement through improved agriculture, and political reform. The teachings were put into practical operation in demonstration areas.

Programs of this sort take on considerable significance at this stage in world history. Under-developed countries have become a matter of great concern to the United States and to many international agencies. Helping such peoples to improve their social and economic status is difficult in direct proportion to the illiteracy of the population. Unfortunately illiteracy is a concomitant of other types of underdevelopment, though with some exceptions. It is also more of a rural than an urban phenomenon. Table 55 shows illiteracy rates in a number of countries, together with urbanization data. Note that the highest illiteracy rates are in the least urbanized areas.

In the United States the organized adult

	REGION OR COUNTRY	PER CENT ILLITERATE	PER CENT OF POPULATION IN CITIES 50,000 AND OVER
TABLE **55** Literacy and Urbanization in Selected Areas	World	50.8	—
	North America	2.5	33.8
	Europe *	9.3	32.1 **
	Oceania	11.5	37.7
	U.S.S.R.	18.8	20.0
	South and Central America	48.6	13.2
	Asia ***	73.4	9.5
	Africa	86.2	6.1
	India and Pakistan (1941)	84.9	5.7
	Burma (1931)	55.5	4.1
	Philippines (1939)	51.1	8.8
	Ceylon (1946)	32.9	6.3
	Indo-China (1936)	90.0	2.5
	Malaya (1947)	56.1	20.2

* Excluding Russia
** Excluding Germany
*** Excluding China

Source: These figures are supplied by Kingsley Davis, Division of Population Research, Bureau of Applied Social Research, Columbia University. The Division will shortly publish a monograph on world literacy and education.

RURAL EDUCATION *Top*: Two-Room Open Country School. *Bottom*: Consolidated School Buses Loading After School. (Photos, Standard Oil Co., N.J.)

COMMUNITY LIFE *Top*: Farmers' Meeting (U.S. Dept. of Agriculture).
Bottom left: Community Repair Shop Sponsored by Vocational School
(Soil Conservation Service, U.S. Dept. of Agriculture). *Bottom right*:
Street Corner Society (Standard Oil Co., N.J.)

COMMUNITY RECREATION *Top*: "Chow Line," Stockman's Barbecue.
Bottom: County Fair. (Photos, U.S. Dept. of Agriculture)

COMMUNITY RECREATION, OLDER RURAL YOUTH
(Extension Service, U.S. Dept. of Agriculture, top photo by Ed Hunton)

education movement is rather new. The American Association for Adult Education was founded barely a quarter of a century ago. It includes a score or more of educational fields, involving vocational, cultural, and recreation activities designed to help in the solution of personal and group problems. Its membership includes both public and private agencies.

The Agricultural Extension Service

The largest and best-financed division of adult education in the United States is entirely rural in nature. This is the tax-supported Coöperative Agricultural and Home Economics Extension Service, the administration and subsidy of which are a joint effort of the United States Department of Agriculture, the State Agricultural Colleges, county governments, and, in a few states, local farmers' organizations. It was organized in its present pattern under the Smith-Lever law in 1914, but had begun to develop a decade before, and expanded enormously during World War I.

The Extension Service is not wholly an adult education agency. About one third of the time of its field staff is given to 4-H Club work. About two million boys and girls are enrolled in tens of thousands of neighborhood 4-H clubs. The 4 H's stand for Heart, Hand, Health, and Head. Each member enlists in definite projects in the home or on the farm, and many clubs also have group projects, often in community service. About one eighth of the counties have full-time workers in this area. These 4-H Clubs are a very important out-of-school educational agency.

Objectives of Extension. The original and still primary objective of the Extension Service is to bring the farmer the knowledge that will enable him to farm more efficiently and thereby increase his income. The Serv-

ice also assists the rural homemaker in all facets of her activities. But these objectives have broadened with the years. The Extension Service is concerned with acquainting farm families with the social, cultural, recreational, and spiritual privileges and possibilities of rural life, and with the means of achieving them. It seeks to develop citizenship among adults and young people. It assists in the development of rural communities. Its aim is to put science at the service of its constituents and substitute it for folklore. The family is increasingly the focus of its interest. Family and farm are increasingly treated in terms of their obvious intimate interrelationship.

Budget and staff. The total budget for this work has steadily increased over the years. In 1951 total appropriations from all sources amounted to over $80,000,000, of which barely 40 per cent came from the federal treasury. On January 1, 1950, the employed professional personnel numbered 12,420 persons, of whom 9500 were county workers. The total staff also includes about 2000 specialists, whose chief functions are to take the technical research findings of colleges of agriculture, put them into teachable, readable form, and train local leaders in this subject matter. The roster of specialties over the years shows how the Extension program has expanded, though about half the specialists are in the areas of agronomy, dairying, poultry, horticulture, animal husbandry, and marketing.[1]

Extension Service democratically organized. Contributions of the Extension Service

---

[1] The remainder are allocated among the following subjects: agricultural engineering, animal diseases, child care and training, clothing, entomology, exhibits, extension schools, farm management, forestry, health and sanitation, home economics (general), home furnishings, home management, nutrition, plant pathology, poultry, rodent pests, rural sociology, recreation, housing, and discussion of public affairs.

are brought to rural people in the counties and communities where they live. Practically every county in the United States, save a few wholly urban ones, has an agricultural adviser, in most states called a county agent. About seven in ten counties also have a home adviser or home demonstration agent. A considerable minority of the counties also have assistant agents. These professional employees are assisted by local leaders who contribute on an average about ten days of their time a year and receive no financial compensation or even expense reimbursement. If valued only at day wages, this contribution exceeds the total grants of federal and state governments to the Service. This is a significant indication of the esteem in which rural people hold the Service.

Supporting the county staff is the state college of agriculture, where there is a director of Extension with his various supervisory assistants. The staff of specialists is also located there, in close touch with college research workers. The state is the basic unit of administration for the Extension Service. Procedures and programs vary by states, but the various systems are similar.

There is a small federal staff headed by a director, but the federal office has no power over the states and functions chiefly as advisor and clearing house. Programs, save in time of war, are determined in the states and, increasingly, the counties. These programs are based on the needs of the people as locally analyzed, usually by committees representing the various communities. With the rapid expansion of various federal agencies, such as the Soil Conservation Service, Farm Credit and Farmers' Home Administration, and others, the Extension Service has more and more come to be regarded as the educational arm of the Department of Agriculture. In its early days the Agricultural Adjustment Program would have had much more difficulty if the Extension Service had not already created the machinery,

the channels, and the contacts for conveying governmental plans to individual farmers. However, preoccupation with that program at the expense of more usual activities was a matter of concern to the Land Grant College Association.

This concern over the effect of new programs of the Department of Agriculture on Agricultural Extension was due not only to the interference of such projects with the routine of Extension activities and teaching, but also to the fact that the AAA and soils program called for action, and there was some fear that county agricultural advisers or agents would be held responsible for getting desired action. This would have interfered with their educational function and with the objective of the Service to bring all pertinent information to bear on subjects of vital concern to the farm population, allowing individuals to reach their own decisions.

This issue is an excellent illustration of the impact of changing conditions upon a social institution and of the demands, resistances, and tensions which are part of the process of reaching decisions. It is worth pointing out that such a clash of opinion as to the function of a tax-supported adult education agency could arise only in a democracy. Under a dictatorship the agency would do what the central government ordered or it would cease to be.

Extension methods varied. The Extension Service uses many educational methods. In its early days much of the teaching was done on a personal, on-the-farm basis. Great reliance was placed upon actual demonstrations of improved methods. With the increasing use of automobiles and acceptance by farm people of this agency, and with the broadening of the program beyond narrowly vocational projects, more and more group work has been done. These groups may be on either a community or a neighborhood basis, or in the case of agriculture, on a commodity or special-interest basis. Lectures, panel or group discussions, moving pictures and film strips are all used extensively. The demonstration technique continues to be important, in terms of both methods and results. Extension Service is an educational agency which dares to put its teachings to the test of practicability on farms, in homes, and in communities.

Results of Extension work. The amount of work accomplished is impressive. County agents actually visit more than a million and a quarter farm homes annually, conduct about a million group meetings, and arrange over a million demonstrations on an almost infinite number of projects. Among the known results of the work are the following: between one third and one half of all farm homes are reached by the Service; several million persons have been assisted in solving agricultural and home-economic problems; millions of changed agricultural and home practices have resulted, and the increased efficiency of American agriculture may be partly ascribed to it; coöperative action has been stimulated; increasing attention has been paid to marketing problems, local leadership has been developed, and community improvements have been furthered. Of late, the Extension Service has attempted interesting excursions into recreational or cultural fields, in music and drama, and to some extent in literature and art. Most of the states are also interested in the discussion of public affairs and some — Iowa, Michigan, and Wisconsin among others — have considerable programs in this area. Careful summaries of factual materials on various issues and impartial statements of the most important points of view on each issue are sent to hundreds of discussion groups. The intent is to enable citizens to come to a reasoned opinion on public issues. This is a great need in a democracy. The Extension Service has shown that a tax-supported agency can supply objective and impartial information on controversial public issues.

Future program. The program, by design and tradition, is largely vocational, though new developments are more largely in nonvocational areas.

In 1946 a committee of the federal extension staff defined its field of teaching as follows:

1. Economic problems and public policies
2. Marketing and distribution
3. Social relationships, adjustments, and cultural values
4. Farm homes and buildings
5. Health
6. Conservation of natural resources
7. Farm and home management
8. Rural organization and leadership development
9. Agricultural production.[2]

Most of these headings are self-explanatory, but a few comments are in order. Numbers 7 and 9, the heart of the vocational program, must of course be maintained but need less increase in the committee's judgment, than the other areas. Changing conditions, as well as consumer needs and attitudes, require teaching of efficient business and trade practices, market demands and outlets, effective organization, and price relationships. The great increase in rural interest in cultural and community development, together with problems of adjustment to social change, are producing heavy demands in this area. The increased agricultural income of the 1940's, and the availability of certain types of credit for home construction and modernization, have brought the need for information on func-

[2] E. deS. Brunner and Hsin Pao Yang, *Rural America and the Extension Service* (New York: Bureau of Publications, Teachers College, 1949), pp. 195–199.

tional requirements of dwellings, beautification of farmsteads, relation of investment and income, financing, technical, and other available services. In the field of health, help in analyzing problems, services, and facilities, ways in which these can be improved, and methods of organizing for group action to improve medical care and facilities, are increasingly called for.

Rural Extension sociology. In a text in rural sociology it is appropriate to mention that rural organization and sociology has a recognized place as a specialized field in the Coöperative Extension Service. The federal staff and half the states have one or more workers in this field. A quarter of these states have added this activity since the close of World War II, but a third of them have had it for over twenty years. Extension sociologists deal with the problem of developing methods of social organization and leadership for reaching maximum numbers of rural people with ever-enlarging Extension programs, with community organization and development, with assistance to rural social institutions and agencies, with improving procedures in existing organizations, and with developing groups and group discussion methods. In coöperation with research workers in this field, they make available social data and information influencing the organization of, and participation in, Extension programs.

Coverage of Extension Service. It is obvious from the foregoing that the Extension Service is a nationwide enterprise high in the confidence of rural, and especially farm, people. It is also clear that to reach the millions of people involved there must be careful organization. Obviously the people of any given community do not participate equally in its organized social life. As a tax-supported agency, the Extension Service is interested in how well it reaches its poten-

tial constituency. Numerous studies of this problem [3] demonstrate beyond any doubt that such factors as economic and educational status, owner or tenant operation, and age influence the amount and quality of participation in the educational program of the Extension Service. Based on one or more of these studies, and often on personal observation, sometimes cursory or biased, the charge is often made that the Extension Service fails to reach the lower one third of the farm population.

This is undoubtedly true in specific counties, but it is a generalization which needs to be examined critically before it can be generally accepted. The low-income farmer may be a sharecropper whose farm management procedures are dictated by the owner of the plantation. He may be a part-time farmer operating a few acres to improve the family standard of living and supplement wages earned elsewhere. He may be one of several other types noted earlier in the discussion of social patterns of farming. The needs of each of these farmers differ. If he fails to participate in a given Extension program it may be not because of his social, educational, or economic status but because he is uninterested. In few counties can the average Extension staff of less than three persons conduct educational work of equal value to all patterns of farming represented in the county.

In one study in Washington, still unpublished at this writing, the proportion of farmers who knew about the Extension Service and participated in its program was very large, over 90 per cent; but the number of contacts which part-time and small-acreage operators had with the Service was only about half that of their neighbors with larger holdings which took their full time.

[3] For a summary and discussion of research on this topic see E. deS. Brunner and Hsin Pao Yang, *Rural America and the Extension Service,* pp. 148–159.

This was obviously a reflection of need rather than status. In Vermont it was found that Extension reached the indigenous Yankee stock in significantly higher proportions than it did recently arrived French-Canadian immigrant farmers. In a county in a neighboring state, however, Portuguese immigrant farmers and their native-born sons who were operating farmers participated more fully in Extension activities than their Yankee neighbors. The reverse was true with the women in the home-making program, not only because of the social distance between native and immigrant, but also because of cultural factors within their own group which retarded the acculturation of women in comparison with their men.

The social skill of the agent is also often important. In a group of counties in one state a relatively new immigrant group had been almost impervious to the Extension program for some years. But when an agent of their own nationality was employed, himself an immigrant who conformed to the cultural practices and understood the cultural values of the group, both men and women soon became loyal and interested participants in the educational program of Extension.

In the main, the surveys indicate that a large group lying between those at the very top of the socio-economic scale and those toward the bottom participate more fully in, and provide more leadership for, the Extension Service than the others. On an over-all basis owner-operators are a bit more likely to participate than tenants, [4] family farms than others, and farmers with medium-sized holdings than those with very large or quite small acreages. Where several nationality groups are present the native group is apt to participate more than the immigrant stock, and among those of foreign birth or extraction, the longer settled groups more than the recent. Several important surveys have shown that farmers under 35 years of age are reached by the Extension Service less than those in any other category selected.

Exceptions can be found to all these generalizations. The Extension Service has been notably successful in counties with a very low score on the Hagood Family Level of Living Indexes, [5] and yet may not secure much participation among the lower fifth or fourth of the families in a prosperous county, even though this fraction may outscore the poorer county. It must be remembered that often those who do participate pass on what they have learned to neighbors who consistently look to them for such help. Surveys have regularly shown that such "indirect influence" is one of the most effective means of securing changed practices used by the Extension Service. Such diffusion is a well-recognized phenomenon in human affairs, and the channels by which it takes place are of great importance to those who expect to work with people in their communities. This, and the very fact that there are significant exceptions to the generalizations given above, emphasize again the need for understanding each local community and its culture.[6]

University extension. Somewhat akin to the Extension Service of the colleges of agriculture, because also under academic auspices, is university extension. Fifty-two

---

[4] M. C. Wilson and R. J. Baldwin, *Extension Results as Influenced by Various Factors* (Washington, D.C.: United States Department of Agriculture, 1929). This study, based on sixteen states, showed the proportions reached by Extension to be 81 for owner and 77 for tenant families.

[5] Margaret Hagood, "Farm Operator Level of Living Indexes for Counties of the United States, 1940 and 1945" (Washington, D.C.: Bureau of Agricultural Economics, 1947), mimeographed.

[6] E. deS. Brunner, "Summary of the Conference," *The Contribution of Extension Methods and Techniques Toward the Rehabilitation of War-Torn Countries* (Washington, D.C.: United States Department of Agriculture, 1945).

institutions belong to a national university extension organization. Together they conduct over 100,000 off-campus classes a year and a considerably smaller number of institutes and lecture courses. Some offer correspondence courses. A few have been interested in helping communities organize for specific projects, supplying materials and advice. Many offer materials, such as reading lists, pamphlet or even book collections, to study groups or departments of women's clubs. Some have radio programs. There is a considerable interest in educational broadcasting "to bring the classroom into the home." There is no way, from existing records, of separating urban and rural data on this work. Some states have broad programs, energetically promoted. Of the 140 village-centered communities referred to many times, it was found that in several in one state from a fifth to a half of the adult population had some contact with the extension division of their state university, in addition to what they were receiving from the Agricultural Extension Service. In other communities studied no impact from university extension was found. In a few states there are coöperative arrangements between agricultural and university extension. This seems to result in increased use of the latter, and its resource possibilities are brought to the attention of rural people by the former.

The Public School

Increasing adult education interest in schools. One of the marked trends in schools over the last twenty-five or thirty years has been increased activity in adult education. In 1924 only two states, California and Delaware, had vigorous and extensive programs of adult education through the public schools, rural as well as urban. In 1950 there were specialists in this area on the staffs of a number of state boards of education and more or less close coöperation be-

tween schools and the state university, as well as agricultural and home economic extension services in some states. Several states have increased aid to consolidated school districts that conducted adult education and community service activities.

In 1924 only nine high schools in the 140 village-centered rural communities were offering courses for adults. In 1936 three out of ten had such offerings. In the school year 1947–48 the United States Office of Education conducted an inquiry as to the extent of adult education in public schools of various sized communities. Of the districts responding, the following proportions reported having classes for adults and/or out-of-school youth:

Districts with a population of
2501 to 10,000   74.9% of 1207
Districts with a population of
2500 or less   80.8% of 316
County unit districts   88.9% of 160

Even if it is assumed that all school districts failing to reply to the inquiry had no adult education activity, which is hardly likely, it is clear that the proportion of schools with offerings in this area has markedly increased.[7]

Enrollments in adult education in 1947–48 were impressive, considering the relative newness of adult education as an organized

---

[7] Homer Kempfer, *Adult Education Activities of the Public Schools* (Washington, D.C.: Office of Education, 1949). These data, the author states, cannot be taken as completely representative of the national situation. It is possible that some county districts and some with populations close to 10,000 may have been urban. The assertion that adult education has made large gains since 1936 is substantiated by the fact that approximately half the rural high schools have vocational education offerings. A great majority of federally subsidized vocational teachers, especially in agriculture, have adult classes. If it is assumed that this is true in only one third of the districts of 2500 and under, which failed to respond to the inquiry, there would still be 60 per cent of these smallest groups of school districts with some adult education, twice the proportion found in the 140 communities in 1936.

school activity. They averaged 175 per district for those with populations of 2500 to 10,000; 101 for small districts of 2500 and less population, and 549 for county-wide systems. These last included an undetermined number of schools.

The curriculum for adults has also grown in richness. In 1936, though twenty topics were listed, four fifths of all courses were vocational in nature, and were available through the federally subsidized vocational education program. Of 24 groups of topics used in the 1947–48 Office of Education inquiry just mentioned, every one was represented by at least a few schools in each size group. While no data are available on numbers of courses, it is quite evident that vocational education, though still the most frequently reported activity, was not the sum total of work for adults.

This is not to underrate the importance of adult vocational education. In the formal agriculture classes of eight or more sessions offered adults by Smith-Hughes teachers, 500,000 adults participated in 1948. While it is not possible to separate home economics enrollment between urban and rural schools, it is probable that rural enrollment in this area was several hundred thousand. As

with Extension, these courses relate instruction to problems and conditions in the homes and on the farms of the students.

The following data, taken from the Office of Education report just referred to, indicate the percentage of school districts with specified programs in vocational education areas and the leading nonvocational topics in the offerings.

Among other topics reported are civic and public affairs (3.5 per cent of all districts in the three size categories), consumer education (4.3 per cent), health education (6.6 per cent), dramatics (5.2 per cent), safety (7 per cent), family life and parent education (8.7 per cent), preparation for marriage (2.1 per cent).

There are several items of special interest in this table. The population base was school districts, not incorporated areas. The fact that two fifths of the districts with populations of 2501 to 10,000 offered vocational agriculture to adults indicates that many of these were consolidated rural districts, doubtless centering in a village or town. The proportion of schools offering industrial or business education is also interesting. Some of these may have been located in the "urban fringe," and others may reflect the

TABLE 56 Percentage of School Districts and Adult-Education Offerings		POPULATION OF SCHOOL DISTRICT		
	VOCATIONAL	2501 to 10,000	2500 and under	Counties
	Agricultural education	40.3	47.5	53.8
	Homemaking	26.2	29.1	30.0
	Industrial education	18.3	10.1	35.6
	Business education	17.6	9.5	23.8
	NON–VOCATIONAL			
	Recreation	37.4	31.3	33.8
	Arts and crafts	19.5	13.0	12.5
	Music	15.7	10.1	15.6
	Literary and elementary education	8.3	4.4	25.7
	High school subjects	18.6	13.3	28.1
	Physical education	16.6	15.2	13.1

spread of small industries to rural centers. Some may be attended by young adults as preparation for moving to the city. Probably quite a number are in rural industrial communities, such as textile villages of the South.

The most significant thing, however, is that essentially rural or small-town systems are beginning to offer nonvocational subjects. This indicates both the beginning of an awareness of the importance of adult education on the part of school administrations and lay boards in these districts and a response on the part of the public, both in terms of enrollment and appropriations. Indeed, the response of the public almost certainly indicates a preceding demand. Rural schools do not add activities and expense without real justification. Doubtless the rising level of education, discussed in the previous chapter, sharpening the awareness of need among adults, accounts for some of the increased attention to adult education. Here then is a case illustration of social processes developing within education a new movement clearly of broadening interests. The effects of this in richer lives, wider understanding, and improved local leadership may be significant if the experiences of the Extension Service are any guide.

Significant too is the use of newer methods of teaching and other devices, rarely met with in rural schools fifteen to twenty years ago. Thus 6.7 per cent of the smaller districts were conducting special young adult programs, 5 per cent were members of community councils, 4.6 per cent were maintaining adult guidance services. Perhaps most significant, one school in eight was conducting community center activities. Granting all the limitations of a questionnaire study, this Office of Education report shows encouraging progress and reveals that much remains to be done in the area of public school adult education.

Rural Libraries

Although proof is increasing that in urban communities the public library is a vastly important agency of adult education, rural America has long been largely without library service. An American Library Association study in 1926 stated that 86 per cent of the rural population had no access to public libraries, as opposed to 5 per cent in cities. Since that time some real progress has been made in the country, but the Association puts the proportion of persons still deficient in library service at over 65 per cent.

According to the Office of Education there were 7408 public library systems in the United States in 1945. Of these just over 6000 answered an inquiry from the Office, 2900 of which were in communities of less than 2500 population. An additional 935 served populations of 2500 to 5000. While some of these were doubtless located in suburban communities, it is clear that half the public libraries in the United States are in rural territory.[8] Compared to the number of rural communities, however, this is far from adequate for the needs of rural America. Moreover, many of these rural libraries are small. In 1945 over 2200 libraries had operating expenses of less than $1000 and 71.1 per cent of less than $4000. It is not surprising, therefore, that about a third of them were open only twelve hours or less per week and half less than twenty-five hours. Forty-four per cent had less than 6000 volumes and 86 per cent less than 25,000. A great majority of the rural libraries were undoubtedly included in these categories.[9] Figure 62 gives an overall picture of the inadequacy of rural library service.

[8] Willard O. Meishoff and Emery M. Foster, *Public Library Statistics, 1944–45* (Washington, D.C.: Office of Education, 1947).

[9] *Ibid.*

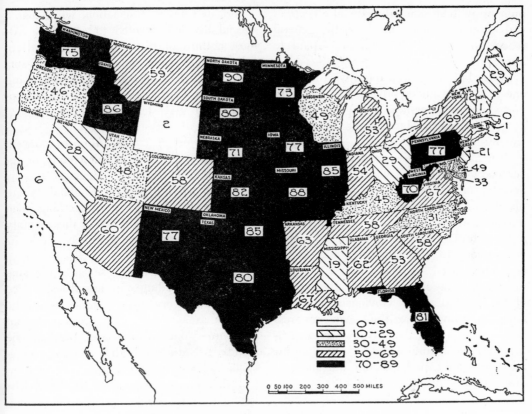

Figure 62. Percentage of Rural Population in Each
State Without Free Public Library Service, 1941.

Source: Anderson and Gross, *Can Towns Have Better Library Service?*
by Rand McNally & Company, Chicago.

Community libraries. Attempts have been made to meet rural library needs in several ways. One is through community libraries. These are especially frequent in New England, where about 1400 libraries are to be found outside of cities, though often these are pathetically inadequate. The unit of service is "the town," or township as it is called elsewhere. In Massachusetts and Rhode Island no town lacks at least one library. One Masachusetts town somewhat above the average, of about 8500 people, with an area of about fifty square miles, has a main library, three branches, over 16,000 books, and an annual circulation of more than 40,000. The budget is over $8000, or

$1 per capita. An article in the weekly newspaper introduces new books to the community, and best-selling fiction and non-fiction books are now topics of conversation. New England, as a matter of fact, has four fifths of all American township libraries. The remainder, about 500 in number, have largely followed the migrant New Englander into New York and some Midwestern states, notably Indiana — an interesting illustration of the migration of a socio-cultural institution.

Elsewhere the problem of rural library service is more difficult; in some states, particularly in the South, it has been helped by opening school libraries to the general public. Such libraries, however, have been

built up with specific educational objectives
and seldom meet the needs of the general
reader unless special attention is paid to
him.

In the 140 villages, of those with libraries
one sixth were under private auspices, supported by memberships and gifts. Judged
by professional standards, these libraries are
usually woefully inadequate. But behind
each is likely to be the devotion and perse-
verance of a Woman's Club, a Ladies' Aid
Society, or a similar organization whose
members keep the library going by their
unpaid continuous volunteer service, year in
and year out. The survival of these libraries
is testimony to the magic of books, to the
communal need for the culture, the rich
mental stimulation, the broadening agency
of the printed page. Obviously, however,
community libraries will not make progress
sufficient to fill up the great vacuum in library service in rural America. Other means
must be sought, perhaps state aid and certainly county library systems.

The county library. The county library
is taxed-supported and maintains a headquarters, branches in towns and villages,
and neighborhood stations to which small
book collections are sent periodically, perhaps to rural schools and stores or even to
homes in more remote areas. Often there is
direct service by "bookmobile." The central library is open to everybody; it usually
serves individuals by mail or telephone, and
secures for serious students any needed book
in county or state libraries.

The first modern county libraries were
established in 1898 in Ohio and Maryland.
From this start, the number grew to 99
counties in 1920, 176 in 1925, 228 in 1936,
and 740 in 1950. Some of these serve more
than one county.

This growth in rural library service has
been due to a number of factors. Perhaps
most important is the persistent effort of the
American Library Association, which has a
special division devoted to extension. Almost a third of the states and several regional groups have undertaken library surveys in the last decade and an increasing
number of legislatures have made appropriations to give state aid to libraries.

Distribution of county libraries uneven.
Forty-two states now permit county or regional libraries by law. Three of the six
which do not are in New England, where
the township library system has long been
established. The distribution of these county
libraries is curiously uneven, as Table 57
shows.

It will be noted that in seven of the nine
divisions the leading state has at least twice
the number of organized counties as has the
division as a whole. It is interesting that
the three southern divisions outrank the
Middle Atlantic and both North Central divisions. The leading state in the West Central division, Louisiana, in 1940 had the
lowest average number of years of schooling completed by the adult farm population
of any state in the Union. Some of the other
leading or high states are in the lower half
of their divisions on economic indices.
The dearth of local libraries in the South
may be one explanation for this record, but
in the main the distribution shows only
slight correlation with economic or educational status. Doubtless the very awareness
of acute need is in part responsible for the
South's record.

Advantages of the county library. The advantages of county libraries lie chiefly in the
fact that the unit of operation is large
enough to obtain support for an adequate
book stock and a trained librarian. Many
reports and records of county librarians read
like romance. Books are sent to remote
ranches and received by people who reach
their rural mail boxes on snowshoes, on

	CENSUS DIVISION	PROPORTION WITH LIBRARY IN	
		Division	Leading State
TABLE **57** Proportion of Counties with County-wide Rural Library Service by Census Divisions and Proportion of Counties So Served in Leading State	New England *	75.7	100.0
	Middle Atlantic	24.3	57.1
	East North Central	30.3	77.2
	West North Central †	9.2	29.0
	South Atlantic †	41.9	82.0
	East South Central	24.4	64.0
	West South Central	16.4	42.8
	Mountain †	16.2	60.9
	Pacific	62.8	86.0

Source: American Library Association data for 1950.
* Includes only 3 states.
† One state in this division which has not yet legalized county library systems omitted.

horseback, or in canoes. Even the statistics are meaningful. The second year after its reorganization a Louisiana parish (county) library operating on a budget of $16,000 in a community having a large percentage of Negroes circulated six books per capita among less than 30,000 population, a high average. This system put deposits into all Negro schools. There can be no question about the response of rural people to library service when it is offered.

Evaluating county libraries. Like other social institutions, libraries are influenced by their physical and social environment. Numerous studies have shown that persons living near a library use it more frequently and in greater proportion than those living farther away. The fact that some village or town public libraries, not parts of a county system, charge persons outside the municipality, though within the trade or community area, is only a partial explanation. Both the factor of distance and the non-resident charge, where it exists, are additional reasons for taking the library to the people by bookmobile or other means.

Again, several studies, especially an exhaustive inquiry into the whole library field by the Social Science Research Council,[10] have shown that members of professional and management groups and their families make more use of libraries than others, as do persons holding positions of leadership in the community. These groups use library facilities two and a half times as frequently as workers and farmers. By some this is interpreted as an evidence that social stratification is a factor in the use of libraries, but there are other explanations. Professional workers make use of a library in part for business reasons; books to them are tools. Many others use the library for recreational purposes only. Again, as is noted below, state colleges of agriculture make technical reading material available to the farmer and

[10] See suggested readings at end of chapter for listing of the main reports of this study.

his wife. They do not need to turn to the library for such material and usually would not find it if they did. Further, as already indicated, library service in rural America, even where found, is a relatively new thing. People who have long been deprived of some social utility, such as a public library, do not learn to use it overnight.

One basis for evaluating the response of people to a social institution is the support they accord it. The 5800 city and rural libraries reporting their operating expenses for 1945 to the Office of Education disbursed almost $62,000,000, or an average of 70¢ per capita. The median expenditure by states was 66¢, the highest $1.14. No state reached the standard of $1.50 set by the American Library Association.

The only extensive data on rural library support concerns those county library systems which do not contract with a city library to furnish the service, or which are not operated by a state library board. There is great variation among these counties, even within states. The top county in Texas, for instance, spent $1.27 per capita; the bottom county — one of the richest in the state — only 10¢. The following data give the state median per capita expenditures for the high and low states by census regions in 1948, the latest year for which data are available.

	NORTH	SOUTH	WEST
High	.99	.66	$1.26
Low	.18	.17	.49
Median	.60	.38	.84

Source: Data furnished by the American Library Association.

An examination of county data shows that counties which have had a county-wide system for a long time rank high in per capita expenditures. It is also interesting that the top state in the South, Louisiana, is one in which some demonstration county libraries were organized some years ago with outside support. It appears that once

the benefits of library service are experienced, rural people are anxious to retain them and are ready to vote tax funds for that purpose.

State colleges and their extension services help. Interesting, too, are the beginnings in several states of additional library services, such as the circulation of pictures, films, periodicals, music and phonograph records, and of coöperation among various rural adult education agencies. Typical of such innovations is the five-year reading project sponsored by the South Dakota Agricultural Extension Service and the South Dakota Library Commission. For the first year's study the state library worker prepared a general outline on "Reading in the Home," mimeographed and distributed by the Extension Service. For the second year a course on the novel was similarly prepared and distributed, and training schools were conducted in thirteen counties to introduce the project to leaders of farm women's clubs organized by the Extension Service. Books were supplied by state traveling libraries and by county and local branches.

The state colleges of agriculture are making other contributions to the problem of furnishing reading materials for rural people. An annual average of over twenty extension bulletins and circulars per year are issued. In few states does the annual distribution fall below a hundred thousand; in some it exceeds a million.

The average Texas farm and village home requests a pamphlet every three weeks. In New York, a request comes from every rural home about six times a month. It should be recalled that publications are sent out only on request, so that the recipient has spent at least one cent for a postal card and the time involved in writing.[11]

[11] E. deS. Brunner and Irving Lorge, *Rural Trends in Depression Years* (New York: Columbia University Press, 1937), p. 215. These comparisons

A number of states conduct book hours over the radio and several promote the organization of libraries. Written requests about what to read on specific subjects have grown so heavy that six states offer what librarians call readers' advisory service.

Next steps in library service. The lines of future development of library service are quite clear on the basis of present developments. The county or regional (district) library system seems to hold the greatest promise. Small libraries under private auspices in villages might well be enlisted in the effort to initiate county-wide library service. New rural school buildings, in view of the present trend toward including space for community activities,[12] should provide for a local library or a branch or depository of the county library, even though the library is not administered by the school. This is a simple economy for the taxpayer. The location of a library is also important. The same sociological techniques that help locate consolidated high schools can be applied. In a county system the county seat is usually the best location. In a regional library the largest trade center of the area, unless far removed from the center of population, is preferable.[13]

The above suggestions deal with the library within its locale. Beyond the county or group of counties is the state. The history of the expansion of rural library service shows that improvement has been rapid in states which extend aid to their public libraries. The American Library Association has urged state as well as federal aid to libraries. In 1938 the President's Advisory Committee drew attention to the deficiences and urged some federal aid to rural libraries in order to begin to remove obvious inequalities. Coupled with the move for more state aid, this step, if it comes, will make for significant progress in rural library service in the decade ahead.

Other Activities in Adult Education

There are many other agencies of rural adult education, some of long standing, some comparatively new. The Grange has for more than fifty years in all its over eight thousand locals stressed its "lecture hour," which is often an open forum of considerable educational value. Materials are specially created for it and leaders are trained. Farm and Home Bureaus in some states have played a large role in rural adult education. In Ohio, for instance, close to 2000 Farm Bureau discussion groups meet regularly to explore issues of public concern and to record their judgments. These discussions are based on carefully prepared materials which give all sides of any question, and define the main issues to be discussed.[14]

The Farmers Union also has a considerable educational program, especially among older rural youth. Women's clubs and certain other agencies, described in another chapter, have their educational features. Churches are beginning to be attracted to adult education. In addition to adult Bible classes, more and more churches, especially in villages, are beginning to arrange for lectures, musicales, or classes.

Radio. In 1945, almost three quarters of the farm homes in the United States had a

include all circulation of state bulletins with no deduction for out-of-state and urban circulation, which is probably relatively small. The circulation of federal bulletins is not included.

[12] Frank Cyr and Harry H. Linn, *Planning Rural Community School Buildings* (New York: Teachers College, Columbia University, 1949).

[13] C. B. Jaeckel, *The Government of the American Public Library* (Chicago: University of Chicago Press, 1935), pp. 318 ff.

[14] John K. Friesen, *The Role of the Ohio Farm Bureau Federation and its Neighborhood Councils in Rural Adult Education,* unpublished doctoral thesis (Teachers College, Columbia University Library, 1948).

radio — 72.8 per cent to be exact — as against 20.8 per cent in 1930 and just under 60 per cent in 1940. In 1950 the proportion was about 90 per cent, more than two thirds of the states exceeding this average. The fourteen which fell below it were in the South and Southwest.

As would be expected, the distribution of radios among rural people varied also according to income and education, though not by age except above thirty years. Thus 86 per cent of farm households with cash incomes of $1750 to $3000 had radios and 93 per cent of those with higher incomes. More than 90 per cent of those who had completed high school and more possessed radios, and 80 per cent of those who had finished grammer school. Even among the more disadvantaged, radio ownership was not inconsiderable. Two in five with cash incomes of less than $750 had radios, and over half of those who had not finished grammar school.

Few agencies of communication have been, and are being, more thoroughly studied than radio. Several national agencies keep constant check on the popularity of programs. The reason, of course, is that most radio programs are sponsored by commercial organizations as a part of their advertising program.

It cannot be assumed that farm and small-town people will conform in all particulars to ratings thus determined. There are even differences among rural people themselves, as developed from a study made by the Bureau of Agricultural Economics [15] as World War II was drawing to a close. Thus religious programs were much more highly valued among both men and women in the South than in other regions, and serial stories were less popular in this area. News re-

[15] *Attitudes of Rural People Toward Radio Service* (Washington, D.C.: 1946). The facts given in this section, unless otherwise noted, are drawn from this study.

ports were by far the most important radio feature for both sexes, but slightly less so in the north central states than in the South or West. One fifth of Southern women said they would miss serials most if their radios gave out. In the other regions the figure was a fourth. On the other hand, the South was less than half as interested in "complete plays" as the West, and popular and "jazz" music would have been missed by less than four per cent. This last type of program called forth a higher proportion of negative responses than any other. More than a fifth said they "did not care" for such programs — twice the proportion of those who expressed dislike for serials or classical music.

Programs designed especially for the farm population were rated as helpful by 84 per cent. Weather forecasts were the most highly valued single feature, but general educational material was mentioned by a third of the respondents and specific informational broadcasts by a fourth. Nonetheless, studies by the Extension Service show that as a teaching method radio alone accounts for relatively few actual changes in practice or behavior, rating eleventh among seventeen teaching methods. There is some indication that it is less effective in producing a change today than it was twenty years ago. Radio broadcasts probably arouse interest by informing people about new developments, but they check from other sources before accepting suggestions from broadcasts.

In general farm listeners select the more "serious" programs, such as news and market reports, religious programs, farm talks, and "good," "classical," or "old-time" music. (The proportion of the farm group with preference for this type of music is almost double that of those preferring other entertainment.) Among the rural non-farm group, entertainment programs are far more popular. In both groups daytime serials — "soap operas" — are the most disliked programs. Classical music, despite the approval many gave it, also rates high on the list of dislikes, largely because of inability to understand it.

Educational status and cultural habits clearly affect listening habits both as to content and preferred time. A study in Pennsylvania showed that Pennsylvania-German farmers and their wives listed as among the twenty programs they most liked only one of the twenty leading programs reported by the commercial radio rating services. Work habits and other cultural factors also affect the amount of time spent in listening.[16]

One of the most interesting uses of the radio for educational purposes is the Canadian Farm Forum of the government-controlled Canadian Broadcasting Corporation. Pertinent issues of rural, social, and economic concern are discussed by farmers and their wives, often with government officials on the panel. Some thousands of discussion groups, scattered all over Canada, listen to the broadcasts and then discuss the issues presented. Materials have also been sent these groups in advance. Their conclusions are recorded and sent to national headquarters. In some cases the government has taken action to meet the expressed desires of Canadian farmers as thus ascertained.

Radio is most welcome in rural America. Over three quarters of those interviewed in the study noted above reported that the loss of radio would make "a great deal of difference" to them, and another ninth said it would mean "some." Only 2 per cent of the men and one per cent of the women never listened to the radio. Rural men listen a median of 2.3 hours daily, rural women 3.7 hours nationally and 5.2 hours in the West. Women, of course, are more in the home than men and can listen while doing other things. A sixth of the men interviewed listened more than four hours a day; in the West the figure rose to a fourth. For the women, 60 per cent in the West and 40 per

16 E. deS. Brunner and Hsin Pao Yang, *op. cit.*, pp. 121–124, 128.

cent nationally fell in this category. It is quite clear, making all allowances for entertainment features, that radio broadcasting contributes to the sum total of adult education in the United States. Except for the broadcasts of the Extension Service, no effort has been made to measure the effects of this vast outpouring of talks, lectures, and the like. Commercial ratings, save on a few experimental projects, go no farther than to measure listening. But it is inevitable that any activity calling forth such investment of time leaves deposits of information and doubtless influences attitudes.

Whether television will add to this influence, and how, it is too early even to guess. The United States Department of Agriculture and a few states are already experimenting with its use as an educational media. Television is obviously well adapted to demonstrations of skills and techniques, as color telecasts of surgical operations to groups of doctors under the technical direction of Peter Goldmark, Ph.D., have shown. The response to telecasts of meetings of the General Assembly of the United Nations indicate still wider possibilities.

The moving picture. Like the radio, the moving picture is both recreational and educational. Conflict is always raging concerning the cultural value of the movies. The film industry is accused of inciting crime and undermining morals, and yet movies are lauded as a great educational force. On the whole, from a sociological standpoint they have been too little studied.

The influence of movies on the dress, customs, morals, and speech of rural people has probably been exaggerated. This influence needs to be studied, however, if proper techniques can be devised. At the same time, it must be remembered that country people have other means of learning about the world at large. Their cars take them frequently to town and city, where they can observe life in urban surroundings. And rural women have learned more about style and dress from Home Demonstration agents than from Lana Turner and Elizabeth Taylor.

Nevertheless, skillful use is being made of educational movies and so-called documentaries. As these have been improved technically, they have been used occasionally in commercial theaters. The United States Department of Agriculture, state colleges of agriculture, and a few commercial or semi-commercial agencies are making increasing use of moving pictures for educational purposes.

All told, there are now thousands of such films available, varying from simple strips illustrating some specific process like picking apples or spraying, to social documentaries like *The River, The Battle for Bread, Give Us the Earth.* Films have been developed to illustrate the operations of coöperatives, the functioning of the modern rural school, the advantages of rural electrification, and so on, through a long and lengthening list. Such films have proved effective in influencing attitudes and as a teaching device.

The newspaper. The newspaper also is an important factor in rural adult education. It has a real function to fill in relaying important local news and in interpreting local meanings of other events. A number of agricultural colleges and state universities are coöperating with rural editors in developing better papers, and the urban daily is finding its way more and more into farm and village homes. Almost four farms in five in the northern region receive a daily newspaper, about half that proportion in the South and seven out of ten in the West. Urban competition has forced many of the poorer rural weeklies to the wall, so that the number has declined from about 16,000 in 1900 and 13,000 in 1930 to something over 9,000 in 1950. The quality of the remaining papers

has improved. While some still give inadequate coverage even to local news and have few or no editorials, many give good attention and editorial comment to political, economic, and socially significant items affecting state, county, and local affairs. Such papers exert real leadership and have undoubted influence.

It is no longer possible, however, to determine the interests of rural people solely as portrayed in their weekly newspapers. The fact that world and national news is omitted from weeklies, save as it has a direct local application, is no evidence that rural people are uninterested in it. Weekly and daily newspapers simply fulfill different functions. The small city daily gives some coverage to events and happenings in outlying areas and usually has regularly appointed part-time reporters in each community in its service area. It does, however, bring some current news of the great society. The weekly is almost exclusively a recorder and mirror of the local community's corporate and political life, its organizational activities, and the personal happenings of significance within the area it serves. Well-edited local newspapers are not only socially significant, they are also usually firmly established.

In this connection the influence of the farm press is not to be ignored. Some farm papers have circulations running into hundreds of thousands, even millions in several cases. The annual analysis of editorial opinion of these papers published each September by the Information Service of the National Council of Churches shows that many are presenting important material dealing with the social and economic issues and events of rural America, as well as with national issues affecting the well-being of agriculture.

Special problems of the education of rural youth. One aspect of rural adult education deserves special attention, though it pervades all those which have been mentioned. During the depression of the 1930's the nation suddenly became worried about its youth. Studies were made and a well-financed national commission was organized. Education was obviously one answer to the problem. A number of colleges of agriculture added youth specialists to their staffs and held conferences and workshops. The work has continued, even though hundreds of thousands of young people went into the armed services during the war and others into war industry, handicapping many projected programs. After World War II this work began to develop further. The Joint Committee of the United States Department of Agriculture and the Land Grant College Association, which studied Extension programs, policies, and goals,[17] called for an expansion of work with older rural young people. The studies noted above and others, together with an analysis of recent programs, show that rural youth were most concerned with getting farms or jobs and next with getting more education. As one young man put it, "More, but none of the same." All over the nation youth seemed to feel that the schooling they had had was weak, or too narrowly vocational; that it had failed to help them fit into or understand their own problems of adjustment. These criticisms are interesting in relation to trends in curriculum described in the previous chapter.

Rural youth also wanted an opportunity to have education for marriage and family life, and asked for information as to how, under existing conditions, homes could be established.

The American Youth Commissions Rural Committee organized what could be called a demonstration program in five states and fifteen counties. State coördinators worked with state and county agencies, and above all with young people, on programs which

youth had a major share in formulating and carrying on. Education was a prominent feature of the programs in most of the counties, though usually "standardized classes" were avoided. Among the leading activities were classes in metal- and wood-working, discussion of personal, local, and national problems and policies, handicrafts, and public speaking.[18]

Adapting the folk-school idea. For rural youth preparing to live on farms, much of traditional education fails to meet the need. In times of rapid social and economic adjustment, a new type of rural citizenship and leadership is required. The informal and dynamic emphasis found chiefly in the folk-school plan of adult education has possibilities which should be explored. As we have seen, the genius of the Danes was shown when they created a new educational spirit and technique to meet a disastrous economic and cultural depression, using an essentially democratic approach. In the classroom the emphasis was upon the "living word" or the inspired lecture, while friendly conversation characterized life about the school and in the homes of teachers. There were no entrance requirements, examinations, or diplomas. The value of vocational subjects was recognized, especially when taught in their social setting, but folk-school leaders concentrated on the so-called humanities; social science, the liberal arts, literature, and above all, history.

While the outward form of the folk school has not seemed to thrive in American and Anglo-Saxon environments, and while any attempt to transplant its mechanics of books, buildings, or curriculum would be foolish indeed, yet there is an interest on the part of educators and thoughtful people in the substance and spirit of this kind of education.

[17] Washington, D.C.: Government Printing Office, 1949, pp. 62–63.

[18] For a full discussion of this project see E. deS. Brunner, *Working with Rural Youth* (Washington, D.C.: American Youth Commission, 1942).

One effort, among others, at adapting and exploring in this area is now in progress at the University of Wisconsin, and has been for 15 years or more. Adaptations have now been made in other institutions, but the Wisconsin plan is described because of its long and successful history. A short course in agriculture, with a typical emphasis on technical and vocational subjects, was reorganized in 1932 to include the social and economic fields of agriculture as well as cultural phases of rural living. This four-month winter course is for young men in their early twenties who live on farms. There are no prerequisites, though a majority have completed high school. The plan of courses is built around the social and cultural, as well as vocational and technical, needs of these young men. In fact, the very essence of this venture is the attempt at synchronizing these two educational objectives. Therefore, in addition to practical training in many features of scientific farming, time and place are found for history, economics, marketing, coöperation, sociology, public speaking and discussion, music, art, and literature. An important feature is the common life in dormitories and dining rooms, a feature which goes far in the personal, social, and cultural development of these rural young people. Another innovation with promise is "evening forums." Two or three times each week throughout the period, stimulating personalities from on and off the campus, leaders not only in agriculture, but also in industry, business, labor, education, government, art, literature, and music, are brought to the auditorium in the dormitory building to talk, but mostly to discuss, in forum fashion, important subjects of the day. The response on the part of young farmers to this new type of educational opportunity has been very gratifying.

Dormitory facilities have been taxed to capacity with about three hundred and fifty young men, coming from every county in the state and from several neighboring states.

This experiment may be summed up in the words of its leader, the dean of the College of Agriculture: "We are trying to give the young men on Wisconsin farms a training which will fit them for active participation in the whole life of a democratic, highly interdependent community. We are trying to educate rural youth not to leave the country for the city, but to give their best to improving rural civilization, including now, as it does, (1) an awakened and enlightened farm population, and (2) a rural leadership capable of manning the affairs of distribution as well as production." [19]

One thing is quite certain. The automobile, giving rural people far greater freedom of movement than they have ever known and permitting therefore more frequent association and group meetings, rural free mail delivery, the telephone, radio, and now television, have in large measure banished the physical and intellectual isolation formerly so characteristic of farm life in many areas. Considerable use is being made of these newer means of communication in rural adult education by many agencies. The earlier isolation caused much concern among rural leaders and reformers in the early days of the country life movement, as early texts in rural sociology make clear. To some these advances in communication may appear a mixed blessing, but the people of rural America would not return to former conditions even if they could

[19] C. L. Christensen, "Significance of the Folk-School Type of Adult Education," *American Coöperation*, 1938. Papers comprising the Fourteenth Annual Session of the American Institute of Coöperation, Washington, D.C.

TOPICS FOR DISCUSSION

1. Describe the activities of the Agricultural Extension Service in your county and indicate what changes you would make in its program and why.
2. Draw up a practical plan for library service for your county or community.
3. List and describe the adult education activities, formal and informal, in your community. Do these activities meet all recognizable needs? What changes would you make in the adult education set up? Why?
4. Write either an affirmative or a negative outline on the question: *Resolved*, that adult education should be included in the public school program at public expense.
5. Should the Extension Service expand its program to include all rural people, farm and non-farm? Defend your opinion.

REFERENCE READINGS

Brunner, Edmund deS., and Hsin Pao Yang, *Rural America and the Extension Service*. New York: Teachers College Bureau of Publications, 1949.

Kelsey, Lincoln D., and Cannon C. Hearne, *Cooperative Extension Work*. Ithaca, N.Y.: Comstock Publishing Company, 1949.

Lynn, C. W., *Agricultural Extension and Advisory Work with Special Reference to the Colonies*. London: His Majesty's Stationary Office (Colonial No. 241), 1949.

McKimmon, Jane S., *When We're Green We Grow*. Chapel Hill: The University of North Carolina Press, 1945.

Organization for European Cooperation, *Agricultural Advisory Services in European Countries*. OEEC, Paris, 1950. In United States, New York: Columbia University Press.

Reid, J. T., *It Happeend in Taos*. Albuquerque: University of New Mexico Press, 1946.

United States Department of Agriculture and Association of Land-Grant Colleges, Joint Committee, "Extension Programs, Policies, and Goals," Washington: 1948.

RURAL LIBRARIES

Goeckel, Carleton, and Amy Winslow, *A National Plan for Public Library Service*. Chicago: American Library Association, 1948.

Humble, M., *Rural America Reads*. New York: American Association for Adult Education, 1938.

Joekel, C. B., *Library Service*, Study No. 11, The President's Advisory Committee on Education. Washington, D.C.: Government Printing Office, 1938.

Leigh, Robert D., *Public Library in the United States*. New York: Columbia University Press, 1950.

RADIO

Bureau of Agricultural Economics, "Attitudes of Rural People Toward Radio Service." Washington, D.C., 1946.

YOUTH

Brunner, Edmund deS., *Working with Rural Youth*. Washington, D.C.: American Youth Commission, 1942.

Kirkpatrick, E. L., *Guideposts for Rural Youth*, chap. III. Washington, D.C.: American Youth Commission, 1940.

FILMS

County Agent. S, 17. Castle, New York.

Under the 4-H Flag. 56. United States Department of Agriculture, Washington.

20   Religion and the Rural Church

PRACTICALLY ALL PEOPLES have contrived systems of faith and practice with respect to the mysteries of life. In these are embodied their values, practices for attaining these ideal values, and the interpretations, rationalizations, or theology by which their faith is systematized and through which approved behavior patterns receive sanction. These systems are known as religions. All religions dignify their beliefs with rituals, often elaborate, which have to do with re-enforcing and illustrating the beliefs, values, and taboos of the group. In the United States religion has its roots in the Judeo-Christian tradition represented by Catholicism, Judaism, and Protestantism. The last named is divided into several hundred bodies, about twoscore of which contain the vast majority of all Protestants. In current parlance, particularly among Protestants, these religious bodies are known as denominations. Many dictionaries use the word sect as a synonym. In the sociology of religion, sect is usually applied to a group "regarded as deviating from the general religious tradition," or a "denomination characterized by insistence on strict qualifications for membership." [1]

The local expressions of religious institutions are churches. In terms of number of units, total amount of current income and capital invested, number of people employed, population enlisted, and attendance secured, the rural church outranks all other

types of rural social organization combined, with the single exception of the public school. In some communities the church is an even greater institution than the school.

This chapter considers the rural church as a social institution. It deals, therefore, with the number of rural churches, their constituencies, organization, leadership, financing, and interrelationships — elements which, although common to all social institutions, are in the church especially influenced, and even conditioned, by the intellectual and religious climate and by the basic policies of national organizations to which local units adhere.

How Many Rural Churches are There?

In 1926 there were, according to the United States Census of Religious Bodies, approximately 175,000 rural churches, including those in both villages and open country. They were distributed over the nation more or less in proportion to the population, but not entirely so, for the lower the density of population, the smaller the number of churches for every 1000 persons. Conversely, the greater the population density, the larger the number of churches for every 1000 people. The problem of over-churching, characteristic of rural America, is mainly a problem peculiar to the older and more thickly settled areas of the East, South, and Middle West. There are about four times as many churches per 1000 persons in the South as in the Rocky Mountain states. Where the density of population exceeds the national average there are about twice

---

[1] The American College Dictionary (New York: Harper, 1948); Dictionary of Sociology (New York: Philosophical Library, 1944).

as many persons per church as where the population density is less than 10 per square mile.

Factors affecting church distribution. Neither population density nor economic prosperity is the final explanation for the great number of Protestant rural churches. Other factors are:

1. The number and strength of non-Protestant churches.

2. The intensity of rivalry among Protestant sects. The stronger this is the more churches there are.

3. The frequency and size of community units. Restriction of the community unit and development of neighborhood life tend to multiply churches.

4. Where population density approaches the extreme in either direction, it operates to affect the number of churches. For example, a very sparse population has difficulty in assembling enough people to establish and maintain a church; the possibilities of church duplication are therefore reduced, and the areas which have no churches at all are more extended. On the other hand, the concentration of a large number of people within a small area makes division along the lines of denominational preference easier and reduces areas unsupplied with churches.

5. In sections where the church is more securely established and where it is most deeply rooted in the affections of the people, as in the South, and perhaps more especially in the Middle Atlantic and Middle Western areas, there tend to be more churches proportionately.

6. Racial groups, like Southern Negroes and large numbers of foreign-born farmers, also tend to increase the number of churches.

General statements such as these give little or no true indication of the importance of the church in local communities. In 1936 the average village-centered locality had 5.6 churches in the village itself and 3.6 churches in the open-country hinterland, a total of 9.2 churches for every community, as opposed to 10 in 1924. This net loss was the product of many church closings and many new organizations. In the village centers deaths and births of churches balanced in this twelve-year period. In the open country there were two churches born for every three that died.[2]

Another view of the decline in the total number of rural churches is to be had from a state-wide study in Indiana.[3] Of the twelve leading denominations, all but one showed a net decline in number of churches from 1926 to 1942, ranging from 7 per cent for Roman Catholics to 33 per cent for one of the Protestant bodies. The median decline was 17 per cent.

There is some evidence in scattered studies since 1936 that both birth and death rates of rural churches declined during the war. Transfer of members from open-country to village churches was halted because of restrictions on automobile travel. Since then, it is probable that the trends described have been reëstablished, though perhaps at a slower tempo.

In the years 1924–36, in which the 140 village-centered communities were subjected to study, nearly 400 of the original 1400 churches were closed, less than a tenth by any planned or coöperative arrangement. There are surely great social losses in this situation, and tragedy for many individuals. True, this gross loss is relatively smaller than among social organizations in the same communities, but the churches presumably have the advantage of overhead leadership and in some cases of financial assistance. Moreover, many of the new churches that have

[2] Edmund deS. Brunner, and Irving Lorge, *Rural Trends in Depression Years* (New York: Columbia University Press, 1937), pp. 299–300.

[3] *Hoosier Churches* (Muncie: Indiana Congregational Christian Conference, 1943).

been born had little if any sociological or economic justification in terms of the population to be served or resources available to support a program and pay for an adequate amount of ministerial service.

Birth and death rates have various explanations. What are the causes of this instability of rural churches, which obviously entails certain hardships and losses to their constituencies?

Population shifts troublesome. The demise of a church is not difficult to understand. It is usually due to population change. More than two fifths of the gross loss of churches occurred in localities which had lost population in preceding years, losses which were traceable, for example, to the departure of Negroes for the North, or of farmers to town or city. The coming of mining or industry into some localities displaced farming population. Poor farming or forestry practices so damaged the land in some neighborhoods that families moved away. A recent study of sixty-two closed Protestant churches in Pennsylvania [4] showed that almost a quarter died because of shifts or declines in population and more than a quarter because of the somewhat related cause of insufficient membership to keep the church performing even minimum functions.

High tenancy ratios serious. Farm tenancy has played its part in the mobility of churches. Where it decreased, the church at least held its own; where it increased, the number of people it reached declined. Studies by the Institute of Social and Religious Research repeatedly demonstrated that when the tenancy ratio exceeds one fifth, the church and other social organiza-

tions begin to decline. In counties where tenants operated half or more of the farms, the church enrolled two to four times more owners than tenants. The causes of this phenomenon have been discussed in another chapter.

Emotional sects unstable. Another large factor in the death of rural churches is the ephemeral character of some denominations, particularly the highly emotional sects so numerous in America. They rise and vanish with the arrival or departure of some extraordinary leader who claims divine eloquence. Such, for example, were the churches inspired by Aimee McPherson and her evangelical radio broadcasting. These bizarre sects seem to attract the economically oppressed, the highly emotional seeking release through religious media — in short, the psychologically unstable. For these reasons their organizations lack the stability and discipline of denominational supervision, which is an important asset of old and traditional sects. Mortality among new sects is high.

Administrative errors. Again, churches die because their administrative arrangements can no longer keep them functioning, because they have become outmoded, like the one-room school. In early days, some of the larger denominations attempted to plant churches in every village and open-country neighborhood. With modern high-speed transportation these isolated congregations are needless. Just as the automobile has enlarged community boundaries and made possible school consolidation, so it has accelerated the marked inclination of rural religious organizations to become centralized in village and town. Too many churches have also been located with no analysis of probable future economic developments or probable population trends in the community.

[4] Theodore C. Scheifele and William G. Mather, *Closed Rural Pennsylvania Churches* (State College: Agricultural Experiment Station, Pennsylvania State College, 1949).

Overchurching. Poor administration is also frequently responsible for the establishment of more churches than a given population can support. This is known among rural religious leaders as overchurching. Methods of mitigating this situation will be described later. In the Pennsylvania study noted above overchurching was deemed to be the chief cause of death of 13 per cent of the sixty-two churches, and a factor in the death of many others. It is interesting to note in this connection that seven in ten of the families that had belonged to closed churches in Pennsylvania lived 2.5 miles or less from the church. After the closing three fourths of the affected families were still within 2.5 miles of an active church.

Disputes within churches and unsatisfactory professional leadership also accounted, almost equally, for a quarter of the closings of these Pennsylvania churches. Underlying the specific causes of church casualties is a trend which has been marked for a generation for village and town churches to grow at the expense of those in open country.

The villageward trend. In 1920, 22.6 per cent of the membership of village churches and 6 per cent in town came from open country. By 1936, 40 per cent of village church members came from the open country and the proportion of open-country members in town churches increased even more sharply, reaching 35.9 per cent. The reasons for this trend are many. It is partly a response to the growing tendency toward grouping rural organizational activities in the village. H. Paul Douglass, in twelve surveys conducted in the 1940's, largely in the Northeast and Middle West, found ten village or town churches in which from 80 to 100 per cent of the members lived in the surrounding open country.[5] Most of these churches had moved to the center because of the convenience of that location for the membership. A sixth of the center churches draw 60 per cent or more of their following from the country and nearly half of the village and town churches drew 40 per cent or more of their membership from the country.

The type of road on which people live has a real and understandable influence on their church affiliation. Professor Rockwell Smith quotes a study of William Mather, Jr., in Allegany County, New York, showing that four fifths of high school youth living in the village were church members, and that two thirds of those from the country who lived on paved roads and less than half of those who lived on dirt roads were church members. With respect to membership in young people's societies the proportions were respectively four, two, and one out of each ten youths. One clue to these data lies in the fact that pastors had visited two thirds of the village homes in the six months prior to the survey, but less than half of the country families living on paved roads and less than two fifths of those living on dirt roads.[6]

It is not only convenience, of course, which draws farm people to village or town churches. The great increase in the number of farm children in the high schools of the center, where they associate with nonfarm youth in extra-curricular and other social activities, plays a part. There is also the desire to enjoy the better-trained ministers and richer programs of village and town churches, to worship in large congregations and thereby benefit from increased social opportunities, and to join in church the village people with whom they participate in other activities. Usually it is the more prosperous families who transfer their memberships from the "little brown church

---

[5] "Some Protestant Churches in Rural America: A Summary and Interpretation," *Town and Country Church* (January, 1950), pp. 2–13. All subsequent references in this chapter to Douglass' studies are based on this report.

[6] Smith, *The Church in Our Town* (Nashville: Abingdon-Cokesbury, 1945), p. 40.

in the vale" to village and town congregations. In this manner the open-country church is undermined and eventually dies, but the farther it is from village or town the more healthy are its roots and the greater its chance of survival. This has been mathematically demonstrated.[7]

Most rural sociologists declare that this trend will continue. The previous edition of this text indicated that this was "likely." While Douglass makes no statement as to the overall percentage of members from the country in center churches, an examination of his data seems to warrant the conclusion that the proportion is no less than the nearly 40 per cent reported above for 1936. Indeed, since he was concerned only with Protestant churches and since very large proportions of Catholic village church members are from the country, the overall proportion is almost certainly larger than in 1936. On the other hand, as with the one-teacher school, there will probably always be some open-country churches. In the Northeast and Midwest, and probably in irrigated sections of the Far West, this movement has come closer to running its course than elsewhere. How rapidly it proceeds depends not only on the availability of good roads, but also on the ability of farmers to buy automobiles. The strength of neighborhood groupings is also important here. As we have seen earlier, the number of neighborhoods in village-centered agricultural communities has declined sharply in the last thirty years; but many remain and strong open-country churches are not only one factor in the survival of many, but in turn draw strength from the neighborhood.

Village and country churches: partners or competitors? The relations of village and town churches with those in the open country have been discussed largely in terms of

effect on the survival of the latter. In this particular, there is both inter- and intra-denominational competition. How parishes overlap and village open-country church competition occurs is shown in Figure 63, which outlines the parishes of churches in Hamilton County, Iowa, in 1947. The Roman Catholic body avoids this dilemma through wise administrative arrangements.

The issue so far as Protestantism is concerned is broader. It is whether there shall be significant and substantial coöperation among farmers and rural non-farm people in religion as there is in education, public health, and other areas of social effort, or whether there shall be competition. The Pennsylvania study [8] showed that 30 per cent of the members of closed churches did not transfer to another, but out of this group half of those 66 years old and over failed to make a new connection. The proportion for those who were younger was exactly half as large. This loss was significantly less when the closing of the church was planned for and it was not allowed to die a lingering death. Even a loss of 25 per cent of formerly active church members is a serious drain. What seems called for is a religious partnership of village and country. This seems to have been best attained where the center has a population of between 1000 and 2000. Culturally and economically these places are closer to farm people than are larger ones. On this point Douglass remarks:

No judgment should be passed upon the individual choices involved in church membership. Each individual is to determine for himself the place of his religious affiliation.

With respect to the community, any judgment on a specific situation must of course consider whether or not there are good alternatives. If there are satisfactory and easily accessible open-country churches within the community areas it will be natural for a larger proportion of

[7] Morse and Brunner, *The Town and Country Church in the United States* (New York: Harper, 1923).

[8] *Op. cit.*

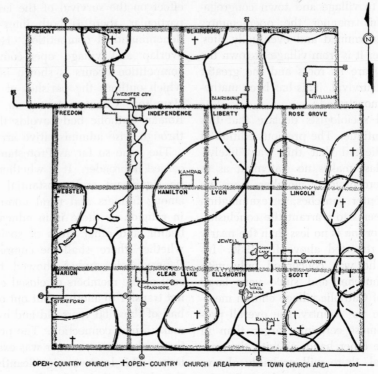

OPEN-COUNTRY CHURCH—✝OPEN-COUNTRY CHURCH AREA════ TOWN CHURCH AREA——and——

Figure 63. Areas of Church Attendance, Hamilton County, Iowa, 1947.

Source: Paul J. Jehlik and Ray E. Wakeley, *Rural Organization in Process,*
Research Bulletin 365 (Ames: Iowa State College Agricultural Experiment
Station, September, 1949).

country people to attend them. This may excuse the town churches for focussing largely on
town people. Denominations with numerous
churches, like the Methodist, seem inclined to
this solution. But where good and convenient
open-country churches are lacking and where
the churches of a given denomination are so
few that there is no alternative but to try to
associate the two groups in the same church, it
seems wholly inexcusable for a town church to
isolate itself, and the church seems sadly inefficient when it fails in its rural outreach. Case
studies show numerous examples of flagrant
failure to bring a due proportion of the country
population into church membership.

Rural Church Membership

Records show that the average surviving
rural church has been growing. It averaged

98 members in 1926 and 133 in 1936.[9] Unfortunately the 1936 religious census is
known to have been quite incomplete, especially in the South, and it is reasonable to
suppose that smaller churches were less
likely than large ones to return their schedules to the Census Bureau. Still more unfortunately, Congress failed to authorize a Census of Religious Bodies in 1946. Douglass
found an average membership of 181 in his
studies in the 1940's, but in these the South
and West were under-represented, both
areas known to have many small churches.
For example, the average membership of
those surveyed in the mountain states was
only 50. The 181 member average he re-

[9] *United States Census of Religious Bodies* (I,
1926; I, 1936).

ports include 25 non-residents, an average of 14 per cent of the roll. In 1936 the average membership of all churches in the 140 communities, 139, agreed closely with the census.[10]

Elimination of the weakest churches, described above, partly accounted for the increase in average church membership, since it obviously tended to lift the average membership in surviving churches. Douglass's study showed that two fifths of the churches he studied had gained 10 per cent or more in membership since 1930, and that an equal proportion had lost 10 per cent or more. The remainder fell between these limits. There was an overall gain of 6.8 per cent in membership. These data concern only existing churches and hence give no effect to such as may have lapsed.

Many factors influence the size of a church in addition to population density and other considerations already mentioned. Program is one, and will be discussed later. The better known and older denominations have more prestige and thus have an advantage. Denominational policy plays a part. Some older religious bodies sought to serve members even in small neighborhoods. Recent developments in transportation have placed many such churches at a disadvantage. Other bodies, notably some of the Lutheran synods and some German sectaries, such as the Amish or Mennonite, frequently founded colonies and moreover tried to keep the land in the control of their group. The average rural Lutheran church exceeds 200 members, while the Methodists and Presbyterians, for example, with different policies, average not much over half that figure. Procedures such as those of the Amish, for instance, illustrate how a cultural value, high regard for land, is given a re-

ligious sanction and in turn reënforces the church as an institution.[11] It has often been shown that there are strong churches in localities where strong characteristics of a folk society continue to exist and where kinship groupings are important.

Some small churches are units of sects with a highly emotional interpretation of religion or with an emphasis upon some one particular doctrine. Frequently, especially in villages, these are literally "on the other side of the tracks." However sincere the religious convictions which separate their members from local churches of better-known denominations, these groups are also an indication of social distance between the various church groups.[12]

There is thus great diversity in numbers and strength among rural churches. Douglass reports that the lowest fifth of those he surveyed had an average membership of 34, the highest fifth of 460. While larger churches tend to be in villages or towns, this is not exclusively true by any means. It is important to remember that while the statistical picture of the rural church indicates, correctly, a weak institution, there are thousands of churches in rural America that are powerful in their communities.

The hold of the rural church on its constituency. The ratio of church attendance to community population is an index of the holding power of the church. So measured there has been a slight but perceptible loosening of church ties among village and farm populations. This is shown by the Indiana study mentioned above. It was quite clear

---

[10] In 1936 the *Census of Religious Bodies* showed an average membership of 382 for rural Roman Catholic churches. The average in the 140 communities was 377.

[11] Walter Kollmorgen, *The Amish Community of Lancaster County, Pennsylvania* (Washington: United States Department of Agriculture, 1939).

[12] Brunner, *Village Communities* (New York: Harper, 1927), p. 221. One of the authors, during a field survey, once asked a young lay leader of an emotional church, "What church is that on the next corner?" Quite matter of factly he replied, "The bosses' church."

in the 140 communities, where between 1924 and 1936 the ratio of church membership to community population declined from 35.3 to 32.8 per cent.

Various surveys by the United States Department of Agriculture on the effect of the war on rural communities, made in 1943 and 1944, indicate that the church lost ground in some respects (though usually less than other social organizations) but gained in others. A state-wide study of Congregational-Christian churches in South Dakota states: "During the war years the Conference has lost strength in every way excepting in financial contributions." [13]

Douglass found that attendance at the main church service averaged 43.6 per cent of the membership — allowing for nonresidents, about one half of the potential audience. A quarter of the churches he studied did not have a service every Sunday. A third of them maintained a second Sunday service most of the year. Assuming that these roughly balance, it would appear that there has been no improvement since 1936. In that year the average church member attended church eight times for every ten times he had in 1924.

Such data, though important, are not the sole measure of the influence of the rural church. Professor Rockwell Smith found in 1938 that the rural churches of one district of the Methodist Church in central Wisconsin were serving 2.5 times as many people as they had members.[14]

Compensating for the small number of southern churches considered in the only recent data on the rural church, the Douglass study, is an interesting piece of research by Dr. S. C. Mayo in North Carolina. He found that rural people continue to give the rural church more than three times as much time as they allot to all other organizations.

Using a weighted scale rating in ascending order, membership, attendance, contribution, committee membership, and office-holding, Mayo found that religious activities accounted for 80 per cent of the total participation in formal organizations by farm people and 75.3 per cent by rural non-farm households.[15]

Population changes affect churches. The hold of the church on its constituency varies greatly according to region. Every church study, from those of Dr. Warren H. Wilson in the 1910's to those of the 140 communities and Dr. Douglass, has shown this. In the main, the older the region the stronger the church. One explanation for this is that the newer states in the western third of the nation have drawn much of their population from the rest of the United States. People of varying habits and cultural heritages have mingled, and in many communities no one strain has become dominant. When the 1926 *Census of Religious Bodies* was published, it revealed that the ratio of adult church members to population varied inversely with the percentage of a state's population born in other states and also with the rate of population increase from 1900 to 1920.

Inequality in the support of religion among the regions is thus in part a phenomenon of unequal population growth and stability. The church as an institution has not yet caught up with more rapidly changing parts of the nation. It has never found a means of ministering adequately to those who live in sparsely settled areas and soon learn to exist without such ministry. Such persons, too, as their very migration showed, were of the restless brood of American pioneers upon whom tradition made but slight impression.[16]

[13] T. A. Tripp, *Congregationalism in South Dakota* (New York: Board of Home Missions, 1945).
[14] *Op. cit.*, p. 36.

[15] Selz C. Mayo, "No. 1 Rural Influence," *Research and Farming* (October, 1949), pp. 3 and 6.
[16] Hooker, *Hinterlands of the Church* (New York: Harper, 1930).

On the other hand, with the more stable populations of the eastern seaboard, loyalty to the church, like other social traditions, has long been ingrained. Church membership is a token of respectability, and for that reason its customs and mores are more binding upon the social group.

The principles here elucidated are true even for local communities, and a consideration of them adds to our knowledge of the influence of population change on church memberships. Church records of villages which gained population more rapidly than the nation as a whole showed that the net membership increase was 4 per cent, or less than a fourth the rate of population gain. On the other hand, in villages which lost more than 10 per cent of their population between 1920 and 1930, church membership declined only 6.2 per cent, while the number of nonresidents simultaneously increased. This tendency for church membership to decline more slowly than population and to increase less rapidly than population may be considered a well-established phenomenon. It has been noted in many studies in both city and country.[17]

With the tremendous increase in migration in this country during and after World War II, it would be interesting to undertake another analysis now. This is impossible because of the failure to carry through the 1946 religious census. The annual compilation of total church membership made in 1950 by *The Christian Herald* indicated that organized religion as a whole enlists a slowly increasing proportion of the total population. How much of this is rural there is no means of knowing.

Other social conditions play a part. It is quite evident thus far that population movements, migration, the villageward trend of rural life, and cultural heritages and differences condition the kind of institution any given church is. It will be apparent later that economic conditions also play a part. So too does the quality and care of the land. Buie distributed 222 Methodist churches in the Piedmont District in South Carolina according to whether they were located in moderately, considerably, or severely eroded areas as determined by technicians of the Soil Conservation Service. He found that membership varied from 160 on the better land, to 132 on land that was considerably eroded, to 105 where the parish area was severely eroded. The percentage of the membership attending service varied similarly, though to a far less degree.[18]

Another indication of the importance of this factor comes from Sewell's work in constructing a Socio-Economic Status Scale, based on 800 Oklahoma farm families. Distributing these families into quartiles, he found the following with respect to the membership and attendance:[19]

	RICHEST	UPPER INTERMEDIATE
Husband Ch. Member	74.0%	53.0%
Husband attends Ch.	77.9%	65.3%
Wife Ch. Member	88.0%	72.4%
Wife attends Ch.	85.9%	74.5%

	LOWER INTERMEDIATE	POOREST
Husband Ch. Member	41.0%	23.5%
Husband attends Ch.	54.5%	40.0%
Wife Ch. Member	57.5%	33.0%
Wife attends Ch.	58.5%	43.0%

[17] See especially, Fry, *Diagnosing the Rural Church* (New York: Harper, 1924); and Sanderson, *The Strategy of City Church Planning* (New York: Harper, 1932). This tendency was first noted by Charles Otis Gill and Gifford Pinchot in their study of churches in one Vermont and one New York county in 1910. Cf. *The County Church* (New York: Macmillan, 1911).

[18] T. S. Buie, *The Land and the Rural Church*, unpublished and undated manuscript furnished by The Town and Country Committee of the Federal and Home Missions Councils. Also quoted by Smith, *op. cit.*, p. 62.

[19] Smith, *op. cit.*, p. 46. The fact that attendance is uniformly higher than membership may reflect above-average mobility among the Oklahoma population.

The Organization and Program of the Rural Church

We have seen that by virtue of the number of its units and an enormous constituency, the rural church is a very important part of the rural social structure, but that because of regional differences, fluctuations in population, and changes in religious attitudes, it is enrolling a slightly smaller proportion of the population than formerly. Here, then, is a great institution facing changes that seem to indicate need for adaptation to altering conditions. What has the rural church done in this exigency? To answer that question, it is necessary to turn first to its program and organization.

Supervision. Each church is part of a denominational body, and each of these bodies in its own way makes suggestions regarding specific activities and goals, and provides supervision. But the supervisory unit can render only small assistance to the local congregation, since its concern is almost wholly with administrative matters. Supervision is far less adequate than for the public school. Some denominations, to be sure, have special rural church departments, but their number is few.

The keystone of church organization is obviously the local minister. The ideal situation and declared objective is a full-time resident minister for every church. This goal has not been attained. About seven tenths of open-country churches have nonresident service, and the same is true of about a fifth of the village churches. Less than a tenth of open-country, and only a few more than two fifths of village churches, have full-time resident clergy. The rest have pastors who give part-time attention to churches elsewhere. The obvious reason for this situation is the large number of churches and resulting small memberships, which are unable, at the present or in any predictable future, to support a full-time minister.

Preaching. The largest part of the church program is preaching. Every effort is made to have at least one service a Sunday, an ideal realized by seven eighths of village and nearly two fifths of country churches, a gain over past performance attributable in part to the automobile, and attained in the face of decreasing attendance and at the expense of other possible features of the program.

Religious education. The traditional Sunday or Church school is the central feature of the nonpreaching program of the church. In 1936, 92 per cent of village and 86 per cent of open-country churches maintained such schools, with enrollments averaging 125 and 75 respectively and an average attendance of two thirds of this. In the 1940's Douglass found that 92 per cent of all churches had such schools, but membership had declined almost 20 per cent in twelve to fifteen years and attendance had dropped to 56.6 of enrollment. Indicative of the difficulties in conducting effective religious education is Dr. Tripp's finding in the South Dakota study, mentioned earlier, that since 1920 Congregational-Christian churches in that state have lost half their Sunday school enrollment; 28.4 per cent of the churches had no Sunday schools. This state lost 13.7 per cent of its rural population between 1930 and 1940. In as sparsely settled a state as South Dakota this loss, shared by over four fifths of its sixty-nine counties, was enough, when distributed among local communities, to account for disproportionate losses in these schools. In an organization so small the removal of only a couple of families may deprive the school of half its teachers and an appreciable proportion of its members.

That the problems of the church and its Sunday school in a state like South Dakota are not ended is indicated by the 1950 census. Although the state gained 1.1 per cent in population in the preceding decade, over two thirds of the counties continued to lose. In half the counties which gained, urban growth was larger than county, indicating that the rural population has continued to drop; almost two thirds of this state's counties had less than 10,000 population, and almost half of these less than 5000, in an average area of nearly 10,000 square miles per county. The problem of effective coverage for the church and all other agencies is obviously difficult under such conditions.

Again, there are great differences among the churches. The highest fifth of Douglass's sample of 1300 Protestant churches had Sunday school enrollments averaging 251, the lowest fifth, 39. These larger, stronger schools naturally are those that are seeking to do an effective job of religious education by modern methods. Thus, Douglass found three schools out of five operating vacation Bible schools; slightly more than half had confirmation or preparatory church membership and mission study classes; about a fourth had week-day religious education, and three in ten, Sunday school teacher training. In each of these, especially the last, the record was as good or better than in 1936.

Other organizations. About 70 per cent of all rural churches possess an average of over two and a half subsidiary organizations, chiefly women's and young people's groups, but also some men's organizations. With the rapid spread of 4-H clubs, boys' and girls' organizations are declining. The presence of subsidiary organizations is influenced by the amount of pastoral service. The Indiana survey alluded to reports that churches with resident pastors had 5.3 of the eight most common program activities, including full-time preaching. Those with nonresident ministers averaged 2.7.

Leadership. This raises the question of leadership in the church, lay and professional. All churches make a considerable point of enlisting the membership both in the conduct of and participation in program activities. Most local churches have two boards, one to manage property and finances, the other to assist the minister in spiritual work and the program of the church. The various subsidiary organizations have their officers, and those for youth and younger children their advisors or leaders. About an eighth of the membership of the Sunday school is made up of adult teachers and officers. But all this work heads up in the minister or pastor, an employed person. Since it is clear that the church has not yet made any considerable adaptation to its emerging problems, the question arises, how competent is its professional leadership to meet new situations as they arise? The handicap under which that leadership works through the necessity of dividing individual attention among a number of churches has already been pointed out. Even resident pastors serve on the average nearly two churches, and nonresidents serve three. Less than half the rural churches have a minister resident in the community and giving his full time to one church. Most of these are village churches.

With respect to professional training of ministers, the data indicate some improvement over the last quarter of a century, but this gain is far more evident in villages and towns than in open-country churches. According to the 1926 *Census of Religious Bodies* only 22.6 of the Protestant rural clergy had standard training, namely, four years of college plus theological training. About 25 per cent had one or the other. Douglass found that slightly more than half the clergy he studied had the full training, but the proportion varied from four out of five in more urbanized counties and the centers down to one in three in the most rural. Practically all Roman Catholic clergy have both college and seminary training.

Conditions of work. A partial explanation of this situation may possibly be found in the conditions under which rural clergy work. The average length of tenure is less than three years, a short time in which to gain the spiritual confidence and respect of a community. The compensation, too, is not large, averaging in 1936 slightly over $1200 a year for Protestant resident village ministers and $858 for all nonresidents. The Census of 1940 covering the labor force of the nation procured data on salaries of 82 per cent of the 136,669 clergymen, rural and urban. Of these, 51 per cent received $1199 a year or less. The great majority of this group were doubtless rural. This compensation is less than the lowest category of federal employees. Slightly over 90 per cent of all clergy received less than $2500. These data, of course, give no effect to the rental value of parsonages, available to two thirds of the Protestant and all the Catholic clergy, nor to income from other occupations. Douglass found that the most typical salary was between $2000 and $3000, though half the ministers reported less than $2000 and 15.6 per cent less than $1000. Among these latter groups about one in four ministers perforce also had part-time secular employment. It is clear that there has been some improvement in ministers' salaries since the depression 1930's, but that it has not kept pace with increased cost of living, nor with improved income of church constituents, especially farmers.

Church Finances

The plight of the clergy raises the question of support for the rural church. Each of the 140 village-centered communities spent an average of $16,000 annually in 1930 for its churches and $10,300 in 1936. Between these years, the average budget fell from $2400 to $1910 in village Protestant churches and from $709 to $560 in the open country, declines of more than 20 per cent.

The Roman Catholic churches spent about $800 and $400 more, respectively, than the Protestant. By the end of World War II, total budgets had come back to the 1930 level.

Douglass reported an average budget of $2645, though there is wide variation among churches. Contrasting the highest and lowest fifths of his sample, the former's annual expenses averaged $5876, the latter's only $784. The lowest fifth were obviously served by part-time nonresident ministers. On the basis of per-member contributions, however, members of these weak and struggling churches spent more to keep what they had, $20.10 per year, than did those belonging to large successful churches. To them each member gave on average $12.77 a year. This tendency for the least effective church to cost more per member than others has been noted in many rural church surveys.

Socio-economic conditions influence giving. As in other matters the social and economic conditions of a community influence both church budget and per capita giving. Buie's study in South Carolina, alluded to earlier, showed that churches located in communities with moderately eroded land had budgets well over double those serving populations on severely eroded soil. The agricultural depression was clearly reflected in per capita giving in the 140 communities. From 1924 to 1930, the average per-member contribution was $16.89. By 1936, this had fallen to $10.45. For open-country churches comparable figures were $8.57 and $5.67. In each case, the largest declines were in the regions most seriously affected, the South and Midwest.

Studies by the Institute of Social and Religious Research repeatedly demonstrated that there is a relation between economic adversity or prosperity and church support. From the mass of available data the following is selected as the simplest.

Where the per capita retail sales in the village community, as determined by the 1930 United States Census of Distribution, amounted to less than $200 a year, average per-member contributions to churches were only $9.84. The remaining figures follow in tabular form:

Sales	Contributions
$200 to $300	$13.05
$300 to $400	14.48
$400 to $500	18.38
Over $500	16.92

The decline when sales passed $500 per person checks with many similar results obtained by using different measuring rods and is probably an index of the highly stereotyped program of the rural church. Since churches are larger in wealthier communities,[20] the per capita cost of the highly standardized program declines. It is in such areas that what people have available for benevolences beyond stated denominational obligations goes into country-wide social and socio-religious agencies with paid executives. Unless subsidized from the outside, such agencies are found only in such wealthier areas.

Benevolences reflect similar influences. Churches place great emphasis on giving. Far-flung missionary, educational, and health enterprises, at home and abroad, are supported by gifts of millions of members. In 1924, 32 cents out of every dollar received by local churches went for such purposes in village and country alike. As the agricultural depression deepened, these causes proved most vulnerable in church budgets. The survival of the church as an institution depended upon the retention of a minister and the upkeep of the building in which activities were carried on. Such expenses became the primary obligation. Benevolences therefore dropped to less than 20 cents of each dollar received. Douglass's and several other less extensive studies show that with the agricultural prosperity of the 1940's, church benevolent enterprises recovered to the point where they received about 28 cents of each dollar.

This analysis has shown that the rural church, especially in the open country, is a small, poorly financed organization, existing under the leadership of a minister who perhaps lacks the desired professional training, and who, more often than not, must divide his services among several congregations. Its program is usually highly stereotyped, and there is some evidence that its hold upon its constituency is slowly diminishing. It is too small to afford better service, and it is difficult to improve the situation without better leadership. Its smallness arises in part from a multiplicity of units, a situation arising out of an administrative policy created before the advent of modern transportation facilities, and out of historic doctrinal differences which have perpetuated themselves in about twoscore major and more than one hundred and fifty minor denominations. These are the things, which, sociologically speaking, place the ministry and the churches on the horns of a very difficult dilemma.

The operation of traditional, sentimental loyalty to a particular church counteracts somewhat the changing material and physical conditions which tend to bring about abandonment of churches, particularly in open country. The church is by nature conservative, the great repository of tradition, slow to change or recognize what is called modernity, so that individual churches are less ready to adapt themselves to change, and die more slowly, than other social insti-

[20] Douglass and Brunner, *The Protestant Church as a Social Institution* (New York: Harper, 1935). Consult also Brunner and Kolb, *Rural Social Trends,* Appendix G; Brunner, Hughes, and Patten, *American Agricultural Villages,* chap. X; Fry, *Diagnosing the Rural Church.*

tutions. But fundamentally the church is closely intertwined with the community; it is therefore important to analyze the relations of rural churches with their communities and with one another.

Effect of Competition

It has already been shown that competition among rural churches is inevitable under present conditions. The national rural church executives of various Protestant denominational boards have declared that one church for each thousand persons of like nationality or tradition is the desirable ideal toward which to strive. The implication of this is a confession that these same denominations are parties to competitive overchurching.

Studies of the 140 village-centered agricultural communities, as well as Douglass's more recent investigations, have shown that where churches enjoyed comparative freedom from competition, in terms of fewer units per 1000 people, they were larger, better manned, better attended, better supported, and registered larger membership gains,[21] than where there was either moderate or severe competition.

On this point Douglass remarks that the burden of "surplus" churches is greatest in the smallest places. Villages with less than 500 population have from two and a half to three times as many churches for each 1000 persons as have large villages and towns. Douglass adds this comment:

All told it is pretty thoroughly established that the common sense expectation is right; namely that where there are more people to draw on the churches will be larger.

Overchurching, as shown by the series of studies, is most obviously present in relatively poor counties which cannot possibly bear the

burden of adequate support of so many churches for so few people. Such a situation does not generally result in a higher Protestant evangelization rate. All the churches put together may not do better in spreading the gospel than relatively fewer do in other counties. The real result is such institutional feebleness that they cannot command more than an ordinary degree of response from the unchurched population.

Social effects of competition. Serious as such conditions are from the standpoint of the church and its moral and spiritual leadership in the community, the social effects within the community are also serious unless the churches have developed coöperative working arrangements. Competition is disruptive of community solidarity and morale. It intensifies instead of healing group divisions. Even such a matter as the location of the annual service for high school graduates has frequently become a matter of bitter controversy. Competition keeps churches small and weak, thus preventing the acquisition of competent and well-trained ministers, and weakening social and ethical aspects of religion in the community.

It must be remembered, however, that church competition is not exclusively a matter of doctrinal differences. In many places the real differentiating factors are economic and social. For example, tenants may gravitate to one church, owners to another, the élite of the community to a third, small business and skilled labor to a fourth, the very poor to a fifth. In areas where the economic make-up consists of farming, industry, and other non-agricultural pursuits, factory people and farmers seldom join the same churches.

Race influences on churching the community. In localities dominated by diverse nationality backgrounds, race heritage determines church affiliation. The Hollander attends the Dutch Reformed Church, the

---

[21] See Brunner and Kolb, *Rural Social Trends* (New York: McGraw-Hill, 1933), pp. 233–236 for detailed analysis on these points.

Rhine German the German Reformed; the Saxon is Lutheran; the North German may be Lutheran or he may join the Evangelical Synod of North America, which was a transplantation of Frederick William the Third's German State Church. In such cases language and customs vary and church connections are the product of ethnic and social variations. The progenitors of such a group, for example, may have come to America partly because they opposed the union of Lutheran and Reformed bodies in Europe. Transition from one church to another, especially where different nationality groups are involved, is not easily effected. In such situations the churches reflect social strata or status groups well recognized within the community.

It is significant to summarize the most important conclusion of the preceding section: in spite of its ideals, the church has had to submit to social and economic factors more often than it has conquered them.

Religious Coöperation in Rural America

The problems of the rural church discussed thus far are well recognized by many of those most concerned. Remedial policies have been worked out, both within and among various Protestant denominations. Frequently those most concerned, the local people, have taken a hand in the situation and moved to solve the problem in terms of the community. These efforts will now be discussed, followed by a discussion of coöperative efforts on denomination-wide state and national levels.

Local efforts to unify the ministry of religion to specific communities have taken the form of seeking to build one strong church to supplant a number of weak ones. Several types of churches growing out of such efforts can be identified.

The nondenominational church. Non-denominational churches are cut off from denominational supervision and leadership and have an uncertain source of ministerial supply. Nevertheless, this severance of sectarian ties has, despite the difficulties it entails, been carried out by more than a hundred existing rural churches.

Affiliated churches. A variation of the nondenominational church is the affiliated type, which remains substantially independent but maintains a loose connection with some denomination to insure a source of ministerial supply and now and then some supervision and suggestion. There are not many churches of this type.

Federated churches. Federated churches are local combinations of congregations of two or more denominations into a single functional organization without severance of the previous denominational ties of combining units. There are perhaps about 400 such churches in rural America, only 10 per cent of which involve more than two denominations. Rural federated churches are about half again as large as the average denominational churches of the bodies generally participating in them, while urban federated churches surpass the average city church in size. Churches federate, in the main, only under great pressure of adverse circumstances.

Federated churches operate as a unit in all local matters but divide benevolences equitably. Frequently the ministers alternate between the bodies represented in the federation. A frequent and highly unsatisfactory aspect of the federated church is the unfederated subsidiary. Minor organizations, such as denominational women's societies, insist on perpetuating themselves, usually because of social cleavages in the community. This does not make for great success within a supposedly united group.

Long-continued successful federation,

however, frequently, though not universally, weakens the desire to maintain separate denominations. A solution for such a condition is sometimes found in a bi-denominational relationship. The church becomes legally one, but is recognized by both denominations to which its members previously belonged. This has proved an acceptable solution for more liberal bodies.

Denominational community churches. The most numerous of united churches, denominational community churches, have been elsewhere defined and described as follows:

A denominational community church is one formally recognized as such by other denominations. A group of coöperating denominations agree to accord an exclusive field to the church of one of their members, usually upon condition that it broadens the terms of membership and maintains a definite community outlook, with or without equivalent exchange of fields. This method remedies past division and prevents future competition.

The act by which a denominational church merely widens the terms of its membership so as to admit members of all denominations without condition, such as assent to a particular creed or re-baptism, is not accepted by the writers as a true criterion of the type. This has always been the theory of the more liberal churches of the congregational type, and has been the actual practice of multitudes of others, as proved by the interchangeable use of denominational churches by large populations.

One needs to recognize the realities behind even so attenuated a version of the community church. It testifies to the softening of denominational asperities and to an atmosphere favorable to integration. Such churches should be kept distinct from those spurious cases where the label "community church" has been adopted for promotional purposes only.[22]

[22] Douglass and Brunner, *The Protestant Church as a Social Institution* (New York: Harper, 1935), chap. XII. For a full discussion of these types of federated churches see Hooker, *United Churches* (Harper, 1927), a study of nearly 1000 cases undertaken in 1924 and 1925 by the Institute of Social and Religious Research.

Many of these churches are quite successful, as several studies by the Home Missions Council show. In the main this type is the most successful of all efforts at local church coöperation.

Larger Parishes. One variation in the type of coöperative effort described above deserves to be noted, though it is largely denominational. It is called the Larger Parish. Under this plan a group of churches of the same denomination are linked in a single organization with a unified staff. This eliminates intradenominational competition. The senior staff member is usually in charge of preaching and worship functions; another staff member specializes in religious education; if there is a third, he may give the bulk of his attention to young people and community service. Such parishes are usually centered in a village or town. Some employ school buses to bring members to the Sunday service. Open-country church buildings may or may not be retained for purposes of religious education, neighborhood meetings, and recreation. A study of Larger Parishes by the Institute of Social and Religious Research in the early 1930's found many instances where the old "circuit" had changed its name to Larger Parish, without, however, greatly changing its operations. On the other hand, it found several hundred which were highly successful and had measurably expanded and improved the service of organized religion to their communities. A few of these were interdenominational. More had a denominational connection but by agreement were solely responsible for their fields in the fashion of the denominational community church described above. The basic theory of the Larger Parish is ministry not to churches but to all the people of an area. The idea is promoted by rural church departments of practically all larger denominations.

Although there are obvious differences in

organization and terminology, in effect this type of parish has always characterized the average rural Roman Catholic church. It has thus avoided most of the problems of the Protestant bodies.

Inter-denominational Protestant Coöperation in Rural America

The rural church departments of larger religious bodies are one of the most encouraging elements in the entire religious situation in rural America. They are concerned chiefly with assisting the churches of their own bodies. They know, however, that often this can best be done by coöperation. They are brought together in a Committee on Town and Country of the National Council of Churches.

This group has promoted with some success chairs of rural church methods and rural sociology in theological seminaries. It conducts summer schools for rural clergy, mostly in coöperation with state colleges of agriculture. It publishes a monthly magazine. It conducts surveys, not only of rural church conditions but also of problems, such as its studies of the church and farm tenancy. It holds an annual national convocation on the church in town and country, which deals not only with the needs of and policies for the rural church but also with ethical and spiritual aspects of rural social and economic problems and national policies. This has become an important means of developing public opinion and, along with the other activities, of building morale among rural clergymen, so that fewer of the successful ones are drained off to city churches.

But the work of this committee, and especially of employed rural church officers within it, has gone beyond such activities and attacked directly one of the most basic of all rural church problems, overchurching. Thousands of rural churches continue to

exist only because they are subsidized by the national body to which they belong. These grants are called home mission aid. Originally this practice developed in an effort to assist the small but growing denominational groups along the western frontier to remain within the sect of their first allegiance. It is sometimes used now to bring a minister to small communities with limited resources. But as the country developed and stabilized, millions of dollars were given annually by the denominations to churches which appeared to be in competitive situations. Since many weaker churches which require such help to keep open are in highly competitive situations, such aid helped to perpetuate an unhealthy situation.[23] The national bodies concerned, in coöperation with their state officers, have visited hundreds of communities and by agreement allocated responsibility to a single church. The denomination yielding at one place was favored elsewhere. In 1934, five denominations prepared and exchanged master lists of aided churches as a basis for withdrawing aid in unjustifiably competitive situations. Some bodies have drawn up criteria which a local church must meet in order to continue to receive aid. These arrangements, of course, are most successfully consummated when the denominations concerned are similar in polity. They have been far more successful in territory administered by national boards than in the so-called self-supporting states and areas which administer their own aid. But despite these limitations, progress has been made. By 1936 the proportion of churches aided in the 140 communities decreased from 13 to 10 per cent for village churches and from 14.2 to 8.6 per cent for open-country churches. Since that time there has undoubtedly been further progress.

Again it should be noted that in the nature of the case this is a problem which does not concern Roman Catholicism. This

[23] Brunner and Lorge, *op. cit.*, pp. 324–328.

body, however, has a National Rural Life Conference which is concerned with the problems of both the rural parish and rural America. Its pronouncements on social and economic problems have been forthright and statesmanlike. It has been especially interested in reducing farm tenancy and in preserving the family-type farm.

Interfaith coöperation. In some particulars, the mutual interests of those concerned with rural religion have brought Protestants, Roman Catholics, and Jews together. There has been coöperation on a few surveys and in efforts to improve the lot of migrating farm labor. A group of clergy and laymen of all three of these major religious groups also recently joined as individuals in a statement of principles and objectives with respect to man and the land which is of high significance. It also is in harmony with many pronouncements on rural life and policy issued by major religious bodies.

The statement declares that land is God's greatest material gift to mankind to use for purposes of human welfare, that land ownership is in fact a stewardship and involves responsibility for the care and enrichment of the soil. Land must become available for families and society must recognize that the family's welfare should have first consideration in economic and social planning. The tiller also has duties as well as rights.

The statement by these religious leaders ends with the following "suggested methods for the practical application" of the various principles laid down:

1. Make use of the land an integral part of socio-economic planning and thinking.
2. Insist that education for land stewardship and the productive home be outstanding features of rural education.
3. Emphasize a special program of enlistment and training in secondary, liberal arts, technical and professional schools for professional service to the rural community.

4. Make the family-type farm operated by the owner a major objective of legislation and planning.
5. Reform the system of taxing land and improvements so as to facilitate access to natural resources, security of tenure and proper land use.
6. Revise land sale and rental contracts, mortgage obligations and other debt instruments so that no loss of ownership or insecurity of tenure be possible except through negligence or injustice on the part of the farmer-operator.
7. Discourage large land holdings as undemocratic and unsocial.
8. Where large-scale production is necessary and advisable, encourage the use of coöperative techniques with local ownership and management.
9. At all times encourage coöperatives as a means of intellectual, moral, and material advancement.
10. Where and when large-scale industrialized farming exists and requires employment of seasonal or year-round labor, demand for such labor groups a living family wage, decent housing conditions and collective bargaining.
11. Urge that wages and housing for the laborer on the small farms be decent and just. (Low wages and poor housing for the farm laborer tend to lower the reward and standards of living of the family-type farmer, bringing his own family labor into competition with the poorly paid hired hand.)
12. Extend social security provisions, particularly health, old age and survivors' insurance, to farm people and other rural dwellers.
13. Develop locally owned and controlled business and industry in rural communities.
14. Encourage development of the "one foot on soil and one foot in city" type of living as greatly advantageous to the family when adequate cash income is secured from work in industry or commerce.
15. Make land settlement possible for returned soldiers and displaced war workers through proper financial and educational planning, provided qualified people so desire and sound arrangements can be made.

Summary. This review of the rural church

as a social institution reveals it as the most powerful of the voluntary agencies of rural society, but with wide divergencies in effectiveness among regions and even within communities. Certain facts and trends seem quite clear.

1. While an increasing proportion of village church-membership resides in the country, the number of country churches has declined.

2. Rural churches, considering village and country together, are somewhat fewer in number, though larger in average membership; yet a smaller proportion of the total population is represented in the membership.

3. While the largest fifth of the rural churches are strong institutions with rich and effective programs, the leadership and activities of the majority give little evidence of change.

4. The financial support of rural churches has recovered from depression levels but not in the same proportion as farm income.

5. Adjustments involving more coöperation are more than ever apparent but inter- and intra-denominational competition is still quite prevalent.

The preceding discussion has shown, too, that the church reflects economic and social determinants. But while this makes it possible to plan for the church effectively in social terms, deep-seated convictions, theological and historical differences, and a sense of the transcendental and eternal as apart from the mundane and temporal may limit the effectiveness of action along such lines. The church has to function as a religious as well as a social body, and the former it regards as its primary value. This may explain some of its dilemmas and seeming contradictions.

TOPICS FOR DISCUSSION

1. Discuss critically Sorokin and Zimmerman's comparison of rural and urban religions.
2. Outline a standard or method by which you would be willing to advise, if asked, whether a particular town-country community had too many or too few churches.
3. Describe the rural service plan and program of some local church, country or village, with which you are acquainted.
4. Describe the rural service plan and policy of some national church body with which you are acquainted.
5. Analyze the program of some rural church you know. How would you change it? Why?
6. Which type of "united church" would you prefer? Why?

REFERENCE READINGS

Brunner, Edmund deS., and Irving Lorge, *Rural Trends in Depression Years*, chap. XII.

New York: Columbia University Press, 1937.

Cain, B. H. *The Church Ministering to Rural Life*. Dayton: The Church of the United Brethren in Christ, 1941. Discusses the program of the local church, including administration, leadership, worship, stewardship, equipment, etc.

Christian Mission Among Rural People, The. New York: Rural Missions Coöperating Committee of the Foreign Missions Conference of North America, 1945. A discussion of the philosophy underlying the program of the church in rural areas at home and abroad.

Felton, Ralph A. *Cooperating Churches*. New York: Home Missions Council of North America, Inc. On problems, experiences, and achievements in church coöperation and consolidation.

Felton, Ralph A. *One Foot on the Land*. New York: Agricultural Missions, Inc., 156 Fifth Avenue, 1947. Stories of sixteen successful rural churches.

Freeman, John D. *Country Church: Its Problems and Their Solution*. Atlanta: Home Mission Board, Southern Baptist Convention,

1943. A statement of some of the ills of rural churches with suggested solutions. Contains a number of illustrations of floor plans for church and parsonage.

Ligutti, L. G. and Rawe, John C. *Rural Roads to Security*. Milwaukee: The Bruce Publishing Company, 1940. A statement of an agrarian philosophy of life written from a Roman Catholic viewpoint.

Lindstrom, David E. *Rural Life and the Church*. Champaign: The Garrard Press, 1946. Presents movements, organizations, and trends in rural America and suggests how the church may influence them.

Manifesto on Rural Life. National Catholic Rural Life Conference. Milwaukee: The Bruce Publishing Company, 1939. Official Roman Catholic teaching.

Mueller, E. W., ed., *Church for the Changing Countryside*. Chicago: National Lutheran Council, various years. A series of monograph surveys on Lutheran strength in ten states.

O'Hara, E. V., *The Church and the Country Community*. New York: Macmillan, 1927. A discussion from the Roman Catholic point of view.

Randolph, Henry S. *A Manual for Town and Country Churches*. New York: Board of National Missions, Presbyterian Church in the U.S.A., 1947. A thorough discussion of the program of the local church as it seeks to be related to total community. Also describes church's program on a functional basis.

Schisler, John Q. *The Educational Work of the Small Church*. Nashville: Abingdon-Cokesbury, 1946. Written with special reference to rural communities.

Smith, Rockwell C. *The Church in Our Town*. Nashville: Abingdon-Cokesbury, 1945. Written for those most concerned about the rural church, considering the church in relationship to rural society and stressing church coöperation with other agencies.

Terry, Paul W., and Verna M. Sims. *They Live on the Land*, chap. VII. University: Bureau of Educational Research, University of Alabama, 1940. A careful case study of religious life in an Alabama community.

Witte, Raymond P., *Twenty-Five Years of Crusading*. Washington: National Catholic Rural Life Conference, 1948. Contains history of Catholic Rural Life Conference.

21 Rural Recreation and the Cultural Arts

RURAL PEOPLE are often reluctant to admit they are not always busy or that they have any "leisure time" for recreation. Nevertheless they are usually ready for a picnic or a party, to stop work and visit for a while, to watch the fishhawk plunge to his prey in a nearby lake or pond, and some even to sketch or paint a little, if not too directly observed. Work and play in rural society have not been sharply separated, nor is work always considered a necessary evil to be endured and strictly divorced from creative experiences.

The cultural arts, including music, drama, dancing, painting, sculpture, architecture, and literature, in many of their various forms, have always been found in rural societies. Their expression was often informal and their character determined by folk origins. The itinerant teller of dramatic tales, especially in rural China, had a sure audience in the small village. Scandinavian rural communities had their rosmaling, their balladry, their costuming and their crafts. American rural pioneers had their tall tales of the lumberjack, their folk dancing, wedding music and dances, their singing schools and festivals. These earlier backgrounds have influenced the emphasis placed upon recreation and the cultural arts in rural society today. They have affected the forms assumed and the organizations and agencies developed for their expression. But emphasis and forms are changing. Recreation is receiving direct attention by most organizations concerned with rural life, and the cultural arts are becoming a people's movement.

Changing Emphasis on Recreation in Rural Life

Rural society has shared, although in its own way, the general movement toward a greater emphasis on recreation which has been designated as one of the significant trends of recent times.[1] This increased emphasis takes so many forms and expresses itself in so many diverse activities that it is difficult to trace, but it penetrates society at every point.

During an earlier period, which might be roughly encompassed by the years 1890 to 1920, rural recreation could be described as largely informal and home-made, carried out on a home and local neighborhood basis. Popular activities included corn husking bees, quilting bees, box socials, picnics, special day celebrations, ring games, and social parties. Play was closely associated with work. Frontier conditions necessitated neighborhood coöperation for such things as threshing or the construction of buildings. "Bees" such as "barn raisings" were a combination of work and play, and the fall threshing was a social occasion for whole families to get together. But the increasing use of agricultural machinery since 1920 has reduced the need for local coöperative labor. Occasions for combining recreation and work have become less frequent. The general use of the automobile and the improvement of roads have provided rural

[1] J. F. Steiner, "Recreation and Leisure Time Activities," *Recent Social Trends* (New York: McGraw-Hill, 1933), II, chap. XVIII.

people with the means for seeking recreation beyond the home and immediate locality.

American pioneer traditions were restrictive. Early Puritan traditions and emphasis upon the virtue of work circumscribed recreation in many rural communities. As Dr. C. J. Galpin pointed out, the "jaunty air of holiday," the "dressed-up costumes of leisure," and "the trappings of indolence," associated with urban life were unwelcome in farm life, where the virtue of hard work had the backing of public opinion and Calvinistic religious doctrines.[2] Despite all this, many kinds of leisure-time activities did develop, and more recently there has been a greatly increased emphasis upon the intelligent use of leisure and the importance of wholesome recreation.

During a later transition period rural leaders claimed that recreation should be a supplement or adjunct to other more useful forms of activity. "People work together better when they learn to play together," they said.[3] A 4–H Club leader in a western state said that the work of the National Recreation Association in his county made it easier to carry on his regular extension program and to enter new communities. It also induced better attendance at all meetings, he thought. An evaluation of recreation by such leaders was expressed in the following terms: "Recreation is a tool in organization work," "coöperation is taught through recreation," "recreation develops experience in group action," and it is "insurance against discontent." In a word, recreation was sugar coating for an otherwise unpalatable educational experience.

More recently recreational activities have been recognized for their own sake, purely as enjoyment for personality development,

group experience, and appreciation in cultural values. Such is the spirit and practice of the Little Country Theatre of North Dakota, the North Carolina Playmakers, and The Wisconsin Rural Writers' Project. Rural leaders urging this changed emphasis express their purposes as follows: "Activities are undertaken for their own sake and not for any reward beyond themselves," "they are relatively free, spontaneous and enjoyable," they foster the "development of socialized personality through self-expression" and "higher ideals and standards in home and community through the cultural arts." Through such motives, many new recreational and cultural activities are being made available to country people, and the response is ample proof of their appreciation.

Specialization by interest and by locality; a national trend. Nationally there has been a steady broadening of recreational activities and a great increase in the number of people taking part in them. Rural people have shared in this general expansion and they have also experienced, although at a considerably slower rate, the tendency toward specialization. Steiner has summarized this trend for urban society: "The supplanting of the more simple pleasures of an earlier day by games and sports and social activities of a more elaborate nature requiring expensive facilities for their enjoyment has ushered in a regime of clubs and associations that have become a characteristic feature of modern recreation. The devotee of sport or the aspirant for social diversions attains his goal most readily by affiliation with organizations that specialize in activities of his choice."[4]

The rise of special interest groups in rural society has been traced in another chapter. It was evident there that recreational and social interests were important in the formation of these groups. Forms of recreation which

[2] *Rural Life* (New York: Century, 1918).
[3] C. B. Smith, "Relationships and Needs in Rural Sociology Extension," *American Sociological Society Papers,* XXIV (1949).

[4] J. F. Steiner, *Americans at Play* (New York: McGraw-Hill, 1933), p. 122.

now prevail in rural society or show a tendency to increase include drama, music and art, social parties, picnics and festivals, group games, and athletics.

Specialization has taken place in the direction of locality as well as of interest. Certain neighborhoods and town-country communities have found pleasure and profit in developing and perfecting distinctive activities. There are abundant illustrations including rose festivals, community fairs, county-wide play days, adult and children's massed musical productions, homecomings, family reunions, annual dramatic events, even the annual presentation of the *Passion Play* or *Wilhelm Tell*, distinctive flower and vegetable gardens, lilac drives, home and school grounds beautification, fish frys, community picnics or dinners featuring locally produced foods or those characteristic of nationality groups.

Wider contacts with larger groups. The tendency for rural people to specialize their formal and informal recreation by interests and localities does not preclude their wider contact with the outside world. First evidence of such wider recreational contacts is the increased participation of country people in village athletics, in musical, patriotic, and youth-serving groups.[5] This friendly and more intimate recreational association of farmer and villager has done much toward the creation of the larger town-country community.

The automobile has made possible an increasing number of rural and urban contacts. City residents in greatly increasing numbers are using the country for hunting, fishing, camping, picnicking, and summer living. Country residents are likewise seeking facilities offered by urban centers for theatricals, musicales, art exhibitions, athletic contests, motion-picture productions,

[5] Brunner and Kolb, *Rural Social Trends* (New York: McGraw-Hill, 1933), p. 250.

and public dancing and amusement places.

Greater opportunities for recreation also bring problems. The old romance triangle — the boy, the girl, the place — has expanded far beyond the neighborhood with its personal and primary controls. The farm boy may seek his companion in another community where he is little known and take her for an evening of entertainment to a distant, impersonal, and commercialized amusement hall. This shifting emphasis requires newer forms of social control, lest the triangle become one of tragedy instead of romance.

Rise of the commercial amusements. Rural people have never been strangers to certain kinds of commercialized sports and entertainment. What country boy has not seen a horse race through the crack in the board fence at the county fair, or had the responsibility for getting the whole family off to the circus under the big tent on the vacant town lots? In the more modern rural world, motion pictures and the radio have probably attained widest popularity. They reach directly into the rural community or the farm home with their programs and their advertising features. Thus rural and urban people are exposed at the same time to the same forms of entertainment.

Radio and motion picture programs are two forms of commercial entertainment more widespread than any others in rural society. Arguments continue as to how well they fulfill the definition set forth for recreation. For example, certain types of motion pictures have been strongly opposed on the ground of morality by such organizations as the Legion of Decency. Agitation has started in certain groups for the return of broadcasting to public control, thus eliminating, as in England and France, private exploitation of this great source of entertainment and education.

Another form of commercial amusement

which is posing a problem for rural people, according to a canvass of farm opinion reported by the magazine *Successful Farming*, is the tavern, with its liquor and its dancing. According to this canvass, both young people and adults were agreed upon the problem. Older forms of local government seem poorly adapted to such modern institutions. Some counties are attempting regulation through zoning ordinances. Business districts are set aside, often in open-country areas, and all business enterprises, including taverns, dance halls, filling stations, and stores, are confined to them. Within the districts, regulations are imposed such as set-back lines for buildings, space for parking, and other provisions intended to insure health, safety, and morals.

In depression years. Rural leaders everywhere are agreed that there was a notable increase in interest during the depression period in local, non-commercial recreation.[6] This came about naturally, because funds were lacking and increased numbers of young people remained in rural communities. Together with adults, these young people developed home-talent activities, rediscovered folk games and dances, and revived out-of-door recreation. The movement was encouraged and stimulated by the Agricultural Extension Service, by leaders employed through WPA, and by the greater attention given to recreation by schools, especially consolidated schools, by churches, and by various other organizations.

Recreation comes of age in war time. With the war-time speeding up of work and the quickening of activity everywhere, it was recognized that recreation was an essential. It was high on priority lists concerned with physical fitness, mental health, emotional

stability, and the building of group morale. Recreation was essential on all fronts, at home and abroad, civilian and military, public and private, rural and urban. Doctor Mark A. McCloskey, speaking in 1944 from the Office of Community War Service, was emphatic in his statement that war-born accelerated programs of all kinds have confirmed recreation as a legitimate public responsibility on a par with such other services as education, health, and welfare.[7] For some communities this point of view meant the assumption of new responsibilities; for others it involved the reorganization of outmoded facilities and programs. For many rural communities, it resulted in more varied activities and in the training of more voluntary local leaders.

Recognition therefore dawned that, like education, recreation is a year-round, cradle-to-grave experience. It need not, indeed cannot and should not, be organized or formalized all the time, but neither can it be ignored or placed low on any priority list. While life goes on, recreation goes on!

Recreation as livelihood and land use. "All over New England a new industry is receiving recognition. The rapid and widespread growth of public, private, and commercial recreation in these states during the last decade indicates that continued expansion may be expected."[8] "The entire cutover area of the three Lake states has recreational possibilities and recreation has been listed as one of the primary land-uses."[9] State-

[6] Dwight Sanderson, *Research Memorandum on Rural Life in Depression Years* (New York: Social Science Research Council, 1937), Bulletin 34.

[7] Introduction to *Community Recreation Comes of Age* (Federal Security Agency, Office of Community War Service, Division of Recreation, 1944).

[8] E. J. Niederfrank and C. R. Draper, *Use of Recreation Sites Developed on Federal Submarginal Land-Purchase Areas in Maine* (College of Agriculture, University of Maine, Maine Bulletin 280, July, 1940).

[9] George S. Wehrwein and Hugh A. Johnson, "A Recreation Livelihood Area," *Journal of Land and Public Utility Economics* (vol. XIX, no. 2, May, 1943); "Zoning Land for Recreation," *Journal of*

ments of this order from two regions of the United States portend future developments which have significance, not only for these areas but for many others. The social implications are far-reaching and involve both private and public interests. It is of special importance to find in the report of the New England study that park areas are used primarily by local people. Lands unsuited to agricultural uses could, therefore, be acquired by towns and made available to their own residents.

The majority of visitors to such recreation areas were, of course, urban residents, but it was not realized what a high proportion was in the medium- or even low-income groups. To provide recreation for them requires reasonable accessibility, equipment, and facilities within their means. It would suggest recreation areas near to urban centers of population.

In the cut-over area, the recreational use of land means that a stage of development has been reached in which agriculture is nearly stable; that is, it is as near to the margin as it can profitably go. It also implies that private enterprise has failed to use the land, once the timber has been removed; therefore, much of it has become county, state, and federally owned. This represents a transition period in which many readjustments are required. For example, with much land in public ownership, the local tax base has been reduced so much that local government finds itself with new responsibilities of land management at the same time that its revenues are more restricted. With new forest-crop laws and the extension of opportunities for recreation as a livelihood, the future holds new prospects.

Consideration must be given to changes in the highway system as well as to the local

Land and Public Utility (February, 1942); Wehrwein and Kenneth H. Parsons, *Recreation as a Land Use* (Madison: Bulletin 422, Agricultural Experiment Station, University of Wisconsin, April, 1932).

school system. Problems of taxation, zoning, and land-use controls must be solved. It might easily be assumed that tourist or resort business could readily supplement a limited farming enterprise. However, closer examination reveals that the two, if combined, require very careful management. The resort season is short and comes in the very months when major farm work must be done. Then, the social habits of "summer boarders" may run counter to the mores of the local people. What commercial amusements will be patronized and how they shall be controlled is one question among many. There will be more recreation for all. That seems assured.

Rising Tide of Cultural Arts with Authentic Rural Values

Expanded and intensified emphasis upon recreation, especially in its recreative and expressive aspects, and upon wholesome use of leisure, leads directly into the wide and varied realm of the cultural arts. These cannot be thought of in any narrow sense; they are not bound by leisure or confined to entertainment but permeate all of life. Beauty and tragedy are everywhere, inside and outside the human frame and its social relationships. The brief discussion which follows can only touch upon the social relations of some of the cultural arts; in no sense can it be considered a review of rural art.

The cultural arts are communicative. They are "forms of human activity one man consciously, by means of certain signs, hands over to others, feelings he has lived through and other people are infected and also experience them." [10] This is Tolstoy's answer to the question, "What is art?" and it seems a strikingly true description of the way a sense of social values, attitudes, and ideals

[10] *What is Art?* (Oxford University Press, 1942), p. 123.

is transmitted in primary group situations, as in neighborhoods. According to one sociologist, Robert E. Park, the social function of art is to "communicate not ideas but sentiments, creating and sustaining in this way a mood in which one's sense of individual and personal differences is lessened and one's sense of mutual understanding and moral solidarity is enhanced." [11]

The American philosopher, John Dewey, gives art a central place in his theory of communication as experience. "Works of art are the only media of complete and unhindered communication between man and man that can occur in a world full of gulfs and walls that limit community of experience." [12] Such interpretations emphasize the fact that the cultural arts cannot exist solely for themselves any more than the sciences can. Their task is larger than providing entertainment or brief respite from reality. On the affirmative side, they point to the need for a better understanding of the importance of the cultural arts in any society. They suggest the interplay of thinking and feeling, of the aesthetic and the practical, of the arts and the sciences.

The arts and sciences, mutually involved in society. In some circles, the arts and the sciences are expected to be different, in opposition to each other, scientific discovery to be isolated from the realm of feeling. Recent reactions to results in atomic research in nuclear physics and in the mass hysteria of war give the lie to any such assumption of isolation. Artists and scientists have often wrestled with similar fundamentals, such as space and time relations. The so-called but inaccurately named "cubists" and "futurists" in painting precipitated a revolution in art and in criticism. The cubists sought to show objects not from a single point of view, not

from one side, but from all sides simultaneously. They dissected their objects into different planes, horizontally and vertically; they even added a fourth dimension — time — to the three traditionally accepted. The futurists may be thought of as research workers in movement. They introduced into painting not only different spatial planes but the concept of motion. Classic examples are Boccioni's "Bottle Evolving in Space" (1912) and Balla's "Speed" (1913). Both groups extended their presentation to familiar and ordinary "objects" such as stones, bowls, glasses, pipes, and bones.

It is significant that the mathematician, Minkowski, at about the same time (1908) was working out his formula of a four-dimensional world with space and time merging to form a continuum, and that Einstein should have been concerned with a definition of "simultaneity," in 1905. [13]

The arts and the sciences are likewise related in modern society, because feelings and emotions are everywhere, in everything. Social systems are built up which must be reconciled with the results of science and industry. Science, particularly social science, in its effort to be scientific, objective, impersonal, has all too frequently neglected these great emotional and moral forces toward human behavior — "motivations," the educators call them. It is at this point that the artists perform a function. They speak with urgency, they declare values, they intend action. Their flourishes of finality are compulsive, at least for those who are able to receive their message.

Common cultural reference important. In any society, artists are concerned with the expression of feelings and emotions deeply embedded in the cultural life of people. Therefore, if the arts are to be communicative in either a personal or a social sense,

[11] "Education and the Cultural Crises," *American Journal of Sociology* (XLVIII, No. 6, May, 1943).
[12] *Art as Experience* (Putnam, 1934), p. 105.

[13] Sigfried Giedion, *Space, Time and Architecture* (Harvard University Press, 1942), p. 357.

they must have, or build, something in common with those to whom they would speak; else, how can they motivate or compel to action?

Cultural arts have a folk basis in primitive forms, earthy in character. Therefore they are fundamental means for expressing creative experiences and for communicating personal and social values. Some artists and scholars forget this. For example, John Barton quotes the Danish scholar, Georg M. Brandes, to the effect that cultural arts could develop only in the great city of Paris, certainly not among the common people of Scandinavia.[14] How mistaken "the scholar" was! In all the Scandinavian countries modern movements in architecture and in the arts and crafts have developed from a long folk tradition.

American society, rural and urban, has a great reservoir of culture groups: Germans, Poles, Irish, Danes, Finns, Norwegians, Swedes, Bohemians, Swiss, Welsh, Cornish, Hungarians, Lithuanians, English, Yugoslavs, Russians, Scots, and many others. These groups did not leave behind them as impedimenta their sense of values or their urge for artistic expression. As people in a new country, they sought for artistic expression of their own. Today they and their descendants are playing rich and diverse roles in our emerging American culture. But they, like other Americans before them, are not and never have been content to rest upon European sources or standards.

With Europe depleted by wars, this is a time for reciprocity in the cultural arts. People in the new country need to develop their own authentic arts, deeply rooted not alone in physical resources but in spiritual ideals and hopes, and to give their accomplishments back to the mother countries as ripened fruits of earlier cultures. Such, for example, is the purpose and the spirit of the *Folk Singer*, a compilation of familiar folk songs belonging to the groups who settled Wisconsin. Its wide use suggests that tuneful songs are enjoyed by everyone, everywhere. They travel unarmed to all countries and are received by all classes of people. To the extent that people use them they are a language universally understood.[15]

The process of cultural communication may also proceed in the opposite order. Artists may reveal values or problems within a society in ways which can be broadly understood and deeply felt by the many who might otherwise be quite oblivious to them. An illustration can be drawn from a current source. While opera came to America from historic Italy, it is now being re-vitalized by Gian Carlo Menotti, "The American-Italian Wizard of the Opera," [16] who "creates Broadway smash hits with high-brow art," and has thus "crashed the gates" of popular experience. Menotti is being comprehended by people in the popular thousands, in the world's most scientific and industrial city. "In a poetic capsule 'The Consul' captures what many serious thinkers consider to be the great tragedy of the Twentieth Century: the plight of the individual overwhelmed by the vast impersonal forces of machine-age organization." This is social analysis as real as the scientist's statistical table. In contrast, there have been many occasions when artists, and for that matter scientists, and their public have been separated by "gulfs" in vital communication. In the middle of the last century Walt Whitman and Henry Thoreau, literary spokesmen, seemed to be voices crying in the wilderness.

Sometimes it may be the artists who are caught in the "cultural lag"; at other times it may be the public. It is not necessary to

[14] *Rural Artists of Wisconsin* (Madison: The University of Wisconsin Press, 1948).

[15] Dan E. Vornholt, editor, *Folk Singer* (Madison: University of Wisconsin, Extension Service, College of Agriculture, Special Circular, February, 1943).

[16] Winthrop Sargent, "Wizard of the Opera," *Life Magazine*, May 1, 1950.

find fault with either the artists, the scientists, or the public, although as the philosopher George Santayana suggests, an art is "poor and melancholy" that is interested only in itself and its techniques rather than in its subject. The same can be said of a science that is interested in its methods rather than in its dicoveries. Whatever the situation, it is only as part of a democratic revolution still in process in many quarters, that any people can develop their own free arts. Similarly, sciences can unfold only in an atmosphere of untrammeled and undirected action.

Recent trends in the arts in America. After exhaustive study, Doctor Frederich P. Keppel came to the conclusion that "where formerly an aesthetic touch would have been considered effeminate and superflous, more and more, art is being treated as an essential and vital element in American life, not something apart." [17] He dated the beginning of this trend as the years between the end of the Chicago World's Fair in 1893 until the beginning of World War I. During this time there was not only increased activity in the arts, but a higher esteem for them. And there was a definite trend toward the belief that beauty, its creation, reproduction, and enjoyment have an essential place in normal life.

Recent strides in mechanical inventions and technical improvements in all sorts of materials and processes have contributed to this trend. Articles of intrinsic beauty and aesthetic value have been made available to masses of people. Rayon, bakelite, cellulose materials, coal-tar dyes, incandescent filaments, color photography, offset lithography, chrome toning, radio, television, and even reinforced steel construction reflect this change in view.

Another trend has been the breaking away from the traditional. Artists and art objects reflect an interest in new subjects, new forms, and new areas of life. At the same time, popular opinion seems less shocked by the new and unfamiliar. Consequently, paintings have found their way out of studios, museums, and private collections into banks, department stores, schools, and other public places — even into magazines and newspapers with circulation in the millions. Business concerns have their art directors or art staffs: United States Steel, Bethlehem Steel, General Electric, Standard Oil, telephone companies, Sears Roebuck, Pennsylvania Railroad. Earlier, this kind of spending would have been considered fantastic. Universities, including agricultural colleges and the United States Department of Agriculture in its Extension Service, have joined the movement for popularizing the arts.

Other factors have contributed to this upswing of interest and activity. An accumulation of wealth has made possible the purchase and display of collections. Traveling exhibits give thousands of ordinary people an opportunity to see many truly great pieces of art. Not to be forgotten is the widespread influence of the WPA cultural arts projects of the 1930's. This enterprise brought about a tremendous release of creative energy in nearly every artistic form known. The President of the United States, in public pronouncement, praised the undertaking. It was the first time in history, declares Horace Kallen, that the head of a state had declared the liberty of the artist.[18]

Like many another social movement, this trend away from the traditional, as with the cubists and the futurists, has not been without its moments of confusion, even hysteria. Doctor Keppel, however, insists that modernism is nothing new. Much depends upon one's point of view and cultural heritage.

[17] "The Arts," *Recent Social Changes in the United States* (June, 1932); F. P. Keppel and R. L. Duffus, *The Arts in American Life* (Knopf, New York, 1932).

[18] *Art and Freedom* (New York: Duell, Sloan & Pearce, 1942) I, p. 30.

Since emotions are deeply involved, violent and "unreasoned" reactions may be expected. These, however, can serve as useful social catharsis in somewhat the same way that certain art techniques are used in therapy for personality disarrangements.

Struggles toward people's arts also a rural movement. Rural values and rural lives have been and are in the midst of the movements and changing emphases we have just described. Rural motifs have served as subjects for writers and artists, from before the days of Currier and Ives to the time of *Tobacco Road* and such paintings as "The Fugitive" by John Steuart Curry. They have also served as a kind of fulcrum in attempts to swing back some of the arts from what was considered too thin, too sophisticated, too urbane to a greater vitality. For example, Grant Wood of "American Gothic" fame, revolted against the city, saying "rural life is not the hinterland of New York," and protested "the thinness of things viewed from outside or from heights," whereas in rural life experience could be from within and in the nearby.[19]

Rural people, too, whether they were always conscious of it or willing to admit it, have long been active in the arts. They have been enveloped in the charms as well as the calamities of nature, as displayed in Curry's paintings "Sunrise" and "The Tornado." They have used native materials in their creation of the graphic arts and the handcrafts. As Allen Eaton has observed, rural people have created the functionally beautiful in their own trimly shaped woodpiles and haystacks, as well as providing subjects for Millet's "Woodpiles," Monet's "Haystacks at Evening," Riviere's "Haystacks in Britany," George Inness' "The Last Load of Hay."[20] Music, pageantry, drama, and folk dancing, have long been the possession of rural people, who have created and enjoyed many original forms of all these kinds of expression.

Professor Lennox Grey of Columbia University pleads for "a new epic of our own, both *urban* and *rural,* communicated not in one art but in all available arts."[21] As has been stressed so often, the rural and urban phases of our society are interdependent. Percy MacKaye puts it in poetic form:[22]

> "What is Culture
> But the seed of Agriculture
> Ripened in the soul of Man?
> Human nature learns of Nature
> All its arts."

Toward the "Little" community theater. There need be no undertone of apology in such terms, as "little," "amateur," "tributary," or "non-professional," as applied to the non-professional theater. The "little" theater has earned its right to identification through the success of such dramatic groups as "The Little Country Theatre" of Arvold fame in Fargo, North Dakota, the Houston "Little Theatre,"; and the Negro "Little Theatre of the Gilpin Players" in Cleveland. A broader comprehension of the community now fixes the truth implicit in the word "little." In order to possess true culture and vitality, drama must be rooted in human situations and needs. Only so can it be genuinely communicative.

How big is "little," as applied to the folk theater? From Percy MacKaye, we have this apt phrasing.[23]

---

19 *Revolt Against the City* (Iowa City: Clio Press, 1935).

20 "Art in Rural Life," *Town and Country Church* (No. 65, November, 1950); *Rural Handicrafts in the United States* (United States Department of Agriculture in coöperation with Russell Sage Foundation, *Miscellaneous Publication* No. 610. Washington, D.C., November, 1946).

21 Lyman Bryson, *The Communication of Ideas* (New York: The Institute for Religious and Social Studies, distributed by Harper, 1949), chap. VIII.

22 Quoted by A. G. Arvold, *The Little Country Theatre* (Fargo, N.D., 1945).

23 Arvold, *Ibid.*

Is this Little Country Theatre
but the epitome of all
The souls that wrought it — Little? Yes
As the Morning Stars are little
Singing together in the prairie
Theatre of our Country's vastness

The story of the Little Country Theatre, an integral part of the College of Agriculture of North Dakota and its state-wide service, is now well known. Its beginnings were meagre, sometimes almost clandestine, in an unused attic, rendezvous of bats and mice. Now housed in a fine log-paneled building known as Lincoln Cabin, it is the workshop and dramatic center, not only of the campus but of the state as well. It is "a mecca where country folks and city folks alike, meet to discuss ways and means to make life in the open country or in the town in which they live more interesting and more human." [24] Each student generation on the campus produces the great Scandinavian classic, *Peer Gynt* by Ibsen, with the music by Grieg, from whose native land many of their own forebears came as pioneers.

This is not only theater, it is a social movement with widespread influence throughout the state. Not only folk-theater activities and outdoor pageantry have developed naturally as an outgrowth of its activities, but such projects as the "Eighty Miles of Lilacs" lining the main roadside of the Red River Valley may be traced to its awakening of community consciousness.

The Carolina Playmakers began in 1918 as a "little" theater, with improvised properties and housing, under the direction of Frederich Koch, who said, "Our Carolina Folk-Plays are plays of common experience and common interest, ranging in scene from the Great Smoky Mountains on the Western border to the shifting shoals of Cape

Hatteras." [25] Such productions were *Job's Kinfolk*, the lives of three generations of mill people in Winston-Salem; *Trista*, a wistful fantasy of fisher folk in the little town of Beaufort; *A Shotgun Splicin'*, a comedy of mountain wedlock; *Off Nags Head,* the tragedy of the lost daughter of Aaron Burr; and *Old Wash Lucas,* a farm tragedy of the stingiest man in Harnett County.

These and other plays have an ever-expanding influence. In the summer of 1950, Paul Green's symphonic drama, *The Lost Colony*, playing annually at Manteo on Roanoke Island, Virginia, attracted 53,000 people. Kermit Hunter's historical drama of the Cherokee Indians, *Unto These Hills*, brought 107,000 people to the gateway of the Smoky Mountains in Cherokee, North Carolina, in that same summer.

As in North Dakota, the Carolina project is no longer concerned solely with play production. There is also the Carolina Dramatic Association, "a means for promoting and encouraging art and stimulating playwriting." [26]

The Wisconsin Idea Theatre also had humble beginnings, though now it is described as "a theater whose walls are the boundaries of the state, whose stage is all of the stages of the state put together, whose audiences number in the millions, and whose participants are the thousands of actors, directors, technicians, and playwriters within the state. This seemingly Bunyanesque institution is, of course, not a theater in the usual sense of the word at all. It should more properly be called a state-wide creative program and service in the theater arts." [27] Services included a two-year re-

[24] Arvold, *op. cit.*; Arvold, *The Soul and the Soil* (New York: National Recreation Association, 1916); and J. H. Kolb, "Twenty-Five Years of the Little Country Theatre," *Rural America* (May, 1939).

[25] "Toward a New Folk Theatre," *Quarterly Journal of the University of North Dakota* (Grand Forks, 1930).

[26] Kai Jurgensen, *Extending a University Theatre* (The Educational Theatre in Adult Education, Division of Adult Education, Washington, D.C., 1951).

[27] Edward L. Kamark, "Wisconsin Idea Theatre, Renaissance of Activity in Drama," *The New York Times*, Sunday Drama Section, (Sept. 25, 1949).

search project for assembling collections of regional materials such as anecdotes, tall tales, yarns, legends, folk lore, and historical incidents which were made available to playwrights. The director has justified this project as follows: "A feeling for place and an understanding of the lore of the people, seem basic to the creative processes of any-one wishing to make a sincere and honest interpretation of regional scenes. People and their experiences are the stuff of comedy in any region; and comedy, although seem-ing to pull and strain away from recorded facts, never really escapes. Because of this realism, comedy expression helps to under-stand the civilization it so well reflects." [28]

There are year-round radio programs over the university-owned radio station, a tour-ing theater which one year played *Wiscon-sin Showtime*, regional and state confer-ences and workshops, extension and correspondence courses in writing and play production, a news letter, a theater quar-terly with four hundred subscribers, a play loan library, the annual State Fair Theatre, and the services of four full-time and some part-time workers. Some results included in the 1950–51 annual report are the writing of about 750 plays in the past four years, the organization of dozens of new community theaters, the participation of over 75,000 persons in play production during the re-ported year, and the witnessing of some form of drama by over a million people. State institutions such as Ohio State Univer-sity, Purdue University, Iowa State College at Ames, and others are also using the radio to good advantage in their various programs of cultural education.

Toward regional interpretations. Chris L. Christensen, a former dean of the University of Wisconsin College of Agriculture, espe-cially sensitive to the cultural values in rural life, brought to his campus in 1937 an "artist in residence," John Steuart Curry. At the seventy-fifth anniversary meeting of the Land Grant Colleges of the United States Christensen said, "Recently a group of artists whose lives and interests are rooted in the soil have attracted the attention of the world by making their paintings the means of expressing the sentiments, the activities, and the thinking of farm people. The at-mosphere and the spirit of farm life are re-corded and preserved on their canvasses. Because their pictures are true to the lives of farm people, these artists are making a def-inite contribution to the culture of Amer-ica." [29] Dean Christensen's purpose in bring-ing Mr. Curry to the College of Agriculture was to help rural people create not only an economy but a culture which would enable them to live upon the land with a full share of joy and satisfaction. Curry, farm-born and reared in Kansas, rose to fame through his paintings of boyhood scenes and surround-ings and was publicly recognized in the Century of Progress Exhibition of the Chi-cago World's Fair in 1933. By then he had completed "Kansas Threshing Outfit," "Bap-tism in Kansas," and "The Tornado," which was awarded second prize at the Carnegie International in Pittsburg. "Sunrise," painted in 1935, was from earlier sketches of Kansas landscapes. Curry's work and that of his contemporaries, Thomas Benton and Grant Wood, began an indigenous art movement in the Middle West which came to be known as "Regionalism." Later, Curry developed his concept of regionalism so as to include psychological and cultural as well as geo-graphical aspects. As Professor Laurence E. Schmeckebier points out, two artistic cur-rents flowed together in Curry, realism and

[28] Robert E. Gard, Director of the Wisconsin Idea Theatre, quoted with permission from an un-published manuscript. (Madison: University of Wisconsin, 1951).

[29]*John Steuart Curry, Artist of Rural Life* (Madi-son: University of Wisconsin, College of Agricul-ture, November, 1937).

romanticism. "His emotional state has none of the sweet melancholy of the 19th Century Romanticism nor the artificial stylization of contemporary New Romanticism in Paris but is held in rigid discipline by realistic fact." [30]

There is rugged power and solidarity of form in his football sketches, in "Fighting Hogs," "Fighting Jack and Stallion," and "Hogs Killing a Rattlesnake." There is likewise tenderness and sympathy in the flower still life he carried to the sickroom of his wife, and in the many portrayals of his mother and his father at home on the farm. His "Good Earth" reveals his real feeling for children and for the land, and "The Fugitive" shows his deep sense of justice and racial understanding. "His art," concludes Schmeckebier, "is not only a product of external Regionalism but it has taken root in a cultural soil which lies psychologically far deeper than the geographic divisions of race and landscape."

Since Curry's death, the spirit and the tradition of the "artist-in-residence" are being carried on by another able American artist, Aaron Bohrod. Services throughout the state of Wisconsin have been expanded by the energetic James Schwalbach through personal travel, regional art shows, and radio programs for children.

Toward racial understanding. The Negro's present success in the American theater is attributed to early dramatic activities of small groups in local communities. When in 1917 the Negro emerged from the segregated theater of Harlem and, with the assistance of sympathetic whites, made himself a real place on the American stage in tragedy as well as in comedy, it was counted a great achievement.

With the help of libraries and other educational agencies, the movement spread to many other Negro sections of New York City, Atlanta, and Cleveland. Under the WPA program more than thirty Negro theater projects were listed. Especially popular were religious plays such as *In Abraham's Bosom* and *The Green Pastures,* and plays like *The Silver Cord.* "The Negro now recognizes the undeveloped potentialities of Negro life and folkways as source material not only for the development of a special Negro drama but for a national drama. One of the Negro's surest contributions to American culture, it seems clear, will be through his dramatic talents and traditions." [31]

Toward creative painting. The rural art movement, at least in Wisconsin, is still a pioneer undertaking. It was only a hundred years ago that European settlers were clearing the land and building their homes in this state. Paintings by their descendants have a folk emphasis, although folk design, dance, festival, or song are difficult to trace, being the accumulation of generations. In spite of variations, most rural artists, at least in their untutored beginnings, tend to use a style that is traditionally primitive. Some are influenced by conventional or modern forms, but even these out-reaching artists tend to acquire a distinctive pattern.

As John Barton observes, the true rural painter compensates for his lack of training and technique by his intimate knowledge and feeling for his subjects. His experiences with people, with plants and animals, seem to give the kind of integrity so necessary for artistic creation. This in itself is reason enough for rural art as an expression of people who live close to the land and are

---

[30] "John Steuart Curry, Artist of Rural Life," address at Seventy-fifth Anniversary of the Land Grant Colleges, Washington, D.C., November, 1937; in *John Steuart Curry's Pageant of America* (New York: American Artists Group, 1943).

[31] Thomas E. Poag, Tennessee Agricultural and Industrial State College, "The Negro Theatre and Adult Education," *Educational Theater in Adult Education* (Washington: Division of Adult Education Service, 1951).

spiritually in tune with its rhythms. The rural art movement in the state has grown until thousands of rural people are painting, having conferences, listening to a university-sponsored radio program for school children, and exhibiting their pictures at community, regional, and state shows. Acting as tutor and friend, the university artist-in-residence, Aaron Bohrod, stimulates and guides the movement and encourages individual painters wherever possible.

Toward creative writing. A rural writers' project in Wisconsin had a thousand members in its first year and continues to bring in hundreds of poems, short stories and plays. The project sponsors fifteen local writers' clubs and has its own publication. Robert Edward Gard, like John Steuart Curry, a rural Kansan, helped in the formation of the writers' project and directs its progress in line with rural values. He has his own unique way of describing its conception: [32]

One day my telephone rang. It was someone from the College of Agriculture. He said, "There are nine people coming to see you."

"What for?"

"They want to talk about writing."

"What kind of writing?"

"They don't know."

"I'm pretty busy."

He said, "One of the women has thirteen children."

"A farm woman with thirteen children has time to come here to talk with me about writing?"

"She's right here."

"All right, I'll see them."

. . . .

They waited for me to say something. As I paused looking at each of them, then all of them together, for no reason at all, I began to remember the happy and carefree life I led as a boy in the Neosho River Valley down in Kansas. It seemed that my early experiences had the unshackled quality of complete freedom, the gaiety, the unreasoned and complete savoring of the goodness of earth and sky, the unquestioned appreciation of neighbors, music and dancing, and a God was, I knew, the source spring of the kind of theater I sought to evolve.

I forgot it was a bare classroom and a hot June morning. They, somehow, became a symbol of a group of my neighbors in Kansas. They symbolized my father who had such impatience with the fabricated theater of the proscenium arch and movie screen. He knew and I knew that at our old home in Kansas there was all about us as about everyone everywhere, the free theater of life for the free appreciation of everyone.

I said to these nine people, "You are like a group of my neighbors when I was a kid down in Kansas."

One said, "You remind me of a neighbor in Manitowoc County. He's a farmer, not a very good one, but he laughs a lot."

"Why did you come?"

"I don't know exactly. We heard that you want people to write about their own places and the folks they know well. I think maybe we could do that."

I said, "Tell me more about yourselves and this place you come from. What kind of place is it?"

Then began one of the most unreasonable experiences I have ever had. These nine people stayed for three days. We talked and talked and talked. We talked about our lives. The struggle in them emerged against the whole fabric of our native places. A kind of fantastic play that was like life itself began to emerge. There were times when we seemed to speak not as ourselves but as imaginative characters that grew from our talk of people and places that was as real as the earth itself. The whole affair was a kind of dramatic ecstasy in which we were both the actors and the audience, the dancers and the music.

When they were ready to leave, we realized we had hardly mentioned the ways of writing at all. But we did have a sense of something that had stirred our lives. We had had an experience together.

[32] Robert E. Gard, *op. cit.* Adapted and quoted by permission.

I said, "I wish there were more persons like yourselves."

One said, "Mr. Gard, there are hundreds and thousands of men and women in our state who live on the land and love the land, and who understand the true meaning of the seasons and man's relationship to man and to his God."

Another said, "If rural people only knew you would encourage them to express themselves in the way they chose, there would be such a rising of creative expression as yet unheard of, and it would be part of the kind of theater we have had these three days. It would be a whole expression of and about ourselves and the places where we live."

There was! After the project was publicly launched our mail boxes were filled with manuscripts for days and days.

Toward a language of the land. How can country people living on the land and in separated valleys communicate, understand one another or even contribute to a nation's culture if they do not have a written language? So questioned the popular poet, Henrik Wergeland of Norway. In 1835 he wrote an essay advocating the inclusion of words and idioms from the various Norwegian dialects into the written language of the country. Some songs and ballads in those dialects had appeared in the eighteenth century but scarcely anyone had ever thought of these expressions as literary. There was, however, a restiveness about having a language in common with Denmark after being separated from the Danish Kingdom in 1814. There was also an upsurge in the national consciousness, and Norway developed her own democratic constitution. A latent unrest among country people found various forms of public expression. They were determined to have a recognized place in the emerging national being. The situation was explained later by Thorstein Veblen, who was Norwegian to the core though born in Wisconsin. Veblen complained bitterly about the earlier Norwegian class system in which townsmen and government officials, includ-

ing church pastors, were set off by Danish tradition in one group and opposed to countrymen and peasants in another.[33] Another reformer, Ivar Aasen, did not believe any permanent good could come from trying to modify a language whose basic grammar and concepts were Danish. Of peasant stock himself, he began a careful study of all the dialects, then decided to construct a written language that would be wholly Norwegian. In 1848 he published his *Folkesprogs* grammar, literally "folk speech," but he called the new language "Landsmaal," a language of the land.

A social movement soon developed, and by the middle of the nineteenth century there were "language conflicts." It was not simply a language for speech and writing that was demanded; the language became a symbol for the self-assertion of Norway's country people, their bid for self-respect and national recognition. Consequently there was set in train a kind of romantic revolution not confined to country people and with an overtone of national feeling. Artists, writers, school men, and professional people took up the cause. Folk dancing was revived, native costumes characteristic of each valley were accepted dress for any occasion, and they were frequently in evidence.

At present both Landsmaal and "Riksmaal," (language of the kingdom) are official; both must be taught in the schools. A university professor may choose the language he prefers, and may take his stand in the larger social conflict which is still a public issue. It is not uncommon to hear succeeding speakers in the same conference or convention use the two languages. However, to hear the American musical comedy *Oklahoma* presented in a Norwegian Landsmaal translation in a public theater, subsidized by a labor government, is to witness

[33] Max Lerner, *The Portable Veblen* (New York: Viking, 1948), and Joseph Dorfman, *Thorstein Veblen and His America* (Viking, 1934).

the fact that a country people's emotional demand is not to be denied.

Toward the organic in architecture. There are two different ways of dealing with the physical environment and of attempting to express spacial relations. The one is toward the so-called rational and the geometric, the other toward the emotional and the organic. Some buildings, even cities, have been planned and built according to regularized schemes; others appear to have grown organically from the soil, in natural surroundings like the trees or shrubs. This is not the place to argue that the one is superior to the other. But there are those who feel keenly that the dominance of classic and gothic in American architecture is little short of tragic. They say that these foreign forms became nothing more than an artificial prop to people whose emotional backgrounds were none too strong. "Behind the screens of their houses — miniature Versailles, Tuscan Villa or medieval manor — or in their skyscrapers in sacred Gothic shapes, these people [Americans] could only hide their inner uncertainty." [34] Architecture, these critics assert, should be an organic interpretation expressing a people's fundamental values.

Frank Lloyd Wright, from the very beginning of his career in 1887, has been the exponent of the organic interpretation. He is not alone architect but advocate of the philosophy that man's relation to land shall be immediate and personal. City organization is to him artificial, arbitrary, and abhorrent. Man must be free to express himself, in his creative impulses in terms of his own natural environment and his organic relations. Mr. Wright's houses reach back in pattern to the early use of the large chimney as a starting point. He spreads his structure out from this massive core. At its base there is always the open fireplace — symbol of home. LePlay

too, we recall, constantly emphasized that the hearth is the heart of the home.

This respect for the organic further explains why Mr. Wright prefers to use materials taken directly from nature — rugged stone for walls, rough granite for floors, and unfinished timbers for frame and even finish. He also likes to work with nature, planning his building in relation to an adjacent valley or stream. If it is a home, the topography is brought within the composition of the dwelling. A tree may have right of way in building a porch, and an opening in the roof may give it growing and breathing space. When asked whether at his own home, Taliesin, he had built up the hill to conform to the contours of the house and garden wall he said, "No, I never build houses on the top of a hill. I build them around it, like an eyebrow." In the light of this explanation, it is easy to see how the house brings into perspective the natural curve of the land.

The organic in architecture is grounded in the union of two fundamentals: *Folk* and *Earth.* Fundamentals are usually simple yet often difficult to communicate except by experience. "The true basis for any serious study of the art of Architecture lies in indigenous structures; more humble buildings everywhere are to architecture what folklore is to literature or folk-song to music . . . In the aggregate of these simple buildings lie traits which make them characteristically Italian, French, Dutch, Spanish or English, as the case may be. It is the traits of these many folk-structures that are of the *soil*." [35]

Mr. Wright explains that no really Italian building seems ill at ease in Italy. "All are happily content with what ornament and color they carry naturally. The native rocks and trees and garden slopes are at one with them." [36] The secret of this charm, he declares, is not to be found in anything scho-

[34] Siegfried Giedion, *op. cit.*, p. 347.

[35] *In the Cause of Architecture* (Spring Green. Wisconsin: Taliesin Press, 1951).

[36] *Ibid.*

lastic or academic. "It all lies close to Earth." In nature itself the artist must seek the source of the beauty he would express.

The organic principle can take many different forms of expression. Above all, nature must be respected, not thwarted. The design may be a farm with fields carefully laid out, "rhythmic" in relation to well-planned buildings, with contour cultivation properly applied not alone to crops and animals but to the people themselves. It may be a well-designed parkway such as the Merritt Parkway in Connecticut, where one feels identified with the landscape, its trees, greenswards and the mountains or sea beyond.

It is definitely the design of "Broadacre City," Mr. Wright's own master model for a modern rurban community. "City," however, is not the word for it. It is rather the composite symbol of space and time, where and when the best of "rural" and "urban" may merge and mingle in the great social movements of centralization and decentralization which have been discussed earlier in this book. Some of the inspiration which brought the plan into being is expressed in the following:

These new Plan-forms were neither Urban nor Rural. They were the outgrowth of use of the Ground as a common human-right equally for the Tiller of the soil, the Poet, the Preacher, and the Makers-of-things, the Shopkeeper and the Trader. So the Broadacre-forms were into the Light out of the Ground.[37]

Every family in Broadacre would have its home on the land and there is provision for industries, utilities, stores, theater, schools, and a social center. The community is related to the Great Society by a multi-lane highway. To the oft-repeated question that this is an enchanting but impractical dream, Mr. Wright replies that industrial society is necessarily moving towards something like it in scope if not in design. Indeed Taliesin itself is growing into the living Broadacre model, as its economic, social and artistic activities develop and expand.

Cultural arts belong together. In the previous discussion, we have perforce considered the different arts separately. Actually they are not separate; they are of one piece. Folk societies indicate this quite clearly, and there are today many efforts to bring them closer together.

The essential and natural unity of the arts, and their folk basis, are most readily seen in native festival and dance. The Maori of New Zealand, one of the most advanced of the Polynesian peoples, still largely rural, have developed a unique harmony and unity in diverse artistic expression. At an all-day festival, the preparation and eating of food is carried on with traditional ceremony; characteristic dress is worn, a grass skirt is made, just as an American country woman might bring her sewing to a picnic; there is dancing and singing; there is oratory and symbolic religious activity. These forms of action are not ordered or successive but spontaneous and carried on simultaneously. Whenever anyone feels moved to dance or sing, to eat or speak, he does so; and others may or may not join him.[38]

Especially significant is the Maori dance in which there is group movement, music, and appropriate costumes. The music suggests the song of the waves cloven by the bow of the canoe. The movement follows the rhythmic dip of the paddles. Songs are the crew's own, the cadence fitted to their breathing as they lift, lower, and pull on their paddles with powerful strokes. The same movement is felt in the "Volga Boat Song" of Russia. Costumes suggest the function of the voyage, whether fishing, journey-

---

[37] *An Autobiography,* Sixth Book, "Broadacre City." Taliesin Press, Spring Green, Wisconsin, 1944.

[38] W. Robert Moore, "New Zealand 'Down Under,'" *The National Geographic Magazine* (LXIX, No. 2, February, 1936).

ing, or fighting. If it is a mission of war, the chant is the blood-curdling, spine-tingling "Haka," in which sticks represent weapons, and the dancers leap from the ground, rolling their eyes, and protrude their tongues in the universal gesture of contempt.

No wonder the Maori canoe and the portal of the meeting house are works of art, carved and painted with the symbols of sacred scenes or historic happenings in their common tribal life. When any part of these artistic expressions is changed, the whole cultural system is affected. This is shown by the degeneration of certain art forms when group or religious ceremonials are greatly modified or discontinued.

Three illustrations will give some evidence of the current tendency for greater coördination of the arts in our own rural society. The Arts Council of Winston-Salem is an organized effort to bring together in administration and in program Little Theatre, Children's Theatre, Civic Oratorio Society, Symphony Society, dance groups, and local arts and crafts. The Council exists not alone for the benefit of the twin cities but for focusing attention and leadership in a wider rural-urban movement represented by the Piedmont Festival.

The Saskatchewan Arts Board formed under an Act of the Provincial Legislature in April, 1949, is given the responsibility for providing "more opportunities for Saskatchewan people in the arts; namely music, the visual arts, handicraft, literature, drama, and other arts; training and information services and maintaining and promoting high standards in these fields." In its third annual report, records of accomplishment and statements of intended activities are found under such headings as music, visual arts, literature, drama, handicraft, and children's art.

A third example of closer coördination of the arts in rural society is the Rhinelander (Wisconsin) Northwoods Arts and Crafts Festival, held in May, 1951, which had for its purpose "a creative interpretation of state and region." There was a united program of music, drama, painting, and crafts for youth and adults. Laymen and professionals alike, farmers, villagers, and townspeople came from a dozen northern counties to participate, talk, and plan. Working with them, helping but not dictating, was the best personnel available at the university and other state educational and cultural institutions.

Recreational and Cultural Activities and Agencies

Against the background of the general discussion in the earlier part of this chapter, let us now briefly enumerate the many forms which recreation and the cultural arts can and do take in rural society, more especially at the local community level. Rural people are most interested in activities which provide actual participation. "Highly commercialized facilities for passive amusement have been more characteristic of city than of country." [39]

From the following enumeration, the inference should not be drawn that all rural communities are equally well cared for, although every activity listed is actually in use in one or more communities. Some of the activities have been discussed in the chapter on adult education, since one reason for the popularity and power of adult education is its appeal to recreational and cultural interests. Many agencies and organizations carrying on these activities have been described in the chapter on the interest groups.

Music — group singing, chorus, glee club, orchestra, band, and festival. In any gathering, public or private, there is nothing that will afford everyone better opportunity for expression and enjoyment than will partici-

[39] J. F. Steiner, *op. cit.*, chap. VIII.

pation in some form of music, especially singing. Music has had and continues to have a very large place in the many organizations and activities of rural life.

The emphasis placed upon group singing during the war gave its development a decided impetus. It is a valuable means of creating group morale. Community leaders say that "sings" are most successful when strictly informal, and when all members of the group join in freely. They say that the matter of leading such singing, sometimes considered a problem, is not difficult to solve.

Choruses are organized on a neighborhood or community basis for adults or for young people or even for children. A children's chorus is an especially attractive form of group singing, and with the wealth of published music now available can easily become a part of the program of most schools, churches, and community clubs.

Orchestral music may blend both string and wind instruments and bring together individuals with varying degrees of skill and training. Many communities have persons qualified to direct an orchestra; others engage the services of a trained director who can come once or twice a month, and who may serve, as well, as private tutor for beginners. Frequently an arrangement is worked out with the local high school whereby one of its teachers can help with a community orchestra.

The band probably has a more popular appeal in many communities than almost any other form of musical organization. Its success depends largely on good leadership and faithful membership. Leadership can be secured on much the same plan as for an orchestra. Many local bands are maintained at partial public expense by village or school districts. One of the factors in the improvement of town-country relations which was repeatedly noticed in the studies of local communities was the band and its weekly concerts. The whole countryside turned out for the concert. Members of the organization were drawn from both farm and village.

The music festival, whether on a large or a small scale, on a community, county, or state basis, is a fitting finale to a season's program. Choral as well as orchestral groups can be brought together in a massed ensemble under skilled leadership. In fact, there is no finer way of bringing country and city people together than through music.

Drama and pageantry — plays, pageants, folk dancing, pantomime, readings, story telling, marionettes, and puppetry. As we have seen, in a number of states there has recently been a great increase in dramatic activity. In addition to its sociability, drama quickens the imagination, cultivates and gives opportunity for the expression of emotions, and provides group experience. The play is probably the most common form of drama to be found in rural communities. The one-act play is especially popular and lends itself to rural groups. The choice of the play and careful attention to the casting of characters are especially important for its success. Much latent talent is available and many stories could be told of how intensive work on such a character as Jean Valjean, for example, had literally transformed a personality by releasing it from suppressions which traced back to boyhood.

The pageant has many possibilities for rural communities since it deals with historical, mythical, or allegorical subjects more commonly than does the play. It is a means of education as well as of entertainment. Many rural groups have presented effective pageants based on local history and produced by the descendants of the original characters. In one community so much enthusiasm was developed in the undertaking and so many things of historic interest were discovered that a local museum was established.

Folk dancing and interpretive dancing may

be considered a form of pantomime. Accompanied by music, they are an effective way of portraying grace and beauty of movement. Folk dancing, especially, has been receiving increased attention in many sections of the country whose residents trace their forbears to foreign lands. Many first generation Americans are anxious to throw off foreign traditions and customs, while those of the second generation often welcome the chance to ransack attics for costumes and to revive folkways in dance, song, play, and story.

Good story-telling is a greatly appreciated art. The country and small town abound with story-tellers who ply their art in small, informal groups, but many communities have not learned how to incorporate them into the more formal meetings, or how to use them for constructive entertainment. Folk tales are a rich source of material. This seems to be a world-wide trait of rural people. The traveling story-teller is still an institution and a social force in parts of Asia.

The art of puppetry has also been revived in recent years in many country districts. A wide range of activity is provided because the ancillary arts of the theater can be practiced — painting drops, making costumes, constructing properties, as well as selecting or writing stories or plays.

Holidays and festivals. Christmas, New Year's, Washington's and Lincoln's birthdays, April Fool's Day, the Fourth of July, Labor Day, Valentine's Day, and Thanksgiving, as well as other special days, are all occasions for rural community programs or festivals. A beautiful and growing custom in rural villages or small towns is the community Christmas celebration. A tree is lighted in the public square, and streets, stores, and homes are decorated with pines and candles. There is often a song festival, a cantata, or a Christmas play, such as Douglas Hyde's *The Nativity*.[40]

[40] A few of the many materials are Edward L.

Social parties and group games. A wide variety of activities are included under the title of group games. During the winter months, social parties and games are especially popular in rural communities. They may be organized around occasions such as holidays, or they may occur informally when neighbors and congenial groups gather for visiting, card playing, dancing, and singing. There are circle games, shuttle relays, table games, checkers, chess, ping pong, croquet, stunts, mixing games, horse-shoe pitching, folk and square dances, and the social dance. Folk games are being revived in some communities and foreign games, especially Oriental ones, are being studied and introduced. There is something creative, even therapeutic, about the moving circle. When people move in a circle, backward and forward with clasped hands to the urge of strong music, the response is strong from playful childhood, romantic youth, and disorganized senescence.

Community athletics and sports. Outdoor and indoor sports and athletics have long been favorites of farm and village people. Baseball, basketball, volley ball, and horseshoes or quoits are probably the most common sports, and the ones which develop the largest groups and stimulate the most community interest and enthusiasm. Teams for contests may be composed of open-country or small-town groups or both. Baseball and quoits are particularly well adapted to the country, while basketball, because it is played indoors during winter months, is usually centered in town or village.

Kamark, "Xmas on the Farm," a comedy in one act (Ithaca, N.Y.: *American Agriculturist*, 1947); Committee on Town and Country, "The Harvest Festival," *Town and Country Church* (No. 36, September, 1947); Helen W. Fritz, "Community Harvest Suppers," *Farm Journal* (Philadelphia, November, 1950); Ralph and Adelin Linton, *We Gather Together*, the story of Thanksgiving (New York: Henry Schuman, 1949).

Automobiles and good roads make it possible to organize inter-community leagues of many kinds: kitten-ball for women, men, girls, or boys; men's baseball leagues; quoit-pitching tournaments; and tug-of-war contests. Amateur rules are drawn and schedules arranged. Plans may include eliminations until a county play-off is arranged in order to select a team to go to state finals, as to the State Fair. This kind of recreational program raises important questions regarding parks and playgrounds in rural areas, which will be discussed briefly in the last section of the chapter.

Graphic arts and handicrafts. Interest in the graphic arts and handicrafts has not been widely developed in all rural areas. Some communities, however, have made much of them and have found in them not only gratifying recreation but profitable sources of auxiliary income. It is sometimes difficult to finance such group projects and to find competent leaders. In some communities, however, older members of the community, grandmothers perhaps, have been induced to revive their early or their old-country crafts, and to teach the younger generation knitting, crocheting, hooking, embroidery, or appliqué work. Many simple and inexpensive ways of learning principles of line, design, and color, as well as rhythm, balance, and harmony can be worked out.

Regional literature and rural-life fiction. Reading is not a lost art. It is a leisure-time activity which presents many possibilities, especially when rural people recognize more fully than they do that a new type of rural literature is developing which has the quality of the older classic novels, and the strong appeal of rural life, the soil, the plain or mountain scene, and the region which one loves best. This type of rural-life fiction pictures the life and the culture of real families and communities, and gives them an emo-

tional flavor and content which may be completely taken for granted by those readers who live in the environments described. Through these novels, rural dwellers gain a sense of belonging in the rural scene and the importance of it in the general scheme. There are countless examples. "One cannot read Ruth Suckow's *The Odyssey of a Nice Girl* without sensing the authentic portrayal of life in a small town of the Middle West. Similarly, we realize the Southern setting of *The Yearling,* the Wisconsin flavor in *Restless Is the River,* the local Maine color in *As the Earth Turns.*"

"In *Old Jules* and *Sod and Stubble* we see the life of pioneer farm people portrayed in new and fascinating biographical form by members of their families, realistic and yet faithful to the lives of the struggling pioneer. Other volumes concern themselves with conflict situations and social adjustment. There are to be found even a number of rural novels about the developing coöperative movement. It all constitutes a wide field, capable of appealing to the interests of many groups." [41]

The more recent writings have their earlier counterparts, and together they become an interpretation of the unfolding life of a pioneering people. There is Rolvaag's *Giants in the Earth,* Hamlin Garland's *Son of the Middle Border,* Willa Cather's *O Pioneers!,* Zona Gale's *Friendship Village,* Martha Ostenso's *Wild Geese.*

Whether in forms of fiction, drama, verse, or biography, rural-life literature offers an enlarging field for cultural activities and for personal enjoyment. These forms of expression are not entirely in the hands of professionals. Writing, as well as reading and acting, holds many possibilities, as the rural writers' project clearly shows.

The foregoing catalogue of varied and

[41] John R. Barton, *Rural Cultural Arts* (Madison: Special Circular, June 1949, Extension Service, College of Agriculture, University of Wisconsin).

widely ranging recreational and cultural activities is evidence of the place they hold in our rural society. These many and varied activities are a sort of democratic guarantee that everyone can share in such creative experiences, and every agency and organization can make some contribution to the enjoyment of rural life. Sources of help and suggestions, lacking in earlier years, are now available.[42] Most rural agencies and organizations are actually giving increased attention to such activities, as the evidence has shown. Attention is varied and the range in programs is wide. This is true of local, state, and national agencies, both public and private. It enlarges their opportunities and at the same time creates problems of coordination for the local community and of administration for the county.

Recreation and cultural activities involve public interests. In whatever way recreation and the cultural arts are approached, it is quite evident that all the people known in democratic societies as "the public" are becoming increasingly concerned and more directly involved. The great rise in commercialized recreation is one result. Profits are the motive of most commercial projects, and when their vested interests are challenged, the public interests must be defined and defended. Recreation must be re-creation, and it is increasingly becoming so, as the evidence has shown. Its expansion is urged by social welfare leaders as one means of preventing juvenile delinquency, and also by health authorities as one form of therapy

42 E. J. Niederfrank, *Planning Recreation for Rural Home and Community* (Agricultural Information Bulletin No. 20, Washington, D.C., November, 1950); Marjorie M. Keller, "Growth Thru Music," *National Educational Journal* (December, 1949); D. M. Hall, "Citizens, End-Product of Education," *County Agent and Vo-Ag Teacher* (May, 1951); Arthur and Verna Katona, "Art Begins at Home," *Design* (March, 1950); William R. Sur, "Mozart and P. S. 36, Music in the Public Schools," *House Beautiful* (August, 1951).

for emotional maladjustments. For these and other reasons social control, involving legal measures and governmental supervision, is increasingly necessary. Such measures include zoning ordinances, set-back lines for buildings and parking areas, building codes for health and safety, and other sanitation provisions, and it would mark a new day if there could be added to such bare minimum standards the terms suggested by the Royal Institute of British Activities and the Town and Country Planning Association, namely, that buildings, playgrounds, and the towns themselves shall be not only convenient but pleasant, attractive, and artistic. It is by such means that youth may keep its romanticism and play-spirit as long as it can, and avoid tragedy where possible.

On the constructive side, public policies are needed to develop the many opportunities for recreation in modern rural life — through parks, playgrounds, scenic and historic spots, wild-life sanctuaries, community buildings and equipment, and most important, trained and competent leadership. Steiner points out that the need for public recreational facilities and policies first arose in congested urban districts, but that the situation at present requires an extended view, reaching beyond either rural or urban interests to a national scope. The invasions of village and open country by new types of organizations modeled on urban patterns and affiliated on a county or nation-wide basis, together with the excursions of urban people into the country, seeking recreation and respite, are not only modifying the leisure-time habits of both rural and urban residents, but are linking them together in the need for national and regional planning.

In rural communities, schools have opportunities which they have thus far not fully realized. They are the public institutions of greatest frequency in rural society; they have the most physical equipment, and the largest paid personnel. Theirs is the task of stimulating greater recognition of recreational need, of directing it into wholesome channels of activity, and of providing in larger measure leadership and equipment for youth, both in school and out, and for the adult members of their communities, as the chapter on adult education has already emphasized.

Local government has opportunities before it also. One of its chief contributions can be in planning beyond local corporate boundaries. The playground of the modern city must extend into surrounding territory. Towns, villages, and the open country are immediately involved. This train of thinking takes one into the whole question of land and policies regarding its most appropriate uses. Several states are definitely attempting land-use planning under various legal forms in which recreation is recognized as a legitimate land use. May it not be considered one of its highest uses?

The importance given to public welfare in modern life is stated very well by a State Supreme Court Justice in the following terms:

In this day none will dispute that government in the exercise of its police power may impose restrictions upon the use of property in the interest of public health, morals, and safety. That the same restrictions may be imposed upon the use of property in promotion of the public welfare, convenience, and general prosperity is perhaps not so well understood, but nevertheless is firmly established by the decisions of this and the Federal Supreme Court.[43]

Thus a consideration of recreation and the cultural arts in rural society, their changing emphasis, their many forms and activities, and their implications for the public interest has led directly to questions of welfare and public policy. This in itself is a significant modern trend, and leads to the further discussion of health and social welfare in the chapters which follow.

[43] Justice Owen, in State *ex rel.* Carter *vs.* Harper, 182 Wis. 148, p. 154.

TOPICS FOR DISCUSSION

The topics suggested below may be assigned to individual students or the class may be divided into committees, each assuming responsibility for one topic. The separate committee reports with recommendations may be presented before the whole class, thus becoming the basis for further discussion.

1. A plan for organizing and carrying to completion a dramatic program for rural groups in a county or district.
2. A plan for organizing and carrying to completion a music program for rural groups in a county or district.
3. A plan for conducting a county-wide baseball tournament in which rural groups participate.
4. A plan for conducting a town-country community fair.

5. A plan whereby a high school may give leadership and direction to a year-around recreation program for a town-country community.
6. A plan for enlisting, encouraging and training rural young people in the arts and crafts by such devices as exhibits, testing aptitudes, or bringing in artists.
7. By use of the ten-point scale of essentials for a public recreation system, rate your own community or any other community, either rural or urban, with which you are familiar, and discuss its merits and its shortcomings: [44]
   a. *Know your community* — the character and distribution of population, the tradi-

[44] The scale is taken from *Community Recreation Comes of Age* (Washington: United States Government Printing Office, Federal Security Agency, Office of Community War Service, Division of Recreation, 1944).

tions, needs, problems, and resources of the community.

b. *Pool your resources.* Work together for full use of all potential assets: from public and private agencies, neighborhood groups, organizations, and individual leaders.

c. *Check your legislation.* Determine what legislation you need and what you have, and then, if necessary, work to get laws that provide an adequate legal base. Authority to develop public recreation depends upon state and local laws.

d. *Establish a legal managing authority* — a responsible lay board with legal authority to administer the program, assuring recreation the community status it warrants.

e. *Get good leadership.* Insist on a trained, full-time executive, responsible to the board, on the job year round, and subordinate leaders chosen with equal care on a basis of qualifications and training. Select and use competent volunteers within this framework of professional leadership.

f. *Make the most of existing facilities* — municipally owned schools, buildings, parks, playfields and playgrounds, and water areas. These may be supplemented by use of privately owned property.

g. *Secure separate budget.* Obtain a definite, adequate amount of public funds through special tax levy or other public appropriations, earmarked for the sole purpose of community recreation.

h. *See that your program is community-wide, year-round, has broad appeal* — with interests for young and old, indoor and outdoor activities, sports, athletics, games, music, arts, crafts, drama, lectures, forums, social recreation, and community events.

i. *Maintain public partnership.* Keep popular opinion abreast of your program. Use all media available to interpret community recreation and win public support for it.

j. *Plan for the future.* Make a place for recreation in long-range town planning.

Good planning should include not only physical facilities, but also program, leadership, and finance.

REFERENCE READINGS

Butler, George D., *Introduction to Community Recreation*, 2nd edition. New York: McGraw-Hill, 1951.

Craven, Thomas, *Modern Art, The Men, The Movements, The Meaning.* New York: Simon & Schuster, 1934.

Flexner, James Thomas, *A Short History of American Paintings.* Boston: Houghton Mifflin, 1950. Pictures and short histories of fifty-one artists.

Gombrich, E. H., *The Story of Art.* New York: Phaidon, Publishers, 1950. An orientation for uninitiated and youthful readers, illustrated and simply written.

Graf, Max, *Modern Music.* New York: Philosophical Library, 1950.

Kargere, Audrey, *Color and Personality.* New York: Philosophical Library, 1950.

Karsh, Jousuf, portfolio of distinguished portraits. *Life*, August 7, 1950.

Alcide De Gasperi   Georges Braque
Jawaharlal Nehru   Harold Wilson
Jean Cocteau   Jean-Louis Barrauls
Henry Bernstein   Jean Sibelius

Meyer, Harold D., and Charles K. Brightbill, *Community Recreation.* Boston: Heath, 1948. A guide to recreation organization and administration with chapters on planning, personnel, programs, and financing.

Mitchell, E. D., and B. S. Mason, *The Theory of Play.* New York: A. S. Barnes, 1941.

Mukerjee, Radhakamal, *The Social Function of Art.* Bombay: Hind Kitabs, Ltd., 1948; New York: Macmillan, 1950. The thesis that great art is used by men to achieve the highest possible degree of understanding of the roles they must play in their various societies.

National Community Recreation pamphlets: *Rural Recreation, Organizing Recreation in a Small Community, Planning a Rural Community Building, The Arts as Recreation, Community Theatre in the Recreation Pro-*

gram, *Roads to Music Appreciation, Enjoying Nature, Nature in Recreation, Fiesta —
The South American Way*. 315 Fourth
Avenue, New York, 1951.

Patten, Marjorie, *The Arts Workshop of Rural
America*. New York: Columbia University
Press, 1937. A study of the rural arts program of the Agricultural Extension Service.

Van de Wall, Willem, *The Music of the People*.
New York: American Association for Adult
Education, 1938.

Wileden, Rockwell, and Borchers, *Dramatics
for Amateur Groups*, Circular 257. Madison:
University of Wisconsin College of Agriculture Extension Service, 1933. Practical suggestions for putting on plays.

Works Progress Administration, *Recreation, A
Selected Bibliography with Annotations*.
Public Administration Recreation Administration, Periodicals, Technical Series Recreation
Circular No. 2, Washington, D.C., June 14,
1937.

FILMS

Christmas Carol Collection. S, 9. Official Films.

Creation of a Portrait. S, C, 11. By the artist
Warsharskey. Encyclopedia Britannica Films.

Folk Dances — American Square Dance. S, 10.
Coronet.

Folk Dances — Norwegian. S, C, 11. American
Film Registry.

Leaders for Leisure. S, 21. Community recreation program and how recreation leaders
should function. Athletic Institute.

Songs of Stephen Foster. S, 10. Teaching Film.

Van Gogh. S, 20. Life story of Vincent Van
Gogh told through his work. Museum of
Modern Art.

What is Modern Art? S, C, 20. Princeton Film
Center.

William Gropper at Work. (Silent) 10. Over
the shoulder of one of America's artists as he
draws a social cartoon. Gutlohn.

William Tell. S, 25. An opera. Official.

"THE GOOD EARTH," BY JOHN S. CURRY

HOMECRAFTS *Top*: Indian Rug Weaving (Soil Conservation Service).
Bottom left: Weaving on a Home Loom (Extension Service, U.S. Dept. of
Agriculture, photo by Ed Hunton). *Bottom right*: Making a Hat of Hand-
plaited Palmetto Strips (Standard Oil Co., N.J.)

Opposite Page: **WORK OF RURAL ARTISTS** *Top*: "Morning Glory," by Lois
Ireland. *Bottom*: Herman Krause at Work. (From Rural Art Exhibit,
University of Wisconsin)

HOMECRAFTS *Top*: Farm Woman Refinishing Antique Furniture. *Center*: County Handicraft Exhibit. *Bottom*: Farm Woman Making Slip Covers. (Extension Service, U.S. Dept. of Agriculture, photos by Ed Hunton)

22 Rural Health and Medical Services

PEOPLE, more especially children, are a nation's most important resource; their health and welfare are its primary concern. Wars and depressions have made this plain. Public attention at every level — local, state and national — has probably never been so strongly focused upon any one social problem, except perhaps education, as it has been recently upon health. During World War II the Selective Service System revealed some startling figures indicating physical and mental unfitness on a broad scale; there were the records of miracles in modern medicine and surgery. More recently there have been programs to improve physical fitness and mental alertness, campaigns for better food and nutrition, and greatly stepped-up efforts to expand health and medical services. Response from the public has been widespread and the efforts of both health and medical people have been extended. Consequently the death, disease, and distress curves continue to swing down on the many measurement charts and graphs recorded by health agencies.

In this as in so many other social movements, rural people and rural problems are close to the general trend, though sometimes above and sometimes below the average. There was a time when rural leaders could point with justifiable pride to the natural advantages of their life — fresh air, sunshine, and direct access to food. They could point to lower mortality and morbidity rates in the country as compared with the city, to longer life expectancy, and to smaller chances of contracting diseases spread by personal con-

tact. Cities were considered breeding places of disease.

Many of these trends began to be reversed soon after the turn of the century. It was not that the rates were increasing in rural areas; they were decreasing in both city and country. But the health of city people improved more rapidly. Determined and enlarged health programs in urban areas began to pay off more quickly. For example, the rural death rate in 1900 was 50 per cent under the urban; in 1940 it was only 10 per cent under. The rural infant mortality rates, to which a good deal of significance will be attached, yielded their preferred position to the more rapidly declining urban rates in about 1928.

Of even greater significance was the fact that death rates from preventable diseases and diseases of remediable causes began to be higher in rural than in urban areas. This would suggest differences in locations, in attitudes, and in individual and group action. These are conditions that people can do something about; they need not bow to what was earlier considered the inevitable. More recently the tendency is for certain country and large city death rates to equalize, but for those in towns of 2500 to 10,000 population to lag behind. These are matters in which the student of rural society has special interest and concern. He may not become expert in the diagnosis of disease, in child care, in public health standards, or in hospital construction. He cannot, however, avoid giving attention to the incidence of death, disease, and accident; to the study of relations of rural people with medi-

405

cal care and health agencies; and to an understanding of the interaction of health with other aspects of rural life. These are fundamental to family life, to community welfare, and to the future of the nation itself. It is to these problems that this chapter will be addressed.

Changing Rural Health Situation — Some Measures and Implications

The quest for good health in rural society, in the past at least, has not been a deliberate thing. Being born, growing up, keeping well, have been more or less taken for granted. When there was trouble too difficult to cope with in the family circle, there was resort to the doctor, or, in dire distress, the hospital. There has not been systematic effort over large areas and with organized agencies to protect health. Promotion of sanitation and control of disease through public measures, such as immunization and quarantine, had to justify themselves in rural society. Public health nurses have had to win their way in country communities just as professionally trained agriculturalists, home economists, and social welfare workers have had to do.

The country doctor, of course, has a fine place in the tradition of rural life. He was a part of the community; he was respected and beloved; and, in fact, he was almost a social institution in himself. Yet he was usually the only doctor in the community or for miles around, and consequently was so busy saving life and responding to emergencies that he had little time or energy, nor did he have the special training, to work in organized ways for promoting better health.

Hospitals, clinics, public health nurses, sanitary engineers, and protection programs have appeared in rural areas during recent years, but not in sufficient quantity and quality to give rural people health parity with urban people.

What is health — how measured? Health is obviously a relative matter, but it is something more than simply staying alive. It is a state of well-being in terms of age, circumstances, and the standards of a society. It is a sort of race between life-building and life-destroying forces, as Professor C. E. Lively suggests.[1] Certainly it is not a simple thing, readily recognized or easily measured; it involves physical, mental, and emotional relations, as the comparatively modern term "psychomatic" implies. And it is not purely an individual matter but a group concern as well. Thus some defects are attributable to inheritance or to poor nutrition in childhood. There are differing susceptibilities, as illustrated by the incidence of cancer and tuberculosis. Some children are born to wealth, others to poverty, some in wholesome environments, some in sordid and disease-infested areas. All these things are of concern to the society as well as to the individual.

Because of these varied relations, measures of health are difficult to devise, and it is difficult to make comparisons from one social situation to another, since there are sure to be many variables. Unfortunately, many measurements have had to be in negative terms, such as mortality, death rate, and morbidity or rate of extent of illness or disease. Life expectancy, a more positive measure, is the relative length of life in terms of the mortality experience of a definite population group during some agreed-upon time period.

Like other social instruments and inventions, indices and scales are perfected through use. For example, before 1930 the Division of Vital Statistics in the Bureau of the Census defined as rural, places of less than 10,000 population, while the Division of Population used less than 2500. Since then, both divisions use the latter figure. It

[1] "Health," *Missouri, Its Resources, People and Institutions* (Columbia, Mo.: University of Missouri, 1950).

	OCCUPATION GROUP	RATE PER HUNDRED EXAMINED		
		White and Negro	White *	Negro
	All occupations	25.4	23.8	45.4
	Professional and semi-professional workers	20.5	20.5	†
Rejection Rates, by	Farmers	41.1	36.4	58.0
Broad Occupational	Proprietors, clerical, sales and kindred workers	21.0	20.9	26.9
Group, of Eighteen- and	Craftsmen, foremen and kindred workers	20.4	19.9	39.6
Nineteen-Year-Old	Operatives and kindred workers	22.2	21.6	39.6
Registrants	Service workers	28.9	25.8	35.9
	Laborers except farm and mine	28.2	25.3	46.0
	Emergency workers and unemployed	37.7	37.2	44.9
	Students	23.3	23.0	31.6

TABLE 58

* Includes all races other than Negro.
† Insufficient data for calculation of rate.
Source: *Journal of the American Medical Association*, September 25, 1943, vol. 123, pp. 181–185.

was not until 1939 that certain mortality statistics were tabulated by place of residence rather than place of occurrence. Not all states were included in what was known as the registration area for vital statistics. Caution must therefore be used in determining long-range trends or in comparing rural and urban data. No readily acceptable social measures have been devised, although some have been proposed. Individual health standards are often set by certain physical and mental reactions, like the ratings of the Selective Service System. It is recognized that conditions vary from place to place, and that the test results depend upon the use to which they are put.

Rejection rates, Selective Service System. Probably the most startling revelation of the disparity between rural and urban health conditions was the publication of rejection rates by the Selective Service System. While its tabulation for rates of health and fitness was not classified into rural and urban, but by broad occupational groups, the figures are

still revealing. One tabulation made for the American Medical Association for 18- and 19-year-old registrants for a certain period is carried in Table 58. It shows that proportionately more farmers were rejected than any other major occupational group — 41 per cent, which is 16 points above the general average of 25 per cent. These figures have been questioned. It has been asked whether the tests were equally applicable to country and city boys, whether the "better" farm boys had migrated into urban occupations, and what had happened to the vaunted rural environment. Whatever the answers, it was clearly evident that all was not well with youth in rural society. The net effect was to focus public attention upon needed improvement.

The seven leading causes of rejection among all white registrants eighteen and nineteen years old were, in the decreasing order of occurrence, eye defects, mental disease, musculo-skeletal defects, cardio-vascular defects, educational defects, underweight, and mental deficiency. Half the rejections of

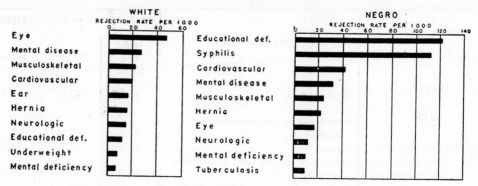

Figure 64. Ten Leading Causes of Rejection by Race, 18- to 19-Year-Old Registrants, December, 1942 – February, 1943.

Negro youths resulted from educational deficiency or from syphilis. These conclusions are drawn from figures based on local board and induction station examinations made during December, 1942, and January and February, 1943. Calculations based on other ages and other periods were somewhat different. For example, mental disease led the list of ten for white registrants for the period from April, 1942, to March, 1943, with 14.2 per cent of all rejections, and for the period from April, 1943, to December, 1943, with 19.2 per cent. Musculo-skeletal defects were second in both periods.[2] Rejections increased in direct relation to increasing age, and from the middle thirties on, reached over 50 per cent of all those examined. There were variations between and within regions. The highest rejection rates were in the South and the lowest in the Northwest. This was largely the result of the differential between white and Negro registrants.

Life expectancy by age — rural and urban. While the accompanying chart showing the trend of life expectancy for all white males in the ten original death registration states does not divide between rural and urban, it does show where the great gains were effected after 1900 (Fig. 65, p. 410). The real gains were in the younger age groups, among infants, children and young adults. This trend continues and its significance is very great, as noted in the chapter on rural families. In four decades, the average length of life in the United States increased nearly one third, or by about 15 years. Tabulations made as comparable as possible show that the life expectancy for those on farms and in small towns was influenced by their advantage at the beginning of the comparison, in 1900.[3] At that time the average length of life for rural white males was 10 years longer and for females 7½ years longer than for corresponding rates in cities. During the ensuing period the average for urban white males increased by 40 per cent while for rural males only by 19 per cent. For urban white females the gain was almost equally impressive. This would seem to indicate that life itself has taken on greater value, since greater efforts and larger expenditures have been made to preserve it. The trend has continued, but, it is anticipated that when the final calculations are made for the half century, rural and urban differences will have vanished or the urban may even have

[2] "Physical Examinations of Selective Service Registrants During Wartime," *Medical Statistics Bulletin* no. 3 (Washington, D.C.: Selective Service System, November 1, 1944).

[3] Frederick D. Mott and Milton I. Roemer, *Rural Health and Medical Care* (New York: McGraw-Hill, 1948), p. 52.

	AREA	TOTAL	RURAL	URBAN
TABLE **59** Infant Mortality by Urban and Rural Areas, 1948. Deaths Under One Year and Infant Mortality Rates, Exclusive of Still Births. Rates per 1000 Live Births	1. United States	32.0	33.2	31.2
	2. New England	27.1	27.6	26.9
	3. Middle Atlantic	27.6	27.9	27.5
	4. East North Central	29.1	28.3	29.5
	5. West North Central	28.1	26.0	30.1
	6. South Atlantic	35.5	36.1	34.7
	7. East South Central	38.3	36.9	40.9
	8. West South Central	40.6	38.8	42.1
	9. Mountain	42.3	46.6	38.5
	10. Pacific	28.1	31.4	26.6

Source: Federal Security Agency, Public Health Service, National Office of Vital Statistics, vol. 35, no. 17, October 16, 1950. Washington, D.C.

a slight advantage, depending on what adjustments are made to arrive at comparable figures. Length of life in the Negro population also has been increasing, but in 1940 was still about 11 years behind the white, or at about the same figure as the white had been 40 years earlier.[4]

Infant mortality — measure of a people's culture. Dr. Enid Charles, distinguished English student of family trends and vital statistics, maintains that infant mortality rates are a true measure of the culture of a people, indicating the real value placed on their human resources. Most health and medical people as well as vital statisticians seem to agree. The rural-urban situation by this measure is given in Table 59 for the year 1948, the latest year for which figures are available. See also Figure 66.

There are variations from the general averages. For example, when the total urban rate of 31.2 is broken down, cities of 100,000 or more population show a rate of only 28.9, while towns of 2500 to 10,000 have the unenviable rate of 36.0, nearly three points higher than the rural of 33.2. There is a

[4] Harold F. Dorn, "Changes in Mortality Rates, 1930 to 1940," Public Health Reports (December 4, 1932), No. 57: pp. 1858–1868.

good deal of variation among the nine regions included in the table; in five the rural rate is higher, and in four, the urban. Differences between white and Negro populations are pronounced: for the former, 29.9; for the latter, 45.7. The state with the lowest rates for whites was Connecticut, with 23.8, and the highest was New Mexico, with 63.2.

All infant mortality rates have declined sharply and steadily since 1900. In 1915, the total rate for the nation was nearly 100. The rate for the white population from that year to 1948 declined from 98.6 to 29.9, a drop of 70 per cent. The Negro rate went down even more, nearly 75 per cent, from 181.2 to 45.7. In 1940 the rural rate stood at 50.7 and the urban at 42.3. Such an array of facts would suggest that the family and society itself still have much to do with the great function of preserving life. Much has already been done and the large cities have outstripped other segments of our society. They have done it by deliberate effort, through social organization and by spending money as an investment in health.

Maternal mortality, a second measure. Authorities seem to agree that a second important index of a nation's health and welfare is the mortality rate for mothers. Like the

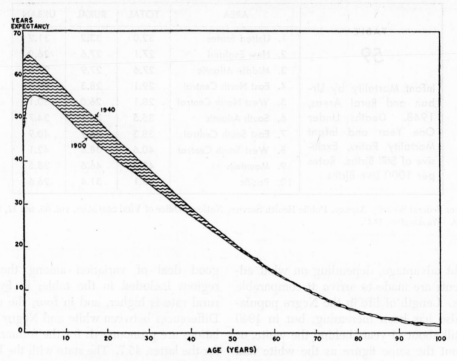

Figure 65. Life Expectancy of White Males in the
Ten Original Registration States, 1900 and 1940.

Shaded area between lines represents the gain in years in life expectancy,
at any age indicated. The greatest gains have been in the lower age levels.
Source: C. E. Lively, "Health," *Missouri, Its Resources, People, and Institutions* (Columbia: University of Missouri Press, 1950).

infant mortality rate, this also has declined
sharply. For the white population, it has
dropped from 6.0 per 1000 live births in
1915 to 0.9 in 1948, or 85 per cent. For the
non-white group, the drop was somewhat
slower, from 10.6 to 3.0, or nearly 73 per
cent. This is not greatly different from the
trend for the infant rate. The total maternal
mortality rate for the United States in 1948
was 1.2, the rural, 1.4, and the urban, 1.0.
Again, when the rural white is combined
with the towns, the rate is 1.4 times the rate
for cities of 100,000 or more population. The
non-white rate is 1.9 times the rate for the
larger cities. Variations among the nine
regions are definitely less than among the
infant rates; in three regions they are the

same, but in only one is the rural less than
the urban.[5]

General mortality rates, too general. General or "crude" death rates, so-called because
no adjustments are made for age or other
differentials, do not have great significance
for analyzing rural society. They show the
same general trends as the infant and maternal rates. In 1948 the rural rate was 8.9
per 1000 and the urban was 10.7; the white
rate was 9.7 and the Negro 11.4.[6] The urban

[5] *Maternal Mortality by Cause, Race and Urban
and Rural Areas,* 1948 (National Office of Vital
Statistics, *op. cit.,* vol. 35, no. 19, December 4,
1950).

[6] *Deaths by Urban and Rural Areas and by Race,*
1948 (National Office of Vital Statistics, *op. cit.,*
vol. 35, no. 5, February 21, 1950).

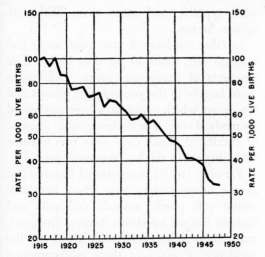

Figure 66. Infant Mortality Rates for the Birth-Registration States: 1915–48.

Source: *Vital Statistics — Special Reports — State Summaries,* XXXIV, No. 50 (Federal Security Agency, Washington, D.C., June 1, 1950).

death rate in 1900 was 50 per cent higher than the rural, but by 1940 it was only 15 per cent higher. In the 1950 calculations, if ages are held constant, differences will tend to disappear, another evidence that the traditional "rural" and "urban" divisions are losing their significance.

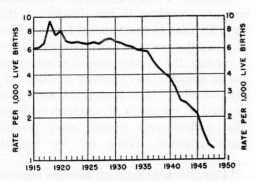

Figure 67. Maternal Mortality Rates for the Birth-Registration States: 1915–48.

Source: *Vital Statistics — Special Reports — State Summaries,* XXXIV, No. 50 (Federal Security Agency, Washington, D.C., June 1, 1950).

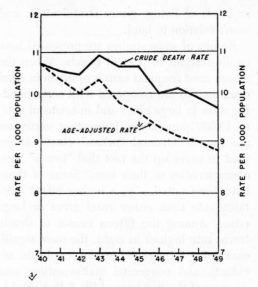

Figure 68. Crude and Age-Adjusted Death Rates for All Causes: United States, 1940–49.

Source: *Current Mortality Analysis,* VII, No. 13 (Federal Security Agency, Washington, D.C., November 29, 1950).

Main causes of death and sickness. The great modern killers are heart disease, cancer, pneumonia, and accidents, and these are not respecters of persons or country and city limits. Death rates alone, however, are not a complete indication of health conditions. There are also the burdens and hazards of sickness. Morbidity rates, intended to measure the extent of sickness, are less exact and less well reported than are mortality rates. No comprehensive analysis of the causes of death and sickness can be attempted but conclusions from some nationwide studies and from many local ones indicate that "by and large rural people appear to get sick from about the same causes as urban people."[7] Other bases for comparison are more meaningful, such as occupation, race, age, environment, and economic status. These are the same kinds of social factors encountered in other areas of analysis such

[7] Mott and Roemer, *op. cit.,* p. 87.

as levels of living, group stratification, and man's relation to land.

Results of some studies are presented here as illustrations of present trends. When the fifteen most frequent causes of death in rural communities are compared with corresponding rates in large cities and in towns of 2500 to 10,000 population, interesting variations are found. General "urban" classifications tend to cover up the fact that "towns" have characteristics of their own. Some of these have been noted, *e.g.*, a higher infant mortality rate than either rural areas or large cities. Among the fifteen causes of death, towns rate highest in eight, the most significant being intracranial lesions, nephritis, accidents, and congenital malformations and diseases of the first year of life.[8] Preventable diseases fatal to both children and adults are highest in certain rural areas. They include typhoid, malaria, pellagra, and hookworm, the very diseases which most large cities have nearly conquered. Chronic diseases were found to be high in certain counties in Missouri. The rates varied directly with age and income. Four fifths of the total days of illness occurred in less than a third of the households contacted.[9]

Chronic illnesses are a drain on people's energies, causing loss of time and money. Many of them trace back to some unremedied defect or untreated heart condition. It is reported that at least one sixth of the defects for which men were rejected by Selective Service could be readily remedied.[10] About 1,500,000 men with major defects were inducted and made fit for military duty, including 1,000,000 with dental defects, more than 250,000 with impaired vision, 100,000 with syphilis, and more than 7000 with serious hernia.

In Ohio residents of poor rural areas had a death rate about 10 per cent higher than residents of prosperous areas. Differences were largely in the younger age groups and for causes which could have been prevented by medical care. For communicable diseases of childhood, death rates were two to three times higher in the low economic areas.[11]

Farming has its occupational hazards just as the urban factory has. These are associated with plants, animals, and soils, and include fungus infections, trauma from animals, anthrax, and tularemia. However, the incidence of many of these environmental hazards is more directly related with sanitation and medical care than with agriculture as such, hookworm disease being the most conspicuous example.[12] Poor health in rural society is also directly related to poverty, which will be evident again and again as medical and hospital care and services are reviewed. Nutritional deficiencies, remedial defects, lack of sanitation, communicable diseases, chronic illnesses — these are the baneful symptoms of rural life wherever it is impoverished.

Accidents. Finally, accidents to American farmers, according to the director of the Farm Division of the National Safety Council, cause the loss of as much time as it takes to produce the average annual wheat crop, and an economic loss of nearly a billion dollars annually.[13] More than 17,000 farm people died as the result of accidents and another million were injured, many permanently crippled. While not the highest

---

[8] *Mortality Summary for Registration States.* National Office of Vital Statistics, Special Reports 16:29–221, July 16, October 12, 1942.

[9] Harold F. Kaufman, *Extent of Illness and Use of Medical Services in Rural Missouri* (Columbia: University of Missouri Progress Report 5, April, 1945).

[10] *Interim Report from the Subcommittee on Wartime Health and Education* (Seventy-eighth Congress Subcommittee Report 3, January, 1945).

[11] Dorn, "Mortality Rates and Economic Status in Rural Areas," *Public Health Reports* (January 5, 1940), no. 55: pp. 3–12.

[12] For an exhaustive analysis, see Mott and Roemer, *Rural Health and Medical Care,* particularly Chapter VI.

[13] M. Coe, "Farm Safety Work," *Better Farming Methods* (May–June, 1945), p. 24.

among all occupations, a rate of 54 deaths by accidents per 100,000 agricultural workers is more than double the rate of 20 deaths for the same number of workers in manufacturing industries. Farm machinery was involved in most of the fatal accidents; therefore, with the advance of technology on the farm must come changes in habits and attitudes.

Mental disorders. It is not possible to make comparisons between rural and urban populations, but it is important to call attention to the high rate of military rejections and discharges for "neuropsychiatric" causes. The Interim Report of the Senate Committee on Wartime Health and Education also points out that about two thirds of the illness encountered in general medical practice is essentially neuropsychiatric in origin, and that half of the patients in hospitals at any one time are there because of serious mental disorders.[14] The report even predicts that in any group of fifteen-year-olds, one out of twenty-two will someday be committed to a mental institution. This is sobering indeed.

Social implications — what are the rural health handicaps? Although the review of the rural health situation is far from complete, it is apparent that whatever the differences between rural and urban ways of life, there are inherent handicaps in some areas of rural society. These can be summed up briefly under three major social categories, population density, ability to pay, and differences in attitudes and traditions, or "the will to have."

1. *Geographic handicaps are readily identified.* For example, in a study of meeting health needs in Michigan, the number of miles to the nearest town with a doctor ranked as the second need; that is, the unmet needs increased with the distance from the

community center.[15] This kind of response bears a close relation to the shift of rural population toward city centers, even toward those of only 5000 population, which was traced in the rural-urban chapter. But distance is not only a physical handicap; it may become an excuse.

Sparsely settled country areas and scattered small villages and towns present a problem for adequate sanitation, sewage disposal, public health services, and hospitalization. While possibilities for travel have been greatly expanded, political inventions to draw people and centers together into workable units of local government and public authority are lagging behind, even though some reorganization is taking place, as the chapter on rural communities has shown.

Finally, climate and soil types may constitute handicaps to good health, as indicated before. For example, in certain southern rural areas the environment is favorable to the spread of malaria and the sandy soil makes it easy to transmit hookworm diseases.

2. *Ability to pay is the paradox in the rural health situation.* Medical care is correlated with income, not with need. Whatever comparative methods are used, it is always evident that, as the income groups go up, the percentage of families included goes down. The opposite is the case for the amount spent for health; it rises directly as income advances. Obviously, the differences do not arise from the relative degree of illness; when people have money, they spend money for health and medical care. This is evident in the budgets of every level-of-living study made. It is clear in the accompanying chart, and it holds for farm, village and city families, so to that extent the relation is not characteristic of rural society. If "wealth is health," from the individual and

[14] Subcommittee Report No. 3 (January, 1945).

[15] Charles R. Hoffer, *et al., Health Needs and Health Care in Michigan* (East Lansing: Michigan State College Special Bulletin 365, June, 1950).

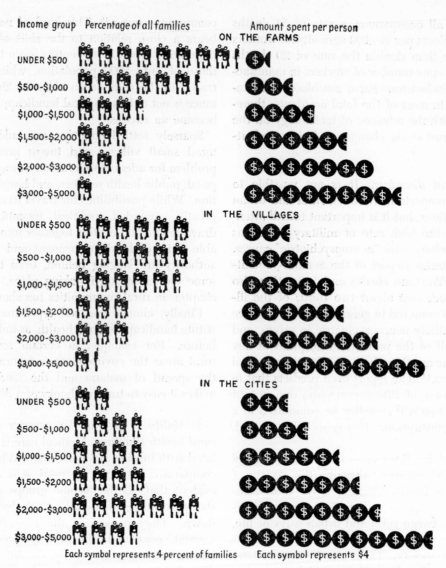

Income group	Percentage of all families	Amount spent per person

ON THE FARMS

IN THE VILLAGES

IN THE CITIES

Each symbol represents 4 percent of families   Each symbol represents $4

Figure 69. What Families Spend for Medical Care.
Source: *Farm Foundation Conference on Rural Health,* April, 1944.

family standpoint, it would seem to follow that from the point of view of social or human resources health is wealth. This was certainly recognized by Dr. Will Alexander, first administrator of the Farm Security Administration. In the early days of its organization, while policies were being formed, he insisted that "it is just plain good business to get rid of the hookworm." Therefore there was a regular item for health in family budgets, and those families that did not have to feed the hookworm could and did pay both principal and interest, and on time.

The joker in the health card-pack is, of

course, that medical expenses are relatively unpredictable. In any one year there are comparatively few families that have large doctor or hospital bills. In an average year about 68 per cent of all rural families, for example, pay only about 23 per cent of the total medical care expenditures of all rural people. But the difficulty arises from the fact that the lower-income groups have to spend a high percentage of their meager incomes in order to pay such bills, and even then they have to be satisfied with less than adequate care. This is probably true not simply because their incomes are low, but because they actually have a greater amount of illness than families in the higher income brackets. It is likewise in these families that the larger number of children are to be found. Both these relationships have been indicated earlier.

To be sure, modern medical care costs money, but many health authorities can show that if the amount of money already spent were spent more wisely, the whole situation could be greatly improved. Likewise, if the costs could be spread over more years and among more people, the burden upon any one family would not be too great. This view will be discussed in the next section. It is a principle which rural people have long since applied to another unforetellable menace — fires.

3. *Psychological handicaps are present among some rural people.* It is evident to those acquainted with the health situation among rural people that factors of attitudes and understanding are involved. Some health deficiencies and some of the lack of good medical care arise from a lack of understanding, failure to recognize early symptoms of trouble, to realize the serious consequences of some kinds of illnesses, and to respond to modern facilities available. The facilities may lie a little beyond the accustomed route of travel — the hospital or clinic in the not-too-far-away urban center. Or public opinion may be too little developed to give the county board courage to hire the second nurse, the full-time, specially trained public health officer, or a sanitary engineer.

Attitudes and traditions must also come in for their share of scrutiny. They are a part of the culture pattern and the system of values which traditionally belong to a people. But it is a mistaken idea to think that they are static or unchangeable. There are some farm people, and village and city people as well, who simply "do not like" doctors, dentists, or hospitals. In some rural communities it is tantamount to a confession of weakness to be seen coming from a doctor's office. Hospitals are places where people "go to die." You can imagine the reply of the frontiersman to the suggestion that he go to a hospital — "Not me. I'll take mine at home and die with my boots on." Reactions change with experience, actual and vicarious, as through education, and frequently the changes come quickly. It is a game of choice, as suggested in the chapter on standards of living. People set about getting what they want, what they value highly, and what they have seen others have. The attitude may soon prevail in rural quarters that you "cannot afford" to be without good medical care.

To sum up. The situation respecting rural health was summarized by a group called together recently to discuss medical care and health services for rural people, in terms of three lacks: (1) lack of adequate health education, facilities, and doctors; (2) lack of financial resources and interest to establish or maintain the necessary medical centers properly equipped and adequately staffed; and (3) lack of sufficient income to afford even the necessary medical services when they are available.[16]

[16] *Medical Care and Health Services for Rural People* (Chicago: Farm Foundation, April, 1944).

Planks in a Rural Health Program

It is agreed by those in the van of the rural health movement that health is not only an individual and family concern, but also a general social responsibility. This means that health and medical care, at least in the broad sense, must be available to all the people regardless of economic status, race, or geography. They maintain that this is the only way people can be efficient and happy. Just how such goals can and should be achieved is a matter of debate. The American tradition in this area of life, as in many others where social responsibility is recognized, has been to expect individuals, families, and voluntary associations to carry the load at first and insofar as they seem able, at least in the initial stages of any plan.[17] When the practical ways and means become established and when generalized needs are recognized, then government at some level — local, state or federal, and often at all three levels at the same time — steps in to help. This trend has been notable in what are now called public health programs of immunization, control of communicable disease, and the providing of public health nurses. The way government steps in to help is known as "grant-in-aid." This policy is employed in many social areas and traces back to 1860, when it was used to establish the land-grant agricultural colleges. It means that the entire nation comes to the aid of its smaller units in order to raise the general level of services to acceptable standards. It means, at least in the case of health, that "some general government programs of today represent special voluntary programs of yesterday." The proportion of medical costs borne by government is steadily increasing, especially in preventive medicine. The trend

will surely continue as efforts are made to level out uneven rural health situations which have been described.

Where public responsibility begins and ends, where the private individual or family has a "right" to public help, and where they must assume the burden are matters not settled once and for all under the American way of life. Conditions change, attitudes and public policies change. Government responsibilities to all private citizens are well established in regard to highways, parks, postal service, education. With the passage of the Social Security Act of 1935, one change took place, as will be traced in the next chapter; public assistance became a recognized "right." As yet social services in the fields of health and medical care are not so well established or defined. Policies are in the process of being hammered out in public and in private debate, as will be evident when compulsory *vs.* voluntary health insurance measures are discussed later in this chapter.

Three general measures or "planks" seem generally agreed upon as essential for a health program in rural society: first, protection and prevention; second, facilities and services; third, the spreading of costs. Such a division is over-simplified, and there are many details which cannot be mentioned here, but it will serve the purpose of the present discussion.

More protection and improved preventive services needed. The health situation in rural areas, described in the previous section, is far from hopeless, even though there are many difficulties and deficiencies. Great advances have been made in the fifty years of this century. Decrease in death rates and increase in length of life and general well-being are the evidence. Greatest promise of further improvement is in those causes of sickness and death which respond to better sanitation and immunization procedures,

---

[17] Roemer, "Government's Role in American Medicine, Brief Historical Survey," *Bulletin of History of Medicine* (18:146–168, July, 1945).

to better nutritional programs, and to earlier diagnosis and medical treatment.

Protection, prevention, and remedial measures are not evenly distributed or equally developed for different classes or locations of families. The Public Health Service lists thousands of communities in rural areas which need new, improved, or expanded water systems, sewage disposal systems, milk pasteurization plants, and health centers equipped for diagnostic and sanitary services. Evidence has accumulated that villages and small towns are increasingly service centers for rural people, both farm and non-farm. Certain health indices have suggested that such centers, even to 10,000 population, are the "forgotten areas" of modern society. They are not as "well off" judged by some tests as are the country or the larger city areas. They are too small for certain urban patterns of organization and too different for the well-organized and publicly supported agricultural services which have been described elsewhere. Here then, would seem to be at least one large area for projects during prosperous times. Profits of both industry and agriculture could well be "plowed back" into both public and private health enterprises which would ultimately raise the levels of living of the individual families, and would also protect and conserve the whole human resource.

1. *Food, shelter, and household facilities rank high in health protection.* Gains have been registered in this department of the rural economy. It has been shown in the chapter dealing with the rural home and its standards of living that "durable goods" have greatly increased. They represent refrigeration facilities made possible by rural electrification service and indoor running water with flush toilets to aid in better sanitation. Provisions of the Public Housing Act are intended to spread them more evenly.

2. *Public health services are important.* Early diagnosis of the cause of trouble and then prompt remedial measures are fundamental, as everyone realizes, but the problem is to make such services much more accessible to more families. It is now generally recognized that effective services of this nature must be organized and offered on a public basis.

As recently as 1935, only 615 counties of the more than 3000 in the United States had full-time public health services. Under the encouragement and assistance provided by the Social Security Act of 1935, the number had nearly tripled by 1942. In 1949, the Public Health Service reported 1242 public health units of various descriptions, the single county unit representing more than half. However, as Table 60 shows, more than a quarter, or 26.2 per cent, of the esti-

TABLE 60 Full-time Local Health Service, June 30, 1949	TYPE OF HEALTH ORGANIZATION	HEALTH UNITS		ESTIMATED POPULATION IN PER CENT
		Number	Per Cent	
	Total	1242	100	100
	Single county	667	53.7	26.7
	Local health district	276	22.2	9.8
	City	242	19.5	30.8
	State health district	57	4.6	6.5
	No health units reporting	—	—	26.2

Source: Report of Local Public Health Resources, 1949. Federal Security Agency, Public Health Service, December, 1950 Prepared by Clifford H. Greve.

mated population were still without the services of such public agencies. More than half the units had populations of less than 50,000, while the average was 86,000, due to some large city and state districts.

Health authorities state that $2 per capita per year is required to provide satisfactory public health services. In rural communities the per capita expenditures are hardly 50 cents annually, and when the most rural states are compared with the urban ones, their expenditures are only about half of that. There is direct correlation between size of community and per capita expenditure for public health services, and the larger the center, the greater the expenditure. This poses a real problem for equalizing health opportunities. Where a child chooses to be born has a direct bearing upon his chances to have a healthy life and live to a ripe old age.

Maps drawn to show distribution of public health services vary in terms of definitions used, but most of them indicate relatively complete coverage for those areas of the South where many diseases and the death rates (noted earlier) were relatively high. Although there is no standardized organization, the average county unit has a health officer, a sanitary inspector, one or more nurses, and a bacteriologist — all under the direction of a trained physician. Organization, of course, is not the only consideration; administration and trained personnel are fully as important. To improve sanitary conditions, it is necessary to have inspections; to detect diseases and their effects at their incipient stages, frequent health examinations are needed; and to secure coöperation from people themselves, continuous health education is essential.

According to representatives of the American Public Health Association, a good health department should have one public health nurse for each 5000 people, a sanitary officer for each 25,000 people, a trained

public health engineer for a unit of 50,000, a veterinarian for every 100,000 population. The smallest operating unit which health authorities advocate is made up of a full-time health officer, a nurse, a sanitarian, and an office clerk. The Association advocates that counties too small to meet such requirements combine with other counties and with the towns in them to compose a district of at least 50,000 people.

Delegates of the farm organizations to the Conference on Medical Care and Health Service, to which reference has been made, pointed out that a program in rural areas should include both the prevention and the care of disease, rather than one limited either to preventive work only or to treatment of illness only.

Many state boards of health, working with a committee of the National Public Health and Medical Associations, are urging legislation whereby their states can be redistricted into smaller units and given more trained personnel. They contend that this is necessary in order to secure more effective discovery of disease, better reporting, and improved sanitation. Federal funds are available to help, but the states must participate. In order for rural people in local communities to gain benefits from such "overhead" organization, they must work out their own plans, programs, and staff, as will be pointed out in the last section of the chapter.

3. *Education and more education.* It is recognized that rural people must become aware of the medical facilities and health services that are now available. This should lead to a greater and better utilization of them. Rural people need to be stimulated to recognize the values of good health and the importance of preventive measures and adequate medical services. Finally, they must be more willing to budget in advance and then to pay more for health purposes. This simply means continuous education.

There are many practical means which can be employed. A primary responsibility lies with the public health service and with the school system. Health authorities say that a local expenditure of one dollar per person is the minimum to spend on education directed toward the protection of health and the prevention of illness. When a local community is willing to spend its own money, it is in a position to ask for help from state and federal sources.

An Agricultural Health Association, in its report on Newton County, Mississippi, urges that more money be spent for educational work, and that Negro leaders should be commissioned to carry information, especially regarding the preventive aspects of rural health programs, to the Negro population of the county, and that when a second nurse is employed, she should be a colored person.[18]

Health programs in the schools need to include not only medical examinations and immunization, but in many situations hot lunches and actual medical and dental services. The directly educational phases need to be related to nutrition, the biological and

social sciences, and to a constructive recreational program in the school and in the community.

More medical care and health facilities. In the second plank of a rural health program many items are included, too many to discuss in detail. Mainly they are medical personnel such as doctors, dentists, and nurses, and medical facilities such as hospitals, centers, and equipment. When Dr. Mott sums up the total picture of rural health and medical care, the shortage of essential health personnel stands out as the most striking deficiency.[19]

1. *More doctors are the crux of the problem.* The doctor is the pivotal person about whom medical and even hospital services are built. Studies of local rural situations suggest that the tradition of dependence upon the family doctor as a source of health information and direct contact services still prevails.[20] Where the number and kind of doctors are adequate, circumstances are also favorable for nurses and technicians as well as for physical facilities. On the other hand,

[18] James E. Montgomery, *Newton County, Mississippi, Agricultural Health Association* (Washington, D.C.: United States Department of Agriculture, August, 1944).

[19] Mott and Roemer, *op. cit.*, p. 149.
[20] Olaf F. Larson and Donald G. Hay, "Family Utilization of Health Resources in Rural Areas," *New York State Journal of Medicine* (vol. 51, no. 3, February, 1951).

TABLE 61 School Physicians Employed by Boards of Education, 1948–49	POPULATION OF CENTERS	NUMBER OF SCHOOL SYSTEMS REPORTING	NUMBER OF PHYSICIANS EMPLOYED (FULL–TIME) EQUIVALENTS	PER CENT OF SCHOOLS REPORTING ONE OR MORE FULL–TIME EQUIVALENTS
	Total	773	256.0	8.7
	100,000 and over	45	151.4	60.0
	30,000 to 99,999	99	39.7	20.2
	10,000 to 29,999	194	44.2	9.3
	5,000 to 9,999	204	15.4	1.0
	2,500 to 4,999	231	5.3	.0

Source: Research Bulletin, "Personnel and Relationships in School Health, Physical Education and Recreation," XXVIII, no. 3, October, 1950, National Education Association, Washington, D.C.

where these are admittedly inadequate, a downward spiral is easily set in motion, for a general practitioner, often beyond the average age, does not attract specialists or well-trained nurses. There is failure to build up the kind and volume of practice necessary to support an up-to-date center for diagnostic and treatment services.

The shortage of well-prepared physicians in rural areas is not new. Even in 1938, strictly rural counties had only a third as many in proportion to population as did urban counties. More recent reports by a federal agency known as the Procurement and Assignment Services indicate that the 141 counties having more than 5000 people per active physician were practically all rural counties. This disparity in distribution is associated with other but related circumstances, as has just been suggested. One factor in the rural situation is the selective movement of physicians. In the past, younger doctors and recent graduates from medical schools have tended to move toward urban centers. Those who remained in rural areas were older, on an average, than city physicians. In four states, the average age was progressively lower as the population of the center increased.

The American Medical Association estimates that a critical level is reached when there is one physician for every 1500 people. Below that, health and productivity are endangered. To meet this standard in rural communities, much hard work will be required. The odds are already against them, since opinion polls taken among young army and navy doctors show that the vast majority wants specialists' training and practice, and preferably with a group. Only 12.5 per cent indicated a desire for rural practice.[21]

However, there is some evidence of a reversal of this trend. In Michigan, the movement of physicians toward Detroit reached its high point about 1930. The dean of the

[21] *Interim Report, op. cit.*

College of Medicine at Syracuse, New York, found about 25 per cent of the 1930 graduates located in communities of less than 5000 population, compared with 18 per cent of the 1925 graduates. A more recent study of the locations of returning armed services medical personnel shows a larger proportion going to rural than to urban communities.[22]

Another factor in securing an adequate supply of doctors in rural areas is the prediction of a general shortage. Rural communities must therefore expect to continue to compete with urban communities. Comparisons made for the total number of physicians and specialists for the whole United States from 1909 to 1949 would indicate that we are losing rather than gaining ground. In 1909 there were 1.49 per 1000 population, in 1949 only 1.37, and the low point of 1.25 was reached in 1929.[23] Estimates of shortages by 1960 would be far in excess of possible supply if ratios which prevailed in 1940 were maintained. There were three more class A medical schools in the United States in 1950 than in 1930, 79 compared to 76, but the enrollment per 10,000 people dropped from 1.75 to 1.65 in the period.

2. Doctors respond to the purchasing power. Again, in 1938 counties with a per capita income of more than $600 had eight times as great a proportion of doctors to population as did counties with a per capita income of less than $100. Another associated factor certainly is the lack of hospi-

[22] Nathan Sinai, *Report of the Committee on Medical Service and Health Agencies* (Lansing: Michigan State Medical Society, 1933). J. W. Mountain, "Relocation of Physicians, a Prerequisite to Better Medical Care," *Journal of the American Medical Association* (Sept. 23, 1944). Virginia Shuler, "Location of Physicians," *Journal of the American Medical Association* (May 17, 1947).

[23] Joseph M. Mountain, *et al.*, "Estimates of Future Physician Requirements, Health Service Areas" (Washington, D.C.: Public Health Bulletin 305, 1949).

tal, diagnostic, and laboratory facilities in rural areas. Hospitals, independently of wealth or size of community, seem to attract doctors. This is suggested by the results of a study by the United States Public Health Service which indicates that among counties with per capita incomes of less than $300, those with no hospital beds had 60 per cent fewer doctors in proportion to population than did those counties with 250 or more general hospital beds. The hospital, it has been pointed out, is a sort of symbol of health in the community just as the school is the symbol of education.[24]

Numerous local and state studies bear out the general trends just reviewed. In North Carolina, for example, the number of doctors in the strictly rural area fell from 1125 in 1914 to 719 in 1940. In the latter year, 73 per cent of the population lived in rural territory, although only 31 per cent of the state's physicians were found there.[25]

The answers to the question, "Is there a doctor in town?" will then depend upon hospital facilities, opportunity for the doctor to be associated with other physicians, and a chance to earn a good living and have a comfortable home.[26] Farmers and villagers will have to revise their family's expenditures for medical care upward if these conditions are to be provided. This should be quite possible in a period of prosperity but it will require deliberate effort and a break from traditional patterns.

3. *More hospitals and medical centers are*

24 *Medical Care and Health Services for Rural People,* Farm Foundation, 600 South Michigan Avenue, Chicago, April, 1944. (Elin Anderson, p. 213).

25 *Medical Care and Hospital Facilities for Rural People in North Carolina,* summary report and recommendations of the Committee on Hospitals and Medical Care for Rural People, submitted to the Governor's Commission on Hospitals and Medical Care, October 11, 1944.

26 *Is There A Doctor In Town?* (Washington, D.C.: Community Health Series no. 5. Federal Security Agency, United States Health Service).

required. Formerly a hospital, at least in most rural areas, was considered a place of last resort for cases of very severe illness or serious accident, and all too often, as has been suggested earlier, as a place in which to die. The modern conception is quite different. It calls for the combining into one institution, or at least in one building or center, the three major functions of medical care — preventive, diagnostic, and therapeutic services. It means bringing together doctors and their offices, needed laboratory equipment, hospital beds for patients, and even the preventive work. It encourages group practice by physicians, surgeons, and dentists. It makes possible research and experimentation, and it stimulates the desire to exchange and to disseminate medical knowledge and better health information.

Doctors, under these circumstances, will not need to become defensive regarding the private ownership of some house which they have transformed into a hospital at their own expense and which they therefore consider their bailiwick for only their own patients. With some of these worries removed, they can concern themselves with some of the preventive health problems of their communities. Such a change in perspective and in motive is likely to have an important effect upon the thinking of the people themselves in regard to health matters. In most cities it has been recognized for a long time that it is in the people's interests to have hospitals and health centers run by the entire community through the municipal government, or by non-profit associations, such as coöperatives, churches, and fraternal or other social groups.

Hospital problems in rural areas tend to pyramid — not enough hospital beds, low occupancy, poor quality in hospital service. There is not complete agreement among hospital and medical authorities as to what should be considered adequate hospital service in rural areas. In recent discussions a standard of 3.5 or four general beds per 1000 population has been considered; five or more beds for that population unit may be required in cities. Most rural areas do not have even two beds per 1000 people, and there are hundreds of rural communities with no hospitals at all. There are 450 counties in which there are only proprietary hospitals — that is, operated for profit — and in these same counties there were only 1.5 beds per 1000 population. Comparing states by percentage of rural population, the range in 1942 was from 4½ beds per 1000 people in six states and the District of Columbia, with less than 30 per cent rural, to two beds per 1000 in eight states with 70 per cent or more rural.[27]

Another disturbing factor is that many hospitals in rural communities are not being used to capacity. This increases the costs per unit or reduces the amount and quality of nurse and attendant services. It is esti-

[27] Mott and Roemer, *op. cit.*, p. 226.

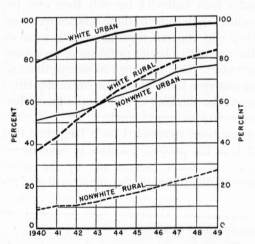

Figure 70. Per Cent of Live Births Occurring in Hospitals by Race for Urban and Rural Areas: United States, 1940–49.

Source: *Vital Statistics — Special Reports — National Summaries*, XXXVI, No. 5 (Federal Security Agency, Washington, D.C., July 2, 1951).

mated that there should be at least an 80 per cent occupancy. But occupancy tends to go down with the percentage of the population which is rural, even approaching 50 per cent in some areas. This is a contradiction difficult to understand: rural people with fewer hospital beds available than urban people occupy them relatively less, despite higher incidence of some diseases. Reasons are not simple; attitudes are involved, as are relative costs, distances, and incomes.

4. *Some rural indices do point upward.* A discriminating index, child births in hospitals and attended by a physician, shows a sharply rising curve among rural white children from 1940 to 1948. The percentage rose from 39 to 82, compared with a rise in urban areas from 80 to 98 per cent. The rate for rural non-whites, including but not exclusively Negroes, was distressingly low, only 28 per cent in 1948, while the urban figure for that year was 78 per cent. Rural and urban distributions for 1949 are shown in Table 62.

5. *Size of hospital and size of rural community must be related.* In 1944 it was reported that the American Medical Association had registered 6655 hospitals. Of the 3300 hospitals not registered, the vast majority were in small towns or rural areas. The American College of Surgeons also has an approval program. Its representatives will not even consider for registration a hospital of fewer than twenty-five beds; experience has shown that it is not worth while to do so. In Ohio only one in six small hospitals of less than fifty beds was able to meet the minimum requirements of this agency.[28]

General agreement as to minimum size for a hospital seems to be changing from thirty to fifty beds. If the upper standard of four

[28] A. R. Mangus, *Hospitals for Rural People in Ohio* (Columbus: Ohio Agricultural Experiment Station Mimeograph Bulletin 184, Feb. 1945).

	REGION	URBAN	RURAL
TABLE	1. United States	94.3	75.8
62	2. New England	98.9	94.3
	3. Middle Atlantic	97.8	90.8
	4. East North Central	96.6	91.3
Proportion of Live Births	5. West North Central	97.0	88.8
in Hospital Attended by	6. South Atlantic	87.0	58.8
Physician, 1949	7. East South Central	81.1	48.5
	8. West South Central	85.8	67.2
	9. Mountain	95.1	87.0
	10. Pacific	98.8	97.5

Source: Births by Person in Attendance, United States, Each Division and State, 1949.   Federal Security Agency, Public Health Service, vol. 36, no. 5, July 2, 1951.

beds per 1000 rural people is assumed, then a population of 12,500 would be required for a fifty-bed hospital, and this is obviously beyond the range of possibility for many rural communities, especially when present high costs of building and equipment are considered.

This argument on the basis of size is not only over-simplified, but it rests on an unsound premise. Not every community can expect to be self-sufficient and supply all the social institutions and services its citizens need. The trends traced in other chapters are in the other direction, the direction of some specialization and of greater interdependence of communities, rural with rural and rural with urban as well. Then, like education, health is not the sole responsibility of local communities and local units of government. The principle of equalization has come to be recognized, and it should be applied to health programs for rural society.

6. *Network of interdependent health centers and hospitals is now possible.* The general plan advocated by the U.S. Surgeon General has now become a reality through the Hospital Survey and Construction Act of August, 1946. He expressed its purpose in the following terms: "For the American people to have good health and medical care, we (the people) must provide the workshops of medicine — modern hospitals and health centers — and they must be distributed geographically throughout the country in proportion to need." The Federal Government, through the principle of grant-in-aid, pays one third of the cost of the survey, and the coöperating states must provide two thirds. Grants for construction are made on the basis of the surveys and the programs submitted. The amount of the grant to the states depends on the number of people and the annual per capita income. This means that the states where people have lower incomes will receive more money per person than the wealthier states.

Actual construction costs are divided according to the same formula as the survey costs, on one-third and two-thirds basis. Since 1948, when the first $75 million was appropriated for the grants to the states, more than 1500 construction projects have been approved. The projects have been mainly for small general hospitals in communities of less than 10,000 population. It is estimated that 75,000 beds have been added to the nation's total by this plan. Centers of this size will benefit greatly, since it will be recalled that by some standards they were in greater need than were rural areas or larger urban centers.

The general plan makes possible an interrelated system which may include four main types of medical units: a local community health center, a rural area hospital, a district hospital, and a base or regional hospital. The hospitals may be public or private non-profit institutions, and may serve for general purposes or for such specialized needs as tuberculosis or mental or chronic diseases. The program does not mean all new construction, since many types of hospitals already exist in many areas, and these may require only remodeling or additions. From the social point of view the plan makes for better organization and closer coordination of all presently available or future facilities.

Community or public health centers are defined as publicly owned facilities for health services, including laboratories, clinics, and offices for professional public health people. They may serve as local centers for diagnosis and emergency purposes and become the directive headquarters for programs of health protection and disease prevention.

The rural hospital might be so located as to be accessible to several local health centers, and in places large enough to warrant larger construction so as to provide additional medical, surgical, obstetrical, and laboratory services. The district hospitals, in turn, might be related to a number of the smaller hospitals so that increased specialization in both medical facilities and personnel could be available. Specialists might visit the small hospitals on occasion or be ready when patients were brought in. Instruction for internes and facilities for group work of various kinds could be provided in the district center.

The base hospital would be the central unit or hub of the whole system. Its service area might include one or two states or a section of one large state. The base hospital would be the teaching hospital, staffed with medical and surgical specialists,

equipped for complete diagnostic services and designed to carry on extensive postgraduate work and important research. Studies would include tuberculosis, nervous and mental diseases, contagious diseases, and orthopedic and chronic diseases. Supplementary facilities of various kinds could be devised. For sparsely settled areas of low income, there must be mobile clinics staffed by a physician and nurse or a dentist and technician. They could undertake services and instruction in maternal and child care, in mental hygiene or immunization. Salaries and equipment could come from public funds or by a group prepayment plan or a combination of both. Ambulance service could also be arranged from out-district clinics to local or regional hospitals. Experiences of the battlefields, with motor equipment, including planes, should prove valuable.

Such a plan for an interdependent network of medical centers constitutes a great ideal or master plan for present and future development. When translated into a state pattern and transferred to a map, the interconnections become more apparent, as the map of Wisconsin shows (Figure 71). On this map the regional boundaries are shown and the routes of referral to area centers. In a more detailed map, boundaries are also indicated for the smaller area hospitals.

Such broad planning should help states and their local communities cope more effectively with their health problems. It should create opportunities which will attract doctors, dentists, and nurses to rural and town communities as they return from duties with the Armed Services or as they are ready to leave the medical schools.

This is not a short-run program, since the Public Health Service estimates that as of January 1, 1950 about double the number of hospital beds were needed as were available and "acceptable." This meant 1,850,000

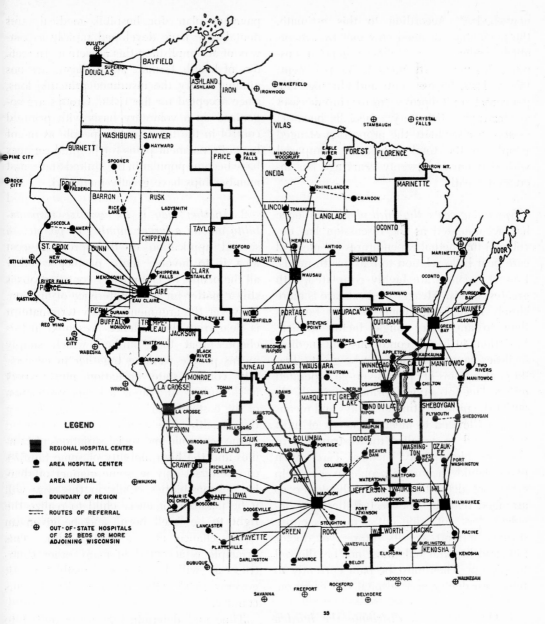

DULUTH
SUPERIOR
DOUGLAS
BAYFIELD
ASHLAND
ASHLAND
IRON
WAKEFIELD
IRONWOOD
VILAS
STAMBAUGH
CRYSTAL
FALLS

WASHBURN
SAWYER
HAYWARD
PINE CITY
BURNETT
SPOONER
PRICE
PARK
FALLS
MINOCQUA-
WOODRUFF
EAGLE
RIVER
FOREST
FLORENCE
IRON MT.

ROCK
CITY
POLK
FREDERIC
BARRON
RICE
LAKE
RUSK
LADYSMITH
CHIPPEWA
TAYLOR
ONEIDA
RHINELANDER
CRANDON
LINCOLN
TOMAHAWK
LANGLADE
MARINETTE

OSCEOLA
AMERY
ST. CROIX
NEW
RICHMOND
DUNN
MENOMONIE
CHIPPEWA
FALLS
CLARK
STANLEY
MEDFORD
MERRILL
ANTIGO
MARATHON
WAUSAU
SHAWANO
OCONTO
MENOMINEE
MARINETTE
DOOR

STILLWATER
RIVER FALLS
PIERCE
HASTINGS
CLAIRE
EAU CLAIRE
WOOD
MARSHFIELD
PORTAGE
SHAWANO
OCONTO
STURGEON
BAY
KEWAUNEE
ALGOMA

RED WING
LAKE
CITY
WABASHA
PEPIN
DURAND
BUFFALO
MONDOVI
TREMPE-
LEAU
JACKSON
NEILLSVILLE
WAUPACA
CLINTONVILLE
NEW LONDON
WAUPACA
APPLETON
BROWN
GREEN
BAY
OUTAGAMIE
KAUKAUNA

WINONA
WHITEHALL
ARCADIA
BLACK
RIVER
FALLS
JUNEAU
ADAMS
WAUSHARA
WAUTOMA
NEENAH
WINNEBAGO
OSHKOSH
CALU-
MET
CHILTON
MANITOWOC
TWO
RIVERS
MANITOWOC

MONROE
LA CROSSE
SPARTA
TOMAH
ADAMS
BERLIN
MARQUETTE
GREEN
LAKE
FOND DU LAC
SHEBOYGAN
PLYMOUTH
SHEBOYGAN

VERNON
VIROQUA
HILLSBORO
MAUSTON
RIPON
FOND DU LAC
WAUPUN

RICHLAND
REEDSBURG
SAUK
BARABOO
COLUMBIA
PORTAGE
DODGE
BEAVER
DAM
WASHING-
TON
WEST
BEND
OZAUK-
EE
PORT
WASHINGTON

CRAWFORD
RICHLAND
CENTER
COLUMBUS
WATERTOWN
HARTFORD

WAUKON
PRAIRIE
DU CHIEN
BOSCOBEL
GRANT
IOWA
DANE
MADISON
DODGEVILLE
STOUGHTON
FORT
ATKINSON
JEFFERSON
OCONOMOWOC
WAUKESHA
WAUKESHA
MIL.
MILWAUKEE

DUBUQUE
LANCASTER
LA FAYETTE
PLATTEVILLE
DARLINGTON
GREEN
MONROE
ROCK
JANESVILLE
BELOIT
WALWORTH
ELKHORN
BURLINGTON
KENOSHA
RACINE
RACINE
KENOSHA

SAVANNA
FREEPORT
ROCKFORD
WOODSTOCK
BELVIDERE
WAUKEGAN

LEGEND

■ REGIONAL HOSPITAL CENTER
● AREA HOSPITAL CENTER
• AREA HOSPITAL
— BOUNDARY OF REGION
--- ROUTES OF REFERRAL
⊕ OUT-OF-STATE HOSPITALS OF 25 BEDS OR MORE ADJOINING WISCONSIN

53

Figure 71. Wisconsin Hospital Construction Plan:
General Hospital Service Areas by Regions.
Source: State Board of Health (Madison, Wisconsin: July 1, 1951).

new beds.[29] According to this estimate, the percentage of need now met by acceptable standards is as follows: general hospital, 51 per cent; mental, 55 per cent; tuberculosis, 55 per cent; and chronic, 11.5 per cent. Hospital provisions for chronic cases are far from satisfactory, especially because, as shown elsewhere, the proportion of aged people in the total population compared with that ten and twenty years ago has increased greatly.

Spreading costs, the third plank. Evidence has accumulated as the discussion has developed that actual expenditures for medical care bear little relation to real health needs. Lowest incomes are highly correlated with greatest needs. Meager medical care is more closely related to income level of families than to any other single factor studied. Variations in health conditions and medical facilities have been shown to be great. Traditional systems of "pay-as-you-go" operated on the "fee-for-service" principle simply do not fit the present situation. Ways and means must be devised to meet the needs of most people and to equalize the distribution of costs of high-quality medical care. Such plans should encourage people to seek help early, not deter them. They should be so arranged that the unexpected illness or accident does not wipe out a family's entire savings or mortgage its future; yet doctor bills and hospital bills must not be allowed to pile up. They must be paid currently so that both doctor and hospital can carry on.

1. *One way is to distribute the burden over longer periods of time.* One application of the principle of spreading the costs of medical care is to distribute them over long periods of time, beginning before the bill is rendered. Health insurance and group prepayment plans for hospital, medical, and dental care have developed rapidly as one way of accomplishing this objective. In matters of health, farmers and villagers are beginning to try the insurance principle long since accepted for fire risks. Groups are organized on a voluntary basis with primary control in the hands of the people as members. Prepayment plans for hospital services have become popular in the United States and memberships have greatly increased.

2. *Another way is to equalize responsibility among a larger number of people.* A second application of the spread-the-cost idea is to involve more people; whether all the people by compulsory contributions is still a matter for wide difference of opinion. However the arguments finally terminate, it is clear from the evidence presented in this chapter that the "public," which simply means people working together in community, county, state, or nation, must expect in the future to assume a larger proportion of the costs of rearing children and keeping them healthy. The wide differences observed in the economic and social situations of families and the high mobility of some families can be offset only by some manner of sharing responsibilities. Only in this way will it be possible for every child to realize the right to be "well born" and be given an equal chance at life and health. This principle is accepted in many other countries, as will be shown directly, and it governs many other areas of life in this country.

Time and determination are required to change fixed social ways and established institutions. This phase of a study of society, rural or urban, is one of the most fascinating as well as the most disturbing, if one is at all personally involved. The histories of social change are interesting tales. For example, Boston nearly burned up three times before public fire protection was effectively

[29] *Public Health Reports* (Washington, D.C.: Federal Security Agency), vol. 65, no. 45, November 10, 1950.

organized [30] and private wells slowly gave way to a central water supply. Sewage systems are frightfully expensive, even in small communities. Sometimes changes are opposed by those who would seem likely to profit most. At other times those with vested interests will not or cannot change because they would lose money or prestige or both. Here society steps in to adjust, regulate, or help equalize the shock of change. This is the service performed by the Hospital Survey and Construction Act just described. Will the costs of insuring adequate hospital and medical care be next?

3. *Voluntary or compulsory?* The crucial argument concerns the voluntary *vs.* the compulsory features of various insurance plans. There is fairly general agreement upon the fundamental aim — medical care for everyone on some coöperative basis. It is probable that any plan finally accepted will not reflect either extreme position, but some combination of several public and private procedures. No one is advocating the "nationalization" of the American Red Cross or the National Tuberculosis Association, and it is probable that many other medical agencies will remain in private hands whatever else may be done.

Health and medical care have now become a major political issue, and this is a sure sign of great public interest. There are two main issues, control and coverage. One view is that health is primarily a state and local concern and that extension of voluntary prepayment plans with state and federal help will solve the problem. This might be considered a voluntary state-federal system. The other view is that health is of national concern and the problem should be solved through nation-wide compulsory insurance to provide comprehensive medical services.

4. *Voluntary prepayment plans.* Advocates of voluntary health insurance, such as the Blue Cross and various medical society prepayment hospitalization plans, contend that such systems will be adequate when they have had time to be fully extended and if supplemented by tax grants for medical care to those who need public assistance. The argument is premised on the belief that medical services by such voluntary means can be extended to at least three fourths of the population, and that no basic change is required in the present organization of medical services. However, they agree that something must be done to enable the low-income families to help themselves provide needed services. While this is considered a state and local problem, the federal government should help by grants-in-aid. It would involve the use of some "means test" by which those who receive the services could prove their poverty. Great emphasis is placed on the idea that health is a very personal matter, primarily a family matter, that the relation of physician and patient must be safeguarded, that the patient must be free to choose his physician and the physician his patients, that any administration must be highly decentralized to localities where people who use the services live, so that such guarantees can be made explicit and sure.

Critics of the voluntary systems contend that they cannot be made universal and indicate that at present over half the population is not covered. They point to budget studies showing that poor rural families simply do not and cannot spend the amounts necessary to join and maintain memberships in such systems. They say that no clear class line separates relief from non-relief recipients, that the health and the economic status of many families change with the business cycle or with unforeseen sickness or accident, and that a free American should not be compelled to take a "means test" whenever he is unable to provide medical care for

[30] Carl Bridenbaugh, *Cities in the Wilderness* (New York: Ronald Press, 1938).

himself and members of his family. There would have to be (and here the question of legality is raised) some means of supervision and control over the private voluntary agencies, since public agencies would be underwriting the deficits involved in their plans for helping low-income families, that is, those who fail to meet the tests. Thus the "con" arguments for the voluntary systems lead directly into the "pro" arguments for national compulsory plans.

The extent of coverage of the voluntary systems in 1950 was summarized by Dr. Dean A. Clark, Director of Massachusetts General Hospital, in a report made to the United States Senate Committee on Labor and Public Welfare.[31] It is estimated that 75,000,000 people had some hospital insurance that year, and that 52,000,000 also had some protection against the cost of medical services. In percentages, this meant that 15 per cent of the population had hospital insurance only, 21 per cent had hospital and surgical, 11 per cent had hospital, surgical, and limited medical, 3 per cent (about 4,000,000) had what was called complete coverage, but 50 per cent had none at all. The proportion of persons carrying hospital insurance was twice as large in urban as in rural states, and twice as high in high-income as in low-income states. Blue Cross subscribers accounted for half of those with hospital insurance.

In his report Dr. Clark emphasized that the general health of people cannot be improved by insurance alone. There must be preventive medicine, early diagnosis, and treatment outside of hospitals in order to reduce hospital and medical care. Other factors also must be considered, such as the economic and emotional condition of families, availability of medical personnel, and attitudes and understanding about health needs and medical service. All fronts must be attacked simultaneously, he said.

5. *Nation-wide compulsory health insurance.* President Truman, in his message to the Congress on a National Health Program in November, 1945, urged the establishment of a national system of compulsory health insurance. It was to have been implemented by the proposed National Health Act introduced in Congress the same day of his message. This bill has been popularly known as the Wagner-Murray-Dingell Bill (1st Sess. S. 1606, 79th Congress). Since then proposals and counter proposals have been made, such as the Flanders Bill, the Taft Bill, the Hill Bill, and the Thomas Bill.

One of the chief proponents of the compulsory plan, Oscar R. Ewing, Federal Security Administrator, summarizes its main provisions as follows:[32]

1. A 3 per cent payroll deduction on annual incomes up to $4800, to be shared equally by employer and employee — on the same principle that old-age and survivor's insurance are operated. Provision is also made for the participation of self-employed persons, (farm laborers and domestic workers with premium collections through a stamp plan.)

2. The insured, in return for these payments, would receive needed medical care for himself and dependents. This care would ultimately cover all services necessary to prevent, diagnose, and cure disease — care by a general practitioner and by specialists, hospital care, laboratory service, X-ray, unusually expensive drugs and medicines, special appliances, and eye glasses. Reasonable limits would be placed on the length of hospital benefits.

3. The administration of the plan would be primarily on a state and a local basis.

---

[31] Dr. Dean A. Clark and Cozette Hapney, "Health Insurance Plans," *Modern Medicine* (July 15, 1951).

[32] With Dr. George F. Lull, "How Shall We Pay for Health Care?" (New York: Public Affairs Pamphlet No. 152, First Edition, 1949).

There would be a National Committee representing the medical profession and other interested groups to advise with the Federal Government on broad standards. The actual community operation would be in the hands of local people — committees of doctors and representative citizens — who would consult with participating doctors to determine a fair scale of fees. Physicians may, if they choose, elect to be paid on a capitation basis, so much per patient per year. Limits would be set on the number of patients per doctor.

4. The patient would be free to choose his own doctor and to change doctors. A doctor would be free to reject patients. No doctor would be required to practice under the plan, or a doctor could combine an independent and an insurance practice. He would in no sense be an employee of the government.

5. Physicians practicing under the plan would have precisely the same amount of paper work as is required of them under voluntary insurance plans. A doctor deals with malingerers and hypochondriacs as he does under voluntary insurance plans.

Critics of compulsory plans raise objections common to any new public service. They say it would "socialize" medicine, regiment doctors, eliminate personalized medical care, and open the way for federal intrusion into other phases of life. They express the fear that it might become a step toward a "welfare state," and they make the term imply some objectional form of government. They argue that government administration is inefficient, and above all that it would be too costly — more than society can afford on top of other social security provisions — and that everyone should not be required to contribute whether or not they need or use the services.

Both rural and urban people have a big stake in these proposed plans for health care and protection. They must decide which of the proposals offers greatest promise of making medical services available to all, and then make their decisions known in legislative circles. That there is still much to be done in the way of familiarizing people with the issues involved is shown by a recent canvass of public opinion in Michigan. About 1100 households, open-country, village and urban, were interviewed. Nearly two thirds said they did not feel that any major health problem existed in their communities. Only 16½ per cent had heard of the Wagner-Murray-Dingell Bill, and only one third were familiar with the term "socialized medicine."

Group Plans in This and Other Countries

There are already many different group plans for financing medical care, some voluntary and some compulsory. A few will be described briefly as a basis for further discussion and comparison with known local situations.

Farm Security Administration medical care program. This plan was the outgrowth of the agency's general rehabilitation efforts and is based on the voluntary prepayment principle. The rates paid were based on the average ability of borrowers in any area to pay, with very little use of subsidy. With few exceptions plans have been worked out in coöperation with local medical societies on the basis of agreements with state medical associations. There is a wide variety of such plans, especially in detail of operation.[33]

At its peak the program covered about 117,000 farm families or over 600,000 persons, and extended into more than a third of the counties of the nation. In 1946 the F. S. A. was abolished by an act of Congress,

[33] *Group Medical Care for Farmers* (Washington, D.C.: Farm Security Administration Publication 75, 1941).

and many of its functions were taken over by a new agency, the Farmers' Home Administration.

Rural health coöperatives.[34] In the middle of 1949, a record of 101 rural health coöperatives had been obtained. Of this number, forty-eight were given special study. Their purpose was stated in very simple terms, quite familiar to those who know rural society: neighbor helping neighbor in time of sickness. The help was organized democratically; there was a board of directors to handle the affairs of the association, and there was a membership on the family basis with initial fees ranging from $25 to $100 and subsequently regular dues. Professional matters were in the hands of the doctors with whom the boards arranged for services. During 1949 there were 24,000 families in active membership. Member families usually lived within ten to twenty-five miles of the coöperative headquarters. These health coöperatives were distributed over twenty-one states, but more than half were in the state of Texas because of encouraging legislation there.

Farmers' Union Hospital Association, Elk City, Oklahoma. One of the pioneer and better-known coöperative hospitals in rural areas is operated by the above-named association. The doctors are on salary, and practice as a group. Families pay a flat rate, with extras for each member beyond four, and there are extra charges for home calls, surgery, and maternity services. The high construction cost of the hospital building prevents this plan from becoming a general one for rural families, and it requires a larger population base.

The association had only an eight-bed health service center in 1931, but now has a 100-bed hospital and a health clinic in an adjoining building. In 1950 the association became involved in a legal battle which has come to have national significance as a test of how such an organization can carry on in the field of medical care. It brought suit against the Beckham County Medical Association in defense of its doctors' rights to practice medicine without discrimination.[35]

Sandhills Region Health Association, Thedford, Nebraska. This association has a voluntary medical care prepayment plan. It allows members to have the services of the physician in their own home at a mileage rate, which is lower to members than to nonmembers, and the fee is less. The organization is also interested in preventive practices. Since it is in a sparsely settled region, and the nearest hospital is sixty miles, interest is growing in plans for a hospital. The physician is employed by the association and receives a base salary and money for travel plus a percentage of the fees for surgery and fracture work.[36]

Coöperative Health Association, Taos County, New Mexico. Taos is one of the oldest settlements in New Mexico and of the United States. Spanish settlers came as early as 1615, and a rather large segment of the population is still what is referred to as Spanish-American. The health association was organized with the help of the University, the Farm Security Administration, and the local doctors. The plan provides for three health centers, each to have a resident graduate nurse, and one ambulance. It also provides for a medical staff on a salary basis, of one full-time medical director, two full-time physicians, two part-time surgeons, and

[34] Helen Johnston, *Rural Health Coöperation* (Washington, D.C.: U.S. Department of Agriculture Bulletin No. 60 and Public Health Service, Federal Security Agency, Bulletin No. 308, June, 1950).

[35] Information Letter, Coöperative League of U.S.A. (Chicago: March–April, 1951).

[36] Elin L. Anderson, "Adequate Medical Care for Rural Families," *Journal of Home Economics,* 36 (September, 1944), 397–400.

a dentist. The hospitals and the druggists of the area participate by contract, and there is provision for coördination with public health and public welfare departments.[37]

Northern Michigan Children's Clinic.[38] In the Upper Peninsula of Michigan, the Children's Fund has provided the Northern Michigan Children's Clinic, which functions as an adjunct to a general hospital. It provides facilities for children eligible for benefits under state laws, particularly crippled children, and medical care for the indigent children of a remote area. Recently there has been expansion in the form of a child guidance clinic under the sponsorship of the State Hospital Commission, and a rheumatic fever program has been conducted in coöperation with the Crippled Children's Commission. Both these services receive federal funds under the provisions of the Social Security Act.

Blue Cross Prepayment Plans.[39] The Blue Cross plans began as a city-wide system of doubtful promise in Dallas, Texas, in 1929. Twenty years later, it accounted for half the hospital insurance coverage, over 37,000,000 persons. Subscribers make regular payments and are assured certain definite hospital benefits. Under a Blue Shield plan, addi-

tional benefits have been arranged in the form of prepayments of doctor bills for services furnished in a hospital. In 1949, 18,000,000 persons were reported in this system and including about 45 per cent of the average costs of physicians' services.[40]

A majority of subscribers are in urban centers, but efforts have been made to extend the plans to farm people. The system has coöperated with the Farm Security Administration, and in some states the Farm Bureau and rural coöperatives have taken over responsibilities for promotion and collection.

American Medical Association.[41] This association has consistently opposed any form of compulsory insurance — in fact, any plan not controlled by the medical profession. It is promoting a twelve-point program, part of which urges expansion of voluntary insurance and wider coverage by hospital and medical plans "to meet costs of illness with extension as rapidly as possible into rural areas." Many local and county medical societies have helped to organize a variety of schemes for the prepayment of hospital and medical bills.

Some systems of compulsory insurance in other countries.[42] Twenty-four countries had systems of compulsory health insurance for all or some of their workers by 1937. Such systems were established in Germany, Austria, and Hungary before 1900, in Norway by 1909, and in Great Britain by 1911. Most of the plans provide for sickness benefits, maternity care, funerals, and medical care.[43]

[37] T. Wilson Longmore and Theodore L. Vaughan, *Taos County Coöperative Health Association* (United States Department of Agriculture), 1942–43; Charles P. Loomis, *Putting Over a Coöperative Health Association to Spanish-Speaking Villagers, or the Organization of the Taos County Coöperative Health Association* (Washington, D.C.: Extension Service and Office of Foreign Agricultural Relations, September, 1944).

[38] Benson Y. Landis, *Rural Welfare Services* (New York: Columbia University Press, 1949), and Copperstock Mostes, "It All Centers on the Children," *Modern Hospital* (May, 1946).

[39] Louis S. Reed, *Blue Cross and Medical Service Plans* (Washington, D.C.: U.S. Public Health Service, Oct., 1947), and Louis H. Pink, *The Story of Blue Cross* (New York: Public Affairs Pamphlet 101, 1945).

[40] Dean A. Clark and Cozette Hapney, *op. cit.*

[41] "Program of American Medical Association for the Advancement of Medicine and Public Health," *Journal of American Medical Association* (December 3, 1949).

[42] Broch Chisholm, *Official Record and Annual Report of the World Health Organization*, No. 30 (Geneva, Switzerland).

[43] Louis S. Reed, *The Next Step in Social Security* (New York: Harper, 1937).

The municipal doctor plan, Canada.[44] In 1921, the Province of Saskatchewan passed legislation permitting a municipality to engage a doctor to take care of the medical needs of a community. Similar measures were enacted within five years in Manitoba, Alberta, and in 1944, in Ontario. The doctor is hired on a salary basis and his duties are the usual ones for a community physician — maternal and child care, minor surgery, and fractures. While the municipality hires the doctor, some control over the general plan is given to the health departments in each province.

Canadian Federation of Agriculture presents principles. In the period of discussion of a Draft Bill for Health Insurance, labor groups and the Farm Radio Forum groups considered the measure, and as a result made suggestions as to how the bill should be altered. The Federation proposed six principles: that this commission should function through a similarly independent commission in each province; that the cost should be derived from the federal consolidated revenue fund; that it should include all citizens; that it should cover all services necessary to positive health, and the prevention and curing of disease (prevention being the primary purpose); and finally, that community effort must have a place in the plan.

In Great Britain.[45] An act passed in 1912 for compulsory health insurance provided for

[44] Rufus C. Roerm, "The Municipal Doctor System in Rural Saskatchewan," Committee on Costs of Medical Care Pub. No. 11 (Chicago: University of Chicago Press, 1931); "Saskatchewan's Air Ambulance Service Sets New Health Style for North America," *Saskatchewan News* (I, no. 19, February 11, 1946).

[45] British Medical Association, Medical Planning Commission, "Interim Report," *British Medical Journal* (I: June 20, 1942), 749–750, and "British National Health Service," *Public Health Reports* (64, no. 6, Feb. 11, 1949), Washington, D.C.: Federal Security Agency, Public Health Service.

what is generally known as "the panel system." It covers manual workers sixteen years of age and over who are under contract, and non-manual workers earning less than $250 per year. Before the war about 18,000,000 workers were included in the plan.

The New National Health Service Act of 1946 came into operation July 5, 1948. Its press announcement read, "The Act will provide you with all medical, dental, and nursing care. Everyone — rich or poor, man, woman, or child — can use any part of it. There are no charges, except for a few special items. There are no insurance qualifications. But it is not 'charity.' You are all paying for it, mainly as taxpayers, and it will relieve your money worries in time of illness."

Under the plan methods of obtaining family doctor services remain virtually unchanged for more than half the English adult population. Since 1912 nearly all employed adults were covered under National Health Insurance for this part of their medical care. The consumer selects a doctor from a local list of those who have agreed to participate. He may change by giving written notice. He visits or is visited by the doctor but pays no fees. Each member of the family over sixteen years of age may make his own selection. Hospital care and treatment by specialists are not included. Voluntary local and private hospitals were taken over by the central government. Those controlled by local units of government had expanded rapidly until the war in 1939. Church hospitals play only a minor role in England. Drugs and appliances, such as eye glasses, are furnished without charge. Preventive health services are provided by local health departments.

In the Scandinavian countries.[46] It is as-

[46] Jorgen S. Dich, "Why has Social Medicine Succeeded in Scandinavian Countries?" An address prepared for the Scandinavian Area Study, Uni-

sumed in the Scandinavian countries that there are basic needs which everyone has the right to satisfy, irrespective of income. This assumption is based upon both moral and practical considerations. The needs are protection of personal freedom, education of children, health of citizens, and care of defectives. Health authorities agree that in matters of health early detection is important for successful treatment. Only a free, or nearly free, medical service can serve as a basis for preventive medicine. However, free medical service is but one aspect of the preventive program. There is also free medical care for expectant mothers, infants, preschool and school children.

For more than a half century Scandinavian countries have had their own systems of social medicine, the backbone of which is the central and district hospital. Admission to a hospital is gained upon presentation of an admission card from a general practitioner. Patients have the privilege of selecting their own doctor. The diagnosis is checked by doctors in the hospital, thus avoiding possible abuses. Hospital doctors are paid yearly salaries, but many have the right to treat private patients also. District hospitals are financed almost exclusively by local taxes, primarily property taxes paid by farmers.

Costs are not considered excessive. For example, Doctor Dich estimated that for Denmark the expenditures for medical care in 1948 were below 3 per cent of the national income, compared with 4.1 per cent for medical care in the United States during the same period. All Scandinavian countries are on their way to a comprehensive compulsory health insurance system which encourages inexpensive and efficient administration and leaves no person unprotected.

In New Zealand.[47] Health insurance is a part of the Social Security Act of 1938. It provides for a system of medical and hospital benefits, as well as for old-age, widows', and other pensions. The benefits include services of a general practitioner, medicines, drugs, and approved appliances, hospitalization, full maternity care, and sickness benefits when a worker is unemployed because of illness.

Costs are included in a special Social Security tax of 5 per cent on all salaries, wages, and other income, including that of business firms. The general plan is fundamental to the whole history of social legislation in the Dominion. New Zealand has been a pioneer in many of these social matters. For example, the public health system has been in effect since 1872, and old-age pensions have been in force since 1898. In fact, New Zealand was the first country to introduce them.

New Zealand is also famous for its child welfare programs, including not only public measures but a unique and highly successful private nursing organization, known as the Plunket Society, founded by Sir Truby King in 1907. Its aim is "to help the mothers save the babies." Its scope can be appreciated when it is realized that well over 70 per cent of the babies born come under the supervision of the Plunket nurses. Through these services and other constructive measures, New Zealand has long enjoyed the distinction of having one of the lowest infant mortality rates in the world.

versity of Wisconsin, Madison, 1950. Professor Dich was visiting professor of Scandinavian Area Studies, University of Wisconsin; Adviser to the Danish Ministry of Social Affairs, Editor of *Socialt Tidsskrift,* Copenhagen, Professor of Public Finance and Public Welfare, University of Aarhus, Denmark.

[47] Walter Nash, *New Zealand, a Working Democracy* (New York: Duell, Sloan & Pearce, 1943).

TOPICS FOR DISCUSSION

1. What do you consider the most serious health problem in your community (either rural or urban)? Present evidence from whatever health records are available to indicate the seriousness and the prevalence of this problem.
2. Select one public and one private agency, local, county, state, or national, which is working with rural health problems, and find out all you can about it. Visit local headquarters, interview officials where possible, or, if necessary, secure information by mail.
3. Organize this information in brief outline form and be prepared to present it to the class. Give particular attention to the following points:
   a. The real purpose of the agency.
   b. Its local forms of organization.
   c. How it serves rural communities.
   d. How you think such service could be improved.
4. Consider one of the "group prepayment" plans described in the chapter. Discuss its workability in some rural situation with which you are well acquainted.

REFERENCE READINGS

Bachmeyer, A. C., and Maurice J. Norby, *Hospital Care in the United States.* New York: The Commonwealth Fund, 1947.

Bureau of Human Nutrition and Home Economics, *What Farm Families Spend for Medical Care,* Miscellaneous Publication 561. Washington, D.C.: United States Department of Agriculture.

Davis, Graham L., "Content and Administration of a Medical Care Program," *American Journal of Public Health,* XXXIV, No. 12, December, 1944.

Department of Rural Sociology, *Medical Care Services in North Carolina,* Progress Report RS-4. College Station: North Carolina Agricultural Experiment Station, December, 1944.

Duncan, O. D., "Rural Health Research," *Rural Sociology,* IX, No. 1, March, 1944.

Farm Security Administration, *Group Medical Care for Farmers.* Washington, D.C.: United States Department of Agriculture.

Galloway, Robert E., and Marion T. Loftin, *Health Practices of Rural Negroes in Bolivar County,* Sociology and Rural Life Series No. 3. State College, Miss.: Mississippi State College Agricultural Experiment Station, April, 1951.

Galloway, Robert E., and Harold F. Kaufman, *Health Practices in Choctaw County,* Sociology and Rural Life Series No. 2. State College, Miss.: Mississippi State College Agricultural Experiment Station, Dec., 1950.

Interbureau Committee on Postwar Programs, *Better Health for Rural America.* Washington, D.C.: United States Department of Agriculture, October, 1945.

Kemp, Jouise, and T. Lynn Smith, *Health and Mortality in Louisiana,* Bulletin 390. Baton Rouge: Louisiana Agricultural Experiment Station, May, 1945.

Kleinschmidt, L. S., "Better Rural Health," *Rural Sociology,* IX, No. 1, March, 1944.

Koos, Earl Lomon, *The Sociology of the Patient.* New York: McGraw-Hill, 1950.

Kraenzel, Carl F., *The Hospitals of Montana,* Bulletin 456. Bozeman: Montana Agricultural Experiment Station, January, 1949.

Larson, Olaf F., and Donald G. Hay, "Rural Health in New York," *Rural Sociology,* XVI, No. 3, September, 1951.

Mangus, A. R., "Personality Adjustment of Rural and Urban Children," *American Sociological Review,* XIII, No. 5, October, 1948.

Mangus, A. R., *Mental Health of Rural Children in Ohio,* Research Bulletin 682. Wooster: Ohio Agricultural Experiment Station, March, 1949.

Mayo, Selz, C. Fullerton, Kie Sebastian, *Medical Care in Greene County,* Bulletin 363. Raleigh: North Carolina Agricultural Experiment Station, November, 1948.

McNamara, Robert L., "Physicians in Rural Ohio," *Rural Sociology,* IX, No. 1, March, 1944.

Mott, F. D., "Rural Health Parity: Federal-State Coöperation," *Land Policy Review,* Spring, 1945.

Paterson, Robert G., *Foundations of Community*

Health Education. New York: McGraw-Hill, 1950.

Plant, James S., M.D., *Personality and the Cultural Pattern.* New York: The Commonwealth Fund, 1937.

Price, Paul H., and Homer L. Hitt, *The Availability of Medical Personnel in Rural Louisiana,* Bulletin 459. Baton Rouge: Louisiana Agricultural Experiment Station, June, 1951.

Proceedings of the Second Psychotherapy Council, Chicago, *Psychotherapy for Children; Group Psychotherapy.* Chicago: Institute for Psychoanalysis, January, 1944.

Reuss, Carl F., *Farmer Views on the Medical Situation,* Circular 20. Pullman: Washington Agricultural Experiment Station V, September, 1944.

Roskelley, R. W., *The Rural Citizen and Medical Care,* Bulletin 495. Pullman: Washington Agricultural Experiment Station, December, 1947.

Stott, Leland H., *Personality Development in Farm, Small-Town, and City Children,* Research Bulletin 114. Lincoln: Nebraska Agricultural Experiment Station, August, 1939.

Thaden, John F., *Distribution of Doctors of Medicine and Osteopaths in Michigan Communities,* Special Bulletin 370. East Lansing: Michigan Agricultural Experiment Station, and Social Research Service, June, 1951.

Treadway, Walter L., *The Place of Mental Hygiene in a Federal Health Program.* Washington, D.C.: United States Public Health Service, 1936.

Washington Committee on Postwar Program for Agriculture, *Prepaid Health Insurance for Farm Families,* Bulletin 316. Pullman: Washington Agricultural Extension Service, October, 1944.

FILMS

Child Care and Development. S, 17. McGraw-Hill.

Doctor (The). S, 10. Work of a community doctor. Encyclopedia Britannica Films.

Doctor (The). S, 14. Busy life of the small town doctor. Castle.

RURAL LIFE IN SOUTH AMERICA *Top*: Market Day in a Colombian Village. *Bottom*: Village Street Scene. (Photos, Standard Oil Co., N.J.)

RURAL LIFE IN SOUTH AMERICA *Top*: Modern Farmhouse Built by the Colombian Government on Long-Term Loan, Farmer's Original Adobe House in Back. *Bottom left*: A Poor Rural Home in Venezuela. *Bottom right*: Streams are Laundries in Underdeveloped Countries. (Photos, Standard Oil Co., N.J.)

**AGRICULTURE IN UNDERDE-
VELOPED ORIENTAL COUNTRIES**
Top: Cultivating Rice Paddy.
Center left: Child Labor in a
Tobacco Field. *Center right*:
Planting Rice Seedlings. *Bot-
tom*: Harvesting Rice. (Photos,
Office of Foreign Agricultural
Relations)

AGRICULTURE IN UNDERDEVELOPED ORIENTAL COUNTRIES *Top*: Plowing Rice Paddy. *Center*: Rice Harvesting. *Bottom left*: Primitive Irrigation. *Bottom right*: Bundling Barley. (Center photo, Government of India Information Services; others, Office of Foreign Agricultural Relations, U.S. Dept. of Agriculture)

23 Rural Welfare and Social Security

THE TRADITION is deeply graven in the social heritage of rural America that no one in distress shall go unaided, but at the same time that no one shall be allowed to depend solely upon others without rendering some service for help received.

Mutual aid among relatives, friends, and neighbors has been the traditional way of meeting personal and family health and social hazards in rural society. It continues to be the accepted way in some areas, although modified in manner to suit changing circumstances. Established agencies, such as school, church, and social club, have also done their share, as previous chapters have shown. While such services continued during the distress which accompanied the onset of the Great Depression, there emerged a broader concept known as "social security." From the standpoint of public attention and legislation, this traces back to a report to the President made by the Committee on Economic Security and to the Social Security Act which became law in August, 1935.

The social security idea, as well as the legislation, comprehends a wide field of activity, including employment assurance, unemployment insurance, old-age pensions and annuities, child welfare, public health, social insurance, and public assistance. It strikes at problems of insecurity, some of which have old and deep roots and some of which stem from more recent difficulties. It is raising issues and causing much discussion because no great scrutiny is necessary to discover that many theories about social security and public welfare are hazy, unrelated to sources of trouble, and even inconsistent with each other.

Here, then, is a relatively new phase in large-scale social organization of rural society. Many queries are involved, the answers to which are not readily apparent. To what extent should society rather than family, for example, assume responsibility for distressed and harassed individuals? Can public welfare services be devised, financed, and administered without disrupting the integrity and self-dependence of individuals and groups, and in fact, of the established order? What is the basis for social legislation and group action which will reflect the will of the majority over sufficiently long periods to make them effective?

The purpose of this chapter is to explore some of the backgrounds from which social difficulties in rural society come, to trace more recent trends, and to examine briefly the social institutions and agencies, public and private, which are attempting to bring about greater social security and welfare. These are appropriate inquiries, since it has been shown elsewhere that there is an increasing interdependence of the various units in a modern society. Uncontrolled sickness, unabated indigence, and far-flung ignorance are public menaces endangering everyone. Many studies make it very evident that there is a close interrelationship among such social maladies as poverty, ill health, unemployment, lack of education, and family disorganization. These represent the seamy side of life, but they are none the less social realities which the student of rural society must face.

The crises in the decade from 1930 to 1940 were so severe in both rural society and general society that actual social revolution was produced. This is the point at which our discussion may well begin. However, it must not obscure the fact that agriculture's depression actually began in the nineteen-twenties when the foreign market collapsed while productive capacity was still greatly expanded in response to wartime demands. Neither should the erroneous conclusion be reached that a social crisis develops quickly and in a vacuum; it has deep roots, long-time causes, and arises out of complicated social situations. To combat the onslaught of the depression, numerous action programs were organized including farm relief, farm blocs, and the alphabetical agencies which are now household terms but continue to be subjects for lively debate and political controversy.

Then Came the Great Depression

About three or three and a half million rural families turned to one or more of the relief agencies for help during the great depression of the early nineteen-thirties. This wholesale breakdown of self-dependency was something new in American rural life. It does not follow, however, that only those on relief were in dire straits. The mores of rural life, as suggested earlier, made rural people reluctant to seek public assistance even when their scale of living fell far below the standards regarded by them and their neighbors as "socially desirable." Many hard-hit families struggled on, hoping against hope that the depression would lift and allow them to get back to "normalcy." Other depressions had done so.

But the notion that rural people have a blind faith in the restorative powers of "natural laws" is open to question, as is the idea

that rural citizens will not accommodate themselves to receiving public help. The effects of federal relief, of social security aids, and of the AAA benefit payments do not seem to point in that direction. After all, subsidy payments are not new in this country. From certain standpoints the AAA might be considered an extension to farmers of the tariff arrangements favoring much of urban industry or as comparable to shipping subsidies. This is not suggested as justification, but by way of possible explanation.

Some classes of rural people were especially distressed, such as the poor tenants and croppers of the South, the migratory and seasonal agricultural workers of the West, the many marginal families on marginal land, or the unskilled and part-time laborers in villages and small towns. These were not all the disadvantaged groups, but the list is enough to give some conception of those whose severe insecurities threatened the security of rural society itself. Some distressed groups were hidden from public view; they were thinly scattered over the whole countryside; they did not form in breadlines as needy urban people often did, nor did they appear at the county agricultural agent's office for a benefit payment or at the county welfare office for a relief grant. Their difficulties, however, were very real, and to overlook them even now when the cloud has lifted is to miss some of the inherent social and economic problems of our times.

Rural insecurities not new. Lest the impression be gained that insecurity is something recent, it is well to glance back for a moment at the history of rural society. From the days of the Pilgrims, there have been rural hazards to threaten the well-being of all. Plagues were not unknown, starvation in some communities followed such crises as the Revolutionary War and the Civil War. There have been many periods of depression. The records of public dependency in rural Massachusetts, extending over three centuries, show that there was no year in which local communities were without relief cases. There were the widows, the orphans, and those families which were "on the town."

While previous distress periods witnessed poverty and dependency, the more recent widespread depression resulted in an unprecedented loss of self-support to both rural and urban families. Other areas had their insecurities, described in other terms, but in those days we were confronted with more intense maladjustments than ever before. The shock reached practically every major social institution and every type of human activity. The question may well be asked why this was so. In part, it was because two "ways out" which had been employed in the past by rural people, especially farm people, could no longer be used with success by some, or to a sufficient extent by others. First, as was stated earlier, the frontier was gone. The social significance of this fact is not always perceived. It meant that older farmers could not make a new start in the West when their farms in the East, Middle West, or South failed. It meant that young farmers could not find good farms easily, or if they did, that the price was beyond their limited resources. Farmers from the drought areas who were wont to seek another chance "in the West" found the struggle too severe, as the novel, *Grapes of Wrath,* so effectively reveals.

Second, the city did not offer its usual avenue of escape. Many ambitious farm and village youths had sought their fortunes in the cities in earlier years. Many, not all, had reported that they had found them there. But in the depression days, every city had its own hordes of unemployed. What opportunities were there for rural youth? There were no jobs in villages, farms were not being turned over to farm youth at the same rate as they were attaining maturity; adults were holding on. Even city young people, especially those with young families and those whose early homes had been in rural areas, sought at least shelter and food there. There was the tendency for certain age groups to accumulate from both city and country, and to pile up in villages and small towns. There was also the push of certain types of families toward the marginal farming areas.

Six rural problem areas. When the rural counties with highest relief loads were plotted on a map of the United States, they formed patterns which have come to be known as "problem areas." They are regions of chronic trouble where poverty has become relatively deep-rooted.[1]

The Appalachian-Ozark area has been cultivated for generations but was a problem area years before the depression began. Forests had been cut, mines abandoned, and hillsides gullied by erosion. The land cannot possibly supply adequate living for the present farm population, which is increasing rapidly because of high birth rates. This population is nearly all native-white. Since the fertility of the land is gone and cultural isolation is great because of poor roads, the level of family and community living is very low by accepted standards of medical care, housing, diet, and mortality.

The eastern and western cotton areas are regions where the fertility of the soil has been depleted by persistent cultivation of a single crop. Expensive commercial fertilizers must be applied in ever-increasing amounts if life is to go on. Traditionally and geographically, the eastern and western

[1] P. G. Beck and M. C. Forster, *Six Rural Problem Areas: Relief, Resources, Rehabilitation* (Washington, D.C.: Research Monograph 1, Works Progress Administration, 1935).

areas are different. In the former, relief rolls were crowded with both whites and Negroes, while Mexicans add to the burden of the latter.

The Lake States cut-over area, like the Appalachian-Ozark area, lost its lumbering and mining resources. A stranded population was left, but later other families moved in. Neither group, however, was able to get far beyond a subsistence basis because of small farms, poor land, and a short growing season. When income from industry went out, relief came in.

The northern and southern Great Plains areas were the last two to be added to the "problem" area map, forced on by the droughts of 1934 and 1936. Droughts have been a constant danger here since the pioneers pushed beyond the irregular twenty-inch annual rainfall line extending from Texas to the Dakotas.[2] The two areas taken together include nearly one tenth of the land area of the nation. Large government subsidies to farmers went into these areas during the seven years of severe depression, 1931 through 1937, and some assistance continues. A recent report of a study of the twenty counties in that southern area known as the "Dust Bowl" recommends that 52 per cent of the area be turned back to nature. Just how Mother Nature is to succor such a prodigal is not suggested.

Permanently disadvantaged classes. The catastrophe of the depression could not have descended with such violence, even in the seven years which are to be described, without some antecedents. Many of the securities, such as they were, before 1930 proved fragile indeed when the crisis came. The

facts were there in the records of the United States Department of Agriculture, but the increasing human risks seem to have passed all but unnoticed. Finally attention was sharply called to the fact that even in 1929, considered a prosperous year, 1,700,000 farm families (7,700,000 persons) lived on farms which yielded a gross income of less than $600 annually; nearly 1,000,000 farms, 15 per cent of the total, yielded less than $400; and nearly 3,000,000, almost 50 per cent, had gross incomes of less than $1000.[3] When there were added to these families those farm laborers and tenants with low incomes, migratory families that move each year, and another 500,000 families on land so poor that the wolf could hardly be kept from the door of the shack in which they lived — then you have a total which agricultural leaders estimated as one third of all farm families — *Disadvantaged Classes in American Agriculture* — trying to live at levels so low as to make security for the nation and self-dependence for the families a fiction.[4]

The extent to which the disadvantages and the handicaps have continued into the present are discussed in the chapter on the agricultural enterprise. There is still poverty in agriculture, that is sure; however, recent studies indicate that many farm families with low incomes from their farming enterprise have secondary sources of support. This is but further indication of interdependence in our modern economy, and the blurring of the lines between rural and urban.

Unprecedented droughts. "Acts of God," as they are sometimes called in legal par-

[2] R. S. Kifer and H. L. Stewart, *Farming Hazards in the Drought Areas* (Washington, D.C.: Research Monograph 16, Works Progress Administration, 1938).

[3] Louis H. Bean and Arthur P. Chew, *Economic Trends Affecting Agriculture* (Washington, D.C.: United States Department of Agriculture, 1933).

[4] Carl C. Taylor, Helen W. Wheeler, and E. L. Kirkpatrick, *Disadvantaged Classes in American Agriculture* (Washington, D.C.: Social Research Report 7, U.S. Department of Agriculture, 1938).

lance, contributed more than their due share to the depression as far as agriculture was concerned. The 1928 Report of the Secretary of Agriculture gave evidence of improvement over the earlier years of the decade, but then came the great industrial collapse of 1929–30. During the depths of that depression, between 1933 and 1937, the series of severe droughts [5] added to the distress of rural people, especially in the Great Plains areas, partly through dust storms and the creation of dust bowls.

The seven lean years. The worst depression years, 1931 through 1937, which Dr. T. J. Woofter has called "the seven lean years," found 3,500,000 rural families — one in four — dependent on relief at some time. There were 4,000,000 urban families in similar plight. At the depth of the depression in 1935, about 2,500,000 rural families — more than 10,000,000 persons — were dependent on some form of relief.[6]

Cost of rural relief reached $3,500,000,-000. The total national relief bill over the seven-year period, paid by both public and private agencies, was estimated as $13,000,-000,000. The rural costs were proportionately less, because of the smaller number of cases and the smaller grants to rural than to urban families. However, rural amounts did not include many of the special loans and benefits for agriculture intended to keep farm families off relief or to reduce the needs of those compelled to apply for public aid. These figures of the numbers of families are bewildering, and the costs in terms of dollars were staggering, yet they cannot be considered a measure of the human waste, suffering, and discouragement involved. Millions of rural people were caught in the sweep of the depression through no fault of their own and could not possibly free themselves without help. Furthermore, some of the misery in rural society did not originate in the recent depression, but, as suggested earlier, traces far back to destructive forces at work in rural life for many years. Finally, distressing rural conditions were closely interrelated with the whole nation-wide situation.

Farmers on relief. It seems almost a contradiction in terms to write of farmers on relief; they are the ones who supply others with food. But as the depression spread wider and cut deeper, farmers sought relief offices for help in feeding their own families.[7] They were farm owners, part-time farmers, share-croppers, and other tenants and laborers.

Farm owners were best able to maintain their self-dependence. Even when the largest number of rural people were on relief, only one farm owner out of every seventeen was on a relief roll. The numbers receiving aid were lowest in the corn belt and in the hay and dairy area, and highest — one in five — in the Lake States cut-over area. When the farm families on relief were compared with neighbors not on relief, some sources of their difficulties became evident. They were larger families, with three or four children and sometimes another relative; they had smaller farms, sometimes less than a third of the average acreage; and they had less livestock and equipment. Some were part-time farmers who had lost their supple-

[5] Francis Cronin and Howard W. Beers, *Areas of Intense Drought Distress, 1930–36* (Washington, D.C.: Works Progress Administration, January, 1937).

[6] The analysis for the first part of the chapter follows closely two summary sources: T. J. Woofter and Ellen Winston, *Seven Lean Years* (Chapel Hill: University of North Carolina Press, 1937), and Rupert B. Vance, *Rural Relief and Recovery* (Washington, D.C.: Social Problems Pamphlet 3, Works Progress Administration, 1939).

[7] Berta Asch and A. R. Mangus, *Farmers on Relief* (Washington, D.C.: Research Monograph 8, Works Progress Administration, 1937); T. C. McCormick, *Comparative Study of Rural Relief and Non-Relief Households* (Research Monograph 2, Works Progress Administration, 1935).

mentary employment, and some, as a result of heavy indebtedness, had lost all.

Farmers without land fared less well than owners. One out of seven tenants was on relief in 1935, and it is considered probable that one fourth have been given public assistance at some time. They were like the owners who experienced trouble, except that they were involved to a greater extent. Their land was poor, holdings small, livestock limited, and debts many. Compared with tenants who did keep their self-dependence, they were distinguished by their lack of education. Those with less than a grade-school education found it very difficult, if not impossible, to live unaided through those lean years.

One share tenant in twelve was on relief during the worst of the troublesome times. There would have been a larger proportion except for the attention given them through rehabilitation loans. The insecurity of this group of families was greatest in the areas where share tenancy itself was greatest, but also where many families were living at very low levels before the depression began. Nearly half the share-croppers on relief were without work of any kind. The relief stipends they received were very low indeed, usually about 9 dollars per month. Attempts to live at that level gave little hope for security or self-dependence. A major problem of long standing lodges here.

Villagers on relief. The second half — or nearly half — of the heads of rural families reported on general relief in February, 1935, had non-agricultural occupations or lived without an occupation in villages. This group of families underwent their own kinds of vicissitudes. Those centers dependent upon the fortunes of agriculture felt the collapse of agriculture's prosperity first. Retail trade fell away, credit limits were broken, workers were unemployed, and business places closed. When 133 of the 140 agricul-

tural villages restudied in 1936 were grouped into four classes on the basis of their relief loads, it was found that high relief loads were associated with decrease in per capita retail sales in three groups, but not in the highest relief group. This highest fourth had the lowest per capita sales even in 1929; the following three or four years seemed merely to intensify their previous problems. Leaders in many of these small communities, although definitely critical of relief as such, admitted that relief grants had actually supported the village.[8]

Families relying on incomes derived from mining, textiles, or lumbering were among those hit especially hard. Some industrial towns were "stranded" as the result of a closed factory or depleted commercial resources. A study of industrial workers in Massachusetts showed that this group was forced to seek relief in greater proportions than any other occupational group, even including the farmers. It was likewise found that industries replacing those closed were all too often exploitive schemes which brought no lasting jobs or permanent income to the towns. Part-time farmers found their income insufficient to carry them through the period when the mills were closed.[9]

Analysis of the reasons given by villagers for seeking relief shows, from another angle, the picture of the village as that in-between group described in the chapter on villages. They became involved in problems of both industry and agriculture. Loss of employment and loss of assets were the prevailing reasons given for distress in villages in every section of the country. Over one half the village workers with any work history, who were on relief from July through October,

[8] Edmund deS. Brunner and Irving Lorge, *Rural Trends in Depression Years* (New York: Columbia University Press, 1937).

[9] John Useem, *A Study of Social Security in the Rural Communities of Massachusetts* (Ph.D. thesis, University of Wisconsin, 1939).

1935, had lost their jobs in private industry. This was a period of supposed business recovery. Two fifths of the villagers on relief were unskilled workers, one fourth reported some agricultural experience, one fifth were skilled or semi-skilled workers. There were few "white-collar" workers on village relief rolls.

A situation peculiar to villages was revealed by the large proportion — 17 per cent — of relief households with women as economic heads or living alone. About 8 per cent of the relief cases were men living alone. Aged people were also numerous, and many families had no person who was employable or considered capable of holding a job.

Plans for rather fundamental readjustments are needed for the many small industrial and agricultural centers if any measure of security is to be found for American villagers. Readjustments will involve not only internal rearrangements but questions of occupational outlook and volume of business necessary to render worth-while services to agricultural communities.

This rather long review of the depression period seems essential to an understanding of what followed. As suggested at the beginning of the chapter, it was a time of national crises. Fundamental fears developed and the determined quest for security brought about revolutionary changes in personal attitudes and in public policies. Social security legislation accepted as public policy twenty years later did not then exist. The period marks a transition in American life from emphasis upon individual responsibility to collective responsibility for important social ills and handicaps.

The Quest for Social Security

The period of the depression left its stamp upon American life and upon rural life especially. Deep fears were aroused; much effort

and legislation was directed, not only toward immediate relief, but was planned so "it would never happen again." It brought farmers into government programs as never before. It stimulated farmer organizations, farm blocs, and pressure groups, beginning in the nineteen-twenties with the MacNary-Haugen agitation. Probably not since the Granger days of the 1870's or the Alliance and Populist movements of the 1880's and '90's have farmers been more involved in political and government activities.

It was a transition period in the rural economy and in the rural social relationships of the nation, just as it was in industry and labor. Before 1933, for example, trade-union agreements gave limited attention to regulating lay-offs. Now every agreement contains such a clause. The focus of demand is for a guaranteed annual wage — the basis for some sense of security.[10] With the greater use of machinery and the wider advance of science and technology on the farms have come problems of social and economic stratification suggested earlier. With them has also come the demand for more security, less of the risk associated with pioneering days. This demand expresses itself in "parity" price demands described in an earlier chapter, and in a variety of other social legislation. The rise in price curves, incomes, and profits has changed some conditions and has directed public attention to other things, but many of the underlying causes for such fears have not been completely removed.

Relief agencies. The federal government in the latter part of 1932 began to lend funds to state and local government units for the relief of the unemployed. By May, 1933, a Federal Emergency Relief Administration was set up and authorized to allocate funds

[10] Jack Chernich and George Hellikson, *Guaranteed Annual Wages* (Minneapolis: University of Minnesota Press, 1945).

to the states for emergency unemployment relief purposes. This was discontinued in December, 1935, when the works program provided for in the Federal Emergency Relief Appropriation Act was inaugurated to furnish employment to the needy and the employable. From its beginning in 1931, unemployment relief tended to overshadow poor relief in this general field of public assistance, while the need for a longer-time program was recognized in 1935.

Prior to 1933, the responsibility for the administration and financing of relief or other forms of public assistance was most frequently placed upon local units of government. Since 1935, however, the prevailing practice has changed until at present the majority of states have laws which provide for state responsibility and direct adminis-

tration or supervision by a single state agency. By January, 1939, very few states did not have legislation which provided for all types of relief and public assistance.[11]

Emergency agencies. Perhaps some conception of the wide variety and complexity of emergency programs can be gained from Figure 72 which shows the trend of public assistance and the earnings of persons employed under federal works programs in the United States from January, 1933, to May, 1944. In the month of May, 1939, for example, earnings of persons employed on works projects operated by the Works Progress Administration amounted to $140,700,-

[11] Robert C. Lowe, *State Public Welfare Legislation* (Washington, D.C.: Research Monograph 20, Works Progress Administration, 1939).

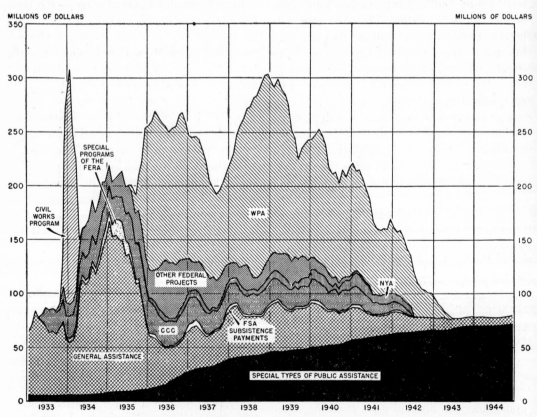

Figure 72. Special Types of Public Assistance.

000, and payments to general relief cases $39,100,000. Together these two types of aid account for nearly 60 per cent of all public assistance in that month. Payments to recipients of old-age assistance, aid to dependent children, and aid to the blind totaled $46,200,000, comprising 15 per cent of the total. Earnings of persons employed on other federal work were $45,700,000, nearly 15 per cent of the total. Earnings of persons enrolled in the Civilian Conservation Corps were $20,400,000, or about 7 per cent of the total. The National Youth Administration's account was $6,700,000, slightly more than 2 per cent of the whole. Emergency subsistence payments certified by the Farm Security Administration were $1,700,000, which was only .6 per cent of the total payment for the month.[12]

The WPA employment program included on the average about 2,285,000 persons, rural and urban, over a six-year period ending June 30, 1941. Its activities were varied, and some of the major ones extended into many rural areas. For example, it erected or improved an average of ten buildings per county and built or improved an average of two hundred miles of roads per county.

Social security, the long-time hope. The Social Security Act passed in 1935, amended in 1939, expanded and liberalized in 1950, is objective evidence of the change in public policy. Social security is now an accepted responsibility of the entire society. Its importance and broad support were shown in the character and extent of the 1950 amendments.[13] This legislation is aimed at those areas of human life which the depression revealed were especially exposed — unem-

ployment, accidents, illness, and disability. Two groups of persons at either end of the age pyramid were particularly vulnerable, children and the aged. Rural sections and classes were not equally provided for in the security program during its early stages but have been increasingly included as amendments have been made. Social security is not a single program but is varied in character, intended to cope with the many kinds of insecurity. In organization, it follows the plan of federal-state and local administration, in which the federal function is grants-in-aid and the maintenance of uniform standards.

In spite of seeming complexities and varieties, the general program is based upon three main principles, namely, *insurance*, *services* and *assistance*. The insurance principle takes the form of old-age and survivors' insurance and unemployment insurance. For the many forms of social services, such as for crippled children, vocational rehabilitation, and child welfare, the federal government grants funds to the states which in turn work with local public agencies. The public assistance program is the only one in which funds go directly to persons, and then only on the basis of the so-called "means tests" and only for specified purposes popularly known as "the categories," three at first, now four. At the national level the whole plan, except unemployment insurance, is organized into the Social Security Administration. This along with Public Health, Education, and some other units, is included within the Federal Security Agency. Unemployment insurance is administered in the Department of Labor and does not include farm workers.

Old-age and survivors' insurance. The plan is described as "a basic system of contributory social insurance." Under the expanded and liberalized provisions of the 1950 amendments which became effective January 1, 1951, about 10,000,000 additional

[12] Donald S. Howard, *The WPA and Federal Relief Policy* (New York: Russell Sage Foundation, 1943).

[13] "Social Security Act Amendments," *Social Security Bulletin* (Washington, D.C.: Federal Security Agency, October, 1950).

workers are included. For the first time, these include about 500,000 regularly employed workers on farms and in farm households. The new provision will bring the total to an estimated 45,000,000, or nearly three fourths of the nation's labor force in an average week. At the end of June, 1950, almost 3,000,000 were already receiving benefits under the plan.

The contributory phase of the plan means that the system is financed by taxes on the worker and the employer, each paying 1½ per cent of the wages to the Collector of Internal Revenue for his district. The rate will increase periodically until the maximum of 3¼ per cent is reached in 1970. The benefits in monthly payments go to the workers on reaching sixty-five years of age, and to their families when they die. In the case of agricultural laborers, there are rules for eligibility including regularity, extent, and kinds of employment.[14]

For the first time, self-employed persons are included under the Social Security Act. They were brought in by the amendments of 1950. However, farmers and certain specified professional people, among them physicians, dentists, lawyers, and clergymen, are not included in the provisions of the Act. It is reported that these groups, especially the farmers, expressed little interest one way or the other, so they were not provided for in the recent revisions. It was the self-employed who are engaged in trade and business who were most active in the hearings and most eager to be included. These are the occupations most characteristic of small towns and villages.

Federal-state partnership in the social services. The principle of the social serv-

ices has taken five forms: (1) maternal and child health, (2) health and medical care, (3) services for crippled children, (4) child welfare, and (5) vocational rehabilitation. These services are spread over both rural and urban areas, though some funds are appropriated on the basis of rural proportions in the states' population. These services represent efforts at protection, prevention, amelioration, and rehabilitation.

Child welfare and maternal and child health services can be used here for illustration. In the case of child welfare, the Children's Bureau administers the funds and helps the states in maintaining standards. States need not match the federal grants, but a part of the costs of the services must come from state and local funds. By the 1946 amendment, the Bureau is directed to grant a minimum of $20,000 to each state, then to apportion the balance of the total grant according to the proportion of a state's rural population to the rural population of the nation as a whole. These funds must be used for services, not for direct personal aids.

In 1935, when the Act was passed in its initial form, eleven states had no general or state-wide plan for services to children. By 1940 there were 735 professional workers whose salaries were paid in whole or in part from federal sources. In most states the emphasis is put upon county systems of welfare service with full-time employment of workers specialized in children's problems. Child welfare workers in rural counties have had to win their way into the confidences of rural people just as county agricultural agents, home economists, and county nurses did in years past. That this takes time, skill, and patience is shown by the fact that many rural counties are still unwilling to assume local support of such programs.

One of the great forces helping to establish and promote the work in this field has been the White House Conferences on the

[14] *Information for County Agents on Social Security* (Washington, D.C.: U.S. Department of Agriculture, Extension Service, January, 1951), and *Agricultural Employers' Social Security Tax Guide. Circular A* (U.S. Treasury Department, January, 1951).

care of children, held every ten years, the last in 1950. These conferences focus public attention on children's problems and needed services. Findings and recommendations are carried back into state and local conferences, whereby a general sense of the importance and value of children is built up. As has been stated repeatedly, what people want and what they value, they will have, treasure, and care for.

Grants for maternal and child health are also made by the Children's Bureau to state departments of health, to be used for state and local services. One half of the national grants must be matched by the states, the balance being allotted according to the number of live births in proportion to the total births in the nation. The Act of 1935 stressed the need for services "in rural areas and in areas suffering from severe economic distress." One phase of the program which has been greatly extended by federal-state coöperation is the child hygiene movement. State workers help to establish local child health centers, promote local conferences, and then provide specialized services. This traveling service in one state is known as "the little red wagon on wheels." The local physicians, dentist, nurse, welfare worker, fathers and mothers, are brought together to consider and act upon problems of nutrition, mental hygiene, and special needs of children.

Public assistance programs — the four categorical aids. The principle of direct assistance takes the form of aids for three defined purposes in the 1935 Act, namely, old-

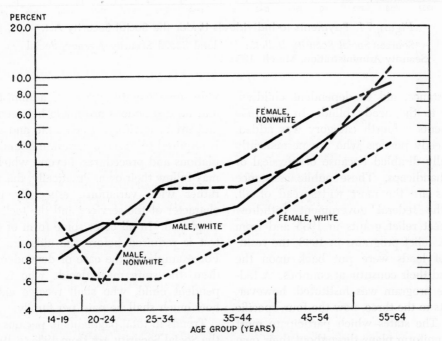

Figure 73. Percentage Disabled in the Civilian Noninstitutional Population Aged 14–64, Whose Disability Had Lasted 7 Months or More, by Age, Sex, and Race, February, 1949.

Source: *Social Security Bulletin* (Federal Social Security Agency, Social Security Administration, November, 1950).

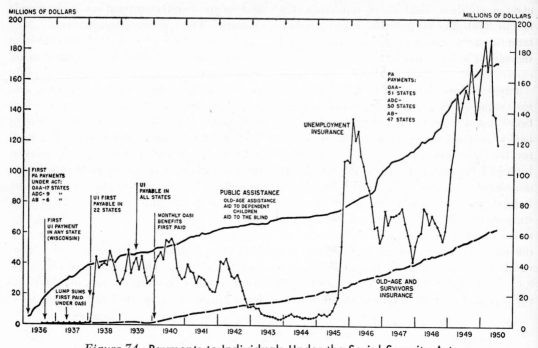

Figure 74. Payments to Individuals Under the Social Security Act.

Source: *Social Security Bulletin* (Federal Social Security Agency, Social
Security Administration, March, 1951).

age assistance, aid to dependent children,
and aid to the needy blind. In the 1950
amendments a fourth category was added,
aid to needy persons who are permanently
and totally disabled because of physical or
mental handicaps. These public assistance
programs are the most widespread of all.
When the federal government withdrew
from direct relief grants in 1935 and from
the work relief programs in 1943, the residual relief loads were put back upon the
states and their constituent counties. A federal-state program was instituted, however,
for grants to the three, now the four, specific
groups. The states which participate must
provide uniform plans throughout their own
areas. They must maintain certain standards
and handle their personnel selection and supervision under an acceptable merit system.
Political activities of workers are forbidden.

More than three fourths of the states pro-

vide some county system of administration
and no distinctions are made between rural
and urban territory. Each state and county
is required to observe certain minimum regulations and procedures, beyond which they
may follow their own. Practically, this means
rather wide variations, especially in the
character of the services and the techniques
employed. In all cases some form of means
test is required before the aids are given.
For example, in the case of dependent children, the state must decide who is a dependent child, who shall receive aid, and
how much shall be paid per family.

Trends in total payments to persons under
the Social Security Act from 1935 to 1950 are
traced in Figure 74. The old-age and survivors' insurance curve and the public assistance curve have been rising at about equal
rates until late 1946 when the latter began
to climb more steeply. The unemployment

insurance curve reflected the mild recession of late 1948 and early 1949, reached an all-time high in January, 1950, but dropped sharply in June of that year.[15]

Farm security. Specialized relief measures for farmers began rather early. Rehabilitation loans were granted instead of direct relief or unemployment relief. This accounts for the low percentage in the May, 1939, budget described above. Three factors were depended upon to enable this form of rehabilitation program to expand: first, the spreading of risk over many borrowers; second, careful selection of borrowers or clients; and, third, close supervision, not

only of the farm operation, but of the family and its household management.

In 1937, after several hundred thousand persons had been removed from the relief rolls by such rehabilitation loans, the proportion of the farm families receiving different kinds of public assistance, exclusive of the Farm Security loans, were as follows: Works Progress Administration, 40 per cent; Farm Security direct grants — not loans — 6 per cent; aid to the aged, to the blind, and to dependent children, 39 per cent; and state and local direct relief, 15 per cent.

It was in 1937 that the Farm Security Administration was reorganized from the Rural Rehabilitation Division of the FERA, made a part of the United States Department of Agriculture, and its services enlarged to include a tenant-purchase pro-

[15] "Social Security at the Midcentury: Report for Year 1950," *Social Security Bulletin* (Washington, D.C.: Federal Security Agency, March, 1951).

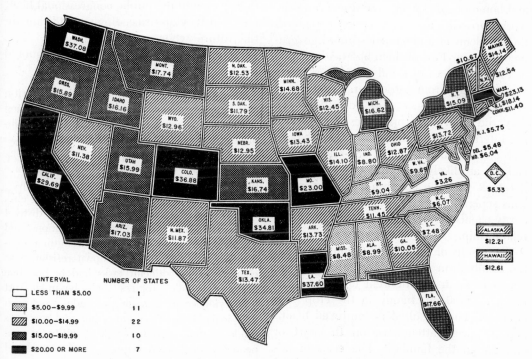

INTERVAL	NUMBER OF STATES
LESS THAN $5.00	1
$5.00–$9.99	11
$10.00–$14.99	22
$15.00–$19.99	10
$20.00 OR MORE	7

Figure 75. Total Amount Expended per Inhabitant for Assistance Payments, Fiscal Year Ending June 30, 1950.

Source: *Social Security Bulletin* (Federal Social Security Agency, Social Security Administration, March, 1951).

gram, homestead projects, and migratory labor camps. The significant function of the agency, as Mr. Wallace — then Secretary of Agriculture — explained, was to lend to low-income farm families unable to get adequate credit elsewhere, and to provide guidance to the borrower by a sound system of farm and home management.[16] The families were also to form coöperatives, including group medical care, and in many cases to change over from a one-crop farming system to a diversified subsistence program. The farm and home plans included the home production of most of the family's food supply and feed for livestock, the development of two or more enterprises which could yield products to sell in the market, and the use of farm practices which would build up the fertility of the soil. Much credit for the success of the plan goes to that group of farm and home advisers who were drawn into the work hurriedly, and who had to cope with the problems of a newly constituted government agency. Few of them had been trained in the techniques of family case work; they came largely from agricultural and home economics experience and education, but they did apply the principles involved in the interrelations of the family and its farm — the man and his land. So-called "specialists" are likely to consider the crops, the livestock, and the children's clothing problems separately. The needs of the Farm Security clients involved the whole family-farm relationship.

The results of the rehabilitation loans and the family-farm plans showed that average net increase in wealth went up steadily, as much as $250 per family in the crop year 1937–38. They resulted in improved health and increased attendance on the part of children in the families. The costs of administration were relatively low compared with work relief, $72 per family per year, contrasted with a range of $350 to $800 for work relief. Reports to Congress in 1944 showed a high degree of solvency in the program with 87 per cent of all loans already paid.[17] Nevertheless, disagreements developed, amendments were introduced, and appropriations were cut. In 1946 the agency was abolished and a substitute agency, known as the Farmers' Home Administration, was formed.

An evaluation of the Farm Security program was made as the result of an intensive study of 600 representative families living in ten selected counties during a four-year period, 1938 to 1942. It stressed the need of families for a sense of security, and made the point that security is not an individual attribute but arises from a feeling of group relations. Such conclusions did not find their way into the public congressional hearings, but they are exceedingly significant for the future welfare of rural society. Two paragraphs from this report are quoted here:

Emotionally these families needed security; they needed to experience the feeling of being wanted; they needed a chance to be contributing members of society. Supervisors in all counties agree that group activities have done more to fulfill these needs — to stimulate production, create unity, and effect social adjustments among the families — than anything else.

To dispel the feeling of inferiority, distrust in humanity, fear of meeting new situations, and so-called relief psychology, to strengthen family solidarity and to break down resistance to change — these difficult tasks had to be done before economic progress could be made. At first, evidences of changing attitudes were seen only in isolated acts — old habits and reactions predominated. Gradually new attitudes appeared with greater frequency and certain old ones were less observable. To contribute to the

---

[16] *Report of the Secretary of Agriculture* (Washington, D.C.: United States Department of Agriculture, 1940).

[17] C. B. Baldwin, *Report of the Administration of the Farm Security Administration* (Washington, D.C., 1940).

welfare of their community and the war gave them new confidence. Better health, clothes, housing, a more cheerful environment and new associations have contributed greatly to a different kind of interplay among personalities in family groups. Explosive or sullen reactions have been replaced by more pleasurable, satisfying and constructive relationships — life has taken on a new meaning, stimulating new hope and greater efforts.[18]

The Farmers' Home Administration Act established by the Seventy-ninth Congress in August, 1946, considers eligible for receiving production and subsistence loans any American citizen who operates a farm not larger than a family-type farm, and is unable to obtain credit from other sources. It is therefore a credit agency and cannot be classed strictly with social security agencies as could its predecessor, the FSA. Its annual report for 1950 indicates that half its loans were advanced to veterans. It administers grants for construction and repairs of farm dwellings and other farm buildings under the Housing Act of 1949.[19]

Public Welfare in Rural Society

Before World War I there was little organized social work in rural counties. Poor relief was carried on for the most part as temporary assistance to keep families out of dire need. During the war the American Red Cross carried on home service work for the families of men who were away. The Red Cross was able to introduce and build up standards of social work in many rural communities which had lacked them entirely before. As the depression came on, it

[18] Rachel Rowe Swiger and Olaf F. Larson, *Climbing Toward Security* (Washington, D.C.: Bureau of Agricultural Economics, U.S. Department of Agriculture, November, 1944).

[19] *Farm Ownership Loans, Farm Housing Loans, Farm Loans to Veterans, Operating Loans for Better Farming, Planning that Pays,* and *Insured Farm Mortgages* (Washington, D.C.: Farmers Home Administration, U.S. Department of Agriculture).

was necessary to organize county or town relief administrations throughout the whole country. It was likewise necessary to devise methods of contacting families. Many counties at first employed local workers with no professional training. Later came an increasing recognition of the importance of good practice by trained social workers to give families adequate care. Scholarships in schools of social work have been obtained and inexperienced workers given an opportunity to carry out and adapt those urban practices of proven worth to rural society.

It is possible that one of the important outcomes of the depression period may be a new conception on the part of rural people and their local welfare officials about the objectives of welfare work through good family case work. They may come to understand the importance of helping those families who sought aid during the depression to become independent and self-reliant again. This emphasis upon the rehabilitation of the family rather than on passing out groceries and fuel for temporary subsistence is basic to public welfare in rural life.

A sketch of public welfare in United States. The laws of Elizabethan England formed the basis for most colonial poor-relief policy. In the New England colonies, responsibility for poor relief was assumed by the towns. The Southern colonies used the county as their administrative unit, while the Middle colonies combined the two systems and placed some responsibility upon counties and some upon towns or other local units. The colonial systems were carried on almost unchanged by the state governments after the revolution.

Specialized care of dependents, defectives, and delinquents developed very slowly during the eighteenth century and the early part of the nineteenth. Classification of dependent persons did not come about to any extent until after 1900. Since that time there has been much improvement in provisions for all groups requiring care, including institutional care. Until relatively recently, however, the only legislation for the public care of needy individuals other than children and war veterans was contained in the state poor laws, and these had undergone very little change since colonial days. "Outdoor" or non-institutional care under the poor laws was not provided to any extent before the last third of the nineteenth century. Those who did receive poor relief were usually designated "paupers," and in some states were deprived even of privileges of citizenship. Eventually, of course, there was an increased acceptance of social responsibility, and state legislatures provided for certain classes of needy persons such as dependent and neglected children or orphans, mothers with dependent children, the blind, or the aged. Aid to dependent children in their own homes was still a later development. The first statute providing for this was not enacted until 1911, but by 1920 the majority of the states had passed some kind of mothers' aid or widows' pension laws. The enactment of the Federal Social Security Act in 1935 required considerable revision in these state statutes.

More recent trends in emphasis. One person who has long been a student and a teacher of social work gives the following conclusions, briefly summarized, after a careful analysis of recent trends: [20]

1. Relative maturity of performance and attitude achieved in the last five to ten years.
2. Acceptance of social work by the man in the street, although he still protests many of its methods. (But not the man in the fields.)
3. Tremendous expansion of public social services including the social insurances and public assistance.
4. Alliance of labor and social work. (As

[20] Helen I. Clarke, "Social Work Today," *Social Forces* (vol. 23, no. 2, December, 1944).

much cannot be said of the farmer or the villager and their organizations. The social worker is still in the process of winning her way, the family case worker probably more than the children's workers.)
5. Extension of social skills into new areas of performance.
6. Expansion of recreation and group work resources for the armed forces and for civilians, particularly for youth.
7. Development of international relief structures.
8. Renewed emphasis upon social planning and social action.

Community organization and county administration. As with health programs, so with welfare and security, the final test of their effectiveness is in the local community. Community organization is now being recognized as a subject for professional consideration in rural as well as in urban circles. One example in the urban field is the rapid expansion in the number of community funds and war chests. Social workers have long been active in community work, but only recently have there been recognized techniques for community analysis of problems and for relating the family to the constructive forces within the community.

At the county level the trend seems to be in the direction of what is called "an Integrated Public Welfare Department." Within such an organization are drawn together the administration of old-age assistance, aid to the needy blind, aid to dependent children, direct relief and medical care, certification to other assistance programs, special aids and services to veterans of military and naval service in coöperation with other designated agencies, family welfare and child welfare activities, as well as maintenance of administration and reporting contacts with state departments involved in any of the programs. This kind of organization involves a legal and working arrangement with the county board of supervisors or other legal authority within the respective counties. Problems of local government to be considered in the next chapter arise at this point, as do those of county-state-federal relationships.

Working with the voluntary and other social agencies. Private or voluntary social services supported by free-will contributions and controlled by citizen boards of various descriptions, like the public services, have increased greatly in recent years. Some have grown up more or less spontaneously, some have been promoted by local lay persons, others by state or national professional workers. They are less uniform from area to area than are the publicly supported and administered agencies. And again, in rural districts including small towns, they are less frequent and less well organized and established than in urban centers.

Mention has been made of the Home Service of the Red Cross. Another nearly universal private "charity" agency in rural communities is the church. The services are often personal and informal and confined to certain groups or classes within the community. In modern public welfare programs the local church may have to modify its traditional lines of relief effort, but it may contribute a great deal to the social and emotional readjustments required to reëstablish self-respect and self-dependence.

Likewise, the school has an important mission to perform in the social welfare and security realm. This can be discharged, not only through class work in the social sciences and in adult education programs, but in the whole attitude and administration of the school as one of the constructive community agencies working along with home, church, club, and government.

Principles and Policies for the Future

Public welfare as a fundamental attack on basic problems of rural destitution has just begun. Social security as a principle in rural society has started a long-time venture. The problems reviewed rapidly in this chapter were characterized by a tone of emergency and a tempo of urgency. The difficulties seemed great and the time short. Many of the problems and difficulties were born of the two great world wars or in the depression which came between. Others were only older ones in aggravated forms.

It must be recognized that insecurities and social problems will always be present, even in so-called "good" or "normal" times. There are sure to be those who through misfortune or mismanagement will need help and guidance. Such help may not, and perhaps should not, be solely in money or in kind, but in services and in the removal of handicaps. The character of a society must be judged by its reaction to such human needs and circumstances.

"Security" and "parity," looking to the future. Both concepts, *security* and *parity*, have arisen during a transition period in American society. Both concepts are ethical in premise, not economic or simply social in character. They have emerged from a deep sense of fair play, equality, and group responsibility. Policies for social security have been designed to give a broader base and a longer perspective to public as well as to private welfare practices. They are aimed to strike at the social and emotional roots of trouble as well as the relief of economic pressures. As the analysis has indicated, the situations from which these problems and difficulties arise involve many conditions besides the economic and the physical. Traditional economic theories or the "input-output" shuttlecock have not brought about a welfare economy.

Social security policies do not go unchallenged. There are people, particularly those with European backgrounds, who decry what is termed excessive social planning to assure security. These arguments are countered by students of modern society (and of American origins) who find adequate justification for these newer developments within our own cultural backgrounds. It does make a difference from what cultural assumptions one begins an analysis of current social situations.[21]

Questions are raised in regard to administration and point of view in approaching so-called "cases." For example, the four categories themselves present special problems in their administration. A farm or village family may not be able to analyze its own difficulty or decide into which category it fits. Therefore the father or the mother starts the rounds of the different agency headquarters, filling out forms and making applications for aid. All these agencies may be housed in the same county court house and have their records there, but there are too few opportunities for cross-reference or for a complete case conference. "Nobody was family minded" is the way one family worker expressed it.[22] These problems arise most readily in regard to caring for children; children are, or should be, in families, and family relations need to be respected. Solutions to administrative complexities are found in better county welfare organization, in family councils or committees, and in the constant reëmphasis upon the central importance of the integrity of the person and of the family, if real rehabilitation is to be effected.

There are others, especially among rural people, who are of the opinion that recipients of social security are losing or have already lost their determination and capacity for individual self-support and for family self-dependence. They say that it is becoming increasingly easy to look to "government" for help or as a scapegoat for one's own failure — a government which some seem to feel lies somewhere beyond them or outside their responsibility and control. As general society matures and as rural society becomes more and more merged into it (and the present analysis indicates that this is happening in America), it would appear that social policies must be revised. The call now is for a wholesome social order where welfare and freedom, security and adventure, responsibility and liberty can dwell together in one household, one community, one nation — perhaps ultimately in one world. How can there be individual freedom or personal liberty without some basic guarantee through group sanction and organized social responsibility? In our time, these are problems of human relations rather than of technical proficiency. Their solution will turn upon our capacity to produce and distribute not only more and better goods and services, but finer human-social beings.

Some principles for assuming social responsibility. With such possibilities in mind, a few simple principles are suggested for consideration in future policies and practices of rural welfare and social security. Goals to be sought are the achievement or the reëstablishment of healthy development and self-dependency for the person in his social relations. But, if the individual suffers a handicap beyond his power to overcome, then the community should assist him. An emphasis upon greater social responsibility appears at this point. Following this thought, it becomes evident that the center of activity for the state or society, whether it be the caring for the disabled, or the aiding of the dependent, or even the handling of the delinquent, hinges upon this matter of the

---

[21] Frederick Hayek, *The Road to Serfdom* (Chicago: University of Chicago Press, 1944); Lawrence K. Frank, "The Rising Stock of Dr. Hayek," *The Saturday Review of Literature* (May 12, 1945).

[22] Gertrude Vaile, *Family Case Work and Public Assistance Policy in Practice of Case Work in Public Agencies* (New York: Family Welfare Association, 1942).

handicap. The handicap may be physical or mental; it may be social or economic, but if it actually exists, society has no choice but to help to correct it. If this view is accepted as a guide to thinking and acting, it will be quickly realized that real strategy for health or for welfare programs is in the direction of prevention, striking at causes before difficulties arise, rather than merely attempting to remedy a problem already existing. This is an emphasis upon conserving and building human resources.

Several corollaries may follow from such an emphasis: [23]

1. Early discovery and diagnosis of remediable defects or social handicaps of an individual, especially of a child, followed by prompt and adequate treatment or training, may save him as a valuable member of society.

2. Difficulties can best be prevented and combated at their source in the local community.

3. Prevention and treatment require that every agency and resource, public or private, be utilized and coördinated.

4. Only skilled and informed personnel can deal with the myriad perplexing problems of health and welfare.

[23] Adapted from Recommendations of Citizens' Committee on Public Welfare, Madison, 1937.

5. Well-organized team work between professionally trained and citizen leaders is necessary — citizen boards to determine policies, professional staffs to execute and administer them.

6. The family should be considered the basic unit for social treatment, and if it becomes necessary to remove a member for special care, a course of treatment should be designed to permit an early return to the home. The family itself may have to be rehabilitated.

7. The county, group of counties, or similar unit should be considered the area for local administration. This unit should be of such population and wealth as to make possible good administration and equitable distribution of costs.

8. State and federal departments should assume such responsibilities as are consistent with local laws and traditions, to insure minimum standards and to equalize the vast inequalities for persons living in different areas.

9. Brick and mortar institutions should be places of last resort, and, even there, treatment should be adapted to individual needs and toward restoring the individual to a useful place in society.

Progress in attaining such goals must depend upon the responsiveness of government to changing social issues at all levels, federal, state and local, but especially local.

TOPICS FOR DISCUSSION

1. What problems in the fields of public welfare and social security do you think are most important in your community? What evidence do you have for your answer?

2. Select one public and one private agency (local, county, state or national) working with welfare and security problems in rural society, and find out all you can about them. Visit local headquarters, interview members of the staff where possible, or if necessary, secure information by mail.

3. Organize this information in brief outline

form and be prepared to present it to the class. Give particular attention to the following points:

   a. The real purpose of agency.

   b. Its local forms of organization.

   c. How it serves rural communities.

   d. How you think such service could be improved.

4. Project a sociodrama for class presentation in which members of the class represent (1) a family case worker, (2) a child welfare specialist, and (3) a public assistance representative. The three are sitting together as a case council. Let the child welfare specialist present "the case" in which a needy child is involved. Through group discussion a de-

cision must be reached as to what should be done.

REFERENCE READINGS

Altmeyer, Arthur J., "Social Security for Farmers," *Land Policy Review,* VIII, No. 1, Spring, 1945.

Arnold, Mildred, "Policies for the Use of Federal Child Welfare Funds," *Social Security Bulletin.* Washington: Federal Social Security Agency, July, 1951.

Biggs, George E., "Federal Grants-in-Aid," *Social Security Bulletin.* Washington: Federal Social Security Agency, November, 1950.

Brown, Josephine C., *The Rural Community and Social Case Work.* New York: Family Welfare Association of America, 1933. Concrete suggestions for immediate steps and for long-time programs in the development of social work in rural communities.

Browning, Grace, *Rural Public Welfare.* Chicago: University of Chicago Press, 1941. Selected records with notes and comments.

Colcord, Joanna C., *Your Community,* Revised Edition. New York: Russell Sage Foundation, 1941. Provisions for health, education, safety, and welfare.

Folsom, Josiah C., *Social Security and Related Insurance for Farm People,* an annotated bibliography. Library List No. 50. Washington: U.S. Dept. of Agriculture, November, 1949.

Gillin, J. L., *Poverty and Dependency,* Revised Edition. New York: Century, 1937. Contains historical and current materials for this and other countries.

Hill, George W., Walter Slocum, and Ruth Hill, *Man-Land Adjustment,* Research Bulletin 134. Madison: Wisconsin Agricultural Experiment Station, 1938. A study of family and interfamily aspects of land retirement in the Central Wisconsin Land Purchase Area.

Howard, Donald S., *The WPA and Federal Relief Policy.* New York: Russell Sage Foundation, 1943.

Landis, B. Y., *Rural Welfare Services.* New York: Columbia University Press, 1949.

Lasseter, Dillard B., *Planning That Pays.* Washington: U.S. Department of Agriculture, July, 1949. Achievements of farm families who are teaming up with the Farmers Home Administration.

Miles, Arthur P., *An Introduction to Public Welfare.* Boston: Heath, 1949. The history, philosophy, structure, and administration of modern public welfare.

Mott, F. D., "Rural Health Parity," *Land Policy Review,* VIII, No. 1, Spring, 1945.

Prentice-Hall, *The 1950 Social Security Act,* with explanation. New York: Prentice-Hall, 1950.

Smith, Marjorie J., *Rural Casework Services.* New York: Family Public Welfare Association, 1943.

Social Security Board, *A Brief Explanation of the Social Security Act,* Information Survey Circular 1. Washington, D.C., 1938. One of a number of popularly written pamphlets which can be readily secured.

Wilson, M. L., *Farm People and Social Security,* Extension Circular 458. Washington: U.S. Department of Agriculture, June, 1949.

FILMS

Canine Eyes for the Blind. S, C, 10. Grubbs.

Problem of Relief. S, 9. Illustrated by the acute relief crisis in New Jersey in 1936. March of Time.

Valley Town. S, 24. Typical American town where in normal times life was good. Then a depression. New York University.

24 Local Government — A Social Institution

GOVERNMENT, and particularly local government, comes well within the purview of "social institution" as defined earlier. It is the more or less regular and recognized way of doing things. In this case it is the more rather than the less regular, since local government has probably changed less in form and organization than any other of the local social institutions with which our study of rural society has been concerned. Yet there have been many changes in the methods by which local units perform their services, and in the relation which such local units bear to state and nation and to rural people themselves. There have also been many new agencies and authorities established in rural areas.

A significant trend is the increased assumption of various social responsibilities by different units of government, as in matters of education, health, welfare, recreation, and services to needy groups. Sometimes this is done by having local units and officials assume larger responsibilities; at other times it is accomplished by the creation of separate administrations for special tasks such as fire protection, library service, health, welfare, irrigation, sewage disposal, or public utilities. In the past decade especially, services have been extended locally by state and federal agencies. The actual number of local units of government did not change significantly as a following section will show, although there was a tendency for the number of small school districts and townships to decrease.

Questions about the future are being pressed in numerous quarters. When much of living was within the country neighborhood, many local government units, such as towns, townships, parishes, villages, and even counties, were necessarily small and locally controlled. Now, with the demand for government to take on an increasing number and amount of functions, there is need for reorganization and realignment. Population is more mobile; group relationships are changing; attitudes are shifting; costs need to be equalized over wider areas and larger numbers of people. These are all concerns for the student of rural society. But, first, it is important, especially in times of uncertainty and when some traditions are being shaken from their moorings, that we should reëxamine the basis for our conception of government here in the United States of America.

America — A B C of Its Law and Government

Assumptions fundamental to all government in this country, are and always have been — not only in phrase but in fact — that our government should be of, for, and by the people. Fuller comprehension of this concept should have a steadying effect.

Backgrounds of our law and government are found in the development of the English common law upon the soil of America. It is important to remember that it was derived from and adapted to a society which was predominantly rural and agricultural. The common law developed slowly and has been influenced along the way by many social, economic, civic, and even ecclesiastical forces. "But running through it all, as warp runs through cloth, were the customs, habits, and traditions of the English race. The enjoyment of political freedom which meant equality before the law was the dominant desire of that race." [1] It is recognized, of course, that other peoples and other traditions have made significant contributions; they have contributed to, not substituted for, the basic principles. Moreover, these very principles and backgrounds became a selective force to determine who came from the Old World into the New. While this theory of government was developing, society was undergoing many changes and the story of the inter-influence of the two is most interesting.

The rural order of things has been greatly altered with the oncoming industrial movement, and many readjustments have been necessary, some of which were tardy in their legal reference. Chief Justice Rosenberry points out that equality before the law does not produce economic equality, and that political freedom does not insure the weaker against oppression by the stronger. In the long run, he suggests, "substantive law is mainly the crystallization of social experiences." This he illustrates in several fields. The common law of master and servant is not adequate in a highly industrial situation. Laws have been made to authorize collective bargaining, agencies have been set up to curb irresponsible activities. The Interstate Commerce Commission is an illustration. Regulations have been made for bringing about a fairer distribution of the proceeds of industry. The common law dealt with nuisances, but now standards must be maintained by both legal and agency means whereby good health can be not only pro-

tected but encouraged. The Pure Food and Drug Act is an example. The free school along with free church and free government came to us from this heritage. In a technical and interdependent society, education is not only desirable, it is necessary; therefore, it was made compulsory and at public expense. The list could be expanded, but the point is that the functions of government are social control and social services, and that the functions of government change and expand as society changes and develops.

In England, the history of social legislation is similar, although in certain fields, as has been pointed out recently, it has often preceded by two or more decades similar enactments in the United States.[2]

Controls of government in the United States were guaranteed to the people in the Constitution by an elaborate system of checks and balances, as they are called, and through the three separate branches of government: legislative, judiciary, and executive. England gave up this system after brief trial. Likewise, the long and intricate provisions by which local, "home rule" government and state's rights shall be protected from the federal authority constitute further basis for popular control. This is quite a different tradition and setting from that of those peoples whose countries have long been committed to state control — statism, as it is termed. Some Americans, particularly in times of distress or depression, may not realize that they are still in control. But those are the very periods when they need to be encouraged to exercise most vigorously the responsibilities of citizenship.

Trends in Local Forms and Functions

With these assumptions, backgrounds, and controls in mind, we may now turn to the

[1] Marvin B. Rosenberry, Chief Justice of the Supreme Court of Wisconsin. "The Development of Substantive Law on Social as Distinguished from Purely Governmental Lines," *Annals of the American Academy of Political and Social Science* (Philadelphia: March, 1928).

[2] Helen Merrell Lynd, *England in the Eighteen-Eighties* (New York: Oxford University Press, 1945).

more recent trends in the local forms and functions of government.

The major fields of local legal and governmental services are three: general political, including election machinery, assessment and collection of taxes, administration of justice, protection of persons and property, and the recording and custody of legal documents; education, agriculture, health and welfare — "charities and corrections" were the early terms; and public services, including highways, bridges, parks, conservation, and control of natural resources. One of the more recent means of control is zoning, under the "police powers." All these functions cannot be considered here; only those which have particular reference to the social as contrasted with the political relations in rural society.

Changes in the number of units. Professor William Anderson's condensed definition of a local unit of government is very useful, and gives ample proof of its social institutional character:

A unit of government may be defined as a resident population occupying a defined area that has a legally authorized organization and a governing body, a separate legal identity, the power to provide certain public or governmental services, and a substantial degree of autonomy, including legal and actual power to raise at least a part of its own revenue.[3]

According to the last decennial census enumeration of 1942, governmental units totaled 155,116.[4] This large number of units, their wide distribution among counties, townships, municipalities, and school and other special districts, and their inter-relations, present a puzzling picture to the uninitiated and often to the professional as well. The distribution of all types of units follows no definite rule either as to population served, extent of areas covered, or taxable base for support. Different regions have

[3] William Anderson, *The Units of Government in the United States* (Chicago: Publication 83 [revised edition], Public Administration Service, 1949).
[4] *A Census of Governments* (formerly called *Wealth, Debt* and *Taxation*) is taken in the years ending in "2."

REGION	ALL GOVERN- MENTAL UNITS †	COUNTIES	TOWNSHIPS AND TOWNS
United States total	155,116	3,050	18,919
Northeast	17,085	205	4,184
North Central	96,595	1,051	14,667
South	25,130	1,396	---
West	16,305	408	68

TABLE 63

Summary of Governmental Units, by Region, 1942

REGION	MUNICIPALITIES			SCHOOL DISTRICTS	SPECIAL DIS- TRICTS
	Total	Urban *	Rural		
United States total	16,220	3,332	12,888	108,579	8,299
Northeast	2,144	834	1,310	9,369	1,174
North Central	7,721	1,099	6,622	70,297	2,847
South	4,756	999	3,757	17,061	1,911
West	1,599	400	1,199	11,852	2,367

* Includes the federal government and the 48 state governments.
† Incorporated places having more than 2500 inhabitants.
Source: *Governmental Units in the United States,* 1942. Washington, D.C.: Bureau of the Census, United States Department of Commerce, 1944.

TABLE 64	REGION	NUMBER OF UNITS PER 1,000 SQUARE MILES	NUMBER OF UNITS PER 100,000 INHABITANTS	AVERAGE NUMBER OF INHABITANTS PER UNIT
Governmental Units Distributed by Population and Areas Served, 1942	United States total	52.1	117.8	848.8
	Northeast	104.4	47.5	2,105.8
	North Central	109.8	231.8	431.3
	South	33.3	62.6	1,597.6
	West	13.8	117.5	851.4

Source: *Governmental Units in the United States*, 1942. Washington, D.C.: Bureau of the Census, United States Department of Commerce, 1944.

different combinations as Tables 63 and 64 clearly indicate. These combinations are not the results of demography or of geography but of the traditions and the movements of the settlers, surveyors' systems, and social and political ideas and patterns.

The town is the distinguishing local unit of New England, and its democratic procedures are an American tradition.[5] The township system, characteristic of New York, spread to the Northwest with westward settlement and took on its regular geographic pattern with the rectangular survey. In Southern states the township and common school districts were unknown. It is a bit of interesting history and fortuity that in territorial days Wisconsin, being a part of Virginia, had the Southern forms of government. Through an election in 1841, the New York system was adopted.[6]

The trend of major changes. A general trend is toward fewer local units, in fact, more than 20,000 fewer, if comparison is made between the 1942 census figures and estimates made by Professor Anderson for 1930–33. Greatest decrease was among school districts and townships. School districts represented more than 70 per cent of

[5] Clarence M. Webster, *Town Meeting Country* (New York: Duell, Sloan and Pearce, 1945, American Folkways Series).

[6] George W. Wehrwein, *Local Government* (Manitowoc, Wisconsin: 1911).

the total. The autonomous school district organized separately from other systems of local administration is uniquely an American institution, although some of these existed in England at one time, and there are also examples in Canada and elsewhere. As has been emphasized in other chapters, the founding fathers in America placed a very high value upon education. They made it universal, compulsory, and at public expense. This was a radical departure from Old World tradition and practice. They were also determined that education be democratically controlled and free from political entanglements; consequently, they devised the small, independent "district system." Like the New England town or the Midwestern township, the early American school district was self-government in its most basic sense. All citizens were expected to assemble in annual meetings, elect board members, determine policies, and vote taxes.

It is interesting by way of comparison to note that in some other countries of English background, Australia, for example, a highly centralized plan of school administration was organized with the same democratic motive in mind. It is claimed that only by a complete system of equalization of rural and urban areas, and of poor and wealthy ones, can every child have an equal opportunity at education.

There are eleven states in which the

county is the principal school unit and ten in which towns or townships perform this function; the other twenty-seven use the district system from the city down to the small rural school district. Among the two latter groups of states, the downward trend in number of school units continued. In a number of states, there have been systematic and determined efforts to combine, consolidate, or reorganize local districts as described in the chapter on education. Professor Anderson has made estimates from official sources for twelve states as given in Table 65.

Illinois, for example, has reduced the number of separate units by nearly one half, Kansas by almost a third. Other states, such as New York, Wisconsin, and Minnesota are in the same process through action by three levels of government: state, county, and local, by townships or school districts.

The elimination of all townships in Oklahoma accounted for three fourths of the total reduction in townships. Other states, in order, were Minnesota, North Dakota, South Dakota, Illinois, Nebraska, and Maine.

The trend is upward for incorporation of centers (cities, villages, boroughs, and towns) although somewhat mixed from state to state or region to region. As recorded elsewhere, shifts in population to suburban areas and to new industrial and residential areas have been accompanied by new incorporations. There is also a tendency for more established villages, small towns, and cities to incorporate to provide their own municipal services, and sometimes to avoid annexation to large cities. Incorporation, however, is no longer the single criterion for inclusion in the "urban" classification of census counts for centers of 2500 or more population.

Special districts for special purposes. The tendency toward special interest groups and the formation of privilege-seeking blocs has been traced in other chapters. One result of such trends, from the standpoint of local government, can be found in special *ad hoc* districts created for the administration of special interests, such as health and sanitation, mosquito abatement, drainage, public assistance, and other services. A locality in the East was found to have eleven different elections each year, some on the township basis, but the majority on the special district basis. Apparently under many local conditions it is easier to organize a special district for a special purpose than it is to reorganize existing units to perform new duties.

Another example is reported in a recent study of local government in the state of Washington. There the taxpayers face a

	STATES	1942 CENSUS FIGURE	OFFICIALLY REPORTED 1948 OR 1949 TOTAL	DECREASE
TABLE	California	2,809	2,342	467
	Idaho	1,148	505	643
65	Illinois	12,138	5,735	6,403
	Kansas	8,632	5,500	3,132
	Missouri	8,613	8,326	287
Decrease in Numbers of	Montana	1,932	1,500	432
School Districts in Twelve	Oklahoma	4,518	2,400	2,118
States	Oregon	1,844	1,363	481
	New York	6,064	4,568	1,496
	Ohio	1,655	1,520	135
	Texas	6,159	4,412	1,747
	Wisconsin	6,569	6,038	531

total of nearly three thousand governmental units empowered to levy taxes and incur debts, and all but about 260 of them are special purpose districts.[7] Nationally, special districts for control of rural roads, bridges, and water are the largest in number. They present many problems. State and county authorities are often unaware of their existence. Their actions, their proposed tax levies, and even their metes and bounds are difficult to record. Their boundaries and often their functions overlap with those of other units.

Urban and rural municipalities also have a tendency to disregard county lines. Local government is, therefore, not a simple arrangement, but rather an intermesh of functions and forms. County and community, as following paragraphs will suggest, must struggle to give it some sense of system and meaning for the local citizen.

Increased social functions bring demands for reorganized systems. Changes in the social functions of a government unit can occur without necessarily altering its form or structure. This process has been developing in recent decades. However, with the increasing load of duties upon public officials and the expanding demands for government action which have been noted has come the demand for reform and reorganization of local government. The many shifts in the characteristics and distribution of population, economic and social changes in group organization, interdependence of country, village, and city, and the greater emphasis upon public education, health, and welfare have made this inevitable. Local units of government as presently constituted, even with the changes which have been described, no longer conform to the social and economic groups in rural society, if indeed

[7] Carl F. Ruess, *County Government in Washington* (Pullman: Washington Agricultural Experiment Station Bulletin 400, May, 1941).

they ever did in some of the middle western states. The civil boundaries of the town, for example, were laid out on quite artificial and arbitrary township lines. The New England town idea may have been in the minds of the pioneering planners, but their engineers set up their transits and laid out the township lines uniformly six miles square. The lines often cut across physical barriers and they were no respecters of the natural groupings of people. A citizen might cast his ballot at a town hall with one group of people and be associated in his educational, religious, and recreational activities with quite another. Certainly this is one reason for the impotence of local government in many rural areas.

During the past few years discussions and studies have turned toward improvement and reorganization of local government. The belief is apparently growing, and with a good deal of strength, that the tens of thousands of local units are a factor in the mounting tax burdens described in an earlier chapter and in the increasing difficulties and problems of local government. Evidence of this rising tide of dissatisfaction is to be found in discussions at meetings of such organizations as the American Country Life Association, Institute of Public Affairs, University of Virginia, Public Administration Service, Chicago, and taxpayers' leagues.

The Governor's Commission of New York for the study of New York and the bill passed in that state for recodification of the century-old town law are examples of reorganization movements. There have been many investigations, some private, others official or quasi-official, of government in rural areas and in such states as New Jersey, Mississippi, Michigan, Wisconsin, Minnesota, and North Carolina. The National Municipal League, the American Public Health Association, and other national organizations have become increasingly interested in local government reform.

Discussion has passed on into action in a number of states. Reorganization seems to be taking two general forms. First is the tendency toward consolidation of existing units or the formation of larger units adjusted to expanded needs. This inevitably involves the abolition of certain local units, especially townships and local districts. Second is the tendency for certain functions and services to pass from local units to county, state, or even to federal control. This involves questions of administration, finance, personnel, and even of constitutional changes. Social considerations need their due share of attention, for it must be emphasized that principles for the reorganization of local government will have to be anchored to heavier arguments than the immediate interests of administrative efficiency and financial economy, important as these are.

Tendencies toward centralization and consolidation. The question of centralized control versus local control, or "home rule" as is often called, has been debated with much fervor. It has gone even to the highest courts of the land. Originally the state legislature had complete power over counties, but the question of local control was raised again and again until the Supreme Court of the United States only a few decades ago ruled that "the state made it [the county] and could, in its discretion, unmake ." [8]

In spite of all this, people continually insist upon their right to circumscribe state and federal rule in their own localities. They fear betrayal of local interests by central authority. Rural people fear domination by urban interests. Constitutions, therefore, are filled with clauses and amendments pre-

venting most states from modifying local functions and units of government unless constitutional limitations are first removed. Centralized tendencies on the part of states have been checked at many points by city home rule legislation. Villages have incorporated and set themselves off from the town government so that they may do as they choose within their boundaries, and in some states they have done so for the specific purpose of securing direct representation on county boards.

States, however, are steadily assuming more and more control over local functions and agencies. For the most part this is accomplished within the framework of existing governmental organizations in one of two ways: through the direct assumption of local functions and by means of various grants-in-aid or subventures which carry certain supervisory or controlling powers. Local units including counties, under the heavy pressure of property taxes, have given way to arguments of economy and efficiency.

Grants-in-aid for education, housing, health, hospitals, social security, and welfare have been reviewed in other chapters. The plan has become increasingly popular as a way for state and federal governments to participate in local affairs and to exert influence. The granting of subsidies by a central government to local units has long been practiced in the Old World, but in the United States it is only within the last fifty years that there has been a notable expansion in the amounts, purposes, and contingent provisions for such grants. The trend has an important bearing on county and community organization policies.

Between 1910 and 1930 the amount of state grants for education increased more than four times, but the total amount of state revenues and expenditures during the same time increased at about the same rate. Consequently the subsidies for education remained in about the same proportion to

[8] Howard P. Jones, "Constitutional Barriers to the Improvement in County Government," *National Municipal Review* (August, 1932, Supplement).

total state expenditures.[9] To be sure, since 1930 there has been a great increase in all state and federal aids, but no estimates are available to indicate the extent to which local budgets have been relieved or augmented in order to assure equality for rural groups. Local communities in many states continue to struggle on as best they can in the face of uncertain or changing state and national policies or in their absence. As suggested earlier, in our American system of government final responsibility rests with the local units. They must assume the residual expense load in caring for their own citizens or allow them to suffer by comparison with others.

Grants for highways come from both state and federal sources; the same holds true for social security, health, and welfare. Not so, however, for general education, it should be noted; only for vocational and other special programs. Many state and some federal specialized services have also increased during recent years. These include laboratories, clinics, diagnostic centers, hospitals for special groups such as veterans, and specialized professional personnel. Their purpose is to relieve local institutions of special problems and expense and to implement the principle of equalizing social opportunities despite wide economic differences in local situations. The centralizing and equalizing trend under review is much less advanced in such matters as fire and accident protection, recreation, parks and playgrounds, and adult education than in other fields of local activity.

Newer forms and working relationships. Recently new types of authority have

[9] John A. Fairlie, "Subsidies to Local Governments," *Proceedings of the Chicago Exploratory Research Conference on the Reorganization of the Areas and Foundation of Local Government* (New York: Social Science Research Council, 1932). See the chapter on education and the schools for other figures regarding proportions of state aid.

appeared for setting up local units of government, encouraged and backed by substantial appropriations from the national government. Examples are the United State Housing Authority and the Soil Conservation Service in the United States Department of Agriculture. The latter is the federal government's first venture into the arena of local government, and as Professor Anderson points out, has resulted in increasing the number of local units and also in further complicating the structure of local government.

Another interesting development in federal-local government relations is the so called "action" agencies described in an earlier chapter. Under the Agricultural Adjustment Act, for example, an acreage allotment of soil-depleting crops was set for every farmer in the country. Compliance with the allotment was the basis for benefit payments. The point of interest here is the direct line of contractual agreement from the federal government to the individual farmer. The general administration was given to a national department, and locally to county and community committees whose activities have been detailed in a previous chapter. A similar direct contract relationship was set up through the Farm Home Administration in the tenant-purchase program. The Pope-Jones Water Facilities Act provides for direct aid to individual farmers and ranchers in the development of facilities for water on private lands. This is definitely something new under the governmental sun.

Some new forms have also been devised looking toward conservation and coördination rather than expansion and specialization. The soil-conservation district cited above is one, but another is the principle of zoning applied to land-use. This is in the sphere of what may be called state-local relations. The state, by passing an enabling act, encourages counties to set up a zoning ordinance which becomes operative when

e local units, townships, or other munici-
alities vote it. This is in conformity with
he idea of social uses for land, also ex-
lained in an earlier chapter. Certain sec-
ons of land are "zoned" against agriculture
ecause it is considered that there are better
ocial uses; that is, better from the standpoint
f public policy. Such uses might be for-
stry, recreation, wild-life refuge, or water
onservation.

Developments such as those briefly re-
iewed can become, as two political scien-
sts have pointed out, opportunities for
artisan prizefights or for collaboration by
arious levels of local governments in order
o strengthen and improve their position.[10]
ew techniques are needed to bring about
uch improvement.

One experiment has been the land-use
lanning committees, both at the commu-
ity and the county level, to which reference
as been made. It is not a new technique
or farmers to meet together and plan, but
nce 1933, when the action programs came
to use, the opportunity has been greatly
xpanded. There is no general agreement
n how well some of the experiments have
ucceeded. In some states the areas for
ctivity were extended from land-use to gen-
ral over-all planning for agriculture, includ-
g social activities.[11] At least one of the
otives, according to M. L. Wilson, director
f the Federal Agricultural Extension Service,
as to intensify and extend the democratic
rocess in rural America. He said, "We must
attle for a renaissance of democracy and

for new democratic patterns in farm life and
in the rural community." [12]

Consideration of the agricultural extension services brings to attention an important federal-state-county government relationship often overlooked or perhaps taken
for granted. It is the system of enabling
legislation, appropriation, and personnel selection whereby the three levels of government — national, state, and county — work
as one in the hiring and the services of agricultural representatives; "county agents"
they are called locally in many states. The
agents may be employed to do agricultural,
home economics, junior, or even specialized
work within the county. It means "the agricultural agent, himself a combination of
federal, state, and local official," carries on
in the county, in the community, and on the
farms.[13]

The agricultural and home economics
teachers in the rural community high schools
are another example of national-state-com-
munity relationships in local government.
They have the unique opportunity, to which
frequent reference has been made, to give
leadership through the high school to local
community development. The hope is registered here that in the future the two lines of
relationship can be more closely coördinated, both officially and practically; namely,
the Smith-Lever provision for county agents
and the Smith-Hughes and the George Dean
provisions for agricultural and home economics teachers.

The TVA is itself an experiment in federal-local governmental relations. Mr. Lilienthal explains that there is a sound distrust of
bigness and of remote control among the
rank and file of local citizens. Therefore he
believes the decentralized administration of

[10] John M. Gaus, address at Association of Land
rant Colleges and Universities, Chicago, Novem-
er 14, 1938; and Leon Wolcott, "National Land-
se Program and the Local Governments," *Na-
onal Municipal Review* (vol. XXVII, no. 2, Feb-
uary, 1939).
[11] Neal C. Gross, "Post Mortem on County Plan-
ing," *Journal of Farm Economics* (vol. XXV, no. 3,
ugust, 1943); Robin M. Williams and Howard W.
eers, *Farmers on Local Planning Committees in
hree Kentucky Counties, 1939–1940* (Lexington:
ulletin 443, Kentucky Agricultural Experiment
tation, 1943).

[12] *Land Policy Review* (January-February, 1939).
[13] David E. Lilienthal, "The T.V.A.: An Experiment in the 'Grass Roots' Administration of Federal
Functions." Address, Southern Political Science
Association, Knoxville, Tennessee, November 10,
1939.

federal functions which lend themselves to such techniques and the coördination in the field of such decentralized activities is one answer. Such activities in the TVA have included use of farm equipment, community refrigeration, operation of power systems, wild-life conservation, and population transfers.[14]

Finally, local units of government may discharge powers and duties by coöperative methods. This may be done by joint employment of trained personnel and the construction, or at least the use by contract or other arrangement, of social institutions, such as sanitaria, fire-fighting equipment, or library services. There may be construction and maintenance on a contract basis of such public services as highways, sewers, or breakwaters. There can be coöperative purchasing of supplies or equipment or the inspection of plumbing or of weights and measures.[15] It is pointed out that savings can accrue from such joint arrangements as well as real improvement in services and facilities.

Where there is a will, a way can frequently be found, and, as has been suggested elsewhere, social practice may need to precede legal sanction. Added opportunities are, therefore, given to local government authorities, and they increase the importance of good county and community organization and administration.

Government in Local Action

The discussion thus far should lead to the conclusion that the issue is not local govern-

ment versus state or federal government but that the real task is to bring into local action all government in all its phases and services. The theory of conflict is giving way, even in the courts, and in its place the realization is slowly growing that the function of government is the welfare and happiness of the citizens; that there are common interests, and that these can best be served by giving attention to local situations where problems arise.[16] Poverty, delinquency, ignorance, unemployment, are problems of local origin and import, but they are no respecters of government units or boundary lines. Protection is prevention at source has proved the best motto. To conclude the chapter, therefore, brief discussion will be given to three phases of government service which may help to reach such local objectives.

The state, the equalizing and servicing unit. The state, and in similar reference the nation, may be regarded, from this one standpoint of local government, as a unit for bringing about a better equalization throughout rural society. The function would include not only equalizing of tax burdens, but of standards in services and contracts, the qualifications of personnel through training and certification in some civil service system in the central custody of records, and in the "orders in council" of state departments.

More vigorous service can be rendered in terms of grants-in-aid and specialized services, materials, laboratories, and personnel which cannot possibly be available in the smaller units. Of course, many complications can easily develop if the principles suggested above are not followed meticulously by all parties involved. For example, it was suggested in the Washington State Report referred to earlier, that a generous State

[14] Lilienthal, *op. cit.,* and *Democracy on the March* (New York: Harper, 1944); Herman Finer, *The T.V.A.: Lessons for International Application* (Montreal: International Labor Office, 1945); Philip Selznick, *T.V.A. and the Grass Roots, a Study in the Sociology of Formal Organization* (Berkeley: University of California Press, 1949).

[15] "Joint Municipal Services," *The Municipality* (Madison: the League of Wisconsin Municipalities, August, 1944).

[16] John R. Mashek, "The Changing Nature of Federalism," *Iowa Farm Economist* (September, 1944).

Claus could later assume the proportions of a Trojan Horse. In changed metaphor, but with the same meaning, the *Municipal Bulletin* of that state describes the situation in which some cities, and it could as well be counties, find themselves. "Through the back door of unemployment relief, the federal government entered the cities and now occupies a seat in the parlor." Well, perhaps the local government house needs both a back door and a parlor, but, more important, it requires some kind of management and also integration with other units in the community and nation. It cannot be a dwelling apart from the rest of society and have even its own household members adequately served. It is an excellent example of how easy it is to get into the "either-or" attitude, the need for the choice between this and that authority, rather than the coöperative position of "both-and" for local and nation-state responsibility for common problems.

The county, the administering unit. A case has been deliberately made for the suggestion that the county serve as the administrative and the community as the working unit for the many public services needed in modern rural society. It could well be an extension of TVA principles to local government practice, namely centralized policy but decentralized administration. Whether this shall be made the prevailing pattern rests ultimately upon rural leaders and upon rural people themselves. There is evidence of an increase in and a concentration of agencies and services at the county level: county health units, many agencies concerned with farm and family including county agricultural and home demonstration extension services; movements toward county administration of education; the urge and legislation for county library service; the increase of county park and recreation places; and an accumulation of social security and welfare functions on the county basis. Further-

more, the Anderson study of trends in government units definitely indicates that the number of counties in the United States has stabilized at about 3000. The county is evidently here to stay.

There is also evidence of renewed effort on the part of county officials and citizens to keep pace in thinking and in control of this mounting tide of public agencies and services. That problems arise is not surprising, but that they are recognized and grappled with is hopeful. Pressures for more central controls and the multiplication of agencies are sure to place the operations of government farther and farther from the understanding of the run-of-the-mill citizen. He may be inclined to throw up his hands in despair or, even worse, in disgust, and feel that government has passed beyond his responsibility or control. Such is not the case in certain areas where sample studies have been made by Councils on Intergovernmental Relations working on three levels: federal, state and county.[17]

In this connection, committees of citizens and public officials tried first to analyze their problems at the local level, then to establish policies, and finally to institute practices. In Henry County, Indiana, they discovered 327 units and agencies purporting to serve their citizens — 110 local, 111 state, and 106 federal. There was little planned coördination, some units working in related fields quite unaware of the presence of other agencies and programs. Many misconceptions were encountered on the

[17] John O. Walker, *Grass Roots*, a report and an evaluation on five experimental programs: Blue Earth County, Minnesota, Henry County, Indiana, Colquitt County, Georgia, Santa Clara County, California, Skagit County, Washington (Washington, D.C.: Council on Intergovernmental Relations, September, 1946); Henry County Council, Indiana, *Adventures in Governmental Gearing*, a progress report of the county demonstration (New Castle: County Council on Intergovernmental Relations, 1946); T. Hamp McGibony, *Government Cooperation in Greene County, Georgia* (Washington, D.C.: Council on Intergovernmental Relations, 1945).

part of people who did not understand local
conditions, and there were criticisms, some
based on facts and some on fiction, arising
out of rumor and gossip.

Popular policy statements arrived at after
studying the problems and discussing their
consequences took the following form:

1. Less centralized control — more federal-state counsel and technical assistance.
2. Furthering citizen participation — civic
   education.
3. Self-help by enabling legislation, plus
   more local doing; less ducking.
4. More central-local shared revenue
   plans — fewer doles.
5. Elimination of duplication — more coordination.
6. Property assessment revisions.

Putting recommendations into practice
proved even more interesting. The Agricultural Committee in the Governmental Co-
operation plan for Greene County, Georgia,
found six agencies in addition to the agricultural extension service. They were working together quite informally but there was
no county-wide farm program. After many
conferences with the coöperation of state
and federal representatives, a United Farm
Program was formally organized. One of
the first undertakings was a land-use planning survey. Each community selected a
committee of local farmers to study and map
their own areas. Their findings were pooled
and a map for the whole county was made.
From this it was agreed which land should
be cultivated, where erosion projects would
be needed, which lands should be terraced
and which retired to pastures or forests. Not
only was the program concerned with the
land, but with improving living conditions
of the people on the land. More and better
education was considered necessary, so five
teachers were added by the County Board

of Education, making a total of seven white
and six colored vocational and home economics teachers in the county.

Encouraged by their success on the farm
front, a United County Program was started
Featured were regular monthly meetings of
all federal, state and local representatives
of public agencies in the county, under the
chairmanship of the county agricultural
agent. The group included the home demonstration agent, teachers of vocational agriculture and home economics, the director
of the county welfare department, county
nurses, county superintendent of schools
representatives of the Soil Conservation
Service, Forest Service, Farm Home Administration, and the chairman of the County
Commissioners.

Another effort to bring about better coördination of effort and to give some sense of
direction is the county council. The idea
harks back nearly forty years to the Councils of National Defense of World War I
Likewise, during World War II, county
agencies assumed large responsibilities and
coördinating policies were put into practice
An especially interesting five-year experiment with a county council was carried on
in Greenville County, South Carolina.[18]

There are those who feel that county government must be something more than administrative; that it should be empowered
to perform services similar to a city municipality; and that it should have an executive
head. The county-manager plan, an adaptation of the city-manager plan, has been advocated for this purpose, but it has had
little acceptance apart from a few largely
urban counties.

Details of county-wide administration for
rural services cannot be given here, but a
summary under six general functions is suggested. They appear to be more and more
dependent for promotion and administration
upon the county or similar local unit.

[18] Edmund deS. Brunner, *Community Organiza-*

1. Education: youth and adult, vocational and cultural, including schools and libraries.

2. Agriculture: services to farm, family, and youth.

3. Health: physical and mental, remedial and preventive.

4. Welfare: social security, child welfare, corrections.

5. Public services: roads, bridges, parks, conservation, zoning for land-uses.

6. Political: elections, tax levy and collection, protection and justice.

Counties unable to perform at least a majority of such functions may be considered not worthy and not capable of permanent county status.

The community, the working unit. The community idea is posited on the theory that rural people can and wish to join together locally, to determine their common weal. Field workers in rural communities reported that local people insist that some form of local organization is necessary. They argue that the county is too large and the county seat too far away. They want local officials whom they "can know and trust." Many town chairmen and clerks as well as many village officials are familiar to their constituencies and go far beyond narrow legal or semi-legal duties. They are truly "representatives of the people." Unfortunately, not all the declarations of local politicians are sincere. Just as city people turn to their ward leaders for help in untangling difficulties arising out of conflicts in governmental jurisdiction, so rural people turn to their own local officials. This is simply to say what Professor William B. Munro has expressed more emphatically thus: "They [people of educated and propertied classes] have been obsessed with a faith in political mechanics and have been enslaved to the conviction that government is an affair of laws, not of men." [19]

The administrative unit for many functions may be the county; but there is need for more localized working units. For example, in some states, like California and Ohio, where the county library plan has wide usage, a local branch is often maintained in the high school, not only for the pupils, but for the residents of the larger community. There may be a branch in the village also, but the whole system, both of finance and of personnel, is integrated. Needless duplications, often found among country district schools, or between country and village schools, or again between school and village libraries, are avoided.

County health units were also visited in which community groups of interested adults formed the real working unit of the organization. Prevention and therapeutic work was all correlated with plans carried out through the schools. Agencies for recreation, child welfare, social service, credit, and fire prevention were found working according to similar arrangements.

Church leaders are talking of the "larger parish," the central idea of which they say is "a group ministry over areas as well as churches." They point out that this is really a return to the original English practice where churches are responsible for definite and assigned "parishes." Promotion of the plan in this country is proceeding definitely upon the theory of a town-country community.

The school has been repeatedly emphasized for the part it may play in community leadership for both youth and adult. The conclusion of the South Carolina Report, to which reference has already been made, is pertinent. "A developing concept of the community school holds greatest hope for the future of a creative rural life."

---

ion and Adult Education (Chapel Hill: University of North Carolina Press, 1942).

[19] Quoted from *Information Service* (New York, October 31, 1931).

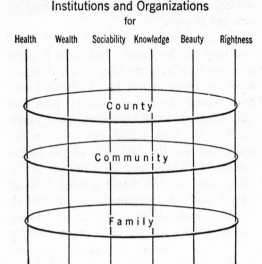

Institutions and Organizations
for

Health   Wealth   Sociability Knowledge   Beauty   Rightness

County

Community

Family

in
Rural Society

Figure 76. Chart Suggesting Perpendicular Type of Organization for Social Institutions in Rural Society.

A complete governmental unit on the community basis has even been proposed. Its advocates suggest that it could be flexible enough to accommodate different local situations in all of their essential functions.[20]

The problem of coördination and the importance of local action can perhaps be illustrated with a simple diagram. The trends toward specialization and segregation of groups and functions which have been traced herein can very easily lead to a perpendicular type of social organization. The familiar either-or view is weak; there is need for some means of deliberate integration and cross-reference. It makes very little difference where one begins or what set of agencies one chooses. The tendency can be illustrated by the chart in Figure 76, in which Doctor A. W. Small's six elementary inter-

ests are used.[21] Institutions and agencies are bearing down upon rural society with a great deal of independence of action and with much pressure from the top down, "the top" being state, regional, or national headquarters. This trend toward centralized control for many agencies has already been pointed out in earlier chapters.

The three rings in the diagram suggest the necessity for some linkage or integration at various levels, the family, the community, and the county. If the picture were to be completed, it would probably be necessary to introduce additional rings for personality and state. However, the concern here is more largely with local organization policies. In discussions of the increasing importance attached to group relationships in a modern and changing society, individual and state interests receive much attention. To be sure, the reconciliation of the demands and impulses of personality with the requirements of a complex society is important; yet it is to be remembered that much of life is lived in an area which is the domain of neither the individual nor the state. As a matter of fact, some of the most important and socializing experiences occur between these two spheres.

The importance of the rural family and the problems centering on its children have been detailed elsewhere. The point at issue here is whether the rural community can, with courage and foresight, forge a link which will bind into a unity of action those agency arrows which are bearing down upon it? Traditionally, the rural community had elements of individualism and of competitive independence. Under modern conditions it has an opportunity to work out another way of living. It might even be argued that collective action is necessary as a means of self-defense, lest independent institutions disrupt local life. From a more

[20] Theodore B. Manny, *The Rural Municipalities* (New York: Century, 1930).

[21] *General Sociology* (Chicago: University of Chicago Press, 1905), p. 198.

constructive standpoint, however, the opportunity is present for a greater awareness of local needs and for coördinated efforts to meet them. To accomplish this, as Sanderson says, a desire for unified action is imperative.[22] The promotion of the common welfare can be made the goal of the community only as it becomes more self-conscious and gradually assumes self-direction.

The county link binding the arrows into a sheaf brings us back to the trends and policies already discussed and to the place which the county can legitimately hope to maintain in public and in voluntary forms of social control and social action. It must be urged once more that local governmental and social organization is not for the purposes of limiting or hemming in, but rather of introducing and relating rural society to the larger society.

This chapter began with the statement that there had been little recent change in the forms of local government, but there have been recorded here many changes in governmental activities and devices. The interesting thing is that the form and structure of local government have not changed significantly under the impact of all this changing activity. State and federal agencies have simply caught on where and how they could. Sometimes, when finding nothing to tie to locally, they have dealt directly with individuals. However, the very contact of local people with representatives of larger units must have modified their conceptions of the purposes of social action under the aegis of this institution which we call government.

Questions arise, of course, which cannot be answered now, as to the long-time effects of this movement upon small local units. The movement may influence the attitudes of rural people as to the uses of government.

It is certainly sharpening the division between those who welcome and those who resent the increased power of state and nation. But whatever their reactions, most rural citizens now find themselves in an intermesh of governmental relationships that have been set up because of some need. They may not be logical and they may not follow existing jurisdictions, but there they are. Soil-conservation districts, for example, were made to follow geological and geographical, not political, lines, although in some instances they have been pressed into present county patterns.

The way to get things done is to get things done. That is the way American society works, and has worked for some time. It is a striking fact that each county council working on intergovernmental relations to which reference has been made, reached the conclusion that there was greater fluidity and flexibility about government, and more interplay among its agencies and other groups in society than they were inclined to believe at the time they began their work. These are characteristics which the Frenchman Alexis de Tocqueville observed and took into account in his analysis of *Democracy in America* more than 75 years ago.[23] They are fundamental to our way of life, for as Professor R. M. MacIver stresses so firmly, society and the state must not be confused nor the one identified as the other.[24] It is necessary to distinguish between the multigroup, uncentralized relationships of society which have been detailed in this discussion, and government with its centrally coördinated activities and agencies, lest we set foot upon a dangerous road leading away from the ABC principles of government with which we started.

[22] Dwight Sanderson, *The Rural Community* (Boston: Ginn, 1932).

[23] Ed. Phillip Bradley (New York: Alfred A. Knopf, 1945).

[24] *The Web of Government* (New York: Macmillan, 1947).

TOPICS FOR DISCUSSION

1. Describe the general plan of local government which is operative in your state. Indicate the relation of local units to each other.
2. Enumerate the functions performed by the local units of government in your state and the officials or boards responsible for each.
3. In establishing or maintaining a rural high-school program, what unit requirements, such as number of people, size of district, and wealth of area, need to be considered? How do these units compare with similar units required for libraries, hospitals, townships, and counties?
4. To the support of what local rural institutions must county, state, or nation contribute? On what principles can you justify such support?
5. Describe evidences which you have observed of the break-down of local units of government, or of efforts (successful or otherwise) to reorganize local functions and units on larger scales.
6. Plans may be worked out for organizing all or part of the class as a county board to consider the needed programs and finances for the year. Committees presenting different phases of work such as health, agriculture, education, recreation, public welfare, and so on, would present their claims. The final adoption of a complete program and budget would rest with the class as a whole or, if organized on the small commission plan, with those members who are appointed to act as commissioners.

REFERENCE READINGS

Bentley, Arthur F., *The Process of Government, A Study of Social Pressures*. Bloomington, Ind.: The Principia Press, 1951.

Beuscher, J. H., *Farm Law in Wisconsin*. Appleton, Wisc.: C. C. Nelson, 1951.

Brownlow, Louis, and Charles S. Ascher, *Less Government or More?* Chicago: American Library Association, 1933.

Conservation Department, *From Public Burden to Public Benefit, The Story of Marinette County's Land Program and Zoning Plans,* Bulletin 483. Madison: Wisconsin Agricultural Experiment Station, 1949.

Council of State Governments, *Federal Grants-in-Aid, Report of Committee* (No. L28). Chicago: Public Administration Service, 1949.

Field, Oliver, Pressly Sikes, and John Stover, *State Government*. New York: Harper, 1949.

Fisher, Marguerite J., and Edith E. Starratt, *Parties and Politics in the Local Community*. A Community Study series prepared for School of Citizenship and Public Affairs, Syracuse University, for use of teachers and community leaders. Washington: National Council for Social Studies, 1945.

Gaus, John M., *Political Science Back Home*. An address to the New York State Political Science Association, Utica, N.Y., October 21, 1951.

Jones, Howard P., "Reorganization of County Government in New York State." Charlottesville: University of Virginia Institute of Public Affairs, 1934.

Kumlien, W. F., *Basic Trends of Social Change in South Dakota*, Chap. vii, "Local Government," Bulletin 347. Brookings: South Dakota Agricultural Experiment Station, February, 1941.

Lancaster, Lane W., *Government in Rural America*. New York: D. Van Nostrand, 1937. Analysis of town and county governments in the several states.

Parsons, K. H., "Local Government Adjustments to Land Programs." Supplementary Report of Land Planning Committee, Section IV, National Resources Board, titled "Certain Aspects of Land Problems and Government Land Policies." Washington, 1935.

Raushenbush, Stephen, *Our Conservation Job*, Report No. 4. Washington: Public Affairs Institute, 1941.

Stein, Clarence S., *Toward New Towns for America*. An account of the development of America's new towns, including Radburn, Chatham Village, the Greenbelt towns, and Baldwin Hills Village. Chicago: Public Administration Service, 1951.

Wehrwein, George S., "Village Government in

Wisconsin." Madison: Wisconsin Blue Book, 1940.

FILMS

Law and Social Controls. S, 10. Three social controls: law, custom, and moral codes. *Coronet.*

Our Government. S, 11. English tradition, state constitutions, current philosophies. Knowledge Builders.

TVA. S, 20. Tennessee Valley Authority.

Wisconsin Makes Its Laws. S, C, 30. Document of the social processes by which needs for laws arise. How the proposed law is discussed, introduced, referred to committee, given public hearings, engrossed, voted upon, signed or vetoed by the governor, and tested before the Supreme Court. University of Wisconsin.

Rural Welfare in Underdeveloped Countries

THIS ANALYSIS of rural society has given major attention to the United States. Those who live in North America, or for the most part wherever the Euro-American culture is dominant, often forget that this is still a rural world. Three fifths, if not two thirds, of the inhabitants of the earth live on farms, close to a billion in Asia alone. The problems and unsatisfied aspirations of these peoples are the root cause of many of the questions that disturb the statesmen of the world.

The close relationship between poverty and rurality is strikingly borne out by a study of the Food and Agriculture Organization, the essence of which is given in Table 66. It will be noted that in 1949 only twelve countries exceeded a per capita income of $500 in United States money. Twelve more fell between $300 and $500. Twenty-one were between $100 and $300. Twenty-five, more than a third, failed to reach $100! Included in this group are some of the most populous nations — China, India, Pakistan. The forty-six countries on the lower part of the scale have for the most part the highest proportions of farm population.

The means to poverty.[1] Obviously the contrasts in income and rurality among these groups of countries are not the only differences between them. A century and a half ago, had records for the comparison given in this table been available, the contrasts would have been far less striking. A cen-

tury ago there was perhaps 1.8 horsepower available per agricultural worker in the United States. Even half a century ago this had risen only to 2.2. By 1930 the figure was 12.7, but by 1940 it had more than doubled, to 27.8 horsepower per farm worker. Today it is probably well over 30.[2] In China there has been no such change. In fact, the Chinese farm worker today has less power available than the North American had in 1800. Hence the shift from agriculture to secondary and tertiary industries has been greatly retarded.

Small size of farms. But there are other "means to poverty." One is the very small average size of farm, 3.3 acres in China, 2.5 acres in Japan, 2.6 in Korea, 5 to 8 in India under British rule, and so on.[3] Since the average size of the farm family is about 5.5 persons, it is clear that income from such farms would be low and provide little surplus for a higher standard of living, let alone for any capital savings. Only unceasing toil by the whole family staves off economic catastrophe, even starvation. Yields per acre in the Orient are often phenomenally high, yields per worker pathetically low judged by western figures. The number of males per 1000 acres employed in agriculture in Japan is thirty-five times as high as in the United States.

[2] Estimates by Professor Erich W. Zimmerman. Cf. his *World Resources and Industries* (New York: Harper, 1951), chap. XII.

[3] Very few references are given in the rest of this chapter. All factual statements made are taken from one or another of the books listed in Appendix II, "Bibliography of Rural Life in Foreign Lands."

[1] This phrase is borrowed from Professor Horace Belshaw, University College, Wellington, New Zealand.

TABLE 66

Per Capita Income in United States 1949 Dollars for Selected Countries Compared with Per Cent Farm Population or Per Cent Labor Force, Both Sexes, in Agriculture*

COUNTRY	PER CAPITA INCOME	% FARM POPULATION	% LABOR FORCE IN AGRICULTURE
United States	$1453	16	x
Canada	870	27	x
New Zealand	856	x	20
Switzerland	849	20	x
Sweden	780	22	x
Great Britain	773	6	x
Denmark	689	26	x
Australia	679	x	11
Norway	587	25	x
Belgium	582	15	x
Luxemburg	553	17	x
Netherlands	502	18	x
France	482	25	x
Iceland	476	31	x
Ireland	420	x	49
Israel	389	56	x
Czechoslovakia	371	28	x
Finland	348	50	x
Argentine	346	x	x
Uruguay	331	x	x
Venezuela	322	x	50
Germany (West)	320	18	x
Soviet Union (Russia)	308	57	x
Poland	300	60	x
Cuba	296	x	41
Hungary	269	49	x
South Africa	264	x	64
Portugal	250	40	x
Italy	235	45	x
Austria	216	87	x
Chili	188	39	x
Panama	183	71	x
Yugoslavia	146	x	22
Colombia	132	x	62
Greece	128	42	x
Costa Rica	125	x	x
Turkey	125	x	82
Lebanon	125	x	x
Mexico	121	x	65
Brazil	112	x	67
N. Rhodesia	101	x	x
Egypt	100	x	x
Japan	100	47	70
Syria	100	x	x
Peru	92	x	x
El Salvador	89	x	75
Nicaragua	85	x	73
Iran	85	x	x
Iraq	84	x	x
Paraguay	83	x	x
Honduras	77	x	71
Guatemala	75	x	x
Dominican Republic	67	x	77
Ceylon	57	x	x
India	55	67	x
Bolivia	51	x	x
Pakistan	50	x	x
Afghanistan	44	x	x
Philippines	40	x	65
Ecuador	40	x	x
Saudi Arabia	40	x	x
Yemen	40	x	x
Haiti	38	x	x
Ethiopia	36	x	x
Burma	36	x	68
Thailand (Siam)	35	x	88
Korea (South)	27	x	x
China	25	73	x
Indonesia	25	x	66

* These data are based on the most recent censuses or official estimates ranging from 1939 to 1948.

x Not available.

Source: *Yearbook of Food and Agricultural Statistics.* Food and Agriculture Organization, Washington, 1951.

Pressure of population. As would be expected from these facts, the pressure of population on the land is heavy in many of the poorer countries. Cultivated area per capita in the United States is about 2.3 acres, permitting exports of food and fibre. In Japan it is only one tenth as much, forcing the importation of food. In China it is .4 acre per person. This, of course, makes land a very valuable commodity. Even in 1927 one of the authors engaged in field research in the Japanese Empire found rice land selling at from $500 an acre for upland fields to $1500 an acre for irrigated paddy land. Ownership, save by inheritance, had become very difficult by the time of World War II. It is estimated that the population of India tripled between 1850 and 1950, and that the average size of farms declined 66 per cent in the same period.

Landless men. Under these circumstances the proportion of owner-operator farmers declined steadily. The ratios differ with different countries, but it is evident from a number of surveys that less than half the farmers of Asia, and in some lands less than a third, own the land they till. Moreover, as the Sino-American Commission on Chinese Agriculture pointed out, tenancy contracts were a mockery. They could be altered or cancelled at the whim of the landlords.

Not only has farm tenancy increased rapidly in many countries as a result of these conditions, but the number of landless men has mounted. Between 1911 and 1931 the number of laborers per 1000 cultivators in India rose from 254 to 417,[4] over a fifth of the total labor force. No wonder one of the first acts of the new Indian Government was to break up the large estates in order to get land for the farmers. It must not be forgotten that in at least three successful revolutions in this century, those in Mexico, Russia, and

[4] Manilal Nanavati and J. J. Anjenia, *The Indian Rural Problem,* rev. ed. (Bombay: 1947).

China, the leaders captured the necessary agrarian support by promises of land reform. They played up a cultural trait common to the farmers of the world: the dominant desire to own the acres they tilled, to share the products of their toil with no man. There is mounting evidence that in Russia and China these promises have turned to dust and ashes. But the realization of that fact has come too late to undo the results of peasant support for the revolution, without which all three of these revolutions would have failed.

Fragmentation. Not only are farms small, but in many underdeveloped countries they are broken into many tiny fields. In India the median range in the number of tracts per farm is five to eight. In one intensively studied village 584 farm operators cultivated 16,000 fields which encompassed only about 2300 acres. The processes of inheritance, mortgage foreclosures, sale of some land to satisfy debts or meet some emergency, account for this condition. Fragmentation results in loss of time as the farmer moves from tract to tract. In one village area covering barely a square mile, the average farmer had to walk two miles to reach each of his parcels of land and return to his home in the village. Under these conditions it is difficult to guard against cattle damage and stealing. Disputes over boundaries multiply and the boundaries themselves take up valuable land.

High rents, taxes, and interest. Not only are considerable proportions of farmers laborers or tenants, but those who achieve the latter status have to pay very high rents, in large part because of the competition for land. Scores of studies in a considerable number of countries report rents ranging from 50 per cent of the gross product up to 75 or 80 per cent of the net. Even in Japan, where some effort was eventually made to control the situation, the government acknowledged over 2000 tenant strikes a year in the latter 1920's rising to over 6000 in 1936. Taxes were also universally high in proportion to the services rendered by government. Buck estimated the tax on wheat land in China in 1929 at United States $1.40, rice land at $3.47, and for China as a whole at $2.40.[5] This is more than average per-acre taxes in the United States have ever been. Usurious interest rates in much of Asia, quite normally 3 per cent per month and often rising to 60 to 100 per cent per year, were noted in the discussion of rural credit.

Lack of capital. The difficulty of saving in such an economy has been mentioned. The problem of lack of capital goes deeper. On such small holdings the house area takes up a larger proportion of the only available basic capital resource, land, than in more fortunate countries. There is no capital to secure any but the crudest tools. Hence, according to the Sino-American Agricultural Mission report in 1947, the man-labor per acre of wheat in China is twenty-six days, against 1.2 days in the United States. Inadequate capital also makes it impossible to protect harvested crops from weather or rodents, because of lack of proper storage facilities. It also makes for inadequate protection from floods, poor drainage, and inefficient irrigation.

Transportation difficult. Even taking to market the small surplus, above what the farm family requires for itself, presents problems. In 1940 the United States had ten times as many miles of railroad per million of population as Japan, twelve times as many as India, 125 times as many as China. It had a mile of automobile highway for each square mile of area as opposed to

a mile for five square miles in Korea, for seventy-five square miles in China, and thirty to eighty in most of South America. Yang Ching-Kim's survey of a *North China Local Market Economy* [6] estimated that 39.3 per cent of the agricultural produce was taken to market on human backs, 46.4 per cent by wheelbarrow, and only 14.3 per cent by pack animal or cart. One result of such transportation difficulties is that there may be surplus food in one district, famine in another close by, and little chance that the surplus can be moved where needed.

Inadequate care of the soil. The conditions already described interact with poor care of the soil. Conservation practices are difficult to initiate on small, fragmented parcels. The low income leaves nothing over for fertilizer. There are few cattle, as the land cannot sustain both human and animal population. What manure there is, because of lack of other fuel, is often used for fuel, along with plant stalks. In some countries untreated human waste is substituted for manure and humus. In others, as in India, the culture prevents this. The health hazard from "night soil" is of course great, but where it is used, especially when combined with plowed under soya bean vines, as in China, soil fertility has been largely sustained. In India and other countries it has deteriorated.

Lack of non-farm employment. In densely populated countries where industrial development has lagged, there are inadequate opportunities for non-farm employment. The society has not produced enough capital for secondary industries to expand in proportion to population growth. Thus a labor surplus keeps wages low and reduces the incentive for rural youth to migrate.

In a number of countries there has been

---

[5] J. Lossing Buck, *Land Utilization in China* (Chicago: University of Chicago Press, 1937).

[6] Reported by the International Secretariat, Institute of Pacific Relations Proceedings, 10th Conference, Stratford-upon-Avon, England, 1947.

some development of cottage industries. The expansion of such enterprises has been unanimously advocated by economists of the largely agrarian countries, as it has been for North American Indians, whose pottery, blanket weaving, and jewelry add appreciably to the income of some tribes and many villages, especially among the Pueblo group.[7] In Japan and Mexico, surveys have shown that considerable proportions of rural families have some such supplementary sources of income. In much of monsoon Asia, however, studies mention the idleness of the population for almost half a year as a great problem.

Cultural Factors

A number of factors which contribute to rural poverty in underdeveloped countries are more obviously cultural than those just listed, though cultural traits in such matters as inheritance and fragmentation must not be overlooked. Moreover, to classify any one factor in rural poverty as either cultural, economic, or technical overlooks the very interrelations among them.

High proportion of children. Throughout the world a high proportion of children in the total population is a recognized rural cultural trait. Surveys in Latin America and the Orient indicate that on the average only around a third of the population is in the active production force. Among the farm population in the United States this proportion is over one half. The high proportion of children in the other areas accounts for the relatively low labor force.

Uneconomic use of lands. Some cultural practices, such as the large burial mounds

and surrounding plots in China, contribute to poverty. Where the pressure of population on land is severe even the 2 per cent of available land estimated by Buck to be used in this way has a disadvantageous effect.

Religion and taboos. Again and again local values or taboos interfere with what a westerner would call common-sense measures for improving income or health. Tilling a certain tract of land would offend the gods. Culling out and butchering unproductive cows or fowls offends one of the deepest values of the Hindu religion, namely that all life, even that of the tiniest insect, is sacred. Though the ratio of cattle to human population in India is low, large but undetermined proportions of the cows give less return to their owners than they cost in the products of the land they consume. Again, ancestor worship in China is one factor making for a high birth rate.

Some of the tribes in the Pacific islands will not eat one or another indigenous fruit because of an assumed relationship. Said one Polynesian leader in the hearing of one of the authors, "We do not eat bananas because they are our cousins and we are not cannibals."

Conspicuous consumption. Veblen's theory of conspicuous consumption is not inapplicable in somewhat different terms to many underdeveloped countries. Borrowing for ceremonies related to death, marriage, and birth, which relate to the social status of the farmer in his community, is frequent. Professor Buck estimates that in China three fourths of the outstanding debt of farm families was chargeable to these and other unproductive purposes. Surveys in other countries have shown similar results, though in varying proportions.

Lack of thrift versus hoarded capital. There

[7] Henrietta Burton, *The Reëstablishment of the Indians in Their Pueblo Life Through the Revival of Traditional Crafts* (New York: Bureau of Publications, Teachers College, Columbia University, 1936).

are two somewhat paradoxical, but quite understandable, problems in some underdeveloped countries. On the one hand, there seems to be a lack of thrift, quite probably due to the grinding poverty under which tens of millions of rural people live. Many have become hopeless that any effort on their part could greatly lighten the burden. The incentive to save has atrophied. Toward the other end of the economic scale untold wealth is tied up in precious stones and metals. The aggregate value of the bracelets and anklets of the women of India has been estimated at hundreds of millions of dollars. This is not only a cultural phenomenon. In thousands of towns and villages the banking and credit facilities a westerner takes for granted are completely lacking. Moreover, the use of capital wealth as a means of commercial or industrial expansion, while understood and acted on in the cities, is a relatively new concept in many of the rural areas of the world.

Deficiency in education. Part of the remedy for some of these problems lies in education, but in most underdeveloped countries this is a weak reed to lean upon. Even under Japanese rule in Korea only half the communities had schools. In many provinces in India a similar situation existed under British rule. Public schools were concerned only with literacy, and the curriculum bore all too little relation to life problems. As in the western world until relatively recent decades, school education was for the professions. Other types of learning went on through the home, thus perpetuating traditional behaviors. Even where there were schools, the necessity of charging tuition reduced enrollment to a fraction of the youth population. Because of the attitude toward women, small proportions of girls attended. In most countries there was until very recently no equivalent of the Agricultural Extension Service.

Local Consequences of Rural Poverty

As can be readily imagined, social consequences of the situation described are serious. They can be documented many times over and are little more than catalogued here. One of the most serious is the inability of the rural population to make any considerable contribution of food and fibre to the non-farm population. This limits the growth of industrial production, discourages rural-urban migration, and retards capital formation.

In fact, it may also retard the very desire for some advance in mechanization. The amount of available labor is large and the wages, therefore, so low that the relatively few larger land owners find it pays to continue antiquated methods of production. The wages of ten men are less than the cost of maintaining, servicing, and fueling a tractor with one man to operate it.

Expenditures for health services under the conditions outlined are close to nothing. Hookworm, pellagra, and a number of other diseases are endemic. Death rates are very high, with infant mortality rates double to quadruple those in the dozen countries with the highest per capita incomes. The nutritional level is also low, and the lowered vitality of the population not only feeds the death rate but day after day reduces the labor productivity of the workers.

Famine is an ever present danger. Flood or drought can eliminate the small surplus available for the non-farm population and can even bring the farmers themselves to starvation. Famines in recent years in both China and India, costing millions of lives, document this sombre fact.

The level of education is low, as already indicated, and other social services are all but non-existent, unless supplied by missions or other private agencies in a relatively few places. Education is a prerequisite for establishing even the most simple improvements in agricultural techniques, such as crop rotation, strip or contour plowing, the use of improved seed, and the like.

These and other consequences aggravate the whole problem of rural poverty in the twenty-five countries with per capita incomes of less than $100 and high proportions of their people on farms. They are only somewhat less acute in the twenty-one nations with between $100 and $299 per capita.

It must be recognized that the consequences of rural poverty and the means to poverty as outlined are not so neatly separated in actuality. They are interactive, both becoming both cause and effect. This becomes clear to anyone who has observed areas of rural poverty in the United States; for, as shown earlier in the text, they exist here too.

The totality of rural poverty and of the measures to combat it may be compared to a circle. A fruitful attempt to encompass the whole circle has been made by the FAO in the pamphlet, *Essentials of Rural Welfare.*[8] The assumption in this work is that the opposite of rural poverty is rural welfare. Well being is the objective of the attack on poverty. It may be useful to summarize the FAO attempt to view the problem as a whole. There are at least seven elements which determine rural welfare: health; levels of living and consumption, including income, diet, housing, savings, etc.; conditions of work, including both amount and working relations; level of literacy and skills, including all forms of expression; social adjustment; individual security in terms of person, income, property and emotions; and finally, the standards of individual and social behavior explicit in the mores.

These elements have determinants, including necessary facilities. The first of these is agricultural production, including a host of things like soil fertility, size of farms, tenure, power, techniques, supplementary occupa-

[8] New York: Columbia University Press, 1949.

tions in and out of agriculture, markets and marketing, transport, credit, and services. Second is the division of the product, used, exchanged, or marketed, the allocation of income, the position of labor, the matters of debt, inheritance, and investment. Third are the community services of transportation, communication, health, education, recreation, and security. Fourth among the determinants comes the social structure, kinship and neighborhood groups, the utilization of which in coöperative work groups raised the income of some experimentally used villages in Japan 14 per cent; social classes; semiformal and formally organized institutions; and government, local and central. Both the elements and the determinants include economic, social, cultural, and technological items. For many it is possible to find both indicators of the element and indicators of the determinants in both quantitative and theoretical terms.

Remedial Measures

This diagnosis from the Food and Agriculture Organization is properly cast in terms of welfare. Rural welfare, if attained, will bring release from poverty. Throughout the world, governments, private welfare agencies, agricultural missionaries, educational institutions, and others have tried experiments and demonstrations in the attack on poverty. Through both successes and failures some remedial measures can be suggested.

Some general considerations must first be emphasized. The attack on rural poverty is an attack on ways of life and methods of cultivation hallowed by unvarying procedures of generations. Any successful program must develop motivation, erect incentives in terms of the values the people hold, build up social pressures that will impel men to work efficiently. These pressures and incentives cannot be merely economic, for they must both insure a better return for the farmer and prevent his reducing his effort when the improvement satisfies his modest needs.

Science must be applied, physical as well as social. The people concerned must participate in any experimental program as people, not, so to speak, as guinea pigs. Without the coöperation of the mass of the people a program will fail, unless buttressed by the expensive methods of compulsion.

To secure such coöperation requires social "know-how," without which those with only technical know-how may never have the chance to demonstrate what their methods can do. The leader or teacher must understand the habits, customs, and taboos of the people with whom he works and fit his program into their background. The system of values of which such things are part represents the culture. The culture of any people is precious to them; the simpler the culture the more precious it is likely to be. The sense of security of the group and all who make it up is inextricably bound up with the culture.

It follows that though problems may be similar, methods of their solution will vary. The migratory tribes of the Near East are poor. So are the peasants of the Yangtse Valley in China. The approach to the same objective, be it better health or better income, could not be identical and at the same time equally successful. Indeed, this follows even on the community level, for each community has its own variants of the overall culture and has made its own adaptations to the society of which it is a part. The compact type of farm-village community which contributes to this has been discussed in another chapter.

Bearing in mind, then, that the social, economic, and political aspects of any rural welfare program are inseparable and indivisible, we turn to a few of the proposals that have been made or attempted.

Making owners of tenants. One of the first essentials is that the farmer have secure tenure of an adequate holding, preferably as an owner-operator. The programs in Czechoslovakia after Word War I and in India after this nation received its independence have been alluded to.

The United States has approved the same policy in Japan. The Occupation was less than four months old when it gave the Japanese Imperial Government three months to submit a plan "to . . . destroy the economic bondage which has enslaved the Japanese farmer to centuries of feudal oppression." Among other things it was "ordered" that this plan should provide for:

Transfer of land ownership from absentee land owners to land operators, purchase of farm lands from now operating owners; tenant purchase of land; reasonable protection of former tenants against reversion to tenancy status.

As a result the proportion of farm owner-operators today is practically 90 per cent, about double what it was in 1946, but the average size of the farm has increased very slightly. Tenants frequently secured the land they had formerly rented. However, the 300 per cent rise in taxation was burdensome to the new owners. The abolition of primogeniture, also at behest of the Occupation, potentially threatens a reduction in size and further fragmentation of the tiny farms of Japan. This western concept, based on the right of all children to an equal share in their parents' estate, is understandable, but in rural Japan the gain to individuals may result in social loss. There the battle has been joined but not won.

In Mexico great stress has been placed on what is essentially coöperative farming. The Ejido has supplemented the hacienda and plantation.

Professor Belshaw, in a data paper for the 1947 conference of the Institute of Pacific Relations, gave an interesting illustration of another device to accomplish the objective among the Maori.

Many of the lands of the Maori people of New Zealand were under joint, or multiple ownership. As a consequence, there was no clear title to land, and finance could not be obtained for development. Largely as the result of the perception of Maori leaders, the European idea of the joint stock corporation was wedded to the Maori notion of multiple ownership within the tribe. The owners of the land were incorporated and received stock in the corporation in proportion to their share of the land. A clear title could then be obtained and funds borrowed for development and operation. The corporation employed a manager, and the members of the tribe obtained employment as wage earners in their own company, and at the same time learned farming. As shareholders they received dividends out of the profits from the farm. These were diverted, in part, for communal purposes; to build a church or a meeting house; to pay the salary of the village clergyman, or to finance boys and girls through college.

Back of the dilemma so solved lay deep cultural values and practices. The Maori, like many Polynesian tribes, has little or no sense of private property. Attitudes toward land use are in terms of tribal behavior in relation to the land. Obviously, such ideas were utterly foreign to the personal and legal concepts of the dominant, English-stock New Zealanders. In all such situations the building of a bridge between the two cultures is the only answer.

Practicing greater efficiency. No mission from the Food and Agriculture Organization has failed to point out — and the missions to China and the Philippines in which the United States coöperated with these nationals both agree — that more effective use could be made of existing land and techniques, and that by adding tested seed and simple equipment to such procedures yields could be raised 25 to 40 per cent. Some experts give even more optimistic figures. The fact that wheat yields in India have recently been doubled on some experimental plots by relatively slight and inexpensive means and under native cultivation, shows that there are possibilities at this point if enough personnel can be secured to "spread the gospel." This in itself is a limiting factor that must be overcome.

Credit. The expansion of coöperative credit unions limited to loans for productive purposes has considerable possibilities for freeing the peasant farmers of underdeveloped countries from the grip of the professional money lender. Grants or loans by government can accelerate this development. This movement is already of considerable scope, as was pointed out in earlier chapters.

Marketing. The highly uneconomic method by which each farmer brings his produce to market on his own back or in a wheelbarrow and deals individually with the merchant in the market town can be supplanted with profit by a coöperative marketing organization.

Social necessities. The discussion thus far has said nothing about the importance of remedial measures for the improvement of health, education, and social organization. This cannot be accomplished, or even initiated, everywhere in a given country all at once. The personnel for such an effort does not exist. The best procedure seems to be to select specific areas or communities and undertake a demonstration, experiment, or "pilot project," to use the term employed by the United Nations Educational, Scientific and Cultural Organization (UNESCO).

It has been done. One of the most interesting, and perhaps significant, efforts along these lines was the Rural Reconstruction Movement in China under Dr. James Y. C.

Yen. A dedicated and trained staff went to live among the farm people in a number of counties in one province of northern China. Their program concerned illiteracy, health, economic improvement, and better government. Large use was made of volunteer leaders. The literacy campaign was organized on the basis of the thousand characters of the earlier Mass Education Movement. Proficient graduates of the courses and middle (high) school children were sent out to teach others. Simple literature was prepared dealing with day-to-day problems of the people in farming and health. Thus they had an incentive to learn to read. In health, high school children were taught to vaccinate and give inoculations, to show how to combat filth and get rid of flies. Junior doctors were trained to treat the more usual and simple diseases and care for relatively minor accidents. For anything beyond their training they hastened to the fully trained doctor at the county seat, under whom they worked.

On the economic side, better seeds and tillage processes were introduced, wells dug, coöperative credit unions and marketing organizations formed. This effort was ended by the Japanese invasion, but the work was carried on wherever possible. Up to then the improvement in health, educational status, and family income was phenomenal.

Essentially the same system with respect to health has been operating most successfully in the Fijian Island group for about twenty years, where it was initiated by Dr. Sylvester Lambert, of the International Health Board of the Rockefeller Foundation.

In Mexico the so-called cultural mission, discussed earlier as an example of adult education, has been quite successful. Staffed usually with a doctor and/or nurse, an agriculturist, a home economist, an arts and crafts specialist, and perhaps others as needed, this mission settles in a small city for a period of months and works among the surrounding villages, usually through the school, if there is one. The school, which in Mexico is indeed the house of the people, became the focal point of continuing effort and leadership after the mission had gone.

The essential point in these enterprises, as in the pilot projects of UNESCO and the Village Improvement Service in India, has been a community-wide approach, with large use of local leadership, attacking a group of the most important related problems.

A final illustration of a different sort, showing the value of government stimulation, may be drawn from Greece. Here the government announced it would pay at the rate of 73 cents a day those who labored on community development projects approved by communities and the provincial governor. Typical of what has gone on in 1500 villages was the experience of Demestica. It had very fertile land and raised excellent grapes for a wine nationally famous; but the nearest road was about seven miles away, reached only over a rugged mountain path. Getting produce to market took so much time that only half the land was cultivated. The villagers proposed to build a road over the mountain, and they did, with nothing but picks, shovels, their own hands, and dynamite given by the winery. The ECA reports that the seven miles of road cost $787. The cost of marketing was greatly reduced and the time saved was put into doubling the acreage. With a road available the government was ready to supply a teacher when the people built a school.[9]

Other illustrations could be given from the experiences of the International Basic Economy Corporation in Brazil and Venezuela, of the Office of Inter-American Affairs in coöperation with many of the governments in Central and South America, and of the Anglo-American Caribbean Commission.

[9] Glen Leet, "They Did Not Wait for a Tractor," *The Survey* (LXXXVII, no. 3), March, 1951.

Industrialization. Thus far the discussion has concerned only measures directly affecting rural people. One proposal always made in programs for rural welfare is for industrialization. Few, if any, are the agrarian countries which do not have plans for industrial development. Such a program, however, lies outside the scope of a study of rural society. It involves many things — procurement of capital by savings or borrowings, trained technicians to operate the plant, housing for workers, and so on. It may result in serious social problems as well. Many who look hopefully toward this solution point to Japan as justifying their expectations. There are reasons to doubt, however, that the experience of Japan from 1870 to 1940 can be taken as an unfailing guide.[10] Clearly, a large steel plant is more spectacular than a small local industry, a farm-to-market road is commonplace beside a superhighway. But small industry, even cottage industry, may be a surer first step in folk societies rooted in family and village relationships. They may produce smaller economic gains, but they will come sooner. They should not be neglected in the development of rural welfare.

Experience can guide. Efforts to improve the welfare of rural people are not new. Missions, foundations, and governments, both at home and abroad, have had considerable experience, especially in the last half century. The problem of raising the productivity of a population often resolves itself into the problem of raising their ambition. Another problem is what to do about local values which are bound to be destroyed by interference with the accustomed way of doing things. In fact, the intent of such programs is to change these accustomed ways and inevitably attack the values on which

they are based. Hence the program that is not prepared to substitute in socio-psychological terms values and desires for the things it destroys is also likely to fail; a number of foundation projects in the early days did just that, leaving those for whom the benefits were intended worse off than they had been before. The same consideration also applies to levels and standards of living. A mere increase in economic assets without instruction and without the implanting of values that will lead to wise expenditure of increased income results in serious anti-social consequences.

The values of a people designated as underdeveloped by economically advantaged nations are interwoven with systems of social and individual behavior. One or two parts of such a system cannot be changed without affecting the whole. It is the whole to which the people give their allegiance. Thus resistances develop. The national of another land cannot be expected to strive for something which seems desirable to an American if he has never experienced it. A Samoan chieftain, when he finally understood the concept of private property, as opposed to his value of village or communal property, commented: "These Americans are an uncivilized people." Thus it is that technical "know-how" fails without social "know-how."

The strategy of a program must be laid out not only in terms of the culture of those concerned but also in terms of an analysis of actual needs and their interrelations. Often what seems like a roundabout way is the shortest path to the goal. The General Education Board found early in its effort to get better schools in the South that the economic base would have to be strengthened in order to secure the needed local support for the schools. To do this often required an attack on the hookworm or other health problems.[11]

10 Irene Taeuber, "Population Increase and Manpower Utilization in Imperial Japan," *The Milbank Memorial Fund Quarterly* (XXVIII, no. 3), July, 1950.

11 Summary of a statement by Dr. Robert D. Calkins, Director, General Education Board, to Columbia University Seminar on Rural Life, 1950.

All of this, experience shows, can be effectively accomplished to the degree that the local people and their leaders are involved and assume responsibility. If the outsider assumes leadership forsaking the role of leadership by indirection, opposition focuses on him. The defenders of the old order and its values have a clearly visible target. If local leadership is successfully enlisted, events begin to change conditions and attitudes. Then the people will need a leader who seems to know the direction in which the community or society is tending and who can interpret it. At this point more direct contributions by an outsider are welcomed. This often calls for a reversal of the role being played. Such a reversal is just as important to success at later stages of a project as working behind the scenes is at the start.

Granted a fundamental democratic, not dictatorial, approach, these procedures are what the sociologist and social psychologist would expect. They are but the application in concrete situations of the findings of social science.[12]

[12] For a further discussion of tested principles, based on the many years' experience of the Agricultural and Home Economics Extension Service of the United States, see Edmund deS. Brunner and H. P. Yang, *Rural America and the Extension Service* (New York: Teachers College Bureau of Publications, 1949), chap. 11.

TOPICS FOR DISCUSSION

1. Report on and analyze sociologically some one project by an agricultural missionary, school, or government in rural reconstruction.
2. Draw up a practical program for rural welfare in some one described community or area.
3. Discuss the pros and cons of breaking up large land holdings into small owner-operated farms.
4. What suggestions does the farm tenant purchase program of the Farm Security Administration hold for underdeveloped countries?
5. Report on the projects initiated in rural areas abroad by the United States under the Point Four Program.

REFERENCE READINGS

Food and Agricultural Organization, *Educational Approaches to Rural Welfare,* Washington, 1949; *Essentials of Rural Welfare,* New York: Columbia University Press, 1949; *Social Welfare in Rural Communities,* Washington, 1949; *Training Rural Leaders,* Washington, 1949.

International Development Advisory Board, *Partners in Progress.* New York: Simon & Schuster, 1951.

Mukerjee, R., *Races, Lands and Food.* New York: Dryden, 1946.

Patterson, Ernest M., ed., *Formulating a Point Four Program.* Philadelphia: American Academy of Political and Social Science, 1950.

Raushanbush, Stephen, *People, Food, Machines.* Washington: Public Affairs Institute, 1950.

Rority, James, *Engineers of World Plenty.* Washington: Public Affairs Institute, 1950.

United States Department of Agriculture, *Contribution of Extension Methods and Techniques Toward the Rehabilitation of War-Torn Countries.* Washington, 1945.

United States Department of Agriculture, *Extension Experiences Around the World.* Washington, 1951.

Zimmerman, Eric W., *World Resources and Industries.* New York: Harper, 1951.

FILMS

A Trip to Coöperative Europe. C, S, 20. Coöperative League of U.S.A., Washington, D.C.

Food — Secret of Peace. S, 17. Brandon Films, Inc., New York.

World of Plenty. S, 45. British Information Service, New York.

26 Rural Society and the Great Society

IT HAS BECOME A TRUISM that more than half the problems of the American farmer lie outside the line fences of his farms. It is, however, a truth that is not fully recognized, either on the farms or in the cities of the nation. Ours has become an interdependent society. If agriculture is depressed, business sales and profits suffer, and labor has less work. If labor is unemployed or works for low wages in comparison with the cost of food, agriculture suffers.

The complicated mechanisms of the price system, credit, tariffs, and foreign exchange are but social inventions devised by man to match the potentialities of his expanding technology in order the better to exchange goods and services among groups. But all these, and even money itself, only facilitate the bartering of wheat for shoes, eggs for coffee, cotton for schooling. This is likewise a truism not adequately grasped by mankind, as our social behavior shows.

At the moment the world looks forward to only one certainty, change — fundamental change compelled by a war which shattered half the world, destroyed untold wealth, and released secrets of atomic energy. The United Nations have drawn a new plan designed to promote peace and allow men to rebuild their nations and the world of which they are a part. As one of its subsidiary agencies we have The Food and Agriculture Organization, with its sixty-three member nations.

What this means is that mankind is attempting to shape its own future through collective action, and to implement policies which will lift the general level of living throughout the world. Amid all the tensions and alarms of international relations the fact remains that more effort is being put forth toward this goal than ever before.

What is true internationally is true within nations. The destruction caused by World War II and the problems growing out of that conflict have been so great that in most countries only society as a whole, through the institution of government, has seemed able to cope with the situation. Enormous amounts of fact-gathering, research, and planning have gone on. Policies have been arrived at and action has been taken. Many of these actions would have been deemed impossible a few decades ago. Some may well prove to be mistaken. Those resting upon the power and authority of dictatorships are definitely distasteful to the United States and other democratic countries, because they are counter to our values and culture.

The necessity, however, to appraise trends and their direction and to formulate policy designed to achieve predetermined ends has been universally recognized. The United States Department of Agriculture has an interbureau committee concerned with all aspects of rural life — productive, economic, social. State colleges of agriculture, through a committee of the Land Grant College Association, have expressed themselves on desirable policies for agriculture and rural life. Private agencies, such as the great farm organizations, labor unions, the United States Chamber of Commerce, educational and religious bodies, and many others, have been engaged in this task of determining what their objectives should be and how they can be successfully achieved. This activity is reaching to the local level. In many states, farmers and their wives and their village neighbors, with the help of the college of agriculture, are examining their present situation and trying to plan for the future.

This is as it should be. Our nation is a democracy, and its essence is that not only the civil servants of our society in government, but also the citizens themselves, where they live and work, should share in this process, and that it should be a continuous process.

There are those who fear that social planning, so-called, will lead to dictatorship. They point to the dictatorships, past and present, as a terrible warning, forgetting that in those countries there was no democratic tradition built up over centuries of experience. They overlook such recent examples in rural society as the formulation of agricultural policies with the coöperation of the farmers concerned under the Agricultural Adjustment Act, and the country planning conferences in which the best of government plans met the correction of freely expressed opinions of local people, based on their own knowledge of their communities. The problem lies not in planning itself but in how the planning is done and whether by few or by all.

Through all the ages of scarcity, when man produced feverishly to have enough to consume in order that life could be sustained, the myth grew that man was helpless to alter social laws said to be inherent in the structure of the universe. But ever-advancing technology, in the factory and on the farm, has proved that concept to be wrong. So long as raw material lasts, an economy of relative abundance is possible. All that is necessary in terms of the United States is to achieve in peace what we have already achieved in war, when, despite many handicaps, food production increased almost 40 per cent over 1935–39 averages, and industrial production considerably more than doubled.

The so-called economic laws are man's creation. The alternative is not between "submission to impersonal and seemingly irrational forces of the market" and "submission to the arbitrary power of men," as Hayek maintains. The alternative is between social chaos and social control by intelligent, democratic planning. Only if Americans forget that in a democratic government there is the spirit of "we, the people," only if they fail to recognize and to exercise their responsibilities as citizens, will there be danger.

While the social sciences, being newer, have lagged behind the physical, they too are fortifying this changed attitude. Anthropologists have discovered and described successful societies that are coöperative rather than competitive.[1] Economists have found under what conditions capital is most rapidly formed and have shed new light on the behavior of the mechanism of price-making.[2] Psychologists are asking if competition is beneficial or whether it arises from feelings of inferiority. Sociologists are developing knowledge as to how society behaves in its groups, institutions, and in other manifestations. Social psychologists and social psychiatrists are helping the individual better to relate himself to a changing physical and social environment. Such knowledge makes planning possible.

The late President Franklin D. Roosevelt, in his last speech, never delivered, put the challenge in this way: "Today we are faced with the pre-eminent fact that if civilization is to survive we must cultivate the science

[1] See, for instance, Margaret Mead, *Competition and Co-operation Among Primitive People.*

[2] *The Formation of Capital* (Washington, D.C.: Brookings Institution, 1934); and Edwin Nourse, *Price-Making in a Democracy* (Washington, D.C.: Brookings Institution, 1944).

of human relations — the ability of all peoples, of all kinds, to live together and work together in the same world, at peace."

Rural America has had many plans, involving both matters of technical agriculture and human relations, written into law. In post-Civil War days a great national land policy was planned and executed with considerable success under the Homestead Law. In 1863, amid all the confusions and alarms of civil war, we planned to bring the benefits of science to agriculture on a national scale, and therefore founded our Land Grant colleges of agriculture. Under the necessities of a greater conflict, World War I, in which each day saw more mouths to feed and backs to clothe than the day before, we redoubled our efforts to produce ever more by planning. We established and expanded our agricultural extension service, and assisted all rural high schools desiring it to have a teacher of agriculture. The extension-service plan has been copied by other nations. Confronted by the problem of providing adequate credit for agriculture, we planned and created the Federal Land Bank System, which measurably improved credit conditions for agriculture. The Soil Conservation and Agricultural Adjustment Acts are more recent examples. What is true in agriculture is true in other branches of our national economy.

Some of these plans, when legislated, have been helpful both to rural people and to the nation as a whole. Some have had unforeseen effects on other sectors of the economy which have seemed detrimental to those concerned. Hence political controversy has arisen, as over the agricultural acts of 1948 and 1950. Social science is not wholly prepared to accept the challenge to guide society more rigorously in the paths of social wisdom. But that attempt must inevitably be made; indeed, it is even now being made in the United States.

This chapter, then, is designed to sum-marize some of the more important trends in American rural society which have been previously discussed, and to outline a few projected policies. It will not, however, rehash facts so much as raise questions and indicate possible further policies. The assumption is that democratic social planning is essential, and that only through planning and experimentation can a larger measure of social well-being be achieved. Furthermore, what can be done in rural America, however good theoretically, will be conditioned by the general level of well-being and productivity in the nation as a whole, and even in the world. This is but another indication of the interdependent nature of modern social life.

Institutional Changes

First, however, let us recall some of the changes which have occurred in the last decades, essentially in the institutional arrangements within which our society operates.

We have come to be far more reliant upon the basic institution of society — government at the national level — especially with respect to achieving greater security for all people against the calamities of life, whether illness or death, depression or drought.

The handling of the now enormous trust funds designed to implement security, and still more the huge sums spent for defense, have forced government to have a fiscal policy, the operations of which affect every citizen.

Furthermore, whether out of the urge for security, the pressures of selfishness, or efforts at social control for the general welfare — probably from all these and other motives — society, through government, has set limits upon the so-called "law of supply and demand" and the "iron law of wages." In short, the market is free only within limits. There are support prices for agricultural commodities, there are fair trade practices laws, there is minimum wage legislation.

Inevitably, out of these trends has come a great increase in the activity of organized groups seeking to represent the claims of major occupational groups upon society as a whole. Thus we have national farm organizations, labor groups, coöperatives and their national council, and such agencies of business as the National Association of Manufacturers and the United States Chamber of Commerce.

Clashes among these groups, when one or another is deemed to be pushing its own desires to the point of harming another group, result in what the cynic calls government by pressure groups. More importantly, they are evidence of the very interdependence of our society, which has grown so complex that the policy of any major group necessarily affects all others. The social scientist at this point advances the concept of the general welfare as the most important criterion to apply to any policy. But techniques for determining what the general welfare requires in any given situation are neither wholly perfected nor wholly accepted in the heat of controversy. These trends, this situation, set the limits within which any democratically developed policies for rural life must be worked out. The discussion now turns to some of these.

Population Problems and Policies

As we have seen, about two thirds of the world's population live on and till the land. A vast majority are close to bare subsistence, ill-fed, ill-clothed, and ill-housed. Even in the United States such conditions exist. The cotton croppers of the South and the hill-dwellers of the Ozarks and Appalachians are far removed from the vaunted American standard of living. And it is in precisely these areas that there is the largest number of children in comparison with the adult population. These areas also contribute disproportionately, but not exclusively, to rural-urban migration.

Migration implications. It is probable that this migration has seldom been larger than in recent years. Mechanization of agriculture, enlarging farm size, urban opportunities, both economic and social, have all contributed to the net loss through migration of the farm to the city. The farm group, though still very large, is becoming more and more of a minority in the total population, as well as more heterogeneous within itself. Its political importance in the 1930's and 1940's was partly the result of its holding a balance of power, a position which the continuation of present trends could change. Rural strategy with reference to achieving any policy would have to adjust to this fact. The only possible approach would then be in general welfare terms.

We still have too many farm families with holdings too small to provide full employment and with little or no other economic opportunity. Relative to others, this is a disadvantaged group. Should society, through government, assist such families as wish to move to the city? Should their neighbors who remain be helped to acquire their land to the point of having economic units? It has been estimated that such a policy, if adopted, would, over a decade, increase the income of both those who migrated and those on the land by over $2 billion a year in the aggregate.[3]

Can social policy affect the birth rate? But a question perhaps more fundamental than location of population is its rate of growth. A century and a half ago Malthus propounded the idea that population increase would outrun the food and other resources of the world. But birth rates in the western world began to decline and in 1927

[3] Leonard H. Schoff, *A National Agricultural Policy* (New York: Harper, 1950).

a world population conference under League of Nations auspices pointed out that countries sharing the Euro-American culture were not producing enough daughters to maintain the population in the next generation. There were estimates that the United States would cease to grow by 1980. The birth rate plummeted still further during the depression but it rose again as the depression lightened and recent United States rates have been about 50 per cent higher than in the lowest years of the 1930's. Several countries have in this century adopted policies to influence the birth rate, such as old-age pensions, maternity benefits or family allowances, as given in a number of countries, notably in Sweden by its so-called "mothers and children" parliament of 1931, and most recently in Canada, unemployment insurance, cheaper and better housing, increased income, large tax exemptions for children, these are all social policies designed to improve the birth rate and to cut down mortality rates.

As a result the net reproduction index has gained and in the United States is again well above 100. One result has been the emergence of a neo-Malthusian school.

In nonwestern lands, in Puerto Rico, and in much of South America, this index has always been high. In many parts of the world there is real pressure of population on the land. India, for instance, gaining five million persons a year, must now import 12 per cent of her total caloric requirements, where once she exported food. Her net gain from 1920 to 1941 was greater than the total population of England and France. Interrelations between population, improving agricultural technology and war and peace are very real. Problems in this area are acute. Advances in medicine and public health have, in the unemotional language of the biologist, "upset the demographic balance," which kept the population of Japan static for 300 years prior

to the coming of western ideas and practices. Use and development of resources must keep pace with population to stave off famine. Birth control, frequently advocated and now approved even in India by the present prime minister, Mr. Nehru, faces cultural obstacles in many countries. Moreover, it would take years to make its effect felt. Meanwhile the western world is becoming more concerned about the quality than about the quantity of the population.

Population and land. If ever in the United States a conscious population policy is adopted it must be linked with land policy. This is another illustration of the way in which social considerations intermesh.

During the 1930's, some embryonic attempts were made to link population and land policies by moving people from submarginal to better land. With the development of great dams along the Columbia, Colorado, and other rivers, and the resultant irrigation of fertile soil, such a policy could be worked out, and marginal, or at least sub-marginal, lands zoned against agriculture, as they have been in a few states.

There is, of course, not enough reclaimed land to care for all the farm population now on poor soil, even assuming people would wish to move. It would be quite possible, however, for society to produce conditions that would stimulate such migration under guided conditions. The arguments in favor of such projects are not merely those often dismissed as "idealistic." During the 1930's there was an appreciable number of counties in which the total value of federal and state payments for rural relief and rehabilitation, agricultural adjustment, aid to rural schools, and the like, exceeded the value of products produced.

Land Use and Human Welfare

This consideration raises squarely the whole issue of relationship between land use and human welfare. Under all is the land, but on the land are people, and without this human factor the best land in the world is unproductive. It is also true that the best land in the world can be ruined by over-cropping, overgrazing, and other bad farm management practices. Our basic capital resource, the soil, can be wasted and destroyed: what is worse, it often has been. Dramatic evidences of wind erosion were the dust storms of the Great Plains during the droughts of 1934 and 1936, which even darkened the streets of eastern seaboard cities on some days. Less dramatic, but just as alarming, are evidences of water erosion in the muddy waters of a thousand rivers and creeks after heavy rains, in the silt shoals fanning out for many a square mile at the mouth of the Mississippi River, made up of the precious top soils of the huge territory it drains. In McLean County, Illinois, land cleared of its first-growth timber and planted to corn for the first time in 1941 produced one hundred and twenty bushels to the acre against a county average of fifty-seven bushels, the difference being a measure of the land's decline.[4] The land we settled was so rich that we assumed it was inexhaustible. We are slowly learning that it is not. The problem is not the soil but the man.

Social action to conserve soil. In the United States in 1935 Congress passed the Soil Conservation Act, providing federal, state, and local coöperation in setting up soil conservation districts when and where voted by the people concerned. On January 1, 1951, there were 2306 such districts in the various states, territories, and insular possessions. They included about 80 per cent of all farms and ranches, and perhaps 70 per cent of all agricultural land. The local agency is a committee elected by the farmers concerned. On the basis of surveys plans are laid out for the district as a whole and

for each farm, field by field. It is, of course a long way from forming a district to putting the plans in operation on every acre it contains: That has thus far been done on perhaps a tenth to an eighth of the land in these districts.

This program is important for several reasons. It is an illustration of planning to meet a severe national problem, on a basis that requires local participation and coöperation. While the act enabled federal coöperation, its implementation involves local, indeed, individual, action on each farm. Procedures are, and must be, democratic, not dictatorial. The Soil Conservation Service reported in 1951:

Group action is the best and cheapest method. . . . Experience gained thus far indicates that the family-type neighbor-group approach is not only a natural way to work with farmers . . . it is also the best method. . . . A variety of family-type interests binds the group together: customs, religion, nationality, backgrounds, type of farming, hobbies, co-operation in . . . farming operations, sports, social activities, educational interests, and kinship. . . . The leaders have acquired leadership because they have won the confidence and respect of the group's members.[5]

The human side. There cannot be too much emphasis in all this program-building upon the human aspects, as emphasized in the discussion of the social-economics of agriculture. People live in families, neighborhoods, communities. They require social institutions. They must maintain adequate standards of living. No land policy can succeed unless it provides this for rural people.

Some Basic Problems of an Agricultural Program

Agricultural policies discussed in this text face some unsolved problems. We have ap-

[4] Arthur Moore, *The Farmer and the Rest of Us,* chap. V (Boston: Little, Brown & Co., 1945).

[5] Quoted from a provisional report on *Family Farm Policy* made to the Secretary of Agriculture by twelve agencies of the Department of Agriculture, June, 1951.

arently decided in the United States that one function of government shall be to promote economic well-being among our rural population. We have not, however, determined on the definition of economic well-being, nor, indeed, on who shall define it. We have a high-grade research agency in the Bureau of Agricultural Economics. Legislative bodies, however, are swayed by political as well as scientific considerations. Thus far the major pieces of agricultural legislation, especially those dealing with prices, have made no major contribution to the economic well-being of the small and under-employed farmer. This is a problem which presses for solution.

Another problem which has not been solved is that of giving needed economic support to agricultural commodities and at the same time maintaining flexibility in farm management. Rather, our programs have tended to perpetuate, not to correct, maladjustments in land use. We know much more about nutrition than we did fifty years ago. The food habits of the nation have changed significantly, and for the better. Historic fibres like cotton, flax, and wool, face severe competition from synthetic fabrics. Shall the objective of policy be to achieve a good level of living for all the rural population or a good level for existing producing units in terms of what they now produce? If the function of the free market in working out adjustments has been supplanted by government action, must government develop devices whereby that function can be administratively performed? This, indeed, is counter to American tradition, though there was of necessity some effort in that direction during World War II. Is a far more intensive educational effort among farmers called for, based on the annual outlook information but geared to the needs of the total population? Physical defects caused by nutritional deficiencies revealed by the draft lend point to this query.

America can take justifiable pride in the participation of the farm population in planning and executing farm programs under the Production and Marketing Administration, Soil Conservation Service, Extension Service, and other agencies. But, by admission of the Secretary of Agriculture, there is doubt if these truly democratic procedures have gone far enough in assisting the poorer farmers, many still on sub-marginal land, farm tenants, and share croppers. Steps to bring them fully into such programs, and to make farmer participation invariably the two-way proposition it is designed to be, are still to be perfected.

Again, each of the present agencies of the United States Department of Agriculture was organized to meet a specific and recognized major need, in soil conservation, agricultural adjustment, education, credit, and so on. Each, therefore, with the tradition and practice of the Department, is so organized as to have local participation and contracts for its own particular interest. But farmers obviously do not organize their operations with respect to agencies. The farm itself is the unit. Operations on a given farm, however, often involve several agencies, and the farmer has frequently been given conflicting advice as to what to do. Local committees of various agencies compete for his time for their meetings, perhaps for his service as a leader. There is sometimes misunderstanding and lack of cooperation among professional representatives of the agencies themselves. Farm organizations have sometimes favored more power, or even sole direction, for one or another agency. Local lay committees have organized state and national associations independent of their local and primary functions, which can become pressure groups in behalf of a single agency. The county war boards of the War Food Administration brought official agencies together with measurable success. Recent administrative directives have had the same objective. In some counties it has been possible to house all agency offices in the same building. In some there is a council of employed officers which attempts to look at the county and its needs as a whole and see where each fits in. But the problem is not solved. Any lack of coöperation among agencies of the Department is uneconomical. Conflicts in advice are confusing and may be costly to the farmer. The solution may well be in terms of the philosophy back of the employed officers councils, though it may come through setting up a single local agency through which all local work of the United States Department of Agriculture would be conducted, in coöperation with the state colleges of agriculture.

Finally, there are problems caused by the great and increasing heterogeneity of agriculture. The corporation farm with tens of thousands of acres has little in common with the share cropper or subsistence farmer. The social patterns of farming require different approaches by the professional servants of agriculture. The Eastern poultryman who buys his feed is interested in cheap corn or feed. The Midwestern corn or cereal farmer has quite different ideas. The problem of developing a program that will distribute its benefits equitably among all patterns of farming and all types of farms must be worked at in the years ahead.

The Farmer and the General Welfare

The original agricultural adjustment legislation was considered necessary both for the farmer and for society as a whole. It was defended in terms of general welfare. A fundamental reason for price supports and legislation which will use governmental machinery to adjust production up or down as needed lies in the farmer's memory of the long agricultural depression. Above everything else he fears a return of the days when

there were bread lines in cities and rotting food and foreclosed mortgages on farms in rural America. He wants machinery ready to combat a depression at its inception. He remembers that it took more than a decade of agitation and effort to get the first Agricultural Adjustment Act.

What price food? The foregoing paragraph explains the farmer's interest in the parity formula, discussed earlier, and in some protection for the prices of his products.[6] He points out that business can have "administered prices" independent of government action, and indeed has had such prices, that, since agriculture is made up of millions of separate units, government itself must administer farm prices. In a democracy, government is not an entity apart from the people, but the organized expression of the will of the people, the tool which society uses to get certain things done.

If, then, government becomes an agency for the support or administration of farm prices, it does so as a recognition of the basic interest which society has in farm incomes. But government has an equal interest in determining that no group receives a disproportionate share of the national income. It must, therefore, take cognizance of the interdependencies of our major occupational groups. The interest society has in adequate farm income is that such income be used, as Schultz says, "to maximize social benefits. The governing criteria are found in social welfare." [7]

These criteria are not met when payments to agriculture are tied to income parity, with payments made according to previous pro-

---

[6] During the war, some farm leaders put themselves in the illogical position of demanding that prices of farm products be allowed to go to their "natural level," but at the same time insisting on government guarantees of prices not less than 10 per cent below parity after the war.

[7] T. W. Schultz, *Redirecting Farm Policy* (New York: Macmillan, 1944), p. 64.

luction records. This results in the more prosperous farmers getting the larger sums and the poorer farmers, who most need help in raising their standard of living, getting the smaller payments. Improvement in their income would result in larger purchases of goods and services of other segments of society, of which medical care is a conspicuous example. Schultz would have any payments by the government to the farmer available on equal terms, as is elementary education and rural free delivery of mail. "This would preserve certain democratic values." [8]

It is at this point that economics and sociology meet. Clearly, if such a program gains adherents, the policies finally adopted must be determined in part by population trends and policies. As noted several times, it is the more economically disadvantaged states and families with low incomes that bear a disproportionate share of feeding, clothing, educating — in short, rearing the nation's children — and their children are as likely to spend their productive years in the city as on the farm. The fact that rural America is the nation's "seed-bed" is in itself one justification for federal policies in aid of agriculture.

Family and farm. This suggests again the central place of the family in rural life. It is a social group; the farm is its economic base. Farming is a way of life and a way of making a living for the family on the land. This interrelation of family and farm in rural society is not built around a single motif or idea. It is a complex of a number of motivations and attitudes. Land gives security to many; it offers not only an economic base, but profit and success as well, especially to the skilled. It presents an opportunity to children for the health that contact with sun, air, and good earth can give. It lures those who love growing things and have a "feel" for the land. It offers so-

[8] *Ibid.*, p. 67.

cial relations in neighborhood and community far more personal and elemental than in cities. These factors, of course, influence different families in different degrees. They change in strength and compulsion as the family moves through its life cycle. This is aptly illustrated by the story of the past-middle-age farmer who was interviewed by a farm-management specialist while cultivating a large flower garden. When suggestions were made for changing his farming practices in order to make more profits, the farmer replied: "Yes, I know, but you don't understand. I have no son, and ma, she likes flowers."

Lessons of the 1940's. In all this discussion, the experiences of the agricultural depression of the 1920's and 1930's are evident. But the 1940's lifted farm incomes to unprecedented levels. Rationing in the war years was caused not so much by Lend-Lease shipments to our allies or by the fact that Americans in uniform ate more than they did as civilians, though these were factors, as by the fact that for the first time in the modern era millions of Americans had enough money to buy an adequate diet. Dramatic is a weak word for that changed situation.

The implication is clear. Full employment in the cities means full pocketbooks on the farm. The prewar years proved that the city has a larger stake in rural prosperity than was suspected. The war years proved that rural America has a high stake in urban prosperity. The interdependencies in our society are therefore clearer than they ever were before. Policies which urban and rural groups alike advocate must take this fact into account. Selfish promotion of group interest by agriculture, labor, or business will bring difficulty, if not ruin, to all.

Confessional. It must not be forgotten that we so mismanaged our economy in the early 1930's that scarcity, hunger, and nakedness were our intimate companions. Labor and agriculture will not readily permit a recurrence of conditions which deprived us as a society of goods and services to an amount equal to our share of the cost of World War II.[9] The need is obvious for the formulation of a social theory and policy regarding the use of wealth based on consumption rather than on production, and on considerations of public welfare rather than on those of maximum profit for corporate bodies or individuals. The cake must be eaten to be kept.

In so doing there appears a reasonable chance for capital to have its just due and for both agriculture and labor to have adequate shares of the national income. But if one or more major groups overreach themselves, if the interdependencies within our economy are forgotten, if inflation melts down the capital values built up by past toil and savings, the future will have a longer, sadder confessional than the present. One possibility here for agriculture would be to go back to the principle of the first Agricultural Adjustment Act, which provided that benefits should cease when any given commodity achieved parity.

The permanent American revolution. The din along the crowded ways of life, the daily strivings and struggles, the pursuit of goals ever enlarging, as they should in a dynamic, developing, democratic society, sometimes cause Americans to forget the way the nation has come. In August, 1951, the Department of Commerce announced that our per capita income was approaching $1500, or about $5000 for each family; even allowing for the changing value of money, that is close to twice that of the once fabulous year

1929. Farm income in the latter half of the 1940's and beyond topped all previous records by billions. The full-time, fully employed American family farm is prosperous as no other farmer in the world is prosperous. Organized workers and organized farmers have political power. Their voices are listened to, even if not always heeded, in legislative halls. True, there is still poverty in America, still exploitation, still racial discrimination. But laws, courts, and public opinion are weakening the last. Each annual survey of the Federal Reserve Board emphasizes the lessening proportion of the population in the lower income levels. With all its admitted faults, if America had done only half as well as it has in the first half of this century, it would still negate every basic assumption of Marxism. Nor does the American at mid-century admit that the record cannot be still further improved. This is what *Fortune* calls the permanent American revolution.

World influences. True, the rich endowment of natural resources in North America has helped both the United States and Canada to their present positions. Despite all the prodigal waste, they were used by those from all over the world who came to this continent. The result is evident from the income data given in the previous chapter. The average American has more resources at his disposal than those of any other nation. Wealth and power bring their responsibilities, responsibilities new to a people who have been for three centuries intent on the development of what they found in their continent, a people who came to America to be rid of the world which now intrudes upon them. These responsibilities cannot be dodged, even though they are unwelcome.

These responsibilities are of concern to rural people, and not simply because they are Americans. They are of concern because

[9] Harold Loeb, *et al., The Chart of Plenty: A Study of America's Product Capacity Based on the Findings of the National Survey of Potential Product Capacity* (New York: Viking Press, 1935).

those who look to us for help or in envy, are themselves so largely tillers of the soil.

Said William O. Douglas, Associate Justice of the Supreme Court of the United States, in a report to the Rotary Club of Tucson, Arizona, about his 1950 trip to the east:

The revolutions which are brewing are not, however, Communist in origin nor will they end even if Soviet Russia is crushed through war. . . . If we undertook to match the Soviets in a program of political action, the chances of success would be considerable. One reason is that the revolutions which sweep Asia are basically incompatible with Communism. . . . The peasants of this area (and they comprise the vast majority of the population) want to be rid of their landlords; they want to own their land — to fence it and call it theirs, to cultivate it and keep the produce for themselves and their families. The Communists merely substitute one landlord (the state) for another.

Paul Hoffman, recent head of the Economic Coöperation Administration, makes the same point:[10] "Land is a social, political and mathematical problem," he says.

The aspirations stirring in the hearts of farmers of the world are in part of our own making.

As one of the authors has said elsewhere, our missionaries have preached the gospel of the infinite value of the individual personality. Our professors and the students from abroad whom they have taught here expounded the doctrines of freedom and democracy. To peoples exploited equally by their own few rich and powerful or by colonial powers, who have worked for a pittance while their masters lived in the ultimate of luxury, these teachings have been heady wine.

This is why Justice Douglas, in the address quoted above, said:

[10] Paul Hoffman, *Waging the Peace* (New York: Doubleday, 1951).

The fact is that America has been so engrossed in providing a defense against Communism that we have lost the initiative. Our great weakness has been our negative attitude. . . . We have thought we could save the world from Communism by dollars. It is, however, ideas not dollars that count the more in this campaign. Dollars are secondary.

This situation underlines the importance of the Point IV program, so called from the fourth point of President Truman's Inaugural Address of January, 1949. He called for a "bold new program" to "make available to peace-loving peoples the benefits of our store of technical knowledge." As a result some hundreds of Americans are at work from India and Iran to Paraguay helping the people to make better use of their resources in agriculture, to improve education, to attack the problems of sanitation and disease.

The world being as largely rural as it is, this method of attack is basic. The espousal of agrarian reform by Communist parties in these rural lands shows their diagnosis of the situation. The long struggle against the philosophy of dictatorship can perhaps be won on the tiny fields of the world's farmers.

The nations of the world collectively have recognized the great importance of agriculture and rural people. Even before the United Nations was organized what is now one of its subsidiaries, The Food and Agriculture Organization, came into being, as noted in the previous chapter.

This Food and Agriculture Organization — FAO — will be the main agency of agriculture in this new era of international coöperation. Its purposes, broadly stated, are to raise the level of nutrition and the standard of living of all peoples; to secure improvements in efficiency of production and distribution of the world's food and fiber; and to better the condition of all rural people. In achieving these ends, it will rely on fact finding and education. It is not an action agency and has no authority over a member nation. It has been compared to our own Agricultural Extension Service on an international scale. It will help nations to help themselves, and should become a force in shaping world public opinion. It has sent "missions" of experts to six member nations asking for assistance. One of its important tasks is to get at the roots of international difficulty in matters pertaining to nutrition and food and to try to find solutions. It has held numerous conferences dealing with coöperatives, rural welfare, extension service, and problems of specific commodities. It is sponsoring a world agricultural census. The Food and Agriculture Organization is a step in economic and social coöperation, without which political agreements have little meaning. If, as it hopes, it can help to increase agricultural production to the right amounts of needed products in the right places, it will improve industrial activity and business, and help to remove causes of agrarian and industrial unrest.

Clearly, there is a theoretical knowledge as to how to reconstruct an adequate national economy. Clearly, the world is determined to rebuild a better structure on the ruins of the old. Whether success is attained depends upon whether nations and groups within them can rid themselves of fears, fostered through centuries of struggle, for resources inadequate to their needs because not yet touched by the magic of technology or the power of atomic energy. Should these efforts end in failure, the sheer weight of human need will force planning and policies beyond anything yet experienced in this nation.

Social Problems of Today and Tomorrow

The importance of international affairs to rural people and to the nation does not, of course, minimize the need for developing rural life and its institutions in the United States. Indeed, a strong and democratic America, city and country alike, is essential in meeting the international responsibilities thrust upon us. Neither can be neglected.

Many reports issued since 1944 by farm organizations, church bodies, and other groups, notably the Post-War Policy Committee of the Land Grant College Association, contain a large measure of agreement on such matters as follow.

Improving rural education. Rural education needs strengthening everywhere. If there is in this land the equality of opportunity which was a cardinal principle of the founding fathers, rural children should have as good education as nonrural children. This includes not only basic curriculum, but also guidance, broadened vocational training, special training for those handicapped physically, mentally, or emotionally, an enriched curriculum for those unable to continue their education beyond high school, and college preparatory work for others. To accomplish this, salaries of rural teachers must be raised, buildings improved in a long-time program, administrative units enlarged, attendance units made to conform to the social boundaries of communities. Adult education must be improved in vocational, family life, social and cultural areas, and this should include development of adequate community library service through county or district organization plans. The value of these policies is already attested by experience, especially in the more advantaged states.

A program of this character cannot be financed by rural America unaided, nor should it be, since half the rural youth migrate to cities and therefore are the cities' equal responsibility. State and federal aid are necessary. The latter should be extended without surrendering state and local control, in a way comparable to federal grants to colleges of agriculture for their research

ınd extension programs, which have oper-
ıted for decades.

Expanding health facilities. The problem
of adequate medical care for rural people
ıas been a serious one for half a century
ınd the need for improvement is admitted.
Various lay and professional programs have
been advanced. Federal assistance has also
been proposed.

Curative medicine, too, must be fortified
by the expansion of county health units to
he one third of the counties not yet so
served, as provided for under the Social
Security Act.

Closely allied to this whole project is the
need of improvement of the nutrition of
rural people. This is proved by the proportion of draft rejections because of physical
inadequacies caused by faulty diet. Educational programs in schools and among
adults are needed in this sphere, and the
balanced school lunch can do much, both
as a corrective and as a demonstration of
how to use a balanced diet.

Better housing is called for. Progress has
been made in improving the housing of rural
America since the end of World War II. The
United States Department of Agriculture
has done considerable work on farm housing, both in terms of plans for efficient
homes suited to regional climate conditions,
and in planning costs. There are still too
many below-standard homes, especially in
poorer farming areas and among share croppers, under-employed farmers, and farm
laborers.

*Recreation and better social organization
needed.* There has been a considerable expansion of social organizations in rural communities as contrasted with the beginning
of the century. But many surveys have
shown that large proportions of rural people
are untouched by this development. Rural
youth especially are critical of recreational

provisions in rural America, especially for
the post-high-school group. Adequate recreational facilities are important factors in
creating satisfaction with rural life. Response to the recreational programs of the
Extension Service in some states justifies
more attention to this area of social life.

The problem, however, goes beyond recreation. It includes the total organizational
structure of rural society. Recent decades
have seen a multiplication of special interest
groups, ranging all the way from national
farm organizations to their local community branches, and breeders' associations, to
service or purely social clubs. Yet fundamental interests remain common to all who
live in the same locality, be it neighborhood
or community; interests such as schools,
roads, health, and the other social utilities.

The question arises whether this tendency
to form special groups will divide rural society into as many parts as there are interests. There is much need for statesmanlike
leadership and better group planning to create a better integrated community life in
which legitimate specialized interests and
total community development will be use-
fully coördinated.

Spiritual leadership essential. Among
many other desirable forward steps in rural
life, perhaps the most important is an improvement in program and leadership of
rural churches. Protestantism is the dominant persuasion of rural America, and its
weakness has been made clear in an earlier
chapter. What the rural church can do as
a whole is shown by hundreds of individually successful rural churches. The problem of expanding this work needs far more
realistic attention than it is receiving. Going far beyond training clergy for rural
parishes, it involves administrative arrangements to retain them for such specialized responsibilities, payment of adequate salaries,
and the reduction of competition and the

partial and fragmented service which results from such scattered effort. There are signs of changing attitudes and policies in the rural life movements among most of the national church bodies — Catholic, Protestant, and Jewish.

The compulsion of institutional change. In essence, these last paragraphs have indicated that social and economic institutions must change and adapt themselves to changing times. The text has given many illustrations of this process. Social institutions are devices whereby men coöperate to accomplish certain agreed-upon purposes. These purposes grow out of recognized needs. As needs change, so do the purposes and objectives of society, and the institutions of society must change comparably. The role of any institution in a dynamic society is to influence, and to be influenced by and adjust to, the changing social trends and forces that operate in any society, whether the social group concerned be neighborhood, community, or nation. Institutions are anchored in the past, but to survive they must be oriented to the future. The social policies suggested for the improvement of rural education, health, and social organization can be made effective only by institutional or agency action. Such action in our democratic society can come only as those concerned are convinced of the necessity of new policies. These principles apply to voluntary associations, whether they be a village women's club or a national farm organization, and also to government from the local level up.

Social Policies Interrelated

A public opinion poll among informed persons would certainly produce a large measure of agreement on a program such as the one outlined in the previous section of this chapter. Implementing such a pro-

gram is another matter. For one thing, it would involve a considerable increase in the number of well-trained professional workers in education, health, religion, and other fields, as well as an increase in the number of skilled artisans in construction, electrification, and other occupations. This in itself would offer expanded employment opportunities.

Again, such a program must be financed. There must be an adequate economic base in rural America to sustain the necessary institutions, or else that base must be strengthened by grants from society as a whole. But that is by no means the whole story. The implementation of such a program will make its own contribution to its cost — a fact that is little realized or understood.

The strongest practical case to be made for an adequate rural health program is economic. A well man pays his way in this world by what he produces and the services he renders. The measurable decline in death rates in counties that have had health units over a period of years shows that tax support for such units has netted society a handsome profit.

Economists by the score have testified to the economic gains for society, to say nothing of the individual, from an adequate educational system.[11] Nor does the case rest on testimony. Data have already been presented on this point in the discussion of education. Compare the low standard of living in the southern Appalachian mountain region with the high standard in mountainous Switzerland. The former has twice the natural resources of the latter, but education in Switzerland is far superior to that in our southern mountains. Its system has produced some of the most skilled workers in the world and a high per capita income. Yugoslavia has average resources. Norway has

[11] Cf. Educational Policies Commission, *Education and Economic Well-Being in American Democracy* (Washington, 1940).

poor soil, a harsh climate, a short growing season, and few natural resources, and yet its yields outstrip those of Yugoslavia, indeed, outstrip all but one of the Balkan countries. Until the German invasion, it had a high per capita income. It also had an unusually high level of education. Switzerland and Norway have invested in their people. They have educated them to make the most intelligent use of the limited resources they possess.[12]

There lies in this and much other data another great social truth which Americans have not sufficiently learned, to judge by their national behavior. It is this: capital invested in human beings earns economic returns just as surely as capital invested in an acre of land, a filling station, or a steel mill. True, the return may not show on next year's balance sheet. This is why society, rather than the individual or a corporation, must share in or make the entire investment. Quarterly and annual statements of profits are not the only ways of measuring economic gain. The production of goods and services over the years is a surer index.

This principle applies even in things of the spirit, and not merely in the sense that Henry Wallace had in mind when he remarked that a strong country church nearby was the best asset a coöperative could have. Liberty Hyde Bailey, one of the greatest deans of agriculture, once remarked that 'the morals of land management are more important than the economics of land." He meant that the right use of the soil is the criterion of whether a nation is civilized. The psalmist who wrote, "The earth is the Lord's and the fullness therof," said essentially the same thing. Here again economics and sociology join hands. The essential unity of the social sciences is the fact that they are social. Social objectives can be buttressed by economic findings just as

sound economic policy can be furthered by wise use of pertinent sociological data.

Criteria for Policy

If there is any validity in the argument in these pages, there should be discernible criteria for judging policy proposals for rural life. There is no final, authoritative source for such criteria, nor can there be in a democracy. But an examination of testimony and literature seems to show the beginnings of a real consensus as to how such policy may be evaluated.

A basic test of any program is whether it safeguards the soil and other natural resources. This criterion met, does the policy provide a fair and adequate share of the total national income for the tillers of the soil, under conditions that call forth efficient production geared to both domestic and foreign needs? In terms of programs in aid of rural society and its institutions the gauge must be whether the benefits of the program justify the cost. Here there is an example from far-away Australia. Its Rural Reconstruction Commission not only declared that the *social* disparities between urban and rural areas were "*economically* insupportable" by the nation, it also attempted to demonstrate the fact.

Implied in these criteria is the all important test of national well-being. The general welfare must be paramount in an interdependent society. There can be no privilege or advantage for any single group that cannot be supported for any other. This means that long term programs based on findings of social science must be kept free from political interference unwarranted by the facts, like appointments to the Civil Service.

Social science can help. If the social sciences are to help, it must be because they have acquired useable knowledge applicable to the field of human relations. This indeed is true. Progress in the last generation has

[12] Cf. Harold Clark, *Teachers College Record* March, 1945), pp. 360–65.

been considerable. Starved as the social sciences have been, relative to the natural sciences, for research funds, they are here and there approaching certitude, if too infrequently in details, at least more often in principles.[13]

Who shall plan for rural America? It has been reiterated in this text that implicit in democracy is the need for citizens to assume their responsibilities in determining policies of the society of which they are a part. As already brought out, rural people have acquired some experience in the art of planning in the last decades in connection with several programs. This experience should be built upon. Probably it should head up, as the Land Grant College Post-War Policy Committee suggests, in a permanent national agricultural policy committee, coöperating with the Department of Agriculture. Similar coöperating bodies could be set up in the states and counties. Labor, business, and consumers should be represented, for the problems of agriculture and rural life are national in scope and implications. Farmers, too, should have their say on policies relating to other large areas of the economy. They should also see how their proposals affect others. Ours is an interdependent society!

What this means is that planning and following action when democratic consensus has been reached, is both vertical and horizontal. It can operate on one level, the local community. The great importance of this level is that people live in communities and in them experience and adapt to broad trends. Planning can also be vertical, from the local community to the nation. Both processes are vitally important.

Essentially what the farmer wants is to feed the hungry, to help answer the prayer for daily bread, on the basis of social and economic equality with other groups in the United States or any other society. This has been called parity, but the parity must be more than economic; it must be social as well. Indeed, it cannot be one without the other, nor can the health of society as a whole be considered sound if any important group suffers from social and economic ills.

Anthropologists declare that periods of stress and social change occur when the mores that control and motivate the behavior of local face-to-face primary groups for some reason or reasons lose their efficacy. Social stability does not return until new mores are accepted as adequate social controls. It is also true that social change is accelerated when major conflicts between important groups develop. The final resolution of these conflicts produces a new equilibrium, a changed social pattern.

Such a period was the Renaissance. Such a period was that of the political and social revolutions in England and France when the machine worker and artisan or handicraftsman joined issue; when the slogan "Liberty, Equality, and Fraternity" challenged monarchy; when the doctrine of *laissez faire* freed the use of capital from ancient restrictions. The present, too, is such a period; two world wars have swept away the savings of generations; science has all but annihilated space and time, made the world interdependent, and given us through mass production undreamed-of potential wealth in goods, displacing entire occupations and speeding up even agricultural processes; and, finally, the ferment of democracy and its hope for the common man has spread to far-off lands. The task of the social scientist today is to plan, work for and achieve the reconciliation of such conflicting social groups and tendencies and the acceptance of new mores befitting our resources, and thus help provide a new equilibrium between nation and nation, capital and labor, city and country.

[13] Stuart Chase, *The Proper Study of Mankind* (New York: Harper, 1949).

TOPICS FOR DISCUSSION

, What values important to the life of the nation do you think are created or fostered in rural society?

, What, if any, is the justification for equalization plans of financing rural social institutions, such as schools, hospitals or libraries, by moneys collected in taxes or otherwise from citizens who do not reside in rural territory?

. What is the main agricultural policy or platform of the National Democratic, Republican, and Socialist parties, as shown by their last statements or conventions?

. Discuss the pros and cons of pertinent sections of the Post-War Policy Report of the Land-Grant College Association in terms either of the nation or your state.

. What are the chief issues on which rural and urban interests are most likely to clash? Can these interests be reconciled in some kind of a national policy? If yes, how? If not, why?

. Name some tests or criteria by which you are willing to judge as to whether changes in rural society are in the direction of progress.

. Outline an adequate land utilization policy for your state; for the nation.

REFERENCE READINGS

Belshaw, Horace, *Foundations of Rural Welfare*. Montreal: International Labor Office, 1945; also in *International Labour Review*, vol. LI, no. 3.

Brandt, Karl, *The Reconstruction of World Agriculture*. New York: W. W. Norton & Co., 1945.

Griswold, A. Whitney, *Farming and Democracy*. New York: Harcourt, Brace & Co., 1948.

Land-Grant College Association, *Post-War Policy Report*, 1944.

Moore, Arthur, *The Farmer and the Rest of Us*. Boston: Little, Brown, 1945.

National Resources Board, A *Report on National Planning and Public Works in Relation to Natural Resources, and Including Land Use and Water Resources, with Findings and Recommendations*, Parts I and II. Washington: Government Printing Office, 1934.

    Agricultural Exports in Relation to Land Policy. 1935.

    Soil Erosion. 1935.

    Regional Factors in National Planning. December, 1935.

    State Planning. June, 1935; December, 1936.

    General Conditions and Tendencies Influencing the Nation's Land Requirements. 1936.

Osborn, Fairfield, *Our Plundered Planet*. Boston: Little, Brown, 1948.

Schultz, T. W., *Agriculture in an Unstable Economy*. New York: McGraw-Hill, 1945.

Shepard, Ward, *Food or Famine*. New York: Macmillan, 1946.

Staff of the Agricultural Economic Research Institute of Oxford University, *Country Planning: A Study of Rural Problems*. London: Oxford University Press, 1944.

Taylor, C. C., *Human Relations in Land Use Planning*. Washington: United States Department of Agriculture, Bureau of Agricultural Economics, 1938 (mimeographed).

Timoshenko, V., *World Agriculture and the Depression*. Ann Arbor: University of Michigan, 1933.

Vogt, William, *Road to Survival*. New York: William Sloane Associates, 1948.

Appendixes

Appendix One

The Book — What It Is, How to Use It

The fourth edition of this book, with revisions and reinterpretations, is now presented because of a sincere and continuing desire to stimulate even greater interest in rural society and to promote still more and better study in the field. More than two thirds of our global population is as yet predominantly rural. In a broad sense progress depends on the harmonious fusion of the best elements of the world's rural and urban cultures. Today's earnest student, teacher, or administrator faces a great opportunity for developing and expanding this area of knowledge.

The title of the book is a true statement of its purpose, *A Study of Rural Society*. It is dedicated to the youth of America, and has been from its first edition. Youth is here considered not in terms of calendar years but in a spirit and attitude of learning and doing. We hope more fully to introduce a greater number of such essentially youthful students to rural society and its people — who they are, where they live, how they live and make a living, how they form and reform their group relations, and how they arrange and rearrange their social institutions.

Society means systems of human relations, people as persons associating with one another in living their lives, making a livelihood, having fun, learning, worshipping, keeping healthy and happy. Association results in various recognized and socially accepted forms or patterns of behavior as groups, institutions and values — what is considered right and wrong, true and false, beautiful and ugly, good and bad. These folkways, technic-ways, group-ways, and state-ways exert strong influences upon members of society. It is all-important then for those living within the society and those wishing to know it better, to understand these influences and how they work. They become effective by means of communication, developing attitudes and opinions, and exerting group controls. On the one hand, this working together gives society a certain toughness and resistance to rapid and radical change, and on the other, it makes change and constant readjustment a requisite to wholesome living and to the continuity of the society itself.

Rural includes both farmers and villagers, as well as other non-farm country dwellers. The modern rural community is made up of country and village or town relationships. But rural society is not separate or apart, it is interrelated within the larger whole or Great Society, as it has come to be known.

What the book is and is not. This is not a "problems" book as such, but plenty of problematical situations and issues will be encountered in the course of the study. These call for many kinds of policies and actions. Education does not end with information or diagnosis but must carry over into decision and action on the part of those who study. Most social problems are group problems; therefore certain group experiences and group methods of study are suggested as helpful to learning. Topics and questions placed at chapter ends call for group work, for evaluation and decision, and for the formulation of principles and policies of action.

Neither is the book a "theory" book as such. Theories are important as means for understanding and as tools for study. Consequently, the materials are organized and the discussion presented within a theoretical frame of reference. Conscious and recognized theories are implicit throughout, although not always explicitly expressed. At present it is doubtful whether there exists a sufficient body of knowledge about rural society so that it can be compressed within a single theoretical system.

The book is quite simply a study of contemporary American rural society. The *theme* or "red thread" about which the presentation is woven is the growing interdependence in our modern society — country and town, rural and urban, agriculture and industry, American and other societies. Historical backgrounds and comparisons with rural society in other lands are considered important. Therefore, a separate chapter on "Rural Welfare in Underdeveloped Countries" is introduced, together with chapter references and a special bibliography in the appendix, "Bibliography of Rural Life in Foreign Lands."

Processes of interdependence involve many movements and numerous procedures. Few of these are simple or one-directional. For example, what has been described in some instances solely as "urbanization," the reaching out of urban interests to control the rural, is actually countered by movements of "ruralization." Rural and urban as aspects of the general society are interdependent. The terms themselves are outmoded and do not represent distinctions they once did. This change has come about not only because of rapid city building and the expansion of city-ways into rural areas, but also through a vast migration of country people with their ways of life to urban areas. Rural-urban interaction and interdependence have developed and multiplied because of greatly increased communication and transportation, and because of progress in science and technology.

Corollaries of the central theme. Several corollaries follow from the central theme:

First, population characteristics change. People move about, seeking employment, pleasure, education, health. Modes of housing and eating are modified. Age distributions shift as science conquers disease. Corresponding accommodations in social arrangements are brought about.

Second, agriculture and manufacturing closely associated with it respond to changed conditions as markets expand or habits, customs of consumers, urban and rural, foreign and domestic, change.

Third, greater freedom of social contact brings about differentiation among groups. A particular person, urban or rural, does not confine his social relations to one kind of group. No single group, even a rural community, however generalized it may be, can possibly compass the whole of social organization. Instead, persons belong to many different groups, all at the same time. Recent research reveals that rural high school pupils, especially, move about freely in a whole mesh of interrelated groups. The theoretical reference therefore is not an independent series of group forms, such as in-group and out-group or primary group and secondary group, but rather persons playing varied roles in various groups within their particular society.

Fourth, while science and technology have taken over in many of the physical realms of agriculture and rural life, there is a great lag in many of the social and institutional forms. Social institutions tend to be tradition-bound, their roots thrust deep into the soil of the past for stability and security. However, to survive, their branches must reach far into the air of the future for flexibility and growth. Many current social inventions, like many early physical inventions, meet with doubts, fears, and open opposition. To the student of present-day rural society, the practical challenge is to deter-nine what was socially desirable in the past, and to bring this into relationship with the design for the future.

Organization into parts and chapters. Such a theme and its corollaries, when formalized, draw the materials and discussion of rural society naturally into four main parts:

1. *Population* — people in their cultural, regional, and demographic aspects.

2. *Agrarian basis of rural society* — ways of earning a livelihood, man's relation to his land.

3. *Group relations* — functions and forms of human association.

4. *Social institutions* — established and recognized ways of getting things done.

Each chapter follows much the same pattern: introduction, situation, changes, trends, comparisons, issues, policies, and conclusions. The order is not always quite the same, but the purpose is.

In class procedure, the sequence should fit the purpose in hand. Parts of the book can be interchanged, even chapters, for good reason. For example, one of the authors begins his course with the study of group relations: neighborhoods, communities, villages, families, then moves on to a consideration of the people who form these groups, their agrarian background and setting, and finally their social institutions.

Some teachers may wish to begin with the agricultural basis, others with social institutions, since these seem so evident, so solid, and so well established. Actually, however, many social institutions are quite fragile and changeable. For this reason, unless there are unusual circumstances, it is wise to lead up to the discussion of institutions, to consider first their group and cultural backgrounds, the reasons for their rise, and the needs for their readjustment in the contemporary scene.

Practical suggestions for class procedures. Suggestions given are based on many years

of teaching. In the process of learning there is no complete substitute for experience. Therefore, every means possible should be devised for exploiting past experiences and for expanding new experiences. Class members and instructor should plan together. This in itself is a learning experience. If the class is large, various committee plans or delegated responsibility can be used; however, the more general the participation, the greater the benefits.

1. *Exploring* one's own experiences. An effort should be made to give them clarity and meaning in terms of the frame of reference and the topics under discussion. This applies to students and to instructor, whether the experience has been in a rural or urban, American or foreign, environment. Topics have been drawn for this purpose and appear at the end of each chapter. To make the best use of past experiences, they should be presented in written form and related to the subject matter under study.

2. *Exchanging* and comparing one's interpretation of past experiences with others. This has double value since careful analysis is required to communicate experiences clearly and interestingly. The exercise also enables the student (or instructor) to compare experiences, to judge their uniqueness, their similarity or difference, and their personal consequences. All this can be accomplished by having members of the class present their papers to the class as a whole or to a section or a committee. Simple sketches on the blackboard or improvised drawings help to make points clear, as well as to relieve self-consciousness.

3. *Reading* as a vicarious or substitute form of experience. This experience can be interesting and exhilarating, especially when materials are selected with discretion and when comparisons can be made with one's own experiences. Reports of readings and conclusions reached should be written for reasons of clarity and stimulation of interest.

If practical, they should be presented orally. Reference readings are listed at the close of chapters. Many footnotes are given which should be explored further. Footnote references are not usually repeated in the list of reference readings.

4. *Writing* as an aid to organization and clarified thinking. The discipline of putting one's ideas into "black and white" has real educational value. It is to be encouraged and guided. Topics suggested at chapter ends may be prepared as short exercises or expanded into term papers or projects. Some may be written individually, some as the work of a committee or a group. Such topics may be an analysis of facts and figures or an explanation of what the facts are considered to mean. The work in hand may be highlighted by an explanation of the experience offered by a field trip or a reference reading.

5. *Analyzing* census or other secondary materials. One variety of reading or research is to examine census reports, year books, world almanac, state agricultural college bulletins, or agency reports. Materials may relate to the student's home county or some local situation of pertinent class interest. Comparisons may be made with another county or subregion in the state, and explanations submitted. Items such as the following may be profitably studied: characteristics of the people, especially with reference to age and sex; educational status of adults; ratio of children to women fifteen to forty-four years of age; size and value of farms; or value of products raised.

This is an age of statistics. It is important therefore for students to acquire an early familiarity in working with figures. Today business concerns, educational institutions, agricultural, social and welfare agencies commonly deal in statistical terms, publish numerical reports, and make factual appeals. A measure of competence in analyzing such reports and evaluating such appeals is essential. This can be achieved only by experience gained from the direct use of statistical materials, which is one reason for including figures, tables and charts in the various chapters. Another reason is that facts and figures help to give the study of rural society the definiteness, concreteness, and tangibility which it merits.

6. *Seeing and hearing,* other substitutes for first-hand or direct experience. Here the wide variety and vast resources of modern audio-visual aids come directly into play. Students and instructor should be encouraged to bring to class or to group or sectional meetings pictures they have taken; in addition, films, colored pictures, stills, and movies are available from many sources. Collections of works of art may be shown or the class as a whole or some of its members may visit exhibits. Careful selection is important. Preparation must be made in advance with discussion of how the pictures relate to class purposes. The seeing experience should be followed by discussion, verbal or in writing, so that the focus and import can be made quite definite.

Educational films are listed at the conclusion of many chapters and in the Bibliography of Rural Life in Foreign Lands. These films have been tested for educational value either by the Bureau of Visual Instruction at the University of Wisconsin, Madison, or by the Institute of Adult Education, Teachers College, Columbia University, New York City, or both.

Most of the films can be secured from state university or college film rental libraries or from local commercial rental libraries. To save space, symbols are used, "S" for sound and "C" for color. Numerals signify the number of minutes the picture requires.

7. *Acting* out a situation. This may be imaginary or authentic, fictional, or factual. Members of the class can present a play, original, classic or contemporary, which deals with some pertinent topic, issue or problem. They can reënact a community

meeting, a committee session, or a family situation which has been observed or read about. They can constitute themselves as a community or a school meeting, a church congregation or a county board, a family case work council or a local health committee, and proceed with appropriate business or consider a particular problem. They should come to some decision as to what should be done, why, and how. The last step is important since group action is involved.

Group discussion of this type is known as *sociodrama* and lends itself to a variety of class purposes. Success depends largely upon the quick and ready response of the actors and their willingness and ability to portray "real life" situations. Presentations may be made with or without rehearsals.

8. *Visiting* communities, neighborhoods, agencies, institutions, homes, or farms. Field trips are an important means for gaining direct experience, even though greatly telescoped. Such trips are to be encouraged whenever possible. If well managed, they give a reality to the class procedure as few other experiences can. Again, success depends greatly on a careful preparation, thorough follow-through, and final review.

Contacts for field visits must be made in advance, and if the instructor and a committee of students can go together, the results are proportionately better than when either goes alone. If a small community is to be visited, initial contacts can be made with a local leader such as a school principal, county agent, church pastor, or coöp manager. Some member of the class may even be a resident of a nearby community which could be visited with profit.

A local community committee may be appointed to meet with the student committee to arrange the details of the visit. The trip itself should follow a prearranged plan for visiting the village center or the country area, attending meetings, inspecting buildings, agencies, or local enterprises. An open forum or dinner meeting with local people and students should follow for a discussion of the local situation. A panel with local and student members may be chosen. By mutual agreement, fields for exploration and discussion can be limited or attention focused on certain issues.

Class members, individually or in groups, may be encouraged to return to the community, gather more facts, make more contacts or even carry on simple schedule studies. Brief reports may be written and presented or made into more ambitious term papers.

9. *Inviting* local leaders or members of high school or adult groups to the class. Such an invitation might well be a reciprocation for a visit made by the class to a community or to a local high school. A high school social science class might be invited to the college campus and a joint class session arranged. The visitors might be taken to a campus eating place and the discussion continued there. Afterwards, if time permits, a brief trip can be made over the campus or into town to visit some agency of mutual interest. If the plan is made in advance, and if school officials are fully informed, a school bus can usually be used for such a trip.

10. *Committee-ing* to gain group experience. This should be done to take advantage of the principle of division of labor, to give informality and provide participation in the class procedure. Committees, sections, or groups can be arranged for many purposes and in a variety of ways. A group product is something different from the sum of its member parts. Group activities invest the class with a sense of its own identity and its own importance. A committee can organize the field trip or the visit to the class of some chosen community representatives. Committee reports can be prepared and presented to the class in panel discussion or in sociodrama form. Committees can help to plan class work, even to devise examinations.

11. *Coöperating* to make the class procedure real educational experience. Basically, education is collective experience. Unless the class can be converted into a working group with the mutual confidence and coöperation of class members and instructor, little of educational value will result. An instructor can dispense information but he cannot substitute for student thinking and acting. He cannot force education upon others. He can only help to provide an opportunity for learning, and create situations where differing personalities yield to educational influences and appropriate to themselves what is communicable. Nor can he monitor honesty in thinking or in the writing of examinations; those who would learn must also assume responsibilities. Only by mutual effort can those qualities of integrity and scholarship be gained which befit students of society.

Appendix Two

Bibliography of Rural Life in Foreign Lands

An increasing amount of work in rural sociology and research is being carried on in foreign lands, especially in Asia and Latin America. Much of it is of value, especially to graduate students in American institutions. Moreover, an increasing number of foreign students interested in rural sociology are attending American colleges and universities. Technical assistance missions of the United Nations and efforts of the United States under the so-called Point IV program and the Economic Coöperation Administration lend further interest to studies of the social life and culture of other countries. A brief bibliography is, therefore, appended on rural life in foreign lands.

Only a few of the references are to articles; but those interested will find a considerable source of valuable material in *Rural Sociology, Journal of Farm Economics,* and *Foreign Agriculture.* This last is a publication of the Office of Foreign Agricultural Relations of the United States Department of Agriculture. *The Far Eastern Survey* of the Institute of Pacific Relations sometimes carries articles of rural interest or general articles with rural references and implications. So does the semimonthly *Bulletin* and other publications of the Foreign Policy Association. Both of these agencies are in New York City.

No pretense is made that the bibliography which follows is complete, but considerable effort has been expended to select significant books. The sections on South and Central America list a larger number of general books than the others because studies in English are few. All the books selected give

considerable attention to rural life. A few titles of books now fairly old are included because of the basic data given or because of their valuable historic contributions.

No one interested in rural life in foreign lands should overlook the publications of the Food and Agriculture Organization of the United Nations, Viale delle Terme de Caracalla, Rome, Italy. It has issued a number of pertinent publications, some mimeographed. The reports of its technical assistance missions, though dealing largely with agriculture, without exception are also concerned with population, land tenure, and other topics of considerable social importance. The F.A.O. maintains a regional office in Washington, D.C. Current reports and publications of UNESCO, 19 Kléber Avenue, Paris 16, France, and of the Social and Economic Council of the United Nations, New York, New York, should also be consulted.

There are no references except in the General section, to rural life in Europe, where six references have a considerable amount of material on this continent, as do some publications of international agencies mentioned above. There are several reasons for this. In the first place, there is little reliable postwar material with respect to Russia and its satellites. Prewar publications are outdated. Again, there are quite naturally fewer references in English.

It will be noted that many of these books have foreign publishers, but a number of them are obtainable from American sources. For the most part, publications of the Royal Institute of International Affairs can be obtained from the Institute of Pacific Relations in New York City.

The Oxford University Press in New York City carries quite a number of the publications relating to the British Commonwealth. G. E. Stechert and Company, 31 East 10th Street, New York, also carries social science works published abroad, including a number listed in this bibliography.

GENERAL

American Philosophical Society, "Population and the Further Spread of Industrial Society," *Proceedings,* CXCV, No. 1, Philadelphia, February, 1951.

Belshaw, Horace, *Essentials of Rural Welfare.* New York: Columbia University Press for Food and Agriculture Organization, 1949.

Bigelow, Karl, ed., *Cultural Groups and Human Relations.* New York: Columbia University Teachers College Bureau of Publications, 1951.

Brandt, Karl, *The Reconstruction of World Agriculture.* New York: Norton, 1945.

Brunner, Edmund deS., I. T. Sanders, and D. Ensminger, eds., *Farmers of The World, The Development of Agricultural Extension.* New York: Columbia University Press, 1945.

Butterfield, K. L., *The Rural Mission of the Church in Eastern Asia.* New York: International Missionary Council, 419 Fourth Avenue; or 2 Eaton Gate, London, S. W. 1, England, 1931.

Colonial Office, *Reading List on Colonial Development and Welfare.* New York: British Library, Public Information, 1950. A free bibliography of official reports covering social and economic conditions and postwar reconstruction developments for all British Crown Colonies.

Colonial Office, *The Colonial Territories* (an annual survey). London: H. M. Stationery Office, 1951.

Cressey, George B., *Asia's Lands and Peoples.* New York: McGraw-Hill, 1945.

Lamartine Yates, Paul, and Warriner, Doreen, *Food and Farming in Post-War Europe.* London: Oxford University Press, 1943.

Lasker, Bruno, *Asia on the Move.* New York Holt, 1945.

Mair, L. P., *Welfare in the British Colonies* New York and London: The Royal Institute of International Affairs, 1944.

Mandelbaum, K., *The Industrialization of Backward Areas.* New York and London: Oxford University Press, 1945.

Moomaw, Ira, *Education and Village Improvement.* New York and London: Oxford University Press, 1949.

Mukerjee, R., *Races, Lands and Foods.* New York: Dryden, 1946.

Pelzer, Karl J., *Agriculture and Land Settlement in South-East Asia.* New York: International Secretariat, Institute of Pacific Relations, in coöperation with American Geographical Society, 1943.

Pelzer, Karl J., *Pioneer Settlement in the Asiatic Tropics.* New York: American Geographical Society, 1945.

Pim, Sir Alan, *Colonial Agricultural Production: The Contribution Made by Native Peasants and Foreign Enterprise.* New York and London: Royal Institute of International Affairs, 1947.

United Nations, *Non-Self Governing Territories.* New York: United Nations, 1948. (Issued periodically.)

United Nations Conference on Food and Agriculture, *Final Act and Section Reports.* Washington, D.C.: Government Printing Office, 1943.

United States Department of Agriculture, *Contribution of Extension Methods and Techniques Toward the Rehabilitation of War-Torn Countries.* Washington, D.C., 1946.

United States Department of Agriculture, *Extension Experiences Around the World.* Washington, D.C., 1951.

Wickizer, V. D., and M. K. Bennett, *The Rice Economy of Monsoon Asia.* Stanford University, California: Stanford University Press, 1945.

The *Annual Yearbooks* of the British Commonwealths and of many of the British colonies are very valuable. They usually contain excellent chapters on population, agriculture, standards of living, social services, and the like. They may be secured through the British Library of Public Information, Radio City, New York, New York.

AFRICA

Agriculture in Uganda, Staff, Department of Agriculture, Uganda. London: Oxford University Press, 1940.

Albertyn, J. R., *Sociological Report: The Poor White and Society,* Part V of *The Poor White Problem in South Africa.* Report of the Carnegie Commission, 1932.

Allan, W., *Land Holding and Land Usage Among the Plateau Tonga* (Northern Rhodesia). New York and London: Oxford University Press, 1948.

Batten, T. R., *Problems of African Development.* New York: Oxford University Press, 1947.

Brookes, E., *The Bantu in South African Life.* Johannesburg: South African Institute of Race Relations, 1943.

Campbell, A., *South Africa, What Now?* Cape Town: Stewart, 1947.

Coulten, Charles W., "Problems Arising from Industrialization of Native Life in Central Africa," *American Journal of Sociology,* XL, No. 5, March, 1935.

Grosskopf, J. R. S., *Economic Report: Rural Impoverishment and Rural Exodus,* Part I of *The Poor White Problem in South Africa.* Report of the Carnegie Commission, 1932.

Jones, J. D. Rheinallt, *Farm Labour in the Union.* Johannesburg: South African Institute of Race Relations, 1944.

Kuczynski, R. R., *Cameroons and Togoland: A Demographic Study.* New York and London: Royal Institute of International Affairs, 1939.

Leubuscher, C., *Tanganyika Territory: A Study of Economic Policy Under Mandate.* New York and London: Royal Institute of International Affairs, 1944.

MacCrone, I. D., *Group Conflicts and Race Prejudice.* Johannesburg: South African Institute of Race Relations, 1947.

Malherbe, E. G., *Educational Report: Education and the Poor White,* Part III of *The Poor White Problem in South Africa.* Report of the Carnegie Commission, 1932.

Malinowski, B., *The Dynamics of Culture Change.* New Haven: Yale University Press, 1945.

Marquard, L., *The Native in South Africa.* Witwatersrand University Press, 1945.

Murray, W. A., *Health Report: Health Factors in the Poor White Problem,* Part IV of *The Poor White Problem in South Africa.* Report of the Carnegie Commission, 1932.

Nash, T. A. M., *The Anchan Rural Development and Settlement Scheme* (Northern Nigeria). London: H. M. Stationery Office, 1948.

Reyher, Rebecca H., *Zulu Woman.* New York: Columbia University Press, 1948.

Social and Economic Planning Council Reports. Pretoria: Government Printer.
  Native Reserves and Their Place in the Economy of the Union of South Africa. Union Government 32, 1946.
  Regional and Town Planning. Union Government 34, 1944.
  The Economic and Social Conditions of the Racial Groups in South Africa. Union Government 53, 1948.

Films

People of the Congo. S, 11. Encyclopedia Britannica Films, Inc., Chicago.

South Africa: Riches of the Veldt. S, 20. United World Films, New York.

Watussi of Africa. S, 11. Encyclopedia Britannica Films, Inc., Chicago.

AUSTRALIA AND NEW ZEALAND

Alley, G. T., and D. O. Hall, *The Farmer in New Zealand.* Wellington: Department of Internal Affairs, 1941.

Belshaw, H., and others, *Agricultural Organization in New Zealand.* Melbourne: Melbourne University Press, published for the New Zealand Council of the Institute of Pacific Relations, 1936.

Brunner, Edmund deS., *Rural Australia and New Zealand.* New York: Institute of Pacific Relations, 1938.

Bush, Alice, et al., *A National Health Service.* Wellington: Progressive Publishing Society, 1943.

Campbell, A. E., *The Feilding Community Centre*. Wellington: New Zealand Council for Educational Research, 1945.

Cowan, James, *Settlers and Pioneers*. Wellington: Department of Internal Affairs, 1940.

Doig, W. T., *A Survey of Standards of Life of New Zealand Dairy-Farmers*. Wellington: Department of Scientific and Industrial Research, Bulletin 75, 1940.

Duff, Oliver, *New Zealand Now*. Wellington: Department of Internal Affairs, 1941.

Eggleston, F. W., *Australian Standards of Living*. Melbourne: Melbourne University Press for the Australian Institute of Internal Affairs, 1939.

Garnett, A. Campbell, *Freedom and Planning in Australia*. Madison: University of Wisconsin Press, 1948.

Holt, Alan J., *Wheat Farms of Victoria*. Melbourne: Melbourne University Press, 1946.

Mason, Hon. H. G. R., *Education Today and Tomorrow*. Wellington, 1945.

McIntyre, A. J. and J. J., *Country Towns of Victoria; A Social Survey*. Melbourne: Melbourne University Press, 1944. New York distributors: G. E. Stechert and Company.

New Zealand Department of Internal Affairs, *Making New Zealand*. Wellington: Department of Internal Affairs, 1940.

New Zealand Institute of International Affairs, *Contemporary New Zealand*. Wellington: Whitcombe and Tombs, Ltd., 1938.

"New Zealand Security Program," *Fortune*, July, 1944.

The Peopling of Australia, First and Second Series. Melbourne: Melbourne University Press for the Institute of Pacific Relations, 1928 and 1933.

Radford, W. C., *The Educational Needs of a Rural Community*. Melbourne: Melbourne University Press, 1939.

The Rural Reconstruction Commission, Ministry of Postwar Reconstruction, Canberra, 1944–45:

1. *A General Rural Survey.*
2. *Land Utilization and Farm Settlement.*
3. *Financial and Economic Reconstruction of Farms.*
4. *Rural Amenities.*

Somerset, H. C. D., *Littledene: A New Zealand Rural Community*. Wellington: New Zealand Council for Educational Research, 1938.

Films

Both Australia and New Zealand, especially the former, have a considerable number of films available in the United States. For titles and terms consult the Australian Trade Commission, 636 Fifth Avenue, New York, and the New Zealand Legation, Washington, D.C.

PACIFIC ISLANDS

Belshaw, Cyril S., *Island Administration in the Southwest Pacific: Government and Reconstruction in New Caledonia, the New Hebrides, and the British Solomon Islands*. London: Institute of Pacific Relations, 1950.

Buss, Claude, "Philippines," *Fortune*, December, 1944.

Coulter, John W., *Land Utilization in American Samoa*. Honolulu: Bernice P. Bishop Museum, 1941.

Coulter, John W., *Fiji, Little India of the Pacific*. Chicago: University of Chicago Press, 1942.

Firth, Raymond, *We, The Tikopia*. New York: American Book Company, 1944.

Furnas, J. C., *Anatomy of Paradise*. New York: Sloane, 1949.

Handbook on the Trust Territory of the Pacific Islands. Washington, D.C.: Government Printing Office, Catalog No. M207, 6:P11.

Keesing, Felix M., *The South Seas in the Modern World*. New York: Institute of Pacific Relations, 1941.

Lind, Andrew W., *An Island Community (Hawaii)*. Chicago: University of Chicago Press, 1938.

Malinowski, Bronislaw, *Coral Gardens and Their Magic*. New York: American Book Company, 1944.

Oliver, Douglas L., *The Pacific Islands*. Cambridge: Harvard University Press, 1951.

Spoehr, Alexander, *Mayuro: A Village in the Marshall Islands*. Chicago: Natural History Museum, 1950.

Thompson, Laura, *Guam and Its People,* revised edition. Princeton: Princeton University Press, 1947.

Vander Plas, Charles O., *Recent Developments*

in the Netherlands East Indies. New York: The Netherlands and Netherlands East Indies Council, Institute of Pacific Relations, 1942.

Wenworth, Edna Clark, *Filipino Plantation Workers in Hawaii.* New York: Institute of Pacific Affairs, 1941.

Films

Dutch East Indies. 16. Eastman, Rochester.

Hawaiian Islands. 16. Encyclopedia Britannica Films, Inc., Chicago.

Java: Tropical Mountain Land. S, 22. United World Films, Inc., New York.

Malay Peninsula. S, 10. Coronet Instructional Films, New York.

Malaya: Nomads of the Jungle. S, 21. United World Films, Inc., New York.

Native Earth (New Guinea). 12½ min. Australian News and Information Service, New York.

Pacific Islands (Marshall Group). S, 18. International Film Foundation, New York.

People of Hawaii. S, 11. Encyclopedia Britannica Films, Inc., Chicago.

FAR EAST

China

Buck, J. Lossing, *Agricultural Survey of Szechwan Province.* New York: International Secretariat, Institute of Pacific Relations, 1943. (Mimeographed.)

Buck, J. L., *Farm Economy in China.* Chicago: University of Chicago Press, 1930.

Buck, J. L., *Land Utilization in China,* 3 vols. Chicago: University of Chicago Press, 1938.

Buck, Pearl (Mrs. J. L.), *The Good Earth.* New York, 1931. A novel of rural life in China.

Buck, Pearl, *Tell the People — Mass Education in China.* New York: American Council, Institute of Pacific Relations, 1945.

Chang, Pei-Kang, *Agriculture and Industrialization.* Cambridge: Harvard University Press, 1949.

Chen, H. S., *Frontier Land Systems in Southernmost China: A Comparative Study of Agrarian Problems and Social Organization Among Pai Yi People of Yunnan and the Kamba People of Sinkiang.* New York: International Secretariat, Institute of Pacific Relations, 1949.

Cressey, George B., *China's Geographic Foundations.* New York: McGraw-Hill, 1945.

Fei, Hsiao-Tung, *Peasant Life in China.* New York: Oxford, 1946.

Fei, Hsiao-Tung, and Tse-i Chang, *Earthbound — China.* Chicago: University of Chicago Press, 1945.

Highbaugh, Irma, *Family Life in West China.* New York: Agricultural Missions Foundation, 1948.

Hsu, Francis L. K., *Under the Ancestor's Shadow.* New York: Columbia University Press, 1948.

Hsu, Y. Y., "The Pao-Chia System in China," *Far Eastern Survey,* XXII, No. 24, December 8, 1943.

Kulp, D. H., *Country Life in South China: The Sociology of Familism.* New York: Bureau of Publications, Teachers College, Columbia University, 1925.

Leong, Y. K., and L. K. Tao, *Village and Town Life in China.* London: Allen and Unwin, Ltd., 1915.

Norins, Martin R., *Gateway of Asia, Sinkiang.* New York: International Secretariat, Institute of Pacific Relations, 1945.

Price, Frank W., *The Rural Church in China.* New York: Agricultural Missions Foundation, 1948.

Report of the China-United States Agricultural Mission. Washington, D.C.: Office of Foreign Agricultural Relations, United States Department of Agriculture, Report No. 2, May, 1947.

Shen, T. H., *Agricultural Resources of China.* Ithaca, N.Y.: Cornell University Press, 1951.

Stewart, John R., "Manchurian Agriculture," *Far Eastern Survey,* X, No. 7, April 21, 1941.

Winfield, Gerard F., *China: The Land and the People.* New York: Sloane, 1949.

Yang, Martin C., *A Chinese Village: Taitou, Shantung Province.* New York: Columbia University Press, 1945.

Films

China. S, 18. March of Time, New York.

China: Home Life in Szechwan. S, 20. United World Films, Inc., New York.

Chinese Peasant Goes to Market. S, 10. China Film Enterprises.

Land of Ghengis Kahn (Mongolia). S, 11. Teaching Films Custodian.

People of Western China. S, 11. Encyclopedia Britannica Films, Inc., Chicago.

Tibet. S, 10. Teaching Films Custodians.

Philippine Islands

Bell, D. W., *Economic Survey Mission to the Philippines,* Report to the President. Washington, D.C.: Department of State, 1950.

Hayden, Joseph R., *The Philippines, A Study in National Development.* New York: Macmillan, 1942.

India, Pakistan, Burma and Ceylon

Andrus, J. Russell, *Burmese Economic Life.* New York: Institute of Pacific Relations, 1948.

Brayne, F. L., *Better Villages.* London: Oxford University Press, 1937.

Brown, W. Norman, ed., *India, Pakistan and Ceylon.* Ithaca, N.Y.: Cornell University Press, 1951.

Darling, Malcolm Lyall, *Wisdom and Waste in a Punjab Village.* London: Oxford University Press, 1934.

Davis, Kingsley, *The Population of India and Pakistan.* Princeton: Princeton University Press, 1951.

Dutt, R. P., *A Guide to the Problem of Rural India: A Survey of Agrarian Structure, Poverty, and Overpopulation.* London: Gollancz, 1942.

Hatch, S., *Further Upward in Rural India.* London: Oxford University Press, 1938.

Hatch, S., *Up From Poverty in Rural India.* London: Oxford University Press, 1936.

Hatch, Spencer, *Toward Freedom from Want.* Bombay: Oxford University Press, 1949.

Jathar, Ganesh B., and Beri, Shridhar G., *Indian Economics: A Comprehensive and Critical Survey.* London: H. Milford, Oxford University Press, 1942.

Jennings, William I., *The Economy of Ceylon.* New York: Oxford University Press, 1948.

Krishnaswarin, S. Y., *Rural Problems in Madras.* Madras: Madras Government Press, 1947.

Mehkri, M. G., *Review of the Coöperative Movement in India.* Bombay: Reserve Bank of India, 1950.

Nanavati, M. B., and J. J. Anjaria, *The Indian Rural Problem.* Bombay: Vora & Co., 3d edition, 1947.

Shah, Vinal, and Sarla Shah, *Bhuvel: Socio-economic Survey of a Village.* Bombay: Vora & Co., 1949.

Sovani, N. V., *The Population Problem in India: A Regional Approach.* Poona: Gokhale Institute of Politics and Economics, 1942.

Williams, L. F. R., *India.* Toronto: Oxford University Press, 1940.

Wiser, C. V. and W. H., *Behind Mud Walls.* New York: R. R. Smith, Inc., 1930.

Wiser, W. H., *The Hindu Jajmani System.* Lucknow: Lucknow Publishing House, 1936.

Films

In Rural Maharashtra. S, 10. Film of the Nations.

India. S, 12. March of Time, New York.

India: Ganges Valley. S, 20. United World Films, Inc., New York.

India: Hyderabad. 15. Encyclopedia Britannica Films, Inc., Chicago.

India: Mysore and Ceylon. Encyclopedia Britannica Films, Inc., Chicago.

Japan and Formosa

Borton, Hugh, ed., *Japan.* Ithaca, N.Y.: Cornell University Press, 1951.

Embree, John F., *Suye Mura: A Japanese Village.* Chicago: University of Chicago Press, 1939.

Embree, John F., *The Japanese Nation: A Social Survey.* New York: Farrar & Rinehart, 1945.

Grajdanzev, Andrew J., *Formosa Today.* New York: Institute of Pacific Relations, 1942.

"Japan," *Fortune,* September, 1936, and April, 1944.

Nasu, S., *Aspects of Japanese Agriculture: A Preliminary Survey.* New York: Institute of Pacific Relations, 1941.

Raper, Arthur, *The Japanese Village in Transition.* Natural Resources Section Report No. 136, Supreme Commander for the Allied Powers, Tokyo, 1950.

Steiner, J. F., "Population Trends in Japan,"

American Sociological Review, IX, No. 1, February, 1944.

Trewartha, Glenn T., *Japan: A Physical, Cultural and Regional Geography.* Madison: University of Wisconsin Press, 1945. Especially chaps. IV, V, VII, IX.

Yoder, Fred R., "The Japanese Rural Community," *Rural Sociology,* I, No. 4, December, 1936.

Film

Japan: Island Nation. 30. Encyclopedia Britannica Films, Inc., Chicago.

Korea

Brunner, Edmund deS., *Rural Korea.* New York and London: International Missionary Council, 1928. Also reprinted in vol. VI, Proceedings of the International Missionary Council, 1929, and translated into Japanese by the Governor-General of Chosen.

Grajdanzev, Andrew J., *Modern Korea.* New York: Institute of Pacific Relations, 1944.

Lee, Hoon K., *Land Utilization and Rural Economy in Korea.* Chicago: University of Chicago Press, 1936.

Osgood, Cornelius, *The Koreans and Their Culture.* New York: Ronald, 1951.

Siam (Thailand)

Anderson, J. M., *Siam, Second Rural Economic Survey.* Bangkok: Times Press, 1936.

Deignan, H. G., *Siam — Land of Free Men.* Washington, D.C.: Smithsonian Institution, 1943.

Food and Agriculture Organization, *Report of the FAO Mission for Siam,* 1948.

Thompson, V. M., *Thailand: The New Siam.* New York: Institute of Pacific Relations, 1941.

Zimmerman, Carle C., *Siam, A Rural Economic Survey.* Bangkok: Times Press, 1931.

MIDDLE AND NEAR EAST

Allen, Harold B., *Come Over Into Macedonia.* New Brunswick, N.J.: Rutgers University Press, 1943.

Allen, H. B., *Rural Education and Welfare in the Middle East.* London: H. M. Stationery Office, 1946.

Badeau, John S., *East and West of Suez.* New York: The Foreign Policy Association, 1943.

Bonne, Alfred, *State and Economics in the Middle East: A Society in Transition.* London: Routledge & Kegan Paul, Ltd., 1948.

Dickson, H. R. P., *The Arab of the Desert.* London: Allen and Unwin, 1949.

Dodd, Stuart Carter, *Social Relations in the Middle East.* Beirut: American Press, 1946.

Fisher, W. B., *The Middle East: A Physical, Social and Regional Geography.* London: Methuen, 1950.

Galatoli, A. M., *Egypt in Midpassage.* Cairo: Urwand & Sons, 1950.

Glanville, S. R. K., *The Legacy of Egypt.* Oxford: Clarendon, 1947.

Groseclose, Elgin, *Introduction to Iran.* New York: Oxford University Press, 1947.

Gupta, Raj Narain, *Iran: An Economic Study.* New Delhi: The Indian Institute of International Affairs, 1947.

Haas, William S., *Iran.* New York: Columbia University Press, 1946.

Hourani, Albert H., *Minorities in the Arab World.* London: Oxford University Press, 1947.

Hourani, A. H., *Syria and Lebanon.* New York and London: Royal Institute of International Affairs, 1945.

Infield, H. F., *Co-operative Living in Palestine.* New York: Dryden, 1944.

Issawi, Charles, *Egypt: An Economic and Social Analysis.* New York: Oxford University Press, 1948.

Jamali, M. R., *The New Iraq.* New York: Teachers College, Columbia University, 1934.

Overseas Consultants, Inc., *Report on the Seven Year Plan.* New York, 1949. (Iran.)

Tannous, A. E., "Rural Problems and Village Welfare in the Middle East," *Rural Sociology,* VIII, No. 3, September, 1943.

Tannous, A. E., "Social Change in an Arab Village," *American Sociological Review,* VI, No. 5, October, 1941.

Thornburg, Max Weston, et al., *Turkey: An Economic Appraisal.* New York: Twentieth Century Fund, 1949.

United Nations, *Final Report of the United Nations Economic Survey Mission for the Middle East.* Lake Success, New York: United Nations, 1949.

Wilbur, Donald N., *Iran, Past and Present*. Princeton: Princeton University Press, 1948.

Wilbur, Donald N., *The Middle East: 1948*. London: Europa Publication, 1949.

Film

Israel. S, 20. United World Films, Inc., New York.

CARIBBEAN ISLANDS

Blanshard, Paul, *Democracy and Empire in the Caribbean*. New York: Macmillan, 1949.

Caribbean Research Council, *The Caribbean Land Tenure System Symposium*. Port of Spain, Trinidad, British West Indies, 1947.

Cook, Mercer, *Haiti*. Washington, D.C.: Pan-American Union, 1951.

Cumper, George E., *The Social Structure of the British Caribbean*. Jamaica: Kingston University of the West Indies, 1949.

Fox, Annette Baker, *Freedom and Welfare in the Caribbean*. New York: Harcourt, Brace, 1949.

Gayer, Arthur D., Paul T. Homan, and Earle K. James, *The Sugar Economy of Puerto Rico*. New York: Columbia University Press, 1938.

Hernandez-Ramirer, Martin, *A Socio-economic Study of Southwestern Puerto Rico*. Rio Piedras: University of Puerto Rico, 1947.

Herskovits, Melville, *Life in a Haitian Village*. New York: Knopf, 1937.

Hibben, Thomas, and Rafael Pico, *Industrial Development of Puerto Rico and the Virgin Islands of the United States*. New York: Columbia University Press, 1948.

Leyburn, J. G., *The Haitian People*. New Haven: Yale University Press, 1941.

Perloff, Harvey S., *Puerto Rico's Economic Future*. Chicago: University of Chicago Press, 1950.

Tugwell, R. G., *Stricken Land*. New York: Doubleday, 1946.

United Nations, *Mission to Haiti*. Lake Success, N.Y.: United Nations, 1949.

Film

West Indies. S, 11. Encyclopedia Britannica Films, Inc., Chicago.

SOUTH AND CENTRAL AMERICA

For those especially interested in the southern hemisphere there are three sources of special value: *The Bulletin of the Pan-American Union*, Washington, D.C., a monthly; *Agriculture in the Americas*, Office of Foreign Agricultural Relations, United States Department of Agriculture, Washington 25, D.C., a monthly; and Bernstein, Sylvia P., *Bibliography on Labor and Social Welfare in Latin America*, Pan-American Union, Washington, D.C., 1944.

The bibliography which follows is divided into two main sections: South America and Central America. Those using it are reminded that there is great interest in this area of the world. Important studies are under way. A few are in press. A number of the books listed below may be superseded, and more specifically rural-life studies are likely to appear. These should be watched for.

SOUTH AMERICA

Dunne, Peter Masten, *A Padre Views South America*. Milwaukee: Bruce, 1945.

Economic Commission for Latin America, *Agricultural Requisites in Latin America*, Report of the Joint ECLA-FAO Working Party. New York: Columbia University Press, 1950.

Gordon, Wendell C., *The Economy of Latin America*. New York: Columbia University Press, 1950.

Hanson, Earl Parker, *The Amazon: A New Frontier*. New York: Headline Series, Foreign Policy Association, No. 45, March, 1944.

Inman, Samuel G., *Latin America — Its Place in World Life*. New York: Harcourt, Brace, 1942.

James, Prestone, *Latin America*. New York: Odyssey, 1950.

Latin America and Freedom from Want. Washington, D.C.: National Planning Association, 1942. (328 pages, mimeographed.)

Oakes, Maude, *The Two Crosses of Todos Santos: Survivals of Mayan Religious Ritual*. New York: Pantheon, 1951.

Ribra, A. F., *The Co-operation Movement in Latin America: Its Significance in Hemisphere Solidarity*. Albuquerque: University of New Mexico Press, 1943.

Soule, George, David Efron, and Norman T. Ness, *Latin America in the Future World*. New York: Farrar & Rinehart, 1945.

United Nations, *Economic Survey of Latin America*. New York: Columbia University Press, 1949.

Wythe, George, *Industry and Nationalism in Latin America*. New York: Columbia University Press, 1945.

Argentine Republic

Herron, Francis, *Letters from the Argentine*. New York: Putnam, 1943.

Jefferson, Mark, *Peopling the Argentine Pampa*. New York: American Geographical Society, 1936.

Parsons, Elsie Clews, *Peguche: A Study of Andean Indians*. Chicago: University of Chicago Press, 1945.

Taylor, Carl C., *Argentine Rural Life*. Baton Rouge: Louisiana State University Press, 1946.

Taylor, Carl C., *Programs of Colonization and Resettlement in Argentina*. Washington, D.C.: Library of Congress, 1944.

Taylor, Carl C., "Rural Locality Groups in Argentina," *American Sociological Review*, IX, No. 2, April, 1944.

Weil, Felix J., *Argentine Riddle*. New York: Day, 1944.

Film

Horseman of the Pampas. S, 20. United World Films, Inc., New York.

Bolivia

Leonard, Olen E., *Cantón Chullpas: A Socio-Economic Study in the Cochabamba Valley of Bolivia*. Washington, D.C.: United States Department of Agriculture, Office of Foreign Agricultural Relations Report No. 27, 1948.

Brazil

Cooke, Morris L., *Brazil on the March*. New York: Whittlesey House, 1945.

de Azevedo, Fernando, *Brazilian Culture*. New York: Macmillan, 1950.

Deffontaines, P., "The Origin and Growth of the Brazilian Network of Towns," *Geographical Review*, XXVII, 1938.

Freyre, G., *The Masters and the Slaves: A Study in the Development of Brazilian Civilization*, translated by Samuel Putnam. New York: Knopf, 1946.

Gauld, C. A., "Brazil Takes a Census," *Journal of Geography*, 40 (4), April, 1941.

Hunnicut, B., *Brazil: World Frontier*. New York: Van Nostrand, 1949.

James, P. E., "The Changing Patterns of Population in Sao Paulo State, Brazil," *Geographical Review*, XXVII, 1938.

James, P. E., "The Expanding Settlements of Southern Brazil," *Geographical Review*, XXX, 1940.

Smith, T. Lynn, *Brazil, People and Institutions*. Baton Rouge: Louisiana State University Press, 1946.

Smith, T. Lynn, "The Locality Group Structure of Brazil," *American Sociological Review*, IX, No. 1, February, 1944.

Wagley, Charles, and Eduardo Galvao, *The Tenehara Indians of Brazil: A Culture in Transition*. New York: Columbia University Press, 1949.

Willems, E., "Cultural Conflict in Rural Brazil," *Rural Sociology*, VII, No. 4, December, 1942.

Wythe, George, and others, *Brazil an Expanding Economy*. New York: Twentieth Century Fund, 1949.

Zweig, Stefan, *Brazil, Land of the Future*. New York: Viking, 1941.

Films

Amazon Awakens. C, S, 45. Office of Inter-American Affairs, Washington.

Brazil: Eastern Highlands. 16. Encyclopedia Britannica Films, Inc., Chicago.

Brazil: Lowlands. S, 20. United World Films, Inc., New York.

Brazil: People of the Plantations. 11. Encyclopedia Britannica Films, Inc., Chicago.

Chile

Ellsworth, P. T., *Chile: An Economy in Transition*. New York: Macmillan, 1945.

Hanson, Earl P., *Chile, Land of Progress*. New York: Reynal & Hitchcock, 1941.

McBride, George M., *Chile, Land and Society*.

New York: American Geographical Society, 1936.

Films

Chili. 16. Encyclopedia Britannica Films, Inc., Chicago.

Chili: People of Country Estates. S, 11. Encyclopedia Britannica Films, Inc., Chicago.

Colombia
Films

Colombia and Venezuela. S, 11. Encyclopedia Britannica Films, Inc., Chicago.

Colombia: Cross Roads of the Americas. S, 27. Office of Inter-American Affairs, Washington, D.C.

Ecuador

Leonard, Olen E., *Pichilinque: A Study of Rural Life in Coastal Ecuador.* Washington, D.C.: United States Department of Agriculture, Office of Foreign Agricultural Relations, March, 1947. (Foreign Agricultural Report No. 17.)

Peru

Gillin, John V., *Moche, A Peruvian Coastal Town.* Washington, D.C.: Government Printing Office, 1947.

Films

Peru. S, 20. Office of Inter-American Affairs, Washington, D.C.

Peru: Indians of the Mountains. Encyclopedia Britannica Films, Inc., Chicago.

Venezuela

"Venezuela," *Fortune.* March, 1939.

CENTRAL AMERICA

Biesanz, John and Mavis, *Costa Rican Life.* New York: Columbia University Press, 1944.

Hooper, O., "Rural Panama: Its Needs and Prospects," *Rural Sociology,* VIII, No. 3, September, 1943.

Hooper, O., "The Plight of Education in Rural Panama," *Rural Sociology,* IX, No. 1, March, 1933.

Jones, C. L., "Costa Rica and Civilization in the Caribbean." Madison: *University of Wisconsin Studies,* No. 23, 1935.

Jones, C. L., *Guatemala, Past and Present.* Minneapolis: University of Minnesota Press, 1940.

Suslow, Leo A., *Aspects of Social Reforms in Guatemala, 1944–49.* Hamilton, N.Y.: Colgate University Press, 1949.

Wilson, Charles Morrow, *Central America: Challenge and Opportunity.* New York: Holt, 1941 and 1942.

Wisdom, Charles, *The Chorti Indians of Guatemala.* Chicago: University of Chicago Press, 1936.

Films

Central America. S, 11. Encyclopedia Britannica Films, Inc., Chicago.

Guatemala. S, 20. United World Films, Inc., New York.

Hill Towns of Guatemala. S, 10. Office of Inter-American Affairs, Washington, D.C.

Mexico

Beals, Ralph L., *Cherán: A Sierra Tarascan Village.* Washington, D.C.: Government Printing Office, 1946.

Cook, Katherine M., *House of the People.* Washington, D.C.: Office of Education, 1932.

Cook, S. F., *Soil Erosion and Population in Central Mexico.* Berkeley: University of California Press, 1949.

Foster, George M., *A Primitive Mexican Economy.* New York: J. J. Augustin, 1942. (American Ethnological Society, Monograph No. V.)

Guillermo, Bonilla y Segura, *Report on Cultural Missions of Mexico.* Washington, D.C.: Office of Education, 1945.

Humphrey, N. D., "The Generic Folk Culture of Mexico," *Rural Sociology,* VII, No. 4, December, 1943.

Lewis, Oscar, *Life in a Mexican Village, Tepaztlan Restudied.* Urbana: University of Illinois Press, 1951.

Niggli, Josephina, *Mexican Village.* Chapel Hill: University of North Carolina Press, 1945.

Parsons, Elsie C., *Milta: Town of the Souls.* Chicago: University of Chicago Press, 1936.

Redfield, Robert, *A Village that Chose Progress:*

Chan Kom Revisited. Chicago: University of Chicago Press, 1950.

Redfield, Robert, *The Folk Culture of Yucatan.* Chicago: University of Chicago Press, 1941.

Redfield, Robert, *Tepaztlan, A Mexican Village.* Chicago: University of Chicago Press, 1930.

Sánchez, George I., *Mexico, A Revolution by Education.* New York: Viking, 1936.

Simpson, E. N., *The Ejido: Mexico's Way Out.* Chapel Hill: University of North Carolina Press, 1937.

Tannenbaum, Frank, *Mexico: The Struggle for Peace and Bread.* New York: Knopf, 1950.

Whetten, N. L., *Rural Mexico.* Chicago: University of Chicago Press, 1948.

Films

Arts and Crafts of Mexico. S, 11. Encyclopedia Britannica Films, Inc., Chicago.

Land of Mexico. S, 11. Encyclopedia Britannica Films, Inc., Chicago.

Mexico: Adobe Village. S, 19. United World Films, Inc., New York.

People of Mexico. S, 11. Encyclopedia Britannica Films, Inc., Chicago.

Tomorrow's Mexico. S, 17. March of Time, New York.

Town in Old Mexico. S, 9. Office of Inter-American Affairs, Washington, D.C.

Yucatan. C, S, 20. Office of Inter-American Affairs, Washington, D.C.

Index of Names

Subject Index

Since this work deals with Rural Society, the use of the adjective *rural* has been largely dispensed with in this index. Thus references to *rural health* will be found indexed under *health*.